JEPPESEN®
Sanderson Training Products

INSTRUMENT RATING

FAA

AIRMEN KNOWLEDGE

TEST GUIDE

for
COMPUTER TESTING

- **Questions, Answers, Explanations, References**
- **Keyed to GFD Instrument/Commercial Manual**
- **Explanations Adjacent to Each Question**
- **Organized by Topic, Includes Full-Color Charts**
- **Unique Sliding Mask for Self-Testing**
- **Perforated and 3-Hole Punched Pages**
- **Includes All FAA Airplane Questions**
- **Contains Instrument Instructor Questions**

©Jeppesen Sanderson, Inc., 1993, 1995, 1996, 1997, 1998, 1999, 2000, 2001, 2002
All Rights Reserved
55 Inverness Drive East, Englewood, CO 80112-5498
ISBN 0-88487-307-2

PREFACE _____

Thank you for purchasing this *Instrument Rating FAA Airmen Knowledge Test Guide*. This Test Guide will help you understand the answers to the test questions so you can take the FAA computer test with confidence. It contains all the FAA Instrument airplane test questions. Included are the correct answers and explanations, along with study references. Explanations of why the other choices are wrong have been included where appropriate. Questions are organized by topic, with explanations conveniently located adjacent to each question. The three-hole punched, perforated pages provide flexibility so you can select and remove specific pages for effective study. Full-color charts identical to those on the FAA test are included, plus our unique sliding mask for self-testing. Please note that this Test Guide is intended to be a supplement to your instructor-led flight and ground training, not a stand alone learning tool.

THE JEPPESEN SANDERSON TRAINING PHILOSOPHY

Flight training in the developing years of aviation was characterized by the separation of academics from flight training in the aircraft. For years, ground and flight training were not integrated. There were lots of books on different subjects, written by different authors, which produced a general lack of continuity in training material. The introduction of **Jeppesen Sanderson Training Products** changed all this. Our proven, professionally integrated training materials include extensive research on teaching theory and principles of how people learn best and most efficiently. Effective instruction includes determining objectives and completion standards. We employ an important principle of learning a complex skill using a step-by-step sequence known as the **building block principle**. Another important aspect of training is the principle of **meaningful repetition**, whereby each necessary concept or skill is presented several times throughout the instructional program. Jeppesen training materials incorporate these principles in our syllabi, textbooks, videos, computer-based training (CBT), exercises, exams, PCATD Desktop Simulator, and this Test Guide. When these elements are combined with an instructor's class discussion and the skills learned in the simulator and airplane, you have an ideal integrated training system, with all materials coordinated.

Observation and research show that people tend to retain 10% of what they read, 20% of what they hear, 30% of what they see, and 50% of what they both hear and see together. These retention figures can be increased to as high as 90% by including active learning methods. Videos and textbooks are generally considered passive learning materials. Exercises, stage exams, student/instructor discussions, CBT, and practice in the simulator and airplane are considered to be active learning methods. Levels of learning include rote, understanding, application, and correlation. One of the major drawbacks with test preparation courses that concentrate only on passing the test is that they focus on rote learning, the lowest level of learning. Students benefit from Jeppesen's professional approach through standardized instruction, a documented training record, increased learning **and** increased passing rates. Our materials are challenging and motivating, while maximizing knowledge and skill retention. Nearly 3 million pilots have learned to fly using our materials, which include:

MANUALS — Our training manuals contain the answers to many of the questions you may have as you begin your training program. They are based on the **study/review** concept of learning. This means detailed material is presented in an uncomplicated way, then important points are summarized through the use of bold type and color. The best results can be obtained when the manual is studied as an integral part of the coordinated materials. The manual is the central component for academic study and is cross-referenced to video presentations.

VIDEOS — These motivating, high-quality ground school videos are professionally produced with actual inflight video and animated graphics. They allow you to review and reinforce essential concepts presented in the manual. The videos are available for viewing at flight and ground schools which subscribe to the Jeppesen Sanderson Guided Flight Discovery (GFD) Training System. Call **1-800-621-JEPP** for the names of our Training System dealers in your area.

SUPPORT COMPONENTS — Supplementary items include a training syllabus, stage and end-of-course exams, CBT, PCATD Desktop Simulator, FAR/AIM Manual, FARs Explained, airmen knowledge test and practical test study guides, test preparation software and videos, question banks and computer testing supplements, an aviation weather book, student record folder, computer, plotter, and logbook. Jeppesen Sanderson's training products are the most comprehensive pilot training materials available. In conjunction with your instructor, they help you prepare for the FAA exam and practical test; and, more importantly, they help you become a more proficient and safer pilot.

You can purchase our products and services through your Jeppesen dealer. For product, service, or sales information call **1-800-621-JEPP, 303-799-9090, or FAX 303-328-4153**. If you have comments, questions, or need explanations about any component of our GFD Training System, we are prepared to offer assistance at any time. If your dealer does not have a Jeppesen catalog, please request one and we will promptly send it to you. Just call the above telephone number, or write:

> Manager, Training and Courseware
> Jeppesen Sanderson, Inc.
> 55 Inverness Drive East
> Englewood, CO 80112-5498

Please direct inquiries from Europe, Africa, and the Middle East to:
> Jeppesen & Co., GmbH
> Frankfurter Strasse 233
> 63263 Neu-Isenburg, Germany
> Tel: 011-49-6102-5070
> Fax: 011-49-6102-507-999

UPDATES OF FAA QUESTIONS — You can obtain free updates for the FAA questions in this Test Guide by visiting Jeppesen's web site. These updates are generally valid within one year of book publication; if you are using an older Test Guide, the web site may not update all questions that have changed since the book was printed.

To find updated questions, go to **www.jeppesen.com**, click Online Publications and then click FAA Test Prep Updates. Due to improvements and ongoing reorganization of the web site, the exact location of the updates is subject to change.

The FAA is changing your test. We want you to be ready.

The FAA is concerned that many students are memorizing the answers to the FAA knowledge test. As a result, they are regularly shuffling around the answer choices to most questions in the FAA databases. This means if you have learned the answer to a question based on the letter of the correct answer, or based on the correct answer's position below the question, you will likely miss the question when you take the test. We believe the shuffle will continue on a regular basis, and it will not be possible for test preparation courses to match the sequence of the answer choices.

Jeppesen has never encouraged its students to memorize answers to FAA questions. We provide comprehensive, no-nonsense study material that teaches you what you need to know to determine the correct answers to the tests. And our test prep materials always tell you why the correct answer is correct and if it is not obvious, why the other answers are incorrect. We want you to know the material, not memorize it.

So, be careful how you study this material. While it is possible to memorize the letter and position of the correct answer, it is not in your best interest, either when taking the test, or further in your flight career when this knowledge will be tested in the cockpit. When answering an FAA question, carefully read and evaluate each answer choice and choose the correct answer based on what you know from your study, not from that answer's position.

Jeppesen thanks you for choosing our test preparation materials. We are confident you will be better prepared to pass the FAA test.

TABLE OF CONTENTS

INTRODUCTION

The *Instrument Rating FAA Airmen Knowledge Test Guide* is designed to help you prepare for the Instrument Airplane Computer Test. It covers FAA exam material that applies to airplanes, including pertinent Federal Aviation Regulations (FARs). Questions and answers pertaining to rotorcraft, gliders, balloons, powered-lift, and airships have been omitted.

We recommend that you use this Test Guide in conjunction with the Guided Flight Discovery (GFD) Pilot Training System. The Test Guide is organized like the GFD Instrument/Commercial Manual, with eleven chapters and distinctive sections within each chapter. Questions are covered in the Test Guide in the same sequence as the material in the manual. References to applicable page numbers in the manual are included along with the answers. A separate chapter (Chapter 12) in the Test Guide is devoted to FAR questions and answers.

[1]	[2]	[3]	[4]	[5]	[6]
4-22.	**J14**	**4-22.**	**Answer C.**	**GFDICM 4B**	**(AIM)**
(FAA Question)			*(Explanation of FAA Question)*		

[1]   Jeppesen designated test guide question number. The first number is the chapter where the question is located in the Test Guide. In most cases, this corresponds to the chapter in the GFD manual. The second number is the question number within the chapter. This number may or may not be in sequential order. In this example, the question is in chapter 4 of the Test Guide and it is the 22th question.

[2]   FAA subject matter knowledge code. The reference to this code can be found in the appendix of the Test Guide.

[3]   The Jeppesen test guide number is repeated in the right hand column above the explanation.

[4]   Correct answer to the question, in this case answer C is correct.

[5]   The location where the question is covered in the GFD manual. In this case, the question is covered in chapter 4, section B of the GFD Instrument/Commercial Manual.

[6]   Abbreviation for the FAA or other authoritative source document. In this case, the reference is the Aeronautical Information Manual (AIM). Abbreviations used in the

Test Guide are as follows:

AC	—	Advisory Circulars
A/FD	—	Airport/Facility Directory
AIM	—	Aeronautical Information Manual
AW	—	Aviation Weather, AC 00-6A
AWS	—	Aviation Weather Services, AC 00-45
FAR	—	Federal Aviation Regulation
AFH	—	Airplane Flying Handbook, FAA-H-8083-3
IAP	—	Instrument Approach Procedure
IFH	—	Instrument Flying Handbook, FAA-H-8083-15
GFDICM	—	Guided Flight Discovery Instrument/Commercial Manual
GFDPPM	—	Guided Flight Discovery Private Pilot Manual
NAVWEPS	—	Aerodynamics for Naval Aviators
PHB	—	Pilot's Handbook of Aeronautical Knowledge, AC 61-23
WBH	—	Aircraft Weight and BalanceHandbook, FAA-H-8083-1
TERPS	—	U.S. Standard for Terminal Instrument Procedures

Below the reference line is the FAA question in the left column and the explanation in the right column. The explanation includes the correct answer followed by an explanation of why the answer is correct and why the other answers are wrong. In some cases, the incorrect answers are not explained. Examples include instances where the answers are calculated, or when the explanation of the correct answer obviously eliminates the wrong answers.

The answers in this Test Guide are based on official reference documents and, in our judgment, are the best choices of the available answers. Some questions which were valid when the FAA test was developed may no longer be appropriate due to ongoing changes in regulations or official operating procedures. However, with the computer test format, timely updating and validation of questions is anticipated. Therefore, when taking the FAA test, it is important to answer the questions according to the latest regulations or official operating procedures.

Two appendices from the FAA test materials are included in the back of the Test Guide. These are Appendix 1, Subject Matter Knowledge Codes, which also lists reference material, and Appendix 2, which consists of legend information from the National Aeronautical Charting Office (NACO) Airport/Facility Directory (A/FD). You will need to refer to this legend to answer some questions concerning A/FD information. Appendix 3 in the Test Guide contains a numerical listing of all airplane questions. Included in this listing is a tabulation with the Jeppesen test guide question number, FAA question number, correct answer, and the page number where the question appears in the Test Guide.

Figures in the Test Guide are the same as those that are used in the FAA Computerized Testing Supplement. These figures, that are referred to in many of the questions, are placed throughout the Test Guide as close as practical to the applicable questions. When a figure is not on the same page or facing page, a note will indicate the page number where you can find that figure. In addition, pages in this Test Guide are three-hole punched and perforated to allow you to easily remove any figure for reference while answering a specific question.

HOW TO PREPARE FOR THE FAA TEST
It is important to realize that to become a safe, competent pilot, you need more than just the academic knowledge required to pass a test. For a comprehensive ground training program, we recommend a structured ground school with a qualified flight or ground instructor. An organized course of instruction will help you complete the course in a timely manner, and you will be able to have your questions answered. The additional instruction will be beneficial in your flight training.

Regardless of whether or not you are in a structured ground training program, you will find this Test Guide is an excellent training aid to help you prepare for the FAA computerized test. The Test Guide contains all of the airplane questions as they are presented in the FAA computerized test format. By reviewing the questions and studying the Guided Flight Discovery Pilot Training materials, you should be well equipped to take the test.

You will also benefit more from your study if you test yourself as you proceed through the Test Guide. Cover the answers in the right-hand column, read each question, and choose what you consider the best answer. A sliding mask is provided for this purpose. Move the sliding mask down and read the answer and explanation for that question. You may want to mark the questions you miss for further study and review prior to taking the exam.

The sooner you take the exam after you complete your study, the better. This way, the information will be fresh in your mind, and you will be more confident when you actually take the FAA test.

WHO CAN TAKE THE TEST

When you are ready to take the FAA computerized test, you must present evidence that you have completed the appropriate ground instruction or a home study course. This proof may be in the form of a graduation certificate from a pilot training course, a written statement, or a logbook entry by a certified ground or flight instructor. Although you are encouraged to obtain ground instruction, a home study course may be used. If you cannot provide one of the above documents, you may present evidence of a completed home study course to an FAA aviation safety inspector for approval.

You also must provide evidence of a permanent mailing address, appropriate identification, and proof of your age. The identification must include a current photograph, your signature, and your residential address, if different from your mailing address. You may present this information in more than one form of identification, such as a driver's license, government identification card, passport, alien residency (green) card, or a military identification card.

GENERAL INFORMATION — FAA COMPUTER TESTS

Detailed information on FAA computer testing is contained in FAA Order 8080.6B, Conduct of Airmen Knowledge Tests. This FAA order provides guidance for Flight Standards District Offices (FSDOs) and personnel associated with organizations that are participating in, or are seeking to participate in, the FAA Computer-Assisted Airmen Knowledge Testing Program. You also may refer to FAA Order 8700.1, General Aviation Operations Inspector's Handbook, for guidance on computer testing by 14 CFR Parts 141 and 142 pilot schools that hold examining authority.

As an applicant, you don't need all of the details contained in FAA Orders, but you will be interested in some of the general information about computer testing facilities. A **Computer Testing Designee (CTD)** is an organization authorized by the FAA to administer FAA airmen knowledge tests via the computer medium. A **Computer Testing Manager (CTM)** is a person selected by the CTD to serve as manager of its national computer testing program. A **Testing Center Supervisor (TCS)** is a person selected by the CTM, with FAA approval, to administer FAA airmen knowledge tests at approved testing centers. The TCS is responsible for the operation of the testing center. A **Special Test Administrator (STA)** is a person selected by a CTD to administer FAA airmen knowledge tests in unique situations and remote or isolated areas. A test proctor is a properly trained and qualified person, appointed by a TCS, authorized to administer FAA airmen knowledge tests.

CTDs are selected by the FAA's Airmen Testing Standards Branch. Those selected may include companies, schools, universities, or other organizations that meet specific requirements. For example, they must clearly demonstrate competence in computer technology, centralized database management, national communications network operation and maintenance, national facilities management, software maintenance and support, and technical training and customer support. They must provide computer-assisted testing, test administration, and data transfer service on a national scale. This means they must maintain a minimum of 20 operational testing centers geographically dispersed throughout the United States. In addition, CTDs must offer operational hours that are convenient to the public. An acceptable plan for test security is also required.

TEST MATERIALS, REFERENCE MATERIALS, AND AIDS

You are allowed to use aids, reference materials, and test materials within specified guidelines, provided the actual test questions or answers are not revealed. All models of aviation-oriented computers, regardless of manufacturer, may be used, including hand-held computers designed expressly for aviation use, and also small electronic calculators that perform arithmetic functions. Simple programmable memories, which allow addition to, subtraction from, or retrieval of one number from the memory, are acceptable. Simple functions such as square root or percent keys are also acceptable.

In addition, you may use any reference materials provided with the test. You will find that these reference materials are the same as those in your Test Guide. They include a printed Computerized Testing Supplement with the legend data and the applicable figures. You also may use scales, straight-edges, protractors, plotters, navigation computers, log sheets, and, as already mentioned, electronic or mechanical calculators that are directly related to the test. Permanently inscribed manufacturer's instructions on the front and back of these aids, such as, formulas, conversions, regulations, signals, weather data, holding pattern diagrams, frequencies, weight and balance formulas, and ATC procedures, are permissible.

WHAT TO EXPECT ON A COMPUTER TEST

Computer testing centers are required to have an acceptable method for the "on-line" registration of test applicants during normal business hours. They must provide a dual method, for example, keyboard, touch screen, or mouse, for answering questions. Features that must be provided also include an introductory lesson to familiarize you with computer testing procedures, the ability to return to a test question previously answered (for the purpose of review or answer changes), and a suitable display of multiple-choice and other question types on the computer screen in one frame. Other required features include a display of the time remaining for the completion of the test, a "HELP" function which permits you to review test questions and optional responses, and provisions for your test score on an Airman Computer Test Report.

On computer tests, the selection of questions is done for you, and you will answer the questions that appear on the screen. You will be given a specific amount of time to complete the test, which is based on past experience with others who have taken the exam. If you are prepared, you should have plenty of time to complete the test. After you begin the test, the screen will show you the time remaining for completion. When taking the test, keep the following points in mind:

1. Answer each question in accordance with the latest regulations and procedures. If the regulation or procedure has recently changed, you will receive credit for the affected question. However, these questions will normally be deleted or updated on the FAA computerized exams.

2. Read each question carefully before looking at the possible answers. You should clearly understand the problem before attempting to solve it.

3. After formulating an answer, determine which of the alternatives most nearly corresponds with that answer. The answer chosen should completely resolve the problem.

4. From the answers given, it may appear that there is more than one possible answer; however, there is only one answer that is correct and complete. The other answers are either incomplete or are derived from popular misconceptions.

5. Make sure you select an answer for each question. Questions left unanswered will be counted as incorrect.

6. If a certain question is difficult for you, it is best to proceed to other questions. After you answer the less difficult questions, return to those which were unanswered. The computer-aided test format helps you identify unanswered questions, as well as those questions you wish to review.

7. When solving a calculator problem, select the answer nearest your solution. The problem has been checked with various types of calculators; therefore, if you have solved it correctly, your answer will be closer to the correct answer than the other choices.

8. Generally, the test results will be available almost immediately. Your score will be recorded on an Airman Computer Test Report form. [Figure 1]

```
1
2
3
4
5
6                        Federal Aviation Administration
7                         Airman Computer Test Report
8
9       EXAM TITLE:  Instrument Rating Airplane (IRA)
10
11      NAME:  Jones David John
12
13      ID NUMBER:  123456789        TAKE:  1
14
15      DATE:  08/14/—            SCORE:  82          GRADE:  Pass
16
17
18
19
20      ---------------------------------------------------------------
21
22      Knowledge area codes in which questions were answered incorrectly.
23      See Appropriate FAA-CT-8080 test book. A code may represent more
24      than one incorrect response.
25
26      A21  B08  B09  H04  H05  H06  I02  I03  J58  K53  M51
27
28
29
30
31      EXPIRATION DATE:  08/31/—
32
33
34                        DO NOT LOSE THIS REPORT
35
36      ---------------------------------------------------------------
37      Authorized Instructor's Statement. (If Applicable)
38
39      I have given Mr./Ms._____additional instruction in
40      each subject area shown to be deficient and consider the applicant competent to pass the
41      test.
42
43      Last _____ Initial _____ Cert. No. _____ Type _____
44      (Print Clearly)
45
46
47      Signature _____
48
49
50
51
52
53
54                                                    CTD's Embossed Seal
```

**FIGURE 1. This sample Airman Computer Test Report shows the applicant's test results.
Take 1 indicates this is the first time the applicant has taken this test. Knowledge area codes
for incorrect answers are listed in the center portion of the report, and an additional instruction section is included in the last part.**

The Airmen Computer Test Report includes subject matter knowledge codes for incorrect answers. To determine the knowledge area in which a particular ques tion was incorrectly answered, compare the subject matter knowledge codes on this report to Appendix 1, Subject Matter Knowledge Codes.

Computer testing designees must provide a way for applicants, who challenge the validity of test questions, to enter comments into the computer. The test proctor should advise you, if you have complaints about test scores, or specific test questions, to write directly to the appropriate FAA office. In addition to comments, you will be asked to respond to a critique form which may vary at different computer testing centers. The TCS must provide a method for you to respond to critique questions projected on the computer screen. [Figure 2]

1. Did the test administration personnel give you an adequate briefing on testing procedures?

2. Was the "sign-on" accomplished efficiently?

3. Did you have any difficulty reading the computer presentation of test questions?

4. Was the test supplementary material (charts, graphs, tables, etc.) pre-sented in a usable manner?

5. Did you have any difficulty using the "return to previous question for review" procedure?

6. Was the testing room noise level distracting?

7. Did you have adequate work space?

8. Did you have adequate lighting?

9. What is your overall evaluation of the computer testing experience?

    a. Unsatisfactory

    b. Poor

    c. Satisfactory

    d. Highly satisfactory

    e. Outstanding

FIGURE 2. Critique forms used at different computer testing centers may vary. This sample form contains typical questions.

RETESTING AFTER FAILURE

The applicant shall surrender the previous test report to the test proctor prior to retesting. The original test report shall be destroyed by the test proctor after administering the retest. The latest test taken will reflect the official score.

As stated in 14 CFR section 61.49, an applicant may apply for retesting after receiving additional training and an endorsement from an authorized instructor who has determined the applicant has been found competent to pass the test.

WHERE TO TAKE THE FAA TEST

Almost all testing is now administered via computer at FAA-designated test centers. As indicated, these CTDs are located throughout the U.S. You can expect to pay a fee and the cost varies at different locations. The following is a listing of the approved computer testing designees at the time of publication of this Test Guide. You may want to check with your local FSDO for changes.

Computer Assisted Testing Service (CATS)
1-800-947-4228
Outside U.S. (650) 259-8550

LaserGrade Computer Testing
1-800-211-2754
Outside U.S. (360) 896-9111

BUILDING PROFESSIONAL EXPERIENCE

This textbook chapter introduces some of the training requirements and the opportunities for pilots with instrument ratings and commercial certificates. It presents highlights of aviation history as well.

Each chapter and section in the Instrument Pilot Airmen Knowledge Study Guide directly corresponds to the same chapter and section in Jeppesen's *Instrument/Commercial Manual*, part of the Guided Flight Discovery Pilot Training System. The manual explores in depth each topic presented in this guide, and covers many areas not tested in the computer exam. This additional information is vital to your instrument pilot preparation, and we strongly encourage you to study the manual, in addition to this guide.

SECTION A
INSTRUMENT/COMMERCIAL TRAINING AND OPPORTUNITIES

INSTRUMENT PILOT PRIVILEGES

1. The addition of an instrument rating to your private pilot certificate allows you to fly under instrument flight rules (IFR). These regulations govern flight operations in weather conditions below VFR weather minimums.

OPERATING UNDER IFR

2. When referring to weather conditions, the terms IFR and IMC (instrument meteorological conditions) are often used interchangeably, as are the terms VFR and VMC (visual meteorological conditions). In addition, the terms IFR and VFR can define the type of flight plan under which you are operating.

3. Instrument and visual flight rules are contained in the Federal Aviation Regulations (FARs), which are part of the Code of Federal Regulations, Aeronautics and Space, Title 14 (14 CFR). Some of the FARs are contained in 14 CFR Part 1, 61, and 91).

4. Instrument training enhances your skill at precisely controlling the aircraft, improves your ability to operate in the complex ATC system, and increases your confidence level. Statistics have shown the risk of a weather-related accident declines as pilots gain instrument flying experience.

REQUIREMENTS FOR INSTRUMENT RATING

5. To be eligible for an instrument rating, you must hold a private pilot certificate, be able to read, write, speak, and understand the English language, and complete specific training and flight time requirements described in 14 CFR 61, as well as pass a knowledge and practical test.

6. You must have at least 50 hours of cross-country time as pilot in command (PIC) and 40 hours of actual or simulated instrument time, including at least 15 hours of instrument flight training from an authorized instructor in the airplane.

7. Some of your instrument time may be conducted with a safety pilot who is appropriately rated for the airplane. Part of your instrument training may be provided by an authorized instructor in a flight simulator, flight training device, or a personal computer-based aviation training device (PCATD).

MAINTAINING INSTRUMENT PROFICIENCY

8. To meet recency of experience requirements for instrument flight, you must have intercepted and tracked courses through the use of navigation systems, performed holding procedures, and flown at least six instrument approaches within the preceding six calendar months.

9. If you do not meet the instrument currency requirements within six calendar months or within six calendar months after that, you must pass an instrument proficiency check.

There are no Instrument FAA questions assigned to this section.

SECTION B
ADVANCED HUMAN FACTORS CONCEPTS

AERONAUTICAL DECISION MAKING

1. **Aeronautical decision making** is a systematic approach to the mental process used by aircraft pilots to consistently determine the best course of action in response to a given set of circumstances.
2. Approximately 75% of all aviation accidents are attributed to human factors-related causes. Studies have identified five hazardous attitudes which can interfere with a pilot's ability to make sound decisions and exercise authority properly.

PILOT-IN-COMMAND RESPONSIBILITY

3. As pilot in command, you are the final authority in the airplane you are flying. When only one pilot is in the cockpit, the PIC is obvious, but when two pilots are present, each pilot's responsibilities must be defined before the flight. Within the cockpit, one person is pilot in command, and the other serves to assist the PIC.

RESOURCE USE

4. Resource use is an important part of human factors training. Cockpit resources increase as you fly more complex aircraft with advanced systems. If you are not thoroughly familiar with the equipment in your aircraft or you rely on it so much that you become complacent, flight safety is compromised.
5. The focus of **crew resource management (CRM)** programs is the effective use of all available resources: human resources, hardware, and information. CRM training helps flight crews understand the limitations of human performance, especially under stressful situations, and makes them aware of the importance of crew coordination to combat error.

COMMUNICATION

6. Readback of ATC clearances is crucial in the IFR environment. Do not assume controller silence after a readback is verification of your transmission. Ask for a verbal confirmation.
7. When flying with another pilot, it is important to use standard terminology and verify that your meaning is understood. A breakdown in communication can cause friction and frustration, detracting from important tasks, or lead to a hazardous situation where one pilot believes the other is controlling the airplane, but in reality, neither pilot has control.

WORKLOAD MANAGEMENT

8. Effective workload management directly impacts safety by ensuring that you are prepared for the busiest segments of the flight through proper use of down time. Organizing charts in the order of use, setting radio frequencies, and writing down expected altitudes and route clearances will help you visualize and mentally prepare for what comes next.

SITUATIONAL AWARENESS

9. **Controlled flight into terrain (CFIT)** occurs when an aircraft is flown into terrain or water with no prior awareness on the part of the crew that the crash is imminent.

AVIATION PHYSIOLOGY

10. The study of aviation physiology is an important part of human factors training. How you feel, physically, has a direct impact on how well you fly.

DISORIENTATION

11. When there is a conflict between the information relayed by your central vision and your peripheral vision, you may suffer from **spatial disorientation**. When subjected to the various forces of flight, the vestibular system can send misleading signals to the brain resulting in **vestibular disorientation**.

12. A rapid acceleration during a missed approach can create the illusion of being in a nose-up attitude, and an abrupt change from climb to straight-and-level flight can create the illusion of tumbling backwards. To prevent or overcome spatial disorientation, you must rely on and properly interpret the indications of the flight instruments.

MOTION SICKNESS

13. Nausea, sweating, dizziness, and vomiting are some of the symptoms of motion sickness. To overcome motion sickness without outside visual references, you should focus on the instrument panel, since it is your only source of accurate position information.

HYPOXIA

14. Hypoxia occurs when the tissues in the body do not receive enough oxygen. It can be caused by an insufficient supply of oxygen, inadequate transportation of oxygen, or the inability of the body tissues to use oxygen. **Hypoxic hypoxia** occurs when there are not enough molecules of oxygen available at sufficient pressure to pass between the membranes in your respiratory system.

15. If you are planning a flight with a cruise altitude over 12,500 feet MSL, you should review FAR Part 91 for the requirements regarding supplemental oxygen. Prior to operating a pressurized aircraft with a service ceiling or maximum operating altitude higher than 25,000 feet MSL, you must complete high-altitude training.

16. **Hypemic hypoxia** occurs when your blood is not able to carry a sufficient amount of oxygen to your body's cells. Since it attaches itself to the hemoglobin about 200 times more easily than does oxygen, **carbon monoxide (CO)** prevents the hemoglobin from carrying sufficient oxygen. Even without considering the dangers of incapacitating the flight crew, carbon monoxide poisoning can be fatal. Frequent inspections should be made of aircraft exhaust manifold-type heating systems to minimize the possibility of exhaust gases leaking into the cockpit.

17. **Stagnant hypoxia** is an oxygen deficiency in the body due to the poor circulation of the blood. It can result from pulling excessive positive Gs. The inability of the cells to effectively use oxygen is defined as **histotoxic hypoxia**. This can be caused by alcohol and other drugs such as narcotics and poisons.

HYPERVENTILATION

18. Hyperventilation is a physiological disorder that develops when too much carbon dioxide (CO_2) has been eliminated from the body, usually caused by breathing too rapidly or too deeply. To overcome the symptoms of hyperventilation, you should slow your breathing rate.

DECOMPRESSION SICKNESS

19. Decompression sickness (DCS) is a painful condition that can occur if flying too soon after diving. It is very important that you allow enough time for the body to rid itself of excess nitrogen absorbed during diving.

FITNESS FOR FLIGHT

20. Stress is the body's reaction to the physical and psychological demands placed upon it, and it can adversely affect your ability to fly safely. When you are fatigued, you are more prone to error in the cockpit. Getting adequate rest and improving your overall fitness will help you perform at your best.

21. Preflight use of the **I'm Safe Checklist** will help ensure you are fit for flight. Consider illness, and medication that might affect your safety as a pilot. Factors such as rest, a good breakfast, and issues at work can interfere with your concentration level in the airplane. If you have any reservations about your ability to make the flight, save the trip for another time.

1-1 H800

Without visual aid, a pilot often interprets centrifugal force as a sensation of

A — rising or falling.
B — turning.
C — motion reversal.

1-1. Answer A. GFDICM 1B (IFH)

A level turn that produces a load factor, such as 1.5 positive Gs, can give you the illusion of a climb. Answer (B) is incorrect because centrifugal force is normally interpreted as rising or falling, not turning. Motion reversal (answer C) usually is experienced when a change in bank angle creates the sensation of rotation in the opposite direction.

1-2 J31

Abrupt head movement during a prolonged constant rate turn in IMC or simulated instrument conditions can cause

A — pilot disorientation.
B — false horizon.
C — elevator illusion.

1-2. Answer A. GFDICM 1B (IFH)

During prolonged constant-rate turns, abrupt head movements may set fluid in more than one semicircular canal in motion. This creates the strong sensation of turning or accelerating in an entirely different axis. The sensation, known as Coriolis illusion, causes serious disorientation. Answer (B) is incorrect; the false horizon illusion results from distorted outside visual cues such as sloping cloud layers. The elevator illusion (answer C) is associated with abrupt vertical accelerations.

1-3 J31

A sloping cloud formation, an obscured horizon, and a dark scene spread with ground lights and stars can create an illusion known as

A — elevator illusions.
B — autokinesis.
C — false horizons.

1-3. Answer C. GFDICM 1B (IFH)

A sloping cloud formation, an obscured horizon, a dark scene spread with ground lights and stars, and certain geometric patterns of ground lights can provide inaccurate visual information for aligning the aircraft correctly with the actual horizon. This illusion is known as a false horizon. Answer (A) is incorrect because the elevator illusion is associated with abrupt vertical accelerations. Autokinesis (answer B) is associated with a stationary light that appears to move about when you stare at it for several seconds.

1-4 J31

An abrupt change from climb to straight and level flight can create the illusion of

A — tumbling backwards.
B — a nose up attitude.
C — a descent with the wings level.

1-4. Answer A. GFDICM 1B (IFH)

The inversion illusion can occur when you abruptly change from a climb to straight-and-level flight. This abrupt change can create the feeling of tumbling backward. Answer (B) is incorrect; a nose-up attitude usually is associated with the somatographic illusion. It can be caused by rapid acceleration such as during takeoff. The illusion of a descent with wings level (answer C) is associated with the graveyard spiral illusion. It can result from an observed loss of altitude during a coordinated constant-rate turn that has ceased stimulating the motion sensing system.

1-5 J31

A rapid acceleration during takeoff can create the illusion of

A — spinning in the opposite direction.
B — being in a nose up attitude.
C — diving into the ground.

1-5. Answer B. GFDICM 1B (IFH)

This somatographic illusion usually is associated with rapid acceleration such as that encountered on takeoff and gives you a feeling of being in a nose-up attitude. Answer (A) is incorrect, this sensation usually is associated with the graveyard spin illusion. Diving into the ground (answer C) is a type of somatographic illusion which is associated with rapid deceleration. An abrupt downward vertical acceleration, the result of a downdraft, also can create the illusion of diving.

1-6   J31

Why is hypoxia particularly dangerous during flights with one pilot?

A — Night vision may be so impaired that the pilot cannot see other aircraft.

B — Symptoms of hypoxia may be difficult to recognize before the pilot's reactions are affected.

C — The pilot may not be able to control the aircraft even if using oxygen.

1-6. Answer B. GFDICM 1B (AIM)

An early symptom of hypoxia is impaired judgment. When the onset of hypoxia is rapid, your judgment may be so impaired that you will not recognize other symptoms. While night vision (answer A) begins to deteriorate at altitudes as low as 5,000 feet MSL, this is not the primary danger in single-pilot flying. Besides, an aircraft's anticollision lights are more easily identifiable than other objects not lighted. Answer (C) is incorrect because recovery from hypoxia usually occurs rapidly after you have been given oxygen.

1-7   J31

The sensations which lead to spatial disorientation during instrument flight conditions

A — are frequently encountered by beginning instrument pilots, but never by pilots with moderate instrument experience.

B — occur, in most instances, during the initial period of transition from visual to instrument flight.

C — must be suppressed and complete reliance placed on the indications of the flight instruments.

1-7. Answer C. GFDICM 1B (IFH)

Spatial disorientation can occur anytime there is a lack of outside visual cues. In the absence of reliable visual information you become more aware of information provided by your body's motion and position sensing systems. These systems can be misleading and the only way to overcome spatial disorientation is to rely on the flight instruments. Answer (A) is incorrect because spatial disorientation results from a lack of visual cues, not pilot experience. Answer (B) is not correct since spatial disorientation can occur at any time as a result of a variety of factors.

1-8   J31

How can an instrument pilot best overcome spatial disorientation?

A — Rely on kinesthetic sense.
B — Use a very rapid cross-check.
C — Read and interpret the flight instruments, and act accordingly.

1-8. Answer C. GFDICM 1B (IFH)

Spatial disorientation can occur anytime there is a lack of outside visual cues. In the absence of reliable visual information referenced to the natural horizon, you must read and interpret the flight instruments, and act accordingly. Answer (A) is incorrect because your kinesthetic sense can only feel G forces, but your brain can't tell the difference between gravity or G forces caused by maneuvering. Answer (B) is not correct because unless the flight instruments are read, and interpreted correctly, a very rapid cross-check will do little to help disorientation.

1-9   J31

How can an instrument pilot best overcome spatial disorientation?

A — Use a very rapid cross-check.
B — Properly interpret the flight instruments and act accordingly.
C — Avoid banking in excess of 30°.

1-9. Answer B. GFDICM 1B (IFH)

This question is identical to 1-8. The correct answer (B) is nearly the same, and answer (A) is the same. Answer (C) is not correct; although smaller bank angles may help to minimize the effects of spatial disorientation, reading and interpreting flight instruments will do more to help overcome disorientation.

1-10   J31

A pilot is more subject to spatial disorientation if

A — kinesthetic senses are ignored.
B — eyes are moved often in the process of cross-checking the flight instruments.
C — body signals are used to interpret flight attitude.

1-10. Answer C. GFDICM 1B (IFH)

In the absence of reliable visual information, you become more aware of information provided by your body's motion and position sensing systems. Conflicting information is transmitted to the brain, creating spatial disorientation, especially when the body signals are used to interpret flight attitudes. Answer (A) is incorrect because ignoring the body's kinesthetic sense will help overcome disorientation. Answer (B) is incorrect because a good instrument scan will help overcome spatial disorientation.

1-11   J31

Which procedure is recommended to prevent or overcome spatial disorientation?

A — Reduce head and eye movements to the extent possible.
B — Rely on the kinesthetic sense.
C — Rely on the indications of the flight instruments.

1-11. Answer C. GFDICM 1B (IFH)

See the explanation for Question 1-8. You need to rely on your flight instruments, interpret them properly, and act accordingly. Answer (A) is incorrect; although reducing head movements can help prevent the onset of spatial disorientation, reducing the required eye movements for an instrument scan can affect your ability to read and interpret the flight instruments. Answer (B) is incorrect because when you rely on your kinesthetic sense, you are subject to illusions which can cause spatial disorientation.

1-12   J31

What action should be taken if hyperventilation is suspected?

A — Breathe at a slower rate by taking very deep breaths.
B — Consciously breathe at a slower rate than normal.
C — Consciously force yourself to take deep breaths and breathe at a faster rate than normal.

1-12. Answer B. GFDICM 10A (AFH)

The treatment for hyperventilation involves restoring the proper carbon dioxide level to the body. Slowing the breathing rate down to a normal level is both the best prevention and the best cure. You also can breathe into a paper bag or talk aloud to overcome hyperventilation. Breathing too deep (answers A and C) or too rapidly (answer C) lowers the carbon dioxide level, thus increasing symptoms.

PRINCIPLES OF INSTRUMENT FLIGHT

SECTION A
FLIGHT INSTRUMENT SYSTEMS

1. The instruments which provide information about the airplane's attitude, direction, altitude, and speed are collectively referred to as the flight instruments.

GYROSCOPIC INSTRUMENTS

2. Gyroscopic instrument operation is based on rigidity in space and precession.
3. The gyroscopic instruments are the attitude indicator, heading indicator, and turn coordinator.
4. Prior to engine start, check the turn-and-slip indicator to determine if the needle is approximately centered and the tube is full of fluid. Turn on the master switch and listen for unusual noises from the electrically powered gyro. During taxi turns, the ball should move to the outside of the turn, and the needle should deflect in the direction of the turn.
5. Give the vacuum-driven heading indicator and attitude indicator 5 minutes to spin up during taxi. Make sure that the horizon bar on the attitude indicator tilts no more than 5° during taxi turns, and that the heading indicator maintains proper alignment with the magnetic compass.

ATTITUDE INDICATOR

6. The attitude indicator, or artificial horizon, is the only instrument that gives you an immediate and direct indication of the airplane's pitch and bank attitude.
7. **Pendulous vanes** on vacuum-powered attitude indicators control the outflow of air from ports on the side of the gyro's shaft and near the bottom. Their purpose is to help erect the gyro.
8. Errors in pitch and bank occur because the pendulous vanes act on the attitude indicator's gyro in an undesirable way during turns. These errors are minor; they are most noticeable as the aircraft rolls out of a 180° turn, and cancel after 360° of turn.
9. Acceleration and deceleration also may induce precession errors. During acceleration, the horizon bar moves down, indicating a climb, and during deceleration, the instrument may indicate a slight descent.

HEADING INDICATOR

10. When properly set, the heading indicator is your primary source of heading information.
11. You must align the heading indicator with the magnetic compass before flight and recheck it periodically during flight.

TURN INDICATORS

12. Turn indicators allow you to establish and maintain standard-rate turns of three degrees per second, or in the case of certain high performance aircraft, half-standard-rate turns.
13. Both **turn coordinators** and **turn-and-slip indicators** indicate rate of turn, but because of the improved design of the turn coordinator, this instrument also indicates rate of roll as you enter a turn.
14. One advantage of an electric turn coordinator is that it serves as a backup in case of vacuum system failure.
15. During a constant-bank level turn, an increase in airspeed results in a decreased rate of turn, and an increased turn radius.
16. The inclinometer is the part of the turn indicator that tells whether you are using the correct angle of bank for the rate of turn. Step on the ball to correct a slipping or skidding condition.

MAGNETIC COMPASS

17. The magnetic compass is the only direction-seeking instrument in most light airplanes.
18. **Magnetic dip** is responsible for the most significant compass errors, including **northerly turning error**.
20. To compensate for northerly turning error in the northern hemisphere, you must roll out early on turns to the north, and turn past the compass-indicated heading on turns to the south. Remember the acronym, OSUN (Overshoot South, Undershoot North).
21. If it is necessary to make turns without the aid of a gyroscopic heading indicator, the most accurate way is make a standard-rate timed turn.
22. Another magnetic dip error, **east-west acceleration error** is described by the acronym, ANDS (Accelerate North, Decelerate South). When accelerating on an east-west heading the compass turns to the north and when decelerating, it turns to the south.
23. **Magnetic deviation** is error due to magnetic interference with metal components in the aircraft, as well as magnetic fields from aircraft electrical equipment. It varies for different headings of the same aircraft.

PITOT-STATIC INSTRUMENTS

24. The pitot-static instruments are the airspeed indicator, altimeter, and vertical speed indicator. Blockages in either the pitot or static systems affect the airspeed indicator, while the remaining instruments are affected only by static system blockage.
25. The altimeter and static system, as well as the transponder, must have been inspected within the preceding 24 calendar months before flying IFR.

AIRSPEED INDICATOR

26. The airspeed indicator operates by comparing ram air (pitot) pressure to ambient (static) pressure. Indicated airspeed is the result of this raw measurement.
27. Calibrated airspeed (CAS) is indicated airspeed corrected for installation and instrument errors. Equivalent airspeed (EAS) is calibrated airspeed corrected for compressibility. True airspeed (TAS) is the actual speed your airplane moves through undisturbed air. Mach is the ratio of the aircraft's true airspeed to the speed of sound at the temperature and altitude in which the aircraft is flying.
28. You should use the same indicated airspeed for takeoff, approach and landing at higher elevation airports, even though the corresponding groundspeed is faster.
29. If, while maintaining a constant indicated altitude, you are able to maintain constant power as outside air temperature increases, true airspeed will increase.
30. Design maneuvering speed (V_A) is one important value not shown by the color coding of an airspeed indicator. During operations in turbulence, you should slow the airplane below this speed.
31. If you are flying in visible moisture and your airplane is equipped with pitot heat, it should be on to prevent pitot tube icing. Complete blockage of the pitot tube can cause the airspeed indicator to react opposite of normal, showing runaway airspeed as you climb, and extremely low airspeed in a descent.

ALTIMETER

32. The most common altimeter error is failure to keep it set to the current barometric pressure.
33. It indicates high when the actual pressure is lower than what is set in the window. The altimeter also indicates high when in colder than standard temperature conditions.
34. Before an IFR flight, verify that the altimeter indicates within 75 feet of the actual field elevation when set to the current altimeter setting.
35. Pressure altitude is displayed on the altimeter when it is set to the standard sea level pressure of 29.92 in. Hg. However, to provide for proper vertical separation of aircraft up to 17,999 feet MSL, all pilots should use the local altimeter setting so that their altimeters approximately indicate true altitude. At or above 18,000 feet MSL, all pilots must set their altimeters to 29.92 in. Hg.

VERTICAL SPEED INDICATOR

36. Although the VSI is a very useful instrument, it is not legally required for IFR flight. If this instrument erroneously indicates a climb or descent during taxi, you can simply use the observed value as a zero indication during flight.

2-1 **B07**

Who is responsible for determining that the altimeter system has been checked and found to meet 14 CFR part 91 requirements for a particular instrument flight?

A — Owner.
B — Operator.
C — Pilot in command.

2-1. Answer C. GFDICM 2A (FAR 91.7)

In order for an aircraft to be airworthy for a flight in instrument conditions, the altimeter system must have been inspected within the previous 24 calendar months. Since the pilot in command is responsible for determining the airworthiness of an aircraft, the PIC is also responsible for determining that the altimeter system has been checked. Answers (A) and (B) are wrong because the owner or operator is primarily responsible for maintaining the aircraft in an airworthy condition. FAR 91.7 only references the pilot in command as being responsible for determining an aircraft's airworthiness.

2-2 **B13**

Your aircraft had the static pressure system and altimeter tested and inspected on January 5, of this year, and was found to comply with FAA standards. These systems must be reinspected and approved for use in controlled airspace under IFR by

A — January 5, next year.
B — January 5, 2 years hence.
C — January 31, 2 years hence.

2-2. Answer C. GFDICM 2A (FAR 91.411)

The static pressure and altimeter systems must be tested and inspected every 24 calendar months. If the date of the last inspection was January 5, of this year, the systems must be reinspected by January 31, 2 years hence. Answer (A) is wrong because the time is considerably shorter than the required time. Answer (B) is wrong because it indicates 24 months exactly, not 24 calendar months.

2-3 **B13**

An aircraft altimeter system test and inspection must be accomplished within

A — 12 calendar months.
B — 18 calendar months.
C — 24 calendar months.

2-3. Answer C. GFDICM 2A (FAR 91.411)

See explanation for Question 2-2.

2-4 **B11**

An aircraft operated under 14 CFR part 91 IFR is required to have which of the following?

A — Radar altimeter.
B — Dual VOR system.
C — Gyroscopic direction indicator.

2-4. Answer C. GFDICM 2A (FAR 91.205)

For operations under IFR, the required aircraft equipment includes the instruments and equipment required for visual flight rules plus a two-way radio, navigational equipment appropriate to the ground facilities to be used, a gyroscopic rate-of-turn indicator, a slip-skid indicator, a sensitive altimeter adjustable for barometric pressure, a clock displaying hours, minutes, and seconds with a sweep-second pointer or digital presentation, a generator or alternator of adequate capacity, a gyroscopic pitch and bank indicator, and a gyroscopic direction indicator (directional gyro or equivalent). Answers (A) and (B) are wrong because neither a radar altimeter nor a dual VOR system is required.

2-5   H814

You check the flight instruments while taxiing and find that the vertical speed indicator (VSI) indicates a descent of 100 feet per minute. In this case, you

A — must return to the parking area and have the instrument corrected by an authorized instrument repairman.

B — may take off and use 100 feet descent as the zero indication.

C — may not take off until the instrument is corrected by either the pilot or a mechanic.

2-5. Answer B. GFDICM 2A (IFH)

If the vertical speed indicator (VSI) indicates a descent of 100 feet per minute while taxiing, you may use the 100-foot descent as the zero indication. Answers (A) and (C) are wrong because you can continue your flight and are not required to have repairs made immediately. However, it's a good idea to have this corrected as soon as possible. The VSI should indicate zero during the taxi check.

2-6   I22

Under what condition is pressure altitude and density altitude the same value?

A — At standard temperature.

B — When the altimeter setting is 29.92″ Hg.

C — When indicated, and pressure altitudes are the same value on the altimeter.

2-6. Answer A. GFDICM 2A (IFH)

Density altitude is pressure altitude corrected for nonstandard temperature. Pressure altitude is read on your altimeter when it is set to standard sea level pressure (29.92 in. Hg.). True altitude is the actual height of an object above mean sea level. When standard temperature and pressure exist at a given level, pressure altitude, density altitude, and true altitude will be equal. Answer (B) is wrong because an altimeter setting of 29.92 makes no adjustment for nonstandard temperature. Answer (C) is wrong because indicated and pressure altitudes can only be equal when standard temperature and pressure prevail.

2-7   I22

Under which condition will pressure altitude be equal to true altitude?

A — When the atmospheric pressure is 29.92″ Hg.

B — When standard atmospheric conditions exist.

C — When indicated altitude is equal to the pressure altitude.

2-7. Answer B. GFDICM 2A (IFH)

See explanation for Question 2-6.

2-8   I22

Which condition would cause the altimeter to indicate a lower altitude than actually flown (true altitude)?

A — Air temperature lower than standard.

B — Atmospheric pressure lower than standard.

C — Air temperature warmer than standard.

2-8. Answer C. GFDICM 2A (IFH)

In temperatures that are warmer than standard, your true altitude will be higher than your indicated altitude. In contrast, colder than standard temperatures will result in true altitude being lower than indicated altitude. Answer (A) is wrong because a temperature lower than standard will cause the altimeter to indicate an altitude higher than actual. Answer (B) is wrong because a lower atmospheric pressure will result in a higher indicated altitude.

2-9   I22

When an altimeter is changed from 30.11″ Hg to 29.96″ Hg, in which direction will the indicated altitude change and by what value?

A — Altimeter will indicate 15 feet lower.
B — Altimeter will indicate 150 feet lower.
C — Altimeter will indicate 150 feet higher.

2-9. Answer B. GFDICM 2A (IFH)

In the lower atmosphere, pressure decreases approximately 1″ Hg. for each 1,000-foot increase in altitude. In this case, the indicated altitude will decrease by 150 feet. You can compute this by taking the difference, in inches, between the two altimeter settings and multiplying it by 1,000 (30.11 - 29.96 = .15 × 1,000 = 150). Since the pressure has fallen, the altimeter will also indicate lower with the new setting. Answer (A) is wrong because .15 in. Hg. change is equal to 150 feet, not 15 feet. Answer (C) is wrong because the altimeter will indicate lower, not higher.

2-10   I22

Under what condition will true altitude be lower than indicated altitude with an altimeter setting of 29.92″ Hg?

A — In warmer than standard air temperature.
B — In colder than standard air temperature.
C — When density altitude is higher than indicated altitude.

2-10. Answer B. GFDICM 2A (IFH)

The memory aid, "When flying from a high to a low or hot to cold, look out below," applies in this situation. In air temperatures below standard, true altitude is lower than indicated. At higher than standard temperatures, true altitude is higher than indicated (answer A). Answer (C) is wrong because when the density altitude is higher than indicated altitude, the temperature is higher than standard.

2-11   I22

Which of the following defines the type of altitude used when maintaining FL 210?

A — Indicated.
B — Pressure.
C — Calibrated.

2-11. Answer B. GFDICM 2A (FAR 91.121)

When operating at or above 18,000 feet MSL, you must set the altimeter to 29.92. The altimeter then indicates pressure altitude. Answer (A) is wrong because indicated altitude is what the altimeter reads when the current, local altimeter setting is used. Answer (C) is wrong because calibrated altitude is indicated altitude corrected for instrument error. This error is not routinely compensated for by the pilot.

2-12   H808

Altimeter setting is the value to which the scale of the pressure altimeter is set so the altimeter indicates

A — true altitude at field elevation.
B — pressure altitude at field elevation.
C — pressure altitude at sea level.

2-12. Answer A. GFDICM 2A (AW)

Altimeter setting is the value to which the scale of the pressure altimeter is set so the altimeter indicates true altitude at field elevation. This is important because airport elevations, terrain, and obstructions are charted in true altitude. Answers (B) and (C) are wrong because the correct altimeter setting (below 18,000 feet) should provide an accurate indication of true (not pressure) altitude.

						Form Approved: OMB No. 2120-0034

U.S. DEPARTMENT OF TRANSPORTATION
FEDERAL AVIATION ADMINISTRATION

FLIGHT PLAN

(FAA USE ONLY)	☐ PILOT BRIEFING	☐ VNR	TIME STARTED	SPECIALIST INITIALS
	☐ STOPOVER			

1. TYPE	2. AIRCRAFT IDENTIFICATION	3. AIRCRAFT TYPE/ SPECIAL EQUIPMENT	4. TRUE AIRSPEED	5. DEPARTURE POINT	6. DEPARTURE TIME		7. CRUISING ALTITUDE
VFR X IFR DVFR	N132SM	C 182/	155 KTS	MFR	PROPOSED (Z)	ACTUAL (Z)	8,000

8. ROUTE OF FLIGHT

GNATS 1, MOURN, V121 EUG

9. DESTINATION (Name of airport and city)	10. EST. TIME ENROUTE		11. REMARKS
MAHLON/SWEET FIELD, EUGENE, OR.	HOURS	MINUTES	INSTRUMENT TRAINING FLIGHT

12. FUEL ON BOARD		13. ALTERNATE AIRPORT(S)	14. PILOT'S NAME, ADDRESS & TELEPHONE NUMBER & AIRCRAFT HOME BASE	15. NUMBER ABOARD
HOURS	MINUTES			
			17. DESTINATION CONTACT/TELEPHONE (OPTIONAL)	
		N/R		

16. COLOR OF AIRCRAFT	CIVIL AIRCRAFT PILOTS. FAR Part 91 requires you file an IFR flight plan to operate under instrument flight rules in controlled airspace. Failure to file could result in a civil penalty not to exceed $1,000 for each violation (Section 901 of the Federal Aviation Act of 1958, as amended). Filing of a VFR flight plan is recommended as a good operating practice. See also Part 99 for requirements concerning DVFR flight plans.

FAA Form 7233-1 (8-82)   CLOSE VFR FLIGHT PLAN WITH _____ FSS ON ARRIVAL

AIRCRAFT INFORMATION

MAKE CESSNA   MODEL 182

N 132SM   Vso 57

AIRCRAFT EQUIPMENT/STATUS**

**NOTE: X= OPERATIVE   INOP= INOPERATIVE   N/A= NOT APPLICABLE
TRANSPONDER: X (MODE C) X ILS: (LOCALIZER) X (GLIDE SLOPE) N/A
VOR NO. 1 X (NO. 2) X ADF: X RNAV: N/A
VERTICAL PATH COMPUTER: NA DME: X
MARKER BEACON: (AUDIO) INOP (VISUAL) Inop.

FIGURE 27.—Flight Plan and Aircraft Information.

2-13   H342

(Refer to figures 27 and 28.) What CAS must be used to maintain the filed TAS at the flight planned altitude if the outside air temperature is -5°C?

A — 134 KCAS.
B — 139 KCAS.
C — 142 KCAS.

2-13. Answer B. GFDICM 2A (PHB)

This question requires you to compute knots calibrated airspeed (KCAS). To do this, use the following steps.

1. Enter pressure altitude (8,000 feet).
2. Enter true airspeed (155 kts.).
3. Enter outside air temperature (-5°C).
4. Compute CAS, 139 knots.

Assuming other conditions are the same, answer (A) is wrong since it would require a TAS of 150 knots. Answer (C) is wrong because it would require a TAS of 159 knots.

FLIGHT LOG

MEDFORD - JACKSON CO. AIRPORT TO HAHLON/SWEET FIELD, EUGENE, OR.

CHECK POINTS		ROUTE	COURSE	WIND	SPEED-KTS		DIST	TIME		FUEL	
FROM	TO	ALTITUDE		TEMP	TAS	GS	NM	LEG	TOT	LEG	TOT
MFR	MERLI	GNATS 1 CLIMB	270°		155			:11:0			
	MOURN	V121 8000	333°			AVER. 135					
	RBG	V121 8000	287°								
	OTH	V121 8000	272°								
	EUG	APPROACH DESCENT	026°								
APPROACH & LANDING								:10:0			
	SWEET FIELD										

OTHER DATA: NOTE:				FLIGHT SUMMARY	
	TIME	FUEL (LB)			
MAG. VAR. 20° E.				EN ROUTE	
AVERAGE G.S. 135 KTS. FOR GNATS 1				RESERVE	
DEPARTURE CLIMB.				MISSED APPR.	
				TOTAL	

FIGURE 28.—Flight Planning Log.

2-14   H342

(Refer to figure 32 on page 2-8.) What CAS must be used to maintain the filed TAS at the flight planned altitude if the outside air temperature is +8°C?

A — 154 KCAS.
B — 157 KCAS.
C — 163 KCAS.

2-14. Answer B. GFDICM 2A (PHB)

This question requires you to compute knots calibrated airspeed (KCAS). To do this, use the following steps.

1. Enter pressure altitude (8,000 feet).
2. Enter true airspeed (180 kts.).
3. Enter outside air temperature (+8°C).
4. Compute CAS, 157 knots.

Assuming other conditions are the same, answer (A) is wrong since it would require a TAS of 176 knots. Answer (C) is wrong because it would require a TAS of 186 knots.

FIGURE 32.—Flight Plan and Aircraft Information.

2-15   H342
(Refer to figure 38.) What CAS must be used to maintain the filed TAS at the flight planned altitude if the outside air temperature is +05°C?

A — 129 KCAS.
B — 133 KCAS.
C — 139 KCAS.

2-15. Answer A. GFDICM 2A (PHB)
This question requires you to compute knots calibrated airspeed (KCAS). To do this, use the following steps.

1. Enter pressure altitude (11,000 feet).
2. Enter true airspeed (156 kts.).
3. Enter outside air temperature (+5°C).
4. Compute CAS, 129 knots.

Assuming other conditions are the same, answer (B) is wrong since it would require a TAS of 160 knots. Answer (C) is wrong because it would require a TAS of 167 knots.

Form Approved: OMB No. 2120-0034

U.S. DEPARTMENT OF TRANSPORTATION FEDERAL AVIATION ADMINISTRATION **FLIGHT PLAN**	(FAA USE ONLY)	☐ PILOT BRIEFING ☐ STOPOVER	☐ VNR	TIME STARTED	SPECIALIST INITIALS

1. TYPE	2. AIRCRAFT IDENTIFICATION	3. AIRCRAFT TYPE/ SPECIAL EQUIPMENT	4. TRUE AIRSPEED	5. DEPARTURE POINT	6. DEPARTURE TIME		7. CRUISING ALTITUDE
VFR					PROPOSED (Z)	ACTUAL (Z)	
X IFR DVFR	N4321P	C402/	156 KTS	BGS			11000

8. ROUTE OF FLIGHT

DIRECT BGS, V16 ABI, ABI.AQN2

9. DESTINATION (Name of airport and city)	10. EST. TIME ENROUTE		11. REMARKS
DALLAS FT. WORTH DFW	HOURS	MINUTES	

12. FUEL ON BOARD		13. ALTERNATE AIRPORT(S)	14. PILOT'S NAME, ADDRESS & TELEPHONE NUMBER & AIRCRAFT HOME BASE	15. NUMBER ABOARD
HOURS	MINUTES			
		N/A	17. DESTINATION CONTACT/TELEPHONE (OPTIONAL)	2

16. COLOR OF AIRCRAFT	CIVIL AIRCRAFT PILOTS. FAR Part 91 requires you file an IFR flight plan to operate under instrument flight rules in controlled airspace. Failure to file could result in a civil penalty not to exceed $1,000 for each violation (Section 901 of the Federal Aviation Act of 1958, as amended). Filing of a VFR flight plan is recommended as a good operating practice. See also Part 99 for requirements concerning DVFR flight plans.
RED/BLUE/WHITE	

FAA Form 7233-1 (8-82)   CLOSE VFR FLIGHT PLAN WITH _____ FSS ON ARRIVAL

AIRCRAFT INFORMATION

MAKE Cessna   MODEL 402C

N 4321P   Vso 71

AIRCRAFT EQUIPMENT/STATUS**

**NOTE: X= OPERATIVE   INOP= INOPERATIVE   N/A= NOT APPLICABLE
TRANSPONDER: X (MODE C) X ILS: (LOCALIZER) X (GLIDE SLOPE) X
VOR NO. 1 X (NO. 2) X ADF: X RNAV: X
VERTICAL PATH COMPUTER: N/A DME: X
MARKER BEACON: X (AUDIO) X (VISUAL) X

FIGURE 38.—Flight Plan and Aircraft Information.

2-16   H342

(Refer to figure 44 on page 2-10.) What CAS must be used to maintain the filed TAS at the flight planned altitude if the outside air temperature is +5°C?

A — 147 KCAS.
B — 150 KCAS.
C — 154 KCAS.

2-16. Answer A. GFDICM 2A (PHB)

This question requires you to compute knots calibrated airspeed (KCAS). To do this, use the following steps.

1. Enter pressure altitude (12,000 ft.)
2. Enter true airspeed (180 kts.)
3. Enter outside air temperature (+5°C)
4. Compute CAS, 147 kts.

Assuming other conditions are the same, answer (B) is wrong since it would require a TAS of 184 kts; answer (C) is wrong because it would require a TAS of 154 knots.

```
                                                        Form Approved: OMB No. 2120-0034
┌─────────────────────────────────────────────────────────────────────────────────┐
│ U.S. DEPARTMENT OF TRANSPORTATION  (FAA USE ONLY)  □ PILOT BRIEFING  □ VNR  TIME STARTED  SPECIALIST │
│ FEDERAL AVIATION ADMINISTRATION                                                    INITIALS │
│ FLIGHT PLAN                        □ STOPOVER                                       │
└─────────────────────────────────────────────────────────────────────────────────┘
```

1. TYPE	2. AIRCRAFT IDENTIFICATION	3. AIRCRAFT TYPE/ SPECIAL EQUIPMENT	4. TRUE AIRSPEED	5. DEPARTURE POINT	6. DEPARTURE TIME		7. CRUISING ALTITUDE
VFR					PROPOSED (Z)	ACTUAL (Z)	
X IFR							
DVFR	N3678A	PA31/	180 KTS	YKM			12000

8. ROUTE OF FLIGHT

GROMO 2, HITCH, V468 BTG, DIRECT

9. DESTINATION (Name of airport and city)	10. EST. TIME ENROUTE		11. REMARKS
PORTLAND INTL. AIRPORT PDX	HOURS	MINUTES	INSTRUMENT TRAINING FLIGHT

12. FUEL ON BOARD		13. ALTERNATE AIRPORT(S)	14. PILOT'S NAME, ADDRESS & TELEPHONE NUMBER & AIRCRAFT HOME BASE	15. NUMBER ABOARD
HOURS	MINUTES		17. DESTINATION CONTACT/TELEPHONE (OPTIONAL)	2
		N/A		

16. COLOR OF AIRCRAFT	CIVIL AIRCRAFT PILOTS. FAR Part 91 requires you file an IFR flight plan to operate under instrument flight rules in controlled airspace. Failure to file could result in a civil penalty not to exceed $1,000 for each violation (Section 901 of the Federal Aviation Act of 1958, as amended). Filing of a VFR flight plan is recommended as a good operating practice. See also Part 99 for requirements concerning DVFR flight plans.
GOLD/WHITE	

FAA Form 7233-1 (8-82)   CLOSE VFR FLIGHT PLAN WITH _____ FSS ON ARRIVAL

AIRCRAFT INFORMATION

MAKE Piper   MODEL PA-31

N 3678A   Vso 77

AIRCRAFT EQUIPMENT/STATUS**

**NOTE: X= OPERATIVE   INOP= INOPERATIVE   N/A= NOT APPLICABLE
TRANSPONDER: X (MODE C) X ILS: (LOCALIZER) X (GLIDE SLOPE) X
VOR NO. 1 X (NO. 2) X ADF: X RNAV: X
VERTICAL PATH COMPUTER: N/A DME: X
MARKER BEACON: X (AUDIO) INOP (VISUAL) X

FIGURE 44.—Flight Plan and Aircraft Information.

2-17   H342
(Refer to figure 50.) What CAS must be used to maintain the filed TAS at the flight planned altitude? (Temperature 0°C).

A — 136 KCAS.
B — 140 KCAS.
C — 147 KCAS.

2-17. Answer B. GFDICM 2A (PHB)
This question requires you to compute knots calibrated airspeed (KCAS). To do this use the following steps.

1. Enter pressure altitude (8,000 ft.).
2. Enter true airspeed (158 kts.).
3. Enter outside air temperature (0°C).
4. Compute CAS, 140 kts.

Assuming other conditions are the same, answer (A) is wrong since it would require a TAS of 153 kts. Answer (C) is wrong because it would require a TAS of 166 kts.

Form Approved: OMB No. 2120-0034

FLIGHT PLAN

| U.S. DEPARTMENT OF TRANSPORTATION FEDERAL AVIATION ADMINISTRATION **FLIGHT PLAN** | (FAA USE ONLY) | ☐ PILOT BRIEFING   ☐ STOPOVER | ☐ VNR | TIME STARTED | SPECIALIST INITIALS |

1. TYPE	2. AIRCRAFT IDENTIFICATION	3. AIRCRAFT TYPE/ SPECIAL EQUIPMENT	4. TRUE AIRSPEED	5. DEPARTURE POINT	6. DEPARTURE TIME		7. CRUISING ALTITUDE
VFR					PROPOSED (Z)	ACTUAL (Z)	
X IFR DVFR	N2468	A36/	158 KTS	SBA			8000

8. ROUTE OF FLIGHT

HABUTI GVO, V27 MQO, V113 PRB

9. DESTINATION (Name of airport and city) PASO ROBLES MUNI PRB	10. EST. TIME ENROUTE		11. REMARKS
	HOURS	MINUTES	IFR TRAINING FLIGHT

12. FUEL ON BOARD		13. ALTERNATE AIRPORT(S)	14. PILOT'S NAME, ADDRESS & TELEPHONE NUMBER & AIRCRAFT HOME BASE	15. NUMBER ABOARD
HOURS	MINUTES		17. DESTINATION CONTACT/TELEPHONE (OPTIONAL)	2
		N/A		

| 16. COLOR OF AIRCRAFT GOLD/WHITE | CIVIL AIRCRAFT PILOTS. FAR Part 91 requires you file an IFR flight plan to operate under instrument flight rules in controlled airspace. Failure to file could result in a civil penalty not to exceed $1,000 for each violation (Section 901 of the Federal Aviation Act of 1958, as amended). Filing of a VFR flight plan is recommended as a good operating practice. See also Part 99 for requirements concerning DVFR flight plans. |

FAA Form 7233-1 (8-82)   CLOSE VFR FLIGHT PLAN WITH _____ FSS ON ARRIVAL

AIRCRAFT INFORMATION

MAKE Beechcraft   MODEL A-36

N 2468   Vso 52

AIRCRAFT EQUIPMENT/STATUS**

**NOTE: X= OPERATIVE   INOP= INOPERATIVE   N/A= NOT APPLICABLE
TRANSPONDER: X (MODE C) X ILS: (LOCALIZER) X (GLIDE SLOPE) X
VOR NO. 1 X (NO. 2) X ADF: X RNAV: X
VERTICAL PATH COMPUTER: N/A DME: X
MARKER BEACON: X (AUDIO) X (VISUAL) INOP

FIGURE 50.—Flight Plan and Aircraft Information.

2-18   H342

(Refer to figure 69 on page 2-12.) What CAS should be used to maintain the filed TAS if the outside air temperature is +05°C?

A — 119 KCAS.
B — 124 KCAS.
C — 126 KCAS.

2-18. Answer A. GFDICM 2A (AFH)

This question requires you to compute knots calibrated airspeed (KCAS). To do this, use the following steps.

1. Enter pressure altitude (5,000 ft.)
2. Enter true airspeed (128 kts.)
3. Enter outside air temperature (+5°C)
4. Compute CAS, 119 kts.

Assuming other conditions are the same, answer (B) is wrong since it would require a TAS of 133 kts. Answer (C) is wrong because it would require a TAS of 136 kts.

U.S. DEPARTMENT OF TRANSPORTATION FEDERAL AVIATION ADMINISTRATION	(FAA USE ONLY)	☐ PILOT BRIEFING	☐ VNR	TIME STARTED	SPECIALIST INITIALS

FLIGHT PLAN   Form Approved: OMB No. 2120-0034

☐ STOPOVER

1. TYPE	2. AIRCRAFT IDENTIFICATION	3. AIRCRAFT TYPE/ SPECIAL EQUIPMENT	4. TRUE AIRSPEED	5. DEPARTURE POINT	6. DEPARTURE TIME		7. CRUISING ALTITUDE
VFR				GREENWOOD LAKE	PROPOSED (Z)	ACTUAL (Z)	
X IFR							
DVFR	N2142S	C172/	128 KTS	4N1			5000

8. ROUTE OF FLIGHT

DIRECT SHAFF INT., V213 HELON INT., V58 JUDDS INT., JUDDS2

9. DESTINATION (Name of airport and city)	10. EST. TIME ENROUTE		11. REMARKS
	HOURS	MINUTES	
BRADLEY INTL. BDL			INSTRUMENT TRAINING FLIGHT

12. FUEL ON BOARD		13. ALTERNATE AIRPORT(S)	14. PILOT'S NAME, ADDRESS & TELEPHONE NUMBER & AIRCRAFT HOME BASE	15. NUMBER ABOARD
HOURS	MINUTES			
			17. DESTINATION CONTACT/TELEPHONE (OPTIONAL)	2
		N/A		

16. COLOR OF AIRCRAFT	CIVIL AIRCRAFT PILOTS. FAR Part 91 requires you file an IFR flight plan to operate under instrument flight rules in controlled airspace. Failure to file could result in a civil penalty not to exceed $1,000 for each violation (Section 901 of the Federal Aviation Act of 1958, as amended). Filing of a VFR flight plan is recommended as a good operating practice. See also Part 99 for requirements concerning DVFR flight plans.
BROWN/TAN/WHITE	

FAA Form 7233-1 (8-82)   CLOSE VFR FLIGHT PLAN WITH _____ FSS ON ARRIVAL

AIRCRAFT INFORMATION

MAKE Cessna   MODEL 172

N 2142S   Vso 33

AIRCRAFT EQUIPMENT/STATUS**

**NOTE: X= OPERATIVE   INOP= INOPERATIVE   N/A= NOT APPLICABLE
TRANSPONDER: X (MODE C) X ILS: (LOCALIZER) X (GLIDE SLOPE) X
VOR NO. 1 X (NO. 2) X ADF: X RNAV: N/A
VERTICAL PATH COMPUTER: N/A DME: X
MARKER BEACON: X (AUDIO) INOP (VISUAL) X

FIGURE 69.—Flight Plan and Aircraft Information.

2-19   H342

(Refer to figure 74.) What CAS should be used to maintain the filed TAS at the flight planned altitude if the outside air temperature is +5°C.

A — 129 KCAS.
B — 133 KCAS.
C — 139 KCAS.

2-19. Answer B. GFDICM 2A (PHB)

This question requires you to compute knots calibrated airspeed (KCAS). To do this, use the following steps.

1. Enter pressure altitude (11,000 feet).
2. Enter true airspeed (160 kts.).
3. Enter outside air temperature (+5°C).
4. Computer CAS, 133 knots.

Assuming other conditions are the same, answer (A) is wrong since it would require a TAS of 155 knots. Answer (C) is wrong because it would require a TAS of 167 knots.

FIGURE 74.—Flight Plan and Aircraft Information.

2-20   J26

How should you preflight check the altimeter prior to an IFR flight?

A — Set the altimeter to 29.92″ Hg. With current temperature and the altimeter indication, determine the true altitude to compare with the field elevation.

B — Set the altimeter first with 29.92″ Hg and then the current altimeter setting. The change in altitude should correspond to the change in setting.

C — Set the altimeter to the current altimeter setting. The indication should be within 75 feet of the actual elevation for acceptable accuracy.

2-20. Answer C. GFDICM 2A (IFH)

Set the altimeter to the current altimeter setting. If it is within 75 feet of the actual elevation of your location, the altimeter is acceptable for use. Answer (A) is incorrect because temperature is used to determine density altitude, not true altitude. Answer (B) is incorrect because you are trying to determine the accuracy of your altimeter relative to field elevation, not a change in altitude or setting.

2-21   J26

What is the procedure for setting the altimeter when assigned an IFR altitude of 18,000 feet or higher on a direct flight off airways?

A — Set the altimeter to 29.92″ Hg before takeoff.
B — Set the altimeter to the current altimeter setting until reaching the assigned altitude, then set to 29.92″ Hg.
C — Set the altimeter to the current reported setting for climbout and 29.92″ Hg upon reaching 18,000 feet.

2-21. Answer C. GFDICM 2A (FAR 91.121)

FAR Part 91.121 states that below 18,000 feet MSL, you must set your altimeter to the ". . . current reported altimeter setting of a station along the route and within 100 n.m." or use the ". . . current reported altimeter setting available before departure." Above 18,000 feet MSL, you must set your altimeter to 29.92 in. Hg. Answers (A) and (B) are incorrect since they do not comply with the regulatory requirements.

2-22   J26

En route at FL 290, the altimeter is set correctly, but not reset to the local altimeter setting of 30.57″ Hg during descent. If the field elevation is 650 feet and the altimeter is functioning properly, what is the approximate indication upon landing?

A — 715 feet.
B — 1,300 feet.
C — Sea level.

2-22. Answer C. GFDICM 2A (IFH)

One inch of pressure altitude equals 1,000 feet, and .65 (the difference between 30.57 and 29.92), equals 650 feet. Since your altimeter was not properly reset, you would be 650 feet lower then your actual altitude. For a landing at a field elevation of 650 feet, your indication would be zero (650 feet – 650 feet), or sea level. Answer (A) is wrong since it is 65 feet higher than the field elevation. Answer (B) is also wrong; it is 650 feet higher than the field elevation.

2-23   J26

While you are flying at FL 250, you hear ATC give an altimeter setting of 28.92″ Hg in your area. At what pressure altitude are you flying?

A — 24,000 feet.
B — 25,000 feet.
C — 26,000 feet.

2-23. Answer B. GFDICM 2A (IFH)

When above 18,000 feet MSL, your altimeter should be set to 29.92. In this case, 29.92 provides a pressure altitude of 25,000 feet which is FL 250. Answers (A) and (C) are wrong because they imply an adjustment for the local altimeter setting. By definition, pressure altitude is the indicated altitude when 29.92 in. Hg. is set in the altimeter setting window.

2-24   H808

How can you obtain the pressure altitude on flights below 18,000 feet?

A — Set your altimeter to 29.92″ Hg.
B — Use your computer to change the indicated altitude to pressure altitude.
C — Contact an FSS and ask for the pressure altitude.

2-24. Answer A. GFDICM 2A (IFH)

Pressure altitude is displayed on your altimeter when it is set to the standard sea level atmospheric pressure of 29.92 in. Hg. Answer (B) does not make sense because you need the local altimeter setting to compute pressure altitude. Answer (C) is incorrect because the FSS does not routinely provide pressure altitude information.

2-25   I04

How can you determine the pressure altitude at an airport without a tower or FSS?

A — Set the altimeter to 29.92″ Hg and read the altitude indicated.
B — Set the altimeter to the current altimeter setting of a station within 100 miles and correct this indicated altitude with local temperature.
C — Use your computer and correct the field elevation for temperature.

2-25. Answer A. GFDICM 2A (IFH)

See explanation for Question 2-24. Answer (B) is incorrect because this would result in true altitude. Answer (C) is incorrect because the field elevation is a true altitude. Also, pressure altitude corrects for nonstandard pressure, not temperature.

2-26   H808

Which altitude is indicated when the altimeter is set to 29.92" Hg?

A — Density.
B — Pressure.
C — Standard.

2-26. Answer B. GFDICM 2A (IFH)

See explanation for Question 2-24. Answer (A) is incorrect because density altitude is pressure altitude corrected for nonstandard temperature. Answer (C) is incorrect because there is no such thing as standard altitude. However, you can have standard atmospheric conditions. In this case, true altitude and pressure altitude are equal only when standard atmospheric conditions exist.

2-27   J26

If you are departing from an airport where you cannot obtain an altimeter setting, you should set your altimeter

A — on 29.92" Hg.
B — on the current airport barometric pressure, if known.
C — to the airport elevation.

2-27. Answer C. GFDICM 2A (IFH) (FAR 91.121)

See explanation for Question 2-24. At an airport where you cannot get the current altimeter setting, adjust your altimeter so it shows the field elevation. Answer (A) is wrong since it would give you a pressure altitude. Answer (B) is wrong because even if you knew the barometric setting, you would still have to correct it for the elevation of the airport to get an accurate altimeter setting.

2-28   J26

En route at FL 290, your altimeter is set correctly, but you fail to reset it to the local altimeter setting of 30.26" Hg during descent. If the field elevation is 134 feet and your altimeter is functioning properly, what will it indicate after landing?

A — 100 feet MSL.
B — 474 feet MSL.
C — 206 feet below MSL.

2-28. Answer C. GFDICM 2A (IFH)

The question indicates your altimeter is set correctly at FL 290, meaning it was set at 29.92 in. Hg. The difference between 30.26 and 29.92 (30.26 – 29.92) equals .34. If one inch equals 1,000 feet, .34 equals 340 feet. Since you are still on 29.92, your altimeter would be showing 340 feet below field elevation, or 206 feet below mean sea level (MSL) (134 feet – 340 feet). Pressure altitude is what you read on your altimeter when it is set to the standard sea level setting, 29.92. Local altimeter settings adjust for field elevation above mean sea level. Answer (A) is incorrect because .34 represents 340 feet, not 34 feet. Answer (B) is incorrect because 340 feet is subtracted, not added, to the field elevation of 134 feet.

2-29   J26

How does a pilot normally obtain the current altimeter setting during an IFR flight in Class E airspace below 18,000 feet?

A — The pilot should contact ARTCC at least every 100 NM and request the altimeter setting.
B — FSS's along the route broadcast the weather information at 15 minutes past the hour.
C — ATC periodically advises the pilot of the proper altimeter setting.

2-29. Answer C. GFDICM 2A (AIM)

When an aircraft is enroute on an instrument flight plan, ATC will furnish this information to the pilot at least once while the aircraft is in each controller's airspace. Answer (A) is incorrect because ATC routinely provides IFR aircraft with an altimeter setting. Answer (B) is incorrect because the FSS does not routinely broadcast weather information at 15 minutes past the hour.

2-30   H808
(Refer to figure 83.) Which altimeter depicts 12,000 feet?

A — 2.
B — 3.
C — 4.

2-30. Answer C. GFDICM 2A (IFH)
The depicted altimeter has three hands. The longest has a triangular tip and it indicates 10,000-foot increments; the short, thick hand shows 1,000-foot increments; and the long, thin hand shows 100-foot increments. The 12,000-foot indication is displayed by altimeter 4. Answer (A) is incorrect because the altimeter reads 21,000 feet. Answer (B) is incorrect because the altimeter reads 11,200 feet. You may also notice that the cross-hatched area is improperly displayed in these figures. It should appear only when the altimeter reads below 10,000 feet.

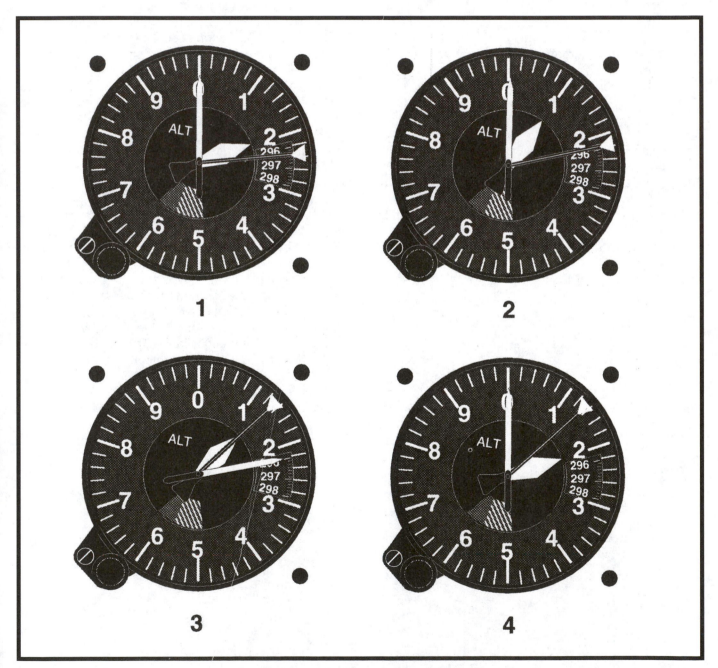

FIGURE 83.—Altimeter/12,000 Feet.

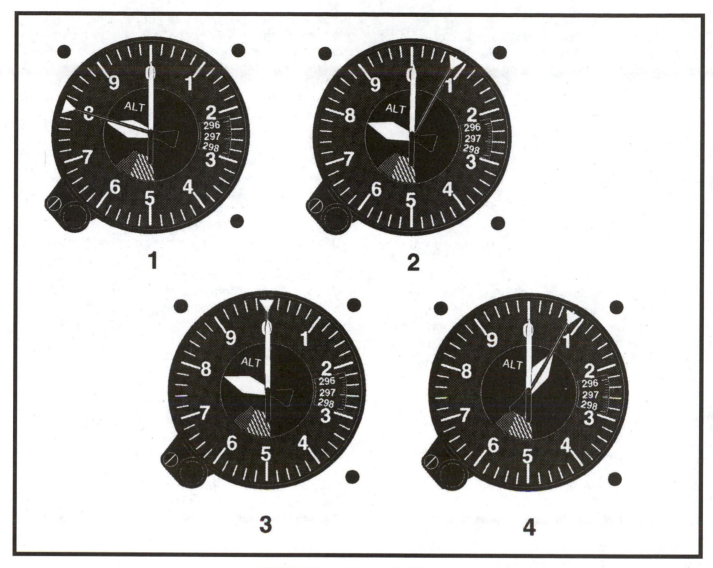

FIGURE 84.—Altimeter/8,000 Feet.

2-31   H808

(Refer to figure 84.) Which altimeter depicts 8,000 feet?

A — 1.
B — 2.
C — 3.

2-32   L57

If both the ram air input and drain hole of the pitot system are blocked, what airspeed indication can be expected?

A — No variation of indicated airspeed in level flight even if large power changes are made.
B — Decrease of indicated airspeed during a climb.
C — Constant indicated airspeed during a descent.

2-31. Answer B. GFDICM 2A (IFH)

See explanation for Question 2-30. Answer (A) shows 88,000 feet, and answer (C) shows an altitude which is below sea level.

2-32. Answer A. GFDICM 2A (AC 91-43)

When both the ram air inlet and drain hole become clogged, the air pressure in the line is trapped and there will be no variation of indicated airspeed, even if large power changes are made. If the static port is open, the airspeed indicator will react the same as an altimeter, showing an increase in airspeed as altitude increases and a decrease in airspeed as altitude decreases. During a climb (answer B), the airspeed will increase, not decrease. During a descent (answer C), the airspeed will decrease instead of remain constant.

2-33   L57
If both the ram air input and the drain hole of the pitot system are blocked, what reaction should you observe on the airspeed indicator when power is applied and a climb is initiated out of severe icing conditions?

A — The indicated airspeed would show a continuous deceleration while climbing.
B — The airspeed would drop to, and remain at, zero.
C — No change until an actual climb rate is established then indicated airspeed will increase.

2-34   H812
What indication should be observed on a turn coordinator during a left turn while taxiing?

A — The miniature aircraft will show a turn to the left and the ball remains centered.
B — The miniature aircraft will show a turn to the left and the ball moves to the right.
C — Both the miniature aircraft and the ball will remain centered.

2-35   H812
On the taxi check, the magnetic compass should

A — swing opposite to the direction of turn when turning from north.
B — exhibit the same number of degrees of dip as the latitude.
C — swing freely and indicate known headings.

2-36   H812
Which condition during taxi is an indication that an attitude indicator is unreliable?

A — The horizon bar tilts more then 5° while making taxi turns.
B — The horizon bar vibrates during warmup.
C — The horizon bar does not align itself with the miniature airplane after warmup.

2-37   H810
What does the miniature aircraft of the turn coordinator directly display?

A — Rate of roll and rate of turn.
B — Angle of bank and rate of turn.
C — Angle of bank.

2-33. Answer C. GFDICM 2A (AC 91-43)
When both the ram air inlet and drain hole become clogged, the air pressure in the line is trapped. There will be no variation of indicated airspeed even with large power changes. In addition, if the static port is open, the airspeed indicator will react the same as an altimeter, showing an increase in airspeed as altitude increases and a decrease in airspeed as altitude decreases. Answer (A) is incorrect since airspeed will increase (not decrease) with altitude. Answer (B) is incorrect since a zero airspeed would indicate that the ram air input is blocked and the drain hole is opened.

2-34. Answer B. GFDICM 2A (IFH)
During taxi turns, the turn coordinator and heading indicator should display a turn in the correct direction. The ball in the inclinometer should swing to the outside of the turn. Therefore, in a left turn, the miniature aircraft shows a turn to the left and the ball moves to the right. Answer (A) is incorrect because the ball in the inclinometer should move freely and swing to the outside of the turn. Answer (C) is more representative of an inoperative instrument and is incorrect.

2-35. Answer C. GFDICM 2A (IFH)
Prior to flight, make sure the compass is full of fluid. During taxi, the compass should swing freely and indicate known headings while taxiing straight or stopped. Answers (A) and (B) are incorrect because magnetic dip (which causes northerly turning error) becomes effective only when the compass card is tilted from the horizontal plane. This an only occur in flight.

2-36. Answer A. GFDICM 2A (IFH)
After starting the engines the gyros normally reach full operating speed in approximately five minutes. During this time, it is common to see some vibration in the instruments. After warmup and during normal taxi turns, the attitude indicator should not tilt more than 5° while on level ground. Answer (B) is incorrect since vibration during warmup is common and should be considered a normal occurrence. Answer (C) is incorrect because the miniature airplane often does not align with the horizontal bar after warmup. When this is the case, you should use the manual adjustment on the miniature airplane to align it.

2-37. Answer A. GFDICM 2A (IFH)
The gimbal in the turn coordinator is set at an angle, or canted. This allows gyro precession to sense both rate of roll and rate of turn. Answers (B) and (C) are not correct because information about angle of bank is not provided by the turn coordinator.

2-38   H812

What pre-takeoff check should be made of the attitude indicator in preparation for an IFR flight?

A — The horizon bar does not vibrate during warmup.
B — The miniature airplane should erect and become stable within 5 minutes.
C — The horizon bar should erect and become stable within 5 minutes.

2-39   H807

During a skidding turn to the right, what is the relationship between the component of lift, centrifugal force, and load factor?

A — Centrifugal force is less than horizontal lift and the load factor is increased.
B — Centrifugal force is greater than horizontal lift and the load factor is increased.
C — Centrifugal force and horizontal lift are equal and the load factor is decreased.

2-40   H810

What indications are displayed by the miniature aircraft of a turn coordinator?

A — Rate of roll and rate of turn.
B — Direct indication of bank angle and pitch attitude.
C — Indirect indication of bank angle and pitch attitude.

2-41   L57

What indication should a pilot observe if an airspeed indicator ram air input and drain hole are blocked?

A — The airspeed indicator will react as an altimeter.
B — The airspeed indicator will show a decrease with an increase in altitude.
C — No airspeed indicator change will occur during climbs or descents.

2-38. Answer C. GFDICM 2A (IFH)

See explanation for Question 2-36. After starting the engines the gyros normally reach full operating speed in approximately five minutes. During this time, it is common to see some vibration in the instruments. When the gyros have stabilized, the horizon bar in the attitude indicator should stop vibrating and remain level within 5° while the airplane is stopped or taxiing straight ahead on level ground. Vibration during warmup (answer A) is common and should be considered a normal occurrence. Answer (B) is incorrect since the miniature airplane is connected to the face of the instrument and not the gyro. With the exception of the vertical adjustment for correct pitch reference, it does not move.

2-39. Answer B. GFDICM 2A (IFH)

During a skid, centrifugal force exceeds the horizontal component of lift. This will make the rate of turn too great for the angle of bank. As a result the ball of the inclinometer moves to the outside of the turn, and load factor increases. Answer (A) is wrong because in situations where centrifugal force is less than the horizontal component of lift, a slip (not skid) would result. Also, the load factor would decrease. When centrifugal force and the horizontal component of lift are equal (answer C), the aircraft is in a coordinated turn so there would be no slip or skid, and the load factor would not change.

2-40. Answer A. GFDICM 2A (IFH)

The gimbal in the turn coordinator is set at an angle, or canted. This allows gyro precession to sense both rate of roll and rate of turn. Answer (B) corresponds more to an attitude indicator and is incorrect. The turn coordinator indirectly displays bank information. Answer (C) is incorrect because although the miniature aircraft on the turn coordinator provides an indirect indication of bank angle, it does not provide information on pitch.

2-41. Answer A. GFDICM 2A (AC 91-43)

If both the ram air input and the drain hole of a pitot tube become blocked simultaneously, the airspeed indicator will react like an altimeter. This means that a climb will result in an increase in indicated airspeed, while a descent will result in a decrease in indicated airspeed. Answer (B) is wrong because indicated airspeed will increase with an increase in altitude. Answer (C) is wrong because indicated airspeed varies with changes in altitude.

2-42   H816

What indication is presented by the miniature aircraft of the turn coordinator?

A — Indirect indication of the bank attitude.
B — Direct indication of the bank attitude and the quality of the turn.
C — Quality of the turn.

2-43   H810

During normal operation of a vacuum-driven attitude indicator, what attitude indication should you see when rolling out from a 180° skidding turn to straight-and-level coordinated flight?

A — A straight-and-level coordinated flight indication.
B — A nose-high indication relative to level flight.
C — The miniature aircraft shows a turn in the direction opposite the skid.

2-44   I04

During normal coordinated turns, what error due to precession should you observe when rolling out to straight-and-level flight from a 180° steep turn to the right?

A — A straight-and-level coordinated flight indication.
B — The miniature aircraft would show a slight turn indication to the left.
C — The miniature aircraft would show a slight descent and wings-level attitude.

2-45   H810

What information does a Mach meter present?

A — The ratio of aircraft true airspeed to the speed of sound.
B — The ratio of aircraft indicated airspeed to the speed of sound.
C — The ratio of aircraft equivalent airspeed, corrected for installation error, to the speed of sound.

2-42. Answer A. GFDICM 2A (IFH)

The turn coordinator gives an indirect indication of the aircraft's bank attitude, while the miniature airplane of a turn coordinator provides a direct indication of an aircraft's rate of turn. When the miniature airplane is aligned with the turn index, you are in a standard-rate turn (3° per second). The inclinometer portion of the turn coordinator displays the quality of a turn (answers B and C).

2-43. Answer C. GFDICM 2A (IFH)

In attitude indicators, a skidding turn precesses the gyro to the inside of the turn. When an aircraft returns to straight-and-level flight from a skidding turn, the miniature airplane will show a turn in the direction opposite the skid. Answer (A) is wrong because is doesn't account for the precession of the gyro. Answer (B) is wrong because a slight climb is experienced after rollout to straight-and-level flight from a normal coordinated turn, not a skidding turn.

2-44. Answer B. GFDICM 2A (IFH)

Centrifugal force in a turn can cause some attitude indicators to precess, creating errors in both pitch and bank. The effect is greatest in a 180° steep turn. For example, when rolling out of a 180° steep turn to straight-and-level flight, the attitude indicator will show a slight climb and turn in the opposite direction. Answer (A) is wrong because it does not account for the effects of precession. Answer (C) is wrong because a slight climb would be shown, not a slight descent, and a wings-level attitude would not be indicated.

2-45. Answer A. GFDICM 2A (IFH)

In high performance aircraft, some limiting airspeeds are based on a relationship to the speed of sound. These aircraft usually have a Mach indicator or Mach meter in addition to an airspeed indicator. Mach indicators simply show the ratio of the aircraft's true airspeed to the speed of sound at the flight altitude. Answers (B) and (C) are wrong because neither indicated airspeed nor equivalent airspeed are taken into consideration.

2-46   H807

What is the relationship between centrifugal force and the horizontal lift component in a coordinated turn?

A — Horizontal lift exceeds centrifugal force.
B — Horizontal lift and centrifugal force are equal.
C — Centrifugal force exceeds horizontal lift.

2-46. Answer B. GFDICM 2A (IFH)

During a turn lift can be divided into two components, a vertical component and a horizontal component. Weight opposes the vertical component of lift while centrifugal force opposes the horizontal component. Once established in the turn, the horizontal component of lift and centrifugal force will be equal. Answer (A) is wrong because the horizontal component of lift exceeds centrifugal force during a slip. Answer (C) is wrong because centrifugal force exceeds the horizontal component of lift during a skid.

2-47   H807

What force causes an airplane to turn?

A — Rudder pressure or force around the vertical axis.
B — Vertical lift component.
C — Horizontal lift component.

2-47. Answer C. GFDICM 2A (IFH)

During a turn lift can be divided into two components, a vertical component and a horizontal component. The vertical component of lift, (answer B), opposes weight, while the horizontal component, which opposes centrifugal force, causes the airplane to turn. Answer (A) is wrong because rudder pressure controls yaw around the vertical axis and helps improve the quality of a turn.

2-48   H809

What should be the indication on the magnetic compass as you roll into a standard rate turn to the left from an east heading in the Northern Hemisphere?

A — The compass will initially indicate a turn to the right.
B — The compass will remain on east for a short time, then gradually catch up to the magnetic heading of the aircraft.
C — The compass will indicate the approximate correct magnetic heading if the roll into the turn is smooth.

2-48. Answer C. GFDICM 2A (IFH)

In the northern hemisphere, compass turning errors are most apparent when turning from a heading of north or south. For example, when making a turn from a northerly heading, the compass will give an initial indication of a turn in the opposite direction (answer A). When making a turn from a southerly heading, the compass will give an indication of a turn in the correct direction, but it will lead the actual heading. On headings of east or west, these turning errors are minimized. Answer (B) is wrong because the compass will not remain on an east heading and then gradually catch up.

2-49   H808

What would be the indication on the VSI during entry into a 500 FPM actual descent from level flight if the static ports were iced over?

A — The indication would be in reverse of the actual rate of descent (500 FPM climb).
B — The initial indication would be a climb, then descent at a rate in excess of 500 FPM.
C — The VSI pointer would remain at zero regardless of the actual rate of descent.

2-49. Answer C. GFDICM 2A (IFH)

If the static port is iced over, the airspeed indicator will still indicate changes in airspeed, but they will not be correct. When operating above the altitude where the static port became clogged, the airspeed will read lower than it should. Conversely, when you are operating below that altitude, the indicator will read higher than the correct value. A blocked static port will also freeze the altimeter at the altitude the blockage occurred, and the vertical speed indicator (VSI) will freeze at zero showing no indication of a descent or a climb. Answers (A) and (B) are wrong because a descent would not be indicated on the VSI.

2-50   H812
How should you preflight check the altimeter prior to an IFR flight?

A — Set the altimeter to the current temperature. With current temperature and the altimeter indication, determine the calibrated altitude to compare with the field elevation.
B — Set the altimeter first with 29.92″ Hg and then the current altimeter setting. The change in altitude should correspond to the change in setting.
C — Set the altimeter to the current altimeter setting. The indication should be within 75 feet of the actual elevation for acceptable accuracy.

2-51   L59
Which practical test should be made on the electric gyro instruments prior to starting an engine?

A — Check that the electrical connections are secure on the back of the instruments.
B — Check that the attitude of the miniature aircraft is wings level before turning on electrical power.
C — Turn on the electrical power and listen for any unusual or irregular mechanical noise.

2-52   L59
Prior to starting an engine, you should check the turn-and-slip indicator to determine if the

A — needle indication properly corresponds to the angle of the wings or rotors with the horizon.
B — needle is approximately centered and the tube is full of fluid.
C — ball will move freely from one end of the tube to the other when the aircraft is rocked.

2-53   L59
What indications should you observe on the turn-and-slip indicator during taxi?

A — The ball moves freely opposite the turn, and the needle deflects in the direction of the turn.
B — The needle deflects in the direction of the turn, but the ball remains centered.
C — The ball deflects opposite the turn, but the needle remains centered.

2-54   H807
Which instrument indicates the quality of a turn?

A — Attitude indicator.
B — Heading indicator or magnetic compass.
C — Ball of the turn coordinator.

2-50. Answer C. GFDICM 2A (IFH)
Prior to taking off, you should check the altimeter for the proper reading. To do this, set the altimeter to the current altimeter setting and check to see that the indicated altitude is within 75 feet of the actual field elevation. If it is, the altimeter is generally considered acceptable for use, provided other required inspections have been accomplished. Answer (A) is wrong because you cannot set the altimeter to the current temperature and there is no need to compute the calibrated altitude. Answer (B) is wrong because there is no need to set the altimeter to 29.92 and compare pressure altitude to field elevation.

2-51. Answer C. GFDICM 2A (AC 91-46)
Prior to starting an engine, turn on the electrical power and listen for any unusual noises from the electrical gyros. Answer (A) is wrong because only a certified technician or mechanic should check electrical connections behind the instrument panel. Answer (B) is wrong because checking for a wings-level attitude on the miniature airplane of the turn coordinator requires electrical power.

2-52. Answer B. GFDICM 2A (AC 91-46)
Prior to starting an aircraft, check to make sure the needle of the turn-and-slip indicator is centered and the inclinometer is full of fluid. Answer (A) is wrong because the needle should be approximately centered, regardless of the angle of the wings. Answer (C) is wrong because the inclinometer should be checked during taxi.

2-53. Answer A. GFDICM 2A (IFH)
When turning during ground operations, centrifugal force will cause the gyro in a turn-and-slip indicator to precess and deflect the needle in the direction of the turn. In addition, the centrifugal force also will cause the ball in the inclinometer to move in the opposite direction of the turn. Answer (B) is wrong because centrifugal force will deflect the ball to the outside of the turn. Answer (C) is wrong because the needle will deflect in the direction of the turn.

2-54. Answer C. GFDICM 2A (PHB)
The inclinometer (ball of the turn coordinator) shows the relationship between the opposing horizontal forces in a turn. This provides an indication of the quality of a turn. Answer (A) is wrong because the attitude indicator indicates pitch and bank, not the coordination or quality of a turn. Answer (B) is wrong because the heading indicator and magnetic compass indicate direction in relationship to magnetic north.

2-55 **H812**

What pretakeoff check should be made of a vacuum-driven heading indicator in preparation for an IFR flight?

A — After 5 minutes, set the indicator to the magnetic heading of the aircraft and check for proper alignment after taxi turns.

B — After 5 minutes, check that the heading indicator card aligns itself with the magnetic heading of the aircraft.

C — Determine that the heading indicator does not precess more than 2° in 5 minutes of ground operation.

2-56 **H314**

What should be the indication on the magnetic compass as you roll into a standard rate turn to the right from an easterly heading in the Northern Hemisphere?

A — The compass will initially indicate a turn to the left.

B — The compass will remain on east for a short time, then gradually catch up to the magnetic heading of the aircraft.

C — The compass will indicate the approximate correct magnetic heading if the roll into the turn is smooth.

2-57 **H314**

What should be the indication on the magnetic compass as you roll into a standard rate turn to the right from a south heading in the Northern Hemisphere?

A — The compass will indicate a turn to the right, but at a faster rate than is actually occurring.

B — The compass will initially indicate a turn to the left.

C — The compass will remain on south for a short time, then gradually catch up to the magnetic heading of the aircraft.

2-58 **H314**

On what headings will the magnetic compass read most accurately during a level 360° turn, with a bank of approximately 15°?

A — 135° through 225°.

B — 90° and 270°.

C — 180° and 0°.

2-55. Answer A. GFDICM 2A (IFH)

Once the aircraft is started, the vacuum-driven gyros should reach full operating speed within 5 minutes. After this time, set the heading indicator to the magnetic heading as indicated on the compass. While taxiing, make sure the heading indicator maintains its proper alignment after each turn. Answer (B) is wrong because, unless the heading indicator is slaved to the magnetic compass, it must be initially set to the correct heading. Answer (C) is wrong because it is normal for the heading indicator to precess and, therefore, it should be checked and reset, if necessary every 15 minutes during flight.

2-56. Answer C. GFDICM 2A (IFH)

In the northern hemisphere, compass turning errors are most apparent when turning from a heading of north or south. For example, when making a turn from a northerly heading, the compass will give an initial indication of a turn in the opposite direction (answer A). When making a turn from a southerly heading, the compass will give an indication of a turn in the correct direction, but it will lead the actual heading. On headings of east or west, these turning errors are minimized. Answer (B) is wrong because the compass will not remain on an east heading and then gradually catch up to the magnetic heading of the aircraft.

This is similar to Question 2-48.

2-57. Answer A. GFDICM 2A (IFH)

See explanation for Question 2-56. During turns from a heading of south, in the northern hemisphere the compass will lead the actual heading of the aircraft. Answer (B) is wrong because the compass initially indicates a turn in the opposite direction and then lags behind the heading of the aircraft when turning from a heading of north. Answer (C) is wrong because the compass will not remain on south and then catch up to the aircraft's heading.

2-58. Answer B. GFDICM 2A (IFH)

See explanation for Question 2-56. In the northern hemisphere, compass turning errors are most apparent when turning from a heading of north or south (answer C). On easterly or westerly headings, the compass turning errors are minimal. Answer (A) is wrong because 135° and 225° are southeasterly and southwesterly headings.

2-59   H809

What causes the northerly turning error in a magnetic compass?

A — Coriolis force at the mid-latitudes.
B — Centrifugal force acting on the compass card.
C — The magnetic dip characteristic.

2-59. Answer C. GFDICM 2A (IFH)

In the northern hemisphere, compass turning errors are most apparent when turning from a heading of north or south. This error increases as you near the poles due to magnetic dip and the vertical component of the earth's magnetic field. Answer (A) is wrong because Coriolis force is a factor in wind direction, not compass indications. Answer (B) is wrong because centrifugal force is unrelated to compass northerly turning errors.

2-60   H314

What should be the indication on the magnetic compass when you roll into a standard rate turn to the left from a south heading in the Northern Hemisphere?

A — The compass will indicate a turn to the left, but at a faster rate than is actually occurring.
B — The compass will initially indicate a turn to the right.
C — The compass will remain on south for a short time, then gradually catch up to the magnetic heading of the aircraft.

2-60. Answer A. GFDICM 2A (IFH)

In the northern hemisphere, compass turning errors are most apparent when turning from a heading of north or south. For example, when making a turn from a southerly heading, the compass will give an indication of a turn in the correct direction, but it will lead the actual heading. When making a turn from a northerly heading, the compass will give an initial indication of a turn in the opposite direction (answer B). On headings of east or west, these turning errors are minimized. Answer (C) is wrong because the compass will not remain on a south heading and then gradually catch up to the magnetic heading of the aircraft.

This is similar to Question 2-57.

2-61   H314

What should be the indication on the magnetic compass as you roll into a standard rate turn to the right from a westerly heading in the Northern Hemisphere?

A — The compass will initially show a turn in the opposite direction, then turn to a northerly indication but lagging behind the actual heading of the aircraft.
B — The compass will remain on a westerly heading for a short time, then gradually catch up to the actual heading of the aircraft.
C — The compass will indicate the approximate correct magnetic heading if the roll into the turn is smooth.

2-61. Answer C. GFDICM 2A (IFH)

In the northern hemisphere, compass turning errors are most apparent when turning from a heading of north or south. On easterly or westerly headings, compass turning errors are minimal. Answer (A) is wrong because it indicates what would happen when making a turn from a northerly heading. Answer (B) is wrong because the compass will not remain on a westerly heading then gradually catch up to the actual heading.

2-62   H314

What should be the indication on the magnetic compass as you roll into a standard rate turn to the right from a northerly heading in the Northern Hemisphere?

A — The compass will indicate a turn to the right, but at a faster rate than is actually occurring.
B — The compass will initially indicate a turn to the left.
C — The compass will remain on north for a short time, then gradually catch up to the magnetic heading of the aircraft.

2-62. Answer B. GFDICM 2A (IFH)

In the northern hemisphere, compass turning errors are most apparent when turning from a heading of north or south. For example, when making a turn from a northerly heading, the compass will give an initial indication of a turn in the opposite direction. When making a turn from a southerly heading, the compass will give an indication of a turn in the correct direction, but it will lead the actual heading (answer A). Answer (C) is wrong because the compass will not remain on a northerly heading and then gradually catch up to the magnetic heading of the aircraft.

2-63   H314

What should be the indication on the magnetic compass as you roll into a standard rate turn to the left from a west heading in the Northern Hemisphere?

A — The compass will initially indicate a turn to the right.

B — The compass will remain on west for a short time, then gradually catch up to the magnetic heading of the aircraft.

C — The compass will indicate the approximate correct magnetic heading if the roll into the turn is smooth.

2-64   H314

What should be the indication on the magnetic compass as you roll into a standard rate turn to the left from a north heading in the Northern Hemisphere.

A — The compass will indicate a turn to the left, but at a faster rate than is actually occurring.

B — The compass will initially indicate a turn to the right.

C — The compass will remain on north for a short time, then gradually catch up to the magnetic heading of the aircraft.

2-65   H810

If a half-standard rate turn is maintained, how long would it take to turn 360°?

A — 1 minute.
B — 2 minutes.
C — 4 minutes.

2-66   I05

If a standard rate turn is maintained, how long would it take to turn 180°?

A — 1 minute.
B — 2 minutes.
C — 3 minutes.

2-67   H810

If a half-standard rate turn is maintained, how much time would be required to turn clockwise from a heading of 090° to a heading of 180°?

A — 30 seconds.
B — 1 minute.
C — 1 minute 30 seconds.

2-63. Answer C. GFDICM 2A (IFH)
See explanation for Questions 2-61 and 2-62.

2-64. Answer B. GFDICM 2A (IFH)
See explanation for Question 2-62.

2-65. Answer C. GFDICM 2A (IFH)
A standard-rate turn is 3° per second. At this rate, you will complete a 180° turn in one minute and a 360° turn in two minutes. A half-standard-rate turn will result in a turn rate of one point five degrees (1.5°) per second. If this is maintained, you will complete a 180° turn in two minutes (answer B) and a 360° turn in 4 minutes. Answer (A) is wrong because in order to complete a 360° turn in one minute, you need a turn rate of six degrees per second, or double that of a standard-rate turn.

2-66. Answer A. GFDICM 2A (IFH)
See explanation for Question 2-65. Answers (B) and (C) are wrong because they require turns that are less than standard rate.

2-67. Answer B. GFDICM 2A (IFH)
See explanation for Question 2-65. A clockwise turn from 090° to 180° is 90°. At a standard rate, the turn will be completed in 30 seconds (answer A). If a half-standard-rate turn is used, the same turn will require one minute. Answer (C) is wrong because in order to complete a 90° turn in one minute 30 seconds, you must make the turn at a rate less than half-standard.

2-68   H810

Errors in both pitch and bank indication on an attitude indicator are usually at a maximum as the aircraft rolls out of a

A – 180° turn.
B – 270° turn.
C – 360° turn.

2-68. Answer A. GFDICM 2A (IFH)

Centrifugal force in a turn can cause some attitude indicators to precess, creating errors in both pitch and bank. These errors are usually minor and result in deviations of no more than five degrees of bank and one bar-width of pitch. The effect is greatest in a 180° steep turn. Answers (B) and (C) are wrong because in a turn greater than 180°, precession in the opposite direction will begin to cancel out the precession created in the first 180° of turn.

2-69   H810

If a 180° steep turn is made to the right and the aircraft is rolled out to straight-and-level flight by visual references, the attitude indicator

A – should immediately show straight-and-level flight.
B – will show a slight skid and climb to the right.
C – may show a slight climb and turn.

2-69. Answer C. GFDICM 2A (IFH)

Centrifugal force in a turn can cause some attitude indicators to precess, creating errors in both pitch and bank. These errors are usually minor and result in deviations of no more than 5 degrees of bank and one bar-width of pitch. The effect is greatest in a 180° steep turn. For example, when you roll out of a 180° steep turn to straight-and-level flight. The attitude indicator may show a slight climb and turn.

2-70   H810

One characteristic that a properly functioning gyro depends upon for operation is the

A — ability to resist precession 90° to any applied force.
B — resistance to deflection of the spinning wheel or disc.
C — deflecting force developed from the angular velocity of the spinning wheel.

2-70. Answer B. GFDICM 2A (IFH)

Gyros are affected by two principles — rigidity in space and precession. Rigidity in space means that once a gyro is spinning, it tends to remain in a fixed position and resists external forces applied to it. This principle allows a gyroscope to be used to measure changes in attitude or direction. Answer (A) is incorrect because precession is the reaction to an applied force, not resistance to the force. Answer (C) is wrong because deflective force is applied to the gyro, not developed by it.

2-71   I05

If a standard rate turn is maintained, how much time would be required to turn to the right from a heading of 090° to a heading of 270°?

A — 1 minute.
B — 2 minutes.
C — 3 minutes.

2-71. Answer A. GFDICM 2A (AIM)

A standard-rate turn is a turn at a rate of three degrees per second. At this rate, you will complete a 360° turn in two minutes. Since the heading change in this question is 180° (270 – 090 = 180), it will take one minute to complete the standard-rate turn. Answer (B) is wrong because to make a 180° turn in two minutes, you would have to turn at a rate half that of standard. Answer (C) is wrong because three minutes significantly exceeds the one minute required.

2-72   H807

If a standard rate turn is maintained, how much time would be required to turn to the left from a heading of 090° to a heading of 300°?

A — 30 seconds.
B — 40 seconds.
C — 50 seconds.

2-72. Answer C. GFDICM 2A (AIM)

See explanation for Question 2-71. The degree of heading change in this example is 150° (360 − 300 = 60 + 90 = 150). Since a standard-rate turn results in a turn rate of 3 degrees per second, the time to turn 150° is 50 seconds (150 ÷ 3 = 50). Answer (A) is wrong because it represents the time to make a 90° turn. Answer (B) is wrong because it represents the time to make a 120° turn.

2-73   I04

If a half-standard rate turn is maintained, how long would it take to turn 135°.

A — 1 minute.
B — 1 minute 20 seconds.
C — 1 minute 30 seconds.

2-73. Answer C. GFDICM 2A (AIM)

If a standard-rate turn is 3 degrees per second, a half-standard-rate turn results in a 1-1/2 degrees per second turn. At a half-standard-rate turn, it will take one minute thirty seconds to turn 135° (135 ÷ 1-1/2 = 90 seconds). Answers (A) and (B) are wrong because they represent the times required for a turn rate greater than the half-standard rate.

2-74   H859

If, while in level flight, it becomes necessary to use an alternate source of static pressure vented inside the airplane, which of the following should the pilot expect?

A — The gyroscospic instruments to become inoperative.
B — The altimeter and airspeed indicator to become inoperative.
C — The vertical speed to momentarily show a climb.

2-74. Answer C. GFDICM 2A (IFH)

Due to slipstream, the pressure inside the cabin is less than that of the outside air. If an alternate static source is selected that is inside the aircraft, the altimeter will read a little high, the airspeed a little fast, and the vertical speed indicator (VSI) will initially indicate a climb. Answer (A) is incorrect because gyroscopic instruments are not affected. Answer (B) is incorrect because these instruments will not be as accurate, but will continue to operate.

2-75   H808

During flight, if the pitot-tube becomes clogged with ice, which of the following instruments would be affected?

A — The airspeed indicator only.
B — The airspeed indicator and the altimeter.
C — The airspeed indicator, altimeter, and Vertical Speed Indicator.

2-75. Answer A. GFDICM 2A (IFH)

The airspeed indicator is the only instrument affected by a pitot tube blockage. There are two ways the system can become blocked. First, the ram air inlet can clog, while the drain hole remains open. In this situation, the pressure in the line to the airspeed indicator will vent out the drain hole, causing the airspeed indicator to drop to zero. The second situation occurs when both the ram air inlet and drain hole become blocked. When this occurs, the air pressure in the line is trapped and, during level flight, the airspeed indicator no longer indicates changes in airspeed. Answers (B) and (C) are wrong because the altimeter and vertical speed indicator are not affected by pitot tube blockage.

2-76   H312

The local altimeter setting should be used by all pilots in a particular area, primarily to provide for

A — the cancellation of altimeter error due to nonstandard temperatures aloft.
B — better vertical separation of aircraft.
C — more accurate terrain clearance in mountainous areas.

2-76. Answer B. GFDICM 2A (IFH)

The altimeter setting system provides you with the means to correct your altimeter for pressure variations. The system is necessary to ensure safe terrain clearance for instrument approaches and landings, and to maintain vertical separation between aircraft during instrument weather. Answer (A) is incorrect because temperature is not corrected by an altimeter setting. Answer (C) is incorrect because it is important to have accurate terrain clearance during all phases of instrument flight, not just in mountainous areas.

2-77   H808

At an altitude of 6,500 feet MSL, the current altimeter setting is 30.42" Hg. The pressure altitude would be approximately

A — 7,500 feet.
B — 6,000 feet.
C — 6,500 feet.

2-77. Answer B. GFDICM 2A (IFH)

To find the current pressure altitude, compute the difference between the current altimeter setting and 29.92. In this example it's .50 inches (30.42 – 29.92 = .50). Since the pressure decreases about one inch for every 1,000-foot increase in altitude, .50 inches is equivalent to about 500 feet. With a current altimeter setting above standard (30.42) you need to subtract 500 feet from the indicated altitude of 6,500 feet. The answer is 6,000 feet (6,500 – 500 = 6,000). Answer (A) is wrong because the current altimeter setting would have to be 28.92 for this answer to be correct. Answer (C) is wrong because the difference between the current setting and standard pressure was not subtracted.

2-78   H808

The pressure altitude at a given location is indicated on the altimeter after the altimeter is set to

A — the field elevation.
B — 29.92" Hg.
C — the current altimeter setting.

2-78. Answer B. GFDICM 2A (AW)

Pressure altitude is always referenced to the standard datum plane where the barometric pressure is 29.92 in. Hg. Answers (A) and (C) are incorrect because field elevation will be indicated when you use the current altimeter setting.

2-79   H808

If the outside air temperature increases during a flight at constant power and at a constant indicated altitude, the true airspeed will

A — decrease and true altitude will increase.
B — increase and true altitude will decrease.
C — increase and true altitude will increase.

2-79. Answer C. GFDICM 2A (IFH)

True airspeed compensates for nonstandard pressure and temperature and represents the true speed of your airplane through the air. As atmospheric pressure decreases or air temperature increases, the density of the air decreases. As the air density decreases at a given indicated airspeed, true airspeed increases.

True altitude is the actual height of an object above mean sea level. Your altimeter displays true altitude only under standard conditions. As temperatures increase, true altitude also increases. Answer (A) is wrong because true airspeed increases with increases in temperature. Answer (B) is wrong because true altitude increases with increases in temperature.

2-80   H66

If severe turbulence is encountered during your IFR flight, the airplane should be slowed to the design maneuvering speed because the

A — maneuverability of the airplane will be increased.
B — amount of excess load that can be imposed on the wing will be decreased.
C — airplane will stall at a lower angle of attack, giving an increased margin of safety.

2-80. Answer B. GFDICM 2A (AFH)

When an aircraft is flown at maneuvering speed, or less, the load that can be placed on the wing before it stalls is within the safe limits. This is a safe speed to fly at, since any combination of maneuver and/or gust loads cannot create damage due to excess G loading. Answer (A) is incorrect because the maneuverability of the aircraft would decrease, not increase. Answer (C) is incorrect because an aircraft will always stall at the same angle of attack (the critical angle of attack), regardless of weight, speed, or attitude.

2-81   I04

When an aircraft is accelerated, some attitude indicators will precess and incorrectly indicate a

A — climb.
B — descent.
C — right turn.

2-81. Answer A. GFDICM 2A (IFH)

In addition to centrifugal force, acceleration and deceleration also may induce precession errors in gyros. For example, while accelerating, the attitude indicator can precess down and indicate a climb. When this occurs, the normal tendency is to lower the pitch attitude. This can be hazardous during a low visibility, low ceiling takeoff and climb. Answer (B) is incorrect. A descent indication on some attitude indicators is due to deceleration, not acceleration. Answer (C) is wrong because the attitude indicator will not indicate a turn when the aircraft accelerates or decelerates.

2-82   I04

When an aircraft is decelerated, some attitude indicators will precess and incorrectly indicate a

A — left turn.
B — climb.
C — descent.

2-82. Answer C. GFDICM 2A (IFH)

See explanation for Question 2-81. Answer (A) is wrong because a turn is not indicated when accelerating or decelerating. Answer (B) is wrong because a climb will be indicated when accelerating.

2-83   H816

The displacement of a turn coordinator during a coordinated turn will

A — indicate the angle of bank.
B — remain constant for a given bank regardless of airspeed.
C — increase as angle of bank increases.

2-83. Answer C. GFDICM 2A (IFH)

The miniature airplane portion of the turn coordinator will be displaced when in a turn. The amount of displacement will vary with the angle of bank. As the angle of bank increases, the amount of displacement also increases. As the angle of bank decreases, the amount of displacement also decreases. Answer (A) is wrong because the turn coordinator gives only an indirect indication of the angle of bank. Answer (B) is wrong because, as airspeed increases, the rate of turn decreases, and then causes the miniature airplane to indicate less bank.

2-84   H808

Altimeter setting is the value to which the scale of the pressure altimeter is set so the altimeter indicates

A — pressure altitude at sea level.
B — true altitude at field elevation.
C — pressure altitude at field elevation.

2-84. Answer B. GFDICM 2A (AW)

When the altimeter is set to the current altimeter setting prior to take off, it should indicate the true altitude at field elevation. Answer (A) is wrong because the pressure altitude at sea level is indicated when at sea level with 29.92 set in the altimeter. Answer (C) is wrong because pressure altitude is indicated when the altimeter is set to 29.92.

2-85   H808

Pressure altitude is the altitude read on your altimeter when the altimeter is adjusted to indicate height above

A — sea level.
B — the standard datum plane.
C — ground level.

2-85. Answer B. GFDICM 2A (IFH)

The altimeter senses the current atmospheric pressure, but it indicates height in feet above the barometric pressure level set in the altimeter setting window. Answer (A) is wrong because the actual altitude above sea level is referred to as true altitude and is displayed only when the altimeter is set to the correct barometric pressure. Answer (C) is wrong because altimeter indications in relation to the ground level are called absolute altitudes.

2-86   H312
If while in level flight, it becomes necessary to use an alternate source of static pressure vented inside the airplane, which of the following variations in instrument indications should the pilot expect?

A — The altimeter will read lower than normal, airspeed lower than normal, and the VSI will momentarily show a descent.

B — The altimeter will read higher than normal, airspeed greater than normal, and the VSI will momentarily show a climb.

C — The altimeter will read lower than normal, airspeed greater than normal, and the VSI will momentarily show a climb and then a descent.

2-87   I04
(Refer to figure 144.) What changes in control displacement should be made so that "2" would result in a coordinated standard rate turn?

A — Increase left rudder and increase rate of turn.
B — Increase left rudder and decrease rate of turn.
C — Decrease left rudder and decrease angle of bank.

2-88   H814
(Refer to figure 144.) Which illustration indicates a coordinated turn?

A — 3.
B — 1.
C — 2.

2-86. Answer B. GFDICM 2A (IFH)
Due to the slipstream around the cabin, the pressure inside the cabin is less than that of outside air. Therefore, when you select an alternate static source inside the cabin, the pressure differential is greater and the altimeter will read a little higher, the airspeed indicator will read a little fast, and the VSI will show a momentary climb. Answer (A) is wrong because none of the indications listed are appropriate. Answer (C) is wrong because the altimeter will not read lower and the VSI will not show a climb and then a descent.

2-87. Answer A. GFDICM 2A (IFH)
Refer to the second (#2) turn-and-slip indicator. The needle shows a turn to the left at a rate less than standard, while the ball in the inclinometer indicates that the aircraft is in a slip. To establish a coordinated standard-rate turn, you must increase left rudder pressure (step on the ball) and increase the rate of turn. Answers (B) and (C) are wrong because if the turn rate or angle of bank are decreased, a less than standard-rate turn will result.

2-88. Answer A. GFDICM 2A (IFH)
The turn-and-slip indicator supplies two types of information. First, the needle indicates a standard-rate turn when aligned with either of the turn indexes. Second, the inclinometer defines the quality of the turn. When the ball is centered, the opposing horizontal forces are in balance and the turn is coordinated. Answer (B) is wrong because it displays a skidding turn. Answer (C) is wrong because it displays a slipping turn.

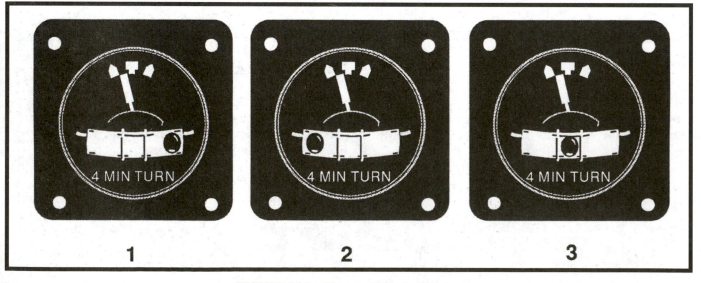

FIGURE 144.—Turn and Slip Indicators.

2-89 **H814**

(Refer to figure 144.) Which illustration indicates a skidding turn?

A — 2.
B — 1.
C — 3.

2-90 **H814**

(Refer to figure 144.) What changes in control displacement should be made so that "1" would result in a coordinated standard rate turn?

A — Increase right rudder and decrease rate of turn.
B — Increase right rudder and increase rate of turn.
C — Decrease right rudder and increase angle of bank.

2-91 **H814**

(Refer to figure 144.) Which illustration indicates a slipping turn?

A — 1.
B — 3.
C — 2.

2-89. Answer B. GFDICM 2A (IFH)

See explanation for Question 2-88. A skidding turn is indicated when the ball of the inclinometer is forced to the outside of the turn. In this case, centrifugal force exceeds the horizontal component of lift. Answer (A) is wrong because it indicates a slipping turn. Answer (C) is wrong because it indicates a coordinated turn.

2-90. Answer B. GFDICM 2A (IFH)

Refer to the first (#1) turn-and-slip indicator. The needle shows a left turn at a rate less than standard, while the ball in the inclinometer indicates that the aircraft is in a skid. To establish a coordinated standard-rate turn, you must increase right rudder pressure (step on the ball) and increase the rate of turn. Answer (A) is wrong because if you decrease the rate of turn, you will be turning at a rate less than standard. Answer (C) is wrong because if you decrease right rudder pressure, the skid will continue.

2-91. Answer C. GFDICM 2A (IFH)

See explanation for Question 2-88. A slipping turn is indicated when the ball of the inclinometer falls to the inside of the turn. In this situation, the vertical component of lift exceeds centrifugal force. Answer (A) is wrong because it indicates a skidding turn. Answer (B) is wrong because it indicates a coordinated turn.

SECTION B
ATTITUDE INSTRUMENT FLYING

FUNDAMENTAL SKILLS

1. Attitude instrument flying consists three fundamental skills. These are **instrument cross-check**, **instrument interpretation**, and **aircraft control**.

2. Instrument cross-check, or scan, requires logical and systematic observation of the instrument panel. The most common scanning errors are fixation, omission, and emphasis.

3. Effective instrument interpretation requires a good working knowledge of how each instrument operates.

4. Aircraft control is the result of instrument cross-check and interpretation. It requires that the airplane be kept properly trimmed so small flight control movements can achieve precise adjustments to pitch, bank, and power.

PRIMARY AND SUPPORTING INSTRUMENTS

5. Primary instruments provide the most pertinent pitch, bank and power information for a given flight condition. Supporting instruments provide additional pitch, bank, and power information to help you maintain the desired indications on the primary instruments.

6. Supporting instruments are no less important than primary instruments. The attitude indicator, although usually a supporting instrument, is essential and central to your scan.

7. The attitude indicator is the primary pitch instrument during any change in pitch and the primary bank instrument during any change in bank. The altimeter is the primary pitch instrument any time your objective is to maintain altitude. The heading indicator is the primary bank instrument any time your objective is to maintain straight flight.

8. The vertical speed indicator (VSI) is the primary pitch instrument any time your objective is to maintain a specific rate of climb or descent. The turn coordinator is the primary bank instrument any time your objective is to maintain a specific rate of turn. The airspeed indicator is the primary power instrument any time your objective is to maintain a constant airspeed during level flight. It is the primary pitch instrument during a constant airspeed climb or descent.

STRAIGHT-AND-LEVEL FLIGHT

9. The three conditions which determine pitch attitude required to maintain level flight are airspeed, air density, and aircraft weight.

10. For maintaining level flight at constant thrust, the attitude indicator would be the least appropriate pitch instrument for determining the need for a pitch change.

11. The altimeter provides the most pertinent information for pitch control. As a rule of thumb, you should make altitude corrections of less than 100 feet using a half-bar width correction on the attitude indicator, and confirm the adjustment on the altimeter and VSI.

12. The instrument which provides the most pertinent information for bank control is the heading indicator. Deviations in heading are not as eye-catching as altitude deviations, and for that reason, require more careful monitoring. When you see a heading deviation, use the attitude indicator to establish an angle of bank equal to the degrees deviation from heading.

13. During level flight you normally adjust pitch to maintain altitude and power to get the desired airspeed. The airspeed indicator provides the most pertinent information for power control.

14. During changes in power, the manifold pressure gauge or tachometer provides the most pertinent power information, since these instruments give you more instantaneous indications and help you make the required adjustments more precisely.

TURNS

15. A **standard-rate turn** is 3 degrees per second. You should use this rate of turn or less for most IFR operations.

16. You can quickly estimate the approximate angle of bank required for a standard-rate turn by dividing the true airspeed in knots by 10 and adding 5 to the result.

17. At steeper banks, the rate of turn increases and the radius decreases. Lowering the airspeed also increases the rate and decreases the radius of turn for a given angle of bank.

18. The primary reason the angle of attack must be increased to maintain a constant altitude during a coordinated turn, is because the vertical component of lift decreases as the result of the bank.

19. When airspeed is increased during a level turn, additional vertical lift is generated. To avoid climbing, you must increase the angle of bank and/or decrease the angle of attack.

20. When airspeed is decreased in a turn, the angle of bank must be decreased and/or the angle of attack must be increased to maintain level flight.

CLIMBS AND DESCENTS

21. In a **constant airspeed climb**, you set climb power, pitch up to get a specific airspeed, and accept the resulting rate of climb. In a **constant rate climb** you maintain a specific vertical velocity in addition to controlling airspeed.
22. The proper way to transition from cruise flight to a climb at a specific speed is to increase back elevator pressure until the attitude indicator shows the approximate pitch attitude for that speed climb.
23. To enter a **constant airspeed descent**, reduce the power, pitch down to maintain airspeed using the attitude indicator as a reference, and accept the resulting rate of descent. In a **constant rate descent** you control the rate of descent with pitch and control airspeed with power.
24. To level off from a descent maintaining the descending airspeed, lead the desired altitude by approximately 10 percent of the vertical velocity. To level off at an airspeed higher than the descent speed, add power at approximately 100 to 150 feet above the desired altitude.

COPING WITH INSTRUMENT FAILURE

25. Although you will become proficient in **partial panel** instrument flying, loss of the attitude indicator in IFR conditions is a potential distress situation under which you should immediately advise ATC.
26. Instrument failures can be subtle. When you suspect an instrument failure, look for corresponding indications among various instruments, and cover the instrument(s) that disagree with the rest.
27. Use the VSI and airspeed indicator to make changes in pitch when flying with inoperative gyroscopic instruments. Use smooth, gradual control inputs and allow a few moments for the change in pitch to be reflected on these instruments.
28. The magnetic compass is the primary bank instrument, during partial panel operations, but it is hard to control the airplane using this instrument. Keeping the wings level, with the ball centered on the turn coordinator, is your best means of maintaining your course without the attitude and heading indicators.
29. Because it can be difficult to perform accurate compass turns, a **timed turn** is the most accurate way to turn to a heading without the heading indicator. In a timed turn, you use the clock instead of the heading indicator to determine when to roll out.

UNUSUAL ATTITUDE RECOVERY

30. When recovering from a nose-high unusual attitude, your objective is to avert a stall. The correct sequence is to add power, lower the nose, level the wings, and return to the original attitude and heading.
31. When recovering from a nose-low, increasing airspeed, unusual attitude, your objective is to avoid overstressing the airplane structure, as well as an excessive loss of altitude. The correct sequence is to reduce power, correct the bank attitude, and raise the nose to a level attitude.
32. When recovering partial panel, use the turn coordinator to stop a turn, and the pitot-static instruments to arrest an unintended climb or descent. An approximate level pitch attitude is first attained when the airspeed and altimeter stop their movement and the VSI reverses its trend

CONTROL AND PERFORMANCE METHOD

33. In the control and performance method, you use the control instruments, such as the manifold pressure gauge and the attitude indicator, to set up power/attitude combinations for specific maneuvers. Then, you check the performance instruments for the desired effect.

2-92   H814
As a rule of thumb, altitude corrections of less than 100 feet should be corrected by using

A — Full bar width on the attitude indicator.

B — Two bar width on the attitude indicator.

C — Half bar width on the attitude indicator.

2-92. Answer C. GFDICH 2B (IFH)
As a rule of thumb use a one-half bar width correction on the attitude indicator for deviations of 100 feet or less. You should use an initial, full-bar width correction for larger altitude deviations.

2-93   H814

The gyroscopic heading indicator is inoperative. What is the primary bank instrument in unaccelerated straight-and-level flight?

A — Magnetic compass.
B — Attitude indicator.
C — Miniature aircraft of turn coordinator.

2-93. Answer A. GFDICM 2B (IFH)

In straight-and-level flight, the heading indicator is normally the primary instrument for bank. It indirectly provides bank information, since banking results in a turn and a changing heading. The only other instrument that provides heading information is the magnetic compass and it should be considered the primary bank instrument when the heading indicator fails. Answers (B) and (C) are incorrect. The attitude indicator and the miniature aircraft on the turn coordinator can help maintain level flight. However, the primary instrument needs to provide heading information and the magnetic compass is the only instrument that will provide heading information when the heading indicator is inoperative.

2-94   H816

When airspeed is decreased in a turn, what must be done to maintain level flight?

A — Decrease the angle of bank and/or increase the angle of attack.
B — Increase the angle of bank and/or decrease the angle of attack.
C — Increase the angle of attack.

2-94. Answer A. GFDICM 2B (IFH)

If you decrease airspeed in a level turn your vertical component of lift will be reduced. To maintain the same vertical lift component required to maintain altitude, you must compensate by either decreasing the angle of bank and/or by increasing the angle of attack. Answer (B) is incorrect since increasing bank will divert more of the vertical lift component to the horizontal component of lift. Also, decreasing the angle of attack will reduce overall lift. Both will decrease the vertical component of lift and the aircraft will descend. Answer (C) is not the most correct answer. At steeper bank angles, increasing the angle of attack may not be practical. You may also need to decrease the angle of bank.

2-95   H815

What instruments are considered supporting bank instruments during a straight, stabilized climb at a constant rate?

A — Attitude indicator and turn coordinator.
B — Heading indicator and attitude indicator.
C — Heading indicator and turn coordinator.

2-95. Answer A. GFDICM 2B (IFH)

The heading indicator is your primary bank instrument during both transition to, and when established in, a straight, constant rate climb. Your supporting bank instruments for an established straight, constant rate climb are the attitude indicator and turn coordinator. Answers (B) and (C) are incorrect because they list the heading indicator (primary bank) as a supporting bank instrument.

2-96   H815

What instruments are primary for pitch, bank, and power, respectively, when transitioning into a constant airspeed climb from straight-and-level flight?

A — Attitude indicator, heading indicator, and manifold pressure gauge or tachometer.
B — Attitude indicator for both pitch and bank; airspeed indicator for power.
C — Vertical speed, attitude indicator, and manifold pressure or tachometer.

2-96. Answer A. GFDICM 2B (IFH)

When transitioning from straight-and-level flight to a constant airspeed climb, the attitude indicator, heading indicator, and tachometer or manifold pressure gauge (MP) are the primary instruments for pitch, bank, and power, respectively. Answer (B) is incorrect because the heading indicator is primary for bank and the tachometer or MP is primary for power. Answer (C) is incorrect because it does not list the heading indicator for primary bank. In addition, the vertical speed indicator is not a primary or supporting instrument when transitioning to a constant airspeed climb.

2-97   H816

What is the primary bank instrument once a standard rate turn is established?

A — Attitude indicator.
B — Turn coordinator.
C — Heading indicator.

2-97. Answer B. GFDICM 2B (IFH)

After the turn is established, the turn coordinator is primary for bank, and the altimeter is primary for pitch control. The attitude indicator is a supporting instrument for both pitch and bank which is why answer (A) is incorrect. The heading indicator (answer C) is neither a primary nor a supporting instrument for an established constant rate turn.

2-98   H813

What is the correct sequence in which to use the three skills used in instrument flying?

A — Aircraft control, cross-check, and instrument interpretation.
B — Instrument interpretation, cross-check, and aircraft control.
C — Cross-check, instrument interpretation, and aircraft control.

2-98. Answer C. GFDICM 2B (IFH)

Three fundamental skills for instrument flying are instrument cross-check, instrument interpretation, and aircraft control in that order. You must first cross-check your instruments, then interpret them correctly so that you can apply the proper control inputs. Answer (A) is incorrect since aircraft control can only be achieved by first cross-checking, and then interpreting the instruments. Answer (B) is incorrect because you cannot have instrument interpretation until you first cross-check the instruments.

2-99   H807

The rate of turn at any airspeed is dependent upon

A — the horizontal lift component.
B — the vertical lift component.
C — centrifugal force.

2-99. Answer A. GFDICM 2B (IFH)

The rate of turn at any given airspeed actually depends on the horizontal component of lift, which is directly proportional to the angle of bank. Answer (B) is incorrect because it is the horizontal (not vertical) component of lift that provides the turning force. Centrifugal force (answer C) is the force which balances the horizontal lift component, resulting in a constant rate of turn.

2-100   H815

As power is increased to enter a 500 feet per minute rate of climb in straight flight, which instruments are primary for pitch, bank, and power respectively?

A — Attitude indicator, heading indicator, and manifold pressure gauge or tachometer.
B — VSI, attitude indicator, and airspeed indicator.
C — Airspeed indicator, attitude indicator, and manifold pressure gauge or tachometer.

2-100. Answer A. GFDICM 2B (IFH)

As power is increased during the transition to a constant rate climb, the attitude indicator is the primary for pitch. When the vertical speed approaches the desired rate of climb the airspeed indicator becomes the primary instrument to maintain the pitch attitude and the rate of climb.

2-101   H815

What is the primary pitch instrument during a stabilized climbing left turn at cruise climb airspeed?

A — Attitude indicator.
B — VSI.
C — Airspeed indicator.

2-101. Answer C. GFDICM 2B (IFH)

A stabilized climbing left turn at cruise climb airspeed is a stabilized constant airspeed climb. As with straight-and-level constant airspeed climbs, the primary instruments are the airspeed indicator for pitch and the turn coordinator for bank. Answer (A) is incorrect because the attitude indicator is the supporting bank instrument when stabilized in the climb. Answer (B) is incorrect since in stabilized constant airspeed climbs or descents, the vertical speed indicator (VSI) is a supporting instrument for pitch. Only during a stabilized constant rate climb or descent is the VSI a primary instrument.

2-102   I05

What is the primary pitch instrument when establishing a constant altitude standard rate turn?

A — Altimeter.
B — VSI.
C — Airspeed indicator.

2-102. Answer A. GFDICM 2B (IFH)

During the roll-in to a constant altitude standard-rate turn, check the altimeter, vertical speed indicator (VSI), and attitude indicator for the pitch adjustments necessary as the vertical lift component decreases with increased bank. The altimeter is the primary pitch instrument while the VSI and attitude indicator are supporting pitch. Answer (B) is incorrect because the VSI is a supporting pitch instrument. Answer (C) is incorrect. If you maintain a constant airspeed, the airspeed indicator becomes primary for power, and the throttle must be adjusted as drag increases.

2-103   H816

What is the initial primary bank instrument when establishing a level standard rate turn?

A — Turn coordinator.
B — Heading indicator.
C — Attitude indicator.

2-103. Answer C. GFDICM 2B (IFH)

When entering a level turn, your primary reference for bank is the bank index on the attitude indicator. Your secondary, or supporting, reference is the turn coordinator (answer A). After a level turn is established, the turn coordinator is primary for bank, and the altimeter is primary for pitch control. The attitude indicator becomes the supporting instrument for both pitch and bank. The heading indicator (answer B) is the primary instrument for bank in straight-and-level flight.

2-104   I05

What instrument(s) is(are) supporting bank instrument when entering a constant airspeed climb from straight-and-level flight?

A — Heading indicator.
B — Attitude indicator and turn coordinator.
C — Turn coordinator and heading indicator.

2-104. Answer B. GFDICM 2B (IFH)

When transitioning from straight-and-level flight to a constant airspeed climb, the attitude indicator, heading indicator, and tachometer or manifold pressure gauge are the primary instruments for pitch, bank, and power, respectively. The supporting instrument for pitch is the vertical speed indicator, while the supporting bank instruments include the attitude indicator and turn coordinator. Answers (A) and (C) are wrong because the heading indicator is primary, not supporting, for bank in straight flight.

2-105   H813

What are the three fundamental skills involved in attitude instrument flying?

A — Instrument interpretation, trim application, and aircraft control.
B — Cross-check, instrument interpretation, and aircraft control.
C — Cross-check, emphasis, and aircraft control.

2-105. Answer B. GFDICM 2B (IFH)

To achieve smooth, positive control of the aircraft during instrument flight maneuvers, you need to develop three fundamental skills. They are instrument cross-check, instrument interpretation, and aircraft control. Answer (A) is wrong because trim application is part of aircraft control. Answer (C) is wrong because emphasis is one of three scanning errors. It identifies the problem of concentrating on one instrument instead of a combination of instruments.

2-106   H816

What is the primary bank instrument while transitioning from straight-and-level flight to a standard rate turn to the left?

A — Attitude indicator.
B — Heading indicator.
C — Turn coordinator (miniature aircraft).

2-106. Answer A. GFDICM 2B (IFH)

When transitioning from straight-and-level flight to a level turn to the left, the altimeter and attitude indicator are the primary instruments for determining pitch and bank, respectively. After the turn is established, the supporting instruments for pitch are the attitude indicator and vertical speed indicator, while the turn coordinator is primary for bank (answer C). Answer (B) is wrong because the heading indicator is primary bank in straight-and-level flight.

2-107   H813

What is the third fundamental skill in attitude instrument flying?

A — Instrument cross-check.
B — Power control.
C — Aircraft control

2-108   H816

During standard-rate turns, which instrument is considered "primary" for bank?

A — Heading indicator.
B — Turn and slip indicator or turn coordinator.
C — Attitude indicator.

2-109   H813

What is the first fundamental skill in attitude instrument flying?

A — Aircraft control.
B — Instrument cross-check.
C — Instrument interpretation.

2-110   H814

As power is reduced to change airspeed from high to low cruise in level flight, which instruments are primary for pitch, bank, and power, respectively?

A — Attitude indicator, heading indicator, and manifold pressure gauge or tachometer.
B — Altimeter, attitude indicator, and airspeed indicator.
C — Altimeter, heading indicator, and manifold pressure gauge or tachometer.

2-111   H814

Which instrument provides the most pertinent information (primary) for bank control in straight-and-level flight?

A — Turn-and-slip indicator.
B — Attitude indicator.
C — Heading indicator.

2-107. Answer C. GFDICM 2B (IFH)

There are three fundamental skills in attitude instrument flying. The first is instrument cross-check (answer A) which requires the logical and systematic observation of the instrument panel. Instrument interpretation, the second fundamental skill, begins with a knowledge of how each instrument operates and what instrument indications represent given flight attitudes. The final fundamental skill, aircraft control, is the result of cross-check and accurate interpretation of the instruments. Answer (B) is wrong because power control is part of aircraft control.

2-108. Answer B. GFDICM 2B (IFH)

For standard-rate turns, the turn and slip indicator or turn coordinator is the primary bank instrument. In this case, the attitude indicator is a supporting instrument, and is essential and central to the scan. It is the only instrument that provides instant and direct aircraft attitude information, and is primary for pitch and bank information.

2-109. Answer B. GFDICM 2B (IFH)

There are three fundamental skills in attitude instrument flying. The first is instrument cross-check which requires the logical and systematic observation of the instrument panel. Instrument interpretation (answer C), the second fundamental skill, begins with a knowledge of how each instrument operates and an awareness of the instrument indications that represent given flight attitudes. The third fundamental skill, aircraft control (answer A), is actually the result of a good cross-check and accurate interpretation of the instruments.

2-110. Answer C. GFDICM 2B (IFH)

When making adjustments in speed, your primary instruments for pitch, bank, and power are the altimeter, heading indicator, and tachometer or manifold pressure gauge, respectively. Supporting pitch instruments include the attitude indicator and VSI, while supporting bank instruments are the attitude indicator and turn coordinator. The supporting power instrument is the airspeed indicator. Answers (A) and (B) are wrong because the attitude indicator is a supporting instrument for both pitch and bank. In addition, the airspeed indicator is a supporting instrument for pitch in straight-and-level flight (answer B).

2-111. Answer C. GFDICM 2B (IFH)

In straight-and-level flight, the altimeter is the primary instrument for determining pitch, the heading indicator is primary for determining bank, and the airspeed indicator is primary for determining power. Secondary instruments for determining pitch include the attitude indicator (answer B) and the vertical speed indicator (VSI). Secondary for determining bank are the attitude indicator and turn coordinator or turn-and-slip indicator (answer A).

2-112   H816

Which instruments are considered primary and supporting for bank, respectively, when establishing a level standard rate turn?

A — Turn coordinator and attitude indicator.
B — Attitude indicator and turn coordinator.
C — Turn coordinator and heading indicator.

2-112. Answer B. GFDICM 2B (IFH)

When establishing a level standard-rate turn, the primary instruments for determining pitch, bank, and power are the altimeter, attitude indicator, and airspeed indicator respectively. The supporting instruments for determining pitch include the attitude indicator and VSI. The supporting instrument for determining bank is the turn coordinator. The tachometer or manifold pressure gauge is the supporting power instrument. Once the turn is established, the turn coordinator becomes primary bank (answers A and C) and the attitude indicator becomes supporting bank (answer A). The heading indicator is primary bank in straight-and-level flight (answer C).

2-113   H818

While recovering from an unusual flight attitude without the aid of the attitude indicator, approximate level pitch attitude is reached when the

A — airspeed and altimeter stop their movement and the VSI reverses its trend.
B — airspeed arrives at cruising speed, the altimeter reverses its trend, and the vertical speed stops its movement.
C — altimeter and vertical speed reverse their trend and the airspeed stops its movement.

2-113. Answer A. GFDICM 2B (IFH)

Recovery from unusual attitudes by partial panel is basically the same as with a full panel, except the turn coordinator is used to stop any turn and the altimeter, airspeed, and vertical speed indicators are used for pitch information. For example, when recovering from a nose-low unusual attitude, an approximate level pitch attitude is indicated when the airspeed indicator and altimeter stop their movement. The VSI will reverse its trend when you begin the initial recovery and will then indicate zero after a few seconds of level flight. Although this is not stated in the answer, choice (A) is the most correct. Choices (B) and (C) are wrong because if the altimeter reverses its trend, you will have passed through level flight.

2-114   H813

Which instruments, in addition to the attitude indicator, are pitch instruments?

A — Altimeter and airspeed only.
B — Altimeter and VSI only.
C — Altimeter, airspeed indicator, and vertical speed indicator.

2-114. Answer C. GFDICM 2B (IFH)

In addition to the attitude indicator, the altimeter, airspeed indicator, and vertical speed indicator all give pitch information. Answers (A) and (B) are wrong because all of the instruments that give pitch information are not listed.

2-115   H814

Which instrument provides the most pertinent information (primary) for pitch control in straight-and-level flight?

A — Attitude indicator.
B — Airspeed indicator.
C — Altimeter.

2-115. Answer C. GFDICM 2B (IFH)

In straight-and-level flight, the primary instruments for pitch, bank, and power are the altimeter, heading indicator, and airspeed indicator respectively. The attitude indicator (answer A) provides supporting information for both pitch and bank. Answer (B) is wrong because the airspeed indicator is primary for power.

2-116   H816

Which instruments are considered to be supporting instruments for pitch during change of airspeed in a level turn?

A — Airspeed indicator and VSI.
B — Altimeter and attitude indicator.
C — Attitude indicator and VSI.

2-116. Answer C. GFDICM 2B (IFH)

Anytime you make a change in airspeed, your primary instruments for pitch and bank are the altimeter and the turn coordinator. The supporting instruments for determining pitch are the attitude indicator and vertical speed indicator. The supporting instrument for bank is the attitude indicator. Answer (A) is wrong because the airspeed indicator is primary for power control. Answer (B) is wrong because the altimeter is the primary pitch instrument.

2-117   H818

If an airplane is in an unusual flight attitude and the attitude indicator has exceeded its limits, which instruments should be relied on to determine pitch attitude before starting recovery?

A — Turn indicator and VSI.
B — Airspeed and altimeter.
C — VSI and airspeed to detect approaching VSI or VMO.

2-117. Answer B. GFDICM 2B (IFH)

If the attitude indicator is unusable, you can determine pitch attitude by referencing the airspeed indicator and altimeter. A nose-down attitude will be indicated by an increasing airspeed and decreasing altimeter. A nose-up attitude will be indicated by a decreasing airspeed and an increasing altimeter. Answer (A) is wrong because the turn indicator gives no pitch information. In addition, vertical speed information lags behind that of the altimeter and airspeed indicator (answers A and C).

2-118   H816

Which instrument is considered primary for power as the airspeed reaches the desired value during change of airspeed in a level turn?

A — Airspeed indicator.
B — Attitude indicator.
C — Altimeter.

2-118. Answer A. GFDICM 2B (IFH)

During the period when airspeed is changing, the tachometer or manifold pressure gauge is your primary instrument for determining power. However, as the airspeed reaches the desired reading, the airspeed indicator becomes the primary instrument for determining power. Answers (B) and (C) are wrong because neither the attitude indicator nor the altimeter indicate power information.

2-119   H818

Which is the correct sequence for recovery from a spiraling, nose-low, increasing airspeed, unusual flight attitude?

A — Increase pitch attitude, reduce power, and level wings.
B — Reduce power, correct the bank attitude, and raise the nose to a level attitude.
C — Reduce power, raise the nose to level attitude, and correct the bank attitude.

2-119. Answer B. GFDICM 2B (IFH)

When recovering from a spiraling, nose-down unusual attitude, the first thing you should do is reduce power to prevent excessive airspeed and loss of altitude. Then, correct the bank attitude with coordinated aileron and rudder pressure to straight flight by referring to the turn coordinator. After this is done, raise the nose to a level flight attitude by applying smooth back elevator pressure. Answer (A) is wrong because increasing the pitch attitude prior to decreasing power and correcting the bank attitude can cause excessive G loading on the airframe. Answer (C) is wrong because the bank attitude should be corrected before the nose is raised to level flight.

2-120   H813

Which instruments should be used to make a pitch correction when you have deviated from your assigned altitude?

A — Altimeter and VSI.
B — Manifold pressure gauge and VSI.
C — Attitude indicator, altimeter, and VSI.

2-120. Answer C. GFDICM 2B (IFH)

In level flight, the altimeter is the primary instrument for pitch information. The supporting instruments are the attitude indicator, airspeed indicator, and vertical speed indicator (VSI). If you deviate from an assigned altitude, you should use the attitude indicator, altimeter, and VSI to correct the deviation. As a guide, adjust the pitch attitude to produce a rate of change which is double the amount of altitude deviation and use power as necessary. Answer (A) is wrong because the attitude indicator is omitted. Answer (B) is wrong because the manifold pressure gauge provides only power information.

2-121   H816

When airspeed is increased in a turn, what must be done to maintain a constant altitude?

A — Decrease the angle of bank.
B — Increase the angle of bank and/or decrease the angle of attack.
C — Decrease the angle of attack.

2-121. Answer B. GFDICM 2B (IFH)

If all other variables remain constant, and your airspeed increases, additional lift will be produced and the aircraft will climb. To prevent this from happening, you must decrease the amount of vertical lift being produced. You can do this by increasing the angle of bank and/or by decreasing the angle of attack. Answer (A) is wrong because decreasing the angle of bank would increase the vertical component of lift even more and cause the airplane to climb. Answer (C) is wrong because you can also increase the angle of bank to maintain a constant altitude.

2-122   H807

During a constant-bank level turn, what effect would an increase in airspeed have on the rate and radius of turn?

A — Rate of turn would increase, and radius of turn would increase.
B — Rate of turn would decrease, and radius of turn would decrease.
C — Rate of turn would decrease, and radius of turn would increase.

2-122. Answer C. GFDICM 2B (IFH)

A specific angle of bank and true airspeed will always produce the same rate and radius of turn, regardless of aircraft type. If you increase the angle of bank in a turn, the rate of turn will increase and the radius will decrease. If you increase the true airspeed in a turn, the radius will increase and the rate will decrease. For a given airspeed, there is no way to achieve an increase (answer A) or a decrease (answer B) in both rate and radius of turn.

2-123   I04

Conditions that determine the pitch attitude required to maintain level flight are

A — airspeed, air density, wing design, and angle of attack.
B — flightpath, wind velocity, and angle of attack.
C — relative wind, pressure altitude, and vertical lift component.

2-123. Answer A. GFDICM 2B (IFH)

Lift is directly proportional to the density of the air, the area of the wings (wing design), and airspeed. Lift is pilot controlled, by modifying the angle of attack.

2-124   H815

Approximately what percent of the indicated vertical speed should be used to determine the number of feet to lead the level-off from a climb to a specific altitude?

A — 10 percent.
B — 20 percent.
C — 25 percent.

2-124. Answer A. GFDICM 2B (IFH)

A rule of thumb for determining the amount of lead to use when leveling off is to lead your level-off point by 10% of the vertical speed. For example, if you are climbing at 1,000 feet per minute, you would begin leveling off 100 feet (1,000 × .1 = 100) prior to the desired altitude. Answers (B) and (C) are wrong because they substantially exceed the suggested 10% rule of thumb.

2-125   H815

To level off from a descent to a specific altitude, the pilot should lead the level-off by approximately

A — 10 percent of the vertical speed.
B — 30 percent of the vertical speed.
C — 50 percent of the vertical speed.

2-125. Answer A. GFDICM 2B (IFH)

See explanation for Question 2-124. The same rule of thumb used for leveling off in a climb can be used for a descent. Lead your desired level-off altitude by 10% of the descent rate. Answers (B) and (C) are wrong because they substantially exceed the suggested 10% rule of thumb.

2-126   H807

Rate of turn can be increased and radius of turn decreased by

A — decreasing airspeed and shallowing the bank.
B — decreasing airspeed and increasing the bank.
C — increasing airspeed and increasing the bank.

2-126. Answer B. GFDICM 2B (IFH)

A specific angle of bank and true airspeed will always produce the same rate and radius of turn, regardless of aircraft type. If you increase your angle of bank, the rate of turn will increase and the radius of the turn will decrease. If you increase your true airspeed, the rate of turn will decrease and the radius of turn will increase. Answer (A) is wrong because decreasing airspeed results in an increased rate of turn and shallowing the bank results in an increased radius. Answer (C) is wrong because increasing the airspeed results in a decreased rate of turn and an increased radius.

2-127   H807

The primary reason the angle of attack must be increased, to maintain a constant altitude during a coordinated turn, is because the

A — thrust is acting in a different direction, causing a reduction in airspeed and loss of lift.
B — vertical component of lift has decreased as the result of the bank.
C — use of ailerons has increased the drag.

2-127. Answer B. GFDICM 2B (IFH)

In a turn, lift can be broken down into two components: a vertical component of lift and a horizontal component of lift. The vertical component of lift supports the weight of the aircraft while the horizontal component causes the aircraft to turn. When you initiate a turn or increase your bank angle, the vertical component of lift decreases and the aircraft tends to descend. Therefore, you must increase the angle of attack, increase the airspeed, or decrease the angle of bank in order to maintain level flight. Answer (A) is wrong because lift supports the aircraft, not thrust. Answer (C) is wrong because aileron drag is not a factor in a coordinated turn, since the ailerons should be in a neutral position.

2-128   H814

For maintaining level flight at constant thrust, which instrument would be the least appropriate for determining the need for a pitch change?

A — Altimeter.
B — VSI.
C — Attitude indicator.

2-128. Answer C. GFDICM 2B (IFH)

According to the primary/support concept of attitude instrument flying, the attitude indicator is the least appropriate instrument for determining the need for a pitch change under these conditions. In straight-and-level flight, the altimeter is the primary pitch instrument since it provides the most pertinent altitude information. If you deviate from the a desired altitude, it is reflected first on the vertical speed indicator (answer B) and next on the altimeter (answer A). By evaluating the initial rate of movement on these instruments, you can estimate the amount of pitch change you need to restore level flight.

2-129   H815

To enter a constant-airspeed descent from level-cruising flight, and maintain cruising airspeed, the pilot should

A — first adjust the pitch attitude to a descent using the attitude indicator as a reference, then adjust the power to maintain the cruising airspeed.
B — first reduce power, then adjust the pitch using the attitude indicator as a reference to establish a specific rate on the VSI.
C — simultaneously reduce power and adjust the pitch using the attitude indicator as a reference to maintain the cruising airspeed.

2-129. Answer C. GFDICM 2B (IFH)

To enter a constant-airspeed descent, simultaneously reduce the power and pitch the nose of the aircraft down. The primary pitch instrument while transitioning to the descent is the attitude indicator. Answer (A) is wrong because if you adjust your pitch first, the aircraft will accelerate and a constant airspeed will not be maintained. Answer (B) is wrong because reducing the power first will cause the aircraft to slow down and a constant airspeed will not be maintained. In addition, in a constant-airspeed descent, the airspeed determines the rate of descent.

2-130   H815

To level off at an airspeed higher than the descent speed, the addition of power should be made, assuming a 500 FPM rate of descent, at approximately

A — 50 to 100 feet above the desired altitude.
B — 100 to 150 feet above the desired altitude.
C — 150 to 200 feet above the desired altitude.

2-131   H815

To level off from a descent maintaining the descending airspeed, the pilot should lead the desired altitude by approximately

A — 20 feet.
B — 50 feet.
C — 60 feet.

2-132   H818

During recoveries from unusual attitudes, level flight is attained the instant

A — the horizon bar on the attitude indicator is exactly overlapped with the miniature airplane.
B — a zero rate of climb is indicated on the VSI.
C — the altimeter and airspeed needles stop prior to reversing their direction of movement.

2-133   H815

While cruising at 160 knots, you wish to establish a climb at 130 knots. When entering the climb (full panel), it is proper to make the initial pitch change by increasing back elevator pressure until the

A — attitude indicator, airspeed, and vertical speed indicate a climb.
B — vertical speed indication reaches the predetermined rate of climb.
C — attitude indicator shows the approximate pitch attitude appropriate for the 130-knot climb.

2-134   H815

While cruising at 190 knots, you wish to establish a climb at 160 knots. When entering the climb (full panel), it would be proper to make the initial pitch change by increasing back elevator pressure until the

A — attitude indicator shows the approximate pitch attitude appropriate for the 160-knot climb.
B — attitude indicator, airspeed, and vertical speed indicate a climb.
C — airspeed indication reaches 160 knots.

2-130. Answer B. GFDICM 2B (IFH)

The level-off from a descent must be started before you reach the desired altitude. The amount of lead depends upon the rate of descent and the desired level-off airspeed. When descending at 500 f.p.m. and leveling off at an airspeed higher than the descent airspeed, begin adding power when you are 100 to 150 feet above the desired altitude. Answer (A) is wrong because 50 to 100 feet above your desired altitude is more appropriate for a level off at the descent airspeed. Answer (C) is wrong because adding power when 150 to 200 feet above your desired altitude could result in a premature level off.

2-131. Answer B. GFDICM 2B (IFH)

See explanation for Question 2-130. To maintain descent airspeed, you should lead the level-off by about 50 feet. Leading the level-off by 20 feet (answer A) would likely cause you to go below the desired altitude. Using 60 feet (answer C) or more may cause you to level off above the desired altitude.

2-132. Answer C. GFDICM 2B (IFH)

During recoveries from unusual attitudes, the attitude indicator (answer A) may become unusable. In this situation, you will know you are passing through level flight when the altimeter and airspeed needles stop and begin to reverse direction. Answer (B) is wrong because the VSI indication lags behind the aircraft's actual vertical speed.

2-133. Answer C. GFDICM 2B (IFH)

When transitioning from straight-and-level flight to a climb, the attitude indicator is primary for pitch and should be used to establish the appropriate pitch attitude for 130 knots. Once the airplane stabilizes at a constant airspeed and attitude, the airspeed indicator is primary for pitch (answer A). The vertical speed indicator (answers A and B) is neither a primary nor supporting instrument when in a constant-airspeed climb.

2-134. Answer A. GFDICM 2B (IFH)

See explanation for Question 2-133. Answers (B) and (C) are wrong because, once you establish the proper pitch attitude, the airspeed indicator will take time to slow to 160 knots.

FIGURE 145.—Instrument Sequence (Unusual Attitude).

2-135   H818

(Refer to figure 145.) What is the correct sequence for recovery from the unusual attitude indicated?

A — Reduce power, increase back elevator pressure, and level the wings.
B — Reduce power, level the wings, bring pitch attitude to level flight.
C — Level the wings, raise the nose of the aircraft to level flight attitude, and obtain desired airspeed.

2-135. Answer B. GFDICM 2B (IFH)

A cross check of the instruments shows that you are in a descending right turn. To recover, immediately reduce power to minimize the loss of altitude and the build up of airspeed. Next, use the turn coordinator and attitude indicator to level the wings. Then increase the pitch attitude to bring the aircraft back to level flight. Answer (A) is wrong because, if you increase back elevator pressure prior to leveling the wings, excessive G loading could result. Answer (C) is wrong because, if you do not reduce the airspeed first, high G loading and an excessive loss of altitude could result.

FIGURE 146.—Instrument Sequence (System Failed).

2-136   I05

(Refer to figure 146.) Identify the system that has failed and determine a corrective action to return the airplane to straight-and-level flight.

A — Static/pitot system is blocked; lower the nose and level the wings to level-flight attitude by use of attitude indicator.

B — Vacuum system has failed; reduce power, roll left to level wings, and pitchup to reduce airspeed.

C — Electrical system has failed; reduce power, roll left to level wings, and raise the nose to reduce airspeed.

2-136. Answer A. GFDICM 2A (IFH)

An increasing airspeed and altitude, plus a moderate climb, indicates that the pitot static instruments are unreliable. Based on the gyroscopic instruments, you are in a nose high attitude and turning right. To recover, lower the nose and level the wings to a level flight attitude. There is no indication that the vacuum system (answer B) has failed, since the attitude indicator and heading indicator appear to be working normally. Also, the recovery procedure listed is for a nose-low attitude. If the electrical system (answer C) has failed, the turn coordinator would be inconsistent with the other instruments. In addition, the recovery procedure listed is for a nose-low attitude.

FIGURE 147.—Instrument Sequence (Unusual Attitude).

2-137   H818

(Refer to figure 147.) Which is the correct sequence for recovery from the unusual attitude indicated?

A — Level wings, add power, lower nose, descend to original attitude, and heading.

B — Add power, lower nose, level wings, return to original attitude and heading.

C — Stop turn by raising right wing and add power at the same time, lower the nose, and return to original attitude and heading.

2-137. Answer B. GFDICM 2B (IFH)

Based on the indications, the aircraft is in a nose-high turn to the right. To recover, add power, lower the nose, and level the wings to return to a level-flight attitude. Answers (A) and (C) are wrong because you should add power and lower the nose before you level the wings.

FIGURE 148.—Instrument Sequence (System Malfunction).

2-138   H818

(Refer to figure 148.) What is the flight attitude? One system which transmits information to the instruments has malfunctioned.

A — Climbing turn to left.
B — Climbing turn to right.
C — Level turn to left.

2-138. Answer B. GFDICM 2B (IFH)

The combination of the altimeter, VSI, attitude indicator, and heading indicator show you in a climbing, right turn. Since the turn coordinator shows wings level, it appears to have failed. Answers (A) and (C) are wrong because both the attitude and heading indicator display right turns. In addition, the aircraft is not in level flight (answer C).

FIGURE 149.—Instrument Interpretation (System Malfunction).

2-139   H818

(Refer to figure 149.) What is the flight attitude? One system which transmits information to the instruments has malfunctioned.

A — Level turn to the right.
B — Level turn to the left.
C — Straight-and-level flight.

2-139. Answer C. GFDICM 2B (IFH)

The combination of airspeed indicator, altimeter, turn coordinator, and VSI indicate level flight. The attitude indicator and heading indicator disagree with each other, which implies that the vacuum system has failed. Answers (A) and (B) are wrong because the aircraft is not turning.

FIGURE 150.—Instrument Interpretation (Instrument Malfunction).

2-140   H826

(Refer to figure 150.) What is the flight attitude? One instrument has malfunctioned.

A — Climbing turn to the right.
B — Climbing turn to the left.
C — Descending turn to the right.

2-140. Answer A. GFDICM 2B (IFH)

The combination of airspeed indicator, altimeter, turn coordinator, heading indicator, and VSI indicate that the aircraft is in a climbing right turn. Both the turn coordinator and heading indicator display a turn to the right. This implies that the attitude indicator has failed. Answer (B) is wrong because the aircraft is not turning to the left. Answer (C) is wrong because you are not descending.

FIGURE 151.—Instrument Interpretation (Instrument Malfunction).

2-141   I05

(Refer to figure 151.) What is the flight attitude? One instrument has malfunctioned.

A — Climbing turn to the right.
B — Level turn to the right.
C — Level turn to the left.

2-141. Answer B. GFDICM 2B (IFH)

The combination of attitude indicator, altimeter, turn coordinator, heading indicator, and VSI show the aircraft in a level turn to the right. Since the attitude indicator, altimeter, and VSI indicate a level pitch attitude, you can assume the airspeed indicator is inoperative. Answer (A) is wrong because the aircraft is not climbing. Answer (C) is wrong because the attitude and heading indicators show a turn to the right.

SECTION C
INSTRUMENT NAVIGATION

VOR NAVIGATION

1. There are various types of indicators for VOR navigation, including the basic VOR indicator, the **horizontal situation indicator** (HSI) and the radio magnetic indicator (RMI).
2. Flying a heading that is reciprocal to the bearing selected on the OBS would result in **reverse sensing** on a conventional VOR indicator.
3. An HSI solves nearly all reverse sensing and other visualization problems associated with a conventional VOR indicator. The HSI display combines the VOR indicator with a heading indicator, so the display is automatically rotated to the correct position for you.
4. Each dot on an HSI or conventional VOR course deviation scale is 2° deviation, or 200 feet per nautical mile, when tuned to a VOR. Station passage is indicated by the first positive, complete reversal of the TO/FROM indicator. Unlike a conventional VOR indicator, an HSI gives information about your aircraft heading and its relationship to your intended course.
5. Although two VOR receivers makes it easier to identify a fix defined by the intersection of radials from two VOR ground stations, one VOR receiver is the minimum equipment needed. If you have only one VOR receiver, then carefully hold the heading that tracks your course from the first VOR while you tune to the second station whose radial intersects your course.

TIME AND DISTANCE TO A STATION

6. You can calculate the time and distance to a station by turning perpendicular to the direct course to the station and measuring the time to move a specific number of degrees to a new radial. [Time to the station] = [Time to move to the new radial x 60] ÷ [Degrees to the new radial]. This formula also works when timing the degrees of change in the magnetic bearing to or from an NDB.
7. Example: If it takes 3 minutes to traverse 10 degrees of DME arc, the time to the station is 3 minutes x 60 ÷ 10 = 18 minutes. If your speed is 120 knots (2 n.m. per minute), the distance to the station is 18 x 2 = 36 n.m.
8. To determine time to a station using the **isosceles triangle method,** turn 10° (or any angle) to the side of your course and twist your course selector the same amount in the opposite direction. Time to station is the same as the time it takes for your CDI to center (assuming no wind).

ADF NAVIGATION

9. To determine time to a station using the isosceles triangle method with an ADF, simply measure the time it takes for the relative bearing (left or right of the aircraft nose) to double while holding a constant heading. This is the time to the station.
10. As you know from your private pilot course, the angle between the nose of the aircraft and an NDB is the **relative bearing. Magnetic heading (MH) plus relative bearing (RB) equals magnetic bearing to the station (MB).**
11. Because **a radio magnetic indicator (RMI)** has a slaved compass card that automatically rotates to the correct heading, it always displays the bearing to a station at the head of the arrow, and the bearing from a station at the tail of the arrow.
12. A movable card ADF also directly indicates bearing to a station when its compass card is adjusted to agree with the aircraft's actual heading.
13. Most RMIs have two bearing pointer needles, either one of which can be set to point to an NDB or VOR station. The tail of an RMI needle set to a VOR station indicates the radial you are on FROM the station, and the arrowhead indicates the course TO the station.
14. Intercepting a bearing to an NDB is easiest if you choose an angle, such as 45°, that is easy to read on the compass card. To establish a 45° intercept, turn so that the bearing to be intercepted appears over the heading indicator reference mark 45° to the left or right of the aircraft nose. Precisely maintain this heading and look for the ADF needle to also point 45° to the left or right of the aircraft's nose.
15. When turned parallel to the course to the station, the needle indicates any deviation by pointing left or right toward the course. If you simply home to the station with a crosswind, you will fly a curved path to the station.
16. If tracking on course to a station and holding a wind correction, the needle indicates the amount of wind correction, but in the opposite direction. If correcting 10° left, the needle points 10° right of the nose.
17. NDB station passage occurs when the needle passes behind the wingtip position and settles at or near the 180° position.

18. When on the desired track outbound with the proper drift correction established, the ADF pointer will be deflected to the windward side of the tail position.

DISTANCE MEASURING EQUIPMENT

19. DME is accurate to within 1/2 mile or 3% (whichever is greater).
20. DME indicates slant-range distance, resulting in greatest error at high altitudes close to a VORTAC. The indication should be 1 n.m. when you are directly over a VORTAC site at approximately 6,000 feet AGL. Slant range error is neglibible when you are at least 1 mile from the DME facility for every 1,000 feet of altitude above the station
21. It is easiest to fly a DME arc procedure using an RMI, although it is possible using a conventional VOR indicator. As you turn toward the VOR to compensate for a crosswind, the bearing pointer moves ahead of the wingtip reference. When correcting away from the VOR, the bearing pointer moves behind the wingtip.
22. Use 10° to 20° of correction if you drift 1/2 nautical mile outside a DME arc.

RADIO NAVIGATION OPERATIONAL CONSIDERATIONS

23. VOR facilities are classified according to their usable range and altitude, or **standard service volume** (SSV). You can find the SSV which applies to a particular VOR in the *Airport/Facility Directory*.
24. At altitudes between 14,500 and 18,000 feet MSL, an **(H) Class VORTAC** has a usable signal range of 100 nautical miles. Therefore, for direct routes off established airways at these altitudes, the facilities should be no farther apart than 200 nautical miles.
25. A **VOR receiver check** is required within 30 days prior to an IFR flight. Written documentation of this check is required.
26. When checking your VOR using a VOT, the CDI should be centered and the OBS should indicate that the aircraft is on the 360° radial, ±4°.
27. When using a VOR ground checkpoint, the CDI must center within ±4°. The allowable error using an airborne checkpoint is ±6°. When you conduct a dual system check, the difference between VOR systems should not exceed 4°.
28. VOR and DME facilities transmit their identifiers on a time sharing basis, with the VOR transmitting several identifiers for each one from the DME. If, when tuning to a VORTAC, you receive a single coded identification approximately once every 30 seconds, it means the DME component is operative and the VOR component is inoperative. The reverse is true if you hear the 1,020 Hz VOR signal several times and the 1,350 Hz DME tone is missing over a 30-second interval.
29. If a station is not transmitting an identifier, it means the station is undergoing maintenance and is unreliable, even if you are receiving navigation indications from that station.

AREA NAVIGATION

30. Area Navigation (RNAV) allows you to fly direct to your destination without the need to overfly VORs or other ground facilities. These systems include VOR/DME RNAV, inertial navigation system (INS), LORAN, and the global positioning system (GPS).
31. GPS provides a 95% probability of horizontal accuracy within 100 meters (328 feet), and a 99.99% probability of accuracy within 300 meters (984 feet).
32. You can determine whether a GPS installation is approved for IFR by checking the appropriate supplement to the airplane flight manual.
33. Aircraft using GPS navigation equipment under IFR must be equipped with an alternate means of navigation appropriate to the flight. You do not have to actively monitor the alternative navigation equipment if the GPS receiver uses RAIM for integrity monitoring. However, if RAIM capability of the GPS equipment is lost, active monitoring of an alternate means of navigation is required.

2-142   B10

When must an operational check on the aircraft VOR equipment be accomplished when used to operate under IFR?

A — Within the preceding 10 days or 10 hours of flight time.

B — Within the preceding 30 days or 30 hours of flight time.

C — Within the preceding 30 days.

2-142. Answer C. GFDICM 2C (FAR 91.171)

In order to operate an aircraft under IFR using the VOR system, the VOR equipment must be operationally checked within the preceding 30 days. Answers (A) and (B) are wrong because there is no flight time requirement.

2-143   B10
Which data must be recorded in the aircraft log or other appropriate log by a pilot making a VOR operational check for IFR operations?

A — VOR name or identification, date of check, amount of bearing error, and signature.
B — Place of operational check, amount of bearing error, date of check, and signature.
C — Date of check, VOR name or identification, place of operational check, and amount of bearing error.

2-144   B10
What record shall be made in the aircraft log or other permanent record by the pilot making the VOR operational check?

A — The date, place, bearing error, and signature.
B — The date, frequency of VOR or VOT, number of flight hours since last check, and signature.
C — The date, place, bearing error, aircraft total time, and signature.

2-145   B10
Which checks and inspections of flight instruments or instrument systems must be accomplished before an aircraft can be flown under IFR?

A — VOR within 30 days, altimeter systems within 24 calendar months, and transponder within 24 calendar months.
B — ELT test within 30 days, altimeter systems within 12 calendar months, and transponder within 24 calendar months.
C — VOR within 24 calendar months, transponder within 24 calendar months, and altimeter system within 12 calendar months.

2-146   B10
When making an airborne VOR check, what is the maximum allowable tolerance between the two indicators of a dual VOR system (units independent of each other except the antenna)?

A — 4° between the two indicated bearings of a VOR.
B — Plus or minus 4° when set to identical radials of a VOR.
C — 6° between the two indicated radials of a VOR.

2-147   B11
What minimum navigation equipment is required for IFR flight?

A — VOR/LOC receiver, transponder, and DME.
B — VOR receiver and, if in ARTS III environment, a coded transponder equipped for altitude reporting.
C — Navigation equipment appropriate to the ground facilities to be used.

2-143. Answer B. GFDICM 2C (FAR 91.171)
When conducting a VOR check, you must record the date and place where the check was done, as well as the bearing error indicated. In addition, you must sign the record indicating that you have completed the check. Answers (A) and (C) are wrong because neither the VOR name nor identification are required to be logged.

2-144. Answer A. GFDICM 2C (FAR 91.171)
See explanation for Question 2-143.

2-145. Answer A. GFDICM 2C (FAR 91.171, 91.411, 91.413)
The VOR system must be checked within 30 days, and the altimeter system and transponder must be inspected within 24 calendar months. None of the systems mentioned except an ELT require an inspection every 12 calendar months. Therefore, answers (B) and (C) are incorrect.

2-146. Answer A. GFDICM 2C (FAR 91.171)
If a dual VOR system is installed in an aircraft, you may check one system against the other. When doing this, both systems must be tuned to the same VOR facility and the maximum permissible variation between the two indicated bearings is 4°. Answer (B) is wrong because both bearing selectors must be indicating the bearing to the station, instead of setting both VORs to the same radial. Answer (C) is wrong because 6° exceeds the 4° maximum.

2-147. Answer C. GFDICM 2C (FAR 91.205, 91.215)
See explanation for Question 2-4. Answers (A) and (B) are wrong because transponders are not considered navigation equipment, and VOR receivers are not listed in the regulation as being required for IFR flight.

2-148   H826

(Refer to figure 30, GNATS ONE on page 10-26.) During the arc portion of the instrument departure procedure (GNATS1.MOURN), a left crosswind is encountered. Where should the bearing pointer of an RMI be referenced relative to the wingtip to compensate for wind drift and maintain the 15 DME arc?

A — Behind the right wingtip reference point.
B — On the right wingtip reference point.
C — Behind the left wingtip reference point.

2-149   J40

(Refer to figures 30 on page 10-26 and 30A.) What is your position relative to GNATS intersection and the instrument departure routing?

A — On departure course and past GNATS.
B — Right of departure course and past GNATS.
C — Left of departure course and have not passed GNATS.

2-148. Answer A. GFDICM 2C (AFH)

In order to compensate for the left crosswind, you must turn the aircraft to the left. Since an RMI always points directly at the station, the bearing pointer will be slightly behind the right wingtip. If there were no wind, the reference point would be on the right wingtip (answer B). Answer (C) is wrong because you would have to be flying in the opposite direction on the arc to get the reference point near the left wingtip.

2-149. Answer B. GFDICM 2C (IFH)

Your heading is 280° and the ADF bearing pointer indicates that VIOLE LMM is directly behind you. This means you are on the 280° bearing FROM VIOLE LMM, which is right of course. On this heading and bearing from the LMM, you would have been at the 216° radial of OED VORTAC when the big needle was 26° behind the right wing. In this example, the needle is 36° behind the right wing indicating that you have passed the 216° radial, or GNATS Intersection. Another way to visualize your position is to note that the tail of the VOR needle indicates 226° which means you have passed the 216° radial. Answer (A) is wrong because you are not on course. Answer (C) is wrong because you are right of course and passed GNATS Intersection.

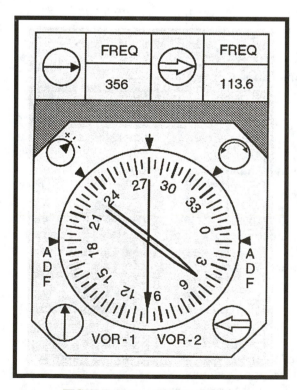

FIGURE 30A.—RMI Indicator.

2-150   J01
(Refer to figures 27 and 30 on pages 2-6 and 10-26.) To which maximum service volume distance from the OED VORTAC should you expect to receive adequate signal coverage for navigation at the flight planned altitude?

A — 100 NM.
B — 80 NM.
C — 40 NM.

2-150. Answer C. GFDICM 2C (AIM)
The *Airport/Facility Directory* contains the notation (H) next to the OED VORTAC. According to Legend 26 in Appendix 2, this indicates a high altitude service volume. This service volume is usable out to 40 n.m. from 1,000 to 14,500 feet MSL, out to 100 n.m. from 14,500 to 18,000 feet MSL, out to 130 n.m. from 18,000 to 45,000 feet MSL, and out to 100 n.m. from 45,000 to 60,000 feet MSL. With a cruising altitude of 8,000 feet (figure 27), you should expect to receive adequate signal coverage out to 40 n.m. Answers (A) and (B) are wrong because they substantially exceed the usable distance.

2-151   J41
(Refer to figures 35 on page 6-2 and 37.) What is your position relative to the CONNY intersection on the BUJ.BUJ3 transition?

A — Left of the TXK R-272 and approaching the BUJ R-059°.
B — Left of the TXK R-266 and past the BUJ R-065.
C — Right of the TXK R-270 and approaching the BUJ R-245.

2-151. Answer A. GFDICM 2C (IFH)
The HSI and RMI in figure 37 have different headings. If you interpret each instrument independently, the RMI indicates you are on the 270° radial of TXK which places the aircraft slightly left, or south, of the 272° radial. The HSI shows a fly right which means you are approaching the BUJ 059° radial. Therefore, answer (A) is correct. Answers (B) and (C) are wrong since the HSI and RMI do not reflect the radials specified in these choices.

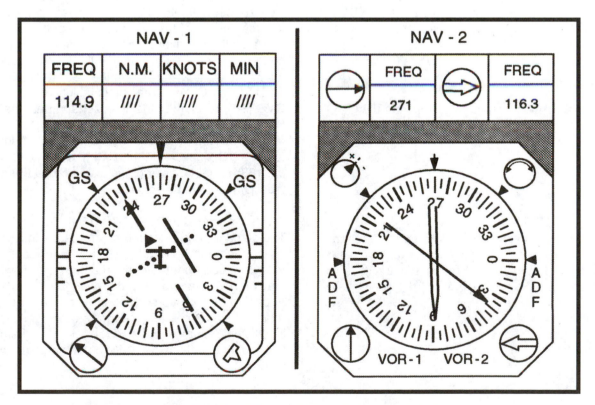

FIGURE 37.—CDI and RMI — NAV1 and NAV 2.

2-152   J42
(Refer to figures 42A and 43 on pages 7-6 and 2-57.) What is your position relative to CHAAR intersection? The aircraft is level at 3,000 feet MSL.

A — Right of the localizer course approaching CHAAR intersection and approaching the glide slope.
B — Left of the localizer course approaching CHAAR intersection and below the glide slope.
C — Right of the localizer course, past CHAAR intersection and above the glide slope.

2-153   J40
(Refer to figures 46 and 48 on pages 10-41 and 2-57.) What is your position relative to the 9 DME ARC and the 206° radial of the instrument departure procedure?

A — On the 9 DME arc and approaching R-206.
B — Outside the 9 DME arc and past R-206.
C — Inside the 9 DME arc and approaching R-206.

2-154   J40
(Refer to figures 52 and 54 on pages 10-45 and 2-58.) What is the aircraft's position relative to the HABUT Intersection? (The VOR-2 is tuned to 116.5.)

A — South of the localizer and past the GVO R-163.
B — North of the localizer and approaching the GVO R-163.
C — South of the localizer and approaching the GVO R-163.

2-155   H832
(Refer to figure 55 on page 6-7.) As a guide in making range corrections, how many degrees of relative bearing change should be used for each one half mile deviation from the desired arc?

A — 2° to 3°.
B — 5° maximum.
C — 10° to 20°.

2-152. Answer A. GFDICM 2C (IFH)
Your CDI is set to the inbound course (353°) for the ILS-1 RWY 36L approach and the course deviation needle is indicating that you are right of course. The DME also indicates that you are 7.5 n.m. from the localizer antenna. Since CHAAR Int. is located 7.2 n.m. from the localizer antenna, you have not reached CHAAR yet. Answer (B) is wrong because you are right of course and below the glide slope until you approach CHAAR Intersection. Answer (C) is wrong because you are not past CHAAR Int.

2-153. Answer A. GFDICM 2C (IFH)
The HSI in figure 48 shows that you are 9.0 nautical miles from the VORTAC. Therefore you are on the 9 DME arc. The 206° radial is dialed in the bearing selector and the CDI deflected to the left. This means that you are approaching the 206° radial. Outside the arc and past the radial (answer B) is incorrect because you are indicating 9 on the DME and the CDI would be deflected to the right if you were past the 206° radial. Inside the arc (answer C) would require a DME readout of less than 9.0 miles.

2-154. Answer B. GFDICM 2C (IFH)
The aircraft is on a heading of 240° tracking the localizer course outbound, which means the CDI has reverse sensing. The right deflection of the CDI indicates the localizer course is to the left, so you are north of the localizer. The tail of the larger needle on the RMI indicates you are on the 130° radial of the GVO VORTAC. Your heading is taking you toward the GVO R-163. South of the localizer and past the GVO R-163 (answer A) is incorrect because the CDI has reverse sensing when flying outbound on the localizer, and the VOR needle on the RMI has not yet crossed the 163° radial. Answer (C) is also incorrect because the CDI has reverse sensing.

2-155. Answer C. GFDICM 2C (IFH)
The standard rule of thumb recommends that you change the relative bearing 10° to 20° for each 1/2-mile deviation from the desired arc. In a crosswind it may be necessary to keep the bearing pointer ahead or behind the wingtip position to remain on the arc. A relative bearing change of 2° to 3° (answer A) is insufficient. A maximum of 5° (answer B) of relative bearing change is also insufficient to maintain most DME arcs.

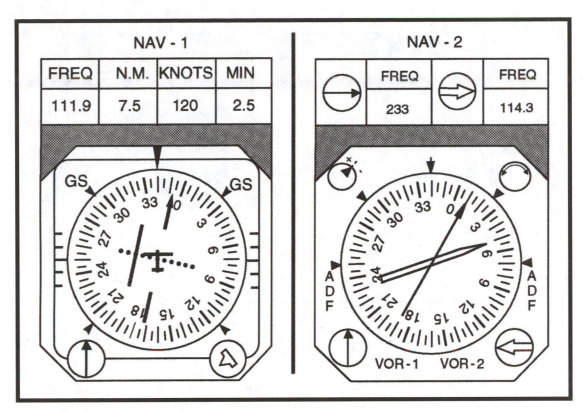

FIGURE 43.—CDI and RMI — NAV1 and NAV2.

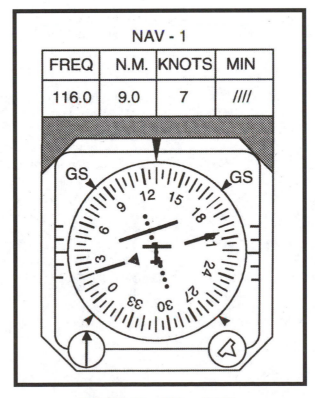

FIGURE 48.—CDI — NAV1.

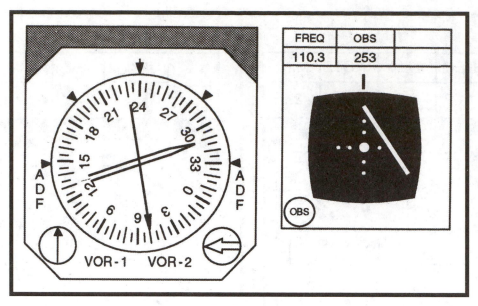

FIGURE 54.—RMI and CDI Indicators.

2-156   J01

(Refer to figure 58.) Which indications on the VOR receivers and DME at the Easterwood Field VOR receiver checkpoint would meet the regulatory requirement for this flight?

VOR TO/FROM   VOR   TO/FROM DME
No. 1   No. 2

A — 097°FROM   101°FROM   3.3
B — 097° TO   096° TO   3.2
C — 277°FROM   280° FROM 3.3

2-157   J42

(Refer to figures 60A and 61 on page 2-60 and 2-61.) What is your position relative to the PLATS intersection, glide slope, and the localizer course?

A — Past PLATS, below the glide slope, and right of the localizer course.
B — Approaching PLATS, above the glide slope, and left of the localizer course.
C — Past PLATS, above the glide slope, and right of the localizer course.

2-156. Answer A. GFDICM 2C (FAR 91.171)

The *Airport/Facility Directory* (A/FD) excerpt in figure 58 lists the details on specific VOR receiver check points, including Easterwood Field at College Station. Included is G for ground check, 097° as the exact radial FROM the station, 3.2 n.m. as the distance from the navaid to the check point, and a description to visually identify the check point. FAR 91.171(b)(2) lists the maximum permissible bearing error of ± 4° for a ground check. Centered CDIs with the bearing selec-tor set on 097° and 096° would meet the requirements with a FROM indication, not a TO indication (answer B). Centered CDI needles with 277° and 280° (answer C) set in the bearing selector do not meet the A/FD specifications for this ground station.

2-157. Answer C. GFDICM 2C (IFH)

The tail of the large RMI needle is past 291°. It indicates you are on the 300° radial FROM VUH VOR. The glide slope indicator is deflected down, showing that you are one dot above the glide slope. The localizer CDI is deflected to the left, showing you are one dot right of course. Below the glide slope (answer A) would be indicated by the upward deflection of the glide slope indicator. The tail of the RMI would be moving clockwise as you approach PLATS Int. In this illustration the needle has already moved past the 291° radial FROM VUH VOR, so you are not approaching PLATS Int. (answer B).

140　　　　　　　　　　　　　　　**TEXAS**

COLLEGE STATION

EASTERWOOD FLD　(CLL)　3 SW　UTC–6(–5DT)　30°35'18"N 96°21'49"W　　　　**HOUSTON**
　320 　B　S4　FUEL 100LL, JET A　OX 2　ARFF Index A　　　　　　　　　**H-2K, 5B, L-17A**
　RWY 16-34: H7000X150 (ASPH–GRVD)　S-70, D-90, DT-150　MIRL　　　　　　　　　**IAP**
　　RWY 16: VASI(V4R)—GA 3.0°TCH 51'. Tree.　　　RWY 34: MALSR.
　RWY 10-28: H5160X150 (CONC)　S-27, D-50, DT-87　MIRL
　　RWY 10: VASI(V4L)—GA 3.0°TCH 50'. Tree.　　　RWY 28: REIL VASI(V4L)—GA 3.0° TCH 54'. Tree.
　RWY 04-22: H5149X150 (CONC)　S-27, D-50, DT-87
　　RWY 04: Tree.　　　RWY 22: Tree.
　AIRPORT REMARKS: Attended 1200-0500Z‡. CAUTION: deer on rwys. CAUTION: Rwy 10-28 taxiway B and taxiway E
　　have uneven surfaces. Birds on and in vicinity of arpt. MIRL Rwy 10-28 preset medium ints when twr clsd, to
　　increase ints and ACTIVATE MIRL Rwy 16–34 and MALSR Rwy 34—CTAF. CLOSED to unscheduled air carrier
　　ops with more than 30 passenger seats except 24 hours PPR call, arpt manager 409-845-4811. Rwy 04–22
　　day VFR ops only. Itinerant acft park North of twr, overnight parking fee. Ldg fee scheduled FAR 135 and all FAR
　　121 ops. For fuel after hours PPR call 409-845-4811/823 –0690 or ctc Texas A and M University police
　　409-845-2345; late ngt fee. Rwy 16–34 grvd except south 200'. Rwy 04–22 deteriorating and vegetation
　　growing through cracks. NOTE: See SPECIAL NOTICE—Simultaneous Operations on Intersecting Runways.
　COMMUNICATIONS: CTAF 118.5　ATIS 126.85 (1200–0400Z‡)　UNICOM 122.95
　　MONTGOMERY COUNTY FSS (CXO) TF 1–800–WX–BRIEF. NOTAM FILE CLL.
　　COLLEGE STATION RCO 122.65 122.2 (MONTGOMERY COUNTY FSS).
　®HOUSTON CENTER APP/DEP CON: 120.4
　　TOWER: 118.5 (1200-0400Z‡) (VFR only)　GND CON: 121.7
　RADIO AIDS TO NAVIGATION: NOTAM FILE CLL. VHF/DF ctc FSS
　　COLLEGE STATION (L) VORTACW 113.3　CLL　Chan 80　30°36'17"N 96°25'13"W　100° 3.1 NM to fld.
　　　370/08E. HIWAS.
　　ROWDY NDB (LOM) 260　CL　30°29'36"N 96°20'16"W　341° 5.9 NM to fld.
　　ILS 111.7 I-CLL Rwy 34 LOM ROWDY NDB. ILS unmonitored when twr closed.

COLLEGE STATION　30°36'17"N 96°25'13"W　NOTAM FILE CLL.　　　　　　　**HOUSTON**
　(L) VORTACW 113.3　CLL　Chan 80　100° 3.1 NM to Easterwood Fld. 370/08E. HIWAS.　**H-2K, 5B, L-17A**
　RCO 122.65 122.2 (MONTGOMERY COUNTY FSS)

VOR RECEIVER CHECK　　　　　　　　259

TEXAS

VOR RECEIVER CHECK POINTS

Facility Name (Arpt Name)	Freq/Ident	Type Check Pt. Gnd. AB/ALT	Azimuth from Fac. Mag	Dist. from Fac. N.M.	Check Point Description
Abilene (Abilene Regional)	113.7/ABI	A/2800	047	10.1	Over silos in center of Ft Phantom Lake.
Alice (Alice International)	114.5/ALI	G	270	0.5	On twy N of hangar.
Amarillo (Amarillo Internationl)	117.2/AMA	G	210	4.5	On east runup pad Rwy 22.
Austin (Robert Mueller Muni)	114.6/AUS	G	118	0.6	On runup area on twy to Rwy 31L.
Beaumont (Jefferson County)	114.5/BPT	G	310	1.0	On runup area for Rwy 12.
Big Spring (Big Spring McMahon-Wrinkle)	114.3/BGS	A/3500	107	10.5	Over red and white water tank.
Borger (Hutchinson Co)	108.6/BGD	G	175	6.7	On intersecting twy in front of terminal.
Brownsville (Brownsville/South Padre Island Intl)	116.3/BRO	G	248	3.2	On NE corner of parking ramp.
Brownwood (Brownwood Muni)	108.6/BWD	A/2600	169	6.2	Over rotating bcn.
Childress (Childress Muni)	117.6/CDS	G	353	3.7	At intersection of edge of ramp at center twy.
College Station (Easterwood Field)	113.3/CLL	G	097	3.2	On W edge of parking ramp
Corpus Christi (Corpus Christi Intl)	115.5/CRP	A/1100	187	7.5	Over grain elevator.
Corpus Christi (San Patricio County)	115.5/CRP	A/1000	318	9.5	Over rotating beacon on arpt.
Daisetta (Liberty Muni)	116.9/DAS	A/1200	195	7.5	Over hangar S of arpt.
Dalhart (Dalhart Muni)	112.0/DHT	G	170	3.9	On SE corner of main ramp
Eagle Lake (Eagle Lake)	116.4/ELA	A/1200	180	4.5	Over water tank 0.4 NM SW

FIGURE 58.—Excerpts from Airport/Facility Directory.

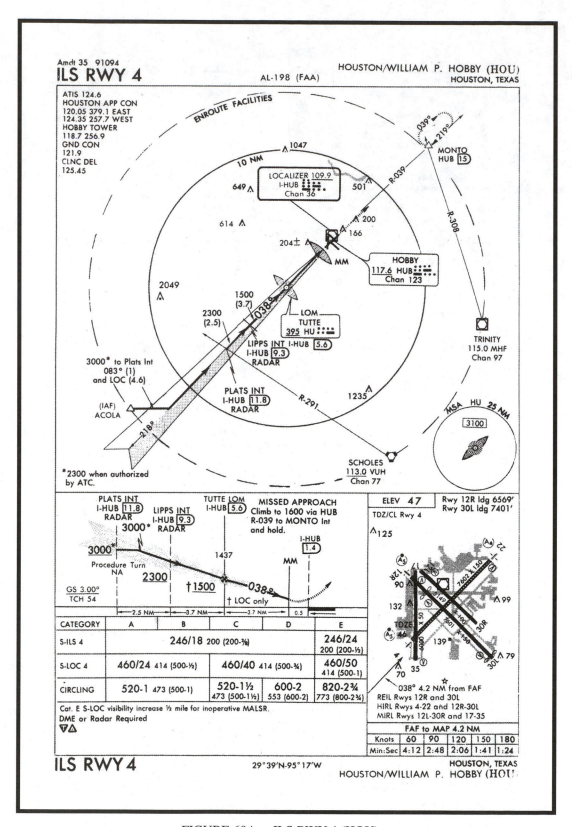

FIGURE 60A.—ILS RWY 4 (HOU).

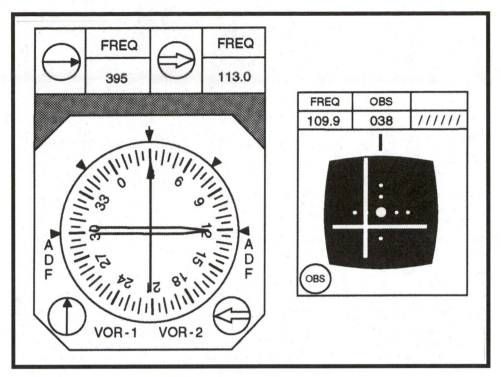

FIGURE 61.—RMI and CDI Indicators.

2-158   J34

(Refer to figure 64 on page 2-62.) The course deviation indicator (CDI) are centered. Which indications on the No. 1 and No. 2 VOR receivers over the Lafayette Regional Airport would meet the requirements for the VOR receiver check?

VOR No. 1	TO/FROM	VOR No. 2	TO/FROM
A — 162°	TO	346°	FROM
B — 160°	FROM	162°	FROM
C — 341°	FROM	330°	FROM

2-159   J35

(Refer to figures 65 and 66 on pages 5-4 and 2-63.) What is your position relative to GRICE intersection?

A — Right of V552 and approaching GRICE intersection.

B — Right of V552 and past GRICE intersection.

C — Left of V552 and approaching GRICE intersection.

2-158. Answer A. GFDICM 2C (FAR 91.171)

The *Airport/Facility Directory* (A/FD) excerpt in figure 64 lists the details on specific VOR receiver check points, including Lafayette Regional Airport. The A/1000 means this is an airborne check at 1,000 feet, 340° is the exact radial FROM the station, the distance is 25 n.m. from the station, and the check point visual description over the rotating beacon is given. FAR 91.171 lists the maximum permissible bearing error of ± 6° when using a designated airborne check point. Centered CDIs must be within 6° of 340° or the reciprocal, 160°. Indications of centered on 162° with TO and centered on 346° with FROM comply with the regulations. With 160° and 162° dialed into the bearing selector (answer B), the ambiguity indicator should read TO. A centered CDI on 330° (answer C) exceeds the maximum airborne VOR check tolerances.

2-159. Answer A. GFDICM 2C (IFH)

The VOR indicator on the left is tuned to the frequency for TBD VORTAC. The bearing selector is set to 116° and the CDI is deflected to the left. This indicates you are right, or south, of V552. The VOR indicator on the right is tuned to the frequency for the ILS that establishes the intersection. The bearing selector is set to the inbound course of 236° and the CDI is also deflected to the left. This indicates that you are approaching GRICE intersection. If you were beyond GRICE int. (answer B) the CDI on the VOR indicator on the right would be deflected to the right. If you were left, or north, of V552 (answer C), the CDI on the VOR indicator tuned to TBD VORTAC would be deflected to the right.

LOUISIANA

VOR RECEIVER CHECK POINTS

Facility Name (Arpt Name)	Freq/Ident	Type Check Pt. Gnd. AB/ALT	Azimuth from Fac. Mag	Dist. from Fac. N.M.	Check Point Description
Baton Rouge (Baton Rouge Metro, Ryan) . . .	116.5/BTR	A/1500	063	7.7	Over water tank W side of arpt.
Downtown	108.6/DTN	A/1500	290	10	Over white water tower.
Esler (Esler Regional)	108.8/ESF	G	151	3.5	On ramp in front of admin bldg.
Hammond (Hammond Muni)	109.6/HMU	G	342	.6	On twy W side app end Rwy 18.
Lafayette (Lafayette Regional)	110.8/LFT	A/1000	340	25	Over rotating beacon.
Lake Charles (Lake Charles Muni)	113.4/LCH	A/1000	253	6.2	Over rotg bcn on atct.
Monroe (Monroe Muni)	117.2/MLU	G	209	0.9	On ramp SE of atct.
Natchez (Concordia Parish)	110.0/HEZ	A/1000	247	10.5	Over hangar NW end of field.
New Orleans (Lakefront)	113.2/MSY	A/1000	081	7.7	Over lakefront atct.
Ruston	112.8/RSN	A/2000	343	14	Over hwy & RR crossing at Dubash.
Shreveport (Shreveport Downtown)	108.6/DTN	G	307	.5	On runup area N side of rwy 14.
Shreveport (Shreveport Regional)	117.4/SHV	A/1200	175	19.3	Over old terminal building.
Tibby (Thibodaux Muni)	112.0/TBD	A/1000	006	5.0	Over railroad bridge off apch end rwy 26.
	112.0/TBD	A/1000	117	10.0	Over intersection of rwys 17-35 and 12-30.

§ **LAFAYETTE REGIONAL** (LFT) 2 SE GMT−6(−5DT) 30°12'14"N 91°59'16"W   **HOUSTON**
42. B S4 FUEL 100LL, JET A OX 1 CFR Index B   **H-4F, L-17C**
   RWY 03-21: H7651X150 (ASPH-GRVD) S-75, D-170, DT-290 HIRL   **IAP**
     RWY 03: REIL. VASI(V4L)──GA 3.0°TCH 35'. Tree.
     RWY 21: MALSR. VASI(V4L)──GA 3.0°TCH 44'. Tree.
   RWY 10-28: H5401X150 (ASPH) S-85, D-110, DT-175 MIRL
     RWY 10: REIL (out of svc indefinitely). VASI(V4L)──GA 3.0° TCH 35.33'. Tree.
     RWY 28: REIL. VASI(V4L)──GA 3.0° TCH 55'. Thld dsplcd 202'. Tree.
   RWY 01-19: H5069X150 (ASPH) S-25, D-45
     RWY 01: VASI(V4R)──GA 3.0°TCH 50'. Tree.
   AIRPORT REMARKS: Attended continuously. Rwy 01-19 closed to air carriers. ACTIVATE MALSR Rwy 21──118.5.
   COMMUNICATIONS: CTAF 118.5   ATIS 120.5 Opr 1200-0500Z‡   UNICOM 122.95
    LAFAYETTE FSS (LFT) on arpt. 122.35, 122.2, 122.1R, 110.8T LD 318-233-4952 NOTAM FILE LFT.
Ⓡ APP/DEP CON 121.1 (011°-190°) 124.0 (191°-010°) (1200-0400Z‡)
    HOUSTON CENTER APP/DEP CON 133.65 (0400-1200Z‡)
    TOWER 118.5, 121.35 (Helicopter ops) (1200-0400Z‡)   GND CON 121.8   CLNC DEL 125.55
    STAGE III ctc APP CON within 25 NM below 7000'
   RADIO AIDS TO NAVIGATION: NOTAM FILE LFT. VHF/DF ctc LAFAYETTE FSS
    (L) VORTAC 110.8 LFT Chan 45 30°08'45"N 91°59'00"W 344° 3.0 NM to fld. 40/06E
    LAFFS NDB (LOM) 375 LF 30°17'21"N 91°54'29"W 215° 5.8 NM to fld
    LAKE MARTIN NDB (MHW) 362 LKM 30°11'33"N 91°52'58"W 270° 5.2 NM to fld
    ILS/DME 109.5 I-LFT Chan 32 Rwy 21 LOM LAFFS NDB. Unmonitored when twr clsd.
   ASR

FIGURE 64.—Excerpts from Airport/Facility Directory(LFT).

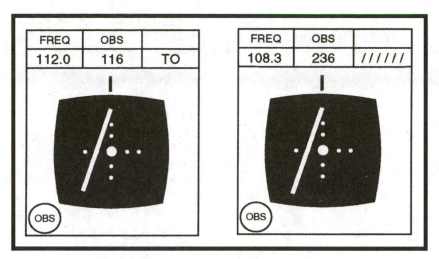

FIGURE 66.—CDI and OBS Indicators.

2-160   J35

(Refer to figures 71 on page 10-50 and 71A.) What is your position relative to the Flosi intersection north-bound on V213?

A — West of V213 and approaching the Flosi intersection.

B — East of V213 and approaching the Flosi intersection.

C — West of V213 and past the Flosi intersection.

2-160. Answer A. GFDICM 2C (IFH)

The VOR indicator on the left is tuned to IGN VOR-TAC and the bearing selector is set to 265° which is the radial that establishes Flosi intersection. The CDI is deflected to the right which indicates that you are south of and approaching Flosi intersection. The VOR indicator on the right is tuned to SAX VORTAC, the bearing selector is set to 029° and the CDI is deflected to the right. This indicates that you are left or west of the 029° radial. Answer (A) is the only correct choice. Answer (B) is incorrect because the VOR indicator tuned to SAX would show a CDI deflection to the left if you were east of V213. Answer (C) is incorrect because the VOR indicator tuned to IGN would show a CDI deflection to the left if you were past Flosi intersection northbound.

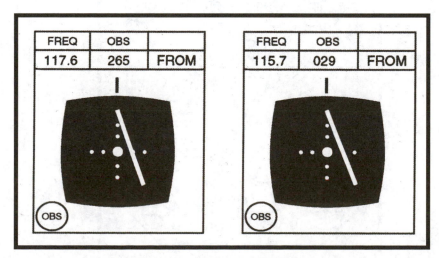

FIGURE 71A.—CDI and OBS Indicators.

2-161   J01
(Refer to figure 76 on page 10-55.) Which indication would be an acceptable accuracy check of both VOR receivers when the aircraft is located on the VOR receiver checkpoint at the Helena Regional Airport?

A — A.
B — B.
C — C.

2-161. Answer C. GFDICM 2C (A/FD Legend) (FAR 91.171)
(Refer to the VOR RECEIVER CHECK portion of the *Airport/Facility Directory* (A/FD) excerpts in figure 76). The VOR receiver check at Helena is a ground checkpoint based on the 237° radial FROM the HLN VORTAC. FAR 91.171 states that a designated VOR check point on the surface has a maximum permissible bearing error of ± 4°. The tails of the two RMI bearing pointers in illustration C are on 235°, well within the ± 4° tolerance. Answers (A) and (B) are wrong because the RMIs are not indicating that the aircraft is anywhere near the 237° radial. The tails of the two RMIs in illustration A are on 175° and 185°. The tails of the two RMIs in illustration B are on 050°.

2-162   J35
(Refer to figures 78 on page 10-57 and 79.) What is your position relative to the VOR COP southeast bound on V86 between the BOZEMAN and LIVINGSTON VORTACs? The No. 1 VOR is tuned to 116.1 and the No. 2 VOR is tuned to 112.2.

A — Past the LVM R-246 and west of the BZN R-110.
B — Approaching the LVM R-246 and west of the BZN R-110.
C — Past the LVM R-246 and east of the BZN R-110.

2-162. Answer C. GFDICM 2C (IFH)
Figure 79 indicates an eastbound heading of 130°. The tail of the thin bearing pointer (VOR-1) is on 239°, indicating that you are past the 246° radial of LVM VORTAC. The tail of the thick bearing pointer (VOR-2) is on 102°, indicating that you are east of the 110° radial of BZN VORTAC. Answer (A) would be correct if the tail of VOR-2 was on a radial greater than 110°. Answer (B) would also require the tail of VOR-1 to be on a radial greater than 246°.

2-163   J01
What is the maximum tolerance allowed for an operational VOR equipment check when using a VOT?

A — Plus or minus 4°.
B — Plus or minus 6°.
C — Plus or minus 8°.

2-163. Answer A. GFDICM 2C (AIM) (FAR 91.171)
The maximum tolerance for a VOR equipment check using a VOT is ± 4°. All VOR equipment checks performed in flight using an airborne checkpoint have a maximum tolerance of ± 6° (answer B). ± 8° (answer C) exceeds the maximum tolerance for any VOR equipment check.

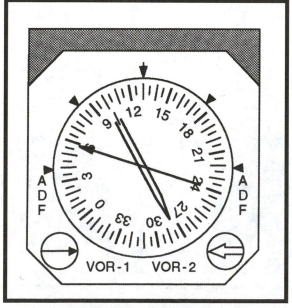

FIGURE 79.—RMI Indicator.

2-164   J01

When using VOT to make a VOR receiver check, the CDI should be centered and the OBS should indicate that the aircraft is on the

A — 090 radial.
B — 180 radial.
C — 360 radial.

2-165   J01

How should the pilot make a VOR receiver check when the aircraft is located on the designated checkpoint on the airport surface?

A — Set the OBS on 180° plus or minus 4°; the CDI should center with a FROM indication.
B — Set the OBS on the designated radial. The CDI must center within plus or minus 4° of that radial with a FROM indication.
C — With the aircraft headed directly toward the VOR and the OBS set to 000°, the CDI should center within plus or minus 4° of that radial with a TO indication.

2-166   J01

When the CDI needle is centered during an airborne VOR check, the omnibearing selector and the TO/FROM indicator should read

A — within 4° of the selected radial.
B — within 6° of the selected radial.
C — 0° TO, only if you are due south of the VOR.

2-167   J01

(Refer to figure 81 on page 2-66.) When checking a dual VOR system by use of a VOT, which illustration indicates the VOR's are satisfactory?

A — 1.
B — 2.
C — 4.

2-168   J01

While airborne, what is the maximum permissible variation between the two indicated bearings when checking one VOR system against the other?

A — Plus or minus 4° when set to identical radials of a VOR.
B — 4° between the two indicated bearings to a VOR.
C — Plus or minus 6° when set to identical radials of a VOR.

2-164. Answer C. GFDICM 2C (AIM) (FAR 91.171)

To use a VOT, tune in the VOT frequency and center the CDI. The OBS should read 360° with the ambiguity indicator showing FROM, meaning you are on the 360° radial. The CDI will not center with the OBS set to 090° (answer A). The CDI will center on 180° (answer B), but the ambiguity indicator will show a TO indication.

2-165. Answer B. GFDICM 2C (AIM) (FAR 91.171)

A ground checkpoint is a designated point on the surface of an airport where you can use a VOR radial to check your VOR receiver. You must first set the OBS to the designated radial and the CDI must center within ± 4° of that radial with the ambiguity indicator showing FROM. Answer (A) is wrong because a ground checkpoint can be based on any designated radial. The heading of the aircraft (answer C) does not matter when using a ground checkpoint. However, you do have to tune in the radial and have a FROM indication.

2-166. Answer B. GFDICM 2C (AIM) (FAR 91.171)

All airborne checkpoints are based on centering the CDI within 6° of a selected radial. All ground based VOR checks have a maximum error of 4° (answer A). Airborne VOR checks are not necessarily based on the 0° radial with a TO indication (answer C).

2-167. Answer A. GFDICM 2C (AIM)

For a VOT check with dual VORs and an RMI, the head of each needle should point toward 180°. In addition, both needles must be within 4° of each other. RMI #2 (answer B) is indicating a 180° difference between the needles. RMI # 4 (answer C) shows the opposite of a proper VOT indication. Both needles should be pointing toward 180°, not 360°.

2-168. Answer B. GFDICM 2C (AIM) (FAR 91.171)

The maximum permissible error between two VOR receivers is 4° between the indicators. Answer (A) is wrong because the two VOR systems do not have to be set to identical radials. ± 6° (answer C) applies to an airborne check of a single VOR.

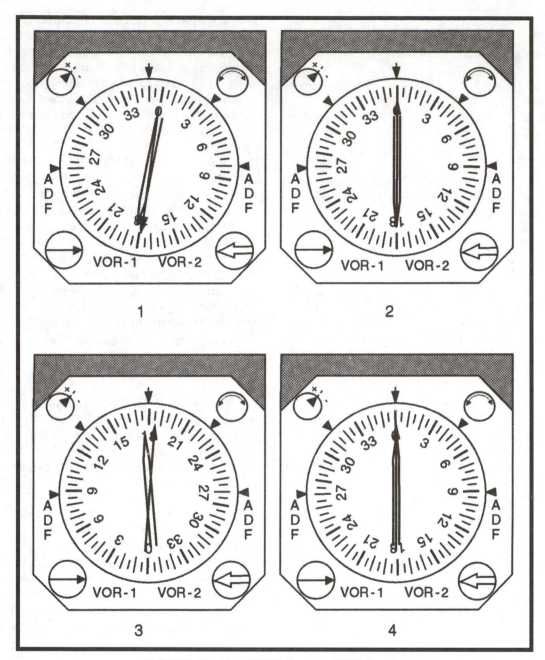

FIGURE 81.—Dual VOR System, VOT Check.

2-169   J01

How should the pilot make a VOR receiver check when the aircraft is located on the designated checkpoint on the airport surface?

A — With the aircraft headed directly toward the VOR and the OBS set to 000°, the CDI should center within plus or minus 4° of that radial with a TO indication.

B — Set the OBS on the designated radial. The CDI must center within plus or minus 4° of that radial with a FROM indication.

C — Set the OBS on 180° plus or minus 4°; the CDI should center with a FROM indication.

2-169. Answer B. GFDICM 2C (AIM) (FAR 91.171)
See explanation for Question 2-165.

2-170   J01
(Refer to figure 82.) Which is an acceptable range of accuracy when performing an operational check of dual VOR's using one system against the other?

A — 1.
B — 2.
C — 4.

2-170. Answer C. GFDICM 2C (AIM) (FAR 91.171)
When using a dual VOR system to complete a VOR accuracy check, tune both VORs to the same frequency and note the bearings to the station. The needles should be within 4° of each other. Indicator #1 (answer A) is displaying a difference of 180° between the RMI needles. Indicator #2 (answer B) shows approximately 10° between needles, which is out of limits.

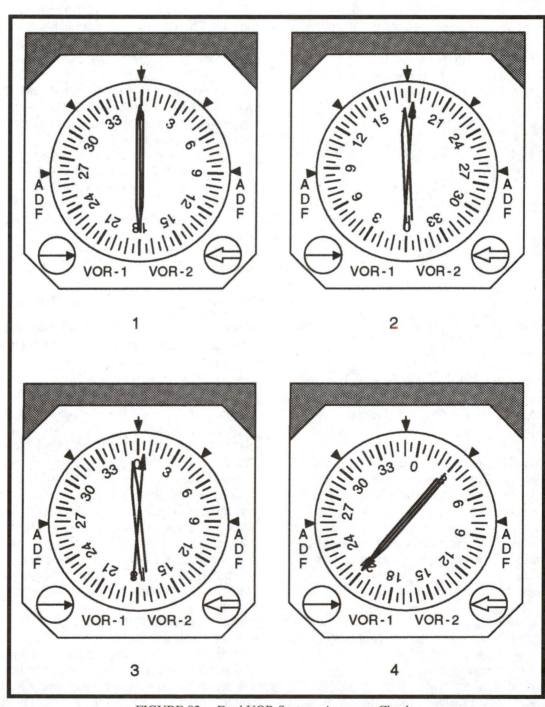

FIGURE 82.—Dual VOR System, Accuracy Check.

2-171   J01
Where can the VOT frequency for a particular airport be found?

A — On the IAP Chart and in the Airport/Facility Directory.
B — Only in the Airport/Facility Directory.
C — In the Airport/Facility Directory and on the A/G Voice Communication Panel of the En Route Low Altitude Chart.

2-172   J01
Which indications are acceptable tolerances when checking both VOR receivers by use of the VOT?

A — 360° TO and 003° TO, respectively.
B — 001° FROM and 005° FROM, respectively.
C — 176° TO and 003° FROM, respectively.

2-173   J01
In which publication can the VOR receiver ground checkpoint(s) for a particular airport be found?

A — Aeronautical Information Manual.
B — En Route Low Altitude Chart.
C — Airport/Facility Directory.

2-174   J01
Which is the maximum tolerance for the VOR indication when the CDI is centered and the aircraft is directly over the airborne checkpoint?

A — Plus or minus 6° of the designated radial.
B – Plus 6° or minus 4° of the designated radial.
C – Plus or minus 4° of the designated radial.

2-175   J01
When making an airborne VOR check, what is the maximum allowable tolerance between the two indicators of a dual VOR system (units independent of each other except the antenna)?

A — 4° between the two indicated radials of a VOR.
B — Plus or minus 4° when set to identical radials of a VOR.
C — 6° between the two indicated radials of a VOR.

2-176   J01
Which distance is displayed by the DME indicator?

A — Slant range distance in NM.
B — Slant range distance in SM.
C — Line-of-sight direct distance from aircraft to VORTAC in SM.

2-171. Answer C. GFDICM 2C (A/FD Legend)
The location and frequency of VOTs are listed near the back of each *Airport/Facility Directory* (A/FD). This information is also in the A/G voice communication panel of NOS enroute low altitude charts. It is not listed on instrument approach procedure charts (answer A). VOT information is included on low altitude enroute charts, not just in the A/FD (answer B).

2-172. Answer C. GFDICM 2C (AIM)
To use a VOT, tune in the VOT frequency and center the CDI. The OBS should read either 360° with a FROM indication or 180° with a TO indication. When conducting a VOT the permissible bearing error is ± 4°. The 360° TO and 003° TO (answer A) is incorrect because the VOT signal would give you 360° (± 4°) with a FROM indication. The CDI centered on 005° with a FROM indication (answer B) exceeds the maximum 4° error for VOT checks.

2-173. Answer C. GFDICM 2C (AIM)
Information on VOR receiver checkpoints can be found in the back of the *Airport/Facility Directory*. This information is not found in the *Aeronautical Information Manual* (answer A), and enroute low altitude charts (answer B) only indicate where VOTs are located.

2-174. Answer A. GFDICM 2C (AIM) (FAR 91.171)
Single VOR checks using an airborne checkpoint allow a maximum error +/- 6°. Answers (B) and (C) are incorrect tolerance limits for an airborne checkpoint.

2-175. Answer A. GFDICM 2C (AIM) (FAR 91.171)
See explanation for Question 2-168. When using a dual VOR system to complete a VOR accuracy check, both VORs should be tuned to the same frequency and the CDIs should be centered with no more than 4° difference between the indicated radials. You do not set identical radials (answer B) in the VOR systems, and you are not allowed ± 4°. An error of 6° (answer C) applies only to the maximum error when testing a single VOR over an airborne checkpoint.

2-176. Answer A. GFDICM 2C (IFH)
Since the airborne interrogator is at altitude, DME distance is the slant range distance in nautical miles between the aircraft and the ground station rather than the actual horizontal distance measured on the earth's surface. Answers (B) and (C) are both wrong because DME distances are measured in nautical miles, not statute miles.

2-177   J01
Where does the DME indicator have the greatest error between ground distance to the VORTAC and displayed distance?

A — High altitudes far from the VORTAC.
B — High altitudes close to the VORTAC.
C — Low altitudes far from the VORTAC.

2-177. Answer B. GFDICM 2C (IFH)
DME displays slant range distance in nautical miles between the aircraft and the ground station, rather than the actual horizontal distance measured on the earth's surface. The higher your altitude and the closer to the station you are, the greater the error. At high altitudes far from the station (answer A), the ratio of altitude to distance from the station becomes smaller and the error is less significant. At low altitudes (answer C), you are closer to the ground distance, so the slant range error is smaller.

2-178   J01
For operations off established airways at 17,000 feet MSL in the contiguous U.S., (H) Class VORTAC facilities used to define a direct route of flight should be no farther apart than

A — 75 NM.
B — 100 NM.
C — 200 NM.

2-178. Answer C. GFDICM 2C (AIM)
The service volume of an (H) class VOR between 14,500 feet AGL up to and including 60,000 feet is 100 n.m. For flights between these altitudes, (H) Class VORs forming an unpublished direct route should be no more than 200 n.m. apart. Answer (A) is wrong because it is less than the 100 n.m. (H) Class VOR. Answer (B) is incorrect because it is the range of one (H) Class VOR, not the maximum reception distance between (H) Class VORs.

2-179   J01
What indication should a pilot receive when a VOR station is undergoing maintenance and may be considered unreliable?

A — No coded identification, but possible navigation indications.
B — Coded identification, but no navigation indications.
C — A voice recording on the VOR frequency announcing that the VOR is out of service for maintenance.

2-179. Answer A. GFDICM 2C (AIM)
The only positive method for identifying a VOR is by its Morse code identification or by a recorded automatic voice identification. During periods of maintenance, the facility may radiate a T-E-S-T code (Morse code), or the code may be removed. There will be no coded identification and no voice recording, therefore answers (B) and (C) are incorrect.

2-180   J01
A particular VOR station is undergoing routine maintenance. This is evidenced by

A — removal of the navigational feature.
B — broadcasting a maintenance alert signal on the voice channel.
C — removal of the identification feature.

2-180. Answer C. GFDICM 2C (AIM)
See explanation for Question 2-179. Answer (A) is wrong because the navigational signal may be transmitted, but it may be unreliable. Answer (B) is also wrong; not all VORs have a voice capability.

2-181   J01
What is the meaning of a single coded identification received only once approximately every 30 seconds from a VORTAC?

A — The VOR and DME components are operative.
B — VOR and DME components are both operative, but voice identification is out of service.
C — The DME component is operative and the VOR component is inoperative.

2-181. Answer C. GFDICM 2C (AIM)
A single, coded identification with a repetition interval of approximately 30 seconds indicates the DME is operative. If the DME is inoperative, the coded identification will be removed even though the distance indications may appear normal. Answer (A) is incorrect because continuous coded identification would be the indication that both VOR and DME were operative. Answer (B) is wrong because, if both were operative, the 30 second interval would not be apparent.

2-182   J01
Which DME indication should you receive when you are directly over a VORTAC site at approximately 6,000 feet AGL?

A — 0.
B — 1.
C — 1.3.

2-182. Answer B. GFDICM 2C (IFH)
DME indicates slant range, not horizontal range. The difference between slant range distance and horizontal distance is slant range error, which is smallest at low altitudes and long range. Slant range error is greatest when the aircraft is directly over the navigational facility. In this case, the DME receiver will display altitude in nautical miles above the facility. One nautical mile is approximately 6,000 feet above the facility (AGL). Answer (B) is the only correct choice.

2-183   J08
Which of the following is required equipment for operating an aircraft within Class B airspace?

A — A 4096 code transponder with automatic pressure altitude reporting equipment.
B — A VOR receiver with DME.
C — A 4096 code transponder.

2-183. Answer A. GFDICM 2C (AIM) (FAR 91.131)
For all operations in Class B airspace, a Mode S or a 4096-code transponder with Mode C automatic altitude reporting is required. Answer (B) is incorrect because a VOR is only required for IFR operations and DME is not required at all. Answer (C) is incorrect because the transponder must have automatic altitude reporting capability.

2-184   H832
As a rule of thumb, to minimize DME slant range error, how far from the facility should you be to consider the reading as accurate?

A — Two miles or more for each 1,000 feet of altitude above the facility.
B — One or more miles for each 1,000 feet of altitude above the facility.
C — No specific distance is specified since the reception is line-of-sight.

2-184. Answer B. GFDICM 2C (IFH)
Slant range error is negligible if the aircraft is one mile or more from the ground facility for each 1,000 feet of altitude above the elevation of the facility. Answer (A) is incorrect because the rule of thumb is based on one, not two or more, miles for each 1,000 feet. Answer (C) is incorrect because reception, although dependent on line-of-sight conditions, is still limited by the rule of thumb, as well as a maximum range of 200 n.m.

2-185   H832
As a rule of thumb, to minimize DME slant range error, how far from the facility should you be to consider the reading as accurate?

A — Two miles or more for each 1,000 feet of altitude above the facility.
B — One or more miles for each 1,000 feet of altitude above the facility.
C — No specific distance is specified since the reception is line-of-sight.

2-185. Answer B. GFDICM 2C (IFH)
See explanation for Question 2-184. Identical question.

2-186   J17

(Refer to figure 87 on page 5-8 and figure 88.) What is your position with reference to FALSE intersection (V222) if your VOR receivers indicate as shown?

A — South of V222 and east of FALSE intersection.
B — North of V222 and east of FALSE intersection.
C — South of V222 and west of FALSE intersection.

2-186. Answer A. GFDICM 2C (Enroute Chart Legend)

The No. 1 VOR indicates that you have tuned the Beaumont VORTAC (BPT, 114.5), the 264° radial is dialed in, and the CDI is deflected to the right. Since you have a FROM indication, the 264° radial (V222) is to the right of your position. In other words, you are to the left or south of V222. The No. 2 VOR indicates that you have Daisetta VORTAC (DAS, 116.9) tuned, the 139° radial dialed in, and the CDI is deflected to the right. As figure 88 shows, you have a FROM indication, the 139° radial is to your right, and you are to the left (east) of the radial. This puts you east of FALSE intersection which is defined by the 142° radial from DAS VORTAC (116.9) and the 264° radial from BPT VORTAC (114.5). Answer (B) is incorrect because the No. 1 CDI needle would have to be to the left, and you would have to be to the right (north). Answer (C) is incorrect because both CDIs would have to be opposite of what is shown.

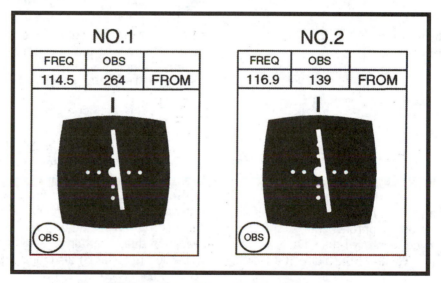

FIGURE 88.—CDI and OBS Indicators.

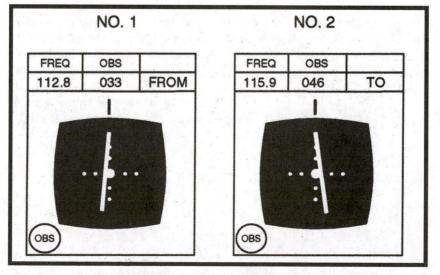

FIGURE 90.—CDI and OBS Indicators.

2-187   J35

(Refer to figures 89 and 90 on pages 5-9, and 2-71.)
What is your relationship to the airway while en route
from BCE VORTAC to HVE VORTAC on V8?

A — Left of course on V8.
B — Left of course on V382.
C — Right of course on V8.

2-188   H831

What angular deviation from a VOR course centerline
is represented by a full-scale deflection of the CDI?

A — 4°.
B — 5°.
C — 10°.

2-189   H831

When using VOR for navigation, which of the following should be considered as station passage?

A — The first movement of the CDI as the airplane
     enters the zone of confusion.
B — The moment the TO-FROM indicator becomes
     blank.
C — The first positive, complete reversal of the
     TO-FROM indicator.

2-190   H831

Which of the following should be considered as station passage when using VOR?

A — The first flickering of the TO-FROM indicator
     and CDI as the station is approached.
B — The first full-scale deflection of the CDI.
C — The first complete reversal of the TO-FROM
     indicator.

2-191   H831

When checking the sensitivity of a VOR receiver, the
number of degrees in course change as the OBS is
rotated to move the CDI from center to the last dot on
either side should be between.

A — 5° and 6°.
B — 8° and 10°.
C — 10° and 12°.

2-187. Answer A. GFDICM 2C (IFH)

VOR No. 1 indicates you are slightly right of the 033°
radial of BCE VORTAC, placing you to the right of
V382. VOR No. 2 indicates that you are slightly left of
the 046° radial of HVE VORTAC, or left of course on
V8. If you were left of course on V382 (answer B), the
CDI on VOR No. 1 would be deflected to the right. If
you were right of course on V8 (answer C), the CDI on
VOR No. 2 would be deflected to the left.

2-188. Answer C. GFDICM 2C (IFH)

Full-scale deflection for VOR on the course deviation
indicator (CDI) is usually 10° on either side of the
course centerline. This may very slightly, depending
on instrument calibration. Answers (A) and (B) are
wrong. For example, 5° represents one-half scale
deflection for a VOR course.

2-189. Answer C. GFDICM 2C (IFH)

Station passage is indicated by a complete and
positive reversal of the TO-FROM indicator. The zone
of confusion (A) is wrong because, at high altitude, the
cone (not zone) of confusion is fairly wide and station
passage would be unlikely. Answer (B) is wrong
because it indicates you have entered the cone of
confusion. This area is also called the no-signal area.

2-190. Answer C. GFDICM 2C (IFH)

Station passage is indicated by a complete and positive reversal of the TO-FROM indicator. Flickering of
the TO-FROM indicator (answer A) indicates you are
entering the cone of confusion. However, if poor
reception is suspected it may indicate poor signal
reception due to terrain or weak signal strength. CDI
deflection (answer B) also indicates entry into the
cone of confusion.

2-191. Answer C. GFDICM 2C (IFH)

You can verify the course sensitivity of your VOR by
rotating the bearing selector knob until the course
deviation indicator (CDI) moves to full deflection. Then
note the number of degrees the course changed. This
figure should be between 10° and 12°. Between 5°
and 6° (answer A) would apply to localizer course
sensitivity, and between 8° and 10° (answer B) would
be less than full deflection.

2-192 H576

A VOR receiver with normal five-dot course sensitivity shows a three-dot deflection at 30 NM from the station. The aircraft would be displaced approximately how far from the course centerline?

A — 2 NM.
B — 3 NM.
C — 5 NM.

2-193 I08

An aircraft which is located 30 miles from a VOR station and shows a 1/2 scale deflection on the CDI would be how far from the selected course centerline?

A — 1 1/2 miles.
B — 2 1/2 miles.
C — 3 1/2 miles.

2-194 H831

What angular deviation from a VOR course centerline is represented by a 1/2 scale deflection of the CDI?

A — 2°.
B — 4°.
C — 5°.

2-195 H831

After passing a VORTAC, the CDI shows 1/2 scale deflection to the right. What is indicated if the deflection remains constant for a period of time?

A — The airplane is getting closer to the radial.
B — The OBS is erroneously set on the reciprocal heading.
C — The airplane is flying away from the radial.

2-196 H576

(Refer to figure 95 on page 2-74.) What is the lateral displacement of the aircraft in NM from the radial selected on the No. 1 NAV?

A — 5.0 NM.
B — 7.5 NM.
C — 10.0 NM.

2-192. Answer B. GFDICM 2C (IFH)

For VOR, each dot of deflection means you are about 200 feet off centerline for each mile away from the station. For example, at 30 miles, one dot equals about one mile from the course centerline (200' × 30 = 6,000'). You can determine your distance from a specific radial if you know how far you are from the station and the number of dots your CDI is deflected. Multiply the number of dots times the distance from the station times 200 feet. In this case, 3 dots × 30 n.m. × 200 feet = 18,000 feet ÷ 6,000 ft./n.m. = 3 n.m. Both 2 n.m. (answer A) and 5 n.m. (answer C) are incorrect.

2-193. Answer B. GFDICM 2C (IFH)

Each dot of deflection means you are 200 feet off centerline for each mile away from the station. You can determine your distance from a specific radial by multiplying the number of dots times the distance from the station times 200 feet. Half scale deflection, or 2-1/2 dots×30 n.m. × 200 feet = 15,000 feet ÷ 6,000 ft./n.m. = 2-1/2 n.m.

2-194. Answer C. GFDICM 2C (IFH)

For VOR, full scale deflection is between 10° and 12°, therefore, a 1/2 scale deflection is approximately 5°. Both 2° (answer A) and 4° (answer B) are less than 1/2-scale deflection.

2-195. Answer C. GFDICM 2C (IFH)

As you travel further from the VOR, the distance between the radials becomes greater since they diverge. At 5 miles from the station, you would be 2,500 feet from the radial, and at 10 miles, you would be displaced about 5,000 feet. Only if you were flying toward the VOR would the airplane be getting closer to the intended radial (answer A). If the bearing selector were set to the reciprocal heading (answer B), you would have reverse sensing on the CDI.

2-196. Answer A. GFDICM 2C (IFH)

Each dot of deflection means you are about 200 feet off centerline for each mile away from the station. You can determine your distance from a specific radial if you know how far you are from the station and the number of dots your CDI is deflected. Multiply the number of dots times distance from the station times 200 feet. Figure 95 shows a 2-1/2 dot deflection and 60 n.m. on the No. 1 NAV (2-1/2 dots×60 n.m.×200 ft = 30,000 ft ÷ 6,000 ft./n.m. = 5.0 n.m.). Both 7.5 n.m. (answer A) and 10 n.m. (answer C) would be indicated by greater deflection of the CDI.

2-197   **H831**
(Refer to figure 95.) On which radial is the aircraft as indicated by the No. 1 NAV?

A — R-175.
B — R-165.
C — R-345.

2-198   **H831**
(Refer to figure 95.) Which OBS selection on the No.1 NAV would center the CDI and change the ambiguity indication to a TO?

A — 175°.
B — 165°.
C — 345°.

2-197. Answer C. GFDICM 2C (IFH)
The TO/FROM indicator (triangular pointer) is showing FROM and with the bearing selector set on 350°; however, the aircraft is flying a heading of 140°. The CDI shows that you are about 5° to the left, or west, of the 350° radial, on the 345° radial. The 175° radial (answer A) is wrong, since it is the reciprocal of 355°. The 165° radial (answer B) is the reciprocal of 345° radial, and also is incorrect. Note that answer (B) would be correct with the TO/FROM indicating TO.

2-198. Answer B. GFDICM 2C (IFH)
The ambiguity indicator is showing a FROM indication, with the bearing selector set on 350°; however, the aircraft is flying a heading of 140°. The 1/2-scale deflection shows a position about 5° to the left or west of the 350° radial. If the bearing selector were set to the reciprocal, 170°, the ambiguity indicator would switch to a TO indication and the CDI would show that you are 5° right, or west, of the 170° course to the station. A 5° adjustment of the bearing selector to 165° would center the CDI. Setting the bearing selector to 175° (answer A) would change the ambiguity indicator to a TO indication but would move the CDI to full right deflection. A bearing selector setting of 345° (answer C) would center the CDI needle, but the ambiguity indicator would still indicate FROM.

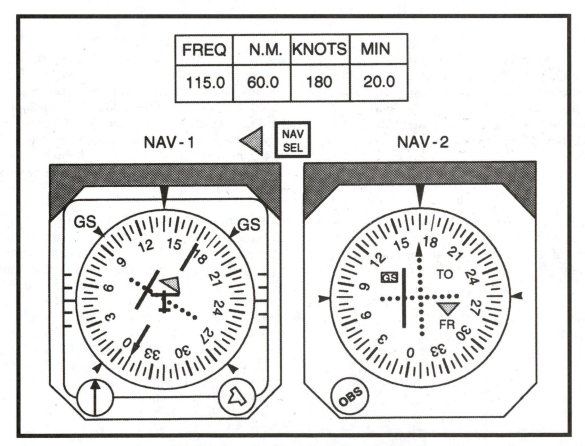

FIGURE 95.—No. 1 and No. 2 NAV Presentation.

2-199   H831
(Refer to figure 95.) What is the lateral displacement in degrees from the desired radial on the No.2 NAV?

A — 1°.
B — 2°.
C — 4°.

2-199. Answer C. GFDICM 2C (IFH)
Each dot represents a 2° displacement. A two dot deflection would indicate a 4° lateral displacement. The choice of 1° (answer A) is wrong, and 2° (answer B) is also wrong; it would be the lateral displacement only if a localizer course were being flown.

2-200   H831
(Refer to figure 95.) Which OBS selection on the No. 2 NAV would center the CDI?

A — 174°.
B — 166°.
C — 335°.

2-200. Answer A. GFDICM 2C (IFH)
The bearing selector is set to 170° with a two dot deflection to the left. With VOR, this indicates that the 170° radial is 4° to the left. Rotating the bearing selector 4° to 174° would center the CDI. Rotating the bearing selector to 166° (answer B) would cause the CDI to move to a four dot deflection to the left, and 335° (answer C) would result in a TO, instead of a FROM indication.

2-201   H831
(Refer to figure 95.) Which OBS selection on the No. 2 NAV would center the CDI and change the ambiguity indication to a TO?

A — 166°.
B — 346°.
C — 354°.

2-201. Answer C. GFDICM 2C (IFH)
The bearing selector is set to 170° with a two dot deflection to the left and FROM on the ambiguity indicator. This indicates that the 170° radial is 4° to the left. Rotating the bearing selector 4° to 174° would center the CDI without changing the FROM indication. The reciprocal of 174°, or 354° would center the CDI with a TO indication. Tuning the bearing selector to 166° (answer A) would result in a FROM indication. Selecting 346° (answer B) on the bearing selector would result in a TO indication, but it would not center the CDI.

2-202   H831
(Refer to figures 98 and 99 on pages 2-76 and 2-77.) To which aircraft position does HSI presentation "D" correspond?

A — 4.
B — 15.
C — 17.

2-202. Answer C. GFDICM 2C (IFH)
The aircraft in position 17 is on a heading of south with the course selector set on 180°. As shown, the CDI would be deflected to the left, and the ambiguity indicator would display FROM. The ambiguity indicator in the aircraft in position 4 (answer A) would be showing TO. The aircraft in position 15 (answer B) would indicate a heading of north.

2-203   H831
(Refer to figures 98 and 99 on pages 2-76 and 2-77.) To which aircraft position does HSI presentation "E" correspond?

A — 5.
B — 6.
C — 15.

2-203. Answer B. GFDICM 2C (IFH)
The aircraft in position 6 is on a heading of north with the course selector set to 360°. The ambiguity indicator shows FROM with the CDI deflected to the left. The aircraft in position 5 (answer A) is on a heading of south on the 360° radial; the CDI would be centered. The ambiguity indicator for the aircraft in position 15 (answer C) would show a TO indication and the CDI would be centered.

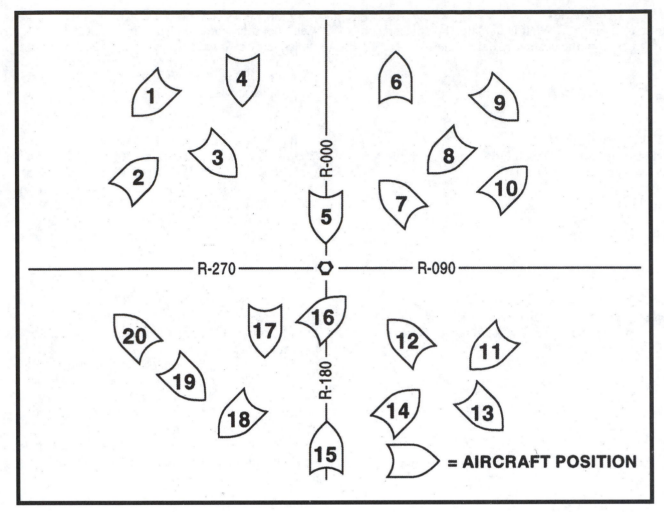

FIGURE 98.—Aircraft Position.

2-204   H831
(Refer to figures 98 and 99.) To which aircraft position does HSI presentation "F" correspond?

A — 10.
B — 14.
C — 16.

2-204. Answer C. GFDICM 2C (IFH)
The aircraft in position 16 is on a northeast heading on the 180° radial. With the bearing selector set to 180°, the CDI should be centered and the ambiguity indicator correctly displays FROM. The aircraft in position 10 (answer A) would have a TO indication with the CDI deflected. The CDI in the aircraft in position 14 (answer B) would also be deflected.

2-205   H831
(Refer to figures 98 and 99.) To which aircraft position does HSI presentation "A" correspond?

A — 1.
B — 8.
C — 11.

2-205. Answer A. GFDICM 2C (IFH)
The aircraft in position 1 is northwest of the station on a southwest heading of 205°. With 090° dialed in the course selector, the ambiguity indicator would show TO, and the CDI would be deflected to the left. The aircraft in position 8 (answer B) is northeast of the station, and would have a FROM indication. The aircraft in position 11 (answer C) would also have a FROM indication.

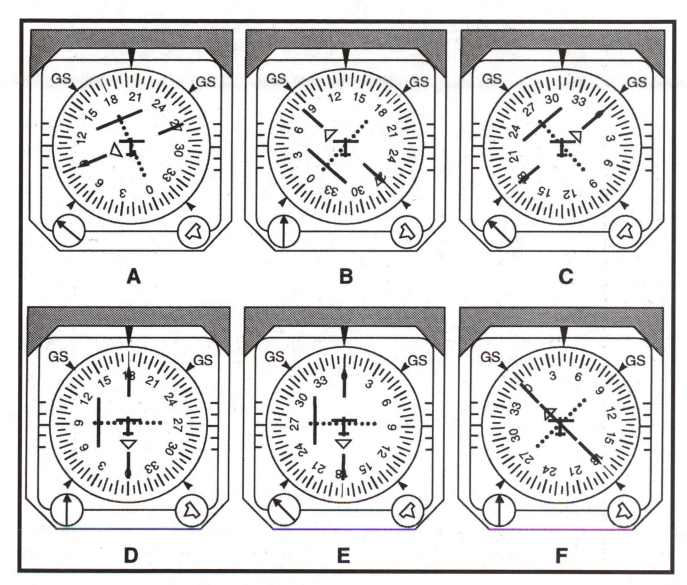

FIGURE 99.—HSI Presentation.

2-206   H831
(Refer to figures 98 and 99.) To which aircraft position does HSI presentation "B" correspond?

A — 9.
B — 13.
C — 19.

2-206. Answer C. GFDICM 2C (IFH)
The aircraft in position 19 is southwest of the station. With the 270° radial dialed in the course selector, the ambiguity indicator would show FROM, and the CDI would be deflected to the left. The aircraft in position 9 (answer A) is northeast of the station and would show a TO indication. The aircraft in position 13 (answer B) is southeast of the station and would show a TO indication.

2-207   H831
(Refer to figures 98 and 99.) To which aircraft position does HSI presentation "C" correspond?

A — 6.
B — 7.
C — 12.

2-207. Answer C. GFDICM 2C (IFH)
The aircraft in position 12 is southeast of the station. With 360° dialed in the bearing selector, the ambiguity indicator would show TO and the CDI would be deflected to the left. The aircraft in position 6 (answer A) is northeast of the station on a heading of north and would indicate FROM. The aircraft in position 7 is also northeast of the station and would indicate FROM.

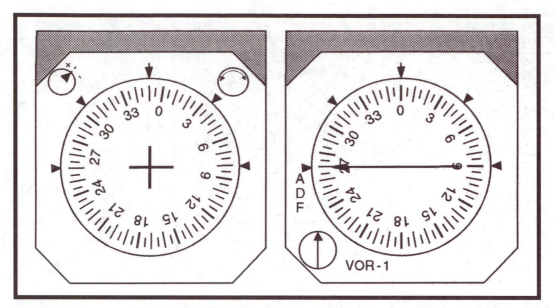

FIGURE 101.—Directional Gyro and ADF Indicators.

2-208   **H830**
(Refer to figure 101.) What is the magnetic bearing TO the station?

A — 060°.
B — 260°.
C — 270°.

2-208. Answer B. GFDICM 2C (IFH)
With a magnetic heading of 350°, plus a relative bearing of 270°, you get a 260° magnetic bearing TO the station (620° − 360° = 260°).

2-209   **H831**
(Refer to figure 100.) Which RMI illustration indicates the aircraft to be flying outbound on the magnetic bearing of 235° FROM the station? (Wind 050° at 20 knots.)

A — 2.
B — 3.
C — 4.

2-209. Answer B. GFDICM 2C (IFH)
With an RMI, the tail of the bearing pointer indicates your magnetic bearing FROM the station. The number 3 RMI indicates the aircraft is on a heading of 235° and shows the tail of the bearing pointer on 235°. RMI number 2 (answer A) indicates a magnetic bearing FROM the station of 055°. RMI number 4 indicates a magnetic bearing FROM the station of 235° but the heading is 285°.

2-210   **H831**
(Refer to figure 100.) What is the magnetic bearing TO the station as indicated by illustration 4?

A — 285°.
B — 055°.
C — 235°.

2-210. Answer B. GFDICM 2C (IFH)
The bearing pointer indicates the magnetic bearing TO the station. In illustration number 4, the bearing pointer indicates 055°.

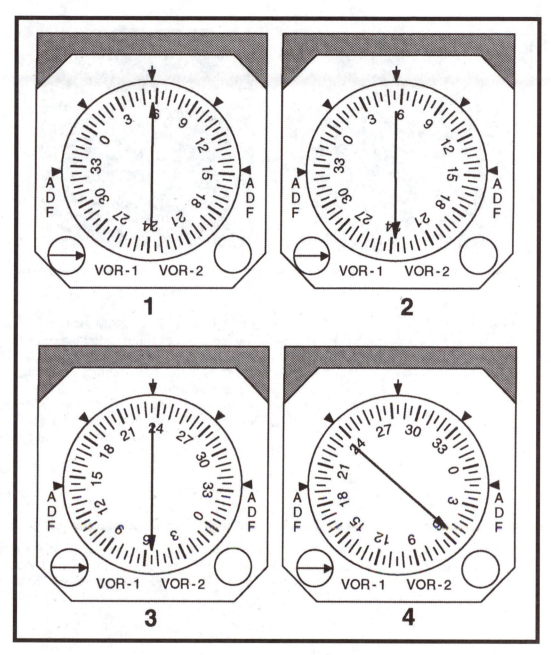

FIGURE 100.—RMI Illustrations.

2-211   H831
(Refer to figure 100.) Which RMI illustration indicates the aircraft is southwest of the station and moving closer TO the station?

A — 1.
B — 2.
C — 3.

2-211. Answer A. GFDICM 2C (IFH)
The tail of the bearing pointer indicates your position FROM the station, and the head indicates the direction to the station. Illustration 1 indicates the aircraft is southwest moving toward the station. Illustration 2 (answer B) indicates the aircraft is positioned northeast of the station moving away. Illustration 3 (answer C) indicates the aircraft is southwest of the station and also moving away.

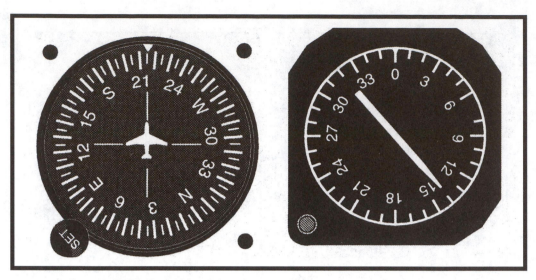

FIGURE 102.—Directional Gyro and ADF Indicators.

2-212   H831
(Refer to figure 100 on page 2-79.) Which RMI illustration indicates the aircraft is located on the 055° radial of the station and heading away from the station?

A — 1.
B — 2.
C — 3.

2-212. Answer B. GFDICM 2C (IFH)
The tail of the bearing pointer indicates the magnetic bearing FROM the station. Illustration 2 indicates the aircraft is on the 055° bearing FROM the station moving away. Illustration 1 (answer A) indicates the aircraft is on the 238° bearing FROM the station moving toward the station. Illustration 3 (answer C) is on the 235° bearing FROM the station moving away.

Note, the term "radial" applies to VOR navigation, and "bearing from" is the approximate equivalent for NDB navigation.

2-213   H830
(Refer to instruments in figure 102.) On the basis of this information, the magnetic bearing TO the station would be

A — 175°.
B — 255°.
C — 355°.

2-213. Answer C. GFDICM 2C (IFH)
With a fixed-card ADF indicator, the magnetic bearing (MB) TO the station equals the magnetic heading (MH) plus the relative bearing (RB) TO the station.

MH + RB = MB

215° + 140° = 355°

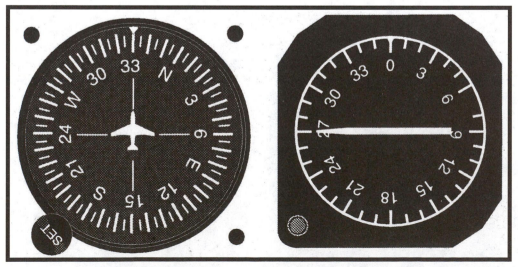

FIGURE 103.—Directional Gyro and ADF Indicators.

2-214   H830
(Refer to instruments in figure 102.) On the basis of this information, the magnetic bearing FROM the station would be

A — 175°.
B — 255°.
C — 355°.

2-214. Answer A. GFDICM 2C (IFH)
With a fixed-card ADF indicator, the magnetic bearing TO the station equals your magnetic heading plus your relative bearing TO the station. An easy way to figure this relationship in this question is to use the standard formula for magnetic bearing to the station and then subtract 180°.

MH + RB = MB

215° + 140° = 355° − 180° = 175°.

2-215   H830
(Refer to instruments in figure 103.) On the basis of this information, the magnetic bearing FROM the station would be

A — 030°.
B — 060°.
C — 240°.

2-215. Answer B. GFDICM 2C (IFH)
With a fixed-card ADF indicator, the magnetic bearing TO the station equals your magnetic heading plus your relative bearing TO the station. An easy way to figure this relationship in this question is to use the standard formula for magnetic bearing to the station and then subtract 180°.

MH + RB = MB

330° + 270° = 600° − 180° = 420°

In this case, you must subtract 360°, since 420° is greater than 360°.

420° − 360° = 060°

2-216   H830
(Refer to instruments in figure 103.) On the basis of this information, the magnetic bearing TO the station would be

A — 060°.
B — 240°.
C — 270°.

2-216. Answer B. GFDICM 2C (IFH)
With a fixed-card ADF indicator, the magnetic bearing TO the station equals your magnetic heading plus your relative bearing TO the station. If the result is greater than 360°, subtract 360°.

MH + RB = MB

330° + 270° = 600° − 360° = 240°

2-217   H831
(Refer to figure 104 on page 2-82.) If the radio magnetic indicator is tuned to a VOR, which illustration indicates the aircraft is on the 115° radial?

A — 1.
B — 2.
C — 3.

2-217. Answer A. GFDICM 2C (IFH)
The tail of the RMI shows the radial that you are on FROM the VOR. Illustration 1 indicates that you are on the 115° radial. Illustration 2 (answer B) indicates that you are on the 315° radial FROM the station. Illustration 3 (answer C) indicates that you are on the 010° radial FROM the station.

2-218   H831
(Refer to figure 104 on page 2-82.) If the radio magnetic indicator is tuned to a VOR, which illustration indicates the aircraft is on the 335° radial?

A — 2.
B — 3.
C — 4.

2-218. Answer C. GFDICM 2C (IFH)
The tail of the RMI shows the VOR radial that you are on. Illustration 4 indicates that you are on the 335° radial. Illustration 2 (answer A) indicates that you are on the 315° radial. Illustration 3 (answer B) indicates that you are on the 010° radial.

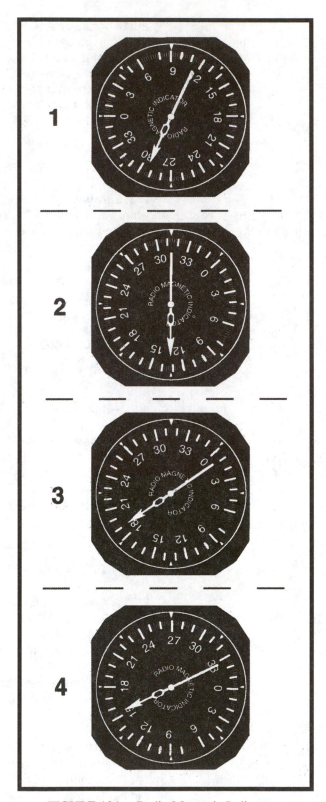

FIGURE 104.—Radio Magnetic Indicators.

2-219   H831
(Refer to figure 104.) If the radio magnetic indicator is tuned to a VOR, which illustration indicates the aircraft is on the 315° radial?

A — 2.
B — 3.
C — 4.

2-220   H831
(Refer to figure 104.) If the radio magnetic indicator is tuned to a VOR, which illustration indicates the aircraft is on the 010° radial?

A — 1.
B — 2.
C — 3.

2-221   H830
(Refer to figure 105 on page 2-84.) If the magnetic heading shown for airplane 7 is maintained, which ADF illustration would indicate the airplane is on the 120° magnetic bearing FROM the station?

A — 2.
B — 4.
C — 5.

2-222   H830
(Refer to figure 105 on page 2-84.) If the magnetic heading shown for airplane 5 is maintained, which ADF illustration would indicate the airplane is on the 210° magnetic bearing FROM the station?

A — 2.
B — 3.
C — 4.

2-219. Answer A. GFDICM 2C (IFH)
The tail of the RMI shows the radial that you are on. Illustration 2 indicates that you are on the 315° radial. Illustration 3 (answer B) indicates that you are on the 010° radial. Illustration 4 (answer C) indicates that you are on the 335° radial.

2-220. Answer C. GFDICM 2C (IFH)
The tail of the RMI shows the radial you are on FROM the VOR. Illustration 3 indicates that you are on the 010° radial. Illustration 1 (answer A) indicates that you are on the 115° radial. Illustration 2 (answer B) indicates that you are on the 315° radial.

2-221. Answer C. GFDICM 2C (IFH)
Even with the fixed-card ADF installation, the ADF bearing pointer always points to the station. Since you're looking for a magnetic bearing of 120° FROM the station, first compute the magnetic bearing TO the station by using the basic formula and add 180°:

MH + RB = MB + 180°

270° + (unknown) = 300°

RB = 30°

Therefore, answer (C) is correct (illustration 5); RB TO the station is 030°, so the aircraft is located on the 120° bearing FROM the station. Illustration 2 (answer A) is wrong since it indicates the aircraft is on the 150° bearing FROM the station. Illustration 4 (answer B) is also wrong because it indicates the aircraft is on the 300° bearing FROM the station.

2-222. Answer C. GFDICM 2C (IFH)
Even with the fixed-card ADF installation, the ADF bearing pointer always points to the station. Since you're looking for a magnetic bearing of 210° FROM the station, first compute the magnetic bearing TO the station by using the basic formula and add 180°:

MH + RB = MB + 180°

180° + (unknown) = 30°

RB = 210°

Therefore, answer (C) is correct (illustration 4); RB TO the station is 210°, so the aircraft is located on the 210° bearing FROM the station. Illustration 2 (answer A) is wrong since it indicates the aircraft is on the 60° bearing FROM the station. Illustration 3 (answer B) is also incorrect; it indicates the aircraft is on the 255° bearing FROM the station.

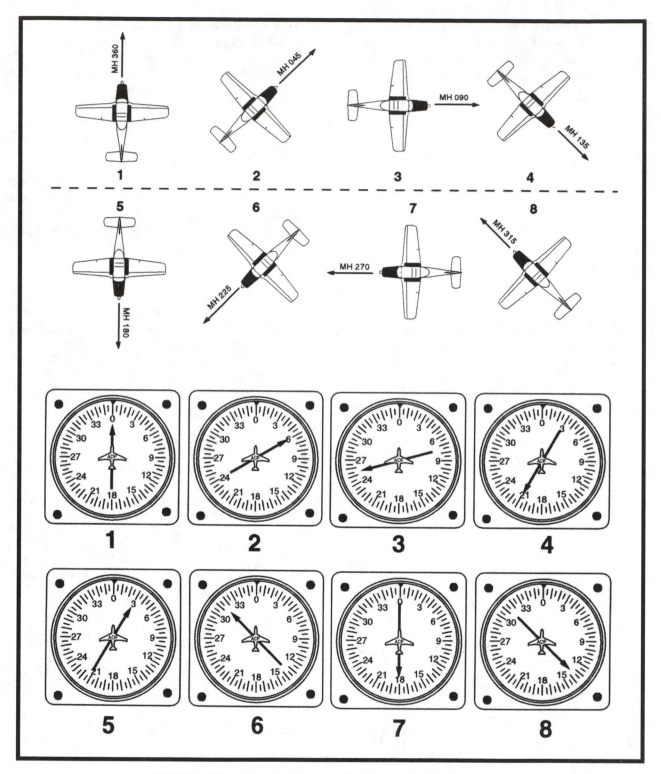

FIGURE 105.—Aircraft Magnetic Heading and ADF Illustration.

2-223   **H830**

(Refer to figure 105.) If the magnetic heading shown for airplane 3 is maintained, which ADF illustration would indicate the airplane is on the 120° magnetic bearing TO the station?

A — 4.
B — 5.
C — 8.

2-224   **H830**

(Refer to figure 105.) If the magnetic heading shown for airplane 1 is maintained, which ADF illustration would indicate the airplane is on the 060° magnetic bearing TO the station?

A — 2.
B — 4.
C — 5.

2-225   **H830**

(Refer to figure 105.) If the magnetic heading shown for airplane 2 is maintained, which ADF illustration would indicate the airplane is on the 255° magnetic bearing TO the station?

A — 2.
B — 4.
C — 5.

2-223. Answer B. GFDICM 2C (IFH)

Even with the fixed-card ADF installation, the ADF bearing pointer always points to the station. Since you're looking for a magnetic bearing of 120° TO the station, first determine the missing information. In this question, it is the relative bearing (RB). Then, use the basic formula:

MH + RB = MB,

090° + (unknown) = 120

RB = 030°

Illustration 5 (answer B), is correct. Illustration 4 (answer A) indicates a 210° relative bearing TO the station which is incorrect. Illustration 8 (answer C) is also wrong since it indicates a 135° relative bearing TO the station.

2-224. Answer A. GFDICM 2C (IFH)

Even with the fixed-card ADF installation, the ADF bearing pointer always points to the station. Since you're looking for a magnetic bearing of 060° TO the station, determine what information is missing — in this case the relative bearing (RB). Then, use the basic formula:

MH + RB = MB

360° + (unknown) = 060°

RB = 060°.

Illustration 2 (answer A) is correct. Illustration 4 (answer B) is wrong; it indicates a 210° relative bearing TO the station. Illustration 5 (answer C) is also wrong, since it indicates a 030° relative bearing TO the station.

2-225. Answer B. GFDICM 2C (IFH)

Even with the fixed-card ADF installation, the ADF bearing pointer always points to the station. Since you're looking for a magnetic bearing of 255° TO the station, determine what information, if any, is needed. In this question, you must compute the relative bearing (RB). Use the basic formula:

MH + RB = MB

045° + (unknown) = 255°

RB = 210°.

Therefore, illustration 4 (answer B) corresponds to this relative bearing. Illustration 2 (answer A) indicates a 060° relative bearing TO the station. Illustration 5 (answer C) indicates a 030° relative bearing TO the station. Both (A) and (C) are incorrect.

2-226   H830

(Refer to figure 105 on page 2-84.) If the magnetic heading shown for airplane 4 is maintained, which ADF illustration would indicate the airplane is on the 135° bearing TO the station?

A — 1.
B — 4.
C — 8.

2-226. Answer A. GFDICM 2C (IFH)

Even with the fixed-card ADF installation, the ADF bearing pointer always points to the station. Since you're looking for a magnetic bearing of 135° TO the station, determine what information is needed. In this case, you'll need to find the relative bearing (RB). Use the basic formula:

MH + RB = MB

135° + (unknown) = 135°

RB = 0°.

Therefore, illustration 1 (answer A) is correct. Illustration 4 (answer B) is wrong; it indicates a 210° relative bearing TO the station. Illustration 8 (answer C) is also wrong, since it indicates a 135° relative bearing TO the station.

2-227   H830

(Refer to figure 105 on page 2-84.) If the magnetic heading shown for airplane 6 is maintained, which ADF illustration would indicate the airplane is on the 255° magnetic bearing FROM the station?

A — 2.
B — 4.
C — 5.

2-227. Answer B. GFDICM 2C (IFH)

Even with the fixed-card ADF installation, the ADF bearing pointer always points to the station. Since you're looking for a magnetic bearing of 255° FROM the station, first compute the magnetic bearing TO the station and subtract 180° (255° − 180° = 075°). Then find RB by using the basic formula:

MH + RB = MB

225° + (unknown) = 075°

RB = 210°

Therefore, answer (B) is correct (illustration 4); RB TO the station is 210°, so the aircraft is located on the 255° bearing FROM the station. Illustration 2 (answer A) is wrong; it indicates the aircraft is on the 105° bearing FROM the station. Illustration 5 (answer C) is also incorrect, since it indicates the aircraft is on the 075° bearing FROM the station.

2-228   H830

(Refer to figure 105 on page 2-84.) If the magnetic heading shown for airplane 8 is maintained, which ADF illustration would indicate the airplane is on the 090° magnetic bearing FROM the station?

A — 3.
B — 4.
C — 6.

2-228. Answer C. GFDICM 2C (IFH)

Even with the fixed-card ADF installation, the ADF bearing pointer always points to the station. Since you're looking for a magnetic bearing of 090° FROM the station, first compute the magnetic bearing TO the station and subtract 180° (090° − 180° = 270°). Then find RB by using the basic formula:

MH + RB = MB

315° + (unknown) − 360° = 270°

RB = 315°

Therefore, answer (C) is correct (illustration 6); RB TO the station is 315°, so the aircraft is located on the 090° bearing FROM the station. Illustration 3 (answer A) is wrong because it indicates the aircraft is on the 30° bearing FROM the station. Illustration 4 (answer B) indicates the aircraft is on the 345° bearing FROM the station and is also wrong.

2-229   H830

(Refer to figure 105 on page 2-84.) If the magnetic heading shown for airplane 5 is maintained, which ADF illustration would indicate the airplane is on the 240° magnetic bearing TO the station?

A — 2.
B — 3.
C — 4.

2-229. Answer A. GFDICM 2C (IFH)

Even with the fixed-card ADF installation, the ADF bearing pointer always points to the station. Since you're looking for a magnetic bearing of 240° TO the station, determine what information, if any, is needed. In this question, you must compute the relative bearing (RB). Use the basic formula:

MH + RB = MB

180° + (unknown) = 240°

RB = 060°.

Therefore, illustration 2 (answer A) corresponds to this relative bearing. Illustration 3 (answer B) indicates a 255° relative bearing TO the station. Illustration 4 (answer C) indicates a 210° relative bearing TO the station. Both (B) and (C) are incorrect.

2-230   H830

(Refer to figure 105 on page 2-84.) If the magnetic heading shown for airplane 8 is maintained, which ADF illustration would indicate the airplane is on the 315° magnetic bearing TO the station?

A — 3.
B — 4.
C — 1.

2-230. Answer C. GFDICM 2C (IFH)

Even with the fixed-card ADF installation, the ADF bearing pointer always points to the station. Since you're looking for a magnetic bearing of 315° TO the station, determine what information, if any, is needed. In this question, you must compute the relative bearing (RB). Use the basic formula:

MH + RB = MB

315° + (unknown) = 315°

RB = 0°.

Therefore, illustration 1 (answer C) corresponds to the relative bearing. Illustration 3 (answer A) indicates a 255° relative bearing TO the station. Illustration 4 (answer B) indicates a 210° relative bearing TO the station. Both (A) and (B) are incorrect.

2-231   H831

(Refer to figure 106 on page 2-88.) The course selector of each aircraft is set on 360°. Which aircraft would have a FROM indication on the ambiguity meter and the CDI pointing left of center?

A — 1.
B — 2.
C — 3.

2-231. Answer B. GFDICM 2C (IFH)

The ambiguity meter, or TO/FROM indicator, shows whether the aircraft would fly toward or away from the station if the selected course is intercepted and flown. A FROM indication places the aircraft north of the VOR. When the CDI is left of center, the aircraft is to the right of course, regardless of the aircraft heading. Therefore, the only correct answer is (B), aircraft 2. Answer (A), aircraft 1, is wrong because the CDI would be to the right of center. Answer (C), aircraft 3, would show the CDI left of center, but the ambiguity meter would indicate TO, not FROM.

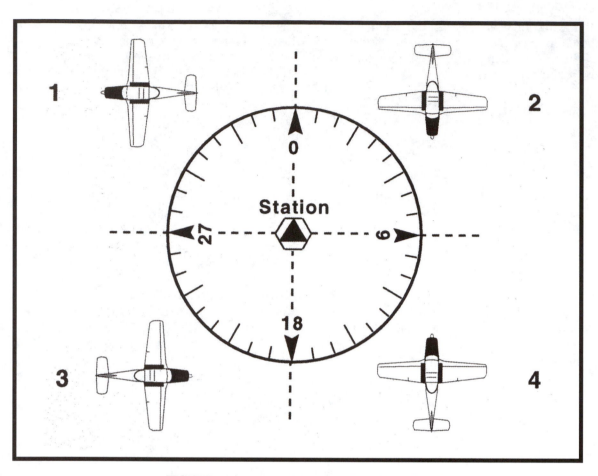

FIGURE 106.—Aircraft Location Relative to VOR.

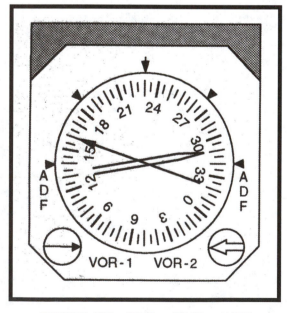

FIGURE 107.—RMI — DME — ARC
Illustration Wind Component.

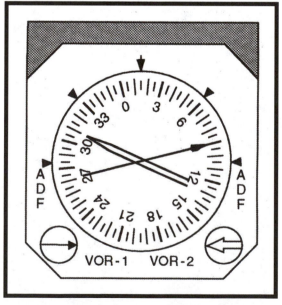

FIGURE 108.—RMI — DME — ARC
Illustration Wind Component.

2-232   H831

(Refer to figure 107.) Where should the bearing pointer be located relative to the wingtip reference to maintain the 16 DME range in a right-hand arc with a right crosswind component?

A — Behind the right wingtip reference for VOR-2.
B — Ahead of the right wingtip reference for VOR-2.
C — Behind the right wingtip reference for VOR-1.

2-233   H831

(Refer to figure 108.) Where should the bearing pointer be located relative to the wingtip reference to maintain the 16 DME range in a left-hand arc with a left crosswind component?

A — Ahead of the left wingtip reference for the VOR-2.
B — Ahead of the right wingtip reference for the VOR-1.
C — Behind the left wingtip reference for the VOR-2.

2-234   H831

(Refer to figure 109 on page 2-90.) In which general direction from the VORTAC is the aircraft located?

A — Northeast.
B — Southeast.
C — Southwest.

2-235   H831

(Refer to figure 110 on page 2-90.) In which direction from the VORTAC is the aircraft located?

A — Southwest.
B — Northwest.
C — Northeast.

2-236   H831

(Refer to figure 111 on page 2-91.) In which general direction from the VORTAC is the aircraft located?

A — Northeast.
B — Southeast.
C — Northwest.

2-237   J15

For IFR operations off of established airways below 18,000 feet, VOR navigational aids used to describe the "route of flight" should be no more than

A — 80 NM apart.
B — 40 NM apart.
C — 70 NM apart.

2-232. Answer B. GFDICM 2C (IFH)

The crosswind would cause you to drift away from the station, so you would need to correct toward the station, placing the VOR-2 needle ahead of the right wingtip. If the VOR-2 bearing pointer was behind the right wingtip (answer A), you would be pointed away from the station, plus the crosswind would cause you to drift farther away from the arc. If the VOR-1 bearing pointer was behind the right wingtip (answer C), the aircraft would be making a left-hand, not right-hand, arc using VOR-1.

2-233. Answer A. GFDICM 2C (IFH)

To prevent the left crosswind from blowing you away from VOR-2, turn toward the station so that the bearing pointer is ahead of the left wingtip reference. For answer (B) you would be in a right-hand, not left-hand, arc around VOR-1. Placing the VOR-2 needle behind the wingtip (answer C) would compound the wind drift and take you further from the station.

2-234. Answer A. GFDICM 2C (IFH)

The diagram shows a selected course of 180° with a TO indication (shown by the head of the triangular arrowhead). This places the aircraft north of the station. Since the aircraft is shown left of the 180° course, it is in the northeast quadrant.

2-235. Answer C. GFDICM 2C (IFH)

The HSI shows a selected course of 060° with a FROM indication. When on course, the aircraft would be northeast of the VORTAC. The course deviation bar shows the aircraft about 6° left of course, or on the 054° radial.

2-236. Answer C. GFDICM 2C (IFH)

The HSI shows a selected course of 360° with a FROM indication. The aircraft is generally north of the VORTAC. It is left of the 360° course by about 8°, so it is northwest of the VORTAC.

2-237. Answer A. GFDICM 2C (AIM)

Air navigation radio aids provide positive course guidance within the standard service volume for the given NAVAID, which is usable for random/unpublished route navigation. In this case, the standard service volume for a low altitude VOR is 40 nautical miles. So, on an off airway flight below 18,000 feet, the VORs used to define a route of flight should be no more than 80 nautical miles apart to insure adequate course guidance.

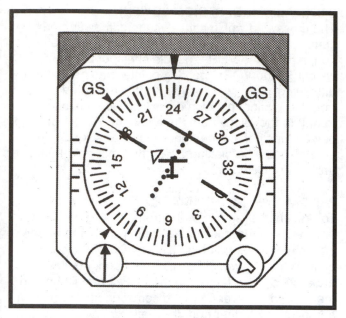

FIGURE 109.—CDI Direction from VORTAC.

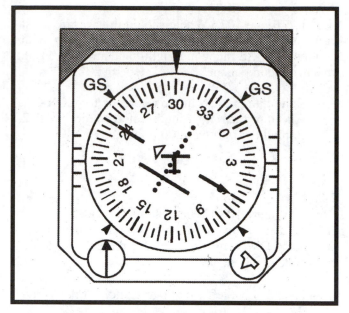

FIGURE 110.—CDI Direction from VORTAC.

2-238   J35

(Refer to figure 47 on page 10-42.) When en route on V448 from YKM VORTAC to BTG VORTAC, what minimum navigation equipment is required to identify ANGOO Intersection?

A — One VOR receiver.
B — One VOR receiver and DME.
C — Two VOR receivers.

2-238. Answer A. GFDICM 2C (IFH)

Using one VOR receiver, you can establish yourself on V448 by tuning it to YKM VORTAC. Maintaining your heading, you can periodically tune the VOR receiver to DLS VORTAC to determine your progress along the airway. As you near ANGOO, select the 330° radial, and when the CDI centers, you are at the intersection. Identification of an intersection is easier when using a VOR and DME (answer B) or two VOR receivers (answer C), but the key word here is "minimum" navigation equipment.

2-239   J01

When a VOR/DME is collocated under frequency pairings and the VOR portion is inoperative, the DME identifier will repeat at an interval of

A — 20 second intervals at 1020 Hz.
B — 30 second intervals at 1350 Hz.
C — 60 second intervals at 1350 Hz.

2-239. Answer B. GFDICM 2C (AIM)

The DME is operative when it transmits an identifier at an interval of approximately 30 seconds. The DME tone is modulated at 1350 Hz, and the VOR or localizer portion is at 1020 Hz. Answer (A) is incorrect for both the interval and the tone frequency, which is a VOR or localizer tone. Answer (C) includes the correct tone (1350 Hz), but the interval of 60 seconds is wrong.

2-240   H831

Full scale deflection of a CDI occurs when the course deviation bar or needle

A — deflects from left side of the scale to right side of the scale.
B — deflects from the center of the scale to either far side of the scale.
C — deflects from half scale left to half scale right.

2-240. Answer B. GFDICM 2C (IFH)

Full scale deflection of a CDI is defined as the deflection from the center to one side of the scale. This indicates 10° or more off course. Answer (A) appears to be plausible; however, full scale deflection is referenced from the center, or courseline, not from one side to the other. Answer (C) is also incorrect because full scale deflection is referenced from the center to one side of the scale.

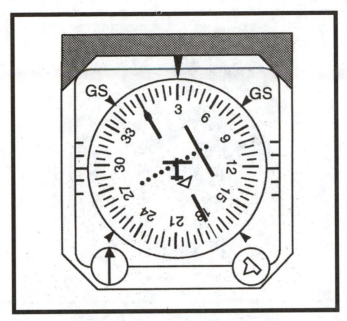

FIGURE 111.—CDI Direction from VORTAC.

2-241   J01

(Refer to figure 128 on page 8-3.) How should a pilot determine when the DME at Price/Carbon County Airport is inoperative?

A — The airborne DME will always indicate "0" mileage.

B — The airborne DME will "search," but will not "lock on."

C — The airborne DME may appear normal, but there will be no code tone.

2-242   H809

(Refer to figure 143 on page 2-92.) The heading on a remote indicating compass is 120° and the magnetic compass indicates 110°. What action is required to correctly align the heading indicator with the magnetic compass?

A — Select the free gyro mode and depress the counter-clockwise heading drive button.

B — Select the slaved gyro mode and depress the clockwise heading drive button.

C — Select the free gyro mode and depress the clockwise heading drive button.

2-241. Answer C. GFDICM 2C (AIM)

Regardless of the DME indication, if there is no coded tone identification, the DME is inoperative. Keep in mind that when it is functioning properly, the coded DME identification is transmitted one time for each three or four times that the VOR or localizer coded identification is transmitted. A single coded identification, repeated at approximately 30-second intervals, indicates the DME is operating, and the VOR is inoperative. Whether the DME indicates "0" (answer A) or is blank, or continues to search (answer B), the coded tone is the key.

2-242. Answer C. GFDICM 2C (IFH)

HSI units utilize a remote indicating compass, which includes a slaving control and compensator unit. The slaving meter deflects from zero when there is a difference between the magnetic heading and the remote indicating compass heading. In this example, your remote indicating compass card has rotated counterclockwise 10°, and reads 120° instead of 110°. To correct it, you would need to select the free gyro mode and depress the clockwise heading drive button. This will rotate the compass card clockwise, correcting the heading from 120° to 110°. Using the counterclockwise heading drive button (answer A) would rotate the compass card counterclockwise, making the remote compass heading greater and increasing the error. Answer (B) is incorrect since, to make an adjustment, you must select the free gyro mode, not the slave gyro mode.

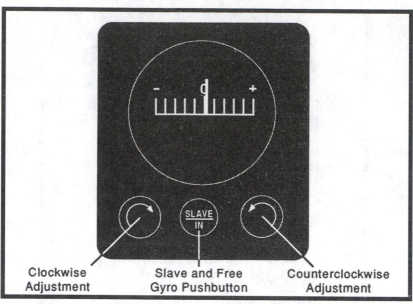

FIGURE 143.—Slaved Gyro Illustration.

2-243   H809

(Refer to figure 143.) When the system is in the free gyro mode, depressing the clockwise manual heading drive button will rotate the remote indicating compass card to the

A — right to eliminate left compass card error.
B — right to eliminate right compass card error.
C — left to eliminate left compass card error.

2-243. Answer A. GFDICM 2C (IFH)

See explanation for Question 2-242. If your compass card had rotated counterclockwise (to the left), you would have a left compass card error. To correct it, you would need to depress the clockwise button, which would rotate the card to the right. Answer (B) is wrong because you would need to rotate the card counterclockwise to correct for right compass card error. Answer (C) is incorrect since the clockwise control rotates the card to the right, not left.

2-244   H809

(Refer to figure 143.) The heading on a remote indicating compass is 5° to the left of that desired. What action is required to move the desired heading under the heading reference?

A — Select the free gyro mode and depress the clockwise heading drive button.
B — Select the slaved gyro mode and depress the clockwise heading drive button.
C — Select the free gyro mode and depress the counter-clockwise heading drive button.

2-244. Answer C. GFDICM 2C (IFH)

See explanation for Questions 2-242 and 2-243. When making an adjustment to correct a compass card that is indicating a heading 5° to the left (a right compass card error), you select the free gyro mode and then depress the counterclockwise manual heading drive button. This will rotate the remote indicating compass card to the left (increasing heading) and eliminate the error. Answers (A) and (B) are incorrect because using the clockwise heading drive button would rotate the compass card to the right, causing the heading to read further left, thereby increasing the error. Also, you must select the free gyro mode, not the slaved gyro mode (answer B).

2-245   J01

During IFR operation using an approved GPS system for navigation,

A — no other navigation system is required.
B — active monitoring of an alternate navigation system is always required.
C — the aircraft must have an approved and operational alternate navigation system appropriate for the route.

2-245. Answer C. GFDICM 2C (AIM)

Aircraft using GPS navigation equipment under IFR must be equipped with an approved and operational alternate means of navigation appropriate to the flight. Active monitoring of alternate systems is not required unless the RAIM capability of the GPS equipment is lost.

CHAPTER 3

THE FLIGHT ENVIRONMENT

SECTION A
AIRPORTS, AIRSPACE, AND FLIGHT INFORMATION

RUNWAY MARKINGS

1. **Precision instrument runways** provide distance information in 500 foot increments. Aiming point markings are located approximately 1,000 feet from the landing threshold.

TAXIWAY MARKINGS

2. Mandatory instruction signs, such as those marking hold lines, consist of white lettering on a red background. A hold line painted on the pavement consists of four yellow lines, with the two dashed lines nearest the runway.
3. When you exit the runway after landing, be sure to cross the **hold line** before stopping to ensure that you are clear of the runway.
4. Remain outside of the **ILS hold line** if asked to hold short of the ILS critical area, and completely pass this line when exiting the runway during ILS operations.

APPROACH LIGHT SYSTEMS

5. Normally, approach lights extend outward from the landing threshold to a distance of 2,400 to 3,000 feet from precision instrument runways and 1,400 to 1,500 feet from nonprecision instrument runways.
6. Some approach light systems incorporate **sequenced flashing lights (SFL)** or **runway alignment indicator lights (RAIL)**, which are moving strobe lights pointing the way to the runway.
7. High intensity white strobe lights on each side of the runway threshold are called **runway end identifier lights (REIL)**, and provide a means of rapidly identifying the approach end of the runway during reduced visibility.

VISUAL GLIDE SLOPE INDICATORS

8. A two-bar **visual approach slope indicator (VASI)** normally has an approach angle of 3°, is visible from 3 to 5 miles during the day and up to 20 miles at night. The near and middle bars of a three-bar VASI provide the same glide path as a standard two-bar VASI installation. The middle and far bars are for high-cockpit aircraft, and provide an upper glide path that is usually .25° steeper than the lower glide path. Remaining on or above the proper glidepath of a VASI assures safe obstruction clearance in the approach area.
9. **Pulsating approach slope indicators (PLASIs)** and **tri-color VASIs** provide glide path guidance from a single light box. The **precision approach path indicator (PAPI)** uses a single row of normally four lights similar to VASI and can indicate the degree of deviation from the glide path by the number of red and white lights.

RUNWAY LIGHTING

10. **Runway edge lights** include high intensity runway lights (HIRL), medium intensity runway lights (MIRL), and low intensity runway lights (LIRL). HIRL and MIRL intensity can be adjusted from the control tower or by the pilot using the CTAF frequency. Runway edge lights are white, except on instrument runways where amber replaces white on the last 2,000 feet or half the runway length, whichever is less, as a caution zone.
11. **Threshold lights** mark the ends of the each runway. They appear green when landing and red when departing the end of the runway. **Displaced threshold lights** are located on each side of the runway. If the displaced runway area is usable for taxi, takeoff, or rollout, the area short of the displaced threshold will have runway edge lights, which appear red taking off toward the displaced threshold and white or amber when rolling out after landing.
12. **Touchdown zone lighting (TDZL)** is a series of white lights flush-mounted in the runway, which help identify the touchdown area during low visibility. **Runway centerline lights (RCLS),** flush-mounted in the runway, initially appear white, changing to alternating red and white when 3,000 feet remain, and all red for the last 1,000 feet of runway.

13. **Land and hold short lights** are a row of five flush-mounted flashing white lights at the hold short point, and are normally on during land and hold short operations.
14. **Taxiway lead-off lights** are flush-mounted alternating green and yellow lights that define the curved path of an aircraft from turning from the runway centerline onto a taxiway. When installed, **taxiway centerline lights** are green and **taxiway edge lights** are blue.

AIRSPACE

CONTROLLED AIRSPACE

15. Controlled airspace includes Class A, B, C, D, and Class E airspace. It is where air traffic control service is available to pilots. When you are operating under IFR, you must comply with ATC clearances.
16. You must have an operating transponder with Mode C (or Mode S) capability in Class A and B airspace and within 30 nautical miles of Class B primary airports. This equipment is also required in and above Class C airspace, and at or above 10,000 feet MSL, except at and below 2,500 feet AGL.
17. Below 10,000 feet MSL, basic VFR visibility is 3 statute miles in controlled airspace and 1 mile in uncontrolled airspace. Cloud clearance requirements within 1,200 feet of the surface in uncontrolled airspace, and in Class B airspace, is simply clear of clouds. Otherwise, you must maintain 1,000 feet above, 500 feet below, and 2,000 feet horizontal distance from clouds. Above 10,000 feet MSL and more than 1,200 feet above the surface, required flight visibility increases to 5 miles in both controlled and uncontrolled airspace with 1 mile horizontal and 1,000-foot vertical separation required from clouds.

Class A Airspace

18. Most **Class A airspace** extends from 18,000 feet MSL up to and including FL600. You are required to use an altimeter setting of 29.92 in. Hg., you must be rated and current for instrument flight, your aircraft must be equipped for IFR and you must be operating on an IFR clearance at an altitude assigned by ATC. DME is required at or above FL 240 where VOR is required, with exceptions for in-flight failure.

Class B Airspace

19. Most Class B airspace is from the surface to 10,000 feet MSL. You must be at least a private pilot, or a student pilot with the appropriate endorsement, and must receive an ATC clearance before you entering this airspace. Some Class B areas completely prohibit student pilot operations.

Class C Airspace

20. **Class C airspace** normally resides in 5 and 10 nautical mile circles extending outward from a primary airport. An outer area with radar coverage outside Class C airspace extends to 20 n.m. From 5 to 10 n.m. from the airport, Class C airspace generally begins at about 1,200 feet above the primary airport surface and extends to approximately 4,000 feet above the airport. Within 5 n.m. of the primary airport, Class C airspace is from the surface to about 4,000 feet AGL.
21. Radio contact is encouraged within the 20 n.m. outer area and required prior to entering Class C airspace. If you depart a satellite airport within Class C airspace, you must establish two-way communication with ATC as soon as practicable after takeoff.

Class D Airspace

22. **Class D airspace** exists at airports with operating control towers which are not associated with Class B or C airspace. Normally, the upper limit of Class D airspace is about 2,500 feet above the surface of the primary airport and the lateral limits are approximately 4 nautical miles from the primary airport.
23. Two-way radio communication with the control tower must be established prior to entering this airspace or taking off from the primary airport. Pilots taking off from satellite airports within Class D airspace must check in with the tower as soon as practicable.
24. At part-time tower locations, Class D airspace normally becomes Class E airspace when the tower is closed, or Class G if weather observations and reporting are not available.

Class E Airspace

25. The remaining controlled airspace includes Federal airways, which are normally 8 nautical miles wide, begin at 1,200 feet AGL, and extend up to 17,999 feet MSL. Transition areas are depicted with magenta shading on sectional charts, for certain airports with approved instrument approach procedures. These areas of Class E airspace typically begin at 700 feet AGL and extend to the overlying controlled airspace.
26. At some nontower airports, Class E airspace extends upward from the surface, and typically encompasses a 4 n.m. circle around the airport, in addition to extensions to accommodate arrivals and departures. These are depicted with dashed magenta lines on VFR charts.
27. At almost all remaining U.S. locations where Class E airspace is not designated at a lower altitude, it begins at 14,500 feet MSL (except within 1,500 feet of the surface) and extends up to 17,999 feet MSL.

Special VFR

28. When the weather is below basic VFR minimums, as indicated by daytime operation of a rotating beacon, you may obtain a **special VFR (SVFR) clearance** from the ATC facility controlling the airspace at selected airports. Ground (or flight) visibility must be at least 1 statute mile and you must remain clear of clouds. An instrument rating and IFR equipped airplane are required for SVFR after sunset and it is not allowed at airports indicating "No SVFR" on aeronautical charts.

CLASS G AIRSPACE

29. **Class G airspace** is that area which has not been designated as Class A, B, C, D, or E airspace. It is uncontrolled by ATC. For example, the airspace below a Class E airspace area or below a Victor airway is normally uncontrolled. Most Class G airspace terminates at the base of Class E airspace at 700 or 1,200 feet AGL, or at 14,500 feet MSL.

AIRCRAFT SPEED LIMITS

30. The speed limit is 250 knots indicated airspeed (KIAS) below 10,000 feet MSL and 200 KIAS within 4 nautical miles of the primary airport of Class C or Class D airspace within 2,500 feet of the surface. The 200 KIAS limit also applies to the airspace underlying Class B airspace or in a VFR corridor through such airspace. Aircraft that cannot safely operate at these speeds are exempt.

SPECIAL USE AIRSPACE

31. An IFR clearance through a **restricted area** is authorization to penetrate that airspace.
32. **Military operations areas (MOAs)** separate certain military training activities from IFR traffic. You may be cleared IFR through an active MOA only if ATC can provide separation.

OTHER AIRSPACE AREAS

33. An **airport advisory area** is within 10 statute miles of an airport with an FSS but no control tower. At these locations, the FSS provides local airport advisory (LAA) service.

FLIGHT INFORMATION

AIRPORT/FACILITY DIRECTORY

34. The *Airport/Facility Directory* (A/FD) is a series of regional books with FAA information for public-use civil airports, associated terminal control facilities, air route traffic control centers, and radio aids to navigation.

AERONAUTICAL INFORMATION MANUAL

35. The *Aeronautical Information Manual* (AIM) contains fundamental information required for both VFR and IFR flight operations within the National Airspace System. It is a major reference for this Study Guide.

NOTICES TO AIRMEN

36. **NOTAM(D)** information is disseminated for all navigational facilities that are part of the National Airspace System, all public use airports, seaplane bases, and heliports listed in the *Airport/Facility Directory*. **NOTAM(L)** information is distributed locally and includes items such as taxiway closures, construction activities near runways, snow conditions, and changes in the status of airport lighting, such as VASI, that do not affect instrument approach criteria. **FDC NOTAMs** are used to disseminate information that is regulatory in nature. Examples are amendments to aeronautical charts, changes to instrument approach procedures, and temporary flight restrictions.

3-1   B11
Where is DME required under IFR?

A — At or above 24,000 feet MSL if VOR navigational equipment is required.
B — In positive control airspace.
C — Above 18,000 feet MSL.

3-1. Answer A. GFDICM 3A (FAR 91.205)
DME is required when flying above 24,000 feet MSL when VOR navigational equipment is required. Both answers (B) and (C) are wrong because DME is not required below 24,000 feet or in all Class A airspace (formerly the positive control area).

3-2   J34

Which sources of aeronautical information, when used collectively, provide the latest status of airport conditions (e.g., runway closures, runway lighting, snow conditions)?

A — Aeronautical Information Manual, aeronautical charts, and Distant (D) Notice to Airmen (NOTAM's).
B — Airport Facility Directory, Distant (D) NOTAM's, and Local (L) NOTAM's.
C — Airport Facility Directory, FDC NOTAM's, and Local (L) NOTAM's.

3-2. Answer B. GFDICM 3A (AIM)

The *Airport/Facility Directory* (A/FD) contains information on runways, communications, and navaids that was current at the time of publication. NOTAMs update publications, such as the A/FD and aeronautical charts, with time-critical information. NOTAM-D information is disseminated primarily by FSSs for all navigational facilities, public use airports, seaplane bases, and heliports listed in the *Airport/Facility Directory*. NOTAM-L information is distributed locally and includes such items as taxiway closures, construction activities near runways, snow conditions, and changes in the status of airport lighting. You must specifically request NOTAM-L information from FSSs having responsibility for the airport concerned. Answer (A) is wrong because the *Aeronautical Information Manual* provides very little information on specific airports, and aeronautical charts do not provide information on current airport conditions. Answer (C) is wrong because FDC NOTAMs are used to disseminate information that is regulatory in nature such as changes in instrument approach procedures.

3-3   J06

What is the purpose of FDC NOTAM's?

A — To provide the latest information on the status of navigation facilities to all FSS facilities for scheduled broadcasts.
B — To issue notices for all airports and navigation facilities in the shortest possible time.
C — To advise of changes in flight data which affect instrument approach procedure (IAP), aeronautical charts, and flight restrictions prior to normal publication.

3-3. Answer C. GFDICM 3A (AIM)

FDC NOTAMs are used to disseminate information that is regulatory in nature. Examples include: amendments to aeronautical charts, changes to instrument approach procedures, and temporary flight restrictions. FDC NOTAMs are kept on file at the FSS until published in the *Notices to Airmen* publication or canceled. FDC NOTAM information is provided to a pilot by an FSS only upon request. Answers (A) and (B) are wrong because the items specified are not regulatory in nature.

3-4   J40

(Refer to figure 30 on page 10-26.) Which restriction to the use of the OED VORTAC would be applicable to the (GNATS1.MOURN) departure?

A — R 333 beyond 30 NM below 6,500 feet.
B — R 210 beyond 35 NM below 8,500 feet.
C — R 251 within 15 NM below 6,100 feet.

3-4. Answer A. GFDICM 3A (A/FD Legend)

The excerpt from the *Airport/Facility Directory* (figure 30) indicates that the VORTAC is unusable in several areas, including between the 280° and 345° radials beyond 30 n.m. and below 6,500 feet. The R-333 falls within this area. Answer (B) is wrong because the R-210 has no restrictions. Answer (C) is wrong because the R-251 is usable until beyond 25 n.m.

3-5   J34

(Refer to figure 29 on page 10-25.) What are the hours of operation (local standard time) of the control tower at Eugene/Mahlon Sweet Field?

A — 0800 - 2300.
B — 0600 - 0000.
C — 0700 - 0100.

3-5. Answer B. GFDICM 3A (A/FD Legend)

The excerpt from the *Airport/Facility Directory* (figure 29) indicates that the tower is open from 1400 to 0800 Zulu time. To convert this to local time subtract 8 hours. The answer is 0600 – 0000 local time. Answer (A) is wrong because it does not represent any time period in the excerpt. Answer (C) is wrong because 7 hours was subtracted instead of 8 hours.

3-6 J34
(Refer to figure 46 on page 10-41.) What are the hours of operation (local time) of the ATIS for the Yakima Air Terminal when daylight savings time is in effect?

A — 0500 to 2100 local.
B — 0600 to 2200 local.
C — 0700 to 2300 local.

3-6. Answer B. GFDICM 3A (A/FD Legend)
Figure 46 shows an A/FD excerpt which notes the ATIS is operated from 1400 through 0600Z. The symbol ‡ indicates that effective times will be one hour earlier during periods of daylight savings time (1300-0500Z). To convert to local time, subtract 7 hours (during daylight savings time). Answer (A) is wrong because −7 hours is the difference between GMT and local daylight savings time, not −8 hours. Times of 0700 to 2300 local (answer C) are inappropriate.

3-7 J34
(Refer to figure 58 on page 2-59.) On which frequencies could you communicate with the Montgomery County FSS while on the ground at College Station?

A — 122.65, 122.2, 122.1, 113.3
B — 122.65, 122.2
C — 118.5, 122.65, 122.2.

3-7. Answer B. GFDICM 3A (A/FD Legend)
The College Station VORTAC is a remote communications outlet (RCO) for the Montgomery FSS. The frequencies for this RCO are 122.65 and 122.2 (answer B).

3-8 J34
(Refer to figures 59 and 60 on pages 3-6 and 3-7.) What are the operating hours (local standard time) of the Houston EFAS?

A — 0600-2200.
B — 0700-2300.
C — 1800-1000.

3-8. Answer A. GFDICM 3A (AIM)
Figure 60 includes a communications outlet for Houston, but no FSS. This area is now covered by the Montgomery County automated FSS. If flying in the Houston area, you would contact Montgomery County between 1200 and 0400Z (0600 – 2200 Local) for enroute flight advisory service.

3-9 J34
(Refer to figure 72 on page 10-51.) How many precision approach procedures are published for Bradley International Airport?

A — One.
B — Three.
C — Four.

3-9. Answer B. GFDICM 3A (A/FD Legend)
The *Airport/Facility Directory* excerpt in figure 72 indicates that there are three ILS approaches to Bradley International Airport.

3-10 J11
When are ATIS broadcasts updated?

A — Every 30 minutes if weather conditions are below basic VFR; otherwise, hourly.
B — Upon receipt of any official weather, regardless of content change or reported values.
C — Only when the ceiling and/or visibility changes by a reportable value.

3-10. Answer B. GFDICM 3A (AIM)
The ATIS broadcast is updated upon the receipt of any official hourly and special weather. A new recording will also be made when there is a change in other pertinent data, such as a change of runway or the instrument approach in use. Answers (A) and (C) are incorrect because ATIS is updated as conditions change, not according to specific weather criteria.

3-11 J11
Absence of the sky condition and visibility on an ATIS broadcast specifically implies that

A — the ceiling is more than 5,000 feet and visibility is 5 miles or more.
B — the sky condition is clear and visibility is unrestricted.
C — the ceiling is at least 3,000 feet and visibility is 5 miles or more.

3-11. Answer A. GFDICM 3A (AIM)
The ceiling/sky condition, visibility, and obstructions to vision may be omitted from the ATIS broadcast if the ceiling is 5,000 feet or higher, and the visibility is 5 miles or more.

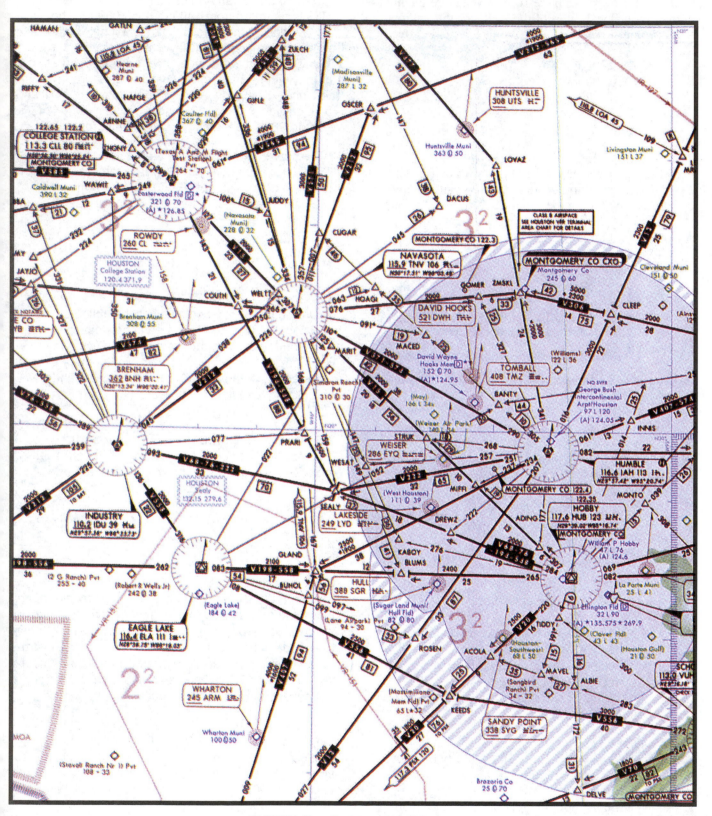

FIGURE 59.—En Route Chart Segment.

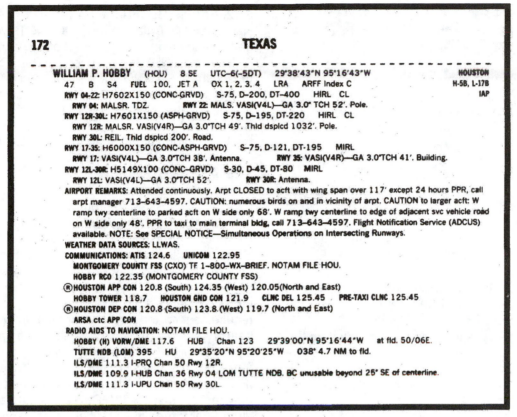

172   **TEXAS**

WILLIAM P. HOBBY   (HOU) 8 SE   UTC-6(-5DT)   29°38'43"N 95°16'43"W   HOUSTON
47   B   S4   FUEL 100, JET A   OX 1, 2, 3, 4   LRA   ARFF Index C   H-5B, L-17B
RWY 04-22: H7602X150 (CONC-GRVD)   S-75, D-200, DT-400   HIRL CL   IAP
  RWY 04: MALSR. TDZ.   RWY 22: MALS. VASI(V4L)—GA 3.0° TCH 52'. Pole.
RWY 12R-30L: H7601X150 (ASPH-GRVD)   S-75, D-195, DT-220   HIRL CL
  RWY 12R: MALSR. VASI(V4R)—GA 3.0°TCH 49'. Thld dsplcd 1032'. Pole.
  RWY 30L: REIL. Thld dsplcd 200'. Road.
RWY 17-35: H6000X150 (CONC-ASPH-GRVD)   S-75, D-121, DT-195   MIRL
  RWY 17: VASI(V4L)—GA 3.0°TCH 38'. Antenna.   RWY 35: VASI(V4R)—GA 3.0°TCH 41'. Building.
RWY 12L-30R: H5149X100 (CONC-GRVD)   S-30, D-45, DT-80   MIRL
  RWY 12L: VASI(V4L)—GA 3.0°TCH 52'.   RWY 30R: Antenna.
AIRPORT REMARKS: Attended continuously. Arpt CLOSED to acft with wing span over 117' except 24 hours PPR, call
  arpt manager 713-643-4597. CAUTION: numerous birds on and in vicinity of arpt. CAUTION to larger acft: W
  ramp twy centerline to parked acft on W side only 68'. W ramp twy centerline to edge of adjacent svc vehicle road
  on W side only 48'. PPR to taxi to main terminal bldg, call 713-643-4597. Flight Notification Service (ADCUS)
  available. NOTE: See SPECIAL NOTICE—Simultaneous Operations on Intersecting Runways.
WEATHER DATA SOURCES: LLWAS.
COMMUNICATIONS: ATIS 124.6   UNICOM 122.95
  MONTGOMERY COUNTY FSS (CXO) TF 1-800-WX-BRIEF. NOTAM FILE HOU.
  HOBBY RCO 122.35 (MONTGOMERY COUNTY FSS)
®HOUSTON APP CON 120.8 (South) 124.35 (West) 120.05(North and East)
  HOBBY TOWER 118.7   HOUSTON GND CON 121.9   CLNC DEL 125.45   PRE-TAXI CLNC 125.45
®HOUSTON DEP CON 120.8 (South) 123.8 (West) 119.7 (North and East)
  ARSA ctc APP CON
RADIO AIDS TO NAVIGATION: NOTAM FILE HOU.
  HOBBY (H) VORW/DME 117.6   HUB   Chan 123   29°39'00"N 95°16'44"W   at fld. 50/06E.
  TUTTE NDB (LOM) 395   HU   29°35'20"N 95°20'25"W   038° 4.7 NM to fld.
  ILS/DME 111.3 I-PRQ Chan 50 Rwy 12R.
  ILS/DME 109.9 I-HUB Chan 36 Rwy 04 LOM TUTTE NDB. BC unusable beyond 25° SE of centerline.
  ILS/DME 111.3 I-UPU Chan 50 Rwy 30L.

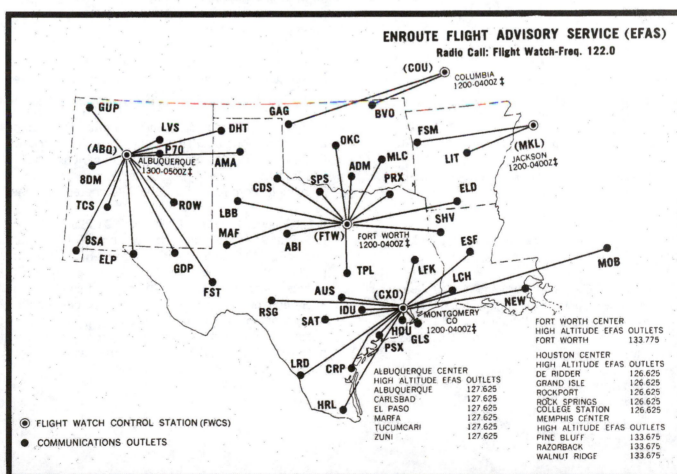

FIGURE 60.—Airport/Facility Directory and Enroute Flight Advisory Service (EFAS).

3-12   J15
From what source can you obtain the latest FDC NOTAM's?

A — Notices to Airmen publications.
B — FAA AFSS/FSS.
C — Airport/Facility Directory.

3-13   J03
The operation of an airport rotating beacon during daylight hours may indicate that

A — the in-flight visibility is less than 3 miles and the ceiling is less than 1,500 feet within Class E airspace.
B — the ground visibility is less than 3 miles and/or the ceiling is less than 1,000 feet in Class B, C, or D airspace.
C — an IFR clearance is required to operate within the airport traffic area.

3-14   J09
MOAs are established to

A — prohibit all civil aircraft because of hazardous or secret activities.
B — separate certain military activities from IFR traffic.
C — restrict civil aircraft during periods of high-density training activities.

3-15   B08
What action should you take if your DME fails at FL 240?

A — Advise ATC of the failure and land at the nearest available airport where repairs can be made.
B — Notify ATC that it will be necessary for you to go to a lower altitude, since your DME has failed.
C — Notify ATC of the failure and continue to the next airport of intended landing where repairs can be made.

3-12. Answer B. GFDICM 3A (AIM)
National Flight Data Center (FDC) NOTAMs are only transmitted once, and then kept on file at the FSS or AFSS until published or cancelled. Therefore, the most current FDC NOTAMs should be on file. The bi-weekly Notices to Airmen publication (answer A) may not include the most recent NOTAMs. The *Airport/Facility Directory* (answer C) will not contain the latest information for planning purposes.

3-13. Answer B. GFDICM 3A (AIM)
The operation of an airport beacon during daylight hours indicates that the ground visibility is less than 3 miles and/or the ceiling is less than 1,000 feet within the surface areas of Class B, C, D, and E airspace. However, you should not rely solely on the beacon as an indication of actual weather conditions. At many airports the beacon is turned on by a photoelectric cell or a time clock. In addition, there is no regulatory requirement for the daylight operation of the airport beacon. Answer (A) is wrong because it specifies inflight visibility (not ground visibility) and 1,500 feet (not 1,000 feet). Answer (C) is incorrect because an IFR clearance may not be required; for example, you may request a special VFR clearance. In addition, airport traffic area is no longer an appropriate term for identification of the airspace surrounding towered airport.

3-14. Answer B. GFDICM 3A (AIM)
MOAs consist of airspace of defined vertical and lateral limits that are established to separate certain military training activities from IFR traffic. If an MOA is not being used, ATC may clear civil IFR traffic through the airspace, as long as IFR separation can be provided. Otherwise, ATC will reroute or restrict nonparticipating IFR traffic. Answers (A) and (C) are incorrect because both imply more restrictive rules than the actual rules.

3-15. Answer C. GFDICM 3A (FAR 91.205)
FAR Part 91.205(e) states that when DME fails at or above FL 240, "...the pilot in command of the aircraft shall notify ATC immediately, and then may continue operations at and above FL 240 to the next airport of intended landing at which repairs or replacements of the equipment can be made". Choice (A) is wrong because you do not have to land short of your planned destination. Answer (B) is also incorrect since you do not have to descend to a lower altitude.

3-16 B08

What is the procedure when the DME malfunctions at or above 24,000 feet MSL?

A — Notify ATC immediately and request an altitude below 24,000 feet.
B — Continue to your destination in VFR conditions and report the malfunction.
C — After immediately notifying ATC, you may continue to the next airport of intended landing where repairs can be made.

3-16. Answer C. GFDICM 3A (FAR 91.205)
See explanation for Question 3-15. These questions are almost identical.

3-17 J08

When are you required to establish communications with the tower, (Class D airspace) if you cancel your IFR flight plan 10 miles from the destination?

A — Immediately after canceling the flight plan.
B — When advised by ARTCC.
C — Before entering Class D airspace.

3-17. Answer C. GFDICM 3A (FAR 91.129)
Class D airspace areas are designated at airports with operating control towers not associated with Class B or C airspace. Before you enter Class D airspace, you must establish and maintain two-way radio communications with the control tower.

3-18 J08

Which airspace is defined as a transition area when designated in conjunction with an airport which has a prescribed IAP?

A — The Class E airspace extending upward from 700 feet or more above the surface and terminating at the base of the overlying controlled airspace.
B — That Class D airspace extending from the surface and terminating at the base of the continental control area.
C — The Class C airspace extending from the surface to 700 or 1200 feet AGL, where designated.

3-18. Answer A. GFDICM 3A (AIM)
Several types of airspace may be designated as Class E. One example is domestic airspace areas which extend upward from 700 feet or more above the surface when designated in conjunction with an airport which has an approved instrument approach procedure (IAP). This type of Class E airspace, which extends up to the overlying controlled airspace, was formerly referred to as a transition area. Class D airspace (answer B) is designated in conjunction with an airport with an operating control tower. Class C airspace is designated in conjunction at airports where ATC provides radar service to all aircraft.

3-19 J08

The vertical extent of Class A airspace throughout the conterminous U.S. extends from

A — 18,000 feet to and including FL 450.
B — 18,000 feet to and including FL 600.
C — 12,500 feet to and including FL 600.

3-19. Answer B. GFDICM 3A (AIM)
Within the conterminous U.S., and within 12 n.m. of the coast, Class A airspace extends from 18,000 feet MSL up to and including FL 600.

3-20 J07

Class G airspace is that airspace where

A — ATC does not control air traffic.
B — ATC controls only IFR flights.
C — the minimum visibility for VFR flight is 3 miles.

3-20. Answer A. GFDICM 3A (AIM)
In the United States, uncontrolled airspace is designated Class G airspace. It is that area which has not been designated as Class A, B, C, D, or E airspace and within which ATC has neither the authority nor the responsibility to exercise control over air traffic. Answer (B) is wrong; ATC has no authority to control traffic in Class G airspace. Answer (C) is also wrong because the visibility minimum for VFR operations is 1 mile when below 1,200 feet AGL.

3-21   J08
What are the vertical limits of a transition area that is designated in conjunction with an airport having a prescribed IAP?

A — Surface to 700 feet AGL.
B — 1200 feet AGL to the base of the overlying controlled airspace.
C — 700 feet AGL or more to the base of the overlying controlled airspace.

3-22   B09
What is the minimum flight visibility and distance from clouds for flight at 10,500 feet with a VFR-on-Top clearance during daylight hours? (Class E airspace)

A — 3 SM, 1,000 feet above, 500 feet below, and 2,000 feet horizontal.
B — 5 SM, 1,000 feet above, 1,000 feet below, and 1 mile horizontal.
C — 5 SM, 1,000 feet above, 500 feet below, and 1 mile horizontal.

3-23   B09
What is the required flight visibility and distance from clouds if you are operating in Class E airspace at 9,500 feet MSL with a VFR-on-Top clearance during daylight hours?

A — 3 SM, 1,000 feet above, 500 feet below, and 2,000 feet horizontal.
B — 5 SM, 500 feet above, 1,000 feet below, and 2,000 feet horizontal.
C — 3 SM, 500 feet above, 1,000 feet below, and 2,000 feet horizontal.

3-24   B09
(Refer to figure 92 on page 3-11.) What is the minimum in-flight visibility and distance from clouds required for a VFR-on-Top flight at 9,500 feet MSL (above 1200 feet AGL) during daylight hours for area 3?

A — 2,000 feet; (E) 1,000 feet; (F) 2,000 feet; (H) 500 feet.
B — 5 miles; (E) 1,000 feet; (F) 2,000 feet; (H) 500 feet.
C — 3 miles; (E) 1,000 feet; (F) 2,000 feet; (H) 500 feet.

3-21. Answer C. GFDICM 3A (AIM)
See explanation for Question 3-18.

3-22. Answer B. GFDICM 3A (AIM) (FAR 91.155)
A VFR-on-Top clearance requires you to follow visual flight rules, including cloud clearance and visibility requirements. Above 10,000 feet MSL, and more than 1,200 feet AGL, you must have 5 miles visibility and remain at least one mile horizontally and at least 1,000 feet above or below the clouds in Class E (controlled) and in Class G (uncontrolled) airspace. Visibility of 3 miles and cloud separation of at least 1,000 feet above, 500 feet below, and 2,000 feet horizontally from any clouds (answer A) applies to flight between 1,200 feet AGL and 10,000 feet MSL (in controlled airspace during the day, and in uncontrolled airspace at night). Answer (C), 5 statute miles, 1,000 feet above, 500 feet below, and 1 mile horizontal is incorrect because of the 500 feet below statement.

3-23. Answer A. GFDICM 3A (AIM) (FAR 91.155)
A VFR-on-Top clearance requires you to follow visual flight rules, including cloud clearance and visibility requirements. Flights in Class E (controlled) airspace above 1,200 feet AGL, but less than 10,000 feet MSL, require a minimum flight visibility of 3 miles and 1,000 feet above the clouds, 500 feet below, and 2,000 feet horizontal. In answer (B), the visibility of 5 miles is incorrect, and the vertical clearance requirements are reversed. The vertical clearance requirements are also reversed in answer (C).

3-24. Answer C. GFDICM 3A (AIM) (FAR 91.155)
A VFR-on-Top clearance requires you to follow visual flight rules, including cloud clearance and visibility requirements. Flights in controlled airspace above 1,200 feet AGL, but less than 10,000 feet MSL, require a minimum flight visibility of 3 miles, 1,000 feet above the clouds, 500 feet below, and 2,000 feet horizontal. In choice (A), the visibility given as 2,000 feet should be 3 miles. In answer (B), the visibility given as 5 miles should be 3 miles.

3-25   B09

(Refer to figure 92.) A flight is to be conducted in VFR-on-Top conditions at 12,500 feet MSL (above 1200 feet AGL). What is the in-flight visibility and distance from clouds required for operation in Class E airspace during daylight hours for area 1?

A — 5 miles; (A) 1,000 feet; (B) 2,000 feet; (D) 500 feet.

B — 5 miles; (A) 1,000 feet; (B) 1 mile; (D) 1,000 feet.

C — 3 miles; (A) 1,000 feet; (B) 2,000 feet; (D) 1,000 feet.

3-25. Answer B. GFDICM 3A (AIM) (FAR 91.155)

A VFR-on-Top clearance requires you to follow visual flight rules, including cloud clearance and visibility requirements. When more than 1,200 feet above the surface and at or above 10,000 feet MSL, you must have 5 miles visibility and remain at least one mile horizontally and at least 1,000 feet vertically from any clouds. A cloud clearance of 1,000 feet above the clouds, 500 feet below, and 2,000 feet horizontal (answer A) applies to flights more than 1,200 feet AGL and below 10,000 feet MSL in controlled airspace during the day and in uncontrolled airspace at night. Answer (C) is wrong because both visibility and horizontal cloud clearance requirements are incorrect.

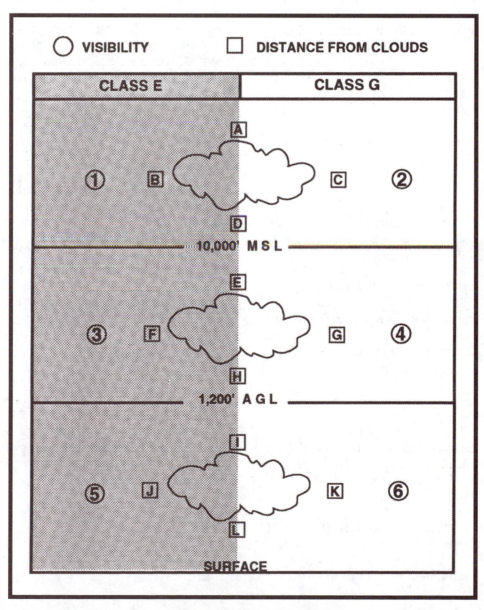

FIGURE 92.—Minimum In-Flight Visibility and Distance from Clouds.

3-26   B09

(Refer to figure 92 on page 3-11.) What is the minimum in-flight visibility and distance from clouds required in VFR conditions above clouds at 13,500 feet MSL (above 1200 feet AGL) in Class G airspace during daylight hours for area 2?

A — 5 miles, (A) 1,000 feet; (C) 2,000 feet; (D) 500 feet.

B — 3 miles; (A) 1,000 feet; (C) 1 mile; (D) 1,000 feet.

C — 5 miles; (A) 1,000 feet; (C) 1 mile; (D) 1,000 feet.

3-26. Answer C. GFDICM 3A (AIM) (FAR 91.155)

In Class G (uncontrolled) airspace at or above 10,000 feet MSL and more than 1,200 feet AGL, you must have 5 miles flight visibility and remain at least one mile horizontally and at least 1,000 feet vertically from the clouds. Answer (A) is wrong because you must remain 1 s.m. (not 2,000 feet) horizontally from clouds. Answer (B) is wrong because the in-flight visibility must be 5 s.m.

3-27   B09

(Refer to figure 92 on page 3-11.) What in-flight visibility and distance from clouds is required for a flight at 8,500 feet MSL (above 1200 feet AGL) in Class G airspace in VFR conditions during daylight hours in area 4?

A — 1 mile; (E) 1,000 feet; (G) 2,000 feet; (H) 500 feet.

B — 3 miles; (E) 1,000 feet; (G) 2,000 feet; (H) 500 feet.

C — 5 miles; (E) 1,000 feet; (G) 1 mile; (H) 1,000 feet.

3-27. Answer A. GFDICM 3A (AIM) (FAR 91.155)

In Class G (uncontrolled) airspace above 1,200 feet AGL and below 10,000 feet MSL, you must have 1 mile visibility and remain 1,000 feet above, 2,000 feet horizontal, and 500 feet below any clouds. Answer (B), 3 miles visibility, applies to night flights below 10,000 feet MSL in uncontrolled airspace. Answer (C) applies to flight more than 1,200 feet above the surface and at or above 10,000 feet MSL.

3-28   B09

(Refer to figure 92 on page 3-11.) What is the minimum in-flight visibility and distance from clouds required for an airplane operating less than 1200 feet AGL during daylight hours in area 6?

A — 3 miles; (I) 1,000 feet; (K) 2,000 feet; (L) 500 feet.

B — 1 mile; (I) clear of clouds; (K) clear of clouds; (L) clear of clouds.

C — 1 mile; (I) 500 feet; (K) 1,000 feet; (L) 500 feet.

3-28. Answer B. GFDICM 3A (AIM) (FAR 91.155)

In uncontrolled airspace below 1,200 feet AGL during the day, you must have 1 mile visibility and remain clear of clouds. Answer (A) applies to flight below 10,000 feet MSL, in uncontrolled airspace at night, and in controlled airspace below 10,000 feet. Answer (C), 500 feet above and 1,000 feet horizontal from any clouds, does not apply to any airspace.

3-29   B09

(Refer to figure 92 on page 3-11.) What is the minimum in-flight visibility and distance from clouds required for an airplane operating less than 1,200 feet AGL under special VFR during daylight hours in area 5?

A — 1 mile; (I) 2,000 feet; (J) 2,000 feet; (L) 500 feet.

B — 3 miles, (I) clear of clouds; (J) clear of clouds; (L) 500 feet.

C — 1 mile, (I) clear of clouds; (J) clear of clouds; (L) clear of clouds.

3-29. Answer C. GFDICM 3A (AIM) (FAR 91.155)

When operating under a special VFR clearance, you must have 1 mile visibility and remain clear of clouds. Answers (A) and (B) do not apply to flight under a special VFR clearance.

3-30   J08
(Refer to figure 93 on page 3-14.) What is the floor of Class E airspace when designated in conjunction with an airway?

A — 700 feet AGL.
B — 1200 feet AGL.
C — 1500 feet AGL.

3-30. Answer B. GFDICM 3A (AIM)
Class E airspace designated as Federal Airways begin at 1,200 feet AGL or higher unless otherwise specified. The 700 feet AGL (answer A) applies to the controlled Class E airspace in the vicinity of some airports, and 1,500 feet AGL (answer C) is inappropriate.

3-31   J08
(Refer to figure 93 on page 3-14.) Which altitude is the normal upper limit for Class D airspace?

A — 1,000 feet AGL.
B — 2,500 feet AGL.
C — 4,000 feet AGL.

3-31. Answer B. GFDICM 3A (AIM)
Class D airspace extends upward to and includes approximately 2,500 feet AGL. Answer (A), 1,000 feet AGL, is inappropriate, and 4,000 feet AGL (answer C) applies to the ceiling of Class C airspace.

3-32   J08
(Refer to figure 93 on page 3-14.) What is the floor of Class E airspace when designated in conjunction with an airport which has an approved IAP?

A — 500 feet AGL.
B — 700 feet AGL.
C — 1200 feet AGL.

3-32. Answer B. GFDICM 3A (AIM)
The Class E airspace surrounding an airport with an instrument approach procedure usually begins at 700 feet AGL. The choice with 500 feet AGL (answer A) is inappropriate, and 1,200 feet AGL (answer C) is the base of Federal Airways.

3-33   J08
(Refer to figure 93 on page 3-14.) Which altitude is the upper limit for Class A airspace?

A — 14,500 feet MSL.
B — 18,000 feet MSL.
C — 60,000 feet MSL.

3-33. Answer C. GFDICM 3A (AIM)
Answer (C), 60,000 feet MSL, is the upper limit of Class A airspace. Answer (A), 14,500 feet MSL, is the base of one portion of Class E airspace. Answer (B), 18,000 feet, is the base of Class A airspace.

3-34   J06
(Refer to figure 93 on page 3-14.) What is the maximum altitude that Class G airspace will exist? (Does not include airspace less than 1,500 feet AGL.

A — 18,000 feet MSL.
B — 14,500 feet MSL.
C — 14,000 feet MSL.

3-34. Answer B. GFDICM 3A (AIM)
The upper limit of Class G airspace (the base of Class E airspace) in some areas is 14,500 feet MSL. Answer (A), 18,000 feet MSL, is the base of Class A airspace.

3-35   J08
(Refer to figure 93 on page 3-14.) What is generally the maximum altitude for Class B airspace?

A — 4,000 feet MSL.
B — 10,000 feet MSL.
C — 14,500 feet MSL.

3-35. Answer B. GFDICM 3A (AIM)
Generally, the maximum altitude for Class B airspace is 10,000 feet MSL, although the configuration of each area is tailored to the specific airport. Answer (A), 4,000 feet MSL, does not apply. The upper limit of Class G airspace in some areas is 14,500 feet MSL (answer C).

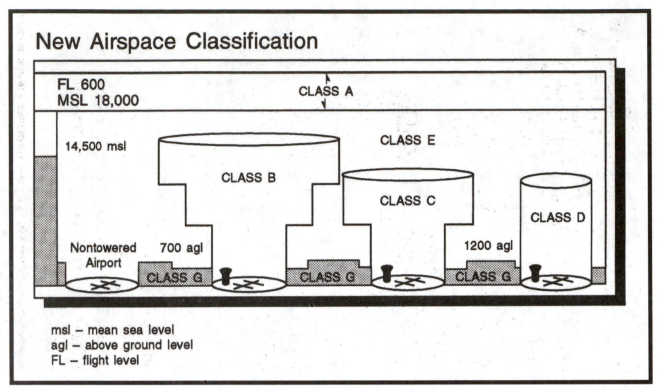

FIGURE 93.—New Airspace Classification.

3-36   J08
(Refer to figure 93.) What are the normal lateral limits for Class D airspace?

A — 3 miles.
B — 4 miles.
C — 5 miles.

3-36. Answer B. GFDICM 3A (AIM) (FAR 91.129)
Although the specific dimensions of the Class D airspace can vary, the NORMAL dimensions are a circle 4 NM in diameter.

3-37   J08
(Refer to figure 93.) What is the floor of Class A airspace?

A — 10,000 feet MSL.
B — 14,500 feet MSL.
C — 18,000 feet MSL.

3-37. Answer C. GFDICM 3A (AIM) (FAR 71.71)
Class A airspace begins at 18,000 feet MSL and extends upward to FL 600. Answer (A), 10,000 feet MSL, is not the floor of any class of airspace. It is the altitude above which a Mode C transponder is required. Answer (B), 14,500 feet MSL, is the base of some Class E airspace.

3-38   J05
(Refer to figure 94 on page 3-15.) Mandatory airport instruction signs are designated by having

A — yellow lettering with a black background.
B — white lettering with a red background.
C — black lettering with a yellow background.

3-38. Answer B. GFDICM 3A (AIM)
Signs with white lettering on a red background are mandatory instruction signs. Signs with yellow lettering on a black background (answer A) are runway and taxiway location signs. Black lettering on a yellow background (answer C) designates a direction sign.

3-39   J05
(Refer to figure 94 on page 3-15.) What sign is designated by illustration 7?

A — Location sign
B — Mandatory instruction sign
C — Direction sign

3-39. Answer B. GFDICM 3A (AIM)
A red sign with white lettering is a mandatory instruction sign, which is used to designate an entrance to a runway or critical area. A location sign (answer A) is black with yellow lettering. A direction sign (answer C) is yellow with black markings.

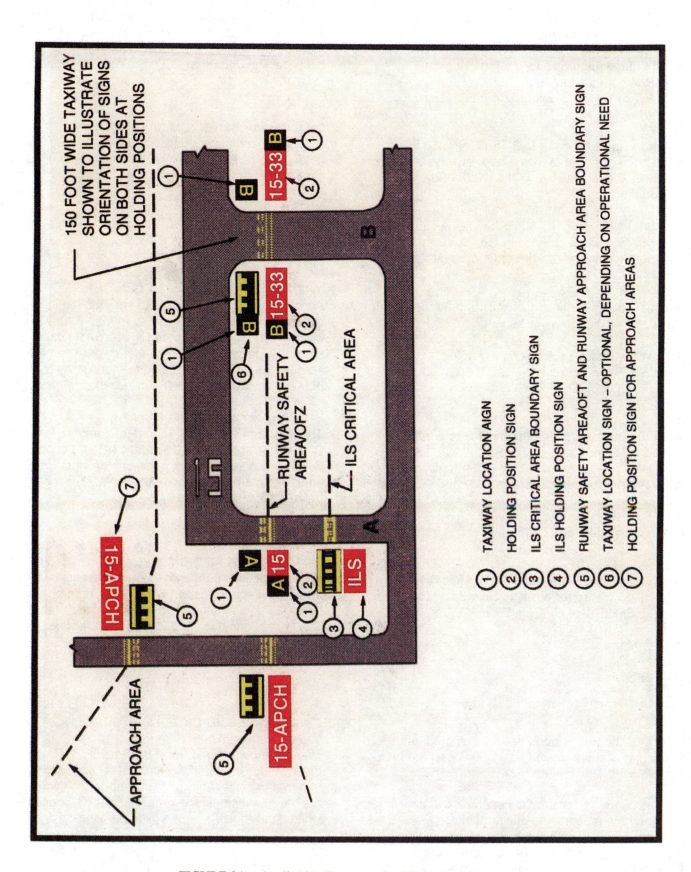

FIGURE 94.—Application Examples for Holding Positions.

3-40   J05
(Refer to figure 94 on page 3-15.) What color are runway holding position signs?

A — White with a red background.
B — Red with a white background.
C — Yellow with a black background.

3-40. Answer A. GFDICM 3A (AIM)
Runway holding position signs have white lettering on a red background. Red markings on a white background (answer B) are not used. Yellow markings on a black background (answer C) are runway and taxiway location signs.

3-41   J05
(Refer to figure 94 on page 3-15.) Hold line markings at the intersection of taxiways and runways consist of four lines that extend across the width of the taxiway. These lines are

A — white and the dashed lines are nearest the runway.
B — yellow and the dashed lines are nearest the runway.
C — yellow and the solid lines are nearest the runway.

3-41. Answer B. GFDICM 3A (AIM)
Hold line markings are yellow, with the dashed lines nearest the runway. Answers (A) and (C) are not applicable, since these markings are not used.

3-42   J13
When should pilots state their position on the airport when calling the tower for takeoff?

A — When visibility is less than 1 mile.
B — When parallel runways are in use.
C — When departing from a runway intersection.

3-42. Answer C. GFDICM 3A (AIM)
According to the the AIM, pilots are required to state their position when ready to depart from a runway intersection. Pilots are not required to state their position (unless requested by the tower) when the visibility is less than one mile (answer A) or when parallel runways are in use (answer B).

3-43   J08
What minimum aircraft equipment is required for operation within Class C airspace?

A — Two-way communications and Mode C transponder.
B — Two-way communications.
C — Transponder and DME.

3-43. Answer A. GFDICM 3A (AIM)
The minimum equipment required to operate in Class C airspace is a two-way radio and a Mode C transponder. Two-way radio communications only (answer B) applies to class D airspace. Answer (C) is wrong because DME is not required.

3-44   J03
(Refer to figure 134 on page 3-17.) Unless a higher angle is necessary for obstacle clearance, what is the normal glidepath angle for a 2-bar VASI?

A — 2.75°.
B — 3.00°.
C — 3.25°.

3-44. Answer B. GFDICM 3A (AIM)
The normal glide path angle for a 2-bar visual approach slope indicator (VASI) is 3°. At some locations, the angle may be higher for obstacle clearance. The normal angle is not 2.75° or 3.25° (answers A and C).

3-45   J03
Which of the following indications would a pilot see while approaching to land on a runway served by a 2-bar VASI?

A — If on the glidepath, the near bars will appear red, and the far bars will appear white.
B — If departing to the high side of the glidepath, the far bars will change from red to white.
C — If on the glidepath, both near bars and far bars will appear white.

3-45. Answer B. GFDICM 3A (AIM)
The on glide path indication for a 2-bar VASI is red over white (far bar red, near bar white). If departing to the high side of the glide path, the far bar will change from red to white. Answer (A) is impossible: you cannot have a white bar over red. Answer (C), white over white, describes the above glide path indication.

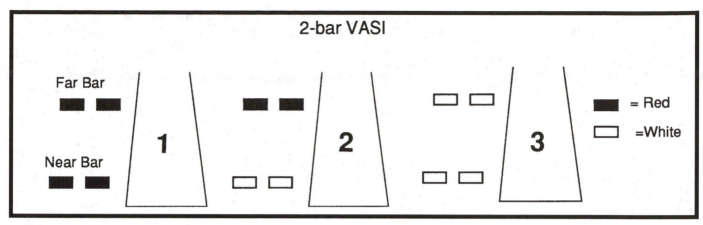

FIGURE 134.—2-BAR VASI.

3-46   J03

The middle and far bars of a 3-bar VASI will

A — both appear white to the pilot when on the upper glidepath.
B — constitute a 2-bar VASI for using the lower glidepath.
C — constitute a 2-bar VASI for using the upper glidepath.

3-46. Answer C. GFDICM 3A (AIM)

Pilots of high-cockpit aircraft use the middle and far bars of a 3-bar VASI to fly the upper glide path. In effect, these two bars constitute a 2-bar VASI for the upper glide path. When on the upper glide path, the far bar is red and the middle bar is white, not both white (answer A). A 2-bar VASI for the lower glide path (answer B) would utilize the near and middle bars.

3-47   J03

Tricolor Visual Approach Indicators normally consist of

A — a single unit, projecting a three-color visual approach path.
B — three separate light units, each projecting a different color approach path.
C — three separate light projecting units of very high candle power with a daytime range of approximately 5 miles.

3-47. Answer A. GFDICM 3A (AIM)

Tri-color VASIs typically are made up of a single light which projects red, green, and amber. Red indicates you are below the glide path, green indicates you are on the glide path, and amber indicates you are above the glide path. If you descend below the proper glide path you may see a dark amber color. A tri-color VASI is not made up of three separate units (answers B and C). The useful range is approximately 1/2 to one mile during the day, and 5 miles at night.

3-48   J03

When on the proper glidepath of a 2-bar VASI, the pilot will see the near bar as

A — white and the far bar as red.
B — red and the far bar as white.
C — white and the far bar as white.

3-48. Answer A. GFDICM 3A (AIM)

See explanation for Question 3-45. The on glide path indication for a 2-bar VASI is red over white (far bar red, near bar white). White over red (answer B) is impossible. White over white (answer C) is the above glide path indication.

3-49   J03

If an approach is being made to a runway that has an operating 3-bar VASI and all the VASI lights appear red as the airplane reaches the MDA, the pilot should

A — start a climb to reach the proper glidepath.
B — continue at the same rate of descent if the runway is in sight.
C — level off momentarily to intercept the proper approach path.

3-49. Answer C. GFDICM 3A (AIM)

If all three bars are red, it means you are below both the upper and lower glide paths. You should level off until you see the indications for the appropriate glide path, and intercept it. If you are at the MDA, you should have obstacle clearance at that altitude, and there is no need to climb (answer A). If you continue at the same rate of descent (answer B), your approach will be below the proper glide path and you may not have obstacle clearance. In addition, you could land short of the runway.

3-50   J03

Which is a feature of the tricolor VASI?

A — One light projector with three colors: red, green, and amber.
B — Two visual glidepaths for the runway.
C — Three glidepaths, with the center path indicated by a white light.

3-51   J03

Which approach and landing objective is assured when the pilot remains on the proper glidepath of the VASI?

A — Continuation of course guidance after transition to VFR.
B — Safe obstruction clearance in the approach area.
C — Course guidance from the visual descent point to touchdown.

3-52   J03

(Refer to figure 135.) Unless a higher angle is required for obstacle clearance, what is the normal glidepath for a 3-bar VASI?

A — 2.3°
B — 2.75°
C — 3.0°

3-53   J03

(Refer to figure 135.) Which illustration would a pilot observe when on the lower glidepath?

A — 4.
B — 5.
C — 6.

3-50. Answer A. GFDICM 3A (AIM)
See explanation for Question 3-47. A tri-color VASI consists of a single light projector with three colors, red, green, and amber. It projects a single glide path, not two or three glide paths (answers B and C). In addition, a green light, not a white light, indicates that you are on glide path.

3-51. Answer B. GFDICM 3A (AIM)
VASI systems are designed to help pilots maintain a safe descent path and to ensure obstruction clearance within ± 10° of the extended centerline and out to 4 n.m. from the runway threshold. VASIs are not intended to provide course guidance (answers A and C).

3-52. Answer C. GFDICM 3A (AIM)
Assuming the normal glide path is the lower one, it is typically 3.0°. It may be higher for obstacle clearance, but not lower (answers A and B). It may help to remember that the second (upper) glide path is about 0.25° steeper than the first.

3-53. Answer B. GFDICM 3A (AIM)
On the lower glide path, you would use the near and middle bars. Illustration 5 shows these two bars as red over white, which is on glide path. Answer (A) shows all three bars dark (red), which is below both glide paths. Answer (C) indicates that you are on the upper glide path, where you use the middle and far bars.

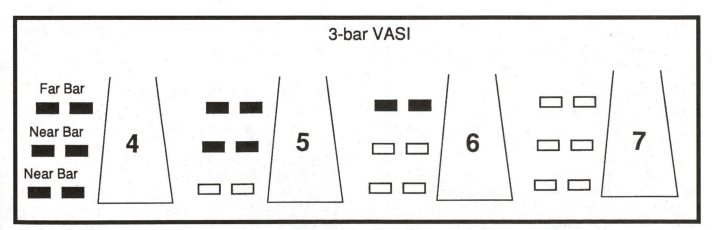

FIGURE 135.—3-BAR VASI.

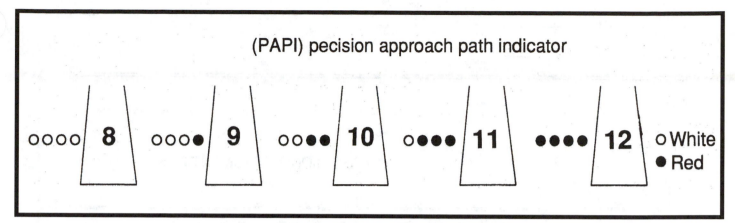

FIGURE 136.—Precision Approach Path Indicator (PAPI).

3-54   J03
(Refer to figure 135.) Which illustration would a pilot observe if the aircraft is above both glidepaths?

A — 5.
B — 6.
C — 7.

3-54. Answer C. GFDICM 3A (AIM)
When above both glide paths, all three bars will be white. Answer (A) shows you on the lower glide path, and answer (B) shows you on the upper glide path.

3-55   J03
(Refer to figure 135.) Which illustration would a pilot observe if the aircraft is below both glidepaths?

A — 4.
B — 5.
C — 6.

3-55. Answer A. GFDICM 3A (AIM)
All three bars will be red if you are below both glide paths. Answer (B) shows you on the lower glide path, and answer (C) shows you on the upper glide path.

3-56   J03
(Refer to figure 136.) Which illustration depicts an "on glidepath" indication?

A — 8.
B — 10.
C — 11.

3-56. Answer B. GFDICM 3A (AIM)
"On glide path" for a PAPI shows two white lights and two red lights. Answer (A), all white lights, is above glide path. Answer (C), one white and three red lights, is the indication for slightly below glide path.

3-57   J03
(Refer to figure 136.) Which illustration depicts a "slightly low" (2.8°) indication?

A — 9.
B — 10.
C — 11.

3-57. Answer C. GFDICM 3A (AIM)
Three red lights and one white light shows "slightly low." Answer (A) shows "slightly high," and answer (B) shows on glide path.

3-58   J03
(Refer to figure 136.) Which illustration would a pilot observe if the aircraft is on a glidepath higher than 3.5°?

A — 8.
B — 9.
C — 11.

3-58. Answer A. GFDICM 3A (AIM)
Assuming the glide path is set at the normal 3° angle, the indication, if you were higher than a 3.5° glide path, would be all white lights. Answer (B), with three white lights and one red light, shows you slightly high, or about 3.2°. Answer (C), three red and one white, shows you slightly low, at about 2.8°.

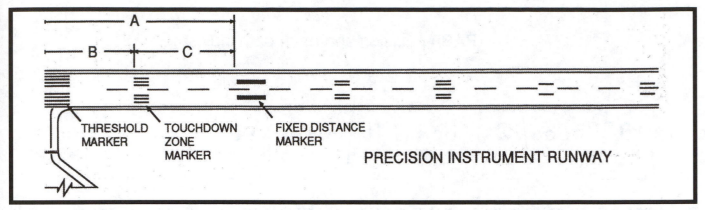

FIGURE 137.—Precision Instrument Runway.

3-59   J03
(Refer to figure 136 on page 3-19.) Which illustration would a pilot observe if the aircraft is "slightly high" (3.2°) on the glidepath?

A — 8.
B — 9.
C — 11.

3-60   J03
(Refer to figure 136 on page 3-19.) Which illustration would a pilot observe if the aircraft is less than 2.5°?

A — 10.
B — 11.
C — 12.

3-61   J05
(Refer to figure 137.) What is the distance (A) from the beginning of the runway to the fixed distance marker?

A — 500 feet.
B — 1,000 feet.
C — 1,500 feet.

3-62   J05
(Refer to figure 137.) What is the distance (B) from the beginning of the runway to the touchdown zone marker?

A — 250 feet.
B — 500 feet.
C — 750 feet.

3-63   J05
(Refer to figure 137.) What is the distance (C) from the beginning of the touchdown zone marker to the beginning of the fixed distance marker?

A — 1,000 feet.
B — 500 feet.
C — 250 feet.

3-59. Answer B. GFDICM 3A (AIM)
Three white lights and one red light indicates you are "slightly high." Answer (A), with 4 white lights, shows you high, above glide path. Answer (C), three red lights and one white light, shows you "slightly low."

3-60. Answer C. GFDICM 3A (AIM)
On a PAPI set to a normal 3° approach angle, you would see all red lights if below a 2.5° glide path. Answer (A) shows you on glide path, and answer (B) shows you slightly low (about 2.8°).

3-61. Answer B. GFDICM 3A (AIM)
The solid bold stripes of the fixed distance marker begin 1,000 feet from the threshold. The touchdown markers begin 500 feet from the threshold (answer A). Additional markings begin every 500 feet thereafter (answer C).

3-62. Answer B. GFDICM 3A (AIM)
The touchdown zone marker begins 500 feet from the threshold. Answers (A) and (C) are incorrect because major runway markers spaced 500 feet apart.

3-63. Answer B. GFDICM 3A (AIM)
The distance between the beginning of the touchdown zone marker and the beginning of the fixed distance marker is 500 feet. Remember that the runway markers are spaced 500 feet apart, not 250 or 1,000 feet apart (answers A and C).

3-64   J05

Which runway marking indicates a displaced threshold on an instrument runway?

A — Arrows leading to the threshold mark.
B — Centerline dashes starting at the threshold.
C — Red chevron marks in the nonlanding portion of the runway.

3-65   J03

Which type of runway lighting consists of a pair of synchronized flashing lights, one on each side of the runway threshold?

A — RAIL.
B — HIRL.
C — REIL.

3-66   J03

The primary purpose of runway end identifier lights, installed at many airfields, is to provide

A — rapid identification of the approach end of the runway during reduced visibility.
B — a warning of the final 3,000 feet of runway remaining as viewed from the takeoff or approach position.
C — rapid identification of the primary runway during reduced visibility.

3-64. Answer A. GFDICM 3A (AIM)

A series of arrows along the runway centerline leading up to a threshold bar indicates a displaced threshold. Answer (B) describes the usable portion of a normal runway, not a displaced threshold. Yellow (not red) chevrons (answer C) depict a blastpad or stopway, not a displaced threshold.

3-65. Answer C. GFDICM 3A (AIM)

These lights identify the runway threshold, and are called runway end identifier lights (REIL). RAIL (answer A) stands for runway alignment indicator lights, which are a series of bright flashing lights leading to the approach end of the runway. Answer (B), HIRL, refers to high intensity runway lights, which are the lights used to outline the edges of the runway.

3-66. Answer A. GFDICM 3A (AIM)

Runway end identifier lights (REILs) help you identify the approach end of the runway during darkness and conditions of low visibility. One way to determine runway remaining distance (answer B) is by the use of colored centerline and runway edge lights. REILs may not always indicate the primary runway (answer C), especially at larger airports.

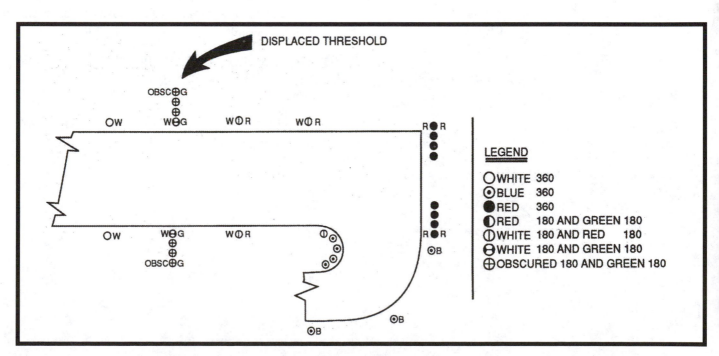

FIGURE 138.—Runway Legend.

3-67A   J05
(Refer to figure 138 on page 3-21.) What night operations, if any, are authorized between the approach end of the runway and the threshold lights?

A — No aircraft operations are permitted short of the threshold lights.
B — Only taxi operations are permitted in the area short of the threshold lights.
C — Taxi and takeoff operations are permitted, providing the takeoff operations are toward the visible green threshold lights.

3-67B   J05
The 'runway hold position' sign denotes

A — intersecting runways.
B — an entrance to runway from a taxiway.
C — an area protected for an aircraft approaching a runway.

3-67C   J05
'Runway hold position' markings on the taxiway

A — identifies where aircraft hold short of the runway.
B — identifies area where aircraft are prohibited.
C — allows an aircraft permission onto the runway.

3-67D   J05
The 'No Entry' sign identifies

A — the exit boundary for the runway protected area.
B — an area that does not continue beyond intersection.
C — paved area where aircraft entry is prohibited.

3-67E   J05
When turning onto a taxiway from another taxiway, the 'taxiway directional sign' indicates

A — direction to the take-off runway.
B — designation and direction of taxiway leading out of an intersection.
C — designation and direction of exit taxiway from runway.

3-67A. Answer C. GFDICM 3A (AC 150/5340-24)
In the area behind the displaced threshold, taxi, take-off, and rollout operations are permitted, as long as takeoffs are toward the green lights. Absence of runway edge lights in this area means that no operations are authorized in this area (answer A), but the white and red lights do allow operations. The red runway edge lights indicate that both taxi and takeoff are permitted from this end, and the white edge lights allow landing rollout to extend into this area (answer B).

3-67B. Answer A. GFDICM 3A (AIM)
Runway holding position signs are located at the holding position on taxiways that intersect a runway or on runways that intersect other runways. It does not in itself denote the entrance to the runway.

3-67C. Answer A. GFDICM 3A (AIM)
Runway hold position markings identify the locations on a taxiway where an aircraft is supposed to stop when it does not have clearance to proceed onto the runway.

3-67D. Answer C. GFDICM 3A (AIM)
The 'no entry' sign prohibits an aircraft from entering an area. Typically, this sign would be located on a taxiway intended to be used in only one direction or at the intersection of vehicle roadways with runway, taxiways, or aprons where the roadway may be mistaken as a taxiway or other aircraft movement surface.

3-67E. Answer B. GFDICM 3A (AIM)
The taxiway directional sign designates the intersecting taxiway or taxiways leading out of the intersection that a pilot would normally be expected to turn onto or hold short of. Each designation is accompanied by an arrow indicating the direction of the turn.

SECTION B
AIR TRAFFIC CONTROL SYSTEM

ATC FACILITIES

1. The air traffic control (ATC) system consists of enroute and terminal facilities. The main enroute facility is air route traffic control center (ARTCC), while approach and departure control, the control tower, ground control, and clearance delivery are terminal facilities.

ARTCC TRAFFIC SEPARATION

2. You must file an IFR flight plan and receive an ATC clearance prior to entering controlled airspace in IFR conditions. IFR flight plans should be filed at least 30 minutes before departure.

3. ATC's first priorities are separating IFR traffic and issuing safety alerts. A safety alert is issued when, in the controller's judgment, an aircraft is in unsafe proximity to terrain, an obstruction, or another aircraft.

4. ATC is not obligated to advise an IFR pilot of conflicting VFR traffic, and may not be aware of all VFR traffic. Whether VFR or IFR, it is your responsibility to see and avoid other aircraft whenever weather conditions permit.

5. Flight plans are processed by the ARTCC in which the flight originates.

6. IFR flight plans are usually deleted from the ARTCC computer if they are not activated within one hour of the proposed departure time. To ensure your flight plan remains active, advise ATC of your revised departure time if you will be delayed one hour or more.

7. Due to weather, unplanned pilot requests, flow control restrictions, etc., controllers may alter your clearance to maintain proper aircraft separation. An ATC request for a speed reduction means you should maintain the new indicated airspeed within 10 knots.

8. If you have a transponder and it has been inspected within the previous 24 months, it must be turned on and squawking Mode C, if available, anywhere in controlled airspace.

ATC WEATHER SERVICES

9. If adverse weather exists or is forecast, an on-site meteorologist at the ARTCC may issue a center weather advisory (CWA).

10. ATC may be able to provide vectors around hazardous weather. However, you should be aware that ATC radar limitations and frequency congestion may limit a controller's capability to provide in-flight weather avoidance assistance.

PROCEDURES AT TOWER-CONTROLLED AIRPORTS

11. Automatic terminal information service (ATIS) broadcasts are updated upon receipt of any official weather information. The absence of the sky condition and visibility on an ATIS broadcast specifically implies the ceiling is more than 5,000 feet AGL and the visibility is more than 5 statute miles.

12. To relieve congestion on ground control frequencies, clearance delivery is used for ATC clearances at busier airports.

13. At airports with an operating control tower, you are required to obtain a clearance before operating in a movement area, which is an area on the airport, other than a parking area and loading ramp, used for taxiing, takeoff, and landing. When departing from a runway intersection, always state your position when calling the tower for takeoff.

14. During a takeoff on an IFR flight plan, contact departure control only after you are advised to do so by the tower controller.

TERMINAL PROCEDURES

15. Terminal radar service for VFR aircraft includes basic radar service, terminal radar service area (TRSA) service, Class C service, and Class B service.

16. Basic radar service for VFR aircraft includes safety alerts, traffic advisories, and limited radar vectoring. Sequencing also is available at certain terminal locations.

17. Departure control provides separation of all aircraft within Class B and Class C airspace.

18. When calling out traffic, controllers describe the position of the traffic in terms of the 12-hour clock. For example, *"traffic at 3 o'clock"* indicates the aircraft lies off your right wing. Traffic advisories from ATC are based on your aircraft's actual ground track, not on your aircraft's heading.

19. A local airport advisory (LAA) is provided by flight service at FSS airports not served by an operating control tower, or when the tower is closed. Although VFR participation LAA service is not mandatory, it is strongly encouraged that you report your position, aircraft type, and intentions when 10 miles from the airport, and request an airport advisory from the FSS.

3-68   J11

When should your transponder be on Mode C while on an IFR flight?

A — Only when ATC requests Mode C.
B — At all times if the equipment has been calibrated, unless requested otherwise by ATC.
C — When passing 12,500 feet MSL.

3-68. Answer B. GFDICM 3B (AIM) (FAR 91.215)

When operating in controlled airspace, transponders must be on, including Mode C if installed, and set to the appropriate code or as assigned by ATC. In uncontrolled airspace, the transponder should be operating while airborne unless otherwise requested by ATC. Mode C should be on unless ATC instructs you
otherwise, not vice versa (answer A). Your Mode C should be turned on just prior to takeoff, not passing through 12,500 feet MSL (answer C).

3-69   J08

What service is provided by departure control to an IFR flight when operating within the outer area of Class C airspace?

A — Separation from all aircraft.
B — Position and altitude of all traffic within 2 miles of the IFR pilot's line of flight and altitude.
C — Separation from all IFR aircraft and participating VFR aircraft.

3-69. Answer C. GFDICM 3B (AIM)

VFR aircraft are separated from IFR aircraft within the Class C airspace by any of the following:

1. Visual separation.
2. 500 feet vertical; except when operating beneath a heavy jet.
3. Target resolution.

Answer (A) is incorrect because separation is only provided from PARTICIPATING VFR aircraft. Even though communication with ATC is mandatory in Class C airspace, there are exceptions. For example, when taking off VFR from a satellite airport a pilot's only obligation is to establish contact "as soon as practicable." Until such contact is made, that aircraft is non-participating and separation is not provided with IFR aircraft. Answer (B) is incorrect because this is not the criteria for providing traffic advisories.

3-70   J11

If a control tower and an FSS are located on the same airport, which function is provided by the FSS during those periods when the tower is closed?

A — Automatic closing of the IFR flight plan.
B — Approach control services.
C — Airport Advisory Service.

3-70. Answer C. GFDICM 3B (AIM)

Local airport advisory (LAA) is a service provided by an FSS physically located on an airport which does not have a control tower or where the tower is operated part-time. Answer (A) is incorrect because an IFR flight plan is automatically closed where there is an operating control tower; however, you must initiate cancellation if the tower is closed. Answer (B) is incorrect because an approach control clearance can only be issued and terminated by ATC.

3-71   J11
Which service is provided for IFR arrivals by a FSS located on an airport without a control tower?

A — Automatic closing of the IFR flight plan.
B — Airport advisories.
C — All functions of approach control.

3-72   J16
During a takeoff into IFR conditions with low ceilings, when should the pilot contact departure control?

A — Before penetrating the clouds.
B — When advised by the tower.
C — Upon completing the first turn after takeoff or upon establishing cruise climb on a straight-out departure.

3-73   J11
During a flight, the controller advises "traffic 2 o'clock 5 miles southbound." The pilot is holding 20° correction for a crosswind from the right. Where should the pilot look for the traffic?

A — 40° to the right of the airplane's nose.
B — 20° to the right of the airplane's nose.
C — Straight ahead.

3-74   J25
Pilots of IFR flights seeking ATC in-flight weather avoidance assistance should keep in mind that

A — ATC radar limitations and frequency congestion may limit the controllers capability to provide this service.
B — circumnavigating severe weather can only be accommodated in the en route areas away from terminals because of congestion.
C — ATC Narrow Band Radar does not provide the controller with weather intensity capability.

3-71. Answer B. GFDICM 3B (AIM)
See explanation for Question 3-70.

3-72. Answer B. GFDICM 3B (AIM)
As a general rule, you should not change to the departure control frequency until instructed to do so. Answer (A) is incorrect because it implies that the timing for a frequency change is based on weather conditions. Answer (C) is wrong since it suggests the frequency change is dependant on flight condition or phase of flight.

3-73. Answer A. GFDICM 3B (AIM)
Traffic advisories are based on the observation of your ground track on the radar. Radar cannot tell which way the nose of your aircraft is pointed. Position of traffic is called in terms of the 12-hour clock. In this example, the aircraft's nose is pointed 20° right of its ground track to compensate for a strong crosswind. In a no-wind situation, the 2 o'clock position would be 60° to the right of the nose. Since the nose is already pointed toward the 2 o'clock position by 20°, you would only have to look further right by 40° to see the controller's advisory. Remember, the controller only sees your ground track on the radar display, not the aircraft's nose position.

3-74. Answer A. GFDICM 3B (AIM)
While ATC's primary function is to provide safe separation between aircraft, center controllers will issue pertinent information on weather and assist pilots in avoiding areas of threatening weather to the extent possible. Keep in mind, the controller's workload is generally heavier than normal when weather disrupts the normal traffic flow. Answer (B) is wrong because radar can be used for circumnavigation of weather in a terminal area. Answer (C) is also incorrect; narrow-band radar is a new system which provides two distinct levels of weather intensity.

3-75   **J19**

What is the pilot in command's responsibility when flying a propeller aircraft within 20 miles of the airport of intended landing and ATC requests the pilot to reduce speed to 160? (Pilot complies with speed adjustment.)

A — Reduce TAS to 160 knots and maintain until advised by ATC.
B — Reduce IAS to 160 MPH and maintain until advised by ATC.
C — Reduce IAS to 160 knots and maintain that speed within 10 knots.

3-75. Answer C. GFDICM 3B (AIM)

You should comply with the requested speed, if able, and reduce your indicated airspeed to 160 kts. When within 20 miles of your destination airport, ATC must obtain pilot concurrence to reduce propeller aircraft speed below 150 knots. You should maintain the assigned airspeed within 10 knots. The airspeed used is indicated (IAS), not true (TAS) (answer A). As indicated in the AIM, IAS is specified in knots, not MPH (answer B).

SECTION C
ATC CLEARANCES

1. An ATC clearance is an authorization for you to proceed under a specified set of conditions within controlled airspace.

PILOT RESPONSIBILITIES

2. You may not deviate from an ATC clearance unless you experience an emergency or the clearance will cause you to violate a rule or regulation. If you deviate from an ATC clearance, you must notify ATC as soon as possible. If you are given priority over other aircraft you may be requested to submit a written report to the manager of the ATC facility within 48 hours.

3. While operating under VFR, if ATC assigns an altitude or heading that will cause you to enter clouds, you should avoid the clouds and inform ATC that the altitude or heading will not permit VFR.

4. Anytime you are in VFR conditions, it is your responsibility to see and avoid all other traffic, even if you have filed an IFR flight plan and are operating under an IFR clearance.

IFR CLIMB CONSIDERATIONS

5. Unless ATC advises "*At pilot's discretion*," you are expected to climb at an optimum rate consistent with your airplane's performance to within 1,000 feet of your assigned altitude. Then attempt to climb at a rate of between 500 and 1,500 f.p.m. for the last 1,000 feet of climb. You should notify ATC if you are unable to maintain a 500 f.p.m. rate of climb.

6. While climbing on an airway, you are required by regulation to maintain the centerline except when maneuvering in VFR conditions to detect and/or avoid other air traffic.

IFR FLIGHT PLAN AND ATC CLEARANCE

7. An IFR flight plan is required before flying into Class A airspace or any other controlled airspace when the weather is below VFR minimums.

8. You must receive an ATC clearance before entering Class A or B airspace regardless of the weather, and in Class C, D, and E airspace when the weather is below VFR minimums.

9. You may cancel an IFR flight plan anytime you are operating under VFR conditions outside of Class A airspace. However, once you cancel IFR, the flight must be conducted strictly in VFR conditions from that point on. If you were to encounter additional IFR weather, it would be necessary to file a new flight plan and again obtain an IFR clearance prior to entering IFR conditions.

TYPES OF IFR CLEARANCES

10. The elements of an ATC clearance are: aircraft identification, clearance limit, departure procedure, route of flight, altitudes/flight levels in the order to be flown, holding instructions, any special information, and frequency and transponder code information.

11. A cruise clearance authorizes you to operate at any altitude from the minimum IFR altitude up to and including the altitude specified in the clearance without reporting changes in altitude to ATC. A cruise clearance also authorizes you to proceed to and execute an approach at the destination airport.

12. An abbreviated clearance can be issued when your route of flight has not changed substantially from that filed in your flight plan. An abbreviated clearance always contains the words "*cleared as filed*" as well as the name of the destination airport or clearance limit; any applicable DP name, number and transition; the assigned enroute altitude; and any addition instructions such as departure control frequency or transponder code assignment.

13. A VFR-on-top clearance can be issued upon pilot request when suitable weather conditions exist. It allows you to fly in VFR conditions and at the appropriate VFR cruising altitudes of your choice. You must remain above the minimum IFR altitude and comply with all instrument flight rules while also maintaining VFR cloud clearances. VFR-on-top is prohibited in Class A airspace.

14. A climb-to-VFR-on-top clearance should be requested in order to climb through a cloud layer or an area of reduced visibility and then continue the flight VFR.

APPROACH CLEARANCES

15. A contact approach must be initiated by the pilot; it cannot be initiated by ATC. In order to fly a contact approach, the reported ground visibility must be at least one statute mile, and you must be able to remain clear of clouds with at least one statute mile flight visibility.

16. A visual approach may be initiated by the controller or the pilot when the ceiling is at least 1,000 feet and the visibility is at least 3 statute miles and the pilot has the airport or the aircraft to follow in sight. During a visual approach, radar service is terminated when ATC tells you to contact the tower.

VFR RESTRICTIONS TO AN IFR CLEARANCE

17. VFR restrictions can be included in an IFR clearance if requested by the pilot. If weather conditions permit, you might request a VFR climb or descent to avoid a complicated departure or arrival procedure.

COMPOSITE FLIGHT PLAN

18. A composite flight plan should be filed when you wish to operate IFR on one portion of a flight and VFR on another portion. Check both the VFR and IFR boxes on the flight plan form, and if the IFR portion of the trip is first, include a clearance limit fix where you anticipate the IFR portion will end. If the VFR portion is first, contact the nearest FSS while still in VFR conditions to close the VFR portion, then contact ATC and request a clearance.

TOWER ENROUTE CONTROL

19. A tower enroute control clearance (TEC) is intended to be used by nonturbojet aircraft at altitudes less than 10,000 feet MSL where the duration of the flight is less than 2 hours. It is available in certain, more densely populated, areas of the United States where it is possible to conduct a flight in continuous contact with local towers and approach control facilities.

DEPARTURE RESTRICTIONS

20. Departure restrictions, such as a release time, hold for release time, and a clearance void time may be imposed to separate IFR departure traffic from other traffic in the area or to regulate the flow of IFR traffic. When departing from a non-tower airport, and receiving a clearance containing a void time, you must advise ATC as soon as possible, and no later than 30 minutes, of your intentions if not airborne by the void time.

CLEARANCE COPYING AND READBACK

21. Shorthand should be used to quickly copy IFR clearances. The type of shorthand you use is not as important as whether you can read the clearance at a later time.
22. You should read back those parts of a clearance which contain altitude assignments, radar vectors, or any instructions requiring clarification.

3-76   J15

When may a pilot file a composite flight plan?

A — When requested or advised by ATC.
B — Anytime a portion of the flight will be VFR.
C — Anytime a landing is planned at an intermediate airport.

3-76. Answer B. GFDICM 3C (AIM)

A composite flight plan is a request to operate under both IFR and VFR on one flight. You can file a composite flight plan anytime a portion of the flight will be in VFR weather conditions. A composite flight plan cannot be requested or advised by ATC (answer A). In addition, since filing a composite flight plan is dependant on weather conditions, you are not required to file one anytime a landing at an intermediate airport is planned (answer C).

3-77   J15

When filing a composite flight plan where the first portion of the flight is IFR, which fix(es) should be indicated on the flight plan form?

A — All points of transition from one airway to another, fixes defining direct route segments, and the clearance limit fix.
B — Only the fix where you plan to terminate the IFR portion of the flight.
C — Only those compulsory reporting points on the IFR route segment.

3-77. Answer A. GFDICM 3C (AIM)

When a composite flight plan is filed, the IFR portion must include all fixes indicating transitions from one airway to another, those defining direct route segments, and the clearance limit. Answer (B) is wrong because if you only filed the clearance limit, ATC would not know how you plan on reaching it. Answer (C) is wrong because ATC needs to know all transitions and fixes you plan on using to reach your clearance limit.

3-78   J15

What is the recommended procedure for transitioning from VFR to IFR on a composite flight plan?

A — Prior to transitioning to IFR, contact the nearest FSS, close the VFR portion, and request ATC clearance.

B — Upon reaching the proposed point for change to IFR, contact the nearest FSS and cancel your VFR flight plan, then contact ARTCC and request an IFR clearance.

C — Prior to reaching the proposed point for change to IFR, contact ARTCC, request your IFR clearance, and instruct them to cancel the VFR flight plan.

3-79   B10

When is an IFR flight plan required?

A — When less than VFR conditions exist in either Class E or Class G airspace and in Class A airspace.

B — In all Class E airspace when conditions are below VFR, in Class A airspace, and in defense zone airspace.

C — In Class E airspace when IMC exists or in Class A airspace.

3-80   B10

Prior to which operation must an IFR flight plan be filed and an appropriate ATC clearance received?

A — Flying by reference to instruments in controlled airspace.

B — Entering controlled airspace when IMC exists.

C — Takeoff when IFR weather conditions exist.

3-81   B10

To operate under IFR below 18,000 feet, a pilot must file an IFR flight plan and receive an appropriate ATC clearance prior to

A — entering controlled airspace.

B — entering weather conditions below VFR minimums.

C — takeoff.

3-82   B10

To operate an aircraft under IFR, a flight plan must have been filed and an ATC clearance received prior to

A — controlling the aircraft solely by use of instruments.

B — entering weather conditions in any airspace.

C — entering controlled airspace.

3-78. Answer A. GFDICM 3C (AIM)

When transitioning from VFR to IFR on a composite flight plan, you must contact the flight service station nearest the VFR to IFR change point, close your VFR flight plan, and then request your IFR clearance. When doing this, keep in mind that you must remain in VFR conditions until you receive an IFR clearance. Answer (B) is wrong because you need to receive an IFR clearance prior to reaching the proposed point of change over to IFR. Answer (C) is wrong because you should close your VFR flight plan through an FSS not ARTCC.

3-79. Answer C. GFDICM 3C (FAR 91.135, 91.173)

An IFR flight plan must be filed prior to flying in Class E airspace in instrument meteorological conditions (IMC). An IFR flight plan is also required prior to flying in Class A airspace. Answer (A) is wrong because an IFR flight plan does not have to be filed prior to flying in Class G airspace with less than VFR weather conditions. Answer (B) is wrong because you do not have to file an IFR flight plan to operate in an air defense identification zone (ADIZ).

3-80. Answer B. GFDICM 3C (FAR 91.173)

See explanation for Question 3-79. Answer (A) is wrong because you can fly by reference to instruments at any time. Answer (C) is wrong because you may takeoff in IFR weather conditions if you are outside of controlled airspace. This can be a dangerous operation since you must provide your own obstruction clearance.

3-81. Answer A. GFDICM 3C (FAR 91.173)

See explanations for Questions 3-79 and 3-80.

3-82. Answer C. GFDICM 3C (FAR 91.173)

See explanation for Question 3-79.

3-83   B10

When is an IFR clearance required during VFR weather conditions?

A — When operating in the Class E airspace.
B — When operating in a Class A airspace.
C — When operating in airspace above 14,500 feet.

3-84   B10

Operation in which airspace requires filing an IFR flight plan?

A — Any airspace when the visibility is less than 1 mile.
B — Class E airspace with IMC and Class A airspace.
C — Positive control area, Continental Control Area, and all other airspace, if the visibility is less than 1 mile.

3-85   B10

When departing from an airport located outside controlled airspace during IMC, you must file an IFR flight plan and receive a clearance before

A — takeoff.
B — entering IFR conditions.
C — entering Class E airspace.

3-86   J15

(Refer to figure 1 on page 3-31.) Which item(s) should be checked in block 1 for a composite flight plan?

A — VFR with an explanation in block 11.
B — IFR with an explanation in block 11.
C — VFR and IFR.

3-87   J15

When may a pilot cancel the IFR flight plan prior to completing the flight?

A — Any time.
B — Only if an emergency occurs.
C — Only in VFR conditions when not in Class A airspace.

3-88   J14

What is the significance of an ATC clearance which reads "... CRUISE SIX THOUSAND ..."?

A — The pilot must maintain 6,000 feet until reaching the IAF serving the destination airport, then execute the published approach procedure.
B — Climbs may be made to, or descents made from, 6,000 feet at the pilot's discretion.
C — The pilot may utilize any altitude from the MEA/MOCA to 6,000 feet, but each change in altitude must be reported to ATC.

3-83. Answer B. GFDICM 3C (FAR 91.135)
See explanation for Question 3-79. Anytime you operate in Class A airspace you must first receive an IFR clearance. Answer (A) is wrong because you do not need an IFR clearance to operate in Class E airspace in VFR conditions. Answer (C) is wrong because you do not need to receive an IFR clearance when operating below 18,000 feet MSL in VFR weather conditions.

3-84. Answer B. GFDICM 3C (FAR 91.135, 91.173)
An IFR flight plan must be filed prior to flying in controlled airspace when instrument meteorological conditions (IMC) exist and prior to flying in Class A airspace. Answers (A) and (C) are wrong because you do not need to file an IFR flight plan when flying in Class G (uncontrolled) airspace, even when the weather is IMC.

3-85. Answer C. GFDICM 3C (FAR 91.173)
See explanation for Question 3-84. Answer (A) is incorrect because an IFR flight plan and clearance are not required until you enter controlled airspace; (B) is wrong for the same reason.

3-86. Answer C. GFDICM 3C (AIM)
When filing a composite flight plan, check both the VFR and IFR boxes in block 1 of the flight plan. Answers (A) and (B) are wrong because both the VFR and IFR blocks should be checked. In addition, no explanation is required in block 11 when filing a composite flight plan.

3-87. Answer C. GFDICM 3C (AIM)
You may cancel an IFR flight plan when in Class G (uncontrolled) airspace, and in VFR conditions in controlled airspace which is outside Class A airspace (formerly the positive control area). Answers (A) and (B) are wrong because, even in an emergency, you are required to be on an IFR flight plan when flying in controlled airspace in instrument meteorological conditions (IMC).

3-88. Answer B. GFDICM 3C (AIM)
The phrase "cruise six thousand" is a cruise clearance that allows altitude changes at the pilot's discretion. You may climb, level off, descend, and cruise at an intermediate altitude when you wish. However, once you begin a descent and report leaving an altitude, you may not climb back to a higher altitude without another clearance from ATC. A cruise clearance does not limit you to maintaining a specified altitude (answer A). You are not required to report changes in altitude to ATC when you are issued a cruise clearance (answer C).

Form Approved: OMB No. 2120-0034

U.S. DEPARTMENT OF TRANSPORTATION FEDERAL AVIATION ADMINISTRATION **FLIGHT PLAN**	(FAA USE ONLY)	☐ PILOT BRIEFING ☐ STOPOVER	☐ VNR	TIME STARTED	SPECIALIST INITIALS

| 1. TYPE ☐ VFR ☐ IFR ☐ DVFR | 2. AIRCRAFT IDENTIFICATION | 3. AIRCRAFT TYPE/ SPECIAL EQUIPMENT | 4. TRUE AIRSPEED   KTS | 5. DEPARTURE POINT | 6. DEPARTURE TIME PROPOSED (Z) | ACTUAL (Z) | 7. CRUISING ALTITUDE |

8. ROUTE OF FLIGHT

| 9. DESTINATION (Name of airport and city) | 10. EST. TIME ENROUTE HOURS | MINUTES | 11. REMARKS |

| 12. FUEL ON BOARD HOURS | MINUTES | 13. ALTERNATE AIRPORT(S) | 14. PILOT'S NAME, ADDRESS & TELEPHONE NUMBER & AIRCRAFT HOME BASE | 15. NUMBER ABOARD |

17. DESTINATION CONTACT/TELEPHONE (OPTIONAL)

| 16. COLOR OF AIRCRAFT | CIVIL AIRCRAFT PILOTS. FAR Part 91 requires you file an IFR flight plan to operate under instrument flight rules in controlled airspace. Failure to file could result in a civil penalty not to exceed $1,000 for each violation (Section 901 of the Federal Aviation Act of 1958, as amended). Filing of a VFR flight plan is recommended as a good operating practice. See also Part 99 for requirements concerning DVFR flight plans. |

FAA Form 7233-1 (8-82)   CLOSE VFR FLIGHT PLAN WITH _____ FSS ON ARRIVAL

FIGURE 1.—Flight Plan.

3-89   J16

When departing from an airport not served by a control tower, the issuance of a clearance containing a void time indicates that

A — ATC will assume the pilot has not departed if no transmission is received before the void time.
B — the pilot must advise ATC as soon as possible, but no later than 30 minutes, of their intentions if not off by the void time.
C — ATC will protect the airspace only to the void time.

3-90   J14

What response is expected when ATC issues an IFR clearance to pilots of airborne aircraft?

A — Read back the entire clearance as required by regulation.
B — Read back those parts containing altitude assignments or vectors and any part requiring verification.
C — Read-back should be unsolicited and spontaneous to confirm that the pilot understands all instructions.

3-89. Answer B. GFDICM 3C (AIM)

The wording, "clearance void if not off by ...," indicates that ATC expects you to be airborne by a certain time. In the event you do not depart by the void time, you must advise ATC of your intentions as soon as possible, but no later than 30 minutes after the void time. Answer (A) is wrong because ATC will assume you have departed if they haven't heard from you before your clearance void time. Answer (C) is also incorrect. Normally, ATC will protect the airspace until they can verify your position whether airborne or still on the ground.

3-90. Answer B. GFDICM 3C (AIM)

Although there is no requirement to read back an ATC clearance, you are expected to read back those parts of any clearance which contain altitude assignments, radar vectors, or any other instructions requiring verification. Regulations (answer A) do not require you to read back a clearance. Answer (C) is incorrect. You should automatically read back only the clearance information that may easily be misunderstood, but ATC may solicit a read back if the controller feels it is necessary.

3-91   J14
Which clearance items are always given in an abbreviated IFR departure clearance? (Assume radar environment.)

A — Altitude, destination airport, and one or more fixes which identify the initial route of flight.
B — Destination airport, altitude, DP Name, Number, and/or Transition, if appropriate.
C — Clearance limit, and DP Name, Number, and/or Transition, if appropriate.

3-91. Answer B. GFDICM 3C (AIM)
ATC may issue an abbreviated clearance by using the phrase "cleared as filed." This clearance will contain the name of your destination airport or clearance limit, the assigned enroute altitude, and DP information if appropriate. Fixes which identify the initial route (answer A) are not included in abbreviated clearances. Answer (C) is wrong because the assigned altitude is not included.

3-92   J14
On the runup pad, you receive the following clearance from ground control: CLEARED TO THE DALLAS LOVE AIRPORT AS FILED — MAINTAIN SIX THOUSAND — SQUAWK ZERO SEVEN ZERO FOUR JUST BEFORE DEPARTURE — DEPARTURE CONTROL WILL BE ONE TWO FOUR POINT NINER.

An abbreviated clearance, such as this, will always contain the

A — departure control frequency.
B — requested enroute altitude.
C — destination airport + route.

3-92. Answer C. GFDICM 3C (AIM)
An abbreviated clearance contains the name of your destination airport or clearance limit; the assigned enroute altitude or altitude to expect; DP information, and route as appropriate; and it may include a departure frequency or transponder code assignment.

3-93   J16
Which information is always given in an abbreviated departure clearance?

A — DP or transition name and altitude to maintain.
B — Name of destination airport or specific fix and altitude.
C — Altitude to maintain and code to squawk.

3-93. Answer B. GFDICM 3C (AIM)
An abbreviated clearance will always contain the name of the destination airport or a clearance limit, any applicable DP, and the assigned enroute altitude. Answer (A) is incorrect because a DP may not always apply. Answer (C) is incorrect because a destination or clearance limit is not included.

3-94   J19
What altitude may a pilot select upon receiving a VFR-on-Top clearance?

A — Any altitude at least 1,000 feet above the meteorological condition.
B — Any appropriate VFR altitude at or above the MEA in VFR weather conditions.
C — Any VFR altitude appropriate for the direction of flight at least 1,000 feet above the meteorological condition.

3-94. Answer B. GFDICM 3C (AIM)
When flying with a VFR-on-Top clearance, you must fly at an appropriate VFR altitude as defined in FAR 91.159. This type of clearance may be issued to a pilot on an IFR flight plan. In this case, you must comply with VFR visibility and cloud clearance requirements, as well as minimum IFR altitude rules. When flying below 18,000 feet MSL, and more than 3,000 feet AGL, you must maintain an odd thousand foot MSL altitude plus 500 feet for easterly magnetic courses (0° through 179°), for example 3,500, 5,500, or 7,500 feet MSL. For westerly magnetic courses (180° through 359°), maintain even thousand foot MSL altitudes plus 500 feet, for example 4,500, 6,500, or 8,500 feet MSL. Refer to the regulation for applicable flight levels above 18,000 feet MSL. Answers (A) and (C) are incorrect because they do not address the requirement to remain above the MEA.

3-95　　　J19

When must a pilot fly at a cardinal altitude plus 500 feet on an IFR flight plan?

A — When flying above 18,000 feet in VFR conditions.
B — When flying in VFR conditions above clouds.
C — When assigned a VFR-on-Top clearance.

3-95. Answer C. GFDICM 3C (AIM) (FAR 91.159)
See explanation for Question 3-94.

3-96　　　J06

You have filed an IFR flight plan with a VFR-on-Top clearance in lieu of an assigned altitude. If you receive this clearance and fly a course of 180°, at what altitude should you fly? (Assume VFR conditions.)

A — Any IFR altitude which will enable you to remain in VFR conditions.
B — An odd thousand-foot MSL altitude plus 500 feet.
C — An even thousand-foot MSL altitude plus 500 feet.

3-96. Answer C. GFDICM 3C (AIM) (FAR 91.159)
Assuming that your flight is below FL 180, and above 3,000 feet AGL, FAR 91.159 specifies that for any magnetic course, 180° through 359°, you will operate at an even thousand foot MSL altitude plus 500 feet, for example 4,500, 6,500, or 8,500 feet MSL. Answer (A) is wrong because IFR altitudes do not apply. Answer (B) is incorrect because odd plus 500 feet is for magnetic courses 0° through 179°.

3-97　　　J14

Which clearance procedures may be issued by ATC without prior pilot request?

A — DP's, STAR's, and contact approaches.
B — Contact and visual approaches.
C — DP's, STAR's, and visual approaches.

3-97. Answer C. GFDICM 3C (AIM)
DPs, STARs, and visual approaches can be initiated by either the pilot or ATC. A contact approach request must be initiated by the pilot; therefore, answers (A) and (B) are incorrect.

3-98　　　J14

What is the significance of an ATC clearance which reads "...CRUISE SIX THOUSAND..."?

A — The pilot must maintain 6,000 until reaching the IAF serving the destination airport, then execute the published approach procedure.
B — It authorizes a pilot to conduct flight at any altitude from minimum IFR altitude up to and including 6,000.
C — The pilot is authorized to conduct flight at any altitude from minimum IFR altitude up to and including 6,000, but each change in altitude must be reported to ATC.

3-98. Answer B. GFDICM 3C (AIM)
A cruise clearance is an authorization by ATC to conduct flight at any altitude from the minimum IFR altitude up to and including the altitude specified, in this case 6,000 feet MSL. Answer (A) is incorrect because you can descend below 6,000 feet, if a lower minimum IFR altitude is prescribed. Answer (C) is incorrect because ATC does not need to be notified on each change in altitude, except once you begin a descent from a specific altitude, you must obtain ATC clearance before climbing back to that altitude.

3-99　　　J08

Where are VFR-on-Top operations prohibited?

A — In a Class A airspace.
B — During off-airways direct flights.
C — When flying through Class B airspace.

3-99. Answer A. GFDICM 3C (AIM) (FAR 91.135)
ATC will not authorize VFR or VFR-on-Top operations in Class A airspace, and you must operate under an IFR flight plan. Answers (B) and (C) are incorrect; VFR-on-Top operations are not prohibited in either area.

3-100   J14

Which rules apply to the pilot in command when operating on a VFR-on-Top clearance?

A — VFR only.

B — VFR and IFR.

C — VFR when "in the clear" and IFR when "in the clouds."

3-100. Answer B. GFDICM 3C (AIM)

VFR-on-Top allows you to fly in VFR conditions and at appropriate VFR cruising altitudes while on an IFR flight plan. In addition to compliance with VFR visibility, cloud clearance, and cruising altitude requirements, you also must observe minimum IFR altitudes. Answer (A) is wrong since you must also comply with certain IFR requirements. Answer (C) is incorrect because you must remain in visual meteorological conditions (VMC) to continue on a VFR-on-Top clearance.

3-101   J14

When can a VFR-on-Top clearance be assigned by ATC?

A — Only upon request of the pilot when conditions are indicated to be suitable.

B — Any time suitable conditions exist and ATC wishes to expedite traffic flow.

C — When VFR conditions exist, but there is a layer of clouds below the MEA.

3-101. Answer A. GFDICM 3C (AIM)

Only the pilot can initiate a VFR-on-Top clearance. In addition, you must maintain VFR flight conditions at all times. Altitude selection must comply with the VFR cruising altitude rules. You may not select an altitude which is less than the minimum IFR altitude prescribed for the route segment. Therefore, answers (B) and (C) are incorrect.

3-102   J14

Which ATC clearance should instrument-rated pilots request in order to climb through a cloud layer or an area of reduced visibility and then continue the flight VFR?

A — To VFR on Top.

B — Special VFR to VFR Over-the-Top.

C — VFR Over-the-Top.

3-102. Answer A. GFDICM 3C (AIM)

Pilots desiring to climb through a cloud, haze, smoke, or other meteorological formation and then either cancel their IFR flight plan or operate VFR-on-Top may request a climb to VFR-on-Top. Answer (B) is wrong because special VFR requires you to remain clear of clouds. Answer (C) is also wrong; the terminology VFR Over-the-Top is not included in the *Pilot/Controller Glossary*.

3-103   J14

When on a VFR-on-Top clearance, the cruising altitude is based on

A — true course.

B — magnetic course.

C — magnetic heading.

3-103. Answer B. GFDICM 3C (AIM)

Altitude selection must comply with the VFR cruising altitude rules which are based on the magnetic course of the aircraft. Choices (A) and (C) are incorrect since neither specify magnetic course.

3-104   J14

In which airspace is VFR-on-Top operation prohibited?

A — Class B airspace.

B — Class E airspace.

C — Class A airspace.

3-104. Answer C. GFDICM 3C (AIM)

See explanation for Question 3-99. Although the answers are somewhat different, the question is the same.

3-105   J14

What cruising altitude is appropriate for VFR on Top on a westbound flight below 18,000 feet?

A — Even thousand-foot levels.

B — Even thousand-foot levels plus 500 feet, but not below MEA.

C — Odd thousand-foot levels plus 500 feet, but not below MEA.

3-105. Answer B. GFDICM 3C (AIM) (FAR 91.159)

When flying on a VFR-on-Top clearance, VFR cruising altitude rules must be followed. On westbound flights (magnetic courses 180° through 359°) above 3,000 feet AGL and below 18,000 feet MSL, you must maintain an even thousand-foot MSL altitude plus 500 feet. The selected altitude must not be less then the applicable MEA. Answer (A) is incorrect since it is an IFR altitude, and answer (C) would apply on magnetic courses of 0° through 179°.

3-106 J14

What minimums must be considered in selecting an altitude when operating with a VFR-on-Top clearance?

A — At least 500 feet above the lowest MEA, or appropriate MOCA, and at least 1,000 feet above the existing meteorological condition.

B — At least 1,000 feet above the lowest MEA, appropriate MOCA, or existing meteorological condition.

C — Minimum IFR altitude, minimum distance from clouds, and visibility appropriate to altitude selected.

3-107 J14

A "CRUISE FOUR THOUSAND FEET" clearance would mean that the pilot is authorized to

A — vacate 4,000 feet without notifying ATC.

B — climb to, but not descend from 4,000 feet, without further ATC clearance.

C — use any altitude from minimum IFR to 4,000 feet, but must report leaving each altitude.

3-108 J14

While on an IFR flight, a pilot has an emergency which causes a deviation from an ATC clearance. What action must be taken?

A — Notify ATC of the deviation as soon as possible.

B — Squawk 7700 for the duration of the emergency.

C — Submit a detailed report to the chief of the ATC facility within 48 hours.

3-109 J19

What responsibility does the pilot in command of an IFR flight assume upon entering VFR conditions?

A — Report VFR conditions to ARTCC so that an amended clearance may be issued.

B — Use VFR operating procedures.

C — To see and avoid other traffic.

3-106. Answer C. GFDICM 3C (AIM) (FAR 91.155, 91.159)

Minimums are set according to the existing weather conditions and follow the appropriate VFR cruising altitude, visibility, and distance from cloud criteria specified in FAR Parts 91.159 and 91.155, respectively. Since there are no set distance requirements above the MEA for VFR-on-Top, answers (A) and (B) are incorrect.

3-107. Answer A. GFDICM 3C (AIM)

The term "cruise" is used by ATC to assign a block of airspace to a pilot from the minimum IFR altitude up to and including the altitude specified in the cruise clearance. You may level off at any intermediate altitude or climb/descend within the block at your discretion. However, once you start descent and verbally report leaving an altitude in the block, you may not return to that altitude without additional ATC clearance. Answers (B) and (C) are incorrect because both contain unnecessary requirements to notify ATC when changing altitudes.

3-108. Answer A. GFDICM 3C (FAR 91.123)

FAR Part 91.123(c) states that, "Each pilot in command who, in an emergency, deviates from an ATC clearance or instruction shall notify ATC of that deviation as soon as possible." Answer (B) is incorrect since it does not include the notification requirement. Answer (C) is wrong because you do not have to submit a detailed report unless you are given priority by ATC during the emergency and ATC requests a report.

3-109. Answer C. GFDICM 3C (FAR 91.113)

FAR Part 91.113(b) states, "When weather conditions permit, regardless of whether an operation is conducted under instrument flight rules or visual flight rules, vigilance shall be maintained by each person operating an aircraft so as to see and avoid other aircraft." Answer (A) is wrong because encountering VFR conditions does not affect IFR operations from ATC's standpoint. Answer (B) is wrong because VFR cloud clearance and visibility requirements do not apply during normal IFR operations.

3-110   J16

An abbreviated departure clearance "...CLEARED AS FILED..." will always contain the name

A — and number of the STAR to be flown when filed in the flight plan.
B — of the destination airport filed in the flight plan.
C — of the first compulsory reporting point if not in a radar environment.

3-111   B08

If, while in Class E airspace, a clearance is received to "maintain VFR conditions on top," the pilot should maintain a VFR cruising altitude based on the direction of the

A — true course.
B — magnetic heading.
C — magnetic course.

3-112   J19

Under which of the following circumstances will ATC issue a VFR restriction to an IFR flight?

A — Whenever the pilot reports the loss of any navigational aid.
B — When it is necessary to provide separation between IFR and special VFR traffic.
C — When the pilot requests it.

3-113.   J14

When operating under IFR with a VFR-On-Top clearance, what altitude should be maintained?

A — An IFR cruising altitude appropriate to the magnetic course being flown.
B — A VFR cruising altitude appropriate to the magnetic course being flown and as restricted by ATC.
C — The last IFR altitude assigned by ATC.

3-114   J18

What are the main differences between a visual approach and a contact approach?

A — The pilot must request a contact approach; the pilot may be assigned a visual approach and higher weather minimums must exist.
B — The pilot must request a visual approach and report having the field in sight; ATC may assign a contact approach if VFR conditions exist.
C — Anytime the pilot reports the field in sight, ATC may clear the pilot for a contact approach; for a visual approach, the pilot must advise that the approach can be made under VFR conditions.

3-110. Answer B. GFDICM 3C (AIM)

An abbreviated clearance will always contain the name of the destination airport or a clearance limit; any applicable SID name, number, and transition; and your assigned enroute altitude. Answers (A) and (C) are incorrect because a STAR or the first compulsory reporting point do not have to be included in an abbreviated clearance.

3-111. Answer C. GFDICM 3C (AIM) (FAR 91.159)

With a VFR-on-Top clearance, you must maintain an appropriate VFR cruising altitude. VFR cruising altitudes are based on magnetic course. Magnetic course is true course corrected for magnetic variation. It does not take into consideration any wind drift correction. True course (answer A) is determined by reference to true north; it must be corrected for magnetic variation before you can use it in flight. Answer (B) is wrong because your cruising altitude is based on magnetic course, not magnetic heading.

3-112. Answer C. GFDICM 3C (AIM)

A restriction to "maintain VFR conditions" may be issued only when requested by the pilot. Loss of any navigational aid (answer A) does not necessarily require a VFR restriction. ATC will not issue a VFR restriction to provide traffic separation (answer B).

3-113. Answer B. GFDICM 3C (AIM)

When flying on an IFR flight plan operating in VFR weather conditions, you may request VFR-ON-TOP in lieu of an assigned altitude. This permits you to select an appropriate VFR cruising altitude or flight level (subject to any ATC restrictions).

3-114. Answer A. GFDICM 3C (AIM)

A contact approach cannot be initiated by ATC; it must be requested by the pilot. Weather minimums need only be one mile flight visibility and clear of clouds. A visual approach may be assigned by ATC if VFR conditions exist. Answers (B) and (C) are wrong because ATC may assign a visual approach, but not a contact approach unless requested by the pilot. To be cleared for a visual approach, you must have either the airport or the preceding aircraft in sight. Since you are expected to remain VFR, you should advise ATC if unable to do so.

See explanations for Questions 3-115, 3-117, and 3-118.

3-115   J18
What are the requirements for a contact approach to an airport that has an approved IAP, if the pilot is on an instrument flight plan and clear of clouds?

A — The controller must determine that the pilot can see the airport at the altitude flown and can remain clear of clouds.
B — The pilot must agree to the approach when given by ATC and the controller must have determined that the visibility was at least 1 mile and be reasonably sure the pilot can remain clear of clouds.
C — The pilot must request the approach, have at least 1-mile visibility, and be reasonably sure of remaining clear of clouds.

3-116   J19
When is radar service terminated during a visual approach?

A — Automatically when ATC instructs the pilot to contact the tower.
B — Immediately upon acceptance of the approach by the pilot.
C — When ATC advises, "Radar service terminated; resume own navigation."

3-117   J18
When may you obtain a contact approach?

A — ATC may assign a contact approach if VFR conditions exist or you report the runway in sight and are clear of clouds.
B — ATC may assign a contact approach if you are below the clouds and the visibility is at least 1 mile.
C — ATC will assign a contact approach only upon request if the reported visibility is at least 1 mile.

3-118   J18
What conditions are necessary before ATC can authorize a visual approach?

A — You must have the preceding aircraft in sight, and be able to remain in VFR weather conditions.
B — You must have the airport in sight or the preceding aircraft in sight, and be able to proceed to, and land in IFR conditions.
C — You must have the airport in sight or a preceding aircraft to be followed, and be able to proceed to the airport in VFR conditions.

3-115. Answer C. GFDICM 3C (AIM)
Only the pilot can initiate a contact approach with a request. You must have 1 mile flight visibility and be able to remain clear of clouds. In addition, you must reasonably expect to be able to remain in these conditions. You do not have to have the airport in sight (answer A), and the controller cannot issue a contact approach unless you request it (answer B).

This question is similar to 3-117.

3-116. Answer A. GFDICM 3C (AIM)
On a visual approach, radar service is automatically terminated, without advising the pilot, when advised by ATC to change to the tower or an advisory frequency. Answer (B) is wrong because radar service is provided for the approach until the pilot is told to switch to the tower or an advisory frequency. ATC does not normally advise that radar service is terminated for a visual approach (answer C).

3-117. Answer C. GFDICM 3C (AIM)
The pilot must request the approach, and the visibility must be at least 1 mile. ATC cannot assign a contact approach (answers A and B) unless the pilot requests it. VFR conditions and visual contact with the runway is not required. You also do not have to be below the clouds, but only remain clear of clouds.

This question is similar to 3-115.

3-118. Answer C. GFDICM 3C (AIM)
The controller may issue a visual approach clearance if you have either the airport or a preceding aircraft in sight. You must also be able to maintain VFR conditions to the airport. Answer (A) is wrong because you can have either the airport or the preceding aircraft in sight. Answer (B) is wrong because you must be in VFR, not IFR, conditions.

See explanation for Question 3-114.

3-119   J18
A contact approach is an approach procedure that may be used

A — in lieu of conducting a SIAP.
B — if assigned by ATC and will facilitate the approach.
C — in lieu of a visual approach.

3-119. Answer A. GFDICM 3C (AIM)
A contact approach may be used instead of the published standard instrument approach procedure (SIAP). Answer (B) is wrong; a contact approach may be approved by ATC only if requested by the pilot, and it replaces the instrument approach rather than facilitate it. Answer (C) is also wrong because a contact approach is used in lieu of the instrument approach, not a visual approach.

See explanations for Questions 3-115 and 3-117.

3-120   J11
If during a VFR practice instrument approach, Radar Approach Control assigns an altitude or heading that will cause you to enter the clouds, what action should be taken?

A — Enter the clouds, since ATC authorization for practice approaches is considered an IFR clearance.
B — Avoid the clouds and inform ATC that altitude/heading will not permit VFR.
C — Abandon the approach.

3-120. Answer B. GFDICM 3C (AIM)
You should not accept a clearance that would cause you to violate an FAR such as entering clouds while operating under VFR. Take the necessary action to avoid the clouds and notify ATC of your situation. Do not enter the clouds (answer A) because you have not been issued an IFR clearance. Avoiding the clouds does not necessarily mean you will need to abandon the approach (answer C).

3-121   J31
Which technique should a pilot use to scan for traffic to the right and left during straight-and-level flight?

A — Systematically focus on different segments of the sky for short intervals.
B — Concentrate on relative movement detected in the peripheral vision area.
C — Continuous sweeping of the windshield from right to left.

3-121. Answer A. GFDICM 3C (AIM)
Only a very small area in the back of the eye can send clear, sharply focused images to the brain. Since the eyes require time to focus on this narrow viewing area, scanning is most effective when using a series of short, regularly spaced eye movements. This will help to bring successive areas of the sky into the central visual field. Although peripheral vision (answer B) picks up motion, an aircraft on a collision course will have little or no relative movement. Continuous sweeping of the windshield (answer C) would not allow time for the eyes to focus.

CHAPTER 4

DEPARTURE

SECTION A
DEPARTURE CHARTS

DEPARTURE PROCEDURES OVERVIEW

1. Instrument departure procedures (DPs) are used after takeoff to provide a transition between the airport and enroute structure.
2. Departure charts help simplify complex clearances, reduce frequency congestion, ensure obstacle clearance, and control the flow of traffic around an airport. They help reduce fuel consumption, and may include noise abatement procedures.
3. Because of the large area covered, most DPs usually are not drawn to scale.
4. Jeppesen and NOS list the airport served by the procedure, the name, and the type of DP at the top of the chart. On NOS DPs, the applicable NOS enroute charts are listed below the navaid information boxes.
5. DPs initial takeoff procedures may apply to all runways, or apply only to the specific runway identified.
6. Since the actual mileage between a given runway and the first fix varies with aircraft performance, pilot technique, and the length of the radar vector, Jeppesen includes the direct distance from the airport to the first fix.
7. DP transition routes are shown with dashed lines on Jeppesen charts and with light, solid lines on NOS charts.

FLIGHT PLANS AND CLEARANCES

8. When you accept a DP in a clearance, or file one in your flight plan, you must possess the DP chart or the textual description.
9. To avoid being issued DPs, enter the phrase "NO DP" in the remarks section of your flight plan.
10. The computer identification code for a transition in your flight plan informs ATC you intend to fly both the DP and the appropriate transition. For example, the DAWNN ONE DEPARTURE (DAWNN1), Louisville transition (IIU), is entered as "DAWNN1.IIU." You will find these abbreviations on the charts.

PERFORMANCE REQUIREMENTS

11. When you are issued a DP, you must ensure your aircraft is capable of achieving the DP performance requirements. Minimum climb gradients are given in feet per nautical mile and must be converted to feet per minute for use during departure.
12. DPs require minimum climb gradients of at least 200 feet per nautical mile, to ensure you can clear departure path obstacles.
13. DPs may specify a minimum ceiling and visibility to allow you to see and avoid obstacles, a climb gradient greater than 200 feet per mile, detailed flight maneuvers, or a combination of these procedures.

PILOT NAV AND VECTOR DPs

14. Pilot nav DPs allow you to navigate along a route with minimal ATC communications. They usually contain instructions to all aircraft, followed by transition routes to navigate to an enroute fix, and may include radar vectors that help you join the DP.
15. Vector DPs exist where ATC provides radar navigation guidance. They usually contain a heading to fly, and an altitude for initial climb. When ATC establishes radar contact, they provide vectors to help you reach fixes portrayed on the chart. When special lost communication procedures are necessary for a DP, they are included on the chart.
16. If you are instructed to maintain runway heading, it means you should maintain the magnetic heading of the runway centerline.

4-1   **J40**

(Refer to figure 77 on page 10-56.) At which point does the basic instrument departure terminate?

A — When Helena Departure Control establishes radar contact.
B — At STAKK Intersection.
C — Over the BOZEMAN VOR.

4-1. Answer B. GFDICM 4A (STAR/DP)

The STAKK Two Departure ends at STAKK Int. as indicated by the end of the heavy black line. From STAKK, a DME arc provides a transition route to five departure routes. The basic DP does not end when Helena Departure Control establishes radar contact (answer A). You will be turned over to departure control within 5 miles of the airport, yet the basic portion of the DP goes out to 15 miles from the airport. The BOZEMAN VOR (answer C) is the end of the Bozeman transition, not the DP.

4-2   **J40**

(Refer to figure 77 on page 10-56.) At which minimum altitude should you cross the STAKK Intersection?

A — 6,500 feet MSL.
B — 1,400 feet MSL.
C — 10,200 feet MSL.

4-2. Answer C. GFDICM 4A (STAR/DP)

You must cross STAKK Int. at or above 10,200 feet MSL. This is listed in the departure route descriptions for runways 9 and 27, as well as in the plan view by the callout *10200*. Both 6,500 feet MSL (answer A) and 1,400 feet MSL (answer B) are below 10,200 feet.

4-3   **J40**

(Refer to figure 77 on page 10-56.) Using an average groundspeed of 140 knots, what minimum rate of climb would meet the required minimum climb rate per NM as specified on the instrument departure procedure?

A — 350 feet per minute.
B — 475 feet per minute.
C — 700 feet per minute.

4-3. Answer C. GFDICM 4A (Rate of Climb Table)

The STAKK TWO DEPARTURE requires a minimum climb of 300 feet per n.m. as indicated by the fourth NOTE in the lower left corner of the plan view. Once you know your groundspeed, there are multiple ways to find the feet per minute climb rate. One way is to use the rate of climb table in Appendix 2. Enter the table with the required climb rate (300 ft/n.m.) and read across to the groundspeed (140 kts.) column to find 700 feet per minute. A second way is the computation method. Divide the groundspeed (140 kts.) by 60 to convert to n.m. per minute. Then multiply by the required climb rate of 300 feet per n.m. The result is 700 feet per minute ($140 \div 60 = 2.33 \times 300 = 700$). Takeoff on runway 9 requires a minimum climb rate of 390 ft./n.m., but this is not the lowest minimum climb rate for this DP. Answers (A) and (B) are wrong because they are less than the 700 feet per minute required.

4-4   **J34**

(Refer to figures 76 and 77 on pages 10-55 and 10-56.) Which en route low altitude navigation chart would cover the proposed routing at the BOZEMAN VORTAC?

A — L-2.
B — L-7.
C — L-9.

4-4. Answer C. GFDICM 4A (A/FD Legend)

Assuming you use the routing listed in figure 75, the entire route is on the same chart as Helena. The A/FD excerpt in figure 76 lists chart L-9 in the upper right-hand corner. Also, if you look at figure 77, the appropriate low altitude enroute chart is indicated below the navaid information boxes and fixes identifying each transition. All five transitions on the STAKK Two Departure are covered on the L-9 low altitude enroute chart. Charts L-2 (answer A) and L-7 (answer B) are inappropriate.

4-5   J40

(Refer to figure 85 on page 4-8.) What route should you take if cleared for the Washoe Two Departure and your assigned route is V6?

A — Climb on the LOC south course to WAGGE where you will be vectored to V6.

B — Climb on the LOC south course to cross WAGGE at 9,000, turn left and fly direct to FMG VORTAC and cross at or above 10,000, and proceed on FMG R-241.

C — Climb on the LOC south course to WAGGE, turn left and fly direct to FMG VORTAC. If at 10,000 turn left and proceed on FMG R-241; if not at 10,000 enter depicted holding pattern and climb to 10,000 before proceeding on FMG R-241.

4-6   J40

(Refer to figure 85 on page 4-8.) What procedure should be followed if communications are lost before reaching 9,000 feet?

A — At 9,000, turn left direct to FMG VORTAC, then via assigned route if at proper altitude; if not, climb in holding pattern until reaching the proper altitude.

B — Continue climb to WAGGE INT, turn left direct to FMG VORTAC, then if at or above MCA, proceed on assigned route; if not, continue climb in holding pattern until at the proper altitude.

C — Continue climb on LOC course to cross WAGGE INT at or above 9,000, turn left direct to FMG VORTAC to cross at 10,000 or above, and continue on assigned course.

4-5. Answer A. GFDICM 4A (STAR/DP)

The Washoe Two Departure requires all flights taking off on RWYS 16 L/R to climb via the I-RNO Localizer south course to WAGGE INT., then via radar vectors to the assigned route. Answers (B) and (C) are incorrect because they include lost communications procedures which are not part of the instrument departure procedure (DP).

4-6. Answer B. GFDICM 4A (STAR/DP)

Lost communications procedures before reaching 9,000 feet are to continue the climb via I-RNO localizer south course to WAGGE INT., turn left, and proceed direct to FMG VORTAC. Cross the FMG VORTAC at or above the published minimum crossing altitude (MCA), then via the assigned route or climb in a holding pattern northeast on the FMG 041° radial, left turns to cross FMG VORTAC at or above the MCA, for the assigned route. Answer (A) is incorrect because it does not specify a left turn to FMG VORTAC. Answer (C) is wrong because it includes an MCA of 9,000 feet at WAGGE INT.

SECTION B
DEPARTURE PROCEDURES

TAKEOFF MINIMUMS

1. IFR takeoff minimums do not apply to private aircraft under IFR and Part 91, but good judgment should dictate compliance.
2. Standard takeoff weather minimums are usually based on visibility. Greater than standard takeoff minimums may be due to terrain, obstructions, or departure procedures.
3. Runway visibility value (RVV) is the distance down the runway you can see unlighted objects or unfocused lights of moderate intensity; it is reported in statute miles or fractions of miles.
4. Runway visual range (RVR) represents the horizontal distance a pilot will see when looking down the runway from a moving aircraft at the approach end. It is always a transmissometer value.
5. When RVR is out of service, convert published RVR values to visibility in statute miles.
6. Prevailing visibility or RVR in the aviation routine weather report should normally be used only for informational purposes. The current visibility at the time of departure is the value you should use for determining compliance with takeoff minimums.

IFR DEPARTURE OPTIONS

7. In general, you have four alternatives when departing an airport on an IFR flight. Your options include a (DP), an IFR departure procedure, a radar departure, or a VFR departure.
8. To accept a clearance with a DP, you must possess the charted DP procedure or at least the textual description. Otherwise, you should file NO DP in your flight plan.
9. IFR departure procedures are not assigned as a portion of your IFR clearance unless required for separation purposes. In general, it is your responsibility to determine if one has been established, then comply with it.
10. Radar departures are often assigned at radar-equipped approach control facilities and require close coordination with the tower.

GENERAL PROCEDURES

11. During the IFR departure, you should not contact departure control until advised to do so by the tower.
12. During departure, terrain and obstruction clearance remains your responsibility until the controller begins to provide navigational guidance in the form of radar vectors.
13. The term *". . . radar contact"* means your aircraft has been identified and radar flight following will be provided until radar identification has been terminated.
14. *"Resume own navigation"* is a phrase used by ATC to advise you to assume responsibility for your own navigation. It generally cancels assigned vectors or other restrictions previously imposed by ATC.

4-7   H342

(Refer to figure 30 on page 10-26.) Using an average groundspeed of 120 knots, what minimum rate of climb must be maintained to meet the required climb rate (feet per NM) to 4,100 feet as specified on the instrument departure procedure?

A — 400 feet per minute.
B — 500 feet per minute.
C — 800 feet per minute.

4-7. Answer C. GFDICM 4B (Rate of Climb Table)

The instrument departure procedure requires a minimum climb rate of 400 feet per n.m. to 4,100 feet as indicated by the note next to the planview. To determine the rate of climb needed, refer to Appendix 2. At an airspeed of 120 knots, the answer is 800 feet per minute. Answers (A) and (B) are wrong because they are substantially less than the rate required.

You also can compute the climb rate in feet per minute. Divide the groundspeed (120 knots) by 60 (to convert to n.m. per minute). Then, multiply by the required
rate per nautical mile, 400 feet, (120 ÷ 60 = 2 × 400 = 800 f.p.m.).

4-8 I10

(Refer to figure 46 on page 10-41.) Using an average groundspeed of 140 knots, what minimum indicated rate of climb must be maintained to meet the required climb rate (feet per NM) to 6,300 feet as specified on the instrument departure procedure?

A — 350 feet per minute.
B — 583 feet per minute.
C — 816 feet per minute.

4-9 J40

(Refer to figure 52 on page 10-45.) Using an average groundspeed of 100 knots, what minimum rate of climb would meet the required minimum climb rate per NM as specified by the instrument departure procedure?

A — 425 feet per minute.
B — 580 feet per minute.
C — 642 feet per minute.

4-10 J14

When ATC has not imposed any climb or descent restrictions and aircraft are within 1,000 feet of assigned altitude, pilots should attempt to both climb and descend at a rate of between

A — 500 feet per minute and 1,000 feet per minute.
B — 500 feet per minute and 1,500 feet per minute.
C — 1,000 feet per minute and 2,000 feet per minute.

4-11 J15

What action is recommended if a pilot does not wish to use an instrument departure procedure?

A — Advise clearance delivery or ground control before departure.
B — Advise departure control upon initial contact.
C — Enter "No DP" in the REMARKS section of the IFR flight plan.

4-8. Answer C. GFDICM 4B (Rate of Climb Table)

If you know the groundspeed, it is easy to find the feet per minute climb rate. One way is to use the rate of climb table in Appendix 2. Enter the table with the required climb rate (350 ft/n.m.) and read across to the known groundspeed (140 kts.) to find 816 feet per minute. The second way is the computation method. Divide the groundspeed (140 kts.) by 60 (to convert to n.m. per minute). Then multiply by the required climb rate of 350 feet per n.m. The result is 816 feet per minute. To maintain a climb rate of 350 feet per n.m. at a rate of 350 feet per minute (answer A), your maximum ground speed would have to be 60 knots. To maintain a climb rate of 350 feet per n.m. at a rate of 583 feet per minute (answer B), your maximum ground-speed would have to be 100 knots.

4-9. Answer C. GFDICM 4B (Rate of Climb Chart)

The minimum climb rate specified in the DP is 385 feet per n.m. Refer to Appendix 2 to convert feet per n.m. into feet per minute. The minimum climb rate of 385 feet per n.m. falls in between 350 and 400 in the far left column. If you follow these two rows across to the 100 kt. groundspeed column. The corresponding numbers are 583 and 667 feet per minute. The only answer that falls between these is 642 feet per minute. If you prefer, you also can easily convert feet per nautical mile to feet per minute. Simply divide the 385 by 60 (385 ÷ 60 = 6.4167) and then multiply by the groundspeed (6.4167 × 100 = 641.66) feet per minute. In addition to using the mathematical method and the tabular method using the legend, you can use the slide graphic computer (CSG). For this problem, first set the speed index to 100 knots. Then, directly above the 385 on the "B" scale, find the answer, 642 feet per minute, on the "A" scale. The CSG works well for all of the rate of climb and descent problems.

4-10. Answer B. GFDICM 4B (AIM)

When ATC has not used the term "at pilot's discretion" nor imposed any climb or descent restrictions, you should climb or descend at an optimum rate to within 1,000 feet of the assigned altitude. Then, you should attempt to maintain a rate between 500 and 1,500 feet per minute. Answer (A), between 500 and 1,000 feet per minute, is less than recommended. Answer (C), 1,000 to 2,000 feet per minute, is greater than recommended.

4-11. Answer C. GFDICM 4B (AIM)

If you do not possess a charted DP or a preprinted DP description or, for any other reason, do not wish to use a DP, you are expected to notify ATC. Notification may be accomplished by filing "NO DP" in the REMARKS section of the filed flight plan. You may notify ATC verbally, but this is the less desirable method. Answers (A) and (B) are incorrect because they are not recommended.

4-12   J40

A particular instrument departure procedure requires a minimum climb rate of 210 feet per NM to 8,000 feet. If you climb with a groundspeed of 140 knots, what is the rate of climb required in feet per minute?

A — 210.
B — 450.
C — 490.

4-12. Answer C. GFDICM 4B (Rate of Climb Table)

Use the rate-of-climb table, Appendix 2, and interpolate between 200 feet per mile and 250 feet per mile at a groundspeed of 140 knots. Since 210 is one fifth of the way between 200 and 250 feet per minute, (583 − 467 = 116 × 1/5 = 23.2). Add 23.2 to 467 and the result is 490.2, rounded to 490.

You can also find the answer with a simple conversion; A groundspeed of 140 knots is 140 ÷ 60, or 2.33 n.m. per minute. Then, 2.33 n.m. per minute × 210 feet per nautical mile equals 490 feet per minute.

4-13   J16

Which procedure applies to instrument departure procedures?

A — Instrument departure clearances will not be issued unless requested by the pilot.
B — The pilot in command must accept an instrument departure procedure when issued by ATC.
C — If an instrument departure procedure is accepted, the pilot must possess at least a textual description.

4-13. Answer C. GFDICM 4B (AIM)

Use of a DP requires the pilot to possess at least the textual description of the DP procedures. Answer (A) is incorrect because a DP can be issued with an ATC clearance, even though it was not originally requested. Since you are not required to accept a DP, (answer B) is incorrect.

4-14   J33

What is meant when departure control instructs you to "resume own navigation" after you have been vectored to a Victor airway?

A — You should maintain the airway by use of your navigation equipment.
B — Radar service is terminated.
C — You are still in radar contact, but must make position reports.

4-14. Answer A. GFDICM 4B (AIM)

This phrase is used by ATC to advise you to resume your own navigational responsibility. It is issued after completion of a radar vector, or when radar contact is lost while your aircraft is being radar vectored. Answer (B) is incorrect because radar service is not necessarily terminated and you will continue to receive radar separation service. Answer (C) is incorrect because you are not required to make position reports while in radar contact.

4-15   J33

What does the ATC term "Radar Contact" signify?

A — Your aircraft has been identified and you will receive separation from all aircraft while in contact with this radar facility.
B — Your aircraft has been identified on the radar display and radar flight-following will be provided until radar identification is terminated.
C — You will be given traffic advisories until advised the service has been terminated or that radar contact has been lost.

4-15. Answer B. GFDICM 4B (AIM)

This term is used by ATC to inform you that your aircraft is identified on the radar display and radar flight following will be provided until radar identification is terminated. Position reports are not required while in radar contact. Answer (A) is incorrect because separation from all aircraft is provided only in certain classes of airspace, such as Class B or Class C. Choice (C) is wrong because advisory service is provided only on a workload permitting basis.

4-16   J33

Upon intercepting the assigned radial, the controller advises you that you are on the airway and to "RESUME OWN NAVIGATION". This phrase means that

A — you are still in radar contact, but must make position reports.
B — radar services are terminated and you will be responsible for position reports.
C — you are to assume responsibility for your own navigation.

4-16. Answer C. GFDICM 4B (AIM)
See explanation for Question 4-14.

4-17   B08

Which procedure is recommended while climbing to an assigned altitude on the airway?

A — Climb on the centerline of the airway except when maneuvering to avoid other air traffic in VFR conditions.
B — Climb slightly on the right side of the airway when in VFR conditions.
C — Climb far enough to the right side of the airway to avoid climbing or descending traffic coming from the opposite direction if in VFR conditions.

4-17. Answer A. GFDICM 4B (FAR 91.181)
FAR Part 91.181 specifies, "... along the centerline of that airway." However, the same regulation does allow deviation in VFR conditions to avoid other traffic. Answers (B) and (C) are wrong; both include climbing on the right side of the airway.

4-18   J16

What does the symbol T within a black triangle in the minimums section of the IAP for a particular airport indicate?

A — Takeoff minimums are 1 mile for aircraft having two engines or less and 1/2 mile for those with more than two engines.
B — Instrument takeoffs are not authorized.
C — Takeoff minimums are not standard and/or departure procedures are published.

4-18. Answer C. GFDICM 4B (Approach Chart Legend)
On NOS charts, the symbol T within a black triangle indicates takeoff minimums are nonstandard and/or IFR departure procedures are published. Answer (A) is incorrect since it lists standard takeoff minimums. Answer (B) is inappropriate, since the airport obviously has published takeoff minimums and/or IFR departure procedures.

4-19   J40

(Refer to figure 85 on page 4-8.) What is the minimum rate climb per NM to 9,000 feet required for the WASH2 WAGGE Departure?

A — 400 feet
B — 750 feet
C — 875 feet

4-19. Answer A. GFDICM 4B (STAR/DP Legend)
The short note (lower right side of the departure sketch) specifies a minimum climb rate of 400 feet per n.m. to 9,000 feet. This climb gradient is required for the WASH2.WAGGE Departure. Answers (B) and (C) are inappropriate.

4-20   J40

(Refer to figure 85 on page 4-8.) Of the following, which is the minimum acceptable rate of climb (feet per minute) to 9,000 feet required for the WASH2 WAGGE departure at a GS of 150 knots?

A — 750 feet per minute.
B — 825 feet per minute.
C — 1,000 feet per minute.

4-20. Answer C. GFDICM 4B (Rate of Climb Table)
If you know the groundspeed, there are two easy ways to find the feet per minute climb rate. One way is to use the rate of climb table in Appendix 2. Enter the table with the required climb rate (400 ft./n.m.) and read across to the known groundspeed (150 knots) to find 1,000 feet per minute. The second way is the computational method. Divide the 150-knot groundspeed by 60 (to convert to n.m. per minute). Then, multiply by the required climb rate of 400 feet per n.m. The result is 1,000 feet per minute. Answers (A) and (B) are inappropriate.

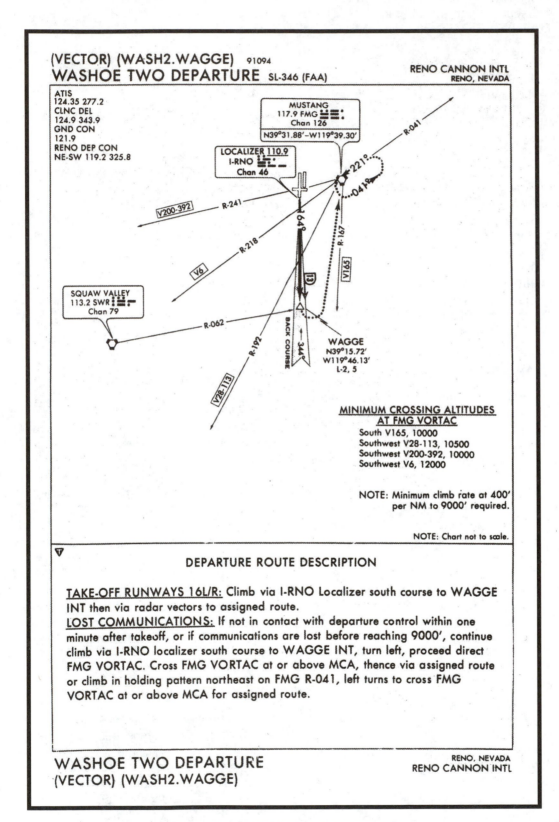

FIGURE 85.—WASHOE TWO DEPARTURE.

4-21   J14

To comply with ATC instructions for altitude changes of more than 1,000 feet, what rate of climb or descent should be used?

A — As rapidly as practicable to 500 feet above/below the assigned altitude, and then at 500 feet per minute until the assigned altitude is reached.

B — 1,000 feet per minute during climb and 500 feet per minute during descents until reaching the assigned altitude.

C — As rapidly as practicable to 1,000 feet above/below the assigned altitude, and then between 500 and 1500 feet per minute until reaching the assigned altitude.

4-22   J14

What is expected of you as pilot on an IFR flight plan if you are descending or climbing in VFR conditions?

A — If on an airway, climb or descend to the right of the centerline.

B — Advise ATC you are in visual conditions and will remain a short distance to the right of the center-line while climbing.

C — Execute gentle banks, left and right, at a frequency which permits continuous visual scanning of the airspace about you.

4-23   J16

Which is true regarding the use of an instrument departure procedure chart?

A — To use an instrument departure procedure, the pilot must possess both the textual and graphic form of the approved departure.

B — To use an instrument departure procedure, the pilot must possess at least the textual description of the approved standard departure.

C — The use of instrument departure procedures is mandatory.

4-21. Answer C. GFDICM 4B (AIM)

Unless ATC advises "At pilot's discretion," you are expected to climb at an optimum rate consistent with your airplane's performance to within 1,000 feet of your assigned altitude. Then attempt to climb at a rate between 500 and 1,500 f.p.m. for the last 1,000 feet of climb. As rapidly as practicable to 500 feet of your assigned altitude (answer A), does not provide safe guidelines for level-off in many high performance turboprop and turbine aircraft, and 1,000 f.p.m. during climb and 500 f.p.m. during descent until reaching the assigned altitude (answer B) is inappropriate.

4-22. Answer C. GFDICM 4B (AIM)

When climbing or descending in VFR conditions, pilots should make gentle turns in both directions in order to scan for other traffic. On an airway (answer A), pilots are expected to fly on the centerline unless maneuvering in VFR conditions to detect or avoid other traffic. Answer (B) implies that you are on an airway where you are required to maintain the airway centerline (not a short distance to the right of the centerline).

4-23. Answer B. GFDICM 4B (AIM)

In order to fly an instrument departure procedure, the pilot must have either the charted procedure or at least the textual description. Use of a DP is not mandatory (answer C). The pilot must possess either the textual description or graphic form of the DP, but is not required to have both (answer A).

CHAPTER 5

ENROUTE

SECTION A
ENROUTE AND AREA CHARTS

AIRWAYS

1. Airways below 18,000 feet MSL are called Victor airways. Airways at and above 18,000 feet MSL are jet routes.
2. Airways are 8 nautical miles wide within 51 nautical miles of a navaid. At distances greater than 51 miles, the airway widens, and is defined by lines diverging at 4.5° from the center of each navaid.

IFR ALTITUDES

3. Since Class A airspace begins at 18,000 feet MSL, it is not shown on low altitude enroute charts. High altitude enroute charts must be used for operations at and above 18,000 feet MSL.
4. The minimum enroute altitude (MEA) generally guarantees both obstruction clearance and navigation signal coverage for the length of the airway segment. It is normally the lowest altitude you can use on an airway.
5. To provide obstruction clearance when flying outside of established airways, NOS and Jeppesen provide off-route obstruction clearance altitudes on enroute low altitude charts. NOS uses the term off-route obstruction clearance altitudes (OROCAs), and Jeppesen calls them minimum off-route altitudes (MORAs).
6. The minimum obstruction clearance altitude (MOCA) has the same terrain and obstruction clearance specifications as MEA and OROCA/MORA, but only promises reliable navigation signal coverage within 22 nautical miles of the facility. A MOCA is preceded by an asterisk on an NOS chart.
7. The maximum authorized altitude (MAA) keeps you from receiving more than one VOR station at a time.
8. The minimum reception altitude (MRA) ensures reception of an off-course navaid that helps define a fix. Below the MRA and above the MEA you still have course guidance, but may not be able to receive the off-course navaid.
9. When an MEA changes to a higher altitude, you normally begin your climb upon reaching the fix where the change occurs. When rising terrain does not permit a safe climb after passing the fix, a minimum crossing altitude (MCA) is published. A flag with an X signifies the MCA on NOS charts. The altitude and applicable flight direction appear near the symbol. Plan your climb so that you will reach the MCA before crossing the fix.
10. In mountainous areas where no other minimum altitude is prescribed, IFR operations must remain 2,000 feet above the highest obstacle within a horizontal distance of 4 nautical miles from the intended course.
11. The MEA along jet routes is 18,000 feet MSL, unless otherwise specified.

SPECIAL IFR POSITIONS

12. Intersections are defined by two navaids, or by a navaid and a DME distance. All intersections can be used as reporting points. Compulsory reporting points are charted as filled triangles.
13. You normally change frequencies midway between navaids, unless a changeover point (COP) is designated. A COP is established where the navigation signal coverage from a navaid is not usable to the midpoint of an airway segment.
14. ARTCC boundaries are shown with distinctive lines on both Jeppesen and NOS charts.

COMMUNICATIONS

15. Most FSSs are able to use 122.2 MHz, as well as the emergency frequency, 121.5. Additional frequencies are shown above navaid boxes.
16. HIWAS is indicated by a small square in the communications box on NOS charts, while Jeppesen places the word HIWAS above the box.
17. Look for ARTCC discrete frequencies in boxes with the name of the controlling center. A remote communications outlet (RCO) for an FSS will have the name of the FSS and the frequency in a communication box.

AIRPORTS, AIRSPACE AND OTHER INFORMATION

18. Colors are used to differentiate between airports with approach procedures and airports without instrument approaches.
19. Basic information about each airport is portrayed on enroute charts using symbols from the chart legend. Additional information about airports with instrument approaches is found on the end panels of the chart.
20. Class G airspace is uncontrolled and shown with gray shading on Jeppesen charts and brown shading on NOS charts. Additionally, airspace below 1,200 feet AGL is uncontrolled, unless designated as Class B, C, D, or E.
21. Area charts are usually larger-scale depictions of major terminal areas. They should be referred to whenever you are in their coverage area, since they may show details that have been omitted from enroute charts.
22. High terrain is sometimes shown with gradient-tinted contours on select Jeppesen area charts.
23. On NOS enroute charts, localizers and back courses are shown only when they serve an enroute ATC function, such as establishing a fix or intersection.
24. On Jeppesen charts, prohibited and restricted areas have maroon hatched outlines, while warning, alert, or military operations areas have green hatching. NOS uses blue hatching around the edges of all special use airspace except military operations areas, which are shown with brown hatched edges.

5-1   J15
Which types of airspace are depicted on the Enroute Low Altitude Chart?

A — Limits of controlled airspace, military training routes, and special use airspace.
B — Class A, special use airspace, Class D, and Class E.
C — Special use airspace, Class E, Class D, Class A, Class B and Class C.

5-1. Answer A. GFDICM 5A (Enroute Chart Legend)
Enroute Low Altitude Charts depict the limits of Controlled airspace, military training routes, and special use airspace. Answers (B) and (C) are wrong because Class A is not depicted. It is also above the area depicted on low enroute charts.

5-2   J17
(Refer to figure 24 on page 10-19.) Proceeding southbound on V187, (vicinity of Cortez VOR) contact is lost with Denver Center. You should attempt to reestablish contact with Denver Center on:

A — 133.425 MHz.
B — 122.1 MHz and receive on 108.4 MHz.
C — 122.35 MHz.

5-2. Answer A. GFDICM 5A (Enroute Chart Legend)
There is a communications box just to the west of Cortez VOR indicating that Denver Center should be contacted on 133.425. Answer (B) is wrong because 108.4 is the frequency of the Cortez VOR. Answer (C) is wrong because 122.35 is an FSS frequency.

5-3   J35
(Refer to figures 22 and 24 on page 10-16 and 10-19.) For planning purposes, what would be the highest MEA on V187 between Grand Junction, Walker Airport and Durango, La Plata Co. Airport?

A — 12,000 feet.
B — 15,000 feet.
C — 16,000 feet.

5-3. Answer B. GFDICM 5A (Enroute Chart Legend)
The highest MEA is 15,000 feet, located on V187 between HERRM and MANCA Intersections. Answer (A) is wrong because it doesn't reflect the highest MEA. Answer (C) is wrong because it is not designated on this route of flight.

5-4   J35
(Refer to figure 24 on page 10-19.) At what point should a VOR changeover be made from JNC VOR to MANCA intersection southbound on V187?

A — 36 NM south of JNC.
B — 52 NM south of JNC.
C — 74 NM south of JNC.

5-4. Answer B. GFDICM 5A (Enroute Chart Legend)
The changeover point is 52 miles south of the JNC VOR as indicated by the changeover symbol and callout. Answers (A) and (C) are wrong because the mileages listed are inappropriate.

5-5   J35
(Refer to figure 24 on page 10-19.) What is the MOCA between JNC and MANCA Intersection on V187?

A — 10,900 feet MSL.
B — 12,000 feet MSL.
C — 13,700 feet MSL.

5-6   J35
(Refer to figure 34 on page 10-31.) At which altitude and location on V573 would you expect the navigational signal of the HOT VOR/DME to be unreliable?

A — 3,000 feet at APINE intersection.
B — 2,600 feet at MARKI intersection.
C — 4,000 feet at ELMMO intersection.

5-7   J35
(Refer to figure 53 on page 10-46.) Where is the VOR COP on V27 between the GVO and MQO VORTACs?

A — 20 DME from GVO VORTAC.
B — 20 DME from MQO VORTAC.
C — 30 DME from SBA VORTAC.

5-8   J35
(Refer to figure 53 on page 10-46.) What service is indicated by the inverse "H" symbol in the radio aids to navigation box for PRB VORTAC?

A — VOR with TACAN compatible DME.
B — Availability of HIWAS.
C — En Route Flight Advisory Service available.

5-9   J35
(Refer to figure 65 on page 5-4.) Which point would be the appropriate VOR COP on V552 from the LFT to the TBD VORTACs?

A — CLYNT intersection.
B — HATCH intersection.
C — 34 DME from the LFT VORTAC.

5-5. Answer C. GFDICM 5A (Enroute Chart Legend)
The minimum obstruction clearance altitude (MOCA) is identified with an "*" in front of the altitude callout. The MOCA between JNC and MANCA Intersection is 13,700 feet MSL. Answer (A) is wrong because 10,900 feet is the MEA between MANCA Intersection and the FMN VOR. Answer (B) is wrong because it is the MEA between JNC and HERRM Intersection.

5-6. Answer A. GFDICM 5A (Enroute Chart Legend)
The MEA normally provides reliable navigation signals. Choices (A) and (B) specify altitudes which are below the MEA. However, the MOCA of 2,600 feet (answer B) ensures a reliable navigation signal within 22 n.m. of the facility. Since MARKI intersection is 21 n.m. from HOT VOR/DME, answer (B) is incorrect. Answer (C) is incorrect since 4,000 feet at ELMMO intersection is at the MEA.

5-7. Answer A. GFDICM 5A (Enroute Chart Legend)
The changeover point (COP) between GVO and MQO VORTACs is 20 n.m. from GVO VORTAC and 34 n.m. from MQO VORTAC. The COP symbol is designed so the mileage on top of the airway refers to the VOR on the right, and the mileage on the bottom of the airway refers to the VOR on the left. Answer B, 20 DME from MQO, is incorrect because the mileage on top of the line refers to the VOR on the right. SBA is the identifier for a localizer (answer C) and has nothing to do with V27 between GVO and MQO VORTACs.

5-8. Answer B. GFDICM 5A (Enroute Chart Legend)
If hazardous inflight weather advisory service (HIWAS) is available on the associated NAVAID frequency, it is indicated by an inverse "H" in the upper corner of the facility box. If a VOR has TACAN capability (answer B) it is identified by the shape of the VOR symbol, and the TACAN channel will be listed in the navaid information box. Enroute flight advisory service (EFAS) (answer C) is provided by select automated flight service stations (AFSSs) controlling multiple remote communications outlets over a large geographical area. EFAS is not broadcast over navaid frequencies, but is broadcast on the common EFAS frequency, 122.0.

5-9. Answer C. GFDICM 5A (Enroute Chart Legend)
If there is no designated changeover point along an airway, you change to the next frequency at the halfway point. In this case, it is 34 DME from LFT VORTAC. CLYNT int. (answer A) and HATCH int. (answer B) are incorrect because COPs at intersections also are depicted by the COP symbol.

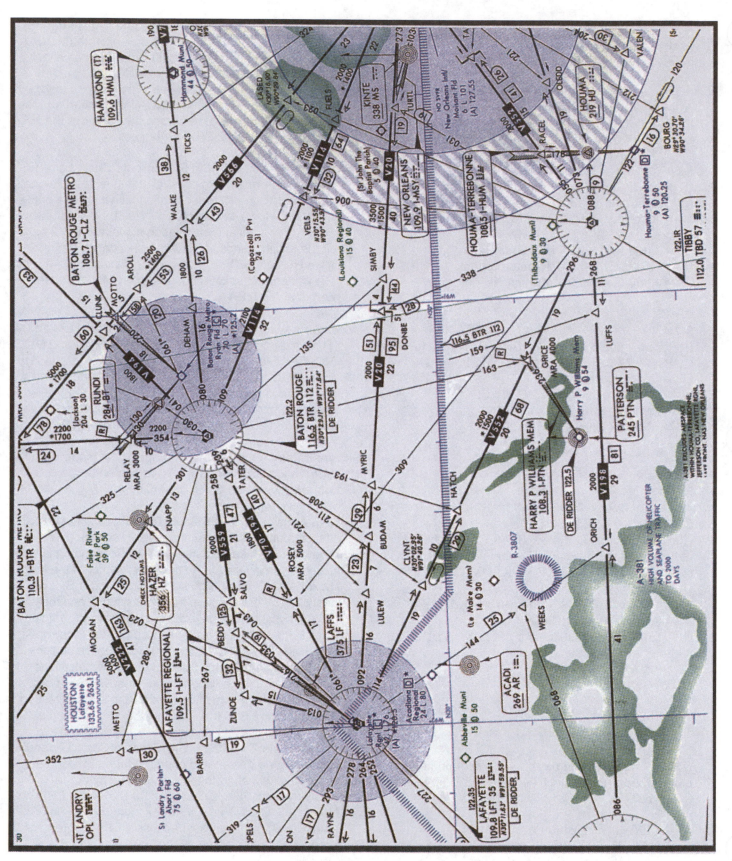

FIGURE 65.—En Route Chart Segment.

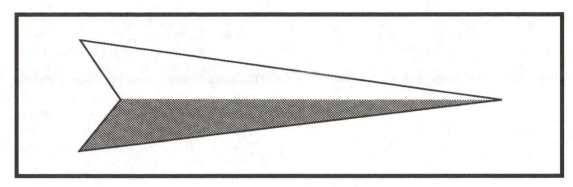

FIGURE 67.—Localizer Symbol.

5-10   J35

(Refer to figures 65 and 67.) What is the significance of the symbol at GRICE Intersection?

A — It signifies a localizer-only approach is available at Harry P. Williams Memorial.

B — The localizer has an additional navigation function.

C — GRICE Intersection also serves as the FAF for the ILS approach procedure to Harry P. Williams Memorial.

5-11   J35

(Refer to figures 70 and 71 on pages 10-49 and 10-50.) Which VORTAC along the proposed route of flight could provide HIWAS information?

A — SPARTA VORTAC.

B — HUGUENOT VORTAC.

C — KINGSTON VORTAC.

5-12   J35

(Refer to figure 78 on page 10-57.) What is the maximum altitude that you may flight plan an IFR flight on V-86 EASTBOUND between BOZEMAN and BILLINGS VORTACs?

A — 14,500 feet MSL.

B — 17,000 feet MSL.

C — 18,000 feet MSL.

5-10. Answer B. GFDICM 5A (Approach Chart Legend)

When the localizer symbol showing the inbound course appears on an enroute chart, it means the facility serves an ATC function. The navaid information box will also be printed near the intersection. On enroute charts, an airport with a localizer-only approach (answer A) does not have a distinctive, feathered localizer symbol. GRICE Intersection is not the FAF for the ILS as specified in answer (C). The FAF for an ILS is the point where you intercept the glide slope at the designated altitude prior to beginning descent to the DH. This information is not depicted on enroute charts.

5-11. Answer C. GFDICM 5A (Enroute Chart Legend)

When hazardous inflight weather advisory service (HIWAS) is transmitted over a VOR, NOS places a small square in the upper left corner of the facility box on enroute charts. The facility boxes for the SPARTA VORTAC (answer A) and the HUGUENOT VORTAC (answer B) do not show the small square which indicates HIWAS.

5-12. Answer B. GFDICM 5A (AIM)

Victor airways extend from 1,200 feet AGL up to but not including 18,000 feet MSL; therefore, the highest IFR cruising altitude is 17,000 feet MSL for an eastbound flight. Also, IFR cruising altitudes are based on even thousands for westbound flights and odd thousands for eastbound flights. An altitude of 14,500 feet MSL (answer A) is well below the maximum available altitude. Flights at and above FL 180 (answer C) are flown in Class A airspace or on jet routes which are depicted on high altitude charts.

5-13   J35

(Refer to figure 78 on page 10-57.) What is the minimum crossing altitude over the BOZEMAN VORTAC for a flight southeast bound on V86?

A — 8,500 feet MSL.
B — 9,300 feet MSL.
C — 9,700 feet MSL.

5-13. Answer B. GFDICM 5A (Enroute Chart Legend)
A flag with an "X" marks the VOR or the intersection where a minimum crossing altitude (MCA) is required. The MCA at BZN VOR, listed above the navaid information box is 9,300 feet MSL for flights southeast bound on V86-365. An altitude of 8,500 MSL (answer A) is the minimum enroute altitude (MEA) on both V86 westbound and V365 northwest bound prior to MENAR Int. The altitude of 9,700 feet MSL (answer C) represents the MEA on V365 from MENAR Int. to HLN VORTAC.

5-14   J07

Unless otherwise prescribed, what is the rule regarding altitude and course to be maintained during an off airways IFR flight over nonmountainous terrain?

A — 1,000 feet above the highest obstacle within 3 NM of course.
B — 2,000 feet above the highest obstacle within 5 SM of course.
C — 1,000 feet above the highest obstacle within 4 NM of course.

5-14. Answer C. GFDICM 5A (FAR 91.177)
Normally you must fly the applicable minimum altitude prescribed in 14 CFR Part 95 or Part 97. However when no minimum altitude is prescribed you may fly an off airways IFR flight over nonmountainous terrain no lower than 1,000 feet above the highest obstacle within a horizontal distance of 4 nautical miles from the course line.

5-15   J07

Unless otherwise prescribed, what is the rule regarding altitude and course to be maintained during an IFR off airways flight over mountainous terrain?

A — 2,000 feet above the highest obstacle within 4 NM of course.
B — 1,000 feet above the highest obstacle within a horizontal distance of 5 NM of course.
C — 7,500 feet above the highest obstacle within a horizontal distance of 3 NM of course.

5-15. Answer A. GFDICM 5A (FAR 91.177)
Normally you must fly the applicable minimum altitude prescribed in 14 CFR Part 95 or Part 97. However when no minimum altitude is prescribed you may fly an off airways IFR flight over mountainous terrain no lower than 2,000 feet above the highest obstacle within a horizontal distance of 4 nautical miles from the course line.

5-16   J33

What is the definition of MEA?

A — The lowest published altitude which meets obstacle clearance requirements and assures acceptable navigational signal coverage.
B — The lowest published altitude which meets obstacle requirements, assures acceptable navigational signal coverage, two-way radio communications, and provides adequate radar coverage.
C — An altitude which meets obstacle clearance requirements, assures acceptable navigation signal coverage, two-way radio communications, adequate radar coverage, and accurate DME mileage.

5-16. Answer A. GFDICM 5A (AIM)
MEA is defined as the lowest published altitude between radio fixes which ensures acceptable navigational signal coverage and meets obstacle clearance requirements between those fixes. Two-way radio, radar coverage, and accurate DME reception are not requirements for an MEA. Therefore answers (B) and (C) are incorrect.

5-17   J33

The altitude that provides acceptable navigational signal coverage for the route, and meets obstacle clearance requirements, is the minimum:

A — enroute altitude.
B — reception altitude.
C — obstacle clearance altitude.

5-18   J33

Reception of signals from an off-airway radio facility may be inadequate to identify the fix at the designated MEA. In this case, which altitude is designated for the fix?

A — MRA.
B — MCA.
C — MOCA.

5-19   J06

Which condition is guaranteed for all of the following altitude limits: MAA, MCA, MRA, MOCA, and MEA? (Non-mountainous area.)

A — Adequate navigation signals.
B — Adequate communications.
C — 1,000-foot obstacle clearance.

5-20   J33

If no MCA is specified, what is the lowest altitude for crossing a radio fix, beyond which a higher minimum applies?

A — The MEA at which the fix is approached.
B — The MRA at which the fix is approached.
C — The MOCA for the route segment beyond the fix.

5-21   J17

Unless otherwise specified on the chart, the minimum en route altitude along a jet route is

A — 18,000 feet MSL.
B — 24,000 feet MSL.
C — 10,000 feet MSL.

5-17. Answer A. GFDICM 5A (AIM)
The Minimum Enroute Altitude (MEA) guarantees obstacle clearance, reception of navigational signals (but not necessarily DME), and two-way communications. It does not guarantee radar coverage. A minimum reception altitude (MRA), answer (B) is established to ensure adequate reception of the navigation signals forming an intersection. Choice (C) is incorrect because a minimum obstruction clearance altitude (MOCA) pertains to obstacles and NAVAID Reception, but only within 22 n.m. of the navigational facility.

5-18. Answer A. GFDICM 5A (AIM)
A minimum reception altitude (MRA) is established to ensure adequate reception of the navigation signals forming an intersection. Answer (B) is wrong because a minimum crossing altitude (MCA) is the lowest altitude you may use to cross a fix when proceeding in the direction of a higher minimum enroute altitude (MEA). Choice (C) is incorrect because a minimum obstruction clearance altitude (MOCA) pertains to obstacles and NAVAID reception, but only within 22 n.m. of the navigational facility.

5-19. Answer C. GFDICM 5A (AIM)
Minimum altitudes for IFR operations are discussed in Part 91.177. Except for takeoff and landing, the minimum IFR altitudes prescribed for operations in non-mountainous areas are 1,000 feet above the highest obstacle within 4 n.m. of the course to be flown. This is the only condition guaranteed for all of the altitude limits, including MAA, MCA, MRA, MOCA, and MEA. Therefore, answers (A) and (B) are incorrect.

5-20. Answer A. GFDICM 5A (AIM)
The minimum altitude at which you can cross a fix, where a higher altitude is subsequently established, is the MEA. Remember, the MEA ensures acceptable navigational signal coverage and meets obstacle clearance requirements. Answer (B) is incorrect because an MRA is established to ensure reception of navigation signals not to provide terrain clearance. Answer (C) is incorrect because minimum altitude to cross a fix without an MCA is determined by the prescribed minimum before crossing the fix, not after.

5-21. Answer A. GFDICM 5A (AIM)
The jet route system is designed for aircraft operating from 18,000 feet MSL to FL 450, inclusive. These routes are depicted on enroute high altitude charts and are identified by the letter "J." Answers (B) and (C) are incorrect because the minimum jet route altitude is 18,000 feet MSL, or FL 180.

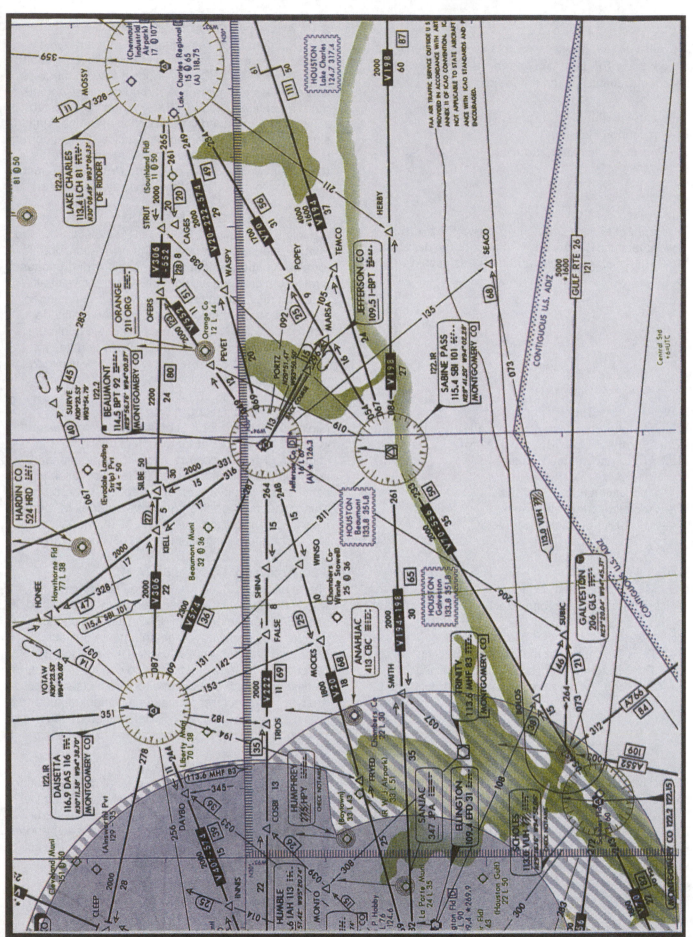

FIGURE 87.—En Route Chart Segment.

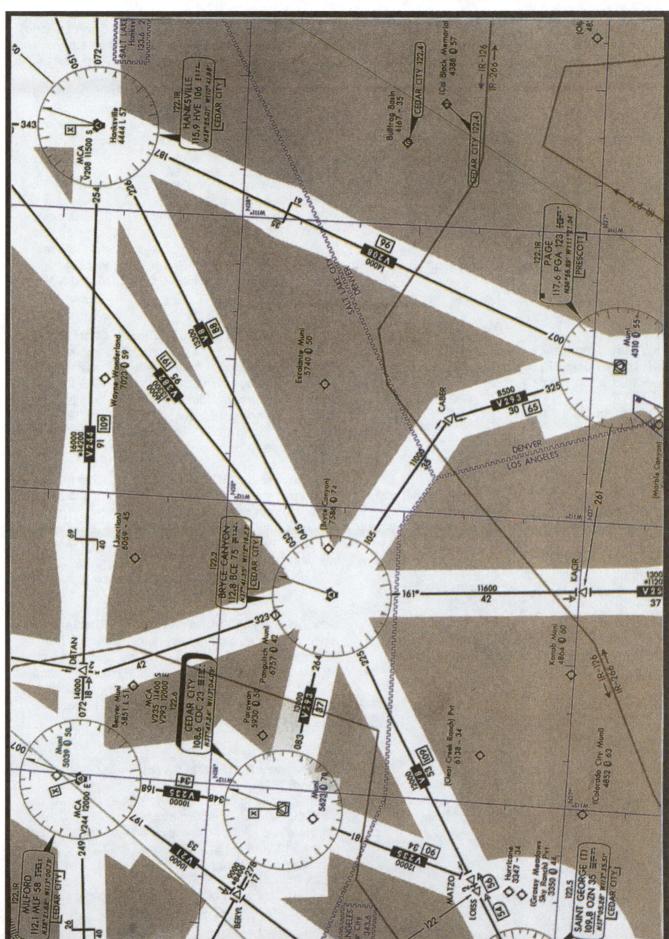

FIGURE 89.—En Route Chart Segment.

5-22   J35
(Refer to figure 87 on page 5-8.) Where is the VOR COP when flying east on V306 from Daisetta to Lake Charles?

A — 50 NM east of DAS.
B — 40 NM east of DAS.
C — 30 NM east of DAS.

5-23   J35
(Refer to figure 87 on page 5-8.) What is indicated by the localizer course symbol at Jefferson County Airport?

A — A published LDA localizer course.
B — A published ILS localizer course, which has an additional navigation function.
C — A published SDF localizer course.

5-24   J35
(Refer to figure 87 on page 5-8.) Which VHF frequencies, other than 121.5, can be used to receive De Ridder FSS in the Lake Charles area?

A — 122.1, 126.4.
B — 123.6, 122.65.
C — 122.2, 122.3.

5-25   J35
(Refer to figure 87 on page 5-8.) Why is the localizer back course at Jefferson County Airport depicted?

A — The back course is not aligned with a runway.
B — The back course has an additional navigation function.
C — The back course has a glide slope

5-26   J35
(Refer to figure 87 on page 5-8.) Where is the VOR changeover point on V20 between Beaumont and Hobby?

A — Halfway point.
B — MOCKS intersection.
C — Anahuac Beacon.

5-27   J35
(Refer to figure 89 on page 5-9.) When flying from Milford Municipal to Bryce Canyon via V235 and V293, what minimum altitude should you be at when crossing Cedar City VOR?

A — 11,400 feet.
B — 12,000 feet.
C — 13,000 feet.

5-22. Answer C. GFDICM 5A (Enroute Chart Legend)
The changeover point (COP), shown by a perpendicular symbol on V306, indicates that it is 30 n.m. east of Daisetta, or 50 n.m. west of Lake Charles. As a double-check, the two changeover distances should add up to the total distance between these VORs — 80 n.m. Answers (A) and (B) do not indicate the correct distances shown by the COP symbol.

5-23. Answer B. GFDICM 5A
The symbol shown on the chart at Jefferson Co. Field indicates the availability of an ILS localizer course with an ATC function, such as identifying a fix or intersection. When the localizer serves an ATC function, the facility identifier, frequency, and inbound course are shown. Answers (A) and (B) are incorrect because there is no distinctive symbology for LDA and SDF courses.

5-24. Answer C. GFDICM 5A (Enroute Chart Legend)
The frequency 122.2 is a standard FSS frequency available even when not indicated. The frequency 122.3 is listed above the Lake Charles VOR facility box, and is another frequency available at this FSS. Answers (A) and (B) are incorrect because 122.1, 126.4, 123.6, and 122.65 are not available in the Lake Charles area.

5-25. Answer B. GFDICM 5A (Enroute Chart Legend)
The large feathered arrow symbol indicates Jefferson County Airport has a back course approach. This portrayal means the localizer provides an ATC function. In this case, the back course is used to form PORTZ intersection.

5-26. Answer A. GFDICM 5A (Enroute Chart Legend)
Since there is no changeover point established on V20, the changeover point will be the halfway point between Hobby and Beaumont VORTACs. Answers (B) and (C) are wrong because no changeover symbol is depicted at either of these locations on V20.

5-27. Answer B. GFDICM 5A (Enroute Chart Legend) (FAR 91.177)
The flag marking Cedar City VOR/DME (near the center of the left side on figure 89) has an "X" in it, meaning there is a minimum crossing altitude (MCA). An MCA of 12,000 feet is noted above the CDC VOR information box for aircraft traveling eastbound on V293. Answer (A), 11,400 feet, is the MCA for crossing the VOR/DME southbound on V235. Answer (C), 13,000 feet, is the MEA along V293.

5-28　　　J35

(Refer to figure 89 on page 5-9.) What VHF frequencies are available for communications with Cedar City FSS?

A — 123.6, 121.5, 108.6, and 112.8.
B — 122.2, 121.5, 122.6, and 112.1.
C — 122.2, 121.5, 122.0, and 123.6.

5-29　　　B11

(Refer to figure 89 on page 5-9.) What are the oxygen requirements for an IFR flight northeast bound from Bryce Canyon on V382 at the lowest appropriate altitude in an unpressurized aircraft?

A — The required minimum crew must be provided and use supplemental oxygen for that part of the flight of more than 30 minutes.
B — The required minimum crew must be provided and use supplemental oxygen for that part of the flight of more than 30 minutes, and the passengers must be provided supplemental oxygen.
C — The required minimum crew must be provided and use supplemental oxygen, and all occupants must be provided supplemental oxygen for the entire flight above 15,000 feet.

5-30　　　J35

(Refer to figure 89 on page 5-9.) What is the ARTCC discrete frequency at the COP on V208 southwest bound from HVE to PGA VOR/DME?

A — 122.1.
B — 122.4.
C — 133.6.

5-31　　　J35

(Refer to figure 89 on page 5-9.) What type airspace exists above Bryce Canyon Airport from the surface to 1,200 feet AGL?

A — Class D airspace.
B — Class E airspace.
C — Class G airspace.

5-32　　　J35

(Refer to figure 91 on page 5-12.) What is the minimum crossing altitude at DBS VORTAC for a northbound IFR flight on V257?

A — 7,500 feet.
B — 8,600 feet.
C — 11,100 feet.

5-28. Answer B. GFDICM 5A (Enroute Chart Legend)
The frequency 122.6 is indicated above the heavy-line Cedar City VOR-DME information box. You can also communicate with Cedar City FSS over the Milford VORTAC frequency by transmitting on 122.1 and receiving on 112.1. These frequencies are in addition to the standard frequency of 122.2, and the emergency frequency of 121.5.

5-29. Answer C. GFDICM 5A (Enroute Chart Legend) (FAR 91.211)
At cabin pressure altitudes above 14,000 feet MSL, the required minimum flight crew must use supplemental oxygen. All passengers must be supplied with oxygen for the entire flight above 15,000 feet MSL. Since the MEA for V382 is 16,000 feet MSL, answer (C) is correct. Answers (A) and (B) are incorrect because they do not apply to flights above 15,000 feet. For flights above 12,500 feet MSL up to and including 14,000 feet MSL, only the required crew must use oxygen for that portion of the flight which is more than 30 minutes.

5-30. Answer C. GFDICM 5A (Enroute Chart Legend)
You are located in the Salt Lake City ARTCC sector. There is an ARTCC remote site with the discrete frequency 133.6 to the east of HVE VORTAC. Answers (A), 122.1 and (B), 122.4 are FSS frequencies.

5-31. Answer C. GFDICM 5A (Enroute Chart Legend)
The surface area at Bryce Canyon Airport is in Class G airspace. The brown lettering indicates that no approved instrument approach procedure exists. The base of the Federal airway (Class E airspace) is 1,200 AGL. Class G (uncontrolled) airspace exists from the surface to 1,200 feet AGL. Answers (A) and (B) are incorrect since they refer to controlled airspace.

5-32. Answer B. GFDICM 5A (Enroute Chart Legend)
An altitude of 8,600 feet (answer B) is the MCA northbound on V257 crossing DBS VORTAC. Answer (A), 7,500 feet, is the MEA for V257 between ROCCA Intersection and DBS VORTAC. Answer (C), 11,100 feet, is the MOCA for flights between DBS VORTAC and DLN VORTAC.

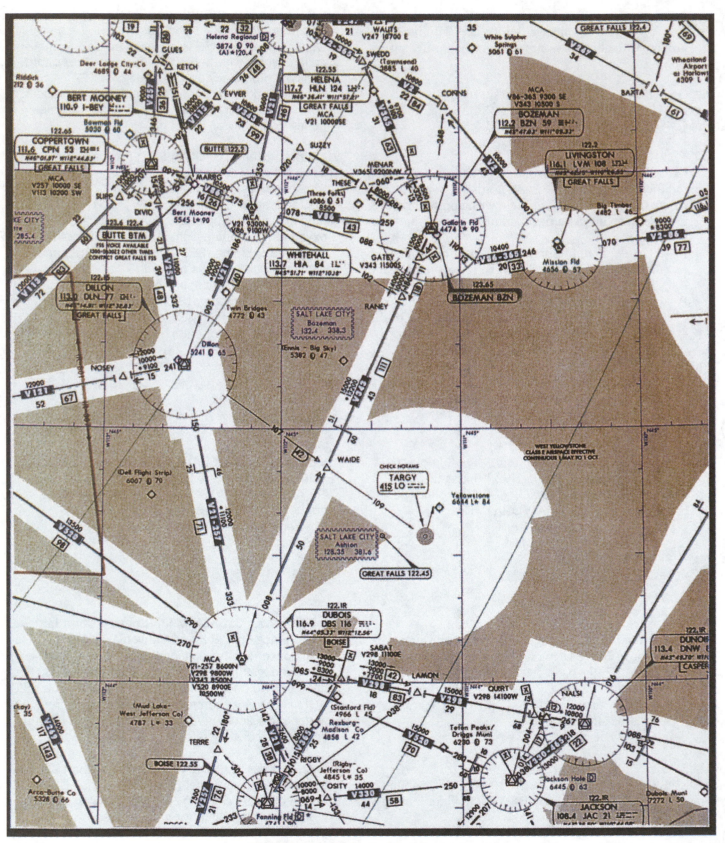

FIGURE 91.—En Route Chart Segment.

5-33 J03

(Refer to figure 91 on page 5-12.) What lighting is indicated on the chart for Jackson Hole Airport?

A — Lights on prior request.
B — No lighting available.
C — Pilot controlled lighting.

5-34 J35

(Refer to figure 91 on page 5-12.) What is the function of the Great Falls RCO (Yellowstone vicinity)?

A — Long range communications outlet for Great Falls Center.
B — Remote communications outlet for Great Falls FSS.
C — Satellite remote controlled by Salt Lake Center with limited service.

5-35 J35

(Refer to figure 91 on page 5-12.) Where should you change VOR frequencies when en route from DBS VORTAC to JAC VOR/DME on V520?

A — 35 NM from DBS VORTAC.
B — 60 NM from DBS VORTAC.
C — 60 NM from JAC VOR/DME.

5-36 J35

(Refer to figure 91 on page 5-12.) What is the minimum crossing altitude at SABAT intersection when eastbound from DBS VORTAC on V298?

A — 8,300 feet.
B — 11,100 feet.
C — 13,000 feet.

5-37 B08

In the case of operations over an area designated as a mountainous area where no other minimum altitude is prescribed, no person may operate an aircraft under IFR below an altitude of

A — 500 feet above the highest obstacle.
B — 1,000 feet above the highest obstacle.
C — 2,000 feet above the highest obstacle.

5-38 J33

MEA is an altitude which assures

A — obstacle clearance, accurate navigational signals from more than one VORTAC, and accurate DME mileage.
B — a 1,000-foot obstacle clearance within 2 miles of an airway and assures accurate DME mileage.
C — acceptable navigational signal coverage and meets obstruction clearance requirements.

5-33. Answer C. GFDICM 5A (Enroute Chart Legend)
The circle around the "L" in the airport information block indicates Pilot Controlled Lighting (PCL). Symbols depicting lights on prior request (answer A) and no lighting available (answer B) are not indicated for Jackson Hole Airport.

5-34. Answer B. GFDICM 5A (Enroute Chart Legend)
The Great Falls remote communications outlet (RCO) is depicted by a circle symbol above the communications box (near the center of figure 91). The circle symbol for an FSS remote communications outlet is depicted in the chart legend (see Appendix 2,). This RCO is used by the Great Falls FSS, as indicated by the communications box. Great Falls Center (answer A) does not exist; the Center for this area is Salt Lake. The RCO is controlled by Great Falls FSS not Salt Lake Center (answer C).

5-35. Answer B. GFDICM 5A (AIM)
Along V520 between DBS VORTAC and JAC VOR/DME, there is a changeover point (COP) close to the JAC VOR/DME at 60 n.m. from DBS VORTAC. Changeover at the halfway point (answer A) would be correct if there were no COP. Answer (C) is incorrect since the COP is 10 n.m. from JAC VOR/DME.

5-36. Answer B. GFDICM 5A (Enroute Chart Legend)
Under the intersection name "SABAT" is the MCA for V298 eastbound, 11,100 feet. An altitude of 8,300 feet (answer A) is the MOCA on V298 from DBS VORTAC to SABAT intersection, and 13,000 feet (answer C) refers to the MEA for flights eastbound on V298.

5-37. Answer C. GFDICM 5A (FAR 91.177)
In mountainous terrain, the minimum altitude for any IFR operation is 2,000 feet above the highest obstacle within a horizontal distance of 4 n.m. of the route to be flown. Answer (A), 500 feet above the highest obstacle, is inappropriate. Answer (B), 1,000 feet above the highest obstacle, applies to instrument flight over non-mountainous terrain.

5-38. Answer C. GFDICM 5A (AIM)
The minimum enroute altitude (MEA) guarantees adequate obstruction clearance and navigation signal reception. It does not guarantee reception from more than one VOR, or adequate DME mileage (answer A). The MEA provides obstruction clearance out to 4 n.m. on either side of the airway centerline, not 2 miles as listed in answer (B).

5-39   J33

Reception of signals from a radio facility, located off the airway being flown, may be inadequate at the designated MEA to identify the fix. In this case, which altitude is designated for the fix?

A — MOCA.
B — MRA.
C — MCA.

5-40   J33

ATC may assign the MOCA when certain special conditions exist, and when within

A — 22 NM of a VOR.
B — 25 NM of a VOR.
C — 30 NM of a VOR.

5-41   J10

Which aeronautical chart depicts Military Training Routes (MTR) above 1500 feet?

A — IFR Planning Chart.
B — IFR Low Altitude En Route Chart.
C — IFR High Altitude En Route Chart.

5-42   J33

Acceptable navigational signal coverage at the MOCA is assured for a distance from the VOR of only

A — 12 NM.
B — 22 NM.
C — 25 NM.

5-43   H842

(Refer to figure 78 on page 10-57.) When eastbound on V86 between Whitehall and Livingston, the minimum altitude that you should cross BZN is

A — 9,300 feet.
B — 10,400 feet.
C — 8,500 feet.

5-44   J35

(Refer to figure 47 on page 10-42.) En route on V112 from BTG VORTAC to LTJ VORTAC, the minimum altitude crossing Gymme intersection is

A — 6,400 feet.
B — 6,500 feet.
C — 7,000 feet.

5-39. Answer B. GFDICM 5A (AIM)

The minimum reception altitude (MRA) is the minimum altitude that guarantees adequate reception of the navaids that form an intersection or other fix. The minimum obstruction clearance altitude (MOCA) (answer A) is the minimum altitude that guarantees obstruction clearance for a published route segment, but not navaid reception. The minimum crossing altitude (MCA) (answer C) is designated when a climb to a higher altitude is required prior to crossing the designated fix. This is generally used for obstruction clearance when necessary for a higher MEA along succeeding segments of an airway.

5-40. Answer A. GFDICM 5A (AIM)

The minimum obstruction clearance altitude (MOCA) provides adequate navaid reception only with 22 n.m. of the VOR. Both answers (B) and (C) are incorrect. However, the AIM definition of MOCA includes both 22 nautical miles and 25 statute miles. Note that these answers are given in nautical miles.

5-41. Answer B. GFDICM 5A (AIM)

Military Training Routes (MTRs) are depicted on NOS IFR low altitude enroute charts. The IFR planning chart (answer A) is designed primarily for planning a flight, and does not show the detail which would include MTRs. Since MTRs are usually established below 10,000 feet MSL, they are not shown on IFR high altitude enroute charts (answer C).

5-42. Answer B. GFDICM 5A (AIM)

See explanation for Question 5-40. The minimum obstruction clearance altitude (MOCA) ensures navaid reception within 22 n.m. of the navaid. Both 12 n.m. (answer A) and 25 n.m. (answer C) are incorrect.

5-43. Answer A. GFDICM 5A (Enroute Chart Legend)

A flag with an "X" marks the VOR or the intersection where a minimum crossing altitude (MCA) is required. The MCA at BZN VOR, listed above the navaid information box is 9,300 feet MSL for flights southeast bound on V86-365.

5-44. Answer C. GFDICM 5A (Enroute Chart Legend)

The MEA for eastbound flights on V112 is depicted as 7,000 feet, both before and after Gymme Intersection. Answer (A), 6,400 feet, is depicted with an asterisk, which is the MOCA. Answer (B), 6,500 feet, is the MEA for westbound flights after Gymme Intersection.

5-45   **J35**
(Refer to figure 47 on page 10-42.) En route on V468 from BTG VORTAC to YKM VORTAC, the minimum altitude at TROTS Intersection is

A — 7,100 feet.
B — 10,000 feet.
C — 11,500 feet.

5-45. Answer C. GFDICM 5A (Enroute Chart Legend)
The flag symbol with an "X" denotes a minimum crossing altitude at TROTS. The restriction "V448 11500 NE" means that flights northeast bound on V448 must be at (or above) 11,500 feet when crossing TROTS. 7,100 feet (answer A) is shown with an asterisk and is the MOCA prior to reaching TROTS. 10,000 feet (answer B) is the MEA for that same portion of the airway.

SECTION B
ENROUTE PROCEDURES

GENERAL COMMUNICATION PROCEDURES

1. During a radar handoff, the controller may advise you to give the next controller certain information, such as a heading or altitude.
2. If you cannot establish contact using a newly assigned frequency, return to the one previously used and request an alternate frequency.

REQUIRED REPORTS

3. You should make the following reports to ATC whether or not you are in radar contact: leaving an altitude, an altitude change if VFR-on-top, time and altitude upon reaching a holding fix or clearance limit, leaving a holding fix or clearance limit, missed approach, inability to climb or descend at a rate of at least 500 feet per minute, and change in true airspeed by 5% or 10 knots (whichever is greater).
4. You are required by regulation to report a loss of airplane navigational capability, unforecast or hazardous weather conditions, and any other information relating to the safety of flight.
5. If radar contact has been lost or radar service terminated, the FARs require you to provide ATC with position reports over compulsory reporting points.
6. The compulsory reporting points on a direct route are those fixes that define the route.
7. A standard position report includes your identification, current position, time, altitude, ETA over the next reporting fix, the following reporting point, and any pertinent remarks.
8. When flying on a VFR-on-top clearance, you should make the same position reports as on any IFR flight, and you should fly at an appropriate VFR cruising altitude.
9. In a nonradar environment, you should report when you reach the final approach fix inbound on a nonprecision approach, and when you leave the outer marker inbound on a precision approach. In addition, a report is necessary when it becomes apparent that an estimated time that you previously submitted to ATC will be in error in excess of 3 minutes.

GPS NAVIGATION

10. To use panel-mounted, IFR enroute-approved GPS as your primary means of point-to-point navigation, your aircraft must be equipped with an alternate means of navigation, such as VOR-based equipment, appropriate to the flight.
11. Active monitoring of alternate navigation equipment is not required if the GPS receiver uses receiver autonomous integrity monitoring (RAIM).

CLEARANCES THROUGH RESTRICTED AREAS

12. ATC usually does not issue an IFR route clearance that crosses an active restricted area, but inactive areas are often released for use.

IFR ALTITUDES

13. Though you may request and be assigned any altitude in controlled airspace, most pilots file flight plan altitudes that correspond to the hemispheric rule.
14. Lowest usable altitudes are specified for use above 18,000 feet MSL when the barometric pressure is below certain values.
15. When you are given a descent clearance " . . . at pilot's discretion," you are authorized to begin the descent whenever you choose, and level off temporarily during the descent, but you cannot return to an altitude once you vacate it.

5-46   J15

For which speed variation should you notify ATC?

A — When the groundspeed changes more than 5 knots.

B — When the average true airspeed changes 5 percent or 10 knots, whichever is greater.

C — Any time the groundspeed changes 10 MPH.

5-47   J15

For IFR planning purposes, what are the compulsory reporting points when using VOR/DME or VORTAC fixes to define a direct route not on established airways?

A — Fixes selected to define the route.

B — There are no compulsory reporting points unless advised by ATC.

C — At the changeover points.

5-48   J35

(Refer to figure 34 on page 10-31.) For planning purposes, what is the highest useable altitude for an IFR flight on V573 from the HOT VORTAC to the TXK VORTAC?

A — 16,000 feet MSL.

B — 14,500 feet MSL.

C — 13,999 feet MSL.

5-49   J35

(Refer to figure 40 on page 10-36.) For planning purposes, what is the highest useable altitude for an IFR flight on V16 between the BGS VORTAC and ABI VORTAC?

A — 17,000 feet MSL.

B — 18,000 feet MSL.

C — 6,500 feet MSL.

5-46. Answer B. GFDICM 5B (AIM)

You must notify ATC if a change in your flight plan occurs or is expected. In addition to changes in altitude, destination, and/or routing, increasing or decreasing the aircraft's true airspeed constitutes a change in your flight plan. Therefore, whenever your average true airspeed at cruising altitude between reporting points changes, or is expected to change by 5% or 10 knots, whichever is greater, ATC should be advised. Answers (A) and (C) are wrong because the change in speed is based on true airspeed and not groundspeed.

5-47. Answer A. GFDICM 5B (AIM)

Any portion of a route which is not flown on radials or courses of established airways, such as a direct route flight, must be defined by indicating the radio fixes over which the flight will pass. Fixes selected must represent a point where your aircraft's position can be accurately determined. These points automatically become compulsory reporting points for your flight, unless advised otherwise by ATC. Answer (B) is wrong because points on a direct flight, which are used to define the route, are compulsory. Answer (C) is wrong because COPs are not required for all navigation systems.

5-48. Answer A. GFDICM 5B (AIM)

Low altitude enroute charts portray the enroute structure from the surface up to, but not including 18,000 feet MSL. In controlled airspace, IFR cruising altitudes are specified by ATC. IFR cruising altitudes in uncontrolled airspace are as prescribed by FAR 91.179. When flying on a heading from 360° to 179°, you must fly at odd thousand-foot altitudes. When on a heading of 180° to 359°, you must fly at even thousand-foot altitudes. While the flight on V573 from HOT VORTAC to TXK VORTAC is in controlled airspace, application of FAR 91.179 would result in a cruising altitude of 16,000 feet MSL. Answers (B) and (C) are wrong because these altitudes have no bearing on an IFR flight along V573.

5-49. Answer A. GFDICM 5B (AIM)

Low altitude enroute charts depict the enroute structure from the surface up to, but not including, 18,000 feet MSL. In controlled airspace IFR cruising altitudes are specified by ATC. In uncontrolled airspace, IFR cruising altitudes are as prescribed in FAR 91.179. When flying on a heading of 360° to 179°, you must fly at odd thousand-foot altitudes. When on a heading of 180° to 359°, you must fly at even thousand-foot altitudes. While the flight on V16 on a heading of 075° from HOT VORTAC to TXK VORTAC is in controlled airspace, application of FAR 91.179 would result in a cruising altitude of 17,000 feet MSL. Answer (B) is wrong because 18,000 feet is considered part of the high altitude structure. Answer (C) is wrong because it is substantially less than the maximum usable altitude.

This question is similar to 5-48.

5-50   J14
What is the recommended climb procedure when a nonradar departure control instructs a pilot to climb to the assigned altitude?

A — Maintain a continuous optimum climb until reaching assigned altitude and report passing each 1,000-foot level.

B — Climb at a maximum angle of climb to within 1,000 feet of the assigned altitude, then 500 feet per minute the last 1,000 feet.

C — Maintain an optimum climb on the centerline of the airway without intermediate level-offs until 1,000 feet below assigned altitude, then 500 to 1,500 feet per minute.

5-51   J14
What reports are required of a flight operating on an IFR clearance specifying VFR on Top in a nonradar environment?

A — The same reports that are required for any IFR flight.

B — All normal IFR reports except vacating altitudes.

C — Only the reporting of any unforecast weather.

5-52   J17
Which report should be made to ATC without a specific request when not in radar contact?

A — Entering instrument meteorological conditions.

B — When leaving final approach fix inbound on final approach.

C — Correcting an E.T.A. any time a previous E.T.A is in error in excess of 2 minutes.

5-53   J35
(Refer to figure 91 on page 5-12.) What are the two limiting cruising altitudes useable on V343 for a VFR-on-Top flight from DBS VORTAC to RANEY intersection?

A — 14,500 and 16,500 feet.

B — 15,000 and 17,000 feet.

C — 15,500 and 17,500 feet.

5-50. Answer C. GFDICM 5B (AIM)
Unless ATC advises "At pilot's discretion," you are expected to climb at an optimum rate to within 1,000 feet of any assigned altitude. Then, attempt to climb at a rate of between 500 and 1,500 feet per minute for the last 1,000 feet of climb. Answers (A) and (B) are incorrect because they do not indicate recommended procedures.

5-51. Answer A. GFDICM 5B (AIM)
When operating in VFR conditions with an ATC authorization to "MAINTAIN VFR-ON-TOP/ MAINTAIN VFR CONDITIONS," pilots on IFR flight plans must:

1. Fly at the appropriate VFR altitude.
2. Comply with the VFR visibility and distance from cloud criteria.
3. Comply with instrument flight rules that are applicable, including minimum IFR altitudes, position reporting, radio communications, course to be flown, and adherence to ATC clearances.

Answer (B) is wrong because the exception is inappropriate. Answer (C) is incorrect because all IFR reports are required, not only unforecast weather.

5-52. Answer B. GFDICM 5B (AIM)
The AIM contains specific guidance on required reports to ATC. This includes reports to be made at all times, as well as reports when not in radar contact. When not in radar contact, you should report leaving a final approach fix inbound on final approach (nonprecision approach). Answers (A) and (C) are incorrect; neither of these reports is required whether you are in radar contact or not.

5-53. Answer C. GFDICM 5B (AIM) (FAR 91.159)
When flying VFR-on-Top you must fly by both visual and instrument flight rules. This requires you to fly at or above the MEA yet below 18,000 feet MSL. You must also follow the VFR cruising altitudes, odd thousand plus 500 feet eastbound, and even thousand plus 500 feet for westbound flights. With this in mind the 15,000 feet MEA along V343 on a heading of 008° between DBS VORTAC and RANEY intersection restricts you to between 15,500 and 17,500 feet.

5-54 J17

During the en route phase of an IFR flight, the pilot is advised "Radar service terminated." What action is appropriate?

A — Set transponder to code 1200.
B — Resume normal position reporting.
C — Activate the IDENT feature of the transponder to re-establish radar contact.

5-54. Answer B. GFDICM 5B (AIM)

While in radar contact, pilots should discontinue position reports. When ATC advises "Radar service terminated," you should resume normal position reporting. The flight is still operating under IFR, but 1200 (answer A) is the code for a VFR flight. Normally, you would continue to use the transponder code assigned by ATC. The IDENT feature (answer C) does not enable the pilot to re-establish radar contact. It is used to help ATC identify a radar target when requested.

5-55 B10

In the case of operations over an area designated as a mountainous area, no person may operate an aircraft under IFR below 2,000 feet above the highest obstacle within a horizontal distance of

A — 3 SM from the course flown.
B — 4 SM from the course flown.
C — 4 NM from the course flown.

5-55. Answer C. GFDICM 5B (FAR 91.177)

In designated mountainous areas, you must remain at least 2,000 feet above the highest obstacle within a horizontal distance of 4 n.m. from the course to be flown. Answers (A) and (B) are in statute miles instead of nautical miles. Remember that most airborne distances are in nautical miles, and statute miles are used almost exclusively for ground visibility.

SECTION C
HOLDING PROCEDURES

PURPOSE OF HOLDING

1. A holding pattern is a time delay used by ATC to help maintain separation and smooth out the traffic flow.
2. You may request a hold, for example, to wait for weather conditions to improve.

FLYING A HOLDING PATTERN

3. Holding pattern size is directly proportional to aircraft speed; doubling your speed doubles the size of your holding pattern.
4. Turns are to the right in standard holding patterns, and to the left in nonstandard holding patterns.
5. Each circuit of the holding pattern begins and ends at the holding fix.
6. Timing for the outbound leg of either a standard or nonstandard holding pattern should begin abeam the holding fix. If the abeam position cannot be identified, start timing the outbound leg at the completion of the turn outbound.
7. Adjust the timing of your outbound leg to make your inbound leg one minute long.
8. When DME is used, the same holding procedures apply, but the turns are initiated at specified DME distances from the station.
9. To correct for crosswind drift in the holding pattern, triple your inbound wind correction angle on the outbound leg.

HOLDING SPEEDS

10. To keep the volume of the protected airspace for a holding pattern within reasonable limits, maximum holding airspeeds are designated according to altitude. The maximum holding speeds for civil aircraft are 200 KIAS up to 6,000 feet MSL, 230 KIAS from 6,001 to 14,000 feet, and 265 KIAS above 14,000 feet.

HOLDING PATTERN ENTRIES

11. The entry procedure for a holding pattern depends on your heading relative to the holding course. The three recommended procedures are direct, teardrop, and parallel.

HOLDING CLEARANCES

12. A holding clearance should always contain the holding direction, the holding fix, and an expect further clearance (EFC) time. If the holding pattern is not published, the clearance also contains the holding course. For nonstandard patterns, left turns are specified. For patterns using DME, the clearance gives the outbound leg length in nautical miles.

5-56   J17
(Refer to figure 87 on page 5-8.) At STRUT intersection headed eastbound, ATC instructs you to hold west on the 10 DME fix west of LCH on V306, what entry procedure is recommended?

A — Direct.
B — Teardrop.
C — Parallel.

5-56. Answer A. GFDICM 5C (Enroute Chart Legend)
It appears that you are to hold on the 265° radial at the 10 DME fix west of LCH. Since you are inbound to the holding fix, on the holding course, you are aligned for a direct entry to the pattern. A teardrop entry (answer B) would require you to be approaching the fix on a southwesterly heading between 195° and 265°. For a parallel entry (answer C), you would be on a heading between 265° and 015°. For additional information, see Questions 5-57 and 5-59.

5-57   J17

(Refer to figure 112 on page 5-22.) You arrive at the 15 DME fix on a heading of 350°. Which holding pattern correctly complies with the ATC clearance below, and what is the recommended entry procedure?

"...HOLD WEST OF THE ONE FIVE DME FIX ON THE ZERO NINE ZERO RADIAL OF THE ABC VORTAC, FIVE MILE LEGS, LEFT TURNS..."

A — 1; teardrop entry.
B — 1; direct entry.
C — 2; direct entry.

5-57. Answer B. GFDICM 5C (AIM)

To answer this question you need to be familiar with holding pattern terminology. (See accompanying illustrations for nonstandard and standard patterns.) Then, you need to have a clear understanding of holding pattern instructions. An ATC clearance with holding instructions at a fix where the pattern is not charted will include the following information:

1. Direction of holding from the fix in terms of the eight cardinal compass points (N, NE, E, SE, etc.).
2. Holding fix (the fix may be omitted if included at the beginning of the transmission as the clearance limit).
3. Radial, course, bearing, airway, or route on which the aircraft is to hold.
4. Leg length in miles if DME or RNAV is to be used (leg length will be specified in minutes on pilot request or if the controller considers it necessary).
5. Direction of turn if left turns are to be made, the pilot requests, or the controller considers it necessary. If the direction of turn is not included, the pattern is standard with right turns.
6. Time to expect further clearance and any pertinent additional delay information.

For entry maneuvering, a key is to visualize your position and heading when you first approach the holding fix. You also have to know where the pattern is in relation to the holding fix. As a general rule, you turn in the shortest direction to get into a position where you can intercept the course of the inbound leg of the holding pattern. Your heading when you initially cross the holding fix determines the type of entry — parallel, teardrop, or direct.

For this question, you first must determine that pattern 1 properly depicts the holding instructions. With an initial heading of 350°, you are approaching the fix within the direct entry sector (340° clockwise to 160°). See accompanying illustration. Therefore, answer (B) is correct. Answer (A) is incorrect because a teardrop entry would apply only if you approach the fix on headings between 270° clockwise to 340°. Answer (C) is wrong because holding pattern 2 does not show the holding fix at the end of the inbound leg.

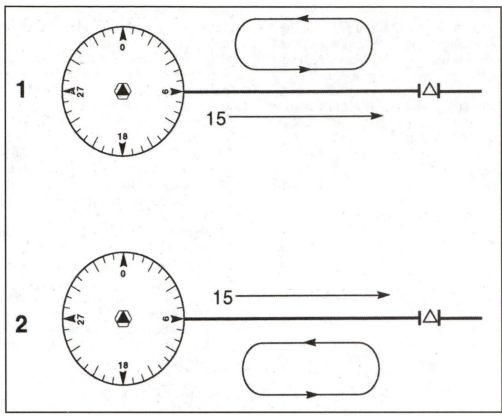

FIGURE 112. — Holding Entry Procedures

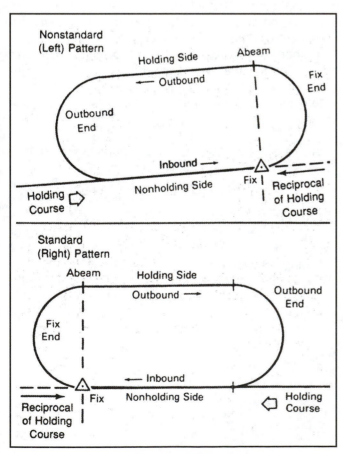

Question 5-57

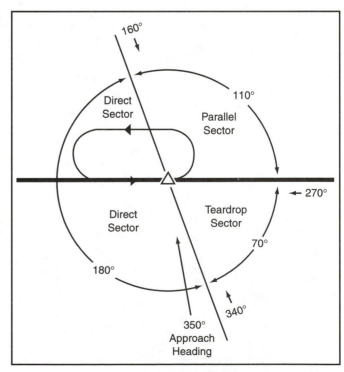

Question 5-57

5-58   J17

(Refer to figure 113.) You receive this ATC clearance:

"...HOLD EAST OF THE ABC VORTAC ON THE ZERO NINER ZERO RADIAL, LEFT TURNS..."

What is the recommended procedure to enter the holding pattern?

A — Parallel only.
B — Direct only.
C — Teardrop only.

FIGURE 113. — Aircraft Course and DME Indicator

5-59   J17

(Refer to figure 113.) You receive this ATC clearance:

"...CLEARED TO THE ABC VORTAC. HOLD SOUTH ON THE ONE EIGHT ZERO RADIAL..."

What is the recommended procedure to enter the holding pattern?

A — Teardrop only.
B — Direct only.
C — Parallel only.

5-58. Answer A. GFDICM 5C (AIM)

Note that the clearance is for a nonstandard (left turns) pattern. The HSI depicts the aircraft on a course of 060°, heading 055°, inbound TO the station, which places it southwest of the VORTAC. An inbound heading between 340° clockwise to 090° will place the airplane in the sector for a parallel entry (answer A). A direct entry (answer B) is wrong because your inbound heading would have to be between 160° clockwise to 340°. The teardrop (answer C) would apply if the inbound heading was between 090° clockwise to 160°.

For additional information, see Question 5-57.

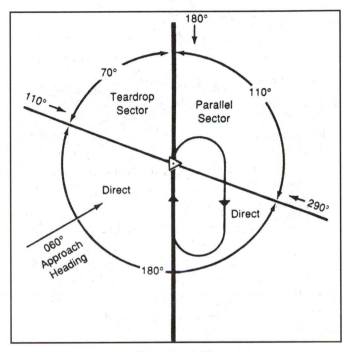

Question 5-59

5-59. Answer B. GFDICM 5C (AIM)

The HSI depicts the aircraft on a 060° course inbound TO the VORTAC (on the 240° radial). The holding pattern is on the 180° radial, right turns implied. As shown in the accompanying illustration, the aircraft is within the 180° of azimuth which requires a direct entry. Answer (A) is wrong because a teardrop would apply only if the inbound heading was between 110° and 180°. Answer (C) is incorrect because the parallel entry would apply only if the inbound heading was between 180° and 290°.

5-60   **J17**

(Refer to figure 113 on page 5-23.) You receive this ATC clearance:

"...CLEARED TO THE XYZ VORTAC. HOLD NORTH ON THE THREE SIX ZERO RADIAL, LEFT TURNS..."

What is the recommended procedure to enter the holding pattern?

A — Parallel only.
B — Direct only.
C — Teardrop only.

5-61   **J17**

(Refer to figure 113 on page 5-23.) You receive this ATC clearance:

"...CLEARED TO THE ABC VORTAC. HOLD WEST ON THE TWO SEVEN ZERO RADIAL..."

What is the recommended procedure to enter the holding pattern?

A — Parallel only.
B — Direct only.
C — Teardrop only.

5-62   **J17**

(Refer to figure 114 on page 5-25.) A pilot receives this ATC clearance:

"...CLEARED TO THE ABC VORTAC. HOLD WEST ON THE TWO SEVEN ZERO RADIAL..."

What is the recommended procedure to enter the holding pattern?

A — Parallel or teardrop.
B — Parallel only.
C — Direct only.

5-63   **J17**

(Refer to figure 114 on page 5-25.) A pilot receives this ATC clearance:

"...CLEARED TO THE XYZ VORTAC. HOLD NORTH ON THE THREE SIX ZERO RADIAL, LEFT TURNS..."

What is the recommended procedure to enter the holding pattern?

A — Teardrop only.
B — Parallel only.
C — Direct only.

5-60. Answer C. GFDICM 5C (AIM)

The HSI depicts the aircraft on a course of 060° inbound TO the VORTAC, on the 240° radial. Since the aircraft is on the nonholding side of the pattern and its heading is within 70° of the outbound course, a teardrop entry is recommended. Answer (A) is wrong because a parallel entry would be correct only if the inbound heading was between 250° and 360°. Answer (B) applies only if the inbound heading was between the 070° clockwise to 250°.

For additional information, see Question 5-57.

5-61. Answer B. GFDICM 5C (AIM)

The HSI depicts the aircraft on a 060° course inbound TO the VORTAC (on the 240° radial), with a heading of 055°. The holding pattern is on the 270° radial, right turns implied. The aircraft heading is within 70° of the inbound holding course of 090°, so a direct entry is recommended. A parallel entry (answer A) applies if the inbound heading is between 270° and 020°. A teardrop entry (answer C) is recommended only if you are inbound on a heading between 200° and 270°.

For additional information, see Question 5-59.

5-62. Answer C. GFDICM 5C (AIM)

The HSI depicts the aircraft on the 330° radial on the 150° course TO the VORTAC, heading 155°. The holding course is on the 270° radial, with standard right turns implied. The aircraft heading is within 110° of the inbound course on the nonholding side, so a direct entry is recommended. Answer (A) is wrong because the only situation where you would have a choice between a parallel or teardrop entry is if you were inbound on a heading of 270°. Answer (B) suggests an inbound heading between 270° and 020°.

For additional information, see Question 5-59.

5-63. Answer C. GFDICM 5C (AIM)

The HSI depicts the aircraft on the 150° course TO the VORTAC on the 330° radial. The inbound heading of 155° is within the 180° sector where a direct entry is recommended. A teardrop (answer A) applies only if the inbound heading is between 360° and 070°. A parallel entry is appropriate only when the inbound heading is between 250° and 360°.

For additional information, see Question 5-57.

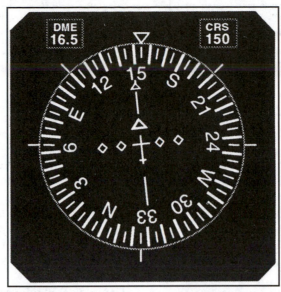

FIGURE 114. — Aircraft Course and DME Indicator

5-64   J17

(Refer to figure 114.) A pilot receives this ATC clearance:

"...CLEARED TO THE ABC VORTAC. HOLD SOUTH ON THE ONE EIGHT ZERO RADIAL..."

What is the recommended procedure to enter the holding pattern?

A — Teardrop only.
B — Parallel only.
C — Direct only.

5-65   J17

To ensure proper airspace protection while in a holding pattern, what is the maximum airspeed above 14,000 feet for civil turbojet aircraft?

A — 200 knots.
B — 265 knots.
C — 230 knots.

5-66   J17

(Refer to figure 115 on page 5-26.) You receive this ATC clearance:

"...HOLD WEST OF THE ONE FIVE DME FIX ON THE ZERO NINE ZERO RADIAL OF ABC VORTAC, FIVE MILE LEGS, LEFT TURNS..."

You arrive at the 15 DME fix on a heading of 350°. Which holding pattern correctly complies with these instructions, and what is the recommended entry procedure?

A — 1; teardrop.
B — 2; direct.
C — 1; direct.

5-64. Answer A. GFDICM 5C (AIM)

The HSI depicts the aircraft on the 330° radial, on the 150° course TO the VORTAC. Since the aircraft is on the nonholding side of the pattern and the heading of 155° is within 70° of the outbound leg, a teardrop entry is recommended. A parallel entry (answer B) applies only if the inbound heading is between 180° and 290°. A direct entry (answer C) requires an inbound heading between 290° clockwise to 110°.

For additional information, see Question 5-59.

5-65. Answer B. GFDICM 5C (AIM)

The maximum airspeed for civil turbojets holding above 14,000 feet MSL is 265 knots. Below 6,000 feet MSL the speed is 200 knots, and above 6,000 through 14,000 feet MSL the maximum holding speed is 230 knots.

5-66. Answer C. GFDICM 5C (AIM)

Since the inbound leg of the holding pattern will always take you to the holding fix, pattern 1 is the only one correctly depicted. The aircraft heading of 350° on the nonholding side places it within 110° of the holding course. A direct entry is recommended.

For additional information, refer to Question 5-57.

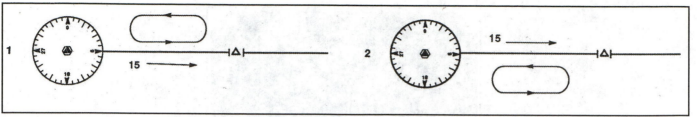

FIGURE 115. — DME Fix with Holding Pattern.

5-67   J17
(Refer to figure 116.) You arrive over the 15 DME fix on a heading of 350°. Which holding pattern correctly complies with the ATC clearance below, and what is the recommended entry procedure?

"...HOLD WEST OF THE ONE FIVE DME FIX ON THE TWO SIX EIGHT RADIAL OF THE ABC VORTAC, FIVE MILE LEGS, LEFT TURNS..."

A — 1; teardrop entry.
B — 2; direct entry.
C — 1; direct entry.

5-67. Answer B. GFDICM 5C (AIM)
Since the inbound leg of the holding pattern will always take you to the holding fix, pattern 2 is the only one correctly depicted. The aircraft heading of 350° on the nonholding side places it within 110° of the holding course. A direct entry is recommended. Answers (A) and (C) are incorrect because the holding fix should always be at the end of the inbound leg.

For additional information, refer to Question 5-57.

5-68   J17
At what point should the timing begin for the first leg outbound in a nonstandard holding pattern?

A — Abeam the holding fix, or wings level, whichever occurs last.
B — When the wings are level at the completion of the 180° turn outbound.
C — When over or abeam the holding fix, whichever occurs later.

5-68. Answer C. GFDICM 5C (AIM)
Outbound leg timing begins over or abeam the holding fix, whichever occurs later. Answer (A) would be correct only if the abeam position cannot be determined, in which case timing begins when the turn to the outbound heading is completed (wings level). The same applies to answer (B), plus the turn outbound is not necessarily 180° for the first leg.

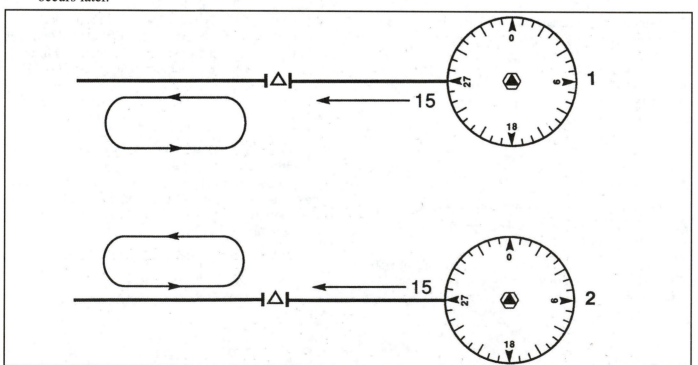

FIGURE 116. — Holding Pattern Procedure.

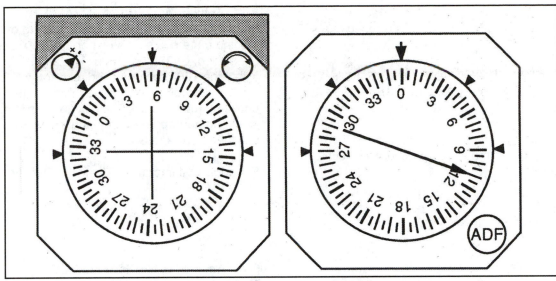

FIGURE 117. — Heading and ADF Indicators.

5-69   J17

(Refer to figure 117.) You receive this ATC clearance:

"...CLEARED TO THE ABC NDB. HOLD SOUTHEAST ON THE ONE FOUR ZERO DEGREE BEARING FROM THE NDB. LEFT TURNS..."

At station passage you note the indications in figure 117. What is the recommended procedure to enter the holding pattern?

A — Direct only.
B — Teardrop only.
C — Parallel only.

5-70   J17

(Refer to figure 117.) You receive this ATC clearance:

"...CLEARED TO THE XYZ NDB. HOLD NORTHEAST ON THE ZERO FOUR ZERO DEGREE BEARING FROM THE NDB. LEFT TURNS..."

At station passage you note the indications in figure 117. What is the recommended procedure to enter the holding pattern?

A — Direct only.
B — Teardrop only.
C — Parallel only.

5-69. Answer C. GFDICM 5C (AIM)

You are crossing the NDB on a heading of 055°. The holding pattern is southeast on the 140° bearing from the station, or 320° inbound. The aircraft is entering on the holding side with a heading greater than 70° from the inbound bearing. Therefore, a parallel entry is recommended. Answer (A) applies to an inbound heading between 210° clockwise to 030°. Answer (B) implies an inbound heading between 140° and 210°.

For additional information, refer to Question 5-57.

5-70. Answer B. GFDICM 5C (AIM)

You are crossing the NDB on a heading of 055°. The holding pattern is northeast on the 040° bearing from the station, or 220° inbound. The aircraft is entering on the nonholding side, within the 70° arc for a teardrop entry. Answer (A) is wrong since it implies an inbound heading between 110° clockwise to 290°. Answer (C) suggests an inbound heading between 290° and 040°.

For additional information, refer to Question 5-57.

5-71   J17

(Refer to figure 117 on page 5-27.) You receive this ATC clearance:

"...CLEARED TO THE ABC NDB. HOLD SOUTHWEST ON THE TWO THREE ZERO DEGREE BEARING FROM THE NDB..."

At station passage you note the indications in figure 117. What is the recommended procedure to enter the holding pattern?

A — Direct only.
B — Teardrop only.
C — Parallel only.

5-72   J17

What timing procedure should be used when performing a holding pattern at a VOR?

A — Timing for the outbound leg begins over or abeam the VOR, whichever occurs later.
B — Timing for the inbound leg begins when initiating the turn inbound.
C — Adjustments in timing of each pattern should be made on the inbound leg.

5-73   J17

When holding at an NDB, at what point should the timing begin for the second leg outbound?

A — When the wings are level and the wind drift correction angle is established after completing the turn to the outbound heading.
B — When the wings are level after completing the turn to the outbound heading, or abeam the fix, whichever occurs first.
C — When abeam the holding fix.

5-74   J17

To ensure proper airspace protection while holding at 5,000 feet in a civil airplane, what is the maximum indicated airspeed a pilot should use?

A — 210 knots.
B — 200 knots.
C — 230 knots.

5-71. Answer A. GFDICM 5C (AIM)

You are crossing the NDB on a heading of 055°. The holding pattern is southwest on the 230° bearing from the station, or 050° inbound. The aircraft heading is within the 180° sector for a direct entry. A teardrop (answer B) would apply if the inbound heading was between 160° and 230°. A parallel entry (answer C) would be appropriate if the inbound heading was between 230° and 340°.

For additional information, refer to Question 5-59.

5-72. Answer A. GFDICM 5C (AIM)

Timing for the outbound leg begins over or abeam the holding fix, whichever occurs later. Timing for the inbound leg (answer B) begins when completing, not initiating, the turn inbound. Adjustments to timing (answer C) should be made on the outbound leg to achieve proper inbound timing.

5-73. Answer C. GFDICM 5C (AIM)

Timing begins abeam the fix, regardless of whether the wings are level or drift correction is established (answers A and B). Only if the abeam position cannot be determined does timing begin at the completion of the turn outbound.

5-74. Answer B. GFDICM 5C (AIM)

The maximum holding speed for civil aircraft (piston and jet) is 200 KIAS up to 6,000 feet MSL, 230 KIAS from 6,001 to 14,000 feet, and 265 KIAS above 14,000 feet.

5-75   J17
(Refer to figure 128 on page 8-3.) What type entry is recommended for the missed approach holding pattern depicted on the VOR RWY 36 approach chart for Price/Carbon County Airport?

A — Direct only.
B — Teardrop only.
C — Parallel only.

5-75. Answer A. GFDICM 5C (AIM)
The inbound heading from the southeast should be within 70° of the inbound holding course, on the holding side of the radial, so a direct entry is recommended. A teardrop entry (answer B) would be recommended only if the inbound heading is from the northwest on the nonholding side. A parallel entry (answer C) is recommended only when entering from the northeast on the holding side. In this case, the inbound heading would have to be greater than 70° from the inbound holding course.

For additional information, refer to Questions 5-57 and 5-59.

5-76   J17
(Refer to figure 129 on page 8-29.) What indication should you get when it is time to turn inbound while in the procedure turn at LABER?

A — 4 DME miles from LABER.
B — 10 DME miles from the MAP.
C — 12 DME miles from LIT VORTAC.

5-76. Answer A. GFDICM 5C (AIM)
Figure 129 depicts a 4 n.m. holding pattern; therefore, the turn inbound begins at 4 DME from LABER IAF. The holding fix (LABER) is 10 DME from the MAP (answer B), but this is not the point to turn inbound. The 4 n.m. holding pattern is measured from the holding fix, not the LIT VORTAC (answer C).

5-77   J17
(Refer to figure 129 on page 8-29.) What type of entry is recommended to the missed approach holding pattern if the inbound heading is 050°?

A — Direct.
B — Parallel.
C — Teardrop.

5-77. Answer C. GFDICM 5C (AIM)
The missed approach holding pattern is at the BENDY waypoint. Note, this is a nonstandard (left turns) holding pattern. When you initially approach the fix from the southwest, heading 050°, you are within the sector where a teardrop entry is recommended. This applies to inbound headings between 042° and 112°. A direct entry (answer A) would be appropriate if approaching the fix on headings between 112° and 292°. Any heading between 292° and 042° would be appropriate for a parallel entry (answer B).

For additional information, refer to Questions 5-57 and 5-59.

5-78   J17
(Refer to figure 133 on page 8-14.) What type of entry is recommended for the missed approach holding pattern at Riverside Municipal?

A — Direct.
B — Parallel.
C — Teardrop.

5-78. Answer A. GFDICM 5C (AIM)
The missed approach holding pattern is shown at the Paradise (PDZ) VOR. From the depicted missed approach path, it is clear that the heading to the VOR is well within the airspace where a direct entry is recommended. A parallel entry (answer B) would be recommended only if arriving from the west through north, on a heading between 078° to 188°. This would not be likely if you flew the missed approach as depicted. A teardrop entry (answer C) is appropriate only when arriving from the southwest on a heading between 008° and 078°.

For additional information refer to Questions 5-57 and 5-59.

5-79   J17

To ensure proper airspace protection while in a holding pattern, what is the maximum indicated airspeed above 14,000 feet?

A — 220 knots.
B — 200 knots.
C — 265 knots.

5-80   J17

Where a holding pattern is specified in lieu of a procedure turn, the holding maneuver must be executed within

A — 10 knots of the specified holding speed.
B — a radius of 5 miles from the holding fix.
C — the 1-minute time limitation or DME distance as specified in the profile view.

5-79. Answer C. GFDICM 5C (AIM)

The maximum holding speed for civil aircraft (piston and jet) is 200 KIAS up to 6,000 feet MSL, 230 KIAS from 6,001 to 14,000 feet, and 265 KIAS above 14,000 feet.

5-80. Answer C. GFDICM 5C (AIM)

The airspace set aside for the holding pattern is based on the published leg length (for DME use) or on an inbound time of 1 minute.

ARRIVAL

SECTION A
ARRIVAL CHARTS

STANDARD TERMINAL ARRIVAL ROUTES

1. Standard terminal arrival routes (STARs) provide a standard method for leaving the enroute structure and entering a busy terminal area. STARs are established to simplify clearance delivery procedures.
2. STARs are grouped along with other airport charts in a Jeppesen subscription, and appear in the front of NOS booklets. Legends are found in the front of the corresponding book.

STARS IN CLEARANCES

3. If you accept a STAR, you must have at least a textual description of the procedure in your possession. A graphic description is preferable.
4. Writing "No STAR" in the remarks section of your flight plan will alert ATC that you do not wish to use these procedures during your flight. You also may refuse a clearance containing a STAR, but avoid this practice if possible.

STAR CHARTS

5. STARs use symbology that is similar to that on SIDs. Altitudes are given in reference to mean sea level, and distances are in nautical miles.
6. A STAR begins at a navaid or intersection where all arrival transitions join.
7. STARs are named according to the point where a procedure begins. They are revised in numerical sequence.
8. Arrival route headings on an NOS STAR are depicted by large numerals within a heavyweight line, while those on Jeppesen STARs are depicted with the abbreviation **hdg** next to the heading in degrees.
9. Frequencies on which to contact the proper approach controller are found in the corner of an NOS chart.
10. Vertical navigation planning information is given for pilots of turboprop and jet traffic, to aid them in making efficient descents from the enroute structure to approach fixes.

6-1   J41
(Refer to figures 35 and 35A on pages 6-2 and 6-3.) At which point does the BUJ.BUJ3 arrival begin?

A — At the TXK VORTAC.
B — At BOGAR intersection.
C — At the BUJ VORTAC.

6-1. Answer C. GFDICM 6A (STAR/DP)
(Refer to Standard Arrival/Departure Chart Legend in Appendix 2.) The Blue Ridge Three Arrival (BUJ.BUJ3) begins at the BUJ VORTAC. This is apparent on the graphic depiction. Arrival routes originating at BUJ are shown with bold lines as opposed to transition routes which are shown with lighter line weights. The arrival routes also are specified in the textual description following the transitions. Answer (A) is wrong because the TXK VORTAC, LIT VORTAC, FSM VORTAC, TUL VORTAC, MLC VORTAC, and ADM VORTAC represent transition routes that allow you to navigate from the enroute structure to the BUJ VORTAC. Answer (B) is wrong because BOGAR Int. is not shown on this STAR.

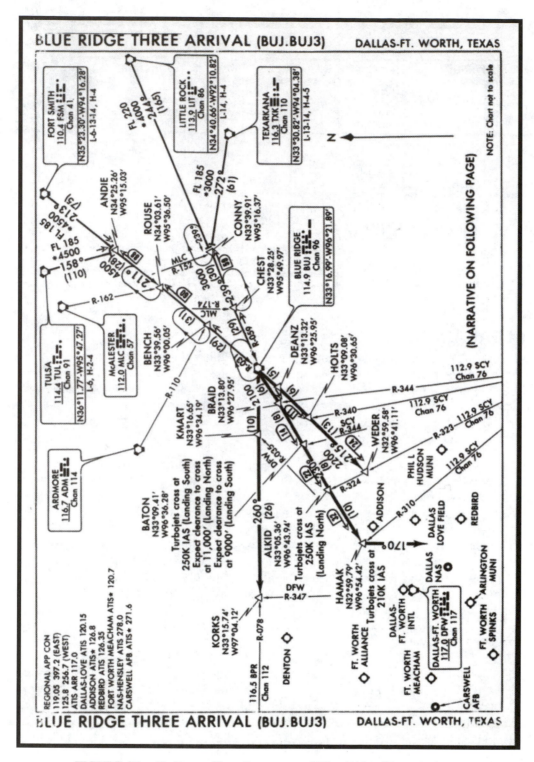

FIGURE 35.—En Route Chart Segment and Blue Ridge Three Arrival.

91094   SL-6039 (FAA)
BLUE RIDGE THREE ARRIVAL (BUJ.BUJ3)   DALLAS-FT. WORTH, TEXAS

ARRIVAL DESCRIPTION

FORT SMITH TRANSITION (FSM.BUJ3): From over FSM VORTAC via FSM R-213
and BUJ R-031 to BUJ VORTAC. Thence . . . .
LITTLE ROCK TRANSITION (LIT.BUJ3): From over LIT VORTAC via LIT R-244
and BUJ R-059 to BUJ VORTAC. Thence . . . .
TEXARKANA TRANSITION (TXK.BUJ3): From over TXK VORTAC via TXK R-272
and BUJ R-059 to BUJ VORTAC. Thence . . . .
TULSA TRANSITION (TUL.BUJ3): From over TUL VORTAC via TUL R-158 and
BUJ R-031 to BUJ VORTAC. Thence . . . .
TURBOJETS LANDING DALLAS-FT WORTH INTL: (Landing South): From over
BUJ VORTAC via BUJ R-230 to HAMAK INT. Expect vectors at BATON INT.
(Landing North): From over BUJ VORTAC via BUJ R-230 to HAMAK INT, thence
heading 170° for vector to final approach course.
NON-TURBOJETS LANDING DALLAS-FT WORTH INTL: (Landing South): From
over BUJ VORTAC via BUJ R-230 to HAMAK INT. Expect vectors at BATON
INT. (Landing North): From over BUJ VORTAC via BUJ R-215 to WEDER INT.
Expect vectors to final approach course.
ALL AIRCRAFT LANDING DALLAS-LOVE FIELD, ADDISON, REDBIRD, NAS
DALLAS, and PHIL L. HUDSON: (Landing South/North): From over BUJ VORTAC
via BUJ R-215 to WEDER INT. Expect vectors to final approach course.
ALL AIRCRAFT LANDING MEACHAM, CARSWELL AFB, ALLIANCE, ARL-
INGTON, DENTON and FT. WORTH SPINKS: (Landing South/North): From over
BUJ VORTAC via BUJ R-260 to KORKS INT. Expect vectors to final approach
course.

FIGURE 35A.—Blue Ridge Three Arrival Description.

6-2   J41
(Refer to figures 41 and 41A on pages 6-4 and 10-37.)
At which point does the AQN.AQN2 arrival begin?

A — ABI VORTAC.
B — ACTON VORTAC.
C — CREEK intersection.

6-2. Answer B. GFDICM 6A (STAR/DP Legend)
The Action Two Arrival (AQN.AQN2) begins at the
ACTION VORTAC. This is apparent on the graphic
depiction. Arrival routes originating at AQN are shown
with bold lines as opposed to transition routes which
are shown with lighter line weights. The arrival routes
also are specified in the textual description following
the transitions. Answer (A) is wrong because ABI
VORTAC, INK VORTAC, TQA VORTAC, MQP VOR-
TAC, and ACT VORTAC represent the beginning of
transition routes that allow you to navigate from the
enroute structure to the AQN VORTAC. Answer (C) is
wrong because it is an intersection that is part of the
arrival.

6-3   J41
(Refer to figures 41 and 41A on pages 6-4 and 10-37.)
Which frequency would you anticipate using to con-
tact Regional Approach Control? (ACTON TWO
ARRIVAL).

A — 119.05.
B — 124.15.
C — 125.8.

**6-3. Answer C. GFDICM 6A (Approach
Chart Legend)**
There is a listing of frequencies pertinent to the arrival
procedure in the upper left hand corner of the Acton
Two Arrival. The first frequency listed is for the
Regional Approach Control. When arriving from the
east, contact approach on 119.05 (answer A). When
arriving from the west, as in this example, contact
approach on 125.8 (answer C). Answer (B) is wrong
because it is not specified in the frequency listing.

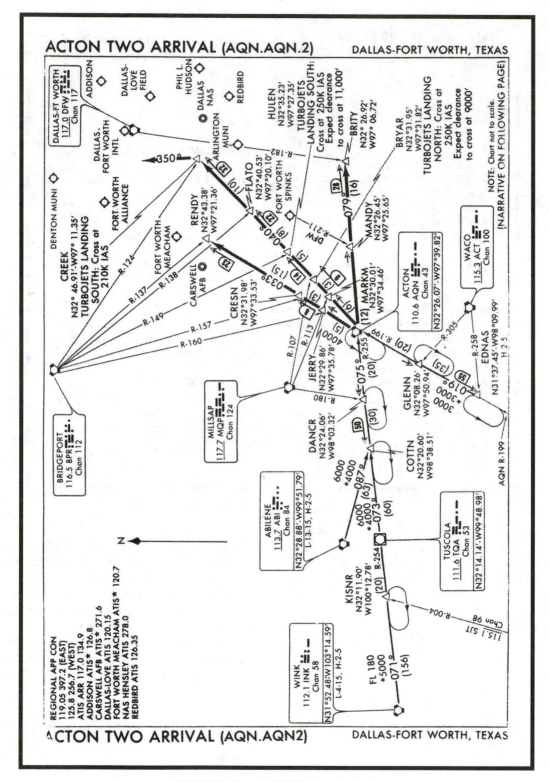

FIGURE 41.—ACTON Two Arrival.

6-4   J41
(Refer to figures 41 and 41A on page 10-37.) On which heading should you plan to depart CREEK Intersection?

A — 010°.
B — 040°.
C — 350°.

6-5   J41
(Refer to figure 72 on page 10-51.) At which location or condition does the IGN.JUDDS2 arrival begin?

A — JUDDS intersection.
B — IGN VORTAC.
C — BRISS intersection.

6-4. Answer C. GFDICM 6A (STAR/DP Legend)
As you depart CREEK Intersection, you should be on a heading of 350°. This is indicated by the heavy solid line and 350° callout in the upper right portion of the chart. It is also specified in the textual description of the procedure. Answer (A) is wrong because no portion of this STAR requires you to fly a 010° heading. Answer (B) is wrong because it represents the inbound heading to CREEK Intersection.

6-5. Answer B. GFDICM 6A (IFH)
The IGN.JUDDS2 begins over IGN VORTAC which is indicated by the bold course line starting from the IGN VORTAC. Both JUDDS Intersection (answer A) and BRISS Intersection (answer C) are intermediate fixes.

SECTION B
ARRIVAL PROCEDURES

1. ATC will issue a STAR when they deem one appropriate, unless you request "No STAR" in your flight plan. It is up to you whether to accept or refuse the procedure.
2. Altitudes and airspeeds published on the STAR are not considered restrictions until verbally given by ATC as part of a clearance.
3. After receiving the arrival clearance, certain tasks can be completed before starting your approach, including gathering weather information and accomplishing the descent and approach checklists.
4. After you determine the approach in use, review the appropriate chart and create a plan of action.
5. A descend via clearance instructs you to follow the altitudes published on the STAR, with descent at your discretion.
6. ATC may issue a descent clearance which includes a crossing altitude. Comply by estimating the distance and rate of descent required.

6-6   I10
(Refer to figure 55.) Using an average groundspeed of 90 knots, what constant rate of descent from 2,400 feet MSL at the 6 DME fix would enable the aircraft to arrive at 2,000 feet MSL at the FAF?

A — 200 feet per minute.
B — 400 feet per minute.
C — 600 feet per minute.

6-7   J18
Which is true regarding STAR's?

A — STAR's are used to separate IFR and VFR traffic.
B — STAR's are established to simplify clearance delivery procedures.
C — STAR's are used at certain airports to decrease traffic congestion.

6-8   J18
How is ATC radar used for instrument approaches when the facility is approved for approach control service?

A — Precision approaches, weather surveillance, and as a substitute for any inoperative component of a navigation aid used for approaches.
B — ASR approaches, weather surveillance, and course guidance by approach control.
C — Course guidance to the final approach course, ASR and PAR approaches, and the monitoring of nonradar approaches.

6-6. Answer A. GFDICM 6B (AFH)
To solve this problem you first need to compute the time required to travel 3 miles at 90 kts, (2 minutes). Simple arithmetic will tell you that in order to descend 400 feet in 2 minutes you must descend at a minimum of 200 feet per minute. At 90 kts. groundspeed, you would descend 800 feet at a rate of 400 feet per minute (answer B), and at 600 feet per minute (answer C) you would descend 1,200 feet.

6-7. Answer B. GFDICM 6B (AIM)
STARs are primarily used to simplify clearance delivery procedures for pilots and controllers. The main purpose of STARs is not necessarily a means of separating air traffic (answer A) or decreasing traffic congestion (answer C).

6-8. Answer C. GFDICM 6B (AIM)
Approach control radar is used for vectors, or course guidance, to the final approach course, for any established instrument approach procedure (IAP). It also may be used to provide guidance to the traffic pattern for a visual approach, or for ASR and PAR approaches, and to monitor nonradar approaches. This does not mean that the radar is available for weather surveillance or as a substitute for inoperative components (answers A and B). Approach control radar is not designed for weather surveillance.

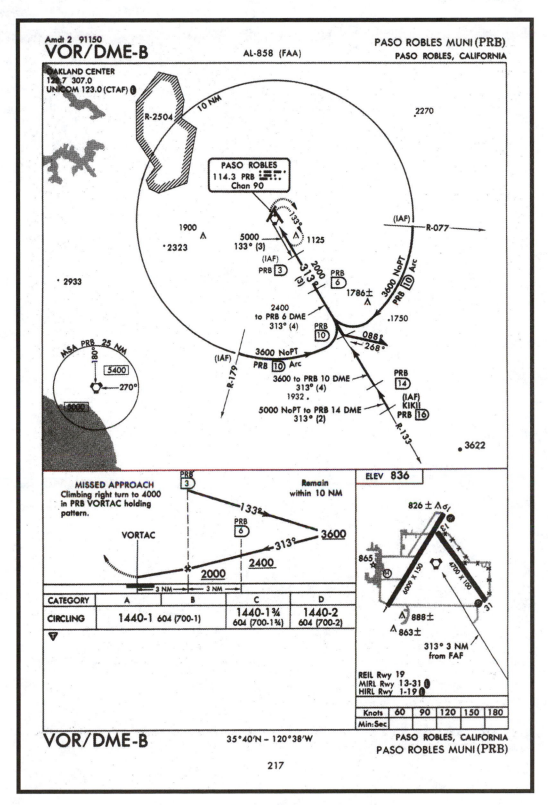

Figure 55.—VOR/DME-B (PRB).

6-9   J18

Under which condition does ATC issue a STAR?

A — To all pilots wherever STAR's are available.

B — Only if the pilot requests a STAR in the "Remarks" section of the flight plan.

C — When ATC deems it appropriate, unless the pilot requests "No STAR."

6-9. Answer C. GFDICM 6B (AIM)

When appropriate, ATC issues standard terminal arrival routes (STARs) to simplify clearance delivery procedures. If you do not wish to use a STAR, you should include the words "No STAR" in the remarks section of the flight plan. A STAR is not always issued when one is available (answer A). Answer (B) is wrong because a STAR may be issued by ATC, anytime, unless you request "No STAR" in the remarks section of the flight plan.

APPROACH

SECTION A
APPROACH CHARTS

OVERVIEW

1. The standard instrument approach procedure (IAP) allows you to descend safely by reference to instruments from the enroute altitude to a point near the runway at your destination from which a landing may be made visually. An IAP may be divided into as many as four segments: initial, intermediate, final, and missed approach.
2. The procedure title indicates the type of approach system used and the equipment required to fly the approach.

PRECISION AND NONPRECISION APPROACHES

3. A precision approach, such as an ILS or Precision Approach Radar (PAR) procedure provides vertical guidance through means of an electronic glide slope, as well as horizontal course guidance. A nonprecision approach, such as a VOR or NDB approach, provides horizontal course guidance with no glide slope information.
4. If the glide slope becomes inoperative during an ILS procedure, it becomes a nonprecision approach, and higher localizer minimums are used.

APPROACH SEGMENTS

5. Feeder routes, also referred to as approach transitions or terminal routes, provide a link between the enroute and approach structures. Flyable routes are indicated with a heavy line arrow on both Jeppesen and NOS charts. Each flyable route lists the radial or bearing, the distance, and the minimum altitude.
6. The letters IAF indicate the location of an initial approach fix. The purpose of the initial approach segment which follows the IAF, is to provide a method for aligning your aircraft with the approach course. The intermediate segment primarily is designed to position your aircraft for the final descent to the airport.
7. The final approach segment allows you to navigate safely to a point at which, if the required visual references are available, you can continue the approach to a landing.
8. The final approach segment for a precision approach begins where the glide slope is intercepted at the minimum glide slope intercept altitude shown on the approach chart. For a nonprecision approach, the final approach segment begins either at a designated final approach fix (FAF) or at the point where you are aligned with the final approach course.
9. If you know the glide slope angle (normally 3°), and if you maintain an average groundspeed on the final approach segment, you can determine the rate of descent to initially establish the airplane on the glidepath for an ILS approach procedure.
10. The missed approach segment takes you from the missed approach point (MAP) to a point for another approach or to another airport.

GENERAL CHART INFORMATION

11. Jeppesen approach charts are filed in a loose-leaf format by state, then by city within each state. NOS charts are published in regional volumes referred to as *Terminal Procedures Publications*, with each airport filed alphabetically by the name of the associated city. Generally, both charts present the same information; however, the symbology and chart layout vary.
12. Jeppesen and NOS present communications frequencies in the normal sequence used by arriving aircraft. Both Jeppesen and NOS use index numbers for chart identification.
13. The plan view is an overhead presentation of the entire approach procedure, including navaid facility boxes and reference points, such as natural or man-made objects.

COURSE REVERSALS

14. A procedure turn is a standard method of reversing your course. When a holding or teardrop pattern is shown instead of a procedure turn, it is the only approved method of course reversal. If a procedure turn, holding or teardrop pattern is not shown, a course reversal is not authorized.
15. The procedure turn, as depicted on the profile view, must be completed within the prescribed distance from the facility.

ALTITUDE INFORMATION

16. Minimum altitudes on approach procedures provide clearance of terrain and obstructions along the depicted flight tracks.
17. The minimum safe altitude, or MSA, provides 1,000 feet of obstruction clearance within 25 nautical miles of the indicated facility, unless some other distance is specified.
18. The touchdown zone elevation (TDZE) is the highest centerline altitude for the first 3,000 feet of the landing runway. The TDZE is depicted on Jeppesen approach charts in the profile view and on NOS charts in the airport sketch.
19. The profile view shows the approach from the side and displays flight path, facilities, and minimum altitudes. Height above touchdown (HAT) is measured from the touchdown zone elevation of the runway. Height above airport (HAA) is measured above the official airport elevation, which is the highest point of an airport's usable runways.
20. Distances between fixes along the approach path and the runway threshold are also shown on the profile view.
21. The threshold crossing height (TCH) is the altitude at which you cross the runway threshold when established on the glide slope.

STEPDOWN FIXES

22. Many approaches incorporate one or more stepdown fixes, used along approach segments to allow you to descend to a lower altitude as you overfly various obstacles. Your ability to identify selected stepdown fixes may permit lower landing minimums in some cases. When you cannot identify a stepdown fix, you must use the minimum altitude given just prior to the fix.
23. A visual descent point (VDP) represents the point from which you can make a normal descent to a landing, assuming you have the runway in sight and you are starting from the minimum descent altitude.

CIRCLING AND SIDESTEP MANEUVERS

24. An approach procedure to one runway with a landing on another is a circling approach, with circle-to-land minimums. Restrictions may apply to circle-to-land procedure. For example, a circle-to-land procedure might not be authorized in a specific area.
25. During a sidestep maneuver, you are cleared for an approach to one runway with a clearance to land on a parallel runway.

AIRPORT INFORMATION

26. The airport diagram plan view portrays an overhead view of the airport, including runways and lighting systems. The airport reference point, or ARP, is where the official latitude and longitude coordinates are derived.

ALTERNATE AIRPORT

27. If the forecast weather at your estimated time of arrival, plus or minus 1 hour, indicates a ceiling of less than 2,000 feet or a visibility of less than 3 miles, you must list an alternate airport on your IFR flight plan.
28. Standard alternate minimums when a precision approach is available are a 600-foot ceiling and 2 statute miles visibility. When only nonprecision approaches are available, an 800-foot ceiling and 2 statute miles apply.

WHEN TO CONDUCT A MISSED APPROACH

29. During a precision approach, the height where you must make the decision to continue the approach or execute a missed approach is referred to in the FARs as the decision height (DH). NOS charts show the decision height as an MSL altitude with the height above touchdown (HAT) listed after the visibility requirement. Jeppesen charts reflect ICAO terminology by showing a decision altitude (height) — DA(H) as an MSL altitude followed by the height above touchdown (HAT) in parentheses.

30. When on the glide slope during a precision approach, the missed approach point is the decision height. The missed approach point for a precision approach is shown on both Jeppesen and NOS charts. Jeppesen also shows the approximate missed approach point when the procedure is flown as a nonprecision approach.

31. Aircraft approach categories used to determine landing minimums are based on approach speed. This speed is 130% of the aircraft's power-off stall speed in the landing configuration at the maximum certificated landing weight ($1.3V_{SO}$). Landing minimums published on instrument approach charts consist of both minimum visibility and minimum altitude requirements for aircraft in various approach categories (A, B, C and D).

32. Visibility is listed on approach charts in statute miles, usually as a prevailing visibility reported by an accredited observer such as tower or weather personnel, or in hundreds of feet determined through the use of runway visual range (RVR) equipment.

33. If Runway Visual Range (RVR) minimums for landing are prescribed for an instrument approach procedure, but RVR is inoperative and cannot be reported for the intended runway at the time, RVR minimums should be converted and applied as ground visibility. For example, RVR 24 translates to 1/2 statute mile visibility.

34. Landing minimums usually increase when a required component or visual aid becomes inoperative. Regulations permit you to make substitutions for certain components when the component is inoperative or is not utilized during an approach.

35. The minimum altitude to which you can descend during a nonprecision approach is shown as a minimum descent altitude (MDA) on NOS charts and as a minimum descent altitude (height) — MDA(H) on Jeppesen charts.

36. For timed approaches, both Jeppesen and NOS use conversion tables to provide various elapsed times to the MAP based on the aircraft's groundspeed.

7-1   J42
(Refer to figure 29 on page 10-25.) What is the TDZ elevation for RWY 16 on Eugene/Mahlon Sweet Field?

A — 363 feet MSL.
B — 365 feet MSL.
C — 396 feet MSL.

7-1. Answer A. GFDICM 7A (Approach Chart Legend)
The touchdown zone elevation (TDZE) can be found on the airport diagram under the "TDZE" callout. Answer (B) is wrong because 365 feet is the airport elevation. Answer (C) is wrong because it is not shown on the chart.

7-2   J42
(Refer to figure 29 on page 10-25.) Using a ground-speed of 90 knots on the ILS final approach course, what rate of descent should be used as a reference to maintain the ILS glide slope?

A — 415 feet per minute.
B — 480 feet per minute.
C — 555 feet per minute.

7-2. Answer B. GFDICM 7A (Rate of Descent Table)
The glide slope is 3°, as indicated on the profile view by "GS 3.00°." To determine the appropriate rate of descent, refer to Appendix 2. At a speed of 90 knots, you must descend at a rate of 480 feet per minute to maintain the glide slope. Answer (A) is wrong because 415 is substantially less than the 480 required. Answer (C) is wrong because it represents the descent rate for a 3.5° glide slope.

7-3   H833
(Refer to figure 36A on page 8-26.) What is the MDA and visibility criteria respectively for the S 33 approach procedure?

A — 1,240 feet MSL; 1 SM.
B — 1,280 feet MSL; 1 and 1/4 SM.
C — 1,300 feet MSL; 1 SM.

7-3. Answer A. GFDICM 7A (Approach Chart Legend)
Using figure 36A, the MDA and visibility criteria for the straight-in landing procedure are 1,240 feet MSL and 1 statute mile, respectively. These minimums apply to category A and B aircraft as well as the availability of the current airport altimeter setting. Answer (B) is wrong because it is not specified anywhere on the chart. Answer (C) is shown on the NOS Chart, but applies only if the Dallas Love altimeter setting is used.

7-4   J18
(Refer to figures 41, 42, 42A on page 6-4, 7-5, and 7-6.)
Approaching DFW from Abilene, which frequencies should you expect to use for regional approach control, control tower, and ground control respectively?

A — 119.05; 126.55; 121.65.
B — 119.05; 124.15; 121.8.
C — 125.8; 124.15; 121.8.

7-5   J42
(Refer to figure 42A on page 7-6.) Which navigational information and services would be available to the pilot when using the localizer frequency?

A — Localizer and glide slope, DME, TACAN with no voice capability.
B — Localizer information only, ATIS and DME are available.
C — Localizer and glide slope, DME, and no voice capability.

7-6   J42
(Refer to figures 42 and 42A on page 7-5 and 7-6.) What is the difference in elevation (in feet MSL) between the airport elevation and the TDZE for RWY 36L?

A — 15 feet.
B — 18 feet.
C — 22 feet.

7-7   J42
(Refer to figure 42A on page 7-6.) What rate of descent should you plan to use initially to establish the glidepath for the ILS RWY 36L approach? (Use 120 knots groundspeed.)

A — 425 feet per minute.
B — 530 feet per minute.
C — 635 feet per minute.

7-4. Answer C. GFDICM 7A (A/FD Legend)
There is a listing of frequencies pertinent to the arrival procedure in the upper left hand corner of the Acton Two Arrival. The first frequency listed is for Regional Approach Control. When arriving from the east, contact approach on 119.05. When arriving from the west, as in this example, contact approach on 125.8. Both the control tower and ground control frequencies can be found in the excerpt from the *Airport/Facility Directory* (figure 42). Since you will be approaching from the west, the frequency for the tower is 124.15, while ground control is 121.8. Answer (A) is wrong because 119.05 and 126.55 represent the approach control and tower frequencies when arriving from the east. Answer (B) is wrong because 119.05 is the approach frequency when arriving from the east.

7-5. Answer C. GFDICM 7A (Approach Chart Legend)
Figure 42A includes ILS in the title, which means both localizer and glide slope are available. Figure 42A shows a DME channel in the localizer identifier box, and DME fixes are shown on the profile view. No voice capability is indicated by the underlined localizer frequency. Answer (A) is wrong because a TACAN is not available on the localizer frequency. Answer (B) is wrong because glide slope is available, and ATIS is not broadcast on the localizer frequency.

7-6. Answer A. GFDICM 7A (Approach Chart Legend)
The touchdown zone elevation (TDZE) is 588 feet. This is indicated on the airport diagram on Figure 42A. The airport elevation is 603 feet and is indicated on the airport diagram (figure 42A). The difference between the airport elevation and the TDZE for RWY/36L is 15 feet. Answers (B) and (C) are wrong because they exceed the difference.

7-7. Answer C. GFDICM 7A (Rate of Descent Table)
The glide slope is 3.0°. This is indicated by the "GS 3.00°" on the profile view of Figure 42A. To determine the rate of descent required to maintain the glide slope, refer to Appendix 2. At 120 knots, you must descend at 635 feet per minute to maintain the glide slope. Answer (A) is wrong because it represents the descent rate for a 2.0° glide slope. Answer (B) is wrong because it represents the descent rate for a 2.5° glide slope.

TEXAS

DALLAS-FORT WORTH INTL (DFW) 12 NW UTC-6(-5DT)32°53'47"N 97°02'28"W · **DALLAS-FT. WORTH**
603 B FUEL 100LL, JET A . OX 1, 3 LRA ARFF Index E H-2K, 4F, 5B, L-13C, A
RWY 17L-35R: H11,388X150 (CONC-GRVD) S-120, D-200, DT-600, DDT-850 HIRL CL IAP
    RWY 17L: ALSF2. TDZ.   RWY 35R: MALSR. TDZ.
RWY 17R-35L: H11,388X200 (CONC-GRVD) S-120, D-200, DT-600, DDT-850 HIRL CL
    RWY 17R: MALSR. TDZ.   RWY 35L: TDZ. VASI(V6L).
RWY 18R-36L: H11,388X150(CONC-GRVD) S-120, D-200, DT-600, DDT-850 HIRL CL
    RWY 18R: ALSF2. TDZ   RWY 36L: MALSR. TDZ
RWY 18L-36R: H11,387X200 (CONC-GRVD) S-120, D-200, DT-600, DDT-850 HIRL CL
    RWY 18L: MALSR. TDZ.   RWY 36R: TDZ. VASI(V6L).
RWY 13R-31L: H9300X150(CONC-GRVD) S-120, D-220, DT-600, DDT-850 HIRL CL
    RWY 13R: MALSR. TDZ.   RWY 31L: TDZ.
RWY 13L-31R: H9000X200 (CONC-GRVD) S-120, D-200, DT-600, DDT-850 HIRL CL 0.5% up NW
    RWY 13L: TDZ. VASI(V6L)—Upper GA 3.25° TCH 93'. Lower GA 3.0° TCH 47'.   RWY 31R: MALSR. TDZ.
RWY 18S-36S: H4000X100 (CONC)
AIRPORT REMARKS: Attended continuously. Rwy 18S-36S CLOSED indefinitely. Arpt under construction, men and
    equipment in movement areas. Partial outages of arpt lgt circuits will occur daily. Prior Permission Required from
    arpt ops for General Aviation acft to proceed to airline terminal gate except to General Aviation Facility. Rwy
    18S-36S located on taxiway G, 4000' long 100' wide restricted to prop acft 12,500 lbs. & below and stol acft
    daylight VFR plus IFR departures. Prior permission required from the primary tenant airlines to operate within
    central terminal area, CAUTION: proper minimum clearance may not be maintained within the central terminal
    area. Landing fee. Helipad H1 on apt 104X104 (CONC) Heliport located at Twy G and Twy 24 intersection,
    daylight VFR. Clearways 500X1000 each end Rwy 17L-35R, Rwy 17R-35L, Rwy 18L-36R and Rwy 18R-36L.
    Flight Notification Service (ADCUS) available.
WEATHER DATA SOURCES: LLWAS.
COMMUNICATIONS: ATIS 117.0 134.9 (ARR) 135.5 (DEP)   UNICOM 122.95
    FORT WORTH FSS (FTW) LC 429-6434, TF 1-800-WX-BRIEF. NOTAM FILE DFW
®REGIONAL APP CON 119.05(E) 119.4(E) 125.8(W) 132.1(W)
    REGIONAL TOWER 126.55 (E) 124.15 (W)   GND CON 121.65 133.15(E) 121.8 (W)   CLNC DEL 128.25 127.5
®REGIONAL DEP CON 118.55 (E) 124.25 (WEST) 127.75 (NORTH-SOUTH)
    TCA: See VFR Terminal Area chart.
RADIO AIDS TO NAVIGATION: NOTAM FILE DFW.
    (H) VORTACW 117.0   DFW   Chan 117   32°51'57"N 97°01'40"W   at fld. 560/08E.
      VOR Portion unusable 045°-050° all altitudes and distances, 350-100° beyond 30 NM below 2100'.
    ISSUE NDB (LOM) 233   PK   32°47'35"N 97°01'49"W   348° 6.2 NM to fld.
    JIFFY NDB (LOM) 219   FL   32°59'44"N 97°01'46"W   179° 6.0 NM to fld.
    ILS/DME 109.5 I-LWN Chan 32 Rwy 13R.
    ILS/DME 109.1 I-FLQ Chan 28 Rwy 17L. LOM JIFFY NDB.
    ILS 111.5 I-JHZ Rwy 17R. LOM JIFFY NDB.
    ILS 111.3 I-CIX Rwy 18L.
    ILS/DME 111.9 I-VYN Chan 56 Rwy 18R.
    ILS 110.9 I-RRA Rwy 31R.
    ILS/DME 109.1 I-PKQ Chan 28 Rwy 35R. LOM ISSUE NDB.
    ILS/DME 111.9 I-BXN Chan 56 Rwy 36L.

FIGURE 42.—ILS-RWY 36L, Dallas-Fort Worth Intl.

7-8   **J42**

(Refer to figure 55 on page 6-7.) Under which condition should a missed approach procedure be initiated if the runway environment (Paso Robles Municipal Airport) is not in sight?

A — After descending to 1,440 feet MSL.
B — After descent to 1,440 feet or reaching the 1 NM DME, whichever occurs first.
C — When you reach the established missed approach point and determine the visibility is less than 1 mile.

7-8. Answer C. GFDICM 7A (Approach Chart Legend)

The missed approach point (MAP) is the PRB VOR-TAC, the minimum descent altitude (MDA) is 1,440 feet MSL for all aircraft categories, and the required visibility is 1 s.m. for Category A and B aircraft. You must initiate a missed approach if you do not have the required visual references in sight at the MAP. Therefore, answer (C) is correct. Answer (A) is incorrect since you should descend to 1,440 feet prior to reaching the MAP. Answer (B) is wrong because the MAP is the VORTAC, not 1 mile from the VORTAC.

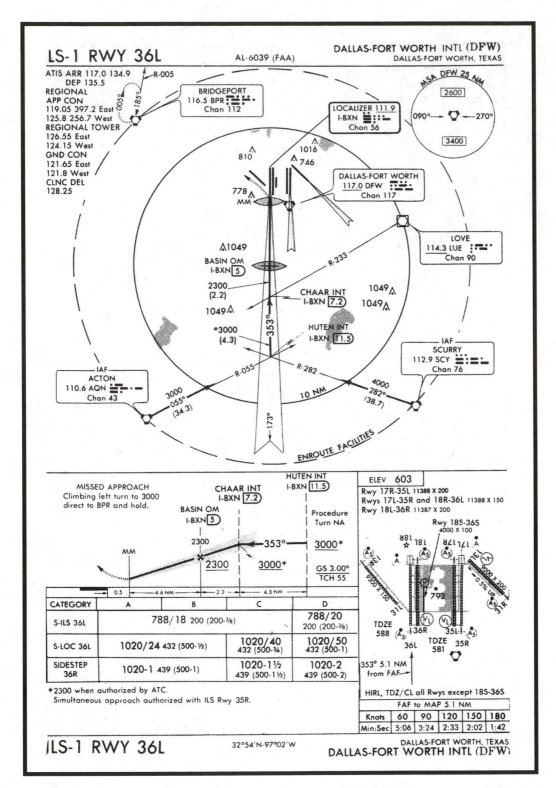

FIGURE 42A.—ILS-RWY 36L, Dallas-Fort Worth Intl.

7-9   J42
(Refer to figure 60A on page 2-60.) What is the elevation of the TDZE for RWY 4?

A — 70 feet MSL.
B — 54 feet MSL.
C — 46 feet MSL.

7-9. Answer C. GFDICM 7A (Approach Chart Legend)
The touchdown zone elevation is 46 feet MSL on runway 4. This is depicted on the airport diagram next to the runway threshold. Answer (A), 70 feet MSL is an inappropriate number. Answer (B), 54 feet, is depicted as the threshold crossing height (TCH).

7-10   J42
(Refer to figure 73 on page 7-9.) What is the minimum altitude at which you should intercept the glide slope on the ILS RWY 6 approach procedure?

A — 3,000 feet MSL.
B — 1,800 feet MSL.
C — 1,690 feet MSL.

7-10. Answer B. GFDICM 7A (Approach Chart Legend)
The published glide slope intercept altitude is the lowest altitude at which you may intercept the ILS glide slope. This minimum altitude is shown on the approach chart profile view near the glide slope, prior to the nonprecision FAF. It is indicated on NOS charts by a lightning bolt symbol. Answer (A), 3,000 feet, is the procedure turn or course reversal altitude. Answer (C), 1,690 feet, is the altitude at which you will cross the outer marker when established on the glide slope.

7-11   J42
(Refer to figure 73 on page 7-9.) At which indication or occurrence should you initiate the published missed approach procedure for the ILS RWY 6 approach provided the runway environment is not in sight?

A — When reaching 374 feet MSL indicated altitude.
B — When 3 minutes (at 90 knots groundspeed) have expired or reaching 374 feet MSL, whichever occurs first.
C — Upon reaching 374 feet AGL.

7-11. Answer A. GFDICM 7A (Approach Chart Legend)
Your missed approach point on an ILS approach is at the decision height (DH) on the glide slope. Timing (answer B) is used to determine the missed approach point on nonprecision approaches, such as a localizer approach when the ILS glide slope is out of service. Answer (C) is wrong because the DH is published in feet MSL, not AGL.

7-12   J42
(Refer to figure 73 on page 7-9.) Using an average groundspeed of 90 knots on the final approach segment, what rate of descent should be used initially to establish the glidepath for the ILS RWY 6 approach procedure?

A — 395 feet per minute.
B — 480 feet per minute.
C — 555 feet per minute.

7-12. Answer B. GFDICM 7A (Rate of Descent Table)
The chart indicates a glide slope angle of 3°. NOS publishes a rate of descent table in the back of each booklet. (See Appendix 2.) To use this table, find the 3.0° glide path angle in the left column, then move right to the 90 kts. groundspeed column to find 480 feet per minute. A 395-foot per minute descent (answer A) is for a 3.0° glide slope flown at 75 kts., and a 555-foot per minute descent (answer C) would apply when flying at a 105-knot groundspeed.

7-13   J42
(Refer to figure 73 on page 7-9.) What is the touchdown zone elevation for RWY 6?

A — 174 feet MSL.
B — 200 feet AGL.
C — 270 feet MSL.

7-14   J42
(Refer to figure 73 on page 7-9.) After passing the OM, Bradley Approach Control advises you that the MM on the ILS RWY 6 approach is inoperative. Under these circumstances, what adjustments, if any, are required to be made to the DH and visibility?

A — DH 424/24.
B — No adjustments are required.
C — DH 374/24.

7-15   J42
(Refer to figure 73 on page 7-9.) Which runway and landing environment lighting is available for approach and landing on RWY 6 at Bradley International?

A — HIRL, REIL, and VASI.
B — HIRL and VASI.
C — ALSF2 and HIRL.

7-16   J42
(Refer to figures 74 and 80 on pages 10-53 and 7-11.) Which aircraft approach category should be used for a circling approach for a landing on RWY 27?

A — A.
B — B.
C — C.

7-17   J42
(Refer to figure 80 on page 7-11.) How many initial approach fixes serve the VOR/DME RWY 27R (Billings Logan) approach procedure?

A — Three.
B — Four.
C — Five.

7-13. Answer A. GFDICM 7A (Approach Chart Legend)
The touchdown zone elevation (TDZE), 174 feet MSL, is shown on the airport diagram of NOS approach charts. Answer (B), 200 feet AGL, is the height above touchdown (HAT). Answer (C), 270 feet MSL, is the height of two obstructions shown in figure 73: the control tower, and an obstacle near the approach end of RWY 6.

7-14. Answer B. GFDICM 7A (Approach Chart Legend)
When using NOS approach charts, you must refer to the inoperative components table in the front of each NOS approach booklet. (See Appendix 2.) Formerly (prior to October 15, 1992), loss of the middle marker raised the DH 50 feet to 424 feet MSL, and the RVR to 2,400 feet. However, the MM-out penalty no longer applies. Answers (A) and (C) are wrong because the landing minimums do not change.

7-15. Answer C. GFDICM 7A (Approach Chart Legend)
NOS indicates the available approach light systems on the airport diagram with an encircled alphanumeric character. To determine the type of lighting installed, you must refer to the Approach Lighting Systems legend in the front of each booklet. The circled A symbol indicates ALSF-2 approach lighting and high intensity runway lighting (HIRL). Answers (A) and (B) are wrong because VASIs are installed on runways 15 and 33, not runway 6. Also, REIL is listed only for runway 15.

7-16. Answer B. GFDICM 7A (Approach Chart Legend)
The approach category is based on 1.3 times the aircraft's stall speed in the landing configuration at maximum gross landing weight ($1.3 \times V_{S0}$). The stalling speed for this aircraft is 72 kts. (figure 74), which suggests an approach speed of 93.6 kts ($72 \times 1.3 = 93.6$). The approach speed range for Category B is 91 to 120 kts. (see Legend 13 in Appendix 2). The approach speed range for Category A (answer A) is up to 90 kts. Category C (answer C) approach speeds range from 121 to 140 kts.

7-17. Answer B. GFDICM 7A (Approach Chart Legend)
There are four initial approach fixes (IAFs) for the VOR/DME RWY 27R approach, as indicated by the "IAF" notations. These fixes are the BIL VORTAC, MUSTY Intersection, and the intersections on the 16 DME arc at the BIL 157° and 040° radials. Answers (A) and (C), three and five respectively, are inappropriate.

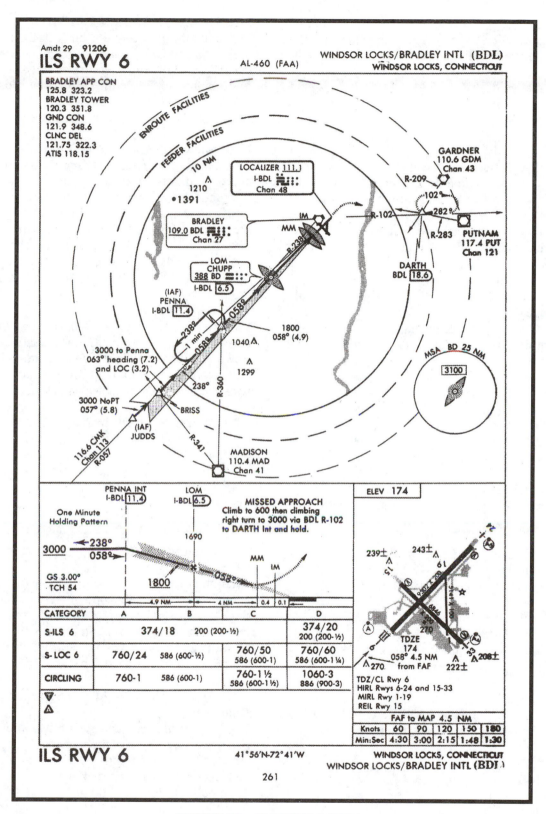

FIGURE 73.—ILS-RWY 6 (BDL).

7-18   J42
(Refer to figure 80 on page 7-11.) What is the TDZE for landing on RWY 27R?

A — 3,649 feet MSL.
B — 3,514 feet MSL.
C — 3,450 feet MSL.

7-19   J18
What obstacle clearance and navigation signal coverage is a pilot assured with the Minimum Sector Altitudes depicted on the IAP charts?

A — 1,000 feet and acceptable navigation signal coverage within a 25 NM radius of the navigation facility.
B — 1,000 feet within a 25 NM radius of the navigation facility but not acceptable navigation signal coverage.
C — 500 feet and acceptable navigation signal coverage within a 10 NM radius of the navigation facility.

7-20   J42
What does the absence of the procedure turn barb on the planview on an approach chart indicate?

A — A procedure turn is not authorized.
B — Teardrop-type procedure turn is authorized.
C — Racetrack-type procedure turn is authorized.

7-21   J42
(Refer to figure 119 on page 7-12.) The final approach fix for the precision approach is located at

A — DENAY Intersection.
B — Glide slope intercept (lightning bolt).
C — ROMEN intersection/locator outer marker.

7-22   J42
(Refer to figure 120 on page 7-13.) Refer to the DEN ILS RWY 35R procedure. The FAF intercept altitude is

A — 7,488 feet MSL.
B — 7,500 feet MSL.
C — 9,000 feet MSL.

7-18. Answer B. GFDICM 7A (IFH)
The touchdown zone elevation (TDZE) for runway 27R at Billings Logan International Airport is identified by the "TDZE 3514" callout in the airport sketch. Answer (A), 3,649 feet MSL, is the airport elevation. Answer (C), 3,450 feet MSL, does not appear on the approach chart.

7-19. Answer B. GFDICM 7A (AIM)
The minimum sector altitudes depicted on instrument approach procedure charts guarantee 1,000 feet clearance within a 25 n.m. radius of the navigational facility shown, but do not guarantee navigational signal or communications coverage at that altitude throughout the 25 n.m. radius area. Acceptable navigational signal coverage (answer A) is not provided. Answer (C), 500 feet within a 10 n.m. radius, is inappropriate.

Minimum sector altitude is referred to as minimum safe altitude in the legend of NOS approach chart booklets. However, definitions in the AIM Glossary indicate that these terms (minimum sector altitude and minimum safe altitude) are practically synonymous.

7-20. Answer A. GFDICM 7A (AIM)
When a procedure turn barb is not depicted, the pilot is expected to fly a straight-in approach, and a procedure turn is not authorized. It does not mean that any other type of course reversal procedure is authorized (answers B and C).

7-21. Answer B. GFDICM 7A (Approach Chart Legend)
On a precision (ILS) approach, the final approach fix is defined as the glide slope intercept point, which is depicted by a lightning bolt on NOS charts. DENAY Intersection (answer A) is an IAF, not the FAF. ROMEN Intersection/LOM (answer C) is the FAF for the nonprecision localizer-only approach.

7-22. Answer B. GFDICM 7A (Approach Chart Legend)
The FAF for an ILS is the glide slope intercept point, designated by a lightning bolt symbol. The FAF intercept altitude is the minimum glide slope intercept altitude, which is shown as 7,500 feet. Above the nonprecision FAF is the number 7,488 (answer A), which is the altitude at which you would cross this fix when on the glide slope centerline. Answer (C), 9,000 feet, is a step-down altitude prior to reaching ENGLE Intersection.

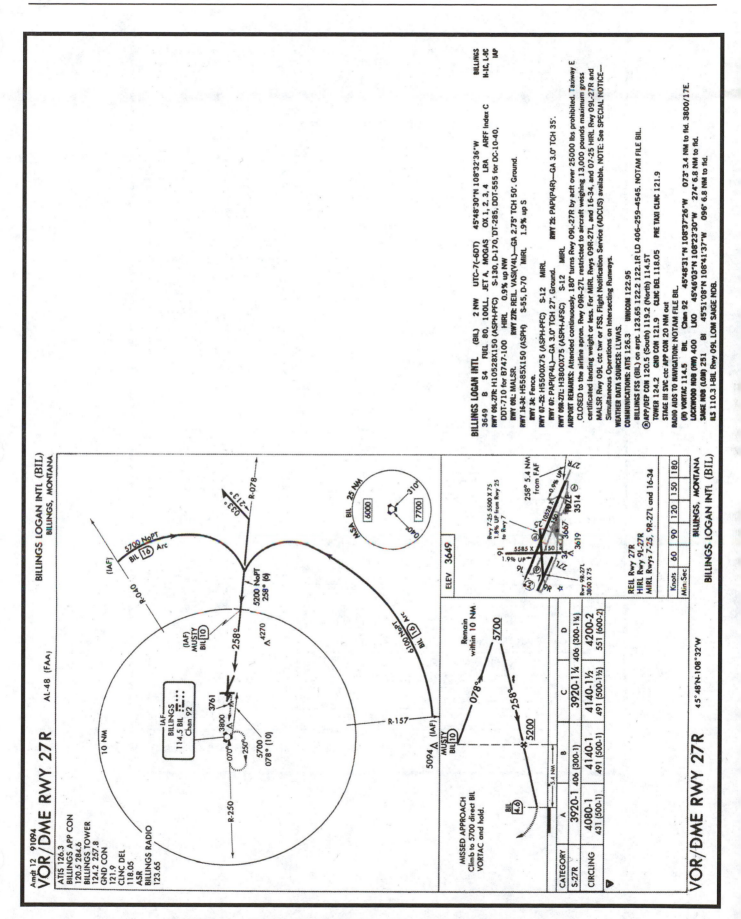

FIGURE 80.—VOR/DME RWY 27R and Airport/Facility Directory (BIL).

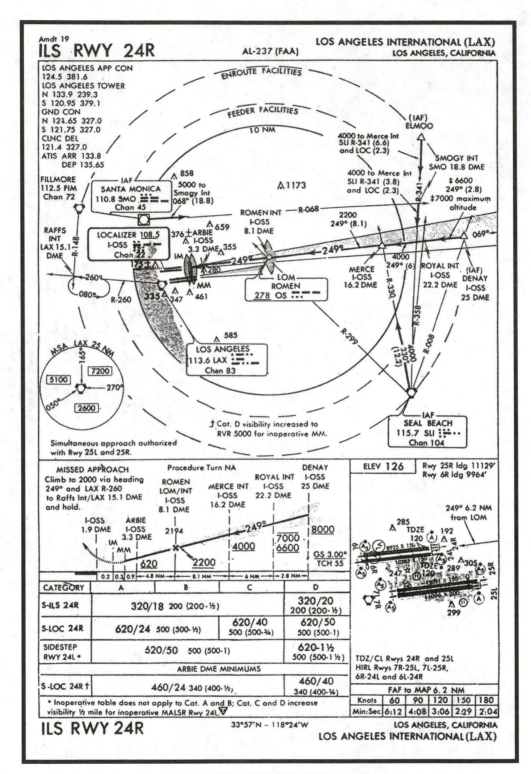

FIGURE 119.—ILS-RWY 24R (LAX).

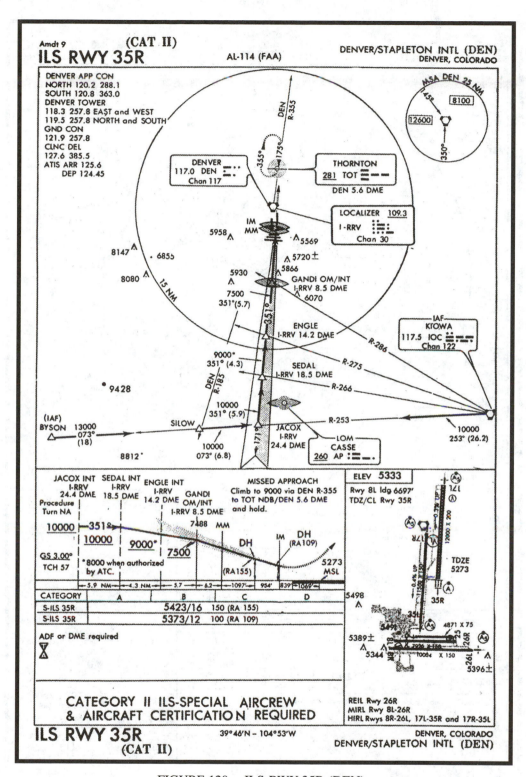

FIGURE 120.—ILS-RWY 35R (DEN).

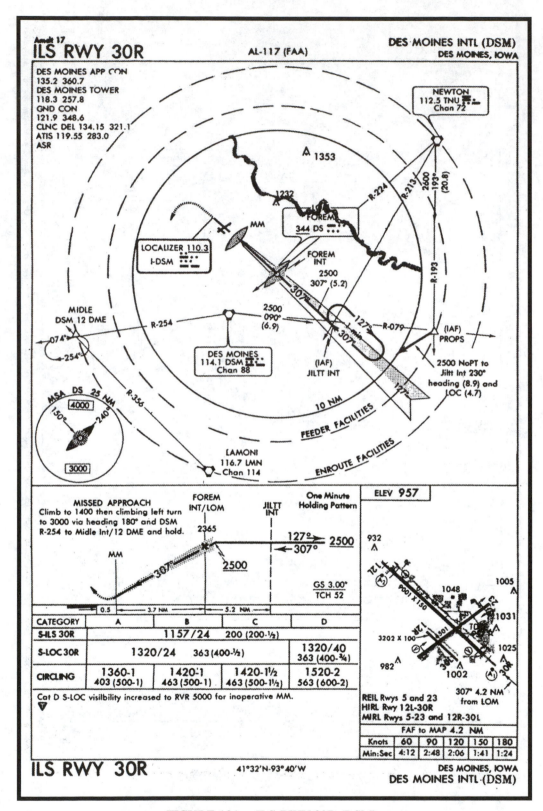

FIGURE 121.—ILS-RWY 30R (DSM).

7-23   J42

(Refer to figure 120 on page 7-13.) The symbol on the planview of the ILS RWY 35R procedure at DEN represents a minimum safe sector altitude within 25 NM of

A — Denver VORTAC.
B — Gandi outer marker.
C — Denver/Stapleton International Airport.

7-24   J42

(Refer to figure 121 on page 7-14.) During the ILS RWY 30R procedure at DSM, the minimum altitude for glide slope interception is

A — 2,365 feet MSL.
B — 2,500 feet MSL.
C — 3,000 feet MSL.

7-25   J42

(Refer to figure 121 on page 7-14.) During the ILS RWY 30R procedure at DSM, what MDA applies should the glide slope become inoperative?

A — 1,157 feet.
B — 1,320 feet.
C — 1,360 feet.

7-26   J42

(Refer to figure 122 on page 7-16.) The missed approach point of the ATL S-LOC 8L procedure is located how far from the LOM?

A — 4.8 NM.
B — 5.1 NM.
C — 5.2 NM.

7-27   J42

(Refer to figure 123 on page 7-17.) What minimum navigation equipment is required to complete the VOR/DME-A procedure?

A — One VOR receiver.
B — One VOR receiver and DME.
C — Two VOR receivers and DME.

7-23. Answer A. GFDICM 7A (AIM)

The minimum safe altitude (MSA) is shown in the upper right corner of this planview and is referenced from the DEN VORTAC (note the DEN identifier above the circle). The MSA usually is based on a VOR, NDB, locator outer marker (LOM) facility, or waypoint, not an outer marker or intersection (answer B), or an airport (answer C).

7-24. Answer B. GFDICM 7A (Approach Chart Legend)

The glide intercept altitude of 2,500 feet is designated by the lightning bolt symbol. Since it is underlined, it is a minimum altitude. Answer (A), 2,365 feet, is the altitude over the nonprecision FAF when on the glide slope centerline. Answer (B), 3,000 feet, is shown as a minimum safe altitude (MSA).

7-25. Answer B. GFDICM 7A (Approach Chart Legend)

When the glide slope becomes inoperative, localizer minimums can be used. The S-LOC MDA is 1,320 for all categories of aircraft. Answer (A), 1,157 feet, is the ILS DH, which requires an operative glide slope. Answer (C), 1,360 feet, is the circling MDA for category A aircraft only. Since circling is not specified in the question, this is not the best answer.

7-26. Answer C. GFDICM 7A (IFH)

The conversion table at the bottom of the chart shows the distance from the nonprecision (LOC) FAF to the MAP. The distance is listed as 5.2 n.m. Answer (A), 4.8 n.m., is shown under the profile view, and is the distance from the nonprecision FAF to the MM. Keep in mind that the depicted missed approach arrow is based on the ILS, not the localizer-only approach. Answer (B), 5.1 n.m., is the total distance from the FAF to the IM, but this is not the nonprecision missed approach point, so this answer is incorrect.

7-27. Answer B. GFDICM 7A (IFH)

VOR/DME on the chart means that both VOR and DME are required for the approach. The -A alphabetic suffix indicates the procedure does not meet criteria for straight-in landing minimums. Since DME is required to determine the FAF and MAP, answer (A) is wrong. Two VOR receivers (answer C) are not required for the "minimum" navigation equipment. The key word here is minimum.

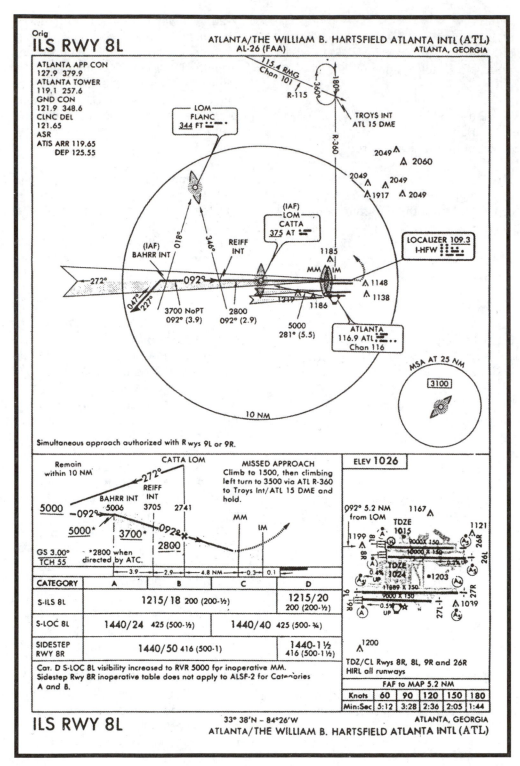

FIGURE 122.—ILS-RWY 8L (ATL).

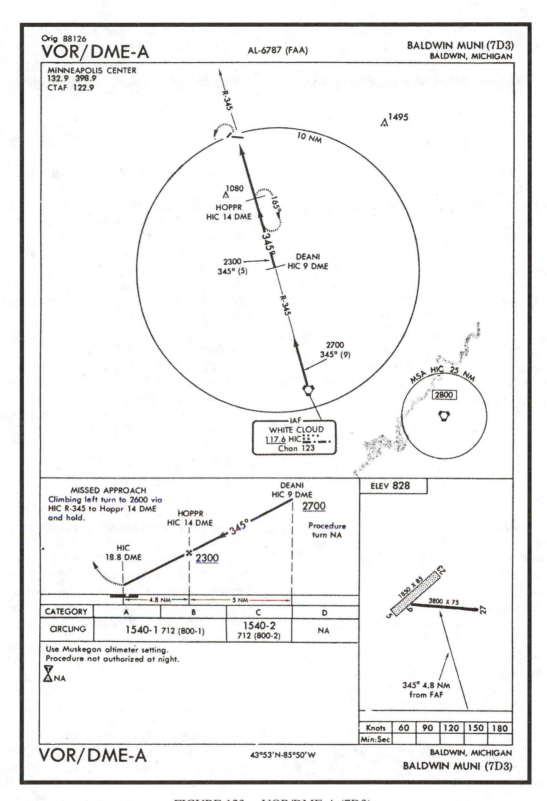

FIGURE 123.—VOR/DME-A (7D3).

7-28   **J42**

(Refer to figure 123 on page 7-17.) The symbol on the planview of the VOR/DME-A procedure at 7D3 represents a minimum safe sector altitude within 25 NM of

A — DEANI Intersection.
B — White Cloud VORTAC.
C — Baldwin Municipal Airport.

7-28. Answer B. GFDICM 7A (AIM)
The letters HIC, above the minimum safe altitude (MSA) circle, identify the White Cloud VORTAC. The MSA is always based upon an NDB or a VOR, not an intersection (answer A) or an airport (answer C).

7-29   **J42**

(Refer to figure 126 on page 7-19.) What landing minimums apply for a 14 CFR part 91 operator at Dothan, AL, using a category C aircraft during a circling LOC 31 approach at 120 knots? (DME available).

A — MDA 860 feet MSL and visibility 2 SM.
B — MDA 860 feet MSL and visibility 1 and 1/2 SM.
C — MDA 720 feet MSL and visibility 3/4 SM.

7-29. Answer B. GFDICM 7A (Approach Chart Legend)
The MDAs given in the answer choices are the published DME minimums for a circling approach. Even if flown at a slower airspeed, aircraft category C must be used. The minimums shown are MDA 860 feet and 1-1/2 s.m visibility. There are no minimums listed as 860-2 (answer A). An MDA of 720 feet is used for the S-LOC (straight-in), not for circling (answer C).

7-30   **J42**

(Refer to figure 126 on page 7-19.) What is the ability to identify the RRS 2.5 stepdown fix worth in terms of localizer circle-to-land minimums for a category C aircraft?

A — Decreases MDA by 20 feet.
B — Decreases visibility by 1/2 SM.
C — Without the stepdown fix, a circling approach is not available.

7-30. Answer A. GFDICM 7A (IFH)
When the RRS 2.5 DME stepdown fix can be identified, the DME minimums apply, and the circling MDA for a category C aircraft is 860 feet. Without DME, you are limited to published circling minimums of 880 feet. Therefore, using DME decreases the MDA by 20 feet. The visibility (answer B) is 1-1/2 s.m. for both DME and non-DME minimums. Answer (C) is wrong because a circling approach with an MDA of 880 feet is available without the stepdown fix.

7-31   **J18**

(Refer to figure 128 on page 8-3.) What is the purpose of the 10,300 MSA on the Price/Carbon County Airport Approach Chart?

A — It provides safe clearance above the highest obstacle in the defined sector out to 25 NM.
B — It provides an altitude above which navigational course guidance is assured.
C — It is the minimum vector altitude for radar vectors in the sector southeast of PUC between 020° and 290° magnetic bearing to PUC VOR.

7-31. Answer A. GFDICM 7A (AIM)
The minimum safe altitude provides at least 1,000 feet of clearance above the highest obstacle in that sector (25 n.m. from the navigation facility). Course guidance from the navaid is not assured (answer B). Minimum vectoring altitudes (answer C) normally are available only to controllers, not pilots.

7-32   **J42**

(Refer to figure 130 on page 7-20.) What are the procedure turn restrictions on the LDA RWY 6 approach at Roanoke Regional?

A — Remain within 10 NM of CLAMM INT and on the north side of the approach course.
B — Remain within 10 NM of the airport on the north side of the approach course.
C — Remain within 10 NM of the outer marker on the north side of the approach course.

7-32. Answer A. GFDICM 7A (AIM)
Both CLAMM Intersection and CNQ NDB are identified on the plan view as initial approach fixes (IAFs). The procedure turn may commence at either fix. The profile view contains a note to remain within 10 n.m. of CLAMM Intersection or the NDB. The plan view also shows the procedure turn on the north side of the final approach course. Unless otherwise specified, the procedure turn distance limit is measured from the procedure turn fix, not the airport (answer B) or the outer marker (answer C).

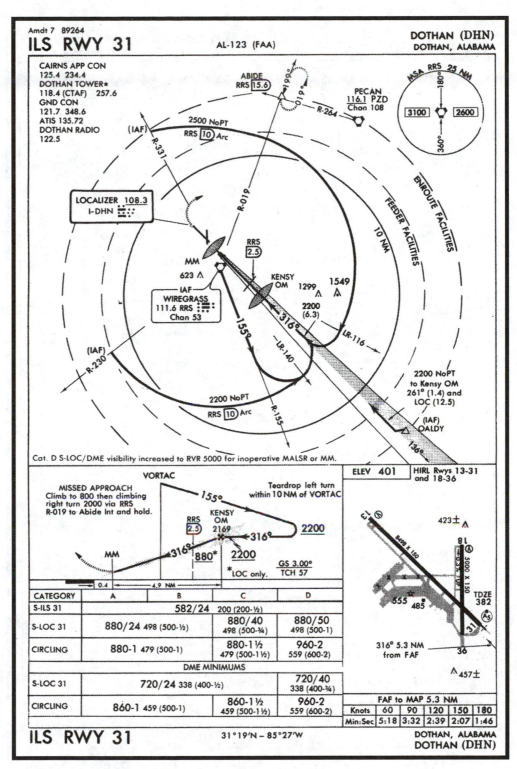

FIGURE 126.—ILS-RWY 31, Dothan, Alabama.

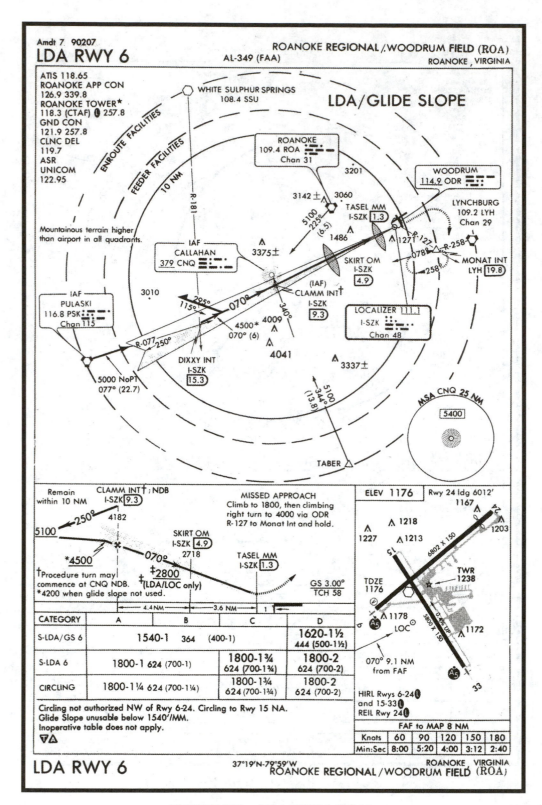

FIGURE 130.—LDA RWY 6 (ROA).

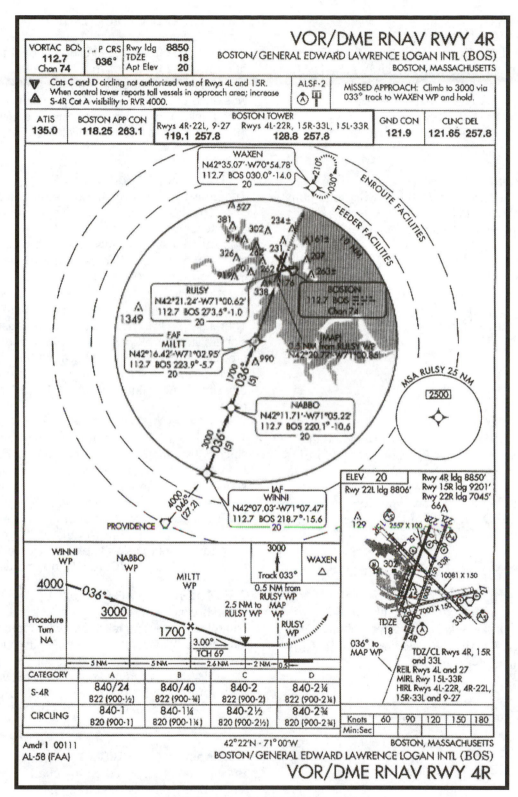

FIGURE 131.—LOC RWY 18 (DEN).

7-33   J42
(Refer to figure 130 on page 7-20.) What are the restrictions regarding circle to land procedures for LDA RWY/GS 6 approach at Roanoke Regional?

A — Circling to runway 24 not authorized.
B — Circling not authorized NW of RWY 6-24.
C — Visibility increased 1/2 mile for circling
      approach.

7-34   J42
(Refer to figure 130 on page 7-20.) At what minimum altitude should you cross CLAMM intersection during the S LDA 6 approach at Roanoke Regional?

A — 4,200 MSL.
B — 4,182 MSL.
C — 2,800 MSL.

7-35   J42
(Refer to figure 130 on page 7-20.) How should the pilot identify the missed approach point for the S LDA GS 6 approach to Roanoke Regional?

A — Arrival at 1,540 feet on the glide slope.
B — Arrival at 1.0 DME on the LDA course.
C — Time expired for distance from OM to MAP

7-36   J42
(Refer to figure 131 on page 7-21.) The control tower at BOS reports "tall vessels" in the approach area. What are the VOR/DME RNAV RWY 4R straight-in approach minimums for Category A aircraft.

A — 890/24.
B — 840/40
C — 890/40..

7-37   J42
(Refer to figure 131 on page 7-21.) What is the landing distance available for the VOR/DME RNAV RWY 4R approach at BOS?

A — 7.000 feet.
B — 10,005 feet.
C — 8,850 feet.

7-33. Answer B. GFDICM 7A (AIM)
Figure 130 contains a note beneath the circling minimums which states that circling is not authorized NW of runway 6-24. Circling to runway 24 is authorized (answer A), as long as you do not circle on the northwest side of runway 6-24. Visibility is listed for the circling minimums, and does not necessarily increase 1/2 mile over the straight-in visibility (answer C).

7-34. Answer A. GFDICM 7A (IFH)
The profile view shows 4,500 feet as the glide slope intercept altitude. It also contains a note (indicated by an asterisk) which shows 4,200 feet when the glide slope is not used. For this reason, a pilot flying a nonprecision approach will cross the FAF at CLAMM Intersection at 4,200 feet MSL. Answer (B) is also plausible. However, the chart lists nonprecision minimums as S-LDA 6, as stated in the question. Therefore, answer (B) is incorrect because the glide slope altitude at CLAMM, 4,182 feet, is used only on a precision approach. Answer (C), 2,800 feet, is a step-down altitude to which the pilot may descend after crossing CLAMM Intersection at 4,200 feet.

7-35. Answer A. GFDICM 7A (IFH)
The S-LDA GS 6 approach requires use of the glide slope, which makes this a precision approach. The missed approach point is the decision height, which is shown as 1,540 feet for category A, B, and C aircraft. Answer (B) is incorrect because a MAP based on DME is for a nonprecision approach. The correct DME is 1.3, not 1.0 DME. Timing (answer C) may also be used for a nonprecision approach, but in this case the time is from the FAF (CLAMM), not the OM.

7-36. Answer B. (FAR 91.175)
In the heading section on figure 131 it states when the control tower reports tall vessels in approach area; increase S-4R Cat A visibility to RVR 4000. The Category A straight in minimums for the VOR/DME RNAV RWY 4R are 840/24, with the tall vessels in the area you should have an RVR of 4000. Answer (A) and (C) are incorrect with a MDA of 890 instead of 840.

7-37. Answer C. (GFDICM 7A)
Runway length depicted on the chart is the physical length of the runway (end-to-end, including displaced thresholds) but excluding areas designated as stopways. Where a displaced threshold is shown and/or part of the runway is otherwise not available for landing an annotation placed above the runway diagram is added to indicated the landing length of the runway. Answer (A) is referring to the total length of runway 9-27. Answer (B) refers to the total runway length of runway 4R.

7-38   J42
(Refer to figure 131 on page 7-21.) During a missed approach from the VOR/DME RNAV RWY 4R approach at BOS, what course should be flown to the missed approach holding waypoint?

A — 036°.
B — Runway heading.
C — 033°.

7-38. Answer C. GFDICM 7A (IFH) (FAR 91.175).
The profile view of the chart shown in figure 131 shows missed approach instructions and a heading of 033° and 3,000 feet to the WAXEN holding fix. Answer (A) is wrong because, 036° is the inbound approach course Answer (B) is wrong because the runway heading of 040° is also incorrect.

7-39   J42
(Refer to figure 131 on page 7-21.) Other than VOR/DME RNAV, what additional navigation equipment is required to conduct the VOR/DME RNAV RWY 4R approach at BOS?

A — None.
B — VNAV.
C — Transponder with altitude encoding and Marker Beacon.

7-39. Answer A. GFDICM 7A (IFH)
The minimum equipment required to fly the approach is indicated by the procedure title and/or notes on the approach chart.

7-40   J18
Which procedure should be followed by a pilot who is circling to land in a Category B airplane, but is maintaining a speed 5 knots faster than the maximum specified for that category?

A — Use the approach minimums appropriate for Category C.
B — Use Category B minimums.
C — Use Category D minimums since they apply to all circling approaches.

7-40. Answer A. GFDICM 7A (IFH)
Obstacle clearance for circling approaches is based on turning radius, which is directly related to speed. Therefore, you should use the approach minimums for the category speeds you are using. If you use Category B minimums (answer B), but fly at a speed for a higher category, you could be outside the circling approach area and would not be guaranteed obstacle clearance. If you fly below Category D airspeeds, there is no point in using Category D minimums (answer C), since the MDA is usually higher than the MDA for lower categories.

7-41   J33
How can an IAF be identified on a Standard Instrument Approach Procedure (SIAP) Chart?

A — All fixes that are labeled IAF.
B — Any fix illustrated within the 10 mile ring other than the FAF or stepdown fix.
C — The procedure turn and the fixes on the feeder facility ring.

7-41. Answer A. GFDICM 7A (AIM)
Initial approach fixes (IAFs) are labeled with the letters "IAF." Answer (B) is incorrect because other fixes within the 10-mile ring may include feeder fixes, missed approach points, and holding fixes. Answer (C) is also incorrect because fixes on the feeder facility ring are not IAFs unless designated by the letters "IAF."

This question is similar to 7-45.

7-42   J42
(Refer to figure 131 on page 7-21.) What determines the MAP for the straight-in VOR/DME RNAV RWY 4R approach at BOS?

A — RULSY waypoint.
B — .5 NM to RULSY waypoint.
C — 2.5 NM to RULSY at 840 feet MSL.

7-42. Answer B. GFDICM 7A (Approach Chart Legend)
The profile view of the VOR/DME RNAV RWY 4R approach chart shows the missed approach profile beginning at .5 NM from RULSY waypoint, There is also a note in the planview, which indicates the MAP is 0.5 NM from RULSY WP.

7-43   B10
RVR minimums for landing are prescribed in an IAP, but RVR is inoperative and cannot be reported for the intended runway at the time. Which of the following would be an operational consideration?

A — RVR minimums which are specified in the procedures should be converted and applied as ground visibility.
B — RVR minimums may be disregarded, providing the runway has an operative HIRL system.
C — RVR minimums may be disregarded, providing all other components of the ILS system are operative.

7-44   J18
Aircraft approach categories are based on

A — certified approach speed at maximum gross weight.
B — 1.3 times the stall speed in landing configuration at maximum gross landing weight.
C — 1.3 times the stall speed at maximum gross weight.

7-45   J18
Which fixes on the IAP Charts are initial approach fixes?

A — Any fix on the en route facilities ring, the feeder facilities ring, and those at the start of arc approaches.
B — Only the fixes at the start of arc approaches and those on either the feeder facilities ring or en route facilities ring that have a transition course shown to the approach procedure.
C — Any fix that is identified by the letters IAF.

7-46   B10
If the RVR is not reported, what meteorological value should you substitute for 2,400 RVR?

A — A ground visibility of 1/2 NM.
B — A slant range visibility of 2,400 feet for the final approach segment of the published approach procedure.
C — A ground visibility of 1/2 SM.

7-43. Answer A. GFDICM 7A (IFH) (FAR 91.175)
When the runway visual range (RVR) equipment is inoperative or not reported, you may covert RVR minimums to ground visibility in statute miles. The conversions are listed in the minimums section of Jeppesen charts, and in a table on NOS Terminal Procedures. Answers (B) and (C) are wrong because you cannot disregard visibility minimums for the approach. You must be able to determine whether you have sufficient visibility to fly the approach.

7-44. Answer B. GFDICM 7A (IFH)
Approach categories are based on computed approach speeds, which are 1.3 V_{S0}. This is 1.3 times the aircraft's power-off stall speed in the landing configuration at the maximum certificated landing weight. Answer (A) does not specify 1.3 times the stall speed (V_{S0}), and maximum gross weight is often different from maximum gross landing weight, especially for larger airplanes. Answer (C) is wrong because it indicates 1.3 time the aircraft's "clean" stalling speed (V_{S1}).

7-45. Answer C. GFDICM 7A (AIM)
Initial approach fixes are specifically indicated on approach procedure charts with the letters "IAF." Other fixes on the chart (answers A and B) are not initial approach fixes, unless they are identified with the letters "IAF."

See explanation for Question 7-41.

7-46. Answer C. GFDICM 7A (Approach Chart Legend) (FAR 91.175)
Jeppesen charts provide both RVR and the equivalent prevailing visibility in miles in the minimums section. NOS Terminal Procedures books contain a table in the front of each volume to convert RVR to miles. Using this table, you will find that 2400 RVR is equivalent to 1/2 s.m. ground visibility. Answer (A) is incorrect because ground visibility is given in statute miles (s.m.), not nautical miles (n.m.). Slant range (answer B) is not reported and cannot be substituted for RVR.

This question is similar to 7-47 and 7-48.

7-47   B10

The RVR minimums for takeoff or landing are published in an IAP, but RVR is inoperative and cannot be reported for the runway at the time. Which of the following would apply?

A — RVR minimums which are specified in the procedure should be converted and applied as ground visibility.
B — RVR minimums may be disregarded, providing the runway has an operative HIRL system.
C — RVR minimums may be disregarded, providing all other components of the ILS system are operative.

7-48   B10

If the RVR equipment is inoperative for an IAP that requires a visibility of 2,400 RVR, how should the pilot expect the visibility requirement to be reported in lieu of the published RVR?

A — As a slant range visibility of 2,400 feet.
B — As an RVR of 2,400 feet.
C — As a ground visibility of 1/2 SM.

7-47. Answer A. GFDICM 7A (Approach Chart Legend) (FAR 91.175)

You would refer to the Jeppesen chart minimums section to find the equivalent prevailing ground visibility, or use the table in the front of the NOS approach chart booklet to convert RVR to prevailing visibility. RVR may not be disregarded (answers B and C), because you must have sufficient visibility to take off or land.

This question is similar to 7-46 and 7-48.

7-48. Answer C. GFDICM 7A (FAR 91.175)

Jeppesen charts provide both RVR and the equivalent prevailing visibility in miles, and NOS approach chart booklets contain a table in the front of each volume to convert RVR to miles. Using this table, you will find that 2400 RVR is equivalent to 1/2 s.m. ground visibility. Answer (A) is incorrect because slant range is not reported and cannot be substituted for RVR. However, you should always keep in mind that slant range visibility is really what you need to acquire the required visual references during an approach. Answer (B) cannot be right because RVR is not available.

See explanations for Questions 7-46 and 7-47.

SECTION B
APPROACH PROCEDURES

PREPARING FOR AN APPROACH

1. After you have been advised as to which approach to expect, you should conduct a thorough approach chart review to familiarize yourself with the specific approach procedure.
2. If ATC does not specify a particular approach but states, *"cleared for approach,"* you may execute any one of the authorized IAPs for that airport.
3. Feeder routes provide a transition from the enroute structure to the IAF or to a facility from which a course reversal is initiated.

STRAIGHT-IN APPROACH AND LANDING

4. The terms straight-in approach and straight-in landing have specific definitions when used in ATC clearances or in reference to landing minimums.
5. A straight-in approach may be initiated from a fix closely aligned with the final approach course, may commence from the completion of a DME arc, or you may receive vectors to the final approach course.
6. A straight-in approach does not require nor authorize a procedure turn or course reversal.
7. A NoPT arrival sector allows flights inbound on Victor airways within the sector to proceed straight in on the final approach course.

RADAR PROCEDURES

8. ATC radar approved for approach control service is used for course guidance to the final approach course, ASR and PAR approaches, and the monitoring of nonradar approaches.
9. Radar vectors to the final approach course provide a method of intercepting and proceeding inbound on the published instrument approach procedure. During an instrument approach procedure, a published course reversal is not required when radar vectors are provided.
10. If it becomes apparent the heading assigned by ATC will cause you to pass through the final approach course, you should maintain that heading and question the controller.

COURSE REVERSALS

11. A course reversal may be depicted on a chart as a procedure turn, a racetrack pattern (holding pattern), or a teardrop procedure. If a teardrop or holding pattern is shown on an approach chart, you must execute the course reversal as depicted. The maximum speed in a course reversal is 200 knots IAS.
12. Course reversals must be completed within the distance specified on the chart which is typically 10 nautical miles from the primary navaid or fix indicated on the approach chart.
13. When more than one circuit of a holding pattern is needed to lose altitude or become better established on course, the additional circuits can be made only if you advise ATC and ATC approves.

TIMED APPROACHES

14. Timed approaches from a holding fix are generally conducted at airports where the radar system for traffic sequencing is out of service or is not available and numerous aircraft are waiting for approach clearance. This can only be conducted at airports which have operating control towers.
15. If more than one missed approach procedure is available, a timed approach from a holding fix may be conducted if none require a course reversal. If only one missed approach procedure is available, a timed approach from a holding fix may be conducted if the reported ceiling and visibility minimums are equal to or greater than the highest prescribed circling minimums for the IAP.
16. When timed approaches are in progress, you will be given advance notice of the time you should leave the holding fix. When making a timed approach from a holding pattern at the outer marker, adjust the holding pattern so you will leave the outer marker inbound at the assigned time.

DESCENDING ON THE APPROACH

17. When you are cleared for an approach while being radar vectored, you must maintain your last assigned altitude until established on a segment of the published approach. If you are above the altitude designated for the course reversal, you may begin descent as soon as you cross the IAF.
18. Normally, you should descend at a rate that allows you to reach the MDA prior to the MAP so that you are in a position to establish a normal rate of descent from the MDA to the runway, using normal maneuvers.

19. To descend below the DH or MDA, you must be able to identify specific visual references, as well as comply with visibility and operating requirements which are listed in FAR 91.175

20. VASI lights can help you maintain the proper descent angle to the runway once you have established visual contact with the runway environment. If a glide slope malfunction occurs during an ILS approach and you have the VASI in sight, you may continue the approach using the VASI glide slope in place of the electronic glideslope.

21. Visual illusions are the product of various runway conditions, terrain features, and atmospheric phenomena which can create the sensation of incorrect height above the runway or incorrect distance from the runway threshold. When landing on a narrower-than-usual runway, the aircraft will appear to be higher than actual, leading to a lower-than-normal approach. An upsloping runway creates the same illusion.

CIRCLING AND SIDESTEP MANEUVERS

22. A circling approach is necessary if the instrument approach course is not aligned within 30° of the runway. In addition, you may find that an unfavorable wind or a runway closure makes a circling approach necessary.

23. Each circling approach is confined to a protected area which varies with aircraft approach category.

24. When executing a circling approach, if you operate at a higher speed than is designated for your aircraft approach category, you should use the minimums of the next higher category.

25. Some approaches have only circling minimums published even when aligned with the runway. You may still execute a straight-in landing if you have the runway in sight in sufficient time to make a normal approach for landing and you have been cleared to land.

26. When cleared to execute a sidestep maneuver, you are expected to fly the approach to the primary runway and begin the approach to a landing on the parallel runway as soon as possible after you have it in sight.

MISSED APPROACHES

27. The most common reason for a missed approach is low visibility conditions that do not permit you to establish required visual cues.

28. If an early missed approach is initiated before reaching the MAP, you should proceed to the missed approach point at or above the MDA or DH before executing a turning maneuver.

29. If you lose visual reference while circling to land from an instrument approach and ATC radar service is not available, you should initiate a missed approach by making a climbing turn toward the landing runway and continue the turn until established on the missed approach course.

VISUAL AND CONTACT APPROACHES

30. If the ceiling is at least 1,000 feet AGL and visibility is at least 3 statute miles, ATC may clear you for a visual approach in lieu of the published approach procedure.

31. ATC can issue a clearance for a contact approach upon your request when the reported ground visibility at the airport is 1 statute mile or greater. ATC cannot initiate a contact approach.

32. Charted Visual Flight Procedures (CVFPs) may be established at some controlled airports for environmental or noise considerations, as well as when necessary for the safety and efficiency of air traffic operations.

7-49   J15

How is your flight plan closed when your destination airport has IFR conditions and there is no control tower or flight service station (FSS) on the field?

A — The ARTCC controller will close your flight plan when you report the runway in sight.

B — You may close your flight plan any time after starting the approach by contacting any FSS or ATC facility.

C — Upon landing, you must close your flight plan by radio or by telephone to any FSS or ATC facility.

7-49. Answer C. GFDICM 7B (AIM)

When landing at an airport without a control tower, you are responsible for closing your IFR flight plan. If the weather conditions are below VFR at the destination airport, you can close your flight plan by radio or telephone to any flight service station or ATC facility. Answer (A) is wrong because an ARTCC controller will not close your flight plan unless you request it. Answer (B) is wrong because you may not close your flight plan until VFR weather minimums can be maintained.

7-50   J17
If only one missed approach procedure is available, which of the following conditions is required when conducting "timed approaches from a holding fix"?

A — The pilot must contact the airport control tower prior to departing the holding fix inbound.
B — The reported ceiling and visibility minimums must be equal to or greater than the highest prescribed circling minimums for the instrument approach procedure.
C — The reported ceiling and visibility minimums must be equal to or greater than the highest prescribed straight-in MDA minimums for the instrument approach procedure.

7-51   J18
Prior to conducting "timed approaches from a holding fix," which one of the following is required:

A — The time required to fly from the primary facility to the field boundary must be determined by a reliable means.
B — The airport where the approach is to be conducted must have a control tower in operation.
C — The pilot must have established two-way communications with the tower before departing the holding fix.

7-52   J18
When making a "timed approach" from a holding fix at the outer marker, the pilot should adjust the

A — holding pattern to start the procedure turn at the assigned time.
B — airspeed at the final approach fix in order to arrive at the missed approach point at the assigned time.
C — holding pattern to leave the final approach fix inbound at the assigned time.

7-53   J18
If the pilot loses visual reference while circling to land from an instrument approach and ATC radar service is not available, the missed approach action should be to

A — execute a climbing turn to parallel the published final approach course and climb to the initial approach altitude.
B — climb to the published circling minimums then proceed direct to the final approach fix.
C — make a climbing turn toward the landing runway and continue the turn until established on the missed approach course.

7-50. Answer B. GFDICM 7B (AIM)
When only one missed approach procedure is available, the weather must be at or above circling minimums for the approach. (A) is wrong because the pilot maintains radio contact with the approach controller until instructed to contact the tower. The weather must be at or above circling, not straight-in, minimums (answer C).

7-51. Answer B. GFDICM 7B (AIM)
A control tower must be in operation at an airport where timed approaches from a holding fix are being conducted. Timing (answer A) is normally determined from the final approach fix to the missed approach point, not the field boundary. Answer (C) is incorrect because the pilot must maintain radio contact with the approach controller until instructed to contact the tower.

7-52. Answer C. GFDICM 7B (AIM)
The pilot is expected to adjust the holding pattern in order to leave the final approach fix inbound at the assigned time. A procedure turn will not be flown (answer A). Pilots should use normal approach airspeeds (answer B). The assigned time is for leaving the final approach fix, not arriving at the missed approach point.

7-53. Answer C. GFDICM 7B (AIM)
An initial climbing turn toward the landing runway should enable the aircraft to remain within the circling and missed approach obstacle clearance areas. The pilot should then intercept and fly the missed approach course. Any other maneuvers (answers A and B) may take the aircraft outside the circling or missed approach protected areas.

7-54   J18

When the approach procedure involves a procedure turn, the maximum speed should not be greater than

A — 180 knots IAS.
B — 200 knots IAS.
C — 250 knots IAS.

7-55   J18

While being radar vectored, an approach clearance is received. The last assigned altitude should be maintained until

A — reaching the FAF.
B — advised to begin descent.
C — established on a segment of a published route or instrument approach procedure.

7-56   J42

(Refer to figure 124 on page 7-30.) What options are available concerning the teardrop course reversal for LOC RWY 35 approach to Duncan/Halliburton Field?

A — If a course reversal is required, only the teardrop can be executed.
B — The point where the turn is begun and the type and rate of turn are optional.
C — A normal procedure turn may be made if the 10 DME limit is not exceeded.

7-57   J42

(Refer to figure 124 on page 7-30.) The point on the teardrop procedure where the turn inbound (LOC RWY 35) Duncan/Halliburton, is initiated is determined by

A — DME and timing to remain within the 10-NM limit.
B — Timing for a 2 minute maximum.
C — Estimating groundspeed and radius of turn.

7-58   J42

(Refer to figure 125 on page 7-31.) If your aircraft was cleared for the ILS RWY 17R at Lincoln Municipal and crossed the Lincoln VOR at 5,000 feet MSL, at what point in the teardrop could a descent to 3,000
feet commence?

A — As soon as intercepting LOC inbound.
B — Immediately.
C — Only at the point authorized by ATC.

7-54. Answer B. GFDICM 7B (AIM)

During a procedure turn, the maximum speed of 200 knots indicated should be observed. Answers (A) and (C) are not maximum airspeed restrictions for a procedure turn.

7-55. Answer C. GFDICM 7B (AIM)

To ensure obstacle clearance, the pilot should maintain the last assigned altitude until established on a segment of a published route or approach procedure. Waiting until the FAF (answer A) may require additional maneuvering to descend in time. When an approach clearance is given, pilots are expected to maintain the published altitudes without being advised to begin descent (answer B).

7-56. Answer A. GFDICM 7B (AIM)

When a tear-drop procedure turn is depicted, as on this chart, and a course reversal is required, the teardrop must be flown. The turn is restricted by the "Remain within 10 n.m." note, and the type and rate of turn are not optional (answer B). The teardrop must be flown as depicted; a normal procedure turn is not an option (answer C).

7-57. Answer A. GFDICM 7B (AIM)

The turn inbound must be initiated in order to remain within the 10 n.m. limit. Either DME or timing may be used. Timing would depend on the aircraft's groundspeed, and is not limited to a 2-minute maximum (answer B). An estimate of the groundspeed and radius of turn (answer C) should be used to calculate the outbound time, but cannot be used alone to determine the turn point.

7-58. Answer B. GFDICM 7B (AIM)

As soon as you cross the IAF to commence the procedure turn, you may start your descent to the procedure turn altitude (3,000 feet). You must maintain the PT altitude until intercepting the localizer inbound. Answer (A) is wrong because you may begin descent prior to this point. Answer (C) is also wrong because when ATC clears you for the approach and does not issue any restrictions, you are expected to fly the approach as published.

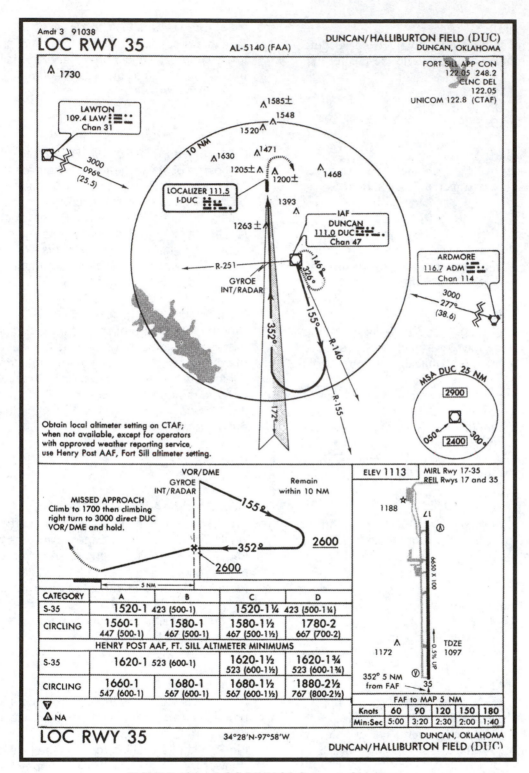

FIGURE 124.—LOC RWY 35, Duncan, Oklahoma.

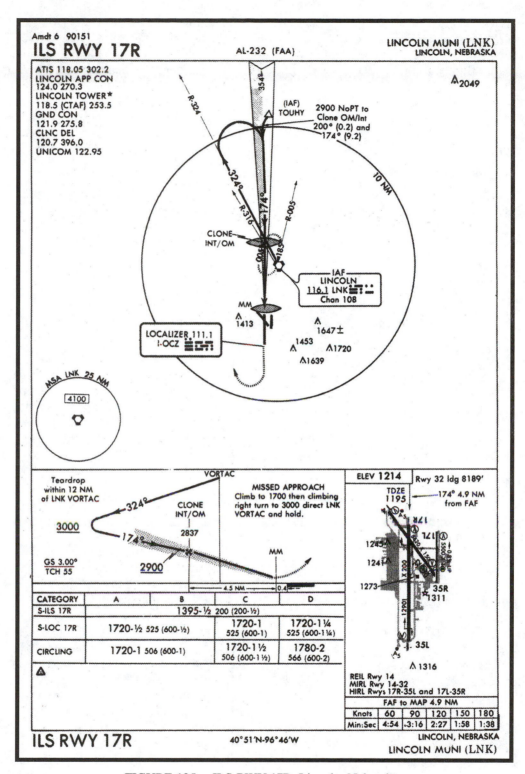

FIGURE 125.—ILS-RWY 17R, Lincoln, Nebraska.

7-59   J18
(Refer to figure 125 on page 7-31.) If cleared for an S-LOC 17R approach at Lincoln Municipal from over TOUHY, it means the flight should

A — land straight in on runway 17R.
B — comply with straight-in landing minimums.
C — begin final approach without making a procedure turn.

7-59. Answer C. GFDICM 7B (AIM)
The route from TOUHY is marked "NoPT," which means that a procedure turn is not authorized. You would intercept the localizer and fly the final approach inbound. An approach clearance at this point does not mean you are cleared to land (answer A), and you may request a different runway than 17R. You may also want to circle to land, and would need to comply with circling minimums instead of straight-in minimums (answer B).

7-60   J33
(Refer to figure 126 on page 7-19.) If cleared for a straight-in LOC approach from over OALDY, it means the flight should

A — land straight in on runway 31.
B — comply with straight-in landing minimums.
C — begin final approach without making a procedure turn.

7-60. Answer C. GFDICM 7B (AIM)
"NoPT" is indicated on the routing from OALDY; a procedure turn is not authorized. See explanation for Question 7-59.

7-61   J18
If an early missed approach is initiated before reaching the MAP, the following procedure should be used unless otherwise cleared by ATC.

A — Proceed to the missed approach point at or above the MDA or DH before executing a turning maneuver.
B — Begin a climbing turn immediately and follow missed approach procedures.
C — Maintain altitude and continue past MAP for 1 minute or 1 mile whichever occurs first.

7-61. Answer A. GFDICM 7B (AIM)
Since obstacle clearance is not guaranteed for a turn prior to the MAP, you should fly the approach to the MAP before turning. Altitude should be at or above the published minimums. Answer (B) is incorrect because an immediate turn before reaching the MAP may not provide adequate obstacle clearance. Answer (C) is also wrong for the same reason. The missed approach should be flown as published.

7-62   J18
When more than one circuit of the holding pattern is needed to lose altitude or become better established on course, the additional circuits can be made

A — at pilot's discretion.
B — only in an emergency.
C — only if pilot advises ATC and ATC approves.

7-62. Answer C. GFDICM 7B (AIM)
When cleared for an approach by ATC, you are expected to commence the approach inbound without additional turns in holding. If extra circuits in the holding pattern are needed, you must receive approval from ATC. To allow ATC to plan for following aircraft, the additional turns in holding are not left to the discretion of the pilot (answer A). An emergency (answer B) is not required; you may ask for extra turns in holding for any reason.

7-63   J18
When simultaneous approaches are in progress, how does each pilot receive radar advisories?

A — On tower frequency.
B — On approach control frequency.
C — One pilot on tower frequency and the other on approach control frequency.

7-63. Answer A. GFDICM 7B (AIM)
At some point on the final approach, pilots are instructed to monitor the tower frequency. The radar controller has the capability to override the tower controller on the tower frequency to issue advisories, if required. The approach control frequency (answer B) is no longer used by the pilot after transfer to the tower frequency. Answer (C) is wrong. Both pilots flying simultaneous approaches should be on tower frequency.

7-64   J18
During an instrument approach, under what conditions, if any, is the holding pattern course reversal not required?

A — When radar vectors are provided.
B — When cleared for the approach.
C — None, since it is always mandatory.

7-65   J18
During an instrument precision approach, terrain and obstacle clearance depends on adherence to

A — minimum altitude shown on the IAP.
B — terrain contour information.
C — natural and man-made reference point information.

7-66   J42
(Refer to figure 133 on page 8-14.) How should a pilot reverse course to get established on the inbound course of the ILS RWY 9, if radar vectoring or the three IAF's are not utilized?

A — Execute a standard 45° procedure turn toward Seal Beach VORTAC or Pomona VORTAC.
B — Make an appropriate entry to the depicted holding pattern at Swan Lake OM/INT.
C — Use any type of procedure turn, but remain within 10 NM of Riverside VOR.

7-67   B10
A pilot is making an ILS approach and is past the OM to a runway which has a VASI. What action should the pilot take if an electronic glide slope malfunction occurs and the pilot has the VASI in sight?

A — The pilot should inform ATC of the malfunction and then descend immediately to the localizer DH and make a localizer approach.
B — The pilot may continue the approach and use the VASI glide slope in place of the electronic glide slope.
C — The pilot must request an LOC approach, and may descend below the VASI at the pilots discretion.

7-64. Answer A. GFDICM 7B (AIM)
When a holding pattern is used in lieu of a procedure turn, it must be followed, except when "NoPT" is shown or when you are given radar vectors. When cleared for the approach (answer B) without any other instructions, you are expected to fly the holding pattern course reversal as depicted. Answer (C) is wrong because of the two exceptions listed above.

7-65. Answer A. GFDICM 7B (AIM)
The instrument approach procedures are designed to provide terrain and obstacle clearance if you observe the depicted altitudes, flight paths, and minimums. Terrain contour information (answer B) is for reference only and would not necessarily provide adequate obstacle clearance. Man-made reference points (answer C) are used to depict the location and altitude of obstacles and would not provide clearance.

7-66. Answer B. GFDICM 7B (IFH)
When not utilizing one of the three IAFs or radar vectors for navigation to the final approach, you are expected to proceed to the holding fix and enter the depicted holding pattern at the Swan Lake outer marker. A solid heavy line indicates that this is a holding pattern used in lieu of a procedure turn. A procedure turn of any kind (answers A and C) is not authorized.

7-67. Answer B. GFDICM 7B (FAR 91.175, 91.129)
When the ILS glide slope fails, you may continue the approach to localizer-only minimums, and, if you have sufficient visual references for the intended runway, may continue the approach visually. In this case, the VASI may be used, and you should follow the VASI glide path. Answer (A) is not correct because a localizer approach has an MDA, not a DH. Answer (C) is wrong because you may continue the approach to localizer minimums, and you must not descend below the visual approach slope indicator (VASI) glide path until necessary for landing.

7-68   J18

You arrive at your destination airport on an IFR flight plan. Which is a prerequisite condition for the performance of a contact approach?

A — A ground visibility of at least 2 SM.
B — A flight visibility of at least 1/2 NM.
C — Clear of clouds and at least 1 SM flight visibility.

7-69   J18

You are being vectored to the ILS approach course, but have not been cleared for the approach. It becomes evident that you will pass through the localizer course. What action should be taken?

A — Turn outbound and make a procedure turn.
B — Continue on the assigned heading and query ATC.
C — Start a turn to the inbound heading and inquire if you are cleared for the approach.

7-70   J18

When cleared to execute a published sidestep maneuver for a specific approach and landing on the parallel runway, at what point is the pilot expected to commence this maneuver?

A — At the published minimum altitude for a circling approach.
B — As soon as possible after the runway or runway environment is in sight.
C — At the localizer MDA minimum and when the runway is in sight.

7-71   J18

When may a pilot make a straight-in landing, if using an IAP having only circling minimums?

A — A straight-in landing may not be made, but the pilot may continue to the runway at MDA and then circle to land on the runway.
B — The pilot may land straight-in if the runway is the active runway and he has been cleared to land.
C — A straight-in landing may be made if the pilot has the runway in sight in sufficient time to make a normal approach for landing, and has been cleared to land.

7-68. Answer C. GFDICM 3C (AIM)

A contact approach cannot be initiated by ATC. This procedure may be used instead of the published procedure to expedite your arrival, as long as the airport has a standard or special instrument approach procedure, and you can remain clear of clouds with a reported visibility of at least 1 statute mile.

7-69. Answer B. GFDICM 7B (AIM)

Sometimes, ATC controllers will vector you through the final approach course to achieve traffic spacing. You should be informed of such an action; if not, maintain your heading and question the controller. Answers (A) and (C) are incorrect because you should not change heading or altitude without clearance from ATC.

7-70. Answer B. GFDICM 7B (AIM)

To enhance traffic separation and obstacle clearance, you should maneuver to the parallel runway as soon as you have it or the runway environment in sight. If the runway environment is not yet in sight, you should descend to the published sidestep minimums, not circling or localizer MDA minimums (answers A and C).

7-71. Answer C. GFDICM 7B (AIM)

Circling minimums only are required when runway and final approach course alignment is exceeded by 30° or more. In this case, straight-in minimums are not published. However, if you have the runway in sight and no excessive maneuvering is required, you may continue straight in for landing. At a tower-controlled airport, you must also be cleared to land. At nontowered airports, it is a good practice to overfly the airport to observe traffic and wind indicators before landing. Answer (A) is wrong because you can make a straight-in landing if the above conditions are met. Answer (B) is incorrect because you must have the runway in sight in time to maneuver for a normal landing.

7-72   J18

While being vectored, if crossing the ILS final approach course becomes imminent and an approach clearance has not been issued, what action should be taken by the pilot?

A — Turn outbound on the final approach course, execute a procedure turn, an inform ATC.

B — Turn inbound and execute the missed approach procedure at the outer marker if approach clearance has not been received.

C — Maintain the last assigned heading and query ATC.

7-73   J17

Which of the following conditions is required before "timed approaches from a holding fix" may be conducted?

A — If more than one missed approach procedure is available, only one may require a course reversal.

B — If more than one missed approach procedure is available, none may require a course reversal.

C — Direct communication between the pilot and the tower must be established prior to beginning the approach.

7-74   J18

Assume this clearance is received:

"CLEARED FOR ILS RUNWAY 07 LEFT APPROACH, SIDE-STEP TO RUNWAY 07 RIGHT."

When would the pilot be expected to commence the side-step maneuver?

A — As soon as possible after the runway environment is in sight.

B — Any time after becoming aligned with the final approach course of Runway 07 left, and after passing the final approach fix.

C — After reaching the circling minimums for Runway 07 right.

7-75   J31

Due to visual illusion, when landing on a narrower-than-usual runway, the aircraft will appear to be

A — higher than actual, leading to a lower-than-normal approach.

B — lower than actual, leading to a higher-than-normal approach.

C — higher than actual, leading to a higher-than-normal approach.

7-72. Answer C. GFDICM 7B (AIM)

Air traffic controllers will occasionally need to increase traffic separation by giving aircraft a vector through the ILS final approach course. You should be notified when this happens, but if not, maintain the last assigned heading and ask the controller for clarification. You should not deviate from a heading issued by approach control as implied by answers (A) and (B).

This question is similar to 7-69.

7-73. Answer B. GFDICM 7B (AIM)

If more than one missed approach procedure is available, none of them can require a course reversal. Presumably, this will prevent conflicts with inbound traffic. Answer (A) is wrong because no missed approach procedure can require a course reversal. You must maintain direct communication with the center or approach controller during the approach (answer C) until instructed to contact the tower.

7-74. Answer A. GFDICM 7B (AIM)

One benefit of a side-step is that it expedites arrivals of aircraft flying an ILS approach. For this reason, you should begin the side-step maneuver as soon as you can after establishing visual contact with the runway environment. Answer (B) is incorrect because you must have the runway environment in sight. Answer (C) is wrong because circling minimums may be different from side-step minimums (normally lower), and you should begin the maneuver as soon as you have the runway environment in sight.

7-75. Answer A. GFDICM 7B (IFH)

A narrower-than-usual runway can create the illusion that you are higher than you actually are, leading to a lower approach. Answer (B) corresponds to a wider than usual runway and is incorrect. Answer (C) is incorrect because a lower-than-normal approach would result.

7-76   J31
What visual illusion creates the same effect as a
narrower-than-usual runway?

A — An upsloping runway.
B — A wider-than-usual runway.
C — A downsloping runway.

7-76. Answer A. GFDICM 7B (IFH)
An upsloping runway can create the illusion that your
aircraft is higher than it actually is, leading to a lower
approach. A wider-than-usual runway (answer B) can
create an illusion that you are lower than you actually
are, leading to a higher approach. A downsloping
runway (answer C) can create the illusion that the
aircraft is lower than it actually is, leading to a
higher approach.

7-77   J42
(Refer to figure 49 on page 8-7.) When conducting the
LOC/DME RWY 21 approach at PDX, what is the
Minimum Safe Altitude (MSA) while maneuvering
between the BTG VORTAC and CREAK intersection?

A — 3,400 feet MSL.
B — 5,700 feet MSL.
C — 6,100 feet MSL.

**7-77. Answer C. GFDICM 7A (Approach Chart
Legend)**
Between 300∞ and 130∞, in the northeast sector, the
MSA on Figure 49 is 6100 feet MSL. 3,400 feet MSL
represents the southwest sector. 5,700 feet MSL rep-
resents the minimum altitude to be flown until reaching
CREAK intersection inbound.

7-78   J42
(Refer to figure 49 on page 8-7.)You have been
cleared to the CREAK intersection via the BTG 054°
radial at 7,000 feet. Approaching CREAK, you are
cleared for the LOC/DME RWY 21 approach to PDX.
Descent to procedure turn altitude should not begin
prior to

A — completion of the procedure turn, and established
on the localizer.
B — CREAK outbound.
C — intercepting the glide slope.

7-78. Answer B. (GFDICM 8B)
Once cleared for the approach, if you are above the
altitude designated for course reversal, you may begin
descent as soon as you cross the IAF, which in this
case, is CREAK Intersection. Answer (A) is incorrect,
because you can descend to procedure turn altitude
once established outbound on the localizer prior to the
procedure turn. Answer (C) request descending to procedure turn altitude upon intercepting the glide slope,
this is incorrect as well.

7-79   J42
(Refer to figure 49 on page 8-7.) What is the usable
runway length for landing on runway 21 at PDX?

A — 5,957 feet.
B — 7,000 feet.
C — 7,900 feet.

7-79. Answer A. GFDICM 8C
Runway length depicted on the chart is the physical
length of the runway (end-to-end, including displaced
thresholds) but excluding areas designated as stopways. Where a displaced threshold is shown and/or
part of the runway is otherwise not available for landing an annotation placed above the runway diagram is
added to indicated the landing length of the runway.
Answer (B) 7,000 feet represents a distance including
displaced thresholds and other parts of the runway not
available for landing. Answer (C) is not a valid distance for runway 21 at PDX.

CHAPTER 8

INSTRUMENT APPROACHES

SECTION A
VOR AND NDB APPROACHES

1. VOR and NDB approaches primarily fall into two categories — those that use an on-airport facility and those with an off-airport facility. On approaches with on-airport navaids, the FAP often serves as the FAF.
2. Preparation to fly an approach should begin well before flying the procedure. Determine which approaches are in use or likely to be in use at the destination airport, and review the approach procedures as early as possible. Obtain weather information, if possible, for the destination airport and analyze whether a successful approach is likely.
3. ATC may clear you to fly the approach of your choice, but they will more likely clear you for a specific approach.
4. A published procedure turn or similar course reversal is mandatory unless you are vectored to the final approach course by ATC, or unless your particular approach transition indicates NoPT. Typically, you accomplish a course reversal by flying outbound for two minutes, turning to a charted heading 45° left or right of your outbound course and flying for one minute, then making a 180° opposite direction turn back to re-intercept the inbound course.
5. When cleared for an approach, you generally should descend promptly to the minimum altitude published for your current route segment or approach transition, or other altitude assigned by ATC.
6. Complete your before landing checklist prior to the FAF, or if there is no FAF, before intercepting the final approach course. If you have retractable landing gear, it is generally best to extend it when starting your descent inbound to the FAF.
7. Make sure you know what rate of descent is required to reach stepdown altitudes or the MDA by the appropriate time.
8. If you do not have the runway environment in sight when reaching the MDA, or if you lose sight of it at any time while circling, it is imperative that you immediately execute the missed approach procedure.
9. If you have the runway environment in sight with the required visibility, you may land. Do not descend below the MDA until you are in a position from which you can safely descend for landing.
10. When executing a missed approach, notify ATC, and, depending on your circumstances, request a clearance to fly the approach again, or request a clearance to your alternate.
11. DME is required on certain approaches that indicate DME in the procedure title. Even on those approaches that do not require DME, using DME to identify stepdown fixes may allow lower minimums.
12. NDB approach procedures are similar to VOR approaches. However, the precision with which you complete the approach is dependent on your skill in ADF tracking and on the accuracy of your heading indicator.

8-1   J42
(Refer to figure 127 on page 8-2.) If cleared for NDB RWY 28 approach (Lancaster/Fairfield) over ZZV VOR, the flight would be expected to

Category A aircraft

Last assigned altitude 3,000 feet

A — proceed straight in from CRISY, descending to MDA after CASER.
B — proceed to CRISY, then execute the teardrop procedure as depicted on the approach chart.
C — proceed direct to CASER, then straight in to S-28 minimums of 1620-1.

8-1. Answer A. GFDICM 8A (AIM)
Near the ZZV VOR is the note "NoPT." This indicates that a procedure turn is not authorized for an approach beginning at the ZZV IAF. You are expected to fly the published routing straight in from CRISY, and descend at the FAF to the S-28 (straight-in) minimums of 1,620 feet, using the published visibility of 1 s.m. Flying the teardrop (answer B) is not authorized unless approved by ATC. The published transition routing from ZZV VOR is to CRISY, then CASER, not direct to CASER (answer C).

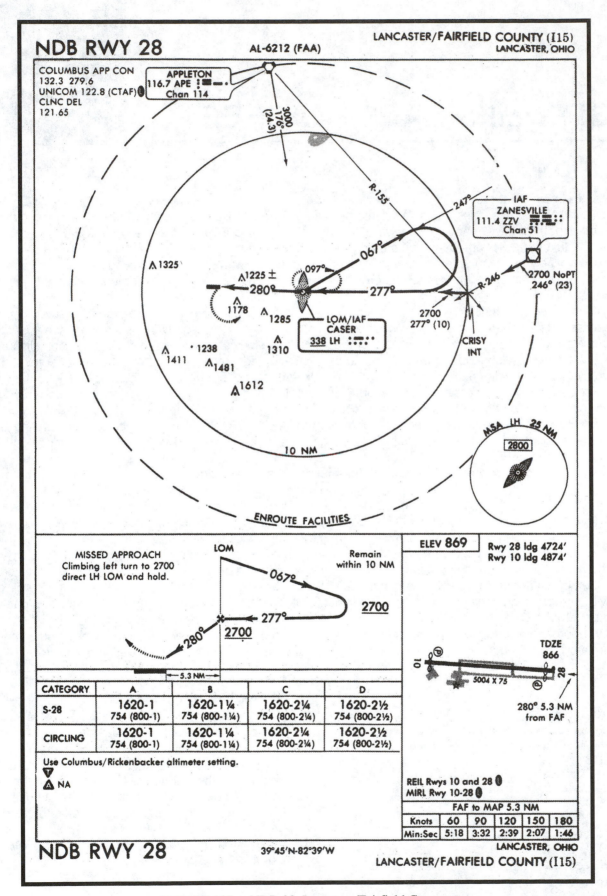

FIGURE 127.—NDB 28, Lancaster/Fairfield County.

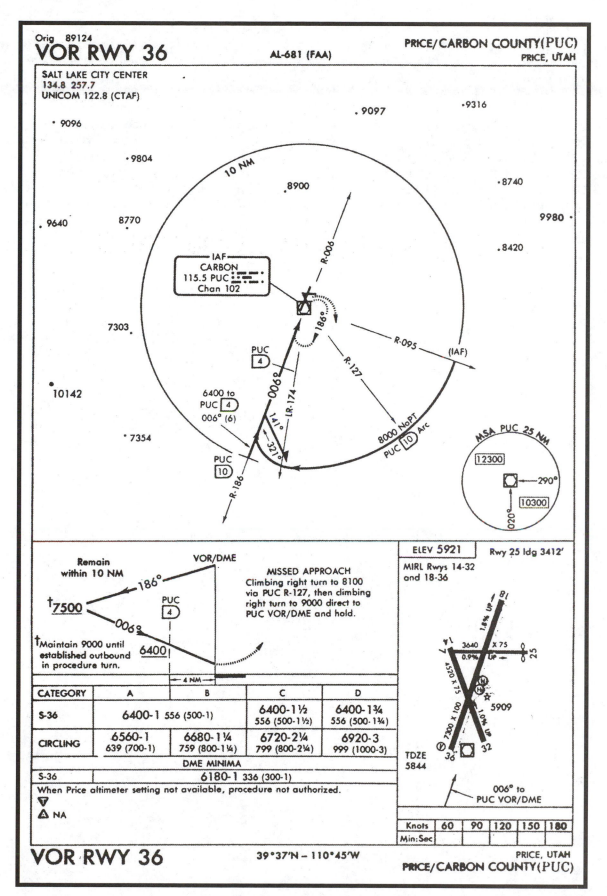

FIGURE 128.—VOR RWY 36 (PUC)

8-2   J42

(Refer to figure 128 on page 8-3.) At which points may you initiate a descent to the next lower minimum altitude when cleared for the VOR RWY 36 approach, from the PUC R 095 IAF (DME operative)?

A — Start descent from 8,000 when established on final, from 7,500 when at the 4 DME fix, and from 6,180 when landing requirements are met.
B — Start descent from 8,000 when established on the PUC R-186, from 6,400 at the 4 DME fix, and from 6,180 when landing requirements are met.
C — Start descent from 8,000 at the R-127, from 6,400 at the LR-127, from 6,180 at the 4 DME fix.

8-2. Answer B. GFDICM 8A (IFH)

You would remain at 8,000 feet while on the arc until established on the 186° radial inbound. Then descend to 6,400 feet until passing the 4 DME fix. At that point, descend to the MDA of 6,180 feet and remain at that altitude until landing requirements are met. Answer (A) includes the 7,500 feet procedure turn altitude, which applies only for a procedure turn, not for the 10 DME arc. Answer (C) is wrong for several reasons: the 127° radial has nothing to do with the descents; it is used for the missed approach, and descent from 6,180 feet is allowed only when landing requirements are met, not at the 4 DME fix.

SECTION B
ILS APPROACHES

OVERVIEW

1. The instrument landing system (ILS) is a precision approach navigational aid which provides highly accurate course, glide slope, and distance guidance to a given runway. ILS approaches are classified as Category I, Category II, or Category III.
2. The ILS localizer transmitter emits a navigational signal from the far end of the runway to provide you with information regarding your alignment with the runway centerline.

GLIDE SLOPE

3. The glide slope signal provides vertical navigation information for descent to the lowest authorized decision height for the associated approach procedure. The glide slope may not be reliable below decision height.
4. If the glide slope is inoperative or fails during your approach, the localizer (GS out) minimums apply. In this case, you may continue the approach to the applicable MDA.
5. Prior to intercepting the ILS glide slope, you should concentrate on stabilizing airspeed and altitude while establishing a magnetic heading which will maintain the aircraft on the localizer centerline. Once your descent rate stabilizes, use power as needed to maintain a constant approach speed.

OTHER ILS COMPONENTS

6. Usually an ILS includes an outer marker (OM) and middle marker (MM). An inner marker (IM) is installed at locations where Category II and III ILS operations have been certified.
7. When a compass locator is installed in conjunction with the outer marker, it is called an outer compass locator (LOM). When a compass locator is collocated with the middle marker, it is referred to as a middle compass locator (LMM). The LOM identifier is the first two letters of the localizer identifier. The LMM identifier is the last two letters of the localizer identifier.
8. A compass locator, precision radar, surveillance radar, or published DME, VOR, or NDB fixes may be substituted for the outer marker.
9. The glide slope centerline normally intersects the middle marker approximately 200 feet above the touchdown zone.
10. When the aircraft passes through the signal array of a marker beacon, a colored light flashes on the marker beacon receiver and a Morse code identification sounds. The outer marker is indicated by a blue light and a series of dashes. The middle marker is an amber light with a higher pitched series of dots and dashes.
11. Certain approach and runway lighting configurations can qualify precision approaches for lower minimums. If an ILS visual aid is inoperative, the visibility requirements are raised on approaches where 1,800 RVR is authorized.
12. Higher landing minimums may be required if some components of an ILS are inoperative. If more than one component is not available for use, you should adjust the minimums by applying only the greatest increase in altitude and/or visibility required by the failure of a single component.

INTERPRETING THE INSTRUMENTS

13. When using a basic VOR indicator, normal sensing occurs inbound on the front course and outbound on the back course. Reverse sensing occurs inbound on the back course and outbound on the front course.
14. You can avoid reverse sensing when using an HSI by setting the published inbound course under the course index. This applies regardless of your direction of travel, whether inbound or outbound on either the front or back course.
15. Full-scale deviation of the glide slope needle is 0.7° above or below the center of the glide slope beam.

FLYING THE APPROACH

16. The rate of descent you must maintain to stay on glide slope must decrease if your groundspeed decreases, and vice versa. If the glide slope and localizer are centered but your airspeed is too fast, your initial adjustment should be to reduce power.
17. Since localizer and glide slope indications become more sensitive as you get closer to the runway, you should strive to fly an ILS approach so that you do not need heading corrections greater than 2° after you have passed the outer marker.

18. On an ILS approach, you must execute a missed approach if you have not established the required visual references at the DH.
19. When advised to change to advisory frequency, you should broadcast your position and intentions on the CTAF.

ILS/DME

20. The procedures you use to fly an ILS/DME approach are essentially the same as any other ILS approach except for the requirement to identify approach fixes using DME.
21. When DME is available through the localizer frequency, Jeppesen charts publish the notation, ILS/DME, on the top of the facility box. On NOS charts, a DME/TACAN channel is shown in the facility box.

PARALLEL AND SIMULTANEOUS APPROACHES

22. Parallel (dependent) ILS approach operations may be conducted on parallel runways with centerlines at least 2,500 feet apart. Simultaneous (independent) parallel ILS approaches may be conducted to airports with parallel runway centerlines separated by 4,300 to 9,000 feet. When certain requirements are met, including the installation of a precision runway monitor, simultaneous close parallel ILS approach procedures may be established at airports with parallel runway centerlines less than 4,300 feet apart.
23. You will be informed by ATC or through the ATIS broadcast if parallel approaches are in progress. A parallel ILS approach provides aircraft with a minimum of two miles separation between successive aircraft on the adjacent localizer course.
24. When simultaneous approaches are in progress, each pilot may receive radar advisories on the tower frequency.

OTHER APPROACH FACILITIES

25. A localizer-type directional aid (LDA) is an approach system which uses a localizer course that is not aligned with the runway centerline. If the final approach course is aligned to within 30° of the runway centerline, straight-in landing minimums may be available. The LDA course width is between 3° and 6°.
26. A simplified directional facility (SDF) course is fixed at either 6° or 12° wide. Since most SDF courses are aligned within 3° of the runway bearing, SDF approaches are typically published with straight-in minimums.
27. The microwave landing system (MLS) offers a precision approach alternative to airports where interference from obstacles and/or high power FM stations makes the installation of ILS difficult or impossible. An MLS is identified by the Morse code for the letter "M" followed by the three-letter identifier for the facility.

8-3   J01
(Refer to figure 73 on page 7-9.) Which sequence of marker beacon indicator lights, and their respective codes, will you receive on the ILS RWY 6 approach procedure to the MAP?

A—Blue — alternate dots and dashes; amber — dashes.
B—Amber — alternate dots and dashes; blue — dashes.
C—Blue — dashes; amber — alternate dots and dashes.

8-3. Answer C. GFDICM 8B (AIM)
When flying this approach, you will cross both the outer and middle markers. Note that you will reach the ILS missed approach point (MAP) prior to the inner marker. The outer marker is identified by continuous dashes at the rate of two per second, and a flashing blue light. The middle marker is identified by alternate dots and dashes and an amber beacon light. Answers (A) and (B) do not have the proper sequence of visual and aural signals.

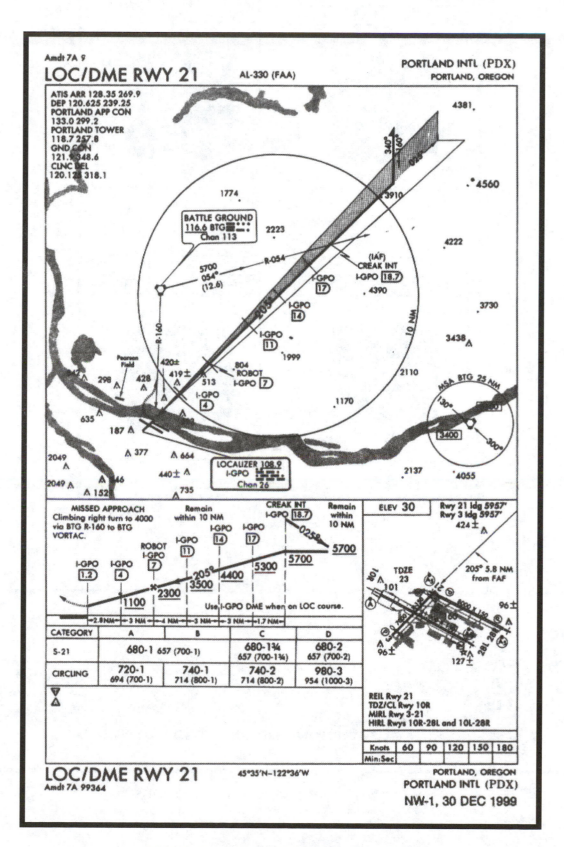

FIGURE 49.—LORAN RNAV RWY 10R (PDX)

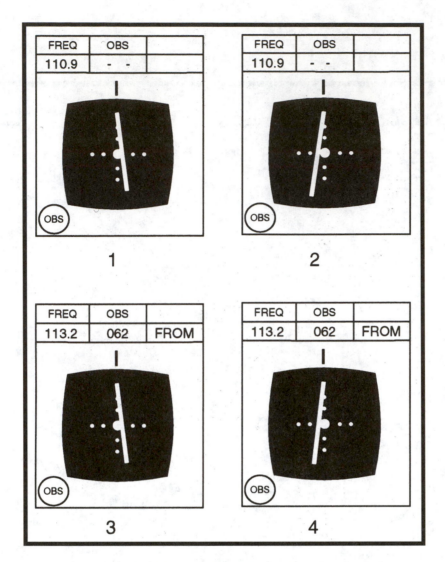

FIGURE 86.—CDI and OBS Indicators.

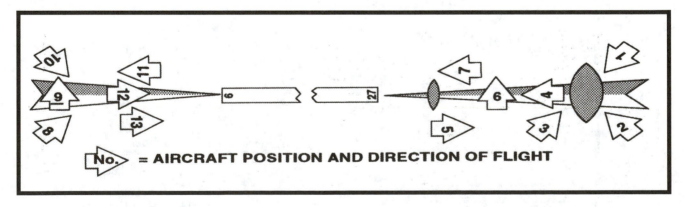

FIGURE 96.—Aircraft Position and Direction of Flight.

8-4   J40

(Refer to figures 85 and 86 on pages 4-8 and 8-8.) Which combination of indications confirm that you are approaching WAGGE Intersection slightly to the right of the LOC centerline on departure?

A — 1 and 3.
B — 1 and 4.
C — 2 and 3.

8-4. Answer C. GFDICM 8B (IFH)

When outbound on the localizer backcourse, you will have correct sensing, so a fly left (CDI 2) is appropriate. When approaching WAGGE, you will have a fly right because you are north of, and approaching, the 062° radial of the SWR VORTAC. CDI 3 indicates you are approaching WAGGE. Answers (A) and (B) are wrong because CDI 1 is showing a fly right, not a fly left.

8-5   H831

(Refer to figures 96 and 97 on pages 8-8 and 8-10.) To which aircraft position(s) does HSI presentation "A" correspond?

A — 9 and 6.
B — 9 only.
C — 6 only.

8-5. Answer A. GFDICM 8B (IFH)

Both aircraft number 9 and 6 are on a heading of north, directly over the extended centerline. This is indicated by the localizer, which from either position, shows a centered CDI. Neither 9 only (B) nor 6 only (C) would be the most correct answer.

8-6   H831

(Refer to figures 96 and 97 on pages 8-8 and 8-10.) To which aircraft position(s) does HSI presentation "B" correspond?

A — 11.
B — 5 and 13.
C — 7 and 11.

8-6. Answer B. GFDICM 8B (IFH)

Both aircraft positions 5 and 13 are on a heading of 090°, the opposite direction of the localizer. Since both of these aircraft are right or south of the localizer course, their CDIs show a deflection to the right. If the HSI had the front course dialed in, the aircraft in positions 5 and 13 would experience proper sensing. The aircraft position 11 (answer A) is incorrect, since it is heading 270°, and aircraft positions 7 and 11 (answer C) are also heading 270° instead of 090°.

8-7   H831

(Refer to figures 96 and 97 on pages 8-8 and 8-10.) To which aircraft position does HSI presentation "C" correspond?

A — 9.
B — 4.
C — 12.

8-7. Answer C. GFDICM 8B (IFH)

The aircraft in position 12 is heading 090° inbound on the back course with the back course set and the CDI is centered. The aircraft in position 9 (answer A) would show a heading of 360°, but the CDI would be centered. The aircraft in position 4 (answer B) would show a heading of 270°, but would get the same CDI indication. The correct procedure for aircraft flying the LOC front course is to have the course selector set on the front course of 270°.

8-8   H831

(Refer to figures 96 and 97 on pages 8-8 and 8-10.) To which aircraft position does HSI presentation "D" correspond?

A — 1.
B — 10.
C — 2.

8-8. Answer C. GFDICM 8B (IFH)

The aircraft in position 2 is the only one on a northwest heading. With the back course of 090° dialed in, reverse sensing would put the CDI behind the aircraft. The aircraft in position 1 (answer A) would indicate a heading toward the southwest. The aircraft in position 10 (answer B) would indicate a heading to the southwest.

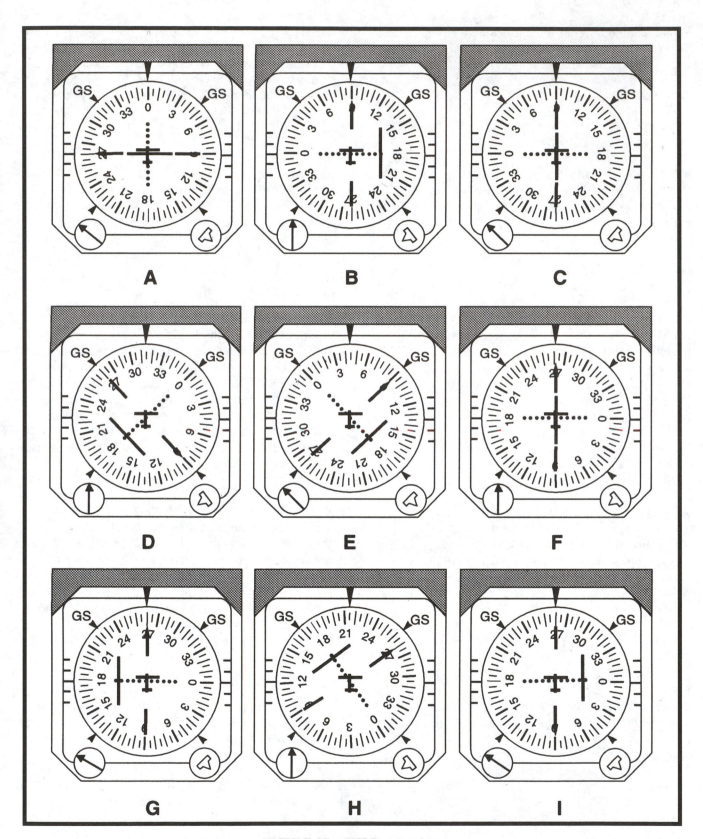

FIGURE 97.—HSI Presentation

8-9   H831
(Refer to figures 96 and 97 on pages 8-8 and 8-10.) To which aircraft position(s) does HSI presentation "E" correspond?

A — 8 only.
B — 3 only.
C — 8 and 3.

8-10   H831
(Refer to figures 96 and 97 on pages 8-8 and 8-10.) To which aircraft position does HSI presentation "F" correspond?

A — 4.
B — 11.
C — 5.

8-11   H831
(Refer to figures 96 and 97 on pages 8-8 and 8-10.) To which aircraft position(s) does HSI presentation "G" correspond?

A — 7 only.
B — 7 and 11.
C — 5 and 13.

8-12   H831
(Refer to figures 96 and 97 on pages 8-8 and 8-10.) To which aircraft position does HSI presentation "H" correspond?

A — 8.
B — 1.
C — 2.

8-13   H831
(Refer to figures 96 and 97 on pages 8-8 and 8-10.) To which aircraft position does HSI presentation "I" correspond?

A — 4.
B — 12.
C — 11.

8-14   J42
(Refer to figure 118 on page 8-12.) During the ILS RWY 12L procedure at DSM, what altitude minimum applies if the glide slope becomes inoperative?

A — 1,420 feet.
B — 1,360 feet.
C — 1,121 feet.

8-9. Answer C. GFDICM 8B (IFH)
Both aircraft in positions 8 and 3 would experience reverse sensing with the course selector set on the back course. Neither position 8 only (answer A) or position 3 only (answer B) would be most correct.

8-10. Answer A. GFDICM 8B (IFH)
The aircraft in position 4 is the only one aligned with the localizer front course and the CDI is centered. The aircraft in position 11 (answer B) is north of the localizer and would have a CDI deflection to the left. The aircraft in position 5 (answer C) would indicate a heading of east, instead of west.

8-11. Answer B. GFDICM 8B (IFH)
Both aircraft in positions 7 and 11 are on the localizer front course heading, but north of course. The aircraft in position 7 (answer A) alone would not be the most correct answer. The aircraft in positions 5 and 13 (answer C) are heading 090°, not 270°, and they are south, not north, of course.

8-12. Answer B. GFDICM 8B (IFH)
The aircraft in position 1 is the only one on a southwest heading of 215°. The CDI indicates that the aircraft is established on a 45° intercept to the inbound localizer course of 270°. The aircraft in position 8 (answer A) is on a northeast heading. The aircraft in position 2 (answer C) is on a northwest heading.

8-13. Answer C. GFDICM 8B (IFH)
The aircraft in position 11 is on a heading of west with the course selector set on the back course of 090°. This results in reverse sensing and a CDI deflection to the right. The CDI for the aircraft in position 4 (answer A) would be centered. The heading of the aircraft in position 12 (answer B) would be 090°, instead of 270°.

8-14. Answer B. GFDICM 8B (Approach Chart Legend)
When the glide slope is inoperative, the nonprecision localizer approach minimums apply. Assuming a straight-in approach, the localizer MDA for this approach is 1,360 feet for all aircraft categories. Answer (A) is the circling MDA for category B and C aircraft, not a straight-in MDA. Answer (C) is the DH for the full ILS.

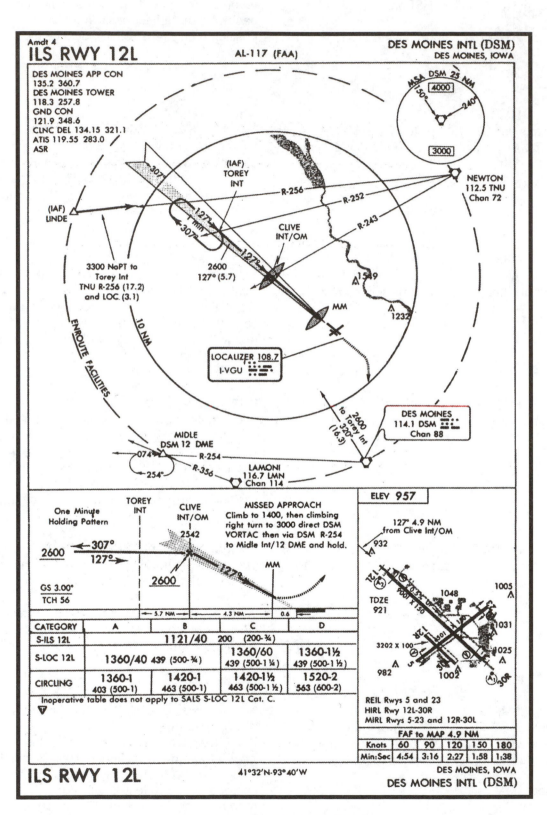

FIGURE 118.—ILS RWY 12L (DSM).

8-15   J01

When installed with the ILS and specified in the approach procedures, DME may be used

A — in lieu of the OM.
B — in lieu of visibility requirements.
C — to determine distance from TDZ.

8-16   J42

How does a pilot determine if DME is available on an ILS/LOC?

A — IAP indicate DME/TACAN channel in LOC frequency box.
B — LOC/DME are indicated on en route low altitude frequency box.
C — LOC/DME frequencies available in the Aeronautical Information Manual.

8-17   H837

(Refer to figure 130 on page 7-20.) How does an LDA facility, such as the one at Roanoke Regional, differ from a standard ILS approach facility?

A — The LOC is wider.
B — The LOC is offset from the runway.
C — The GS is unusable beyond the MM.

8-18   J18

Which of the following statements is true regarding Parallel ILS approaches?

A — Parallel ILS approach runway centerlines are separated by at least 4,300 feet and standard IFR separation is provided on the adjacent runway.
B — Parallel ILS approaches provide aircraft a minimum of 1 1/2 miles radar separation between successive aircraft on the adjacent localizer course.
C — Landing minimums to the adjacent runway will be higher than the minimums to the primary runway, but will normally be lower than the published circling minimums.

8-15. Answer A. GFDICM 8B (FAR 91.175)

When authorized in the approach procedure, DME, VOR, or an NDB may be substituted for the outer marker (OM). The only way DME affects visibility (answer B) is when separate DME minimums are listed, as in the case of a stepdown fix, for example. But DME cannot be used in lieu of the published visibility. Answer (C) can be somewhat misleading. On some (but not all) approaches, depending on the location of the DME facility, the pilot may be able to determine distance from the runway threshold. But this is not the same as the touchdown zone (TDZ), which is the first 3,000 feet of the runway.

8-16. Answer A. GFDICM 8B (Approach Chart Legend)

NOS approach charts include the DME/TACAN channel in the LOC frequency box. An example would be the notation "Chan 79" underneath the frequency and identifier. Note: Jeppesen charts do not display the DME/TACAN channel, but indicate "ILS DME" on the top of the facility box. Enroute low altitude charts (answer B) do not indicate "LOC/DME," but only show a localizer feather symbol to indicate that an ILS and/or localizer procedure is available. The AIM (answer C) contains only general information on frequencies; it does not list specific LOC/DME frequencies available at each facility.

8-17. Answer B. GFDICM 8B (AIM)

A localizer-type directional aid (LDA) is comparable to a localizer, but it is not aligned with the runway. An LDA is similar in accuracy to a localizer, so the LOC is not wider than an ILS (answer A). An LDA is also not part of a complete ILS and does not incorporate a glide slope (GS) (answer C).

8-18. Answer B. GFDICM 8B (AIM)

Aircraft are afforded a minimum of 1.5 miles radar separation diagonally between successive aircraft on the adjacent localizer/azimuth course when runway centerlines are at least 2,500 feet but no more than 4,300 feet apart. Answer (A) is incorrect because parallel ILS approaches may be conducted when runway centerlines are at least 2,500 feet apart. Landing minimums are not based on whether parallel approaches are being conducted (answer C).

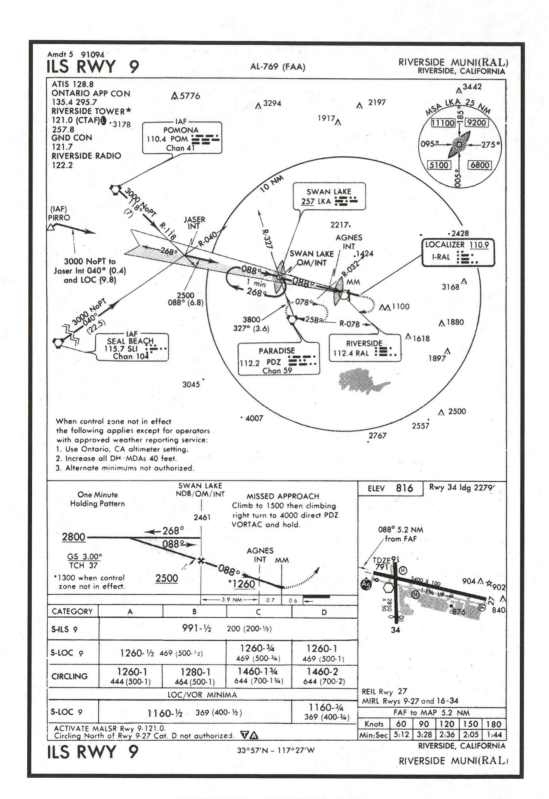

FIGURE 133.—ILS RWY9 (RAL).

8-19　　　　J17

(Refer to figure 133 on page 8-14.) What action should the pilot take if the marker beacon receiver becomes inoperative during the S ILS 9 approach at Riverside Municipal?

A — Substitute SWAN LAKE INT. for the OM and surveillance radar for the MM.

B — Raise the DH 100 feet (50 feet for the OM and 50 feet for the MM).

C — Substitute SWAN LAKE INT. for the OM and use published minimums.

8-20　　　　J42

(Refer to figure 133 on page 8-14.) Why are two VOR/ LOC receivers recommended to obtain an MDA of 1,160 when making an S LOC 9 approach to Riverside Municipal?

A — To obtain R-327 of PDZ when on the localizer course.

B — In order to identify Riverside VOR.

C — To utilize the published stepdown fix.

8-21　　　　J42

(Refer to figure 133 on page 8-14.) What is the minimum altitude descent procedure if cleared for the S ILS 9 approach from Seal Beach VORTAC?

A — Descend and maintain 3,000 to JASER INT, descend to and maintain 2,500 until crossing SWAN LAKE, descend and maintain 1,260 until crossing AGNES, and to 991 (DH) after passing AGNES.

B — Descend and maintain 3,000 to JASER INT, descend to 2,800 when established on the LOC course, intercept and maintain the GS to 991 (DH).

C — Descend and maintain 3,000 to JASER INT, descend to 2,500 while established on the LOC course inbound, intercept and maintain the GS to 991 (DH).

8-19. Answer C. GFDICM 8B (IFH) (FAR 91.175)

Swan Lake Int. or the NDB may be substituted for the outer marker (OM). Prior to October 15, 1992, when the MM was inoperative, ILS DH minimums increased by 50 feet. Currently, the MM-out penalty does not apply. Pilots using NOS charts must refer to the inoperative components table inside the front cover of the U.S. Terminal Procedures for inoperative components. (See Appendix 2.) The new table does not include an increase in the DH for MM out. Answer (A) is incorrect because precision, not surveillance, radar is required to identify the MM. Answer (B) is wrong because the approach would be illegal without an OM (or substitute) and the MM-out penalty no longer applies.

8-20. Answer C. GFDICM 8B (IFH)

On final approach, after the FAF, one VOR/LOC receiver must be continuously tuned to the final approach course frequency. A second receiver is required to identify any VOR radial stepdown fixes. On this approach, the stepdown fix, AGNES, is identified off the PDZ VOR, so a second receiver is necessary. After AGNES, you may descend from 1,260 feet to the straight-in localizer MDA of 1,160 feet. Two VOR/LOC receivers are not required to identify the 327° radial of PDZ (answer A). The FAF may be identified using an ADF receiver for the Swan Lake NDB and a single VOR/LOC receiver to determine that you are on the localizer course. Riverside VOR (answer B) is not required for this approach.

8-21. Answer C. GFDICM 8B (IFH)

From Seal Beach VORTAC (SLI), the published minimum altitude to JASER INT is 3,000 feet. Since this is a NoPT routing at JASER, you would proceed inbound on the final approach course without executing a procedure turn and, when established on the localizer course, descend to the glide slope intercept altitude of 2,500 feet. Then intercept the glide slope and descend to the ILS decision height (DH) of 991 feet. Answer (A) describes a nonprecision localizer approach, except it includes the ILS DH. Answer (B) incorrectly includes the procedure turn altitude of 2,800 feet.

8-22   J01
What is a difference between an SDF and an LDA facility?

A — The SDF course width is either 6° or 12° while the LDA course width is approximately 5°.
B — The SDF course has no glide slope guidance while the LDA does.
C — The SDF has no marker beacons while the LDA has at least an OM.

8-23   J01
What is the difference between an Localizer-Type Directional Aid (LDA) and the ILS localizer?

A — The LDA is not aligned with the runway.
B — The LDA uses a course width of 6° or 12°, while an ILS uses only 5°.
C — The LDA signal is generated from a VOR-type facility and has no glide slope.

8-24   J01
How wide is an SDF course?

A — Either 3° or 6°.
B — Either 6° or 12°.
C — Varies from 5° to 10°.

8-25   J01
What are the main differences between the SDF and the localizer of an ILS?

A — The useable off-course indications are limited to 35° for the localizer and up to 90° for the SDF.
B — The SDF course may not be aligned with the runway and the course may be wider.
C — The course width for the localizer will always be 5° while the SDF course will be between 6° and 12°.

8-26   J01
Which range facility associated with the ILS is identified by the last two letters of the localizer identification group?

A — Inner marker.
B — Outer marker.
C — Middle compass locator.

8-22. Answer A. GFDICM 8B (AIM)
A localizer-type directional aid (LDA) is comparable in use and accuracy to a localizer, but it is not a part of a complete ILS nor is it aligned with the runway center-line. An LDA has a course width between 3° and 6°. A simplified directional facility (SDF) has a fixed course width of either 6° or 12°. Answer (B) is wrong because neither the SDF nor all LDAs have a glide slope. SDF and LDA facilities are not part of a complete ILS, and may or may not include marker beacons (answer C).

8-23. Answer A. GFDICM 8B (AIM)
The primary difference between an LDA and an ILS is that an LDA is not aligned with the runway centerline. Answer (B) is incorrect because an LDA is similar to the ILS localizer in design and accuracy and has a course width between 3° and 6°. An SDF course width is either 6° or 12°. Because the LDA is similar to a localizer, it has a smaller course width than a VOR signal (answer C), and some LDAs have a glide slope.

8-24. Answer B. GFDICM 8B (AIM)
A simplified directional facility (SDF) course is fixed at either 6° or 12° wide. Neither answer (A) or (C) describe an SDF course width.

8-25. Answer B. GFDICM 8B (AIM)
Unlike an ILS, an SDF may be offset from the runway centerline, normally not more than 3°, and no glide slope information is provided. In addition, an SDF course width is either 6° or 12°, while an ILS course is typically 5° wide. Usable off-course indications (answer A) are 35° for both the localizer (up to 10 n.m.) and the SDF. Answer (C) is incorrect because a localizer course width is between 3° and 6° and an SDF course is either 6° or 12° wide.

8-26. Answer C. GFDICM 8B (AIM)
A compass locator at the middle marker transmits Morse code for the last two letters of the localizer identifier. The compass locator at the outer marker transmits the first two letters of the localizer identifier. Marker beacons not combined with a compass locator do not transmit two-letter identifiers. Rather, the inner marker (answer A) transmits a continuous series of dots. The outer marker (answer B) transmits a continuous series of dashes. Although not included here as an answer choice, the middle marker is identified by a series of alternating dots and dashes.

8-27   J01
Which range facility associated with the ILS can be identified by a two-letter coded signal?

A — Middle marker.
B — Outer marker.
C — Compass Locator

8-28   J42
Which pilot action is appropriate if more than one component of an ILS is unusable?

A — Use the highest minimum required by any single component that is unusable.
B — Request another approach appropriate to the equipment that is useable.
C — Raise the minimums a total of that required by each component that is unusable.

8-29   J01
Which substitution is permitted when an ILS component is inoperative?

A — A compass locator or precision radar may be substituted for the ILS outer or middle marker.
B — ADF or VOR bearings which cross either the outer or middle marker sites may be substituted for these markers.
C — DME, when located at the localizer antenna site, should be substituted for the outer or middle marker.

8-30   J42
What facilities, if any, may be substituted for an inoperative middle marker during an ILS approach without affecting the straight-in minimums?

A — ASR.
B — Substitution not necessary, minimums do not change.
C — Compass locator, PAR, and ASR.

8-31   J18
When being radar vectored for an ILS approach, at what point may you start a descent from your last assigned altitude to a lower minimum altitude if cleared for the approach?

A — When established on a segment of a published route or IAP.
B — You may descend immediately to published glide slope interception altitude.
C — Only after you are established on the final approach unless informed otherwise by ATC.

8-27. Answer C. GFDICM 8B (AIM)
See explanation for Question 8-26.

8-28. Answer A. GFDICM 8B (IFH)
When components of an ILS are inoperative, higher minimums may be required, but the effect is not cumulative. You would use the highest minimums required by the inoperative status of any single component. Answer (B) is a possible choice, but is not necessary. You would not add the increased minimums for each inoperative component (answer C).

8-29. Answer A. GFDICM 8B (IFH) (FAR 91.175)
A compass locator or precision radar may be used in place of the outer or middle marker. VOR, ADF (answer B), or DME (answer C) fixes authorized in an instrument approach may be substituted for the outer marker only, not the middle marker.

8-30. Answer B. GFDICM 8B (IFH) (FAR 91.175)
An inoperative middle marker (MM) no longer affects straight-in landing minimums. Therefore, answer (B) is correct. Airport surveillance radar (ASR), answer (A), is not used as a substitute for the MM. A compass locator or precision approach radar (PAR), answer (C), may be substituted for the MM, but there is no change to the minimums with or without the substitution.

This question is similar to 8-32.

8-31. Answer A. GFDICM 8B (AIM)
To ensure obstacle clearance, you must maintain your last assigned altitude until established on a segment of the published routing or approach procedure. If you descend immediately to the glide slope intercept altitude (answer B) while you are not on course, you would not be guaranteed obstacle clearance. Answer (C) is partially correct, but you do not have to wait until on final approach if you are established on a published route to the final approach course.

8-32   J01

Which of these facilities may be substituted for an MM during a complete ILS IAP?

A — Surveillance and precision radar.
B — Compass locator and precision radar.
C — A VOR/DME fix.

8-33   J18

If all ILS components are operating and the required visual references are not established, the missed approach should be initiated upon

A — arrival at the DH on the glide slope.
B — arrival at the middle marker.
C — expiration of the time listed on the approach chart for missed approach.

8-34   K04

The rate of descent required to stay on the ILS glide slope

A — must be increased if the groundspeed is decreased.
B — will remain constant if the indicated airspeed remains constant.
C — must be decreased if the groundspeed is decreased.

8-35   J01

Which indications will a pilot receive where an IM is installed on a front course ILS approach?

A — One dot per second and a steady amber light.
B — Six dots per second and a flashing white light.
C — Alternate dashes and a blue light.

8-36   K04

To remain on the ILS glidepath, the rate of descent must be

A — decreased if the airspeed is increased.
B — decreased if the groundspeed is increased.
C — increased if the groundspeed is increased.

8-32. Answer B. GFDICM 8B (IFH) (FAR 91.175)
Either a compass locator or precision approach radar may be used as substitutes for a middle marker (MM) on an ILS approach. Surveillance radar (answer A) is incorrect and may not be used. A VOR/DME fix (answer C) also may not be substituted for the MM.

See explanations for Questions 8-29 and 8-30.

8-33. Answer A. GFDICM 8B (IFH) (FAR 91.175)
The decision height (DH) is the missed approach point for a precision approach. If you do not have the required visual references at the DH, you must immediately initiate the missed approach. The middle marker (answer B) is often located near the DH point on the glide slope, but is not the missed approach point. Answer (C) would be used for a nonprecision localizer-only approach, not for a full ILS.

8-34. Answer C. GFDICM 8B (AC 00-54)
To maintain a constant glide angle, your vertical speed depends on your speed over the ground. If your groundspeed decreases, you will have to reduce your rate of descent to stay on the glide slope. The rate of descent must be increased when the groundspeed is increased, not decreased (answer A). Even if your indicated airspeed remains constant (answer B), your groundspeed can still change due to winds, and the rate of descent would have to change.

This question is similar to 8-36.

8-35. Answer B. GFDICM 8B (AIM)
An inner marker (IM) is identified by a continuous series of dots at the rate of six per second and a flashing white light. Answers (A) and (C) do not identify any marker beacons. The outer marker transmits dashes at two per second with a blue light, and the middle marker is identified by alternating dots and dashes with an amber light.

See explanation for Question 8-26.

8-36. Answer C. GFDICM 8B (AC 00-54)
When groundspeed increases, you must increase your rate of descent to remain on the glide slope. Answer (A) is wrong because your descent rate is based on groundspeed, not airspeed. If the groundspeed is increased and you decreased the rate of descent (answer B), you would fly above the glidepath.

See explanation for Questions 9-90, 9-92, 9-94, and 8-34 for additional information.

8-37   K04

The rate of descent on the glide slope is dependent upon

A — true airspeed.
B — calibrated airspeed.
C — groundspeed.

8-38   J01

Approximately what height is the glide slope centerline at the MM of a typical ILS?

A — 100 feet.
B — 200 feet.
C — 300 feet.

8-39   H815

The glide slope and localizer are centered, but the airspeed is too fast. Which should be adjusted initially?

A — Pitch and power.
B — Power only.
C — Pitch only.

8-40   B10

If during an ILS approach in IFR conditions, the approach lights are not visible upon arrival at the DH, the pilot is

A — required to immediately execute the missed approach procedure.
B — permitted to continue the approach and descend to the localizer MDA.
C — permitted to continue the approach to the approach threshold of the ILS runway.

8-41   J01

Immediately after passing the final approach fix inbound during an ILS approach in IFR conditions, the glide slope warning flag appears. The pilot is

A — permitted to continue the approach and descend to the DH.
B — permitted to continue the approach and descend to the localizer MDA.
C — required to immediately begin the prescribed missed approach procedure.

8-37. Answer C. GFDICM 8B (Rate of Descent Table)

The rate of descent needed to maintain the glide slope varies with groundspeed. True airspeed (answer A) and calibrated airspeed (answer B) do not take into account changes in wind, which will cause groundspeed to vary.

See explanations for Questions 8-34 and 8-36.

8-38. Answer B. GFDICM 8B (AIM)

Usually the middle marker (MM) is located about 3,500 feet from the landing threshold. At that point, the typical glide slope will be 200 feet above the touchdown zone elevation. Answer (A), 100 feet, is below the normal decision height (DH) and answer (C), 300 feet, is above the normal DH for ILS approaches.

8-39. Answer B. GFDICM 8B (IFH)

The power should be reduced first to begin slowing the airplane. As airspeed decreases, the pitch will tend to decrease, and you should make the necessary corrections to pitch the nose upward in order to maintain the glide slope. If you adjust pitch and power together (answer A) or pitch only (answer C), the aircraft would go above the glide slope.

8-40. Answer A. GFDICM 8B (FAR 91.175)

This question assumes that no other runway visual references are visible. In this case, you may not continue the approach below the DH and must immediately execute the missed approach. At the DH, you would already be below the localizer MDA (answer B). You cannot continue the approach to the runway threshold (answer C), since this would normally take you well below the DH.

This question is similar to 8-33.

8-41. Answer B. GFDICM 8B (AIM)

If the glide slope fails, you are permitted to continue the approach, using localizer-only minimums. You would descend to the MDA and continue to the MAP. If the runway environment is not in sight at the MAP, you must execute a missed approach. With a failed glide slope, you are not able to continue an ILS approach to DH (answer A). There is no need to execute the missed approach (answer C) since you can continue the localizer approach. Also, if you have to execute the missed approach, you should level off and continue to the MAP prior to turning.

8-42   J01

Which substitution is appropriate during an ILS approach?

A — A VOR radial crossing the outer marker site may be substituted for the outer marker.

B — LOC minimums should be substituted for ILS minimums whenever the glide slope becomes inoperative.

C — DME, when located at the localizer antenna site, should be substituted for either the outer or middle marker.

8-42. Answer B. GFDICM 8B (AIM) (FAR 91.175)

When the glide slope becomes inoperative, you may use LOC minimums and fly a nonprecision approach to the LOC MDA. A VOR radial may not be substituted for the outer marker (answer A). Permissible substitutes for the outer marker are: surveillance or precision radar, compass locator, and DME, VOR, or NDB fixes when published on the procedure (answer C).

8-43   K04

During a precision radar or ILS approach, the rate of descent required to remain on the glide slope will

A — remain the same regardless of groundspeed.

B — increase as the groundspeed increases.

C — decrease as the groundspeed increases.

8-43. Answer B. GFDICM 8B (AC 00-54)

See explanations for Questions 8-34, 8-36, and 8-37. When making a precision radar or ILS approach, the aircraft's rate of descent will vary with changes in groundspeed. If your groundspeed increases, the rate of descent required to stay on the glide slope must also increase. If your groundspeed decreases, the rate of descent must also decrease.

8-44   H837

When tracking inbound on the localizer, which of the following is the proper procedure regarding drift corrections?

A — Drift corrections should be accurately established before reaching the outer marker and completion of the approach should be accomplished with heading corrections no greater than 2°.

B — Drift corrections should be made in 5° increments after passing the outer marker.

C — Drift corrections should be made in 10° increments after passing the outer marker.

8-44. Answer A. GFDICM 8B (IFH)

On the narrow localizer course, establish your drift correction prior to the outer marker. Since overcontrolling can be a problem, heading corrections should be no greater than 2° after passing the outer marker. Winds may shift as you descend, but drift corrections in 5° or 10° increments (answers B and C) are usually too large and could result in overcontrolling.

8-45   J01

What international Morse Code identifier is used to identify a specific interim standard microwave landing system?

A — A two letter Morse Code identifier preceded by the Morse Code for the letters "IM".

B — A three letter Morse Code identifier preceded by the Morse Code for the letter "M".

C — A three letter Morse Code identifier preceded by the Morse Code for the letters "ML".

8-45. Answer B. GFDICM 8B (AIM)

A microwave landing system (MLS) is identified by the Morse code for the letter "M" followed by the three-letter identifier for the facility. This system of identification is the same for both the MLS and interim standard MLS facility. The facility identifier is three letters, not two (answer A), and the letter "I" is used with ILS not MLS identifiers. The three-letter identifier is preceded only by the letter "M," not "ML" (answer C).

8-46   H837

(Refer to figures 139 and 140 on page 8-22.) Which displacement from the localizer and glide slope at the 1.9 NM point is indicated?

A — 710 feet to the left of the localizer centerline and 140 feet below the glide slope.

B — 710 feet to the right of the localizer centerline and 140 feet above the glide slope.

C — 430 feet to the right of the localizer centerline and 28 feet above the glide slope.

8-47   H837

(Refer to figures 139 and 141 on page 8-22.) Which displacement from the localizer centerline and glide slope at the 1,300-foot point from the runway is indicated?

A — 21 feet below the glide slope and approximately 320 feet to the right of the runway centerline.

B — 28 feet above the glide slope and approximately 250 feet to the left of the runway centerline.

C — 21 feet above the glide slope and approximately 320 feet to the left of the runway centerline.

8-46. Answer B. GFDICM 8B (IFH)

Figure 140 indicates that the aircraft is 2 dots above the glide slope and 2 dots to the right of the localizer. At 1.9 n.m. this corresponds to 710 feet to the right of the localizer centerline and 140 feet above the glide slope. Answer (A) is incorrect because the CDI indicates right (not left) of course. Answer (C) corresponds to the localizer and glide slope displacements at a distance of 1,300 feet (not 1.9 nm.).

8-47. Answer C. GFDICM 8B (IFH)

Figure 141 indicates that the aircraft is approximately 1-1/2 dots above the glide slope and between 1-1/2 and 2 dots to the left of the localizer. At 1,300 feet, this best corresponds to 21 feet above the glide slope and approximately 320 feet to the left of the runway centerline. Answer (A) is incorrect because the CDI indicates that you are above (not below) glide slope, and to the left (not right) of course. Answer (B), 28 feet above glide slope, would correspond to a 2 dot deflection, not 1-1/2 dots. Also, a localizer displacement of 250 feet would be shown as approximately 1-1/4 dots.

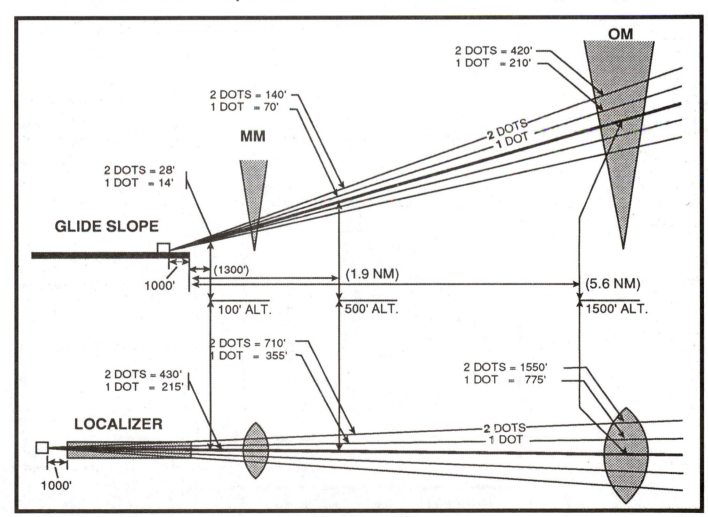

FIGURE 139.—Glide Slope and Localizer Illustration.

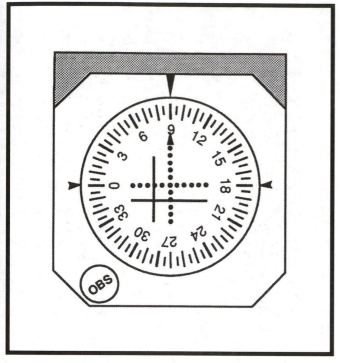

FIGURE 140.—OBS, ILS, and GS Displacement.

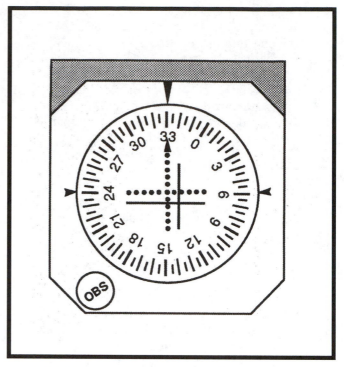

FIGURE 141.—OBS, ILS, and GS Displacement.

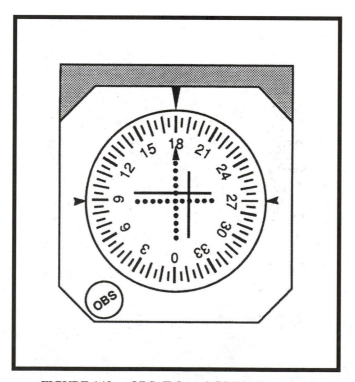

FIGURE 142.—OBS, ILS, and GS Displacement.

8-48   H837

(Refer to figures 139 on page 8-21 and 142.) Which displacement from the localizer and glide slope at the outer marker is indicated?

A — 1,550 feet to the left of the localizer centerline and 210 feet below the glide slope.
B — 1,550 feet to the right of the localizer centerline and 210 feet above the glide slope.
C — 775 feet to the left of the localizer centerline and 420 feet below the glide slope.

8-48. Answer A. GFDICM 8B (IFH)

Figure 142 indicates that the aircraft is approximately 1 dot below the glide slope and 2 dots to the left of the localizer. At the outer marker, this corresponds to 210 feet below glide slope and approximately 1,550 feet to the left of the centerline. Answer (B) is incorrect since the CDI shows you to the left (not right) of course, and below (not above) glide slope. Answer (C) is incorrect because the answer corresponds more to a localizer displacement of 1 dot (not 2 dots) and a glide slope displacement of 2 dots (not 1 dot).

8-49   J42

(Refer to figure 49 on page 8-7.) What determines the MAP on the LOC/DME RWY 21 approach at Portland International Airport?

A — I-GPO 1.2 DME.
B — 5.8 NM from ROBOT FAF.
C — 160° radial of BTG VORTAC.

8-49. Answer A. (GFDICM 8C)

The missed approach point shown on figure 49 is located at I-GPO 1.2 DME. Answer (B) is referring to the nm distance over the ground, not DME, and Answer (C) refers to the intercept radial after reaching the MAP.

8-50   J42

(Refer to figures 44 on page 10-39 and 49 on page 8-7.) What is the MDA and visibility criteria for a straight-in LOC/DME RWY 21 approach at Portland International?

A — 1,100 feet MSL; visibility 1SM.
B — 680 feet MSL; visibility 1SM.
C — 680 feet MSL; visibility 1 NM

8-50. Answer B. GFDICM 7A (AIM)

The provided flight plan and aircraft information lists the VSO at 77 knots. To determine the proper approach category, multiply 1.3 x VSO (1.3 x 77 = 100.1). This falls into the Category B approach minimums (91 to 120 kts.). The approach minimums for Category A and B are 680 feet MSL and 1 statute mile visibility. Answer (A) is not available as a possible MDA or visibility. Answer (C) has the correct MDA of 680 MSL, but the incorrect 1 NM visibility.

8-51   I10

(Refer to figure 49 on page 8-7.) With a groundspeed of 120 knots, approximately what minimum rate of descent will be required between I-GPO 7 DME fix (ROBOT) and the I-GPO 4 DME fix?

A — 1,200 fpm.
B — 500 fpm.
C — 800 fpm..

8-51. Answer C. GFDICM 8C

Traveling at 120 knots between I-GPO 7 DME fix (ROBOT) at 2300 ft MSL to I-GPO 4 DME fix should take you 1-1/2 minutes. To Descend a total of 1,200 feet in a minute and a half you should be descending at 800 f.p.m.

SECTION C
GPS AND RNAV APPROACHES

OVERVIEW

1. Phase II of the overlay program uses existing approach charts, and requires the underlying ground navaids and associated aircraft navigation equipment to be operational, but not monitored during the approach as long as the GPS meets RAIM accuracy requirements. Phase III of the GPS overlay program eliminates the requirement for conventional navigation equipment to be operational during the approach to your destination airport.

2. You are not required to monitor or have conventional navigation equipment for stand alone GPS approaches to your destination airport.

3. You must have conventional navigation equipment aboard your aircraft as a backup for enroute navigation, and to fly to an alternate airport if it becomes necessary. While you can conduct an approach to an alternate airport using GPS, you must have the capability of conducting the approach using conventional equipment.

4. You can determine if a GPS is approved for IFR enroute and approach operations by referring to the supplements section of Airplane Flight Manual (AFM).

RAIM

5. The GPS continuously monitors the reliability of the GPS signal using a system known as receiver autonomous integrity monitoring (RAIM). If RAIM is not available when you set up a GPS approach, you should select another type of navigation and approach system.

NAVIGATION DATA

6. Your GPS receiver is required to have current data before it is used for IFR navigation.

7. A sensor waypoint is included on approaches that do not have a final approach fix defined and usable as the FAWP.

GPS DISTANCE AND VARIATION

8. You may need to compute the along track distance (ATD) to stepdown fixes and other points due to the receiver showing ATD to the waypoint rather than DME to the VOR or other ground station.

9. There may be a variance between the distance displayed on your GPS receiver and the distance published on the accompanying procedure. This occurs because GPS uses a straight line ATD between waypoints while the DME data published on instrument charts is based on slant range to the respective station. The difference between ATD and DME will vary depending on your altitude as well as your proximity to the navaid.

10. While the charted magnetic tracks defined by a VOR radial are determined by the application of magnetic variation at the VOR, GPS computers usually use an algorithm to apply magnetic variation at the current position. Although this process can produce small differences between GPS displayed data and charted information, both operations should produce the same ground track.

NAVIGATION DURING THE APPROACH

11. Normal operation of the GPS unit is referred to as TO-TO navigation. However, when passing a waypoint in hold mode, the external VOR indicator changes from TO to FROM, and the GPS does not autosequence to the next waypoint.

12. Flying from the MAP directly to the MAHWP may not provide sufficient obstacle clearance. You should always fly the full missed approach procedure as published on the approach chart.

13. When you receive radar vectors to final you generally will have to manually sequence ahead and select the leg to which you are being vectored. You should avoid accepting or requesting radar vectors which will cause you to intercept the final approach course within 2 nautical miles of the FAWP.

VOR/DME RNAV

14. Waypoints are predetermined geographical positions used for RNAV routes or approaches. They are marked with special symbols on approach charts.
15. On a VOR/DME RNAV system, you program the offset angle and distance of phantom VORs, or waypoints, with respect to actual VORTACs.
16. An RNAV CDI indicates absolute deviation in nautical miles, rather than angular deviation from course.
17. All VOR/DME RNAV procedures require at least two waypoints; some require six or more waypoints. An approved RNAV receiver is the minimum navigation equipment needed to conduct such an approach.
18. VOR/DME RNAV approach charts provide the final approach angle for equipment with vertical navigation capability. On an NOS approach chart, the glidepath angle for vertical guidance systems appears in the profile view between the FAF and the MAP.

8-52   H862

What is a waypoint when used for an IFR flight?

A — A predetermined geographical position used for an RNAV route or an RNAV instrument approach.
B — A reporting point defined by the intersection of two VOR radials.
C — A location on a victor airway which can only be identified by VOR and DME signals.

8-52. Answer A. GFDICM 8C (AIM)

A waypoint is a predetermined geographical position used to define an RNAV route, instrument approach, or a reporting position. Although they are commonly defined by radials and distances from a VORTAC, they also may be defined by geographical coordinates. Answer (B) is wrong because a waypoint is not defined using two VOR radials. Answer (C) is wrong because waypoints are usually located off victor airways and can also be identified using geographical coordinates. Answer (C) describes a DME fix on an airway, not a waypoint.

8-53   I07

(Refer to figure 36A on page 8-26.) Under which condition should the missed approach procedure for the VOR/DME RNAV RWY 33 approach be initiated?

A — Immediately upon reaching the 5.0 DME from the FAF.
B — When passage of the MAP waypoint is shown on the ambiguity indicator.
C — After the MDA is reached and 1.8 DME fix from the MAP waypoint.

8-53. Answer B. GFDICM 8C (IFH)

When conducting an RNAV approach, you begin the missed approach as soon as you reach the missed approach point (MAP). This is identified by the ambiguity indicator switching from a TO to a FROM indication. Answer (A) is wrong because distances are from the MAP. Answer (C) is wrong because if you arrive at the MDA, 1.8 n.m. from the MAP, you can continue the approach to the MAP at the MDA before initiating a missed approach.

8-54   K26

How can a pilot determine if a Global Positioning System (GPS) installed in an aircraft is approved for IFR enroute and IFR approaches?

A — Flight manual supplement.
B — GPS operator's manual.
C — Aircraft owner's handbook.

8-54. Answer A. GFDICM 8C (AC90-94)

All GPS IFR operations should be conducted in acccordance with the FAA Approved Flight Manual (AFM) or Flight Manual Supplement. The type and degree of authorized operations for a GPS receiver are specified in these documents. Answers (B) and (C) are incorrect because these publications do not specify approval for IFR operations.

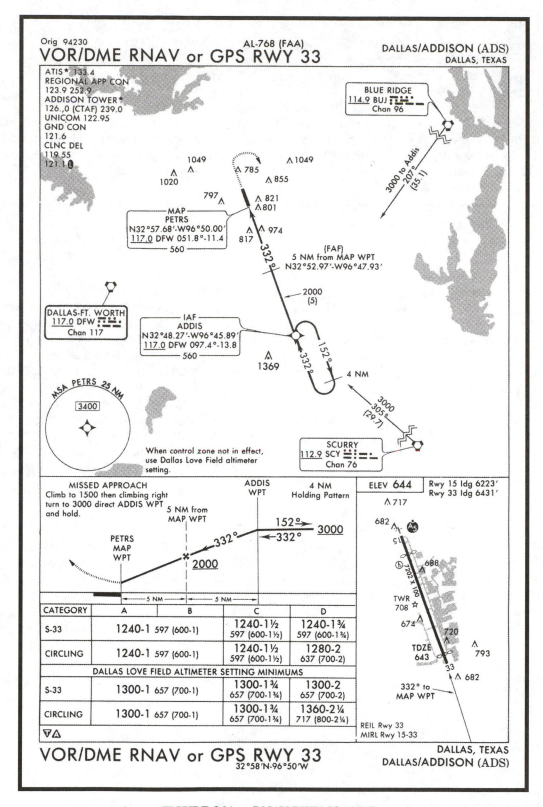

Orig 94230
AL-768 (FAA)
VOR/DME RNAV or GPS RWY 33
DALLAS/ADDISON (ADS)
DALLAS, TEXAS

FIGURE 36A.—RNAV RWY 33 (ADS).

8-55   **J42**
(Refer to figure 36A on page 8-26.) What is the minimum number of waypoints required for the complete RNAV RWY 33 approach procedure including the IAF's and missed approach procedure?

A — One waypoint.
B — Two waypoints.
C — Three waypoints.

8-56   **J42**
(Refer to figure 129 on page 8-29.) How should the missed approach point be identified when executing the RNAV RWY 36 approach at Adams Field?

A — When the TO-FROM indicator changes.
B — Upon arrival at 760 feet on the glidepath.
C — When time has expired for 5 NM past the FAF.

8-57   **J42**
(Refer to figure 129 on page 8-29.) What is the position of LABER relative to the reference facility?

A — 316°, 24.3 NM.
B — 177°, 10 NM.
C — 198°, 8 NM.

8-58   **J42**
(Refer to figure 129 on page 8-29.) What minimum airborne is required to be operative for RNAV RWY 36 approach at Adams Field?

A — An approved RNAV receiver that provides both horizontal and vertical guidance.
B — A transponder and an approved RNAV receiver that provides both horizontal and vertical guidance.
C — Any approved RNAV receiver.

8-55. Answer B. GFDICM 8C (AC 90-45A)
The RNAV RWY 33 approach requires a minimum of two waypoints; the initial approach fix (ADDIS) and the MAP. These two waypoints are indicated in the planview of the approach chart. Answer (A) is wrong because all RNAV approaches require a minimum of two waypoints. Answer (C) is wrong because only two waypoints are required for this approach.

8-56. Answer A. GFDICM 8C (IFH)
With RNAV equipment, waypoint passage is the same as station passage over a VOR: when the TO/FROM indicator changes to FROM. The MAP waypoint will be identified this way. Since this is a nonprecision approach, 760 feet (answer B) is an MDA, not a precision approach DH as implied. If the RNAV system incorporates vertical guidance, it allows you to follow a glide path from the FAF to arrive at the MDA at a specified distance from the MAP, but the approach is still nonprecision. An RNAV approach is not based on timing (answer C), but on miles from the waypoints and waypoint passage.

8-57. Answer C. GFDICM 8C (IFH)
On the planview, the waypoint data box for LABER includes the radial and distance from the reference facility, LIT VORTAC. It is shown as 198° and 8 n.m. Answer (A) does not define a waypoint, rather this is the radial and distance from the Pine Bluff VORTAC to LABER. Answer (B) is the course and distance from the MAP waypoint to LABER.

8-58. Answer C. GFDICM 8C (IFH)
This approach requires an FAA-approved RNAV receiver which provides navigational, or horizontal, guidance. Vertical guidance (answers A and B) is not required. RNAV systems which incorporate vertical guidance enable the pilot to fly the designated glide path angle to arrive at the MDA at a specified distance from the MAP. However, this is a nonprecision approach, and vertical guidance is not a requirement to fly the approach. The requirement for a transponder (answer B) depends on whether the approach is in Class B or Class C airspace.

8-59   J01

If Receiver Autonomous Integrity Monitoring (RAIM) is not available when setting up a GPS approach, the pilot should

A — select another type of navigation and approach system.

B — continue to the MAP and hold until the satellites are recaptured.

C — continue the approach, expecting to recapture the satellites before reaching the FAF.

8-59. Answer A. GFDICM 8C (AIM)

Receiver Autonomous Integrity Monitoring (RAIM) is essential for conducting GPS approaches. Loss of RAIM is like an OFF flag or no identifier on a VOR. This question asks what you should do if loss of RAIM occurs or is predicted to occur, before beginning the approach. The answer is the flight must rely on other approved navigation equipment. Answers (B) and (C) are incorrect because they improperly state the procedure for loss of RAIM after the approach has already begun. Assuming you are not monitoring alternative navigation equipment, or that you are flying a standalone GPS approach, you should proceed to the missed approach waypoint (MAWP) via the final approach waypoint (FAWP), and NOT descend to the MDA. ATC should be notified as soon as possible.

8-60   J01

When using GPS for navigation and instrument approaches, any required alternate airport must have

A — authorization to fly approaches under IFR using GPS avionics systems.

B — a GPS approach that is anticipated to be operational and available at the ETA.

C — an approved operational instrument approach procedure other than GPS.

8-60. Answer C. GFDICM 8C (AIM)

Although you can conduct the actual approach to the alternate using GPS, a non-GPS approach must be available and you must be equipped to fly it.

8-61   J01

Hand-held GPS systems, and GPS systems certified for VFR operation, may be used during IFR operations as

A — the principal reference to determine en route waypoints.

B — an aid to situational awareness.

C — the primary source of navigation.

8-61. Answer B. GFDICM 8C (AIM)

Hand-held GPS systems are not authorized for IFR navigation, instrument approaches, or as a principal flight reference. During IFR operations they may be considered only as an aid to situational awareness.

8-62   J01

During IFR en route and terminal operations using an approved GPS system for navigation, ground based navigational facilities

A — are only required during the approach portion of the flight.

B — must be operational along the entire route.

C — must be operational only if RAIM predicts an outage

8-62. Answer B. GFDICM 8C (AIM)

GPS domestic enroute and terminal IFR operations can be conducted as long as the avionics can receive all of the ground-based facilities appropriate for the route of flight and any required alternates. Ground-based facilities necessary for these routes must also be operational.

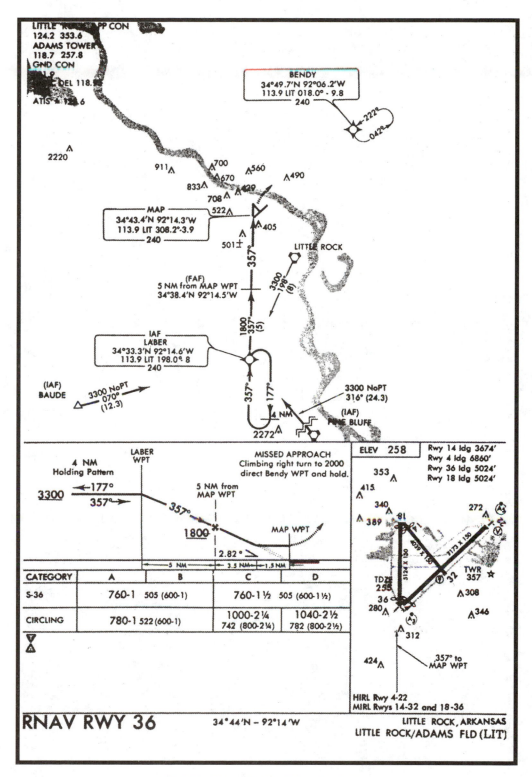

FIGURE 129.—RNAV RWY 36 (LIT).

CHAPTER 9

METEOROLOGY

SECTION A
WEATHER FACTORS

THE ATMOSPHERE

1. The atmosphere commonly is divided into a number of layers according to its thermal characteristics. The lowest layer, the troposphere, is where most weather occurs.

2. In the troposphere, temperatures decrease with altitude up to the tropopause, where an abrupt change in the temperature lapse rate occurs. The average height of the troposphere in the middle latitudes is 36,000 to 37,000 feet. The temperature in the lower part of the stratosphere (up to approximately 66,000 feet) experiences relatively small changes in temperature with an increase in altitude.

ATMOSPHERIC CIRCULATION

3. Uneven heating of the earth's surface is the driving force behind all weather. The special characteristics of water also affect the release of heat into the atmosphere, and dramatically affect the weather.

4. Atmospheric circulation patterns are caused by differences in pressure. Wind flows outward from high pressure areas to low pressure areas.

5. Above the friction layer, the wind does not flow directly from a high to a low because of Coriolis force, which deflects air to the right in the northern hemisphere. The result is a wind that flows in a clockwise direction leaving a high and in a counterclockwise, or cyclonic, direction when entering a low.

6. Near the surface, friction reduces the effects of Coriolis force and causes the wind to flow more directly from a high to low pressure area. This causes the wind to cross the isobars at an angle, rather than flowing parallel to them.

7. A low pressure area, or trough, is an area of rising air, which results in generally unfavorable weather conditions. A high pressure area, or ridge, is characterized by descending air, which encourages dissipation of clouds and results in generally favorable weather conditions. Because of the wind circulation patterns, you will most likely experience a crosswind from the left when flying from a high to a low in the northern hemisphere, with stronger winds as you approach the low.

8. Convective circulation patterns associated with sea breezes are caused by land absorbing and radiating heat faster than water. Cool air must sink to force warm air upward.

9. Moisture is added to a parcel of air by evaporation and sublimation. The amount of water vapor that air can hold increases with temperature. When the temperature cools to the dewpoint, the air is saturated.

10. At 100% humidity, water vapor condenses, forming clouds, fog or dew. Frost forms when the temperature of the collecting surface is below the dewpoint and the dewpoint is below freezing.

11. Precipitation occurs when water vapor condenses out of the air and becomes heavy enough to fall to earth. The type of precipitation is influenced by the temperature and other conditions under which condensation occurs. Upward currents enhance the growth rate of precipitation.

12. The presence of ice pellets normally indicates freezing rain at higher altitudes. The presence of wet snow indicates the temperature is above freezing at your flight altitude.

13. Virga is best described as streamers of rain trailing beneath clouds which evaporate before reaching the ground.

STABILITY

14. When unsaturated air is forced to ascend a mountain slope, it cools at the rate of approximately 3°C per 1,000 feet. When saturated air is lifted, it cools at a lower rate, which could cause it to be warmer than the surrounding air. The standard temperature of the surrounding air at sea level is 15°C, and it decreases at an average rate of 2°C per 1,000 feet.

15. Stability is the atmosphere's resistance to vertical motion. Air is stable when a lifted parcel of air is cooler than the ambient air. Dry air tends to cool more when lifted and tends to be more stable. The ambient lapse rate allows you to determine atmospheric stability.
16. Ambient air with a low or inverted lapse rate tends to be stable. A common type of ground- or surface-based temperature inversion is that which is produced by ground radiation on clear, cool nights with calm or light wind. When humidity is high you can expect poor visibility due to fog, haze, or low clouds.

CLOUDS
17. Clouds occur when water vapor condenses. They are divided into four basic families: low, middle, high, and clouds with vertical development.
18. Cumulus clouds are formed when unstable air is lifted. Stratiform clouds are formed when stable air is lifted. The lifting of moist, unstable air results in good visibility outside the cloud, showery precipitation, and turbulence. However, the lifting of moist, stable air results in continuous precipitation, little or no turbulence, and poor visibility.
19. Towering cumulus clouds indicate convective turbulence. Fair weather cumulus clouds indicate turbulence at and below the cloud level. To estimate the bases of cumulus clouds, in thousands of feet, divide the temperature/dewpoint spread at the surface by 2.5°C (4.4°F). If using the quick estimate method, divide the temperature/dewpoint spread by 4°F (2.2°C).
20. The suffix nimbus, used in naming clouds, means a rain cloud.
21. High clouds are composed mostly of ice crystals.

AIRMASSES AND FRONTS
22. An airmass is a large body of air that covers an extensive area and has fairly uniform temperature and moisture content. A front is a discontinuity between two airmasses. A cold front occurs when cold air displaces warmer air. A warm front occurs when warm air overruns colder air.
23. Cooling from below increases the stability of an airmass and warming from below decreases it. Steady precipitation, in contrast to showers, preceding a front is an indication of stratiform clouds with little or no turbulence.
24. When a cold airmass moves over, or is heated by, a warm surface, the result is cumuliform clouds, turbulence, and good visibility. When the air is moist and unstable, the updrafts are particularly strong, resulting in cumulonimbus clouds.
25. An occlusion occurs when a cold front overtakes another front. In a cold front occlusion, the air ahead of the warm front is warmer than the air behind the overtaking cold front.
26. A frontal cyclone starts as a slow-moving cold front or stationary front and can end as a cold front occlusion with potentially severe weather.

HIGH ALTITUDE WEATHER
27. A jetstream is defined as wind of 50 knots or greater. They are found in bands of strong westerly winds that occur at breaks in the tropopause in the northern hemisphere. While they can provide beneficial winds when flying west to east, they also can be associated with strong turbulence.
28. The strength and location of the jetstream is normally weaker and farther north in the summer. During the winter months in the middle latitudes, the jet stream shifts toward the south and speed increases.

9-1　　　　I21

A common type of ground or surface based temperature inversion is that which is produced by

A — warm air being lifted rapidly aloft in the vicinity of mountainous terrain.
B — the movement of colder air over warm air, or the movement of warm air under cold air.
C — ground radiation on clear, cool nights when the wind is light.

9-1. Answer C. GFDICM 9A (AW)

An inversion means the temperature increases (instead of decreases) with an increase in altitude. When an inversion exists, visibility is often restricted by fog, haze, smoke, and low clouds. One of the most familiar types of ground- or surface-based inversions forms from radiation cooling just above the ground on clear, cool nights when the wind is light. Answer (A) is wrong because rapidly lifted air in the vicinity of mountainous terrain is an example of unstable conditions, not the stable conditions associated with an inversion. Answer (B) is wrong because the movement of air implies somewhat unstable conditions which hinders the development of an inversion.

9-2 I21

The primary cause of all changes in the Earth's weather is

A — variation of solar energy received by the Earth's regions.
B — changes in air pressure over the Earth's surface.
C — movement of the air masses.

9-3 I20

A characteristic of the stratosphere is

A — an overall decrease of temperature with an increase in altitude.
B — a relatively even base altitude of approximately 35,000 feet.
C — relatively small changes in temperature with an increase in altitude.

9-4 I27

Steady precipitation, in contrast to showers, preceding a front is an indication of

A — stratiform clouds with moderate turbulence.
B — cumuliform clouds with little or no turbulence.
C — stratiform clouds with little or no turbulence.

9-5 I24

The presence of ice pellets at the surface is evidence that

A — there are thunderstorms in the area.
B — a cold front has passed.
C — there is freezing rain at a higher altitude.

9-6 I29

Which conditions result in the formation of frost?

A — The temperature of the collecting surface is at or below freezing and small droplets of moisture are falling.
B — When dew forms and the temperature is below freezing.
C — Temperature of the collecting surface is below the dewpoint of surrounding air and the dewpoint is colder than freezing.

9-2. Answer A. GFDICM 9A (AW)

The primary cause of weather is uneven heating of the earth's surface by the sun; solar radiation is the driving force that sets the atmosphere in motion. Answers (B) and (C) are wrong because changes in air pressure and movement of airmasses are both caused by uneven heating of the earth.

9-3. Answer C. GFDICM 9A (AW)

The stratosphere is above the tropopause. The base of the stratosphere varies with latitude and season from about 20,000 feet at the poles to 60,000 feet at the equator. This layer is characterized by relatively small changes in temperature with increasing altitude. Answer (A) is wrong because the temperature actually increases slightly with increases in altitude. Answer (B) is wrong because the base of the stratosphere varies with latitude and season.

9-4. Answer C. GFDICM 9A (AW)

Steady precipitation usually indicates the presence of moist, stable air that supports the development of stratiform clouds with little or no turbulence. Showery precipitation indicates the presence of moist, unstable air which is characterized by cumulus clouds with moderate or greater turbulence. Answer (A) is wrong because moderate turbulence is not associated with stable air and stratiform clouds. Answer (B) is wrong because cumuliform clouds are good indicators of unstable air and turbulent conditions.

9-5. Answer C. GFDICM 9A (AW)

Rain that remains a liquid even though its temperature is below freezing is referred to as freezing rain. Ice pellets result if the rain freezes as it falls. This always indicates freezing rain at some higher altitude and the existence of a layer of warmer air aloft. Answer (A) is wrong because ice pellets are not always an indication of a thunderstorm. Answer (B) is wrong because cold fronts do not necessarily produce ice pellets.

9-6. Answer C. GFDICM 9A (AW)

On cool nights, the surface of an aircraft may cool below the dewpoint of the surrounding air. When this happens, moisture condenses out of the air in the form of dew. If the temperature of the aircraft is at or below the dewpoint and the dewpoint is below freezing, moisture will deposit directly as ice crystals or frost rather than condensing as dew. Answer (A) is wrong because the dewpoint also must be below freezing; also, small droplets of falling moisture are not necessary. Answer (B) is wrong because, if dew forms and later freezes, it will be hard and transparent while frost is white and opaque.

9-7   I24
To which meteorological condition does the term "dewpoint" refer?

A — The temperature to which air must be cooled to become saturated.
B — The temperature at which condensation and evaporation are equal.
C — The temperature at which dew will always form.

9-8   I24
What temperature condition is indicated if wet snow is encountered at your flight altitude?

A — The temperature is above freezing at your altitude.
B — The temperature is below freezing at your altitude.
C — You are flying from a warm air mass into a cold air mass.

9-9   I24
The amount of water vapor which air can hold largely depends on

A — relative humidity.
B — air temperature.
C — stability of air.

9-10   I24
Clouds, fog, or dew will always form when

A — water vapor condenses.
B — water vapor is present.
C — the temperature and dewpoint are equal.

9-11   I23
What causes surface winds to flow across the isobars at an angle rather than parallel to the isobars?

A — Coriolis force.
B — Surface friction.
C — The greater density of the air at the surface.

9-7. Answer A. GFDICM 9A (AW)
When the dewpoint is reached, the air contains all the moisture it can hold at that temperature, and it is said to be saturated. Answer (B) is wrong because evaporation occurs at a higher temperature than condensation. Answer (C) is wrong because once the air cools to its saturation point, clouds, fog, or dew will form.

9-8. Answer A. GFDICM 9A (AW)
Precipitation that forms by sublimation falls as snow if the temperature of the air remains below freezing. Melting snow indicates that the temperature is above freezing at your altitude. Answer (B) is wrong because the temperature needs to be above freezing for the snow to begin melting. Answer (C) is wrong because wet snow does not specifically identify the type of air-mass you are flying through.

9-9. Answer B. GFDICM 9A (AW)
The amount of water vapor which air can hold largely depends on air temperature. Since warm air is not as dense as cold air, it can hold more water vapor than cold air. When the air temperature is the same as the dewpoint, the air is 100 percent saturated. As the air temperature increases above the dewpoint, the saturation percentage decreases below 100 percent. Answer (A) is wrong because the relative humidity is an indication of how saturated the air is at the existing temperature. Answer (C) is wrong because the stability of air is not the primary factor in determining how much water vapor the air can hold.

9-10. Answer A. GFDICM 9A (AW)
Condensation identifies a change in state of water vapor. When this happens in the atmosphere, clouds, fog, or dew will always form. Answer (B) is wrong because the presence of water vapor is not enough to induce condensation. Answer (C) is wrong because clouds, fog, and dew can form when the air is less than 100 percent saturated if sufficient condensation nuclei are present.

9-11. Answer B. GFDICM 9A (AW)
When the pressure gradient force and Coriolis force are balanced, airflow circulation aloft is parallel to the isobars. Within about 2,000 feet of the ground, surface friction slows the wind, and Coriolis force is weakened. Pressure gradient force then predominates, causing the wind to flow at an angle to the isobars. Answer (A) is wrong because Coriolis force causes the wind to flow parallel to the isobars. Answer (C) is wrong because air density at the surface has practically no effect on the pressure gradient.

9-12   I23

Winds at 5,000 feet AGL on a particular flight are southwesterly while most of the surface winds are southerly. This difference in direction is primarily due to

A — a stronger pressure gradient at higher altitudes.
B — friction between the wind and the surface.
C — stronger Coriolis force at the surface.

9-13   I23

What relationship exists between the winds at 2,000 feet above the surface and the surface winds?

A — The winds at 2,000 feet and the surface winds flow in the same direction, but the surface winds are weaker due to friction.
B — The winds at 2,000 feet tend to parallel the isobars while the surface winds cross the isobars at an angle toward lower pressure and are weaker.
C — The surface winds tend to veer to the right of the winds at 2,000 feet and are usually weaker.

9-14   I23

Which force, in the Northern Hemisphere, acts at a right angle to the wind and deflects it to the right until parallel to the isobars?

A — Centrifugal.
B — Pressure gradient.
C — Coriolis.

9-15   I21

The most frequent type of ground- or surface-based temperature inversion is that produced by

A — radiation on a clear, relatively still night.
B — warm air being lifted rapidly aloft in the vicinity of mountainous terrain.
C — the movement of colder air under warm air, or the movement of warm air over cold air.

9-16   I21

What feature is associated with a temperature inversion?

A — A stable layer of air.
B — An unstable layer of air.
C — Air mass thunderstorms.

9-12. Answer B. GFDICM 9A (AW)

See explanation for Question 9-11. Answer (A) is wrong because pressure gradient force is not affected by friction. Answer (C) is incorrect since Coriolis force is weaker at or near the surface.

9-13. Answer B. GFDICM 9A (AW)

See explanation for Question 9-11. At an altitude of about 2,000 feet AGL, the effect of surface friction on the wind decreases. Because of this, Coriolis force strengthens and tends to make the wind blow parallel to the isobars. Answer (A) is wrong because the winds at the surface, and at 2,000 feet, do not flow in the same direction. Answer (C) is wrong because the winds at 2,000 feet (not the surface) tend to be deflected to the right due to the stronger Coriolis force.

9-14. Answer C. GFDICM 9A (AW)

Coriolis force acts at a right angle to the wind and deflects the air to the right in the Northern Hemisphere. Answer (A) is wrong because centrifugal force doesn't act on the wind unless it is turning. With a wind curving to the right, centrifugal force would tend to act outward, or to the left. Answer (B) is wrong because the pressure gradient causes the wind to flow directly (perpendicular to the isobars) from an area of high pressure to an area of low pressure.

9-15. Answer A. GFDICM 9A (AW)

Temperature inversions are usually confined to fairly shallow layers and may occur near the surface or at higher altitudes. They usually develop in stable air with little or no wind and turbulence. One of the most familiar types of a ground- or surface-based inversion is from radiation cooling just above the ground on clear, cool nights when the wind is light. Answer (B) is wrong because rapidly lifted air in the vicinity of mountainous terrain is an example of orographic lifting. Answer (C) is wrong because the movement of air implies somewhat unstable conditions, such as frontal movement. This tends to inhibit the development of an inversion.

9-16. Answer A. GFDICM 9A (AW)

See explanation for Question 9-15. Typical conditions associated with temperature inversions include stable air with little, or no, wind and turbulence. Answers (B) and (C) are wrong because temperature inversions seldom occur with unstable conditions.

9-17   I25
What type of clouds will be formed if very stable moist air is forced upslope?

A — First stratified clouds and then vertical clouds.
B — Vertical clouds with increasing height.
C — Stratified clouds with little vertical development.

9-17. Answer C. GFDICM 9A (AW)
When air is forced aloft from orographic lifting, the stability of the air before it is lifted determines the type of clouds that will form. For example, if stable, moist air is forced up a slope, stratus-type clouds with little vertical development typically form. The stable air resists further upward movement. On the other hand, if unstable, moist air is lifted aloft, clouds with vertical development usually form (answers A and B).

9-18   I27
The general characteristics of unstable air are

A — good visibility, showery precipitation, and cumuliform-type clouds.
B — good visibility, steady precipitation, and stratiform-type clouds.
C — poor visibility, intermittent precipitation, and cumuliform-type clouds.

9-18. Answer A. GFDICM 9A (AW)
Unstable air is usually turbulent, with good surface visibility outside of scattered rain showers and cumuliform-type clouds, including clouds with extensive vertical development. In contrast, stable air is generally smooth, with restricted visibilities in widespread areas of stratiform clouds and steady rain or drizzle. Answers (B) and (C) are incorrect because they indicate some of the characteristics of stable air.

9-19   I27
Which is a characteristic of stable air?

A — Fair weather cumulus clouds.
B — Stratiform clouds.
C — Unlimited visibility.

9-19. Answer B. GFDICM 9A (AW)
See explanation for Question 9-18.

9-20   I25
What type clouds can be expected when an unstable air mass is forced to ascend a mountain slope?

A — Layered clouds with little vertical development.
B — Stratified clouds with considerable associated turbulence.
C — Clouds with extensive vertical development.

9-20. Answer C. GFDICM 9A (AW)
See explanation for Question 9-17.

9-21   I27
What are the characteristics of stable air?

A — Good visibility, steady precipitation, and stratus-type clouds.
B — Poor visibility, intermittent precipitation, and cumulus-type clouds.
C — Poor visibility, steady precipitation, and stratus-type clouds.

9-21. Answer C. GFDICM 9A (AW)
See explanation for Question 9-18.

9-22   I27
What are some characteristics of unstable air?

A — Nimbostratus clouds and good surface visibility.
B — Turbulence and poor surface visibility.
C — Turbulence and good surface visibility.

9-22. Answer C. GFDICM 9A (AW)
See explanation for Question 9-18.

9-23   I25

Stability can be determined from which measurement of the atmosphere?

A — Low-level winds.
B — Ambient lapse rate.
C — Atmospheric pressure.

9-23. Answer B. GFDICM 9A (AW)

The ambient lapse rate is the rate at which the air cools with an increase in altitude. If the lapse rate is large, warm air is encouraged to rise creating unstable conditions. If the lapse rate is small, lifting is suppressed resulting in stable conditions. Low-level winds (answer A) do not measure stability in the atmosphere, and atmospheric pressure (answer C) does not measure stability, it measures the weight of a given parcel of air.

9-24   I25

What determines the structure or type of clouds which form as a result of air being forced to ascend?

A — The method by which the air is lifted.
B — The stability of the air before lifting occurs.
C — The amount of condensation nuclei present after lifting occurs.

9-24. Answer B. GFDICM 9A (AW)

Assuming moisture is present, the stability of the air before lifting occurs plays a major role in determining the structure or type of clouds that form when air is lifted. For example, when stable air is forced aloft, stratus-type clouds with little vertical development commonly form. If unstable air is lifted aloft, clouds with vertical development will usually form. The method by which the air is lifted (answer A) has little to do with determining the type of clouds formed. Further, the amount of condensation nuclei (answer C) can induce condensation or sublimation, but it has a minimal effect on the structure or type of clouds.

9-25   I25

Which of the following combinations of weather producing variables would likely result in cumuliform-type clouds, good visibility, rain showers, and possible clear-type icing in clouds?

A — Unstable, moist air, and no lifting mechanism.
B — Stable, dry air, and orographic lifting.
C — Unstable, moist air, and orographic lifting.

9-25. Answer C. GFDICM 9A (AW)

Unstable, moist air that is lifted orographically usually results in turbulent conditions, with good surface visibility outside of scattered rain showers and cumuliform-type clouds. With temperatures near or below freezing, an accumulation of clear ice is possible. Answer (A) is wrong because a lifting mechanism is required for the production of cumuliform clouds. Answer (B) is wrong because stable, dry air doesn't support the development of stratus clouds or precipitation.

9-26   I25

Unsaturated air flowing upslope will cool at the rate of approximately (dry adiabatic lapse rate)

A — 3°C per 1,000 feet.
B — 2°C per 1,000 feet.
C — 2.5°C per 1,000 feet.

9-26. Answer A. GFDICM 9A (AW)

The adiabatic lapse rate is the rate at which air cools as it is lifted. The rate depends on the amount of moisture present in the air. The dry adiabatic lapse rate is 3°C per 1,000 feet. The moist adiabatic lapse rate varies from 1.1°C to 2.8°C per 1,000 feet. A lapse rate of 2°C per 1,000 feet is the average lapse rate (answer B). Answer (C) is wrong because 2.5°C per 1,000 feet is the rate of temperature and dewpoint convergence in a convective, or lifting, airmass.

9-27   I21

A temperature inversion will normally form only

A — in stable air.
B — in unstable air.
C — when a stratiform layer merges with a cumuliform mass.

9-27. Answer A. GFDICM 9A (AW)

Temperature inversions normally occur in stable air with little, or no, wind and turbulence. Answers (B) and (C) are wrong because temperature inversions are seldom associated with unstable conditions.

9-28   I27
Frontal waves normally form on

A — slow moving cold fronts or stationary fronts.
B — slow moving warm fronts and strong occluded
       fronts.
C — rapidly moving cold fronts or warm fronts.

9-29   I27
Which are characteristics of an unstable cold air mass
moving over a warm surface?

A — Cumuliform clouds, turbulence, and poor visibility.
B — Cumuliform clouds, turbulence, and good visibili-
       ty.
C — Stratiform clouds, smooth air, and poor visibility.

9-30   I26
The suffix "nimbus," used in naming clouds, means a

A — cloud with extensive vertical development.
B — raincloud.
C — dark massive, towering cloud.

9-31   I26
What are the four families of clouds?

A — Stratus, cumulus, nimbus, and cirrus.
B — Clouds formed by updrafts, fronts, cooling layers
       of air, and precipitation into warm air.
C — High, middle, low, and those with extensive ver-
       tical development.

9-32   I27
Which weather phenomenon is always associated with
the passage of a frontal system?

A — A wind change.
B — An abrupt decrease in pressure.
C — Clouds, either ahead or behind the front.

9-28. Answer A. GFDICM 9A (AW)
A frontal wave is a phenomenon which results primarily from the interaction of two contrasting airmasses.
The wave usually begins as a disturbance along a
slow moving cold front or stationary front. Answer (B)
is wrong because slow moving warm fronts do not
promote the development of a frontal wave and an
occluded front typically develops from a frontal wave.
Answer (C) is wrong because a frontal wave rarely
develops ahead of a rapidly moving front.

9-29. Answer B. GFDICM 9A (AW)
The characteristics of an unstable cold airmass are
similar to that of any unstable airmass that is forced
aloft. The unstable air promotes the development of
cumuliform clouds, turbulence, and good visibility
outside of clouds or precipitation. Answer (A) is wrong
because poor visibility is associated with stable
conditions. Answer (C) is wrong because all the elements
listed represent conditions of a stable airmass.

9-30. Answer B. GFDICM 9A (AW)
The term prefix "nimbo" and the suffix "nimbus" are
used to describe a raincloud. "Cumulo" is used to
describe clouds with extensive vertical development
(answer A). "Cumulonimbus" describes massive towering
clouds, such as those in a thunderstorm (answer C).

9-31. Answer C. GFDICM 9A (AW)
The four families of clouds are: high, middle, low, and
those with extensive vertical development. Stratus,
cumulus, nimbus, and cirrus (answer A) are classifica-
tions based on appearance of a cloud. Answer (B) lists
ways in which clouds are developed.

9-32. Answer A. GFDICM 9A (AW)
The most reliable indications that you are crossing a
front are a change in wind direction, wind speed, or
both. Although the exact new direction of the wind is
difficult to predict, the wind always shifts to the right in
the northern hemisphere. Answer (B) is wrong
because, although there will probably be a pressure
change, it can be in either direction and may not be
abrupt. Answer (C) is wrong because, if the air is
relatively dry, clouds may not form near a front.

9-33   I27

What is indicated by the term "embedded thunderstorms"?

A — Severe thunderstorms are embedded within a squall line.
B — Thunderstorms are predicted to develop in a stable air mass.
C — Thunderstorms are obscured by massive cloud layers and cannot be seen.

9-34   I28

Fair weather cumulus clouds often indicate

A — turbulence at and below the cloud level.
B — poor visibility.
C — smooth flying conditions.

9-35   I20

The average height of the troposphere in the middle latitudes is

A — 20,000 feet.
B — 25,000 feet.
C — 37,000 feet.

9-36   I32

A jetstream is defined as wind of

A — 30 knots or greater.
B — 40 knots or greater.
C — 50 knots or greater.

9-37   I26

A high cloud is composed mostly of

A — ozone.
B — condensation nuclei.
C — ice crystals.

9-38   I27

An air mass is a body of air that

A — has similar cloud formations associated with it.
B — creates a wind shift as it moves across the Earth's surface.
C — covers an extensive area and has fairly uniform properties of temperature and moisture.

9-33. Answer C. GFDICM 9A (AW)
When a thunderstorm is obscured by other cloud formations, it is said to be embedded. When IFR conditions exist, this can be particularly hazardous, since you cannot see the thunderstorms. Maximum use of ground and/or airborne radar is recommended when embedded thunderstorms are reported, or even suspected. Answer (A) is wrong because a squall line is a line of severe weather and thunderstorms. Answer (B) is wrong because thunderstorms do not develop in a stable airmass.

9-34. Answer A. GFDICM 9A (AW)
Cumulus clouds form in convective currents resulting from the uneven heating of the earth's surface. Widely spaced cumulus clouds that form in fairly clear skies are called fair weather cumulus and indicate a shallow layer of instability. You can expect turbulence at and below the cloud level, but little icing or precipitation. Answers (B) and (C) are wrong because in order for cumulus clouds to develop, the air must be somewhat unstable, resulting in good visibilities and turbulent flying conditions.

9-35. Answer C. GFDICM 9A (AW)
The height of the tropopause varies from about 20,000 feet to 30,000 feet (answer A) at the poles to 60,000 feet at the equator. For a given latitude, it is higher in the summer than it is in the winter. In the mid-latitudes, it averages about 37,000 feet. Answers (A) and (B) are incorrect because 20,000 to 25,000 feet is an approximate height in the polar regions, not in the mid-latitudes.

9-36. Answer C. GFDICM 9A (AW)
A jetstream can be described as a narrow band of high velocity wind of 50 knots or more which meanders vertically and horizontally around the earth in wave-like patterns. Answers (A) and (B) are wrong because they do not meet the 50 knot criterion.

9-37. Answer C. GFDICM 9A (AW)
Because of the extremely cold temperatures, high clouds are composed mainly of ice crystals. The height of the bases of these clouds ranges from about 16,500 to 45,000 feet MSL. Ozone (answer A) is a layer of unstable oxygen within the stratosphere which extends from a height of about 9 to 22 miles. Answer (B) is wrong because there are fewer condensation nuclei in the upper altitudes.

9-38. Answer C. GFDICM 9A (AW)
An airmass is a large body of air with fairly uniform temperature and moisture content. It usually forms where air remains stationary or nearly stationary for several days. Answer (A) is wrong because a dry airmass may not have any clouds. Answer (B) is wrong because a wind shift is associated with frontal passage.

9-39   I24
What enhances the growth rate of precipitation?

A — Advective action.
B — Upward currents.
C — Cyclonic movement.

9-39. Answer B. GFDICM 9A (AW)
Once a water droplet forms, it grows as it collides and merges with other droplets. This process produces large precipitation particles. If these particles encounter any upward currents, the process will continue and the growth rate will be increased. Precipitation formed by merging drops with mild upward currents can produce light to moderate rain. Strong upward currents support the largest drops and can produce heavy rain and hail. Answer (A) is wrong because advection is the transference of heat by horizontal currents. Answer (C) is wrong because cyclonic movement refers to the counterclockwise movement around a low pressure area.

9-40   I24
Which precipitation type normally indicates freezing rain at higher altitudes?

A — Snow.
B — Hail.
C — Ice pellets.

9-40. Answer C. GFDICM 9A (AW)
Ice pellets result if rain freezes as it falls. This usually indicates freezing rain at some higher altitude and the existence of a layer of warmer air aloft. Answer (A) is wrong because snow normally indicates that the temperature at higher levels is below freezing, not above freezing. Answer (B) is wrong because hail typically develops in the updraft of a thunderstorm.

9-41   I32
The strength and location of the jetstream is normally

A — stronger and farther north in the winter.
B — weaker and farther north in the summer.
C — stronger and farther north in the summer.

9-41. Answer B. GFDICM 9A (AW)
In the mid-latitudes, the jetstream is usually weaker in the summer than in the winter. This is because its mean position shifts north in the summer. As the jet stream moves north, its core descends to a lower altitude, and its average speed usually decreases. Answer (A) is wrong because the jetstream shifts south in the winter. Answer (C) is wrong because the jetstream is stronger in the winter.

9-42   I21
Which weather conditions should be expected beneath a low-level temperature inversion layer when the relative humidity is high?

A — Smooth air and poor visibility due to fog, haze, or low clouds.
B — Light wind shear and poor visibility due to haze and light rain.
C — Turbulent air and poor visibility due to fog, low stratus-type clouds, and showery precipitation.

9-42. Answer A. GFDICM 9A (AW)
In order for a low-level temperature inversion to exist, the air must be stable. This, combined with a high relative humidity, usually results in smooth air with poor visibility in fog, haze, or low clouds. Answers (B) and (C) are wrong because light wind shear, turbulent air, and showery precipitation are characteristics of unstable air.

9-43   I20
Which feature is associated with the tropopause?

A — Absence of wind and turbulent conditions.
B — Absolute upper limit of cloud formation.
C — Abrupt change in temperature lapse rate.

9-43. Answer C. GFDICM 9A (AWS)
The top of the troposphere is called the tropopause and serves as the boundary between the troposphere and the stratosphere. The location of the tropopause is usually characterized by a pronounced change in the temperature lapse rate. In the northern hemisphere there are two breaks in the tropopause; one is between the polar and subtropical airmasses and the other is between the subtropical and tropical airmasses. These breaks define the location of the jet stream (answer A). Although it is rare, clouds may extend above this layer (answer B), but only in extreme cases.

SECTION B
WEATHER HAZARDS

THUNDERSTORMS

1. When sufficient moisture is present, cumulus cloud build-ups indicate the presence of convective turbulence.
2. Thunderstorm formation requires an unstable lapse rate, a lifting force, and a relatively high moisture level.
3. The life cycle of a thunderstorm consists of three distinct stages. The cumulus stage is characterized by continuous updrafts. Thunderstorms reach the greatest intensity during the mature stage, which is signaled by the beginning of precipitation at the surface. As the storm dies during the dissipating stage, updrafts weaken and downdrafts become predominant.
4. Airmass thunderstorms are relatively short-lived storms and are usually isolated or scattered over a large area. They form in convective currents, which are most active on warm summer afternoons when the winds are light. Severe thunderstorms contain wind gusts of 50 knots or more, hail 3/4 inch in diameter or larger, and/or tornadoes.
5. Cumulonimbus clouds by themselves indicate severe turbulence. Other indications of turbulence are very frequent lightning and roll clouds.
6. Some weather hazards associated with thunderstorms, such as lightning, hail, and turbulence are not confined to the cloud itself. Wind shear areas can be found on all sides of a thunderstorm, as well as directly under it.
7. Embedded thunderstorms are particularly dangerous to IFR pilots. Because they are obscured by massive cloud layers, they are more difficult to avoid.
8. Airborne weather radar can help you avoid thunderstorms. However, it provides no assurance of avoiding IFR weather conditions. If using radar, avoid intense radar echoes by at least 20 miles and do not fly between them if they are less than 40 miles apart.
9. A squall line is a narrow band of active thunderstorms that often forms 50 to 200 miles ahead of a fast moving cold front and contains some of the most severe types of weather-related hazards.
10. If you encounter turbulence during flight, establish maneuvering or penetration speed, maintain a level flight attitude, and accept variations in airspeed and altitude. If encountering turbulence during the approach to a landing, it is recommended that you increase the airspeed slightly above normal approach speed to attain more positive control.

WAKE TURBULENCE

11. Wake turbulence is created when an aircraft generates lift. The greatest vortex strength occurs when the generating aircraft is heavy, slow, in a clean configuration, and at a high angle of attack.
12. Wingtip vortices can exceed the roll rate of an aircraft, especially when flying in the same direction as the generating aircraft.
13. Wingtip vortices tend to sink below the flight path of the aircraft which generated them. They are most hazardous during light, quartering tailwind conditions. You should avoid the area below and behind an aircraft generating wake turbulence, especially at low altitude where even a momentary wake encounter could be hazardous.
14. A helicopter can produce vortices similar to wingtip vortices of a large fixed-wing airplane.

OTHER TURBULENCE

15. Turbulence that momentarily causes slight, erratic changes in altitude and/or attitude should be reported as light. Moderate turbulence causes noticeable changes in altitude and/or attitude, but aircraft control remains positive.
16. Mechanical turbulence is often experienced in the traffic pattern when wind forms eddies as it blows over hangars, stands of trees, or other obstructions.
17. Any front traveling at a speed of 30 knots or more produces at least a moderate amount of turbulence.
18. Turbulence that is encountered above 15,000 feet AGL that is not associated with cumuliform cloudiness, including thunderstorms, are reported as clear air turbulence. Clear air turbulence often develops in or near the jet stream, which is a narrow band of high altitude winds near the tropopause.
19. A common location of clear air turbulence is in an upper trough on the polar side of a jet stream. The jet stream and associated clear air turbulence can sometimes be visually identified in flight by long streaks of cirrus clouds.
20. Strong mountain wave turbulence can be anticipated when the winds across a ridge are 40 knots or more, and the air is stable. The crests of mountain waves may be marked by lens-shaped, or lenticular, clouds. The presence of rotor clouds on the lee side of the mountain also indicates the possibility of strong turbulence.

21. The greatest turbulence normally occurs as you approach the lee side of mountain ranges, ridges, or hilly terrain in strong headwinds.

WIND SHEAR

22. Wind shear is a sudden, drastic change in wind speed and/or direction. It can exist at any altitude and may occur in a vertical or horizontal direction.
23. Wind shear is often associated with a strong low-level temperature inversion with strong winds above the inversion, a jet stream, a thunderstorm, or a frontal zone.
24. Wind shear can also occur prior to the passage of a warm front and following the passage of a cold front.
25. During an approach, monitoring the power and vertical velocity required to remain on the proper glideslope is the most important and most easily recognized means of being alerted to possible wind shear. When the wind changes to more of a headwind, the aircraft initially tends to balloon above the glidepath, and then drop below the glidepath because of lower groundspeed. To correct, reduce power momentarily, and then increase it once established in the headwind conditions. The reverse actions are needed if flying into conditions of less headwind or more tailwind.
26. Microbursts are one of the most dangerous sources of wind shear. A microburst is an intense, localized downdraft seldom lasting longer than 15 minutes from the time the burst first strikes the ground until dissipation. The maximum downdrafts encountered in a microburst may be as strong as 6,000 feet per minute.
27. In a microburst, strong wind flows outward in every direction at the surface. An aircraft entering a microburst initially experiences a headwind, with increasing performance, and then a tailwind, with decreasing performance combined with a strong downdraft. If encountering a headwind of 45 knots within a microburst, you would expect a total shear across the microburst of 90 knots.

RESTRICTIONS TO VISIBILITY

28. Restrictions to visibility can include fog, haze, smoke, smog, and dust.
29. Formation of fog is encouraged by the presence of small particles in the air on which condensation can occur. Industrial areas typically produce more fog since the burning of fossil fuels produces more of these condensation nuclei.
30. Radiation fog forms over fairly flat land on clear, calm nights when the air is moist and there is a small temperature/dewpoint spread.
31. Advection fog is most likely to form in coastal areas when moist air moves over colder ground or water. It can appear suddenly during the day or night and is more persistent than radiation fog.
32. Advection fog and upslope fog are both dependent upon wind for their formation. However, surface winds stronger than 15 knots tend to dissipate or lift advection fog into low stratus clouds.
33. Volcanic ash clouds are highly abrasive to aircraft and engines, and they also restrict visibility.
34. Precipitation-induced fog is most commonly associated with warm fronts and is a result of saturation due to evaporation of precipitation.
35. Steam fog forms when very cold air moves over a warmer water surface.
36. Restrictions to visibility, such as haze, create the illusion of being at a greater distance above the runway, which can cause a pilot to fly a lower-than-normal approach.

ICING

37. The three types of structural ice are rime, clear, and mixed.
38. The accumulation of ice on an aircraft increases drag and weight and decreases lift and thrust.
39. Ice pellets usually indicate the presence of freezing rain at a higher altitude. Freezing rain is hazardous because it is most likely to have the highest rate of accumulation of structural icing. The presence of freezing rain at your altitude indicates the temperature is above freezing at some higher altitude.
40 Since high clouds typically do not consist of liquid water, they are least likely to contribute to aircraft structural icing.
41. The freezing level is where the temperature is 0°C. You can estimate the freezing level by dividing the temperature in °C above zero, by the lapse rate of 2°C per 1,000 feet.
42. If frost is not removed from the wings before flight, it may cause an early airflow separation which decreases lift and increases drag. This causes the airplane to stall at a lower-than-normal angle of attack.

HYDROPLANING

43. Hydroplaning occurs when the tires float on top of a thin layer of water on the runway. It results in poor or nil braking action at high speeds, and may result in an aircraft skidding off the side or end of the runway.
44. High aircraft speed, standing water, slush, and a smooth runway texture are factors conducive to hydroplaning.

COLD WEATHER OPERATIONS

45. During preflight in cold weather, crankcase breather lines should receive special attention because they are susceptible to being clogged by ice from crankcase vapors that have condensed and subsequently frozen.
46. It is recommended that during cold weather operations, you should preheat the cabin, as well as the engine.

9-44   I31

Which is true regarding the use of airborne weather-avoidance radar for the recognition of certain weather conditions?

A — The radarscope provides no assurance of avoiding instrument weather conditions.

B — The avoidance of hail is assured when flying between and just clear of the most intense echoes.

C — The clear area between intense echoes indicates that visual sighting of storms can be maintained when flying between the echoes.

9-45   I21

If the air temperature is +8°C at an elevation of 1,350 feet and a standard (average) temperature lapse rate exists, what will be the approximate freezing level?

A — 3,350 feet MSL.
B — 5,350 feet MSL.
C — 9,350 feet MSL.

9-46   I30

Which weather phenomenon signals the beginning of the mature stage of a thunderstorm?

A — The start of rain at the surface.
B — Growth rate of cloud is maximum.
C — Strong turbulence in the cloud.

9-44. Answer A. GFDICM 9B (AC 00-24B)
Airborne weather radar is designed as an aid for avoiding severe weather, not for penetrating it. Weather radar detects precipitation based on echo returns of significant raindrops; it does not detect minute droplets or other phenomenon such as hail, turbulence, and updrafts/downdrafts. Therefore, it should not be relied on to avoid instrument weather associated with clouds and fog or certain other severe weather conditions. Answers (B) and (C) are wrong because areas that appear clear between or near intense echoes may contain severe weather that the radar is unable to detect.

9-45. Answer B. GFDICM 9B (AW)
The standard, or average, temperature lapse rate is approximately 2°C per 1,000 feet. If the temperature at 1,350 feet is 8°C, divide 8°C by 2°C to determine how much higher the freezing level is (8 ÷ 2 = 4). This means the freezing level is 4,000 feet above 1,350 feet, or 5,350 feet MSL. Answers (A) and (C) are wrong because they represent lapse rates of 4° per 1,000 feet and 1° per 1,000 feet, respectively.

9-46. Answer A. GFDICM 9B (AW)
There are three stages for a typical thunderstorm — cumulus, mature, and dissipating. In the cumulus stage, a lifting action initiates the vertical movement of air. As the air rises and cools to the dewpoint, water vapor condenses forming cumuliform clouds. This first stage is dominated by rapid cloud growth (answer B) and the presence of updrafts that can reach speeds of 3,000 f.p.m. Updrafts continue to increase up to speeds of 6,000 f.p.m. early in the mature stage. Thunderstorms reach the greatest intensity during the mature stage, which is signaled by the beginning of precipitation at the surface. A corresponding downdraft is typical and may reach a velocity of 2,500 f.p.m. When the cell becomes an area of predominant downdrafts, it is considered to be in the dissipating stage. Answer (C) is wrong because strong turbulence exists throughout the life cycle of a thunderstorm.

9-47   I28
Which clouds have the greatest turbulence?

A — Towering cumulus.
B — Cumulonimbus.
C — Altocumulus castellatus.

9-48   I28
Standing lenticular clouds (ACSL), in mountainous areas, indicate

A — an inversion.
B — unstable air.
C — turbulence.

9-49   I28
The presence of standing lenticular altocumulus clouds is a good indication of

A — a jetstream.
B — very strong turbulence.
C — heavy icing conditions.

9-50   I29
Which family of clouds is least likely to contribute to structural icing on an aircraft?

A — Low clouds.
B — High clouds.
C — Clouds with extensive vertical development.

9-51   I30
Where can wind shear associated with a thunderstorm be found? Choose the most complete answer.

A — In front of the thunderstorm cell (anvil side) and on the right side of the cell.
B — In front of the thunderstorm cell and directly under the cell.
C — On all sides of the thunderstorm cell and directly under the cell.

9-52   I30
Where do squall lines most often develop?

A — In an occluded front.
B — In a cold air mass.
C — Ahead of a cold front.

9-47. Answer B. GFDICM 9B (AW)
Cumulonimbus clouds usually have the greatest turbulence because of the existence of both up- and downdrafts. Cumulonimbus is synonymous with thunderstorms. Towering cumulus (answer A) and altocumulus castellatus (answer C) consist primarily of clouds with updraft conditions and less turbulence than cumulonimbus.

9-48. Answer C. GFDICM 9B (AW)
Standing lenticular altocumulus clouds are formed on the crests of waves created by barriers in the wind flow. The clouds show little movement and are characterized by their smooth, polished edges. The presence of these clouds is a good indication of very strong turbulence, and they should be avoided. Answer (A) is wrong because a temperature inversion is associated with stratus clouds, not lenticular clouds. Answer (B) is wrong because cumulus, not lenticular, clouds exist in unstable air.

9-49. Answer B. GFDICM 9B (AW)
See explanation for Question 9-48. Answer (A) is incorrect because a jet stream is usually well above the level of lenticulars. Answer (C) is wrong because lenticular clouds may form in hot weather, as well as in cold conditions associated with icing.

9-50. Answer B. GFDICM 9B (AW)
High clouds are the least likely to contribute to structural icing since they are composed mainly of ice crystals. On the other hand, icing is quite common in low clouds (answer A) and clouds with extensive vertical development (answer C), especially when the temperature is between 0°C and −10°C.

9-51. Answer C. GFDICM 9B (AW)
Near the surface, under a thunderstorm, there is typically an area of low-level turbulence which develop as downdrafts emerge and spread out at the surface. These create a shear zone that spreads outward in all directions from the center of the storm. Answers (A) and (B) represent only some of the areas wind shear can be found in the vicinity of a thunderstorm.

9-52. Answer C. GFDICM 9B (AW)
Squall lines are a narrow band of active thunderstorms which normally contain very severe weather. They often form 50 to 200 miles ahead of a fast moving cold front, although the existence of a front is not necessary for a squall line to from. Answers (A) and (B) are wrong because squall lines are not common in occluded fronts or cold airmasses.

9-53   I28

Where does wind shear occur?

A — Exclusively in thunderstorms.
B — Wherever there is an abrupt decrease in pressure and/or temperature.
C — With either a wind shift or a windspeed gradient at any level in the atmosphere.

9-54   I28

What is an important characteristic of wind shear?

A — It is primarily associated with the lateral vortices generated by thunderstorms.
B — It usually exists only in the vicinity of thunderstorms, but may be found near a strong temperature inversion.
C — It may be associated with either a wind shift or a windspeed gradient at any level in the atmosphere.

9-55   I28

Which is a characteristic of low-level wind shear as it relates to frontal activity?

A — With a warm front, the most critical period is before the front passes the airport.
B — With a cold front, the most critical period is just before the front passes the airport.
C — Turbulence will always exist in wind-shear conditions.

9-56   I30

During the life cycle of a thunderstorm, which stage is characterized predominantly by downdrafts?

A — Cumulus.
B — Dissipating.
C — Mature.

9-53. Answer C. GFDICM 9B (AW)
A wind shear is a sudden, drastic shift in wind speed and/or direction that may occur at any altitude in a vertical or horizontal plane. Thunderstorms and abrupt decreases in pressure and/or temperature (answers A and B) are places where wind shear is common, but they do not represent all the places wind shear can occur.

9-54. Answer C. GFDICM 9B (AW)
See explanation for Question 9-53.

9-55. Answer A. GFDICM 9B (AW)
With fronts, the most common places for wind shear is either just before or just after the front passes. With a warm front, wind shear occurs just before the front passes. In a cold front, wind shear occurs just after the front passes. Studies indicate the amount of wind shear in a warm front is generally greater than in a cold front. Answer (B) is wrong because the most critical period for wind shear associated with a cold front is after the front passes. Answer (C) is wrong because turbulence will not always exist in wind shear conditions.

9-56. Answer B. GFDICM 9B (AW)
There are three stages to a thunderstorm — cumulus, mature, and dissipating. In the cumulus stage (answer A), a lifting action indicates the vertical movement of air. As the air rises and cools to the dewpoint, water vapor condenses forming cumuliform clouds. This stage is dominated by rapid cloud growth and the presence of updrafts that can reach speeds of 3,000 f.p.m. Updrafts continue to increase up to speeds of 6,000 f.p.m. in the early mature stage. Thunderstorms reach the greatest intensity during the mature stage (answer C), which is signaled by the beginning of precipitation at the surface. Resulting downdrafts during this stage may reach velocities of 2,500 f.p.m. When the cell becomes an area of predominant downdrafts, it is considered to be in the dissipating stage.

9-57   I30

Which weather phenomenon is always associated with a thunderstorm?

A — Lightning.
B — Heavy rain showers.
C — Supercooled raindrops.

9-58   I30

Which thunderstorms generally produce the most severe conditions, such as heavy hail and destructive winds?

A — Warm front.
B — Squall line.
C — Air mass.

9-59   I30

Which procedure is recommended if a pilot should unintentionally penetrate embedded thunderstorm activity?

A — Reverse aircraft heading or proceed toward an area of known VFR conditions.
B — Reduce airspeed to maneuvering speed and maintain a constant altitude.
C — Set power for recommended turbulence penetration airspeed and attempt to maintain a level flight attitude.

9-60   I30

What is an indication that downdrafts have developed and the thunderstorm cell has entered the mature stage?

A — The anvil top has completed its development.
B — Precipitation begins to fall from the cloud base.
C — A gust front forms.

9-61   I30

What are the requirements for the formation of a thunderstorm?

A — A cumulus cloud with sufficient moisture.
B — A cumulus cloud with sufficient moisture and an inverted lapse rate.
C — Sufficient moisture, an unstable lapse rate, and a lifting action.

9-57. Answer A. GFDICM 9B (AW)

Remember, lightning causes thunder. By definition, lightning is one of the hazards always associated with thunderstorms and it may occur throughout the cloud. While it rarely causes personal injury or substantial damage to the aircraft in flight, it can cause temporary loss of vision, puncture the aircraft skin, or damage electronic navigation and communications equipment. Answer (B) is wrong because heavy rain showers are not always associated with thunderstorms. Answer (C) is wrong because the precipitation that falls from a thunderstorm is not always supercooled.

9-58. Answer B. GFDICM 9B (AW)

A squall line is a nonfrontal band of thunderstorms that contains the most severe types of weather-related hazards including heavy hail and destructive winds. Answers (A) and (C) are wrong because thunderstorms that develop near warm fronts or airmasses are usually isolated and scattered over a large area and not as severe as squall line thunderstorms.

9-59. Answer C. GFDICM 9B (AW)

If you enter turbulence unexpectedly, unintentionally enter a thunderstorm, or expect that you may encounter turbulence, reduce power to slow the airplane to maneuvering speed or less, and attempt to maintain a level flight attitude. You normally should not reverse direction (answer A), since this may result in longer exposure to the thunderstorm hazards. Answer (B), although partially correct, is less correct than answer (C). Trying to maintain a constant altitude in turbulence only increases the stress on the aircraft.

9-60. Answer B. GFDICM 9B (AW)

See explanation for Question 9-56. Answer (A) is incorrect because the anvil top formation is more characteristic of the dissipating stage. Although presence of a gust front (answer C), is commonly associated with the mature stage, the most accurate answer choice is (B).

9-61. Answer C. GFDICM 9B (AW)

There are three conditions necessary to create a thunderstorm. They are an unstable lapse rate, some type of lifting action, and a relatively high moisture content. If these conditions exist, cumulus clouds typically begin to form. Answers (A) and (B) are wrong because neither mention a lifting action. Also the inclusion of an inverted lapse rate in (B) would imply a temperature inversion which normally indicates stable conditions.

9-62   I28

What is an important characteristic of wind shear?

A — It is an atmospheric condition that is associated exclusively with zones of convergence.
B — The Coriolis phenomenon in both high- and low-level air masses is the principal generating force.
C — It is an atmospheric condition that may be associated with a low-level temperature inversion, a jet stream, or a frontal zone.

9-63   I29

Why is frost considered hazardous to flight operation?

A — Frost changes the basic aerodynamic shape of the airfoil.
B — Frost decreases control effectiveness.
C — Frost causes early airflow separation resulting in a loss of lift.

9-64   I29

In which meteorological environment is aircraft structural icing most likely to have the highest rate of accumulation?

A — Cumulonimbus clouds.
B — High humidity and freezing temperature.
C — Freezing rain.

9-65   I29

What is an operational consideration if you fly into rain which freezes on impact?

A — You have flown into an area of thunderstorms.
B — Temperatures are above freezing at some higher altitude.
C — You have flown through a cold front.

9-66   I31

Under which condition does advection fog usually form?

A — Moist air moving over colder ground or water.
B — Warm, moist air settling over a cool surface under no-wind conditions.
C — A land breeze blowing a cold air mass over a warm water current.

9-62. Answer C. GFDICM 9B (AW)
Typically, wind shear is associated with temperature inversions, the jet stream, thunderstorms, and frontal zones. It's also important to remember that wind shear can occur in any direction and at any altitude. Answer (A) is incorrect because zones of convergence are associated with low pressure areas and wind shear can occur in high or low pressure areas. Answer (B) is an obvious wrong choice; Coriolis is unrelated to wind shear.

9-63. Answer C. GFDICM 9B (AW)
Frost is an element which poses a serious hazard. It interferes with smooth airflow over the wings and can cause early airflow separation, resulting in a loss of lift. Frost also increases drag and, when combined with the loss of lift, may prevent the aircraft from becoming airborne. Answers (A) and (B) are wrong because frost normally does not change the basic aerodynamic shape of the wing, nor does it decrease control effectiveness.

9-64. Answer C. GFDICM 9B (AW)
The condition most likely to result in rapid formation of hazardous icing is freezing rain. This occurs as an aircraft flies through the colder air below a frontal surface where the temperature is between 0°C and -15°C. When rain falling from warmer air above strikes the aircraft, it spreads rapidly and freezes, creating a layer of clear ice. Clear ice is the most serious of the various forms of ice because it has the fastest rate of accumulation, adheres tenaciously to the aircraft, and is more difficult to remove than rime ice. Answer (A) is wrong because you will not always accumulate ice in cumulonimbus clouds, especially if the temperature is well above freezing. High humidity with freezing temperatures (answer B) is incorrect; visible moisture is necessary for ice accumulation.

9-65. Answer B. GFDICM 9B (AW)
Freezing rain (rain that freezes on impact with the aircraft's surface) is an indication of warmer air at higher altitudes. It is not necessarily an indication that you have flown into an area of thunderstorms (answer A). Although freezing rain can be associated with a cold front, (answer C), the key is that the rain comes from warmer air aloft.

9-66. Answer A. GFDICM 9B (AW)
Advection fog is caused when a low layer of warm, moist air moves over a cooler surface, which may be either land or water. It is most common under cloudy skies along coastlines where sea breezes transport air from the warm water to cooler land. Answer (B) represents the conditions that are likely to produce radiation fog, not advection fog, while answer (C) represents the conditions needed to produce steam fog.

9-67   I30

If you fly into severe turbulence, which flight condition should you attempt to maintain?

A — Constant airspeed (V$_A$).
B — Level flight attitude.
C — Constant altitude and constant airspeed.

9-67. Answer B. GFDICM 9B (AW)

If you enter turbulence unexpectedly, enter a thunderstorm, or expect that you may encounter turbulence, reduce power to slow the airplane to maneuvering speed V$_A$ or less and attempt to maintain a level flight attitude. Although you want your airspeed to remain somewhat constant, don't keep adjusting the throttle to try and maintain a constant airspeed (answer A). Answer (C) is wrong because trying to maintain a constant altitude could result in unnecessary stress on the aircraft.

9-68   I32

Which weather condition can be expected when moist air flows from a relatively warm surface to a colder surface?

A — Increased visibility.
B — Convective turbulence due to surface heating.
C — Fog.

9-68. Answer C. GFDICM 9B (AW)

When a low layer of warm, moist air moves from a warm surface to a cooler surface, advection fog can be expected. Answer (A) is wrong because this situation is likely to produce fog and increased visibility is not a characteristic of fog. Answer (B) is wrong because the colder surface cools the overlying air. This results in stable rather than the unstable conditions associated with convective turbulence.

9-69   I31

Fog is usually prevalent in industrial areas because of

A — atmospheric stabilization around cities.
B — an abundance of condensation nuclei from combustion products.
C — increased temperatures due to industrial heating.

9-69. Answer B. GFDICM 9B (AW)

Fog requires both sufficient moisture and condensation nuclei on which water vapor can condense. Because there is an abundance of condensation nuclei in industrial areas, fog is common. Answer (A) is wrong because the airmasses around cities are not necessarily more (or less) stable than airmasses in rural areas. Answer (C) is wrong because fog is inhibited by increased temperatures.

9-70   I31

In which situation is advection fog most likely to form?

A — An air mass moving inland from the coast in winter.
B — A light breeze blowing colder air out to sea.
C — Warm, moist air settling over a warmer surface under no-wind conditions.

9-70 Answer A. GFDICM 9B (AW)

Advection fog is caused when a low layer of warm, moist air moves over a cooler surface, which may be either land or water. It is most common under cloudy skies along coastlines where sea breezes transport air from the warm water to cooler land. Answer (B) is wrong because the conditions listed are likely to produce steam fog, not advection fog. Answer (C) is wrong because fog is unlikely to occur under these circumstances.

9-71   I31

In what localities is advection fog most likely to occur?

A — Coastal areas.
B — Mountain slopes.
C — Level inland areas.

9-71. Answer A. GFDICM 9B (AW)

See explanation for Question 9-70.

9-72　　　I31

What types of fog depend upon a wind in order to exist?

A — Steam fog and downslope fog.
B — Precipitation-induced fog and ground fog.
C — Advection fog and upslope fog.

9-73　　　I31

What situation is most conducive to the formation of radiation fog?

A — Warm, moist air over low, flatland areas on clear, calm nights.
B — Moist, tropical air moving over cold, offshore water.
C — The movement of cold air over much warmer water.

9-74　　　I31

Which conditions are favorable for the formation of radiation fog?

A — Moist air moving over colder ground or water.
B — Cloudy sky and a light wind moving saturated warm air over a cool surface.
C — Clear sky, little or no wind, small temperature/dewpoint spread, and over a land surface.

9-75　　　I29

Test data indicate that ice, snow, or frost having a thickness and roughness similar to medium or coarse sandpaper on the leading edge and upper surface of an airfoil can

A — reduce lift by as much as 50 percent and increase drag by as much as 50 percent.
B — increase drag and reduce lift by as much as 25 percent.
C — reduce lift by as much as 30 percent and increase drag by 40 percent.

9-76　　　I67

A pilot reporting turbulence that momentarily causes slight, erratic changes in altitude and/or attitude should report it as

A — light turbulence.
B — moderate turbulence.
C — light chop.

9-72. Answer C. GFDICM 9B (AW)
See explanation for Question 9-70. Upslope fog forms when moist, stable air is forced up a sloping land mass. Like advection fog, upslope fog can form in moderate to strong winds and under cloudy skies. Answer (A) is wrong because steam fog, also known as sea smoke, requires calm conditions to develop. In addition, there is no such thing as downslope fog. Answer (B) is wrong because precipitation-induced fog depends on relatively warm precipitation falling through cooler air, and calm winds are a characteristic associated with ground fog.

9-73. Answer A. GFDICM 9B (AW)
Radiation fog, often called ground fog, forms with warm, moist air over fairly low, level land areas on clear, calm nights. Radiation fog does not develop off-shore (answer B) because water surfaces cool very little from nighttime radiation. Advection fog often forms offshore. Answer (C) is wrong because this condition typically results in the development of steam fog.

9-74. Answer C. GFDICM 9B (AWS)
See explanation for Question 9-73. Answer (A) is wrong because radiation fog does not typically form over water. Answer (B) is wrong because the conditions indicated are those required to produce advection fog.

9-75. Answer C. GFDICM 9B (AC 20-117)
According to AC 20-117, wind tunnel and flight tests indicate that ice, frost, or snow formations on the leading edge and upper surface of a wing, having a thickness similar to medium or course sandpaper, can reduce wing lift by as much as 30% and increase drag by 40%. These changes in lift and drag will significantly increase stall speed, reduce controllability and alter aircraft flight characteristics. Answers (A) and (B) do not reflect these percentages.

9-76. Answer A. GFDICM 9B (AIM)
Light turbulence can be described as turbulence that momentarily causes slight, erratic changes in altitude or attitude. In addition, you should feel slight strains against your seat belt. Light chop (answer C) is identified by slight, rapid bumpiness without appreciable changes in altitude or attitude. Moderate turbulence (answer B) is identified by changes in altitude or attitude, but you are able to maintain positive control of the aircraft at all times. Usually you will experience changes in indicated airspeed and feel definite strains against your seat belt.

9-77   I23

Hazardous wind shear is commonly encountered near the ground

A — during periods when the wind velocity is stronger than 35 knots.
B — during periods when the wind velocity is stronger than 35 knots and near mountain valleys.
C — during periods of strong temperature inversion and near thunderstorms.

9-78   J25

What is the expected duration of an individual microburst?

A — Two minutes with maximum winds lasting approximately 1 minute.
B — One microburst may continue for as long as 2 to 4 hours.
C — Seldom longer than 15 minutes from the time the burst strikes the ground until dissipation.

9-79   J25

Maximum downdrafts in a microburst encounter may be as strong as

A — 8,000 feet per minute.
B — 7,000 feet per minute.
C — 6,000 feet per minute.

9-80   J25

An aircraft that encounters a headwind of 45 knots, within a microburst, may expect a total shear across the microburst of

A — 40 knots.
B — 80 knots.
C — 90 knots.

9-81   J25

(Refer to figure 13 on page 9-21.) If involved in a microburst encounter, in which aircraft positions will the most severe downdraft occur?

A — 4 and 5.
B — 2 and 3.
C — 3 and 4.

9-77. Answer C. GFDICM 9B (AWS)

Wind shear is a sudden and drastic shift in wind speed and/or direction that may occur at any altitude and in any direction. Wind shear is commonly associated with strong temperature inversions, the jet stream, thunderstorms, and along fronts. Wind shear may be present in strong winds (answers A and B), but it is not as common.

9-78. Answer C. GFDICM 9B (AIM)

A microburst is an intense, localized downdraft of brief duration which spreads out in all directions when it reaches the surface. This creates severe horizontal and vertical wind shears which pose serious hazards to aircraft, particularly those near the surface, An individual microburst usually lasts no longer than 15 minutes from the time the burst first strikes the ground until dissipation. Answer (A) is wrong because it is less than the normal time limit. Answer (B) is wrong because it exceeds the normal time limit.

9-79. Answer C. GFDICM 9B (AIM)

An individual microburst typically covers an area of less than two and a half miles in diameter at the surface. Peak winds last two to four minutes and attendant downdrafts can be as strong as 6,000 feet per minute. Answers (A) and (B) are wrong because they substantially exceed the maximum speed.

9-80. Answer C. GFDICM 9B (AIM)

A headwind of 45 knots may result in a 90-knot wind shear (headwind to tailwind change for a traversing aircraft) across the microburst. Answers (A) and (B) are wrong because they are substantially less than the 90 knots that can occur.

9-81. Answer C. GFDICM 9B (AIM)

Positions 3 and 4 represent the center of the microburst where the strongest downdrafts will be experienced. At these points, the strength of downdrafts can reach 6,000 feet per minute. Beyond these points (1, 2, and 5), the downdrafts usually begin to turn outward and slow down (answers A and B).

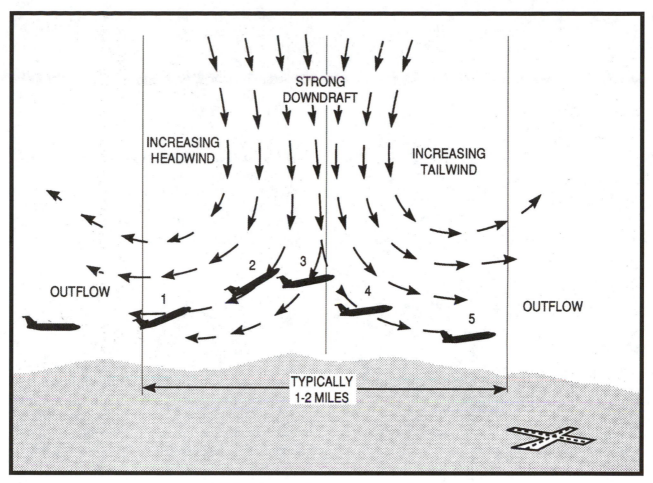

FIGURE 13.—Microburst Section Chart.

9-82   J25
(Refer to figure 13.) When penetrating a microburst, which aircraft will experience an increase in performance without a change in pitch or power?

A — 3.
B — 2.
C — 1.

9-82. Answer C. GFDICM 9B (AIM)
An aircraft will experience an increase in performance without a change in pitch or power whenever a headwind is experienced. When encountering a microburst, an aircraft will experience a headwind on initial entry into the phenomenon. As the aircraft continues through the microburst, the headwind will change into a downdraft (answers A and B). Once the aircraft reaches the opposite end of the microburst it will experience a performance decreasing tailwind.

9-83   J25
(Refer to figure 13.) The aircraft in position 3 will experience which effect in a microburst encounter?

A — Decreasing headwind.
B — Increasing tailwind.
C — Strong downdraft.

9-83. Answer C. GFDICM 9B (AIM)
The center of the microburst represents the area of strongest downdrafts. Just prior to this point the aircraft would experience a decreasing headwind (answer A), while just after passing through the center, the downdraft will start to transition into a tailwind (answer B).

9-84   **J25**
(Refer to figure 13 on page 9-21.) What effect will a microburst encounter have upon the aircraft in position 4?

A — Strong tailwind.
B — Strong updraft.
C — Significant performance increase.

9-85   **J25**
(Refer to figure 13 on page 9-21.) How will the aircraft in position 4 be affected by a microburst encounter?

A — Performance increasing with a tailwind and updraft.
B — Performance decreasing with a tailwind and downdraft.
C — Performance decreasing with a headwind and downdraft.

9-86   **J27**
What wind condition prolongs the hazards of wake turbulence on a landing runway for the longest period of time?

A — Direct headwind.
B — Direct tailwind.
C — Light quartering tailwind.

9-87   **J27**
Wake turbulence is near maximum behind a jet transport just after takeoff because

A — the engines are at maximum thrust output at slow airspeed.
B — the gear and flap configuration increases the turbulence to maximum.
C — of the high angle of attack and high gross weight.

9-88   **J27**
What effect would a light crosswind of approximately 7 knots have on vortex behavior?

A — The light crosswind would rapidly dissipate vortex strength.
B — The upwind vortex would tend to remain over the runway.
C — The downwind vortex would tend to remain over the runway.

9-84. Answer A. GFDICM 9B (AIM)
Position 4 represents the point where downdrafts begin transitioning to strong tailwinds causing aircraft performance to decrease. Answer (B) is wrong because updrafts typically don't exist in microbursts. Answer (C) is wrong because a performance increase would be experienced at position 1.

9-85. Answer B. GFDICM 9B (AIM)
See explanation for Question 9-84. Answer (A) is wrong because aircraft performance will not increase with a tailwind and updrafts typically don't exist in microbursts. Answer (C) is wrong because aircraft performance increases with a headwind.

9-86. Answer C. GFDICM 9B (AIM)
A light, quartering tailwind can move the upwind vortex of a preceding aircraft onto the runway in the touchdown zone. Depending on the wind speed, a direct headwind (answer A) or direct tailwind (answer B) would tend to disperse wake turbulence, and would not push a vortex into the landing zone like a quartering tailwind.

9-87. Answer C. GFDICM 9B (AIM)
Wake turbulence is greatest behind large, heavy aircraft at slow speeds and high angles of attack. Engine thrust provides a type of wake turbulence. It is usually called jet engine blast, but it may be referred to as thrust stream turbulence. Answer (A) is wrong because the most hazardous form of wake turbulence depends on the aerodynamic factors listed above, not jet blast. Answer (B) is somewhat misleading because a clean-configured aircraft (gear and flaps up) contributes to greater wake turbulence, but the maximum turbulence depends on the other factors as well.

9-88. Answer B. GFDICM 9B (AIM)
Since vortices tend to drift at 2 to 3 knots laterally, a light crosswind tends to hold the upwind vortex over the runway. Answer (A) is wrong because a light wind does not dissipate the vortex, but holds it in place. The downwind vortex (answer C) would drift with the crosswind and move away from the runway.

9-89   J27

When landing behind a large jet aircraft, at which point on the runway should you plan to land?

A — If any crosswind, land on the windward side of the runway and prior to the jet's touchdown point.

B — At least 1,000 feet beyond the jet's touchdown point.

C — Beyond the jet's touchdown point.

9-90   K04

When passing through an abrupt wind shear which involves a shift from a tailwind to a headwind, what power management would normally be required to maintain a constant indicated airspeed and ILS glide slope?

A — Higher than normal power initially, followed by a further increase as the wind shear is encountered, then a decrease.

B — Lower than normal power initially, followed by a further decrease as the wind shear is encountered, then an increase.

C — Higher than normal power initially, followed by a decrease as the shear is encountered, then an increase.

9-91   I10

What effect will a change in wind direction have upon maintaining a 3° glide slope at a constant true airspeed?

A — When groundspeed decreases, rate of descent must increase.

B — When groundspeed increases, rate of descent must increase.

C — Rate of descent must be constant to remain on the glide slope.

9-92   K04

While flying a 3° glide slope, a constant tailwind shears to a calm wind. Which conditions should the pilot expect?

A — Airspeed and pitch attitude decrease and there is a tendency to go below glide slope.

B — Airspeed and pitch attitude increase and there is a tendency to go below glide slope.

C — Airspeed and pitch attitude increase and there is a tendency to go above glide slope.

9-89. Answer C. GFDICM 9B (AIM)

Because wake turbulence tends to sink, you should stay above the preceding airplane's glide path and land beyond its touchdown point. Answer (A) is incorrect because a crosswind might keep the vortex over the entire runway, and landing prior to the jet's touchdown point can put you into its wake turbulence. Normally, you can safely land at any point beyond the jet's touchdown point, and 1,000 feet beyond (answer B) is not specified. In addition, with some airplanes, or on a short runway, 1,000 feet beyond may be impractical.

9-90. Answer B. GFDICM 9B (AC 00-54)

As the wind shears to less tailwind, or to a headwind, it will be necessary to lower power to avoid ballooning above the glide slope. Later, increased power will be needed because of slower groundspeed. Both (A) and (C) are wrong because the initial required power is lower, not higher than normal.

This question is similar to 9-92.

9-91. Answer B. GFDICM 9B (AC 00-54)

This question essentially addresses a wind shear situation. As groundspeed increases, you must descend at a greater rate to remain on glide slope. When groundspeed decreases (answer A), the rate of descent must also decrease, not increase. Answer (C) is incorrect because a change in wind direction will usually change the groundspeed, and you will need to change the rate of descent.

9-92. Answer C. GFDICM 9B (AC 00-54)

When a tailwind shears to a calm wind or headwind, indicated airspeed will increase, causing the aircraft to pitch up, and go above the glide slope. The pitch attitude change is caused by the airplane's tendency to seek the trimmed airspeed. Answers (A) and (B) are wrong because indicated airspeed and pitch attitude increase and the tendency is to go above glide slope.

This question is similar to 9-90.

9-93   V14
Under which conditions is hydroplaning most likely to occur?

A — When rudder is used for directional control instead of allowing the nosewheel to contact the surface early in the landing roll on a wet runway.
B — During conditions of standing water, slush, high speed, and smooth runway texture.
C — During a landing on any wet runway when brake application is delayed until a wedge of water begins to build ahead of the tires.

9-94   K04
Thrust is managed to maintain IAS, and glide slope is being flown. What characteristics should be observed when a headwind shears to be a constant tailwind?

A — PITCH ATTITUDE: Increases; REQUIRED THRUST: Increased, then reduced; VERTICAL SPEED: Increases; IAS: Increases, then decreases to approach speed.
B — PITCH ATTITUDE: Decreases; REQUIRED THRUST: Increased, then reduced; VERTICAL SPEED: Increases; IAS: Decreases, then increases to approach speed.
C — PITCH ATTITUDE: Increases; REQUIRED THRUST: Reduced, then increased; VERTICAL SPEED: Decreases; IAS: Decreases, then increases to approach speed.

9-95   K04
While flying a 3° glide slope, a headwind shears to a tailwind. Which conditions should the pilot expect on the glide slope?

A — Airspeed and pitch attitude decrease and there is a tendency to go below glide slope.
B — Airspeed and pitch attitude increase and there is a tendency to go above glide slope.
C — Airspeed and pitch attitude decrease and there is a tendency to remain on the glide slope.

9-96   J31
What affect does haze have on the ability to see traffic or terrain features during flight?

A — Haze causes the eyes to focus at infinity, making terrain features harder to see.
B — The eyes tend to overwork in haze and do not detect relative movement easily.
C — Haze creates the illusion of being a greater distance than actual from the runway, and causes pilots to fly a lower approach.

9-93. Answer B. GFDICM 9B (AC 91-6A)
Standing water, slush, high aircraft speed, and a smooth runway texture all contribute to hydroplaning. Answer (A) is wrong because the nosewheel should not be used for directional control early in the landing roll. Allowing the nosewheel to contact the runway earlier than usual is not a significant factor in hydroplaning. Nosewheel hydroplane speeds are different than the hydroplane speeds for the main wheels. Water can build up under the tires (answer C) whether or not brake application is delayed.

9-94. Answer B. GFDICM 9B (AC 00-54)
This situation would cause a loss in indicated airspeed (IAS) with a resulting decrease in pitch attitude. You would need to increase power (thrust) to regain the lost airspeed, then reduce it again due to the higher groundspeed from the tailwind. The higher groundspeed also requires a higher rate of descent to maintain the glide slope. Answers (A) and (C) are incorrect for the reasons explained here.

See Questions 9-90 and 9-92 for additional information.

9-95. Answer A. GFDICM 9B (AC 00-54)
When a headwind changes to a tailwind, the indicated airspeed will decrease and cause the pitch attitude to decrease. As the nose pitches down, the aircraft will tend to go below glide slope if no corrections are made. Answer (B) describes what would happen in the opposite situation (tailwind shears to a headwind). Answer (C) is incorrect because decreasing airspeed and pitch would cause the aircraft to descend below glide slope.

See explanations for Questions 9-91, 9-94, 8-34, and 8-36.

9-96. Answer C. GFDICM 9B (AIM)
Visual obscuration caused by such elements as rain, haze, or even a dark runway environment can cause you to fly a lower approach. Answer (A) is incorrect because when there is a lack of visual cues such as in haze, your eyes tend to focus on a point three to six feet in front of you, not at infinity. Instead of overworking in hazy conditions (answer B), your eyes tend to relax. In addition, even out-of-focus images can quickly be noticed when relative movement is present.

9-97   **K04**

When a climb or descent through an inversion or wind-shear zone is being performed, the pilot should be alert for which of the following change in airplane performance?

A — A fast rate of climb and a slow rate of descent.
B — A sudden change in airspeed.
C — A sudden surge of thrust.

9-97. Answer B. GFDICM 9B (AW)

Wind shear is a sudden shift in wind speed and/or direction that may occur at any altitude and at any time. Wind shear is associated with temperature inversions, the jet stream, thunderstorms, and frontal inversions. When flying through wind shear, be alert for a sudden change in airspeed and carry an extra margin of speed if you suspect an inversion or wind shear. Answer (A) is incorrect because this type of performance change is beneficial, not hazardous. Answer (C) is incorrect because thrust is not affected by wind shear.

SECTION C
PRINTED REPORTS AND FORECASTS

METARS

1. An aviation routine weather report (METAR) is an observation of surface weather written in a standard format which typically contains 10 or more separate elements.
2. A non-routine aviation weather report (SPECI) is issued when a significant change in one or more of the elements of a METAR has occurred.
3. Prevailing visibility is the greatest distance an observer can see and identify objects through at least half of the horizon.
4. When a squall (SQ) is reported, you can expect a sudden increase in wind speed of at least 15 knots to a sustained wind speed of 20 knots or more for at least 1 minute.
5. Runway visual range (RVR) is based on what a pilot in a moving aircraft should see when looking down the runway. If included in a METAR, RVR is reported following prevailing visibility.
6. A ceiling is the height above ground level of the lowest layer of clouds aloft which is reported as broken (BKN) or overcast (OVC), or the vertical visibility (VV) into an obscuration. For example, VV008 indicates that the sky is obscured with a vertical visibility of 800 feet.
7. If the top of a layer is known, you can easily determine its thickness by adding the airport's elevation (MSL) to the height of the cloud base (AGL) found in a METAR observation, then subtract the height of the cloud tops.
8. The beginning of the remarks section is indicated by the code RMK. The remarks section reports weather considered significant to aircraft operations, which are not covered in the previous sections of the METAR.

RADAR WEATHER REPORTS

9. Radar weather reports (SDs) define general areas of precipitation, particularly thunderstorms.
10. The abbreviation MT is used to denote maximum tops of the precipitation in the clouds. Heights are reported in hundreds of feet MSL followed by the radial and distance in nautical miles from the reporting location.

PILOT WEATHER REPORTS

11. The bases and tops of cloud layers, in-flight visibility, icing conditions, wind shear, and turbulence may be included in a pilot weather report (PIREP).
12. PIREPs are the best source for current weather between reporting stations.

TERMINAL AERODROME FORECASTS

13. Terminal aerodrome forecasts (TAFs) are issued 4 times per day, and predict the weather at a specific airport for a 24-hour period of time. A TAF should be your primary source of weather information for your destination.
14. In a TAF, the contraction VRB indicates that the wind direction is variable. A calm wind (3 knots or less) is indicated by 00000KT.
15. P6SM in terminal aerodrome forecast implies that the prevailing visibility is expected to be greater than 6 statute miles.
16. The letters SKC are used in a terminal aerodrome forecast to indicate "sky clear."
17. The letters WS indicate that low-level wind shear which is not associated with convective activity may be present during the valid time of the forecast. For example, WS005/27050KT indicates that the wind at 500 feet AGL is 270° at 50 knots.
18. The term PROB40 2102 +TSRA in a terminal aerodrome forecast indicates that there is approximately a 40% probability of thunderstorms with heavy rain between 2100Z and 0200Z.

AVIATION AREA FORECASTS

19. Aviation area forecasts are issued three times each day and generally include a total forecast period of 18 hours. They cover a geographical group of states or well known areas.
20. An aviation area forecast (FA) is a good source of information for weather at airports which do not have terminal aerodrome forecasts, as well as for enroute weather.
21. The VFR clouds and weather section of an aviation area forecast summarizes sky conditions, cloud heights, visibility, obstructions to vision, precipitation, and sustained surface winds of 20 knots or greater.
22. When the wind is forecast to be 20 knots or greater the categorical outlook in the aviation area forecast includes the contraction WND.

WINDS AND TEMPERATURES ALOFT FORECASTS

23. An estimate of wind direction in relation to true north, wind speed in knots, and the temperature in degrees Celsius for selected altitudes can be found in the winds and temperatures aloft forecast (FD).
24. A winds and temperatures aloft forecast (FD) does not include winds within 1,500 feet of the station elevation. Likewise temperatures for the 3,000-foot level or for a level within 2,500 feet of the station elevation are omitted.
25. Wind direction and speed information on an FD are shown by a four-digit code. The first two digits are the wind direction in tens of degrees. Wind speed is shown by the second two digits. The last two digits indicate the temperature in degrees Celsius. All temperatures above 24,000 feet are negative and the minus sign is omitted.
26. To decode a forecast of winds between 100 and 199 knots, subtract 50 from the two-digit direction code and multiply by 10. Then, add 100 to the two-digit wind speed code. The code 9900 indicates the winds are light and variable.

SEVERE WEATHER

27. A convective outlook (AC) forecasts general thunderstorm activity for the next 24-hour period.
28. Severe weather watch bulletins (WW) are issued only when required. They outline areas of possible severe thunderstorms or tornadoes.

9-98   I21

How much colder than standard temperature is the forecast temperature at 9,000 feet, as indicated in the following excerpt from the Winds and Temperature Aloft Forecast?

FT   6000   9000

       0737-04   1043-10

A — 3°C.
B — 10°C.
C — 7°C.

9-98. Answer C. GFDICM 9C (AW)

Standard temperature is 15°C at sea level and the standard lapse rate is approximately 2°C per 1,000 feet. To compute standard temperature for 9,000 feet, subtract 2°C for every 1,000-foot increase in altitude. The result is –3°C (15 – [2 x 9]) = –3°C. The forecast temperature at 9,000 feet, as indicated in the winds aloft report, is –10°C. This is 7°C colder than standard.

9-99   I57

If squalls are reported at your destination, what wind conditions should you anticipate?

A — Sudden increases in windspeed of at least 16 knots, rising to 22 knots or more, lasting for at least 1 minute.
B — Peak gusts of at least 35 knots for a sustained period of 1 minute or longer.
C — Rapid variation in wind direction of at least 20° and changes in speed of at least 10 knots between peaks and lulls.

9-99. Anewer A. GFDICM 9C

When a squall (SQ) is reported in an aviation routine weather report, you can expect sudden increases in windspeed of at least 16 knots, the speed rising to 22 knots or more, and lasting at least 1 minute.

9-100   I57

The body of a Terminal Aerodrome Forecast (TAF) covers a geographical proximity within a

A — 5 nautical mile radius of the center of an airport.
B — 5 statute mile radius from the center of an airport runway complex.
C — 5 to 10 statute mile radius from the center of an airport runway complex

9-100. Answer B. GFDICM 9C (AWS)

Terminal aerodrome forecasts are issued four times a day and are normally valid for a 24-hour period. The TAF is a concise statement of the expected meteorological conditions within a 5-statute-mile radius from the center of an airport's runway complex.

9-101   I63
What wind direction and speed is represented by the
entry 9900+00 for 9,000 feet, on an Winds and
Temperatures Aloft Forecast (FD)?

A — Light and variable; less than 5 knots.
B — Vortex winds exceeding 200 knots.
C — Light and variable; less than 10 knots.

9-102   I64
What does a Convective Outlook (AC) describe for a
following 24 hour period?

A — General thunderstorm activity.
B — A severe weather watch bulletin.
C — When forecast conditions are expected to contin-
ue beyond the valid period.

9-103   I57
Which primary source should be used to obtain forecast weather information at your destination for the
planned ETA?

A — Area Forecast.
B — Radar Summary and Weather Depiction Charts.
C — Terminal Aerodrome Forecast (TAF).

9-104   I57
A "VRB" wind entry in a Terminal Aerodrome
Forecast (TAF) will be indicated when the wind is

A — 3 knots or less.
B — 6 knots or less.
C — 9 knots or less.

9-105   I57
When the visibility is greater than 6 SM on a TAF it is
expressed as

A — 6PSM.
B — P6SM.
C — 6SMP.

9-101. Answer A. GFDICM 9C (AWS)
A code of 9900 indicates light and variable winds
(less than five knots). Answers (B) and (C) are wrong
because the winds indicated exceed the five knot
requirement.

9-102. Answer A. GFDICM 9C (AWS)
According to Advisory Circular 00-45D, answer (A) is
correct. A convective outlook (AC) includes areas of
high, moderate, or slight risk of severe thunderstorms.
A severe weather watch bulletin (WW), answer (B), is
not correct because it defines the areas of possible
severe thunderstorms or tornadoes. Answer (C), is
wrong because the convective outlook does not
contain a forecast beyond the 24-hour valid period.

9-103. Answer C. GFDICM 9C (AWS)
The terminal aerodrome forecast (TAF) is the only
printed weather report that gives you forecast information for a 24-hour period at your destination. The terminal aerodrome forecast allows you to select the
most favorable approach, based on the forecast
winds, visibility, and ceiling. You also need this forecast to determine if an alternate airport is required. If
one is required, you need the TAF for the alternate to
see if it qualifies (answer C). The area forecast
(answer A) is a good source of enroute weather and is
your principal source of weather at airports that do not
have terminal aerodrome forecasts. An area forecast
is also a good single reference for information on
frontal movement, turbulence, icing, and other flight
hazards. Answer (B) is wrong because radar summary
charts and weather depiction charts provide current
information instead of a forecast for future conditions.

9-104. Answer A GFDICM 9C (AWS)
A variable wind is encoded as VRB when wind direction fluctuates due to convective activity or low wind
speeds (3 knots or less).

9-105. Answer B. GFDICM 9C (AWS)
Answer (B) is correct. The presence of the "P", which
indicates plus, preceding the visibility entry of a terminal aerodrome forecast specifically implies that the
visibility is greater than 6 statute miles. Answers (A)
and (C) are wrong because they are not in the correct
format.

9-106 I57

"WND" in the categorical outlook in the Aviation Area Forecast means that the wind during that period is forecast to be

A — At least 6 knots or stronger.
B — At least 15 knots or stronger.
C — At least 20 knots or stronger.

9-106. Answer C. GFDICM 9C (AWS)
The contraction "WND" is included in the outlook if winds, sustained or gusty, are expected to be 20 knots or greater (answer C).

9-107 I57

What is the forecast wind at 1800Z in the following TAF?

KMEM 091740Z 091818 00000KT 1/2SM RAFG OVC005=

A — Calm.
B — Uknown.
C — Not recorded.

9-107. Answer A. GFDICM 9C (AWS, AIM)
Answer (A) is correct because a calm wind entry, "00000KT," in a terminal aerodrome forecast specifically implies that the wind is expected to be 3 knots or less.

9-108 I56

What significant sky condition is reported in this METAR observation?

METAR KBNA 091250Z 33018KT 290V360 1/2SM R31/2700FT +SN BLSNFG VV008 00/M03 A2991 RMK RAE42SNB42

A — Runway 31 ceiling is 2700 feet.
B — Sky is obscured with vertical visibility of 800 feet.
C — Measured ceiling is 300 feet overcast.

9-108. Answer B. GFDICM 9C (AWS, AIM)
Answer (B) is correct, because total obscuration of the sky is reported in hundreds of feet preceded by "VV." In this case, the vertical visibility is 800 feet. Answer (A) is wrong because ceiling heights are not reported with reference to a runway. Answer (C) is wrong because the "00/M03" following the vertical visibility is the temperature/dewpoint. The note "M03" indicates that the dewpoint is minus 3°C.

9-109 I57

When are severe weather watch bulletins (WW) issued?

A — Every 12 hours as required.
B — Every 24 hours as required.
C — Unscheduled and issued as required.

9-109. Answer C. GFDICM 9C (AWS)
Answer (C) is correct because severe weather watch bulletins are issued only when required to define an area of possible severe thunderstorms or tornadoes.

9-110 I63

When is the temperature at one of the forecast altitudes omitted at a specific location or station in the Winds and Temperatures Aloft Forecast (FD)?

A — When the temperature is standard for that altitude.
B — For the 3,000-foot altitude (level) or when the level is within 2,500 feet of station elevation.
C — Only when the winds are omitted for that altitude (level).

9-110. Answer B. GFDICM 9C (AWS)
A winds and temperatures aloft forecast (FD) does not forecast winds within 1,500 feet of the station elevation, or temperatures for the 3,000-foot level or for any level within 2,500 feet of the station elevation. Answer (A) is wrong because nonstandard temperatures are also reported. Answer (C) is wrong because winds may be reported near the surface, within 1,500 feet of the station elevation, without corresponding temperature information.

9-111   I63

When is the wind-group at one of the forecast altitudes omitted at a specific location or station in the Winds and Temperatures Aloft Forecast (FD)? When the wind

A — is less than 5 knots.
B — is less than 10 knots.
C — at the altitude is within 1,500 feet of the station elevation.

9-112   I63

Decode the excerpt from the Winds and Temperature Aloft Forecast (FD) for OKC at 39,000 feet.

FT 3000 6000 39000

OKC 830558

A — Wind 130° at 50 knots, temperature -58°C.
B — Wind 330° at 105 knots, temperature -58°C.
C — Wind 330° at 205 knots, temperature -58°C.

9-113   I63

Which values are used for winds aloft forecasts?

A — Magnetic direction and knots.
B — Magnetic direction and MPH.
C — True direction and knots.

9-111. Answer C. GFDICM 9C (AWS)

See explanation for Question 9-110. Answer (A) is wrong because winds less than 5 knots are reported as light and variable, and are coded 9900. Answer (B) is wrong because these winds would be reported, if over 6 knots and at an altitude more than 1,500 feet above the reporting station's elevation.

9-112. Answer B. GFDICM 9C (AWS)

If the wind speed for a specific station is between 100 and 199 knots, 50 should be subtracted from the wind direction code and 100 added to the speed. In this example, "830558" indicates the wind at OKC is from 330° (83 – 50 = 33 or 330°) at 105 knots (05 + 100 = 105 knots). You can recognize this when you see a coded direction that exceeds "36" or 360°. The last two digits of the sequence always represents the temperature. Above 24,000 feet, the "–" is omitted because temperatures are always negative. Answer (A) is wrong because 130° at 50 would be coded as 1350. Note, the wind is less than 100 knots. Answer (C) is wrong because the code for a windspeed greater than 200 knots is "99." This means winds of 330° at 205 knots would be coded "8399."

9-113. Answer C. GFDICM 9C (AWS)

The winds and temperatures aloft forecast (FD) provides an estimate of wind direction in relation to true north, wind speed in knots, and temperature in degrees Celsius for selected stations and altitudes. Answers (A) and (B) are wrong because the wind direction is not reported in magnetic direction nor is wind speed reported in MPH (answer B).

FT	3000	6000	9000	12000	18000	24000	30000	34000	39000
				VALID 141200Z FOR USE 0900-1500Z. TEMPS NEG ABV 24000					
EMI	2807	2715-07	2728-10	2842-13	2867-21	2891-30	751041	771150	780855
ALB	0210	9900-07	2714-09	2728-12	2656-19	2777-28	781842	760150	269658
PSB		1509+04	2119+01	2233-04	2262-14	2368-26	781939	760850	780456
STL	2308	2613+02	2422-03	2431-08	2446-19	2461-30	760142	782650	760559

FIGURE 2.—Winds and Temperatures Aloft Forecast.

9-114   I63

(Refer to figure 2.) What approximate wind direction, speed, and temperature (relative to ISA) should a pilot expect when planning for a flight over PSB at FL 270?

A — 260° magnetic at 93 knots; ISA +7°C.
B — 280° true at 113 knots; ISA +3°C.
C — 255° true at 93 knots; ISA +6°C.

9-114. Answer C. GFDICM 9C (AWS)

If your desired cruising altitude falls between forecast levels, you must interpolate to find the forecast winds. In this example, you must interpolate between the PSB winds aloft forecast at 24,000 feet, "2368-26" and those at 30,000 feet, "781939." The first step is to decode the wind information at 30,000 feet. Refer to the explanation for Question 4190 to do this. Since 27,000 feet is directly between 24,000 and 30,000, add one-half the difference between the wind direction, speed, and temperature at these altitudes to the 24,000 foot information to determine the winds and temperature at 27,000 feet.

Altitude	Wind Dir	Wind Spd	Temp
30,000	280°	119	−39°C
24,000	230°	68	−26°C
	50°	51	13°
27,000	255°	93	−33°C

The International Standard Atmosphere (ISA) temperature at 27,000 feet (FL 270) is approximately −39°C. This is based on a 2°C per 1,000-foot lapse rate. Therefore, −33°C is ISA plus 6°C.

9-115   I63

(Refer to figure 2 on page 9-31.) What approximate wind direction, speed, and temperature (relative to ISA) should a pilot expect when planning for a flight over ALB at FL 270?

A — 270° magnetic at 97 knots; ISA -4°C.
B — 260° true at 110 knots; ISA +5°C.
C — 275° true at 97 knots; ISA +4°C.

9-116   I63

(Refer to figure 2 on page 9-31.) What approximate wind direction, speed, and temperature (relative to ISA) should a pilot expect when planning for a flight over EMI at FL 270?

A — 265° true; 100 knots; ISA +3°C.
B — 270° true; 110 knots; ISA +5°C.
C — 260° magnetic; 100 knots; ISA -5°C.

9-117   I55

The station originating the following weather report has a field elevation of 1,300 feet MSL. From the bottom of the overcast cloud layer, what is its thickness? (tops of OVC are reported at 3,800 feet)

SPECI KOKC 092228Z 28024G36KT 3/4SM BKN008 OVC020 28/23 A3000

A — 500 feet.
B — 1,700 feet.
C — 2,500 feet.

9-115. Answer C. GFDICM 9C (AWS)

For this question, you must interpolate between the ALB winds and temperatures at 24,000 feet and 30,000 feet. See explanation for Question 4192. The answer is 275° true at 97 knots and +4°C above standard.

Altitude	Wind Dir	Wind Spd	Temp
30,000	280°	118	−42°C
24,000	270°	77	−28°C
	10°	41	14°
27,000	275°	97	−35°C

The International Standard Atmosphere (ISA) temperature at 27,000 feet (FL 270) is −39°C; this is based on a 2°C per 1,000-foot lapse rate. Therefore −35° is ISA + 4°C.

9-116. Answer A. GFDICM 9C (AWS)

To solve, you must interpolate between the EMI winds and temperatures at 24,000 feet and 30,000 feet. See explanation for Question 4192. The answer is 265° true at 100 knots and +3°C above standard.

Altitude	Wind Dir	Wind Spd	Temp
30,000	250°	110	−41°C
24,000	280°	91	−30°C
	30°	19	11°
27,000	265°	100	−36°C

The International Standard Atmosphere (ISA) temperature at 27,000 feet (FL 270) is −39°C; this is based on a 2°C per 1,000-foot lapse rate. Therefore −36° is ISA plus 3°C.

9-117. Answer A. GFDICM 9C (AWS, AIM)

Answer (A) is correct. The note indicates the top of the overcast is at 3,800 feet MSL. In the SPECI, the overcast begins at 2,000 feet AGL. By adding the field elevation, 1,300 feet MSL, to the height of the cloud base, 2,000 feet AGL, you can determine that the cloud base is 3,300 feet MSL. Then subtract the height of the cloud base from the reported cloud top. The overcast is calculated to be 500 feet thick (3,800 − 3,300=500).

9-118   I56

Which response most closely interprets the following PIREP?

UA/OV OKC 063064/TM 1522/FL080/TP C172/TA -04/WV 245040/TB LGT/RM IN CLR.

A — 64 nautical miles on the 63 degree radial from Oklahoma City VOR at 1522 UTC, flight level 8,000 ft. Type of aircraft is a Cessna 172.

B — Reported by a Cessna 172, turbulence and light rime icing in climb to 8,000 ft.

C — 63 nautical miles on the 64 degree radial from Oklahoma City, thunderstorm and light rain at 1522 UTC.

9-119   I63

A station is forecasting wind and temperature aloft at FL 390 to be 300° at 200 knots; temperature -54°C. How would this data be encoded in the FD?

A — 300054.
B — 809954.
C — 309954.

9-120   I57

Area forecasts generally include a forecast period of 18 hours and cover a geographical

A — terminal area.
B — area less than 3,000 square miles.
C — area the size of several states.

9-121   I55

A ceiling is defined as the height of the

A — highest layer of clouds or obscuring phenomena aloft that covers over 6/10 of the sky.

B — lowest layer of clouds that contributed to the overall overcast.

C — lowest layer of clouds or obscuring phenomena aloft that is reported as broken or overcast.

9-118. Answer A. GFDICM 9C (AWS)

In this PIREP, which is identified by the letters "UA," the aircraft's position is designated by the letters "OV" followed by the distance, direction, and reference facility. The aircraft is 64 nautical miles from Oklahoma City VOR on the 063° radial. The time is 1522 (TM 1522) and the aircraft is at 8,000 feet MSL (FL080). The type of aircraft is a Cessna 172 (TP C172). The outside air temperature is minus four degrees Celsius (TA–04), the wind is 245° at 40 knots (WV 245040), and the pilot is experiencing light turbulence (TB LGT). The remarks section, which begins with the letters "RM," indicates the aircraft is in clear skies. Answer (B) is wrong because the PIREP does not mention rime icing. Answer (C) is incorrect because the radial and distance are reversed.

9-119. Answer B. GFDICM 9C (AWS)

When the windspeed is forecast at 200 knots or greater, 50 is added to the wind direction and the wind speed is coded as 99. The answer is 809954. The wind direction is encoded as 80 (30 + 50 = 80), the speed as 99 (200 knots or greater), and the temperature as 54 indicating –54°C. All temperatures above 24,000 feet are negative; therefore, the minus sign is omitted for temperatures above 24,000 feet. Answer (A) is wrong because the wind direction should have 50 added to it and the wind speed should be expressed as 99. Answer (C) is wrong because the wind direction should have 50 added to it.

9-120. Answer C. GFDICM 9C (AWS)

An Aviation Area Forecast (FA) is a forecast of general weather conditions over an area the size of several states (answer C). Answer (A) is wrong because a forecast for a terminal area is a terminal aerodrome forecast which is issued four times a day and is valid for a 24-hour period, beginning at 0000Z. Answer (B) is wrong because the specific forecast section gives a general description of clouds and weather which covers an area greater than 3,000 square miles and is significant to VFR flight operations.

9-121. Answer C. GFDICM 9C (AWS)

A ceiling is the AGL height of the lowest broken (BKN) or overcast (OVC) layer, or vertical visibility into an obscuration. Therefore, Answer (C) is the most correct. Answer (A) is wrong because it's the lowest layer, not the highest. However, the sky cover condition for any higher layers represents total sky coverage, which includes any lower layer. Answer (B) is wrong because the lowest layer does not constitute a ceiling if it is few (FEW) or scattered (SCT).

9-122   I57

The reporting station originating this Aviation Routine Weather Report has a field elevation of 620 feet. If the reported sky cover is one continuous layer, what is its thickness? (tops of OVC are reported at 6,500 feet)

METAR KMDW 121856Z AUTO 32005KT 1 1/2SM +RA BR OVC007 17/16 A2980

A — 5,180 feet.
B — 5,800 feet.
C — 5,880 feet.

9-122. Answer A. GFDICM 9C (AWS, AIM)

Answer (A) is correct. The note indicates the top of the overcast is at 6,500 feet MSL. In the METAR, the overcast begins at 700 feet AGL. By adding the field elevation, 620 feet MSL, to the height of the cloud base, 700 feet AGL, you can determine that the cloud base is 1,320 feet MSL. Then subtract the height of the cloud base from the reported cloud top. The overcast is calculated to be 5,180 feet thick (6,500 – 1,320=5180).

9-123   I57

What is the wind shear forecast in the following TAF?

TAF
KCVG 231051Z 231212 12012KT 4SM -RA BR OVC008 WS005/27050KT TEMPO 1719 1/2SM -RA FG FM1930 09012KT 1SM -DZ BR VV003 BECMG 2021 5SM HZ=

A — 5 feet AGL from 270° at 50 KT.
B — 50 feet AGL from 270° at 50 KT.
C — 500 feet A GL from 270° at 50 KT.

9-123. Answer C. GFDICM 9C (AWS)

When wind shear is reported in a TAF, it always comes after the sky conditions group. Following the wind shear indicator (WS), is the altitude of the forecast wind shear reported in hundreds of feet AGL, then the wind direction and speed. In this example, the wind shear is forecast at 500 feet AGL from 270° at 50 knots, answer (C).

9-124   I55

What is meant by the entry in the remarks section of METAR surface report for KBNA?

METAR KBNA 211250Z 33018KT 290V260 1/2SM R31/2700FT +SN BLSNFG VV008 00/M03 A2991 RMK RAE42SNB42

A — The wind is variable from 290° to 360°.
B — Heavy blowing snow and fog on runway 31.
C — Rain ended 42 past the hour, snow began 42 past the hour.

9-124. Answer C. GFDICM 9C (AWS, AIM)

The "RAE42SNB42" in this report indicates rain ended at 42 minutes after the hour and snow began at 42 minutes after the hour. Answers (A) and (B) are wrong because the reference to variable wind and heavy snow are in the body of the report.

9-125   I65

What information is provided by a Convective Outlook (AC)?

A — It describes areas of probable severe icing and severe or extreme turbulence during the next 24 hours.
B — It provides prospects of both general and severe thunderstorm activity during the following 24 hours.
C — It indicates areas of probable convective turbulence and the extent of instability in the upper atmosphere (above 500 MB).

9-125. Answer B. GFDICM 9C (AWS)

The convective outlook (AC) forecasts general thunderstorm activity for the next 24-hour period. Areas with a high, moderate, or slight risk of severe thunderstorms are included, as well as areas where thunderstorms may approach severe limits. Answers (A) and (C) are wrong because icing, turbulence, and atmospheric instability are not forecast on the convective outlook.

9-126   I56

Interpret this PIREP.

MRB UA/OV MRB/TM 1430/FL060/TP
C182/SK BKN BL/WX RA/TB MDT.

A — Ceiling 6,000 feet intermittently below moderate
   thundershowers; turbulence increasing westward.
B — FL 60,000, intermittently below clouds; moderate rain, turbulence increasing with the wind.
C — At 6,000 feet; between layers; moderate turbulence; moderate rain.

9-127   I57

Which weather forecast describes prospects for an
area coverage of both severe and general thunderstorms during the following 24 hours?

A — Terminal Aerodrome Forecast.
B — Convective Outlook.
C — Radar Summary Chart.

9-128   I43

From which primary source should you obtain information regarding the weather expected to exist at your
destination at your estimated time of arrival?

A — Weather Depiction Chart.
B — Radar Summary and Weather Depiction Chart.
C — Terminal Aerodrome Forecast.

9-129   J25

AIRMET's are issued on a scheduled basis every

A — 15 minutes after the hour only.
B — 15 minutes until the AIRMET is canceled.
C — six hours.

9-126. Answer C. GFDICM 9C (AWS)

You can identify this as a pilot report by the notation
"UA." The coding "OV MRB/TM 1430/FL060" indicates
the aircraft is over Martinsburg at 1430Z and 6,000
feet. "SK BKN BL/WX RA/TB MDT" indicates sky
broken, between layers, moderate rain and turbulence.
Answer (A) is wrong because there is no indication of
a ceiling at 6,000 feet or moderate thundershowers.
Answer (B) is wrong because the report was not made
for FL600 and there is no mention of being intermittently below clouds. In addition, the turbulence is not increasing with the wind.

9-127. Answer B. GFDICM 9C (AWS)

The convective outlook (AC) forecasts thunderstorm
activity for a 24-hour period. The forecast includes
areas where thunderstorms may approach severe
conditions, as well as the areas containing a high,
moderate, or slight risk of severe thunderstorms.
Answer (A) is wrong because the terminal aerodrome
forecast predicts thunderstorm activity without regard
to severity. Answer (C) is wrong because severe
weather watch bulletins define areas of possible
severe (not general) thunderstorms or tornadoes.

9-128. Answer C. GFDICM 9C (AWS)

The terminal aerodrome forecast (TAF) is the only
printed weather report that gives you forecast information
for a 24-hour period at your destination. The terminal
aerodrome forecast allows you to select the most
favorable approach, based on the forecast winds,
visibility, and ceiling. You also need this forecast to
determine if an alternate airport is required. If one is
required, you need the TAF for the alternate to see if it
qualifies. The weather depiction chart (answer A) is a
good source of general weather information when you
are flight planning. It can be thought of as an abbreviated surface analysis chart. It provides a simplified station model and graphic depiction of VFR, marginal
VFR, and IFR weather conditions. Answer (B) is wrong
because radar summary charts and weather depiction
charts provide current information instead of a forecast
for future conditions.

9-129. Answer C. GFDICM 9C (AIM)

AIRMETs are issued on a scheduled basis every six
hours and corrected or updated as necessary.
Answers (A) and (B) are inappropriate.

SECTION D
GRAPHIC WEATHER PRODUCTS

SURFACE ANALYSIS CHART
1. The solid lines that depict sea level pressure patterns are called isobars. When they are close together, the pressure gradient is stronger and the wind velocities are stronger.
2. A surface analysis chart is a good source for general weather information over a wide area, depicting the actual positions of fronts, pressure patterns, temperatures, dewpoint, wind, weather, and obstructions to vision at the valid time of the chart.
3. A dashed line on a surface analysis chart indicates a weak pressure gradient.

WEATHER DEPICTION CHART
4. The weather depiction chart provides a graphic display of VFR and IFR weather, as well as the type of precipitation.
5. A ( ]) plotted to the right of a station circle on the weather depiction chart means the station is an automated observation location.
6. When total sky cover is FEW or scattered, the height shown on the weather depiction chart is the base of the lowest layer.

RADAR SUMMARY CHART
7. Radar summary charts are the only weather charts which show lines and cells of thunderstorms as well as other heavy precipitation. You can also determine the tops and bases of the echoes, the intensity of the precipitation, and the echo movement.
8. A radar summary chart is most effective when used in combination with other charts, reports, and forecasts.

CONSTANT PRESSURE ANALYSIS CHART
9. A constant pressure analysis chart provides observed winds aloft, temperature and dewpoint information. You can also use this chart to determine temperatures.
10. Hatching on a constant pressure analysis chart indicates wind speeds between 70 and 110 knots.

WINDS AND TEMPERATURES ALOFT FORECASTS
11. An estimate of wind direction in relation to true north, wind speed in knots, and the temperature in degrees Celsius for selected altitudes can be found in the winds and temperatures aloft forecast (FD).

LOW AND HIGH LEVEL SIGNIFICANT WEATHER PROGNOSTIC CHARTS
12. A low-level significant weather prognostic chart depicts weather conditions forecast to exist at 12, and 24 hours in the future. This chart is valid up to 24,000 feet MSL.
13. In a high-level significant weather prognostic chart the areas enclosed in scalloped lines indicate that you should expect cumulonimbus clouds (CBs), icing, and moderate or greater turbulence.
14. A high-level significant weather prognostic chart forecasts clear air turbulence, tropopause height, sky coverage, embedded thunderstorms, and jet stream velocities between 24,000 feet MSL and 63,000 feet MSL.

COMPOSITE MOISTURE STABILITY CHART
15. A freezing level panel of the composite moisture stability chart is an analysis of observed freezing level data from upper air observations.
16. The difference found by subtracting the temperature of a parcel of air theoretically lifted from the surface to 500 millibars and the existing temperature at 500 millibars is called the lifted index.

9-130 Reserved

9-130. Reserved

9-131 I60

What important information is provided by the Radar Summary Chart that is not shown on other weather charts?

A — Lines and cells of hazardous thunderstorms.
B — Types of precipitation.
C — Areas of cloud cover and icing levels within the clouds.

9-131. Answer A. GFDICM 9D (AWS)

The radar summary chart is unique because it shows areas of precipitation, thunderstorm cells, and lines of cells. In addition, the chart provides echo heights of the tops and bases of associated precipitation areas, size, shape, and intensity of returns, as well as the intensity trend and direction of movement. Radar summary charts do not show types of precipitation (answer B), or cloud cover and icing levels within clouds (answer C).

9-132 I61

What flight planning information can a pilot derive from constant pressure charts?

A — Clear air turbulence and icing conditions.
B — Levels of widespread cloud coverage.
C — Winds and temperatures aloft.

9-132. Answer C. GFDICM 9D (AWS)

The constant pressure analysis chart is an upper air weather map on which all information is referenced to a specified pressure level. The observed data for each reporting location are plotted on the chart. The information includes the observed temperature and temperature/dewpoint spread, the wind direction, the wind speed, the height of the pressure surface, and any changes in height over the previous 12 hours. Answers (A) and (B) are wrong because clear air turbulence, icing conditions, and levels of widespread cloud coverage are not indicated on a constant pressure chart.

9-133 I65

(Refer to figure 9 on page 9-38.) The Severe Weather Outlook Chart depicts

A — areas of probable severe thunderstorms by the use of single hatched areas on the chart.
B — areas of forecast, severe or extreme turbulence, and areas of severe icing for the next 24 hours.
C — areas of general thunderstorm activity (excluding severe) by the use of hatching on the chart.

9-133. Answer NCA.

There is no correct answer. The Severe Weather Outlook Chart has been replaced by the Convective Outlook chart. This chart depicts the probability of thunderstorm activity for a two day period. The chart no longer uses single-hatched, or cross-hatched areas to indicate weather phenomena. Risk levels are indicated as Slight (SLGT), Moderate (MDT), or High (HIGH).

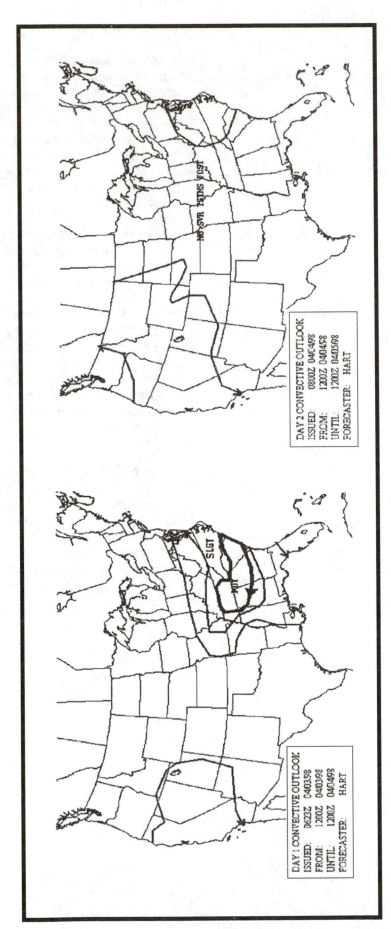

FIGURE 9.—Severe Weather Outlook Charts.

9-134   I59
(Refer to figure 4 on page 9-40.) What is the meaning of a bracket (]) plotted to the right of the station circle on a weather depiction chart?

A — The station represents the en route conditions within a 50 mile radius.
B — The station is an automated observation location.
C — The station gives local overview of flying conditions for a six hour period.

9-135   I59
(Refer to figure 4 on page 9-40.) The Weather Depiction Chart indicates the heaviest precipitation is occurring in

A — north central Florida.
B — north central Minnesota.
C — central South Dakota.

9-136   I59
(Refer to figure 4 on page 9-40.) The Weather Depiction Chart in the area of northwestern Wyoming, indicates

A — overcast with scattered rain showers.
B — 1,000-foot ceilings and visibility 3 miles or more.
C — 500-foot ceilings and continuous rain, less than 3 miles visibility.

9-137   I58
The Surface Analysis Chart depicts

A — actual pressure systems, frontal locations, cloud tops, and precipitation at the time shown on the chart.
B — frontal locations and expected movement, pressure centers, cloud coverage, and obstructions to vision at the time of chart transmission.
C — actual frontal positions, pressure patterns, temperature, dewpoint, wind, weather, and obstructions to vision at the valid time of the chart.

9-138   I64
The Low-Level Significant Weather Prognostic Chart depicts weather conditions

A — that are forecast to exist at a valid time shown on the chart.
B — as they existed at the time the chart was prepared.
C — that existed at the time shown on the chart which is about 3 hours before the chart is received.

9-134. Answer B. GFDICM 9D (AWS)
The sky cover symbols used in the station model are nearly the same as those used for the surface analysis chart. The only exception is that automated stations are depicted with a bracket (]) to the right of the station circle, answer (B). Answer (A) is wrong because the station model represents a general area around the reporting station. Answer (C) is wrong because the weather depiction chart is valid for an 8-hour period and the bracket symbol indicates the station is automated.

9-135. Answer B. GFDICM 9D (AWS)
Answer (B) is correct. In north central Minnesota, the presence of a group of four dots within the shaded area indicates continuous rain, heavy at the time of observation, throughout the area. Answer (A) is wrong because the shaded area over central Florida indicates IFR conditions exist with ceilings less than 1,000 feet and/or visibility less than 3 miles. Answer (C) is wrong because the contoured area without shading indicates MVFR conditions with ceilings 1,000 feet to 3,000 feet and/or visibility 3 miles to 5 miles.

9-136. Answer C. GFDICM 9D (AWS)
The shaded area within the contour indicates the area is IFR with ceilings less than 1,000 feet and visibility less than 3 miles. The solid black station symbol indicates the sky is overcast. Continuous rain is indicated by the two dots. The 5 below the station model indicates a ceiling of 500 feet.

9-137. Answer C. GFDICM 9D (AWS)
The surface analysis chart shows weather conditions as they existed at the observation time shown on the chart. Included are actual frontal positions, sea level pressure patterns, highs and lows, temperature and dewpoint, wind direction and speed, local weather, and obstructions to vision. The surface analysis chart does not show cloud tops (answer A) or expected frontal movement (answer B).

9-138. Answer A. GFDICM 9D (AWS)
The low-level significant weather prognostic chart is valid from the surface to the 400-millibar pressure level (24,000 feet). The chart depicts weather conditions that are forecast to exist during the valid time of the chart. The chart is divided into four different panels: the upper panels are 12- and 24-hour forecasts of weather between the surface and 24,000 feet, while the two lower panels are 12- and 24-hour forecasts of surface weather conditions. Answers (B) and (C) are wrong because a prognostic chart represents forecast information.

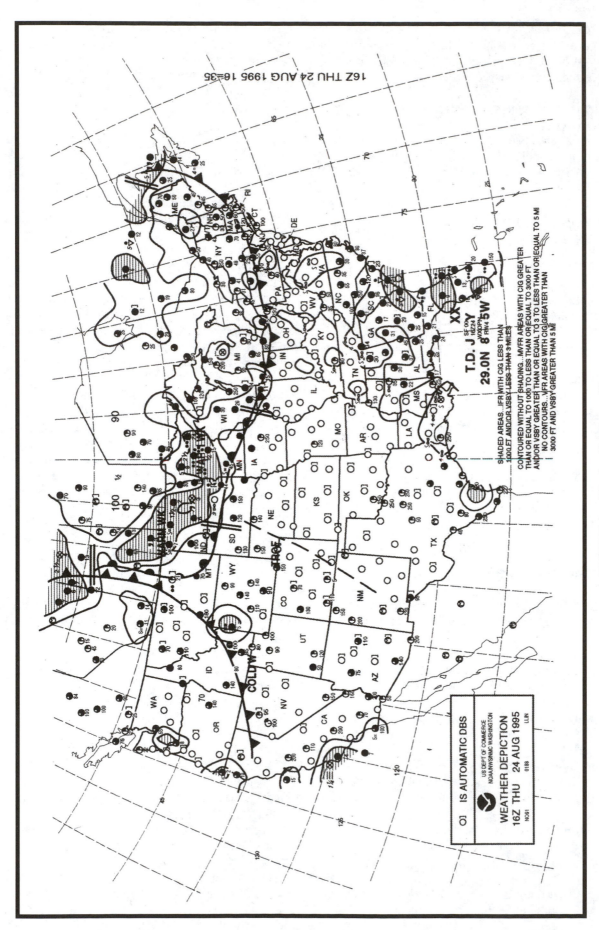

FIGURE 4.—Weather Depiction Chart.

9-139   I64

Which meteorological conditions are depicted by a prognostic chart?

A — Conditions existing at the time of the observation.

B — Interpretation of weather conditions for geographical areas between reporting stations.

C — Conditions forecast to exist at a specific time shown on the chart.

9-139. Answer C. GFDICM 9D (AWS)

See explanation for Question 9-138.

9-140   I64

(Refer to figure 5.) What is the meaning of the symbol depicted as used on the U.S. Low-Level Significant Weather Prognostic Chart?

A — Showery precipitation (e.g. rain showers) embedded in an area of continuous rain covering half or more of the area.

B — Continuous precipitation (e.g. rain) covering half or more of the area.

C — Showery precipitation (e.g. thunderstorms/rain showers) covering half or more of the area.

9-140. Answer A. GFDICM 9D (AWS)

An area which is expected to have continuous or intermittent precipitation is enclosed by a solid line. If only showers are expected, the area is enclosed with a dot-dash line. When precipitation covers one-half or more of the area, it is shaded. The symbols within the circle indicate continuous rain with rain showers. Therefore, the figure represents an area of showery precipitation embedded in an area of continuous rain. Answer (B) is wrong because continuous precipitation is represented by only two dots without the shower symbol. Answer (C) is wrong because no thunderstorm symbol is depicted.

9-141   I64

A prognostic chart depicts the conditions

A — existing at the surface during the past 6 hours.

B — which presently exist from the 1,000-millibar through the 700-millibar level.

C — forecast to exist at a specific time in the future.

9-141. Answer C. GFDICM 9D (AWS)

See explanation for Question 9-138. Answers (A) and (B) are wrong because the conditions are forecast, not existing. Answer (B) is also wrong because conditions are forecast from the surface to the 400-millibar level (24,000 feet), not the 1,000- through the 700-millibar level.

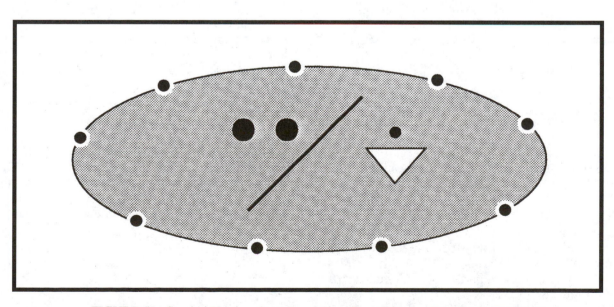

FIGURE 5.—Symbol Used on Low-Level Significant Weather Prognostic Chart.

9-142   I64
(Refer to figure 18, SFC PROG, on page 9-43.) A planned low altitude flight from northern Florida to southern Florida at 00Z is likely to encounter

A — intermittent rain or rain showers, moderate turbulence, and freezing temperatures above 8,000 feet.
B — showery precipitation, thunderstorms/rain showers covering half or more of the area.
C — showery precipitation covering less than half the area, no turbulence below 18,000 feet, and freezing temperatures above 12,000 feet.

9-143   I64
(Refer to figure 18, SFC-400MB, on page 9-43.) The 24-Hour Low Level Significant Weather Prog at 12Z indicates that southwestern West Virginia will likely experience

A — ceilings less than 1,000 feet, visibility less than 3 miles.
B — clear sky and visibility greater than 6 miles.
C —ceilings 1,000 to 3,000 feet and visibility 3 to 5 miles.

9-144   I64
(Refer to figure 18, SFC-400MB, on page 9-43.) The U.S. Low Level Significant Weather Surface Prog Chart at 00Z indicates that northwestern Colorado and eastern Utah can expect

A — moderate or greater turbulence from the surface to FL 240.
B — moderate or greater turbulence above FL 240.
C — no turbulence is indicated.

9-145   I64
(Refer to figure 18, SFC-PROG, on page 9-43.) The chart symbols shown in the Gulf of Mexico at 12Z and extending into AL, GA, SC, and northern FL indicate a

A — tropical storm.
B — hurricane.
C — tornado originating in the Gulf of Mexico.

9-146   I64
(Refer to figure 7 on page 9-44.) What weather conditions are depicted within the area indicated by arrow E?

A — Occasional cumulonimbus, 1/8 to 4/8 coverage, bases below 24,000 feet MSL, and tops at 40,000 feet MSL.
B — Frequent embedded thunderstorms, less than 1/8 coverage, and tops at FL370.
C — Frequent lightning in thunderstorms at FL370.

9-142. Answer B. GFDICM 9D (AWS)
The only panels valid for the proposed departure time are the two panels on the left. The top panel indicates moderate to severe turbulence from the surface to 24,000 feet. The lower panel indicates showery precipitation, thunderstorms and rain showers covering more than half of the state. Answers (A) and (C) are wrong because moderate to severe turbulence is predicted, and the showery precipitation is embedded in an area of continuous rain covering more than half of the area.

9-143. Answer A. GFDICM 9D (AWS)
The 24-hour panels are located on the right. The top panel indicates IFR conditions over southwestern West Virginia. Ceilings less then 1,000 feet and/or visibility less than 3 miles are depicted by the smooth contour line. Answers (B) and (C) are wrong because VFR conditions are not indicated.

9-144. Answer A. GFDICM 9D (AWS)
The 12-hour significant weather prognostic shows northwestern Colorado and eastern Utah enclosed in a dashed line. This indicates an area of moderate or greater nonconvective turbulence is predicted as indicated by the legend between the top two panels. The expected range is shown in hundreds of feet. The number "240/" indicates the turbulence is expected from the surface to 24,000 feet.

9-145. Answer A. GFDICM 9D (AWS)
The symbol in the lower right panel indicates a tropical storm off the southern coast of the Florida panhandle, Alabama, and Georgia. The textual note indicates tropical storm Jerry is located 29.8 degrees north latitude by 84.8 degrees west longitude. Answer (B) is wrong because the hurricane symbol is depicted with a blackened center. Answer (C) is wrong because tornadoes are not depicted.

9-146. Answer A. GFDICM 9D (AWS)
The altitude of the "CB" is "400/XXX." The "XXX" means the bases start below the lower limit of the chart, which is FL240. "Occasional" means 1/8 to 4/8 coverage. Answers (B) and (C) are wrong because the cloud tops extend to FL400.

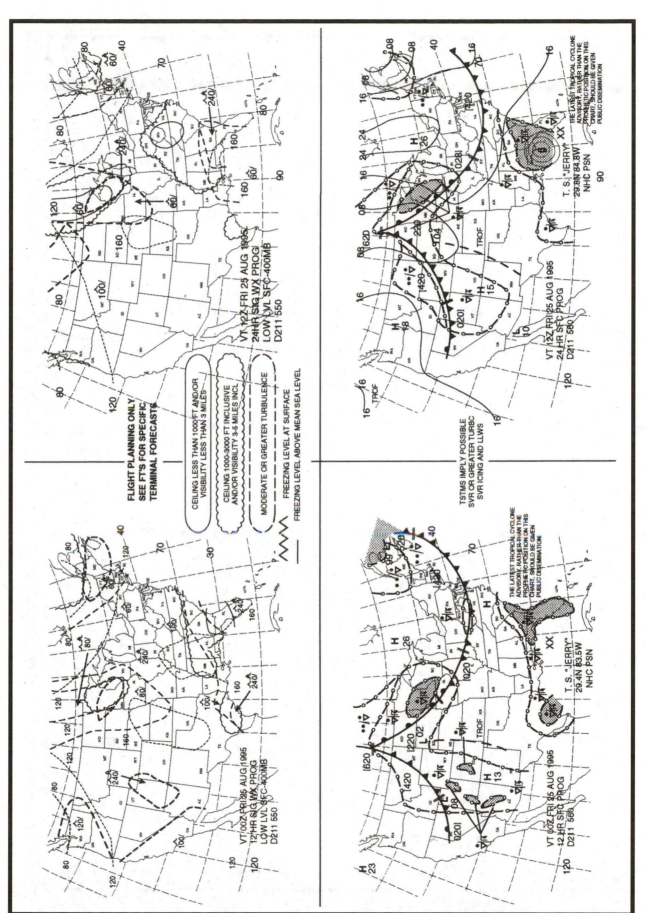

FIGURE 18.—U.S. Low-Level Significant Weather Prognostic Charts.

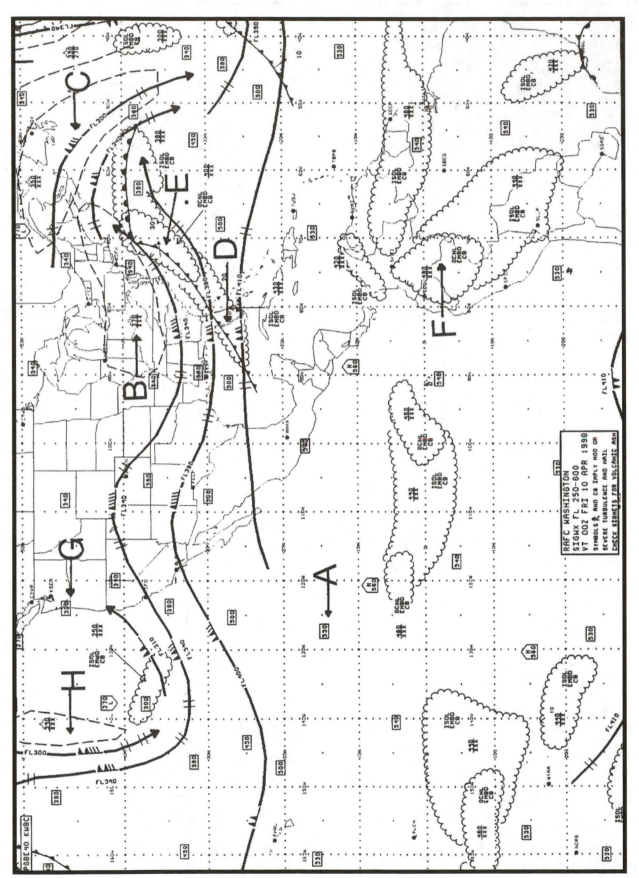

FIGURE 7.—High-Level Significant Weather Prognostic Chart.

9-147   I64

(Refer to figure 7 on page 9-44.) What weather conditions are depicted within the area indicated by arrow D?

A — Forecast isolated thunderstorms, tops at FL 440, more than 1/8 coverage.

B — Existing isolated cumulonimbus clouds, tops above 43,000 feet with less than 1/8 coverage.

C — Forecast isolated embedded cumulonimbus clouds with tops at 43,000 feet MSL, and less than 1/8 coverage.

9-148   I64

(Refer to figure 7 on page 9-44.) What weather conditions are predicted within the area indicated by arrow C?

A — Light turbulence at FL 370 within the area outlined by dashes.

B — Moderate turbulence at 32,000 feet MSL.

C — Moderate to severe CAT has been reported at FL 320.

9-149   I64

(Refer to figure 7 on page 9-44.) What weather conditions are depicted within the area indicated by arrow B?

A — Light to moderate turbulence at and above 37,000 feet MSL.

B — Moderate to severe CAT is forecast to exist at FL 370.

C — Moderate turbulence from below 24,000 feet MSL to 37,000 feet MSL.

9-150   I64

(Refer to figure 7 on page 9-44.) What information is indicated by arrow A.

A — The height of the tropopause in meters above sea level.

B — The height of the existing layer of CAT.

C — The height of the tropopause in hundreds of feet above MSL.

9-147. Answer C. GFDICM 9D (AWS)

The prognostic chart is a FORECAST, not a report of existing conditions. Use a WEATHER DEPICTION CHART to look at existing conditions. "Isolated" means less than one-eighth coverage. The forecast conditions by arrow D show isolated embedded cumulonimbus clouds with tops at 43,000 feet MSL. Answer (A) is wrong because the cloud tops do not exceed FL 440. Answer (B) is wrong because the conditions are forecast, not existing conditions.

9-148. Answer B. GFDICM 9D (AWS)

The dashed line around Area C indicates moderate turbulence from below FL240 up to FL350.

9-149. Answer C. GFDICM 9D (AWS)

The prognostic chart is a FORECAST. Use a WEATHER DEPICTION CHART to look at existing conditions. Heavy dashed lines indicate an area of turbulence. The symbol for moderate turbulence is shown. The altitude of the turbulence is "370/XXX." The "XXX" means the bases start below the lower limit of the chart, which is 24,000 feet MSL. Answer (A) is incorrect because the turbulence extends to, but not above, 37,000 feet MSL. Answer (B) is incorrect because the turbulence is only forecast to be moderate, not severe.

9-150. Answer C. GFDICM 9D (AWS)

The high-level significant prog chart covers the altitude range of 400 millibars (24,000 feet) to 70 millibars (63,000 feet). However, three-digit numbers contained in boxes represent the forecast height of the tropopause in hundreds of feet MSL, or flight levels. Arrow A indicates that the height of the tropopause is 53,000 feet MSL. Answer (A) is wrong because the height is measured in hundreds of feet, not meters. Answer (B) is wrong because the height of any forecast clear air turbulence (CAT) is enclosed within a series of dashed lines.

9-151   I64

(Refer to figure 7 on page 9-44.) What weather conditions are depicted within the area indicated by arrow F?

A — 1/8 to 4/8 coverage, occasional embedded thunderstorms, maximum tops at 51,000 feet MSL.
B — Occasionally embedded cumulonimbus, bases below 24,000 feet with tops to 48,000 feet.
C — 2/8 to 6/8 coverage, occasional embedded thunderstorms, tops at FL 540.

9-152   I60

(Refer to figure 8 on page 9-47.) What weather conditions are depicted in the area indicated by arrow A on the Radar Summary Chart?

A — Moderate to strong echoes; echo tops 30,000 feet MSL; line movement toward the northwest.
B — Weak to moderate echoes; average echo bases 30,000 feet MSL; cell movement toward the southeast; rain showers with thunder.
C — Strong to very strong echoes; echo tops 30,000 feet MSL; thunderstorms and rain showers.

9-153   I60

(Refer to figure 8 on page 9-47.) What weather conditions are depicted in the area indicated by arrow D on the Radar Summary Chart?

A — Echo tops 4,100 feet MSL, strong to very strong echoes within the smallest contour, and area movement toward the northeast at 50 knots.
B — Intense to extreme echoes within the smallest contour, echo tops 29,000 feet MSL, and cell movement toward the northeast at 50 knots.
C — Strong to very strong echoes within the smallest contour, echo bases 29,000 feet MSL, and cell in northeast Nebraska moving northeast at 50 knots.

9-154   I64

(Refer to figure 7 on page 9-44.) The area indicated by arrow H indicates

A — light turbulence below 34,000 feet.
B — isolated embedded cumulonimbus clouds with bases below FL180 and tops at FL340.
C — moderate turbulence at and below 34,000 feet.

9-151. Answer B. GFDICM 9D (AWS)

Scalloped lines enclose areas of expected embedded cumulonimbus (CB) clouds. The altitude of the embedded CB is depicted by 480/XXX which means the tops are 48,000 feet and the bases are below 24,000 which is the lower limit of the chart. "Occasional" means 1/8 to 4/8 coverage.

9-152. Answer C. GFDICM 9D (AWS)

The radar summary chart provides a graphic depiction of certain types of weather phenomena, primarily precipitation. It shows size, shape, and intensity of echo returns with various contour levels. The first contour level indicates weak to moderate echoes, the second contour level indicates strong and very strong echoes, and the third contour level indicates intense and extreme echoes. Tops of echoes are indicated if a number is displayed above a solid line. A base is indicated if a number is displayed below a solid line. Arrow A is pointing out a second contour level of strong to very strong echoes with tops at 30,000 feet MSL. In addition, the notation "TRW" indicates thunderstorms and rain showers. Answers (A) and (B) are wrong because moderate echoes are not illustrated and general movement of this area is toward the northeast.

9-153. Answer B. GFDICM 9D (AWS)

See explanation for Question 9-152. Arrow D is pointing out an area of intense to extreme echoes with echo tops at 29,000 feet MSL. In addition, the arrow pointing to "50" shows the cell is moving toward the northeast at 50 knots. Answers (A) and (C) are wrong because strong to very strong echoes are not indicated and the correct tops and bases are not called out.

9-154. Answer C. GFDICM 9D (AWS)

Heavy dashed lines indicate an area of turbulence. The symbol for moderate turbulence is shown. The altitude of the turbulence is 340/XXX, The "XXX" means the bases start below 24,000 feet MSL, the lower limit of the chart.

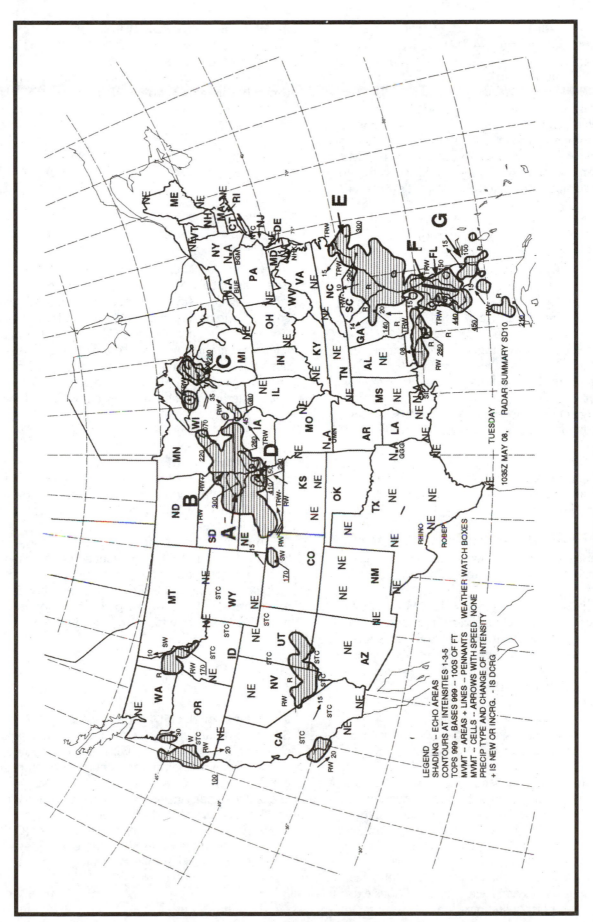

FIGURE 8.—Radar Summary Chart.

9-155   I60
(Refer to figure 8 on page 9-47.) What weather conditions are depicted in the area indicated by arrow C on the Radar Summary Chart?

A — Average echo bases 2,800 feet MSL, thundershowers, and intense to extreme echo intensity.
B — Cell movement toward the northwest at 20 knots, intense echoes, and echo bases 28,000 feet MSL.
C — Area movement toward the northeast, strong to very strong echoes, and echo tops 28,000 feet MSL.

9-155. Answer C. GFDICM 9D (AWS)
See explanation for Question 9-152. Arrow C is pointing to an area of strong to very strong echoes with tops at 28,000 feet MSL. Answers (A) and (B) are wrong because no echo bases are indicated. In addition, intense to extreme echoes are not indicated by the double contour.

9-156   I60
(Refer to figure 8 on page 9-47.) What weather conditions are depicted in the area indicated by arrow B on the Radar Summary Chart?

A — Weak echoes, heavy rain showers, area movement toward the southeast.
B — Weak to moderate echoes, rain showers increasing in intensity.
C — Strong echoes, moderate rain showers, no cell movement.

9-156. Answer B. GFDICM 9D (AWS)
See explanation for Question 9-152. Arrow B is pointing out an area of weak to moderate echoes. Rain showers, increasing in intensity, are indicated by the "RW+" near the cell. Answer (A) is wrong because area movement is not depicted. Also, the "+" sign is used to show increasing intensity, not heavy rain showers. Answer (C) is wrong because strong echoes and moderate rain showers are not indicated.

9-157   I60
(Refer to figure 8 on page 9-47.) What weather conditions are depicted in the area indicated by arrow E on the Radar Summary Chart?

A — Highest echo tops 30,000 feet MSL, weak to moderate echoes, thunderstorms and rain showers, and cell movement toward northwest at 15 knots.
B — Echo bases 29,000 to 30,000 feet MSL, strong echoes, rain showers increasing in intensity, and area movement toward northwest at 15 knots.
C — Thundershowers decreasing in intensity; area movement toward northwest at 15 knots; echo bases 30,000 feet MSL.

9-157. Answer A. GFDICM 9D (AWS)
See explanation for Question 9-152. Arrow E is pointing out an area of weak to moderate echoes in thunderstorms and rain showers (TRW) with tops at 30,000 feet MSL. In addition, the arrow pointing to "15" means the cell is moving to the northwest at 15 knots. Answer (B) is wrong because echo bases, strong echoes, and increasing rain showers are not indicated. Answer (C) is wrong because thundershowers decreasing in intensity would be shown as "TRW-," and echo tops, not bases, are indicated.

9-158   I60
For most effective use of the Radar Summary Chart during preflight planning, a pilot should

A — consult the chart to determine more accurate measurements of freezing levels, cloud cover, and wind conditions between reporting stations.
B — compare it with the charts, reports, and forecasts of a three-dimensional picture of clouds and precipitation.
C — utilize the chart as the only source of information regarding storms and hazardous conditions existing between reporting stations.

9-158. Answer B. GFDICM 9D (AWS)
Since the radar summary chart primarily displays observed conditions at the valid time, it's best to compare it with other charts, reports and forecasts to get a three-dimensional picture of the existing and forecast weather. Answer (A) is wrong because freezing levels, cloud cover, and wind conditions are not indicated on radar summary charts. Answer (C) is wrong because the radar summary chart does not provide information on all hazardous conditions.

9-159   I60

(Refer to figure 8 on page 9-47.) What weather conditions are depicted in the area indicated by arrow G on the Radar Summary Chart?

A — Echo bases 10,000 feet MSL; cell movement toward northeast at 15 knots; weak to moderate echoes; rain.

B — Area movement toward northeast at 15 knots; rain decreasing in intensity; echo bases 1,000 feet MSL; strong echoes.

C — Strong to very strong echoes; area movement toward northeast at 15 knots; echo tops 10,000 feet MSL; light rain

9-160   I60

(Refer to figure 8 on page 9-47.) What weather conditions are depicted in the area indicated by arrow F on the Radar Summary Chart?

A — Line of echoes; thunderstorms; highest echo tops 45,000 feet MSL; no line movement indicated.

B — Echo bases vary from 15,000 feet to 46,000 feet MSL; thunderstorms increasing in intensity; line of echoes moving rapidly toward the north.

C — Line of severe thunderstorms moving from south to north; echo bases vary from 4,400 feet to 4,600 feet MSL; extreme echoes.

9-161   I65

(Refer to figure 9 on page 9-38.) The Severe Weather Outlook Chart, which is used primarily for advance planning, provides what information?

A — An 18-hour categorical outlook with a 48-hour valid time for severe weather watch, thunderstorm lines, and of expected tornado activity.

B — A preliminary 12-hour outlook for severe thunderstorm activity and probable convective turbulence.

C — A 24-hour severe weather outlook for possible thunderstorm activity.

9-159. Answer A. GFDICM 9D (AWS)

The radar summary chart provides a graphic depiction of certain types of weather phenomena, primarily precipitation. It shows size, shape, and intensity of echo returns with various contour levels. The first contour level indicates weak to moderate echoes, the second contour level indicates strong and very strong echoes, and the third contour level indicates intense and extreme echoes. Tops of echoes are indicated if a number is displayed above a solid line. A base is indicated if a number is displayed below a solid line. Arrow G is pointing out an area with weak to moderate intensity with bases at 10,000 feet MSL. In addition, the arrow pointing to "15" means the cell is moving to the northeast at 15 knots. Answer (B) is wrong because strong echoes, decreasing rain, and echo bases of 1,000 feet are not depicted. Answer (C) is wrong because strong to very strong echoes, echo tops, and light rain is not indicated.

9-160. Answer A. GFDICM 9D (AWS)

See explanation for Question 9-152 and 9-159. Arrow F is pointing out a line of echoes and thunderstorms with tops at 45,000 feet MSL and no movement. Answer (B) is wrong because bases varying from 15,000 feet to 46,000 feet, increasing thunderstorms, and rapid movement are not indicated. Answer (C) is wrong because line movement and varying bases are not indicated.

9-161. Answer C. GFDICM 9D (AWS)

The severe weather outlook chart provides a 48-hour outlook for thunderstorm activity as well as severe thunderstorms. This chart is prepared five times a day for the next 24 hours (Day 1 convective outlook) and twice a day for the following 24 hours (Day 2 convective outlook). Answers (A) and (B) are wrong because tornado activity and turbulence are not depicted.

9-162   I65
(Refer to figure 9 on page 9-38) Using the DAY 2
CONVECTIVE OUTLOOK, what type of thunder-
storms, if any, may be encountered on a flight from
Montana to central California?

A — Moderate risk area, surrounded by a slight risk
     area, of possible severe turbulence.
B — General.
C — None.

9-162. Answer B. GFDICM 9D (AWS)
The severe weather outlook chart provides a 48-hour
outlook for thunderstorm activity. A line with an arrowhead depicts forecast general thunderstorm activity.
When facing in the direction of the arrow, thunderstorm activity is expected to the right of the line.
General thunderstorms (non-severe) are outlined, but
with no label on the graphic map.

9-163   I64
(Refer to figure 20.) What is the maximum wind veloci-
ty forecast in the jet stream shown on the high level
Significant Weather Prognostic Chart over Canada?

A — 80 knots.
B — 103 knots.
C — 130 knots.

9-163. Answer C. GFDICM 9D (AWS)
The maximum forecast jet stream core speed, when
more than 80 knots, is depicted by shafts, pennants,
and feathers. In this case the maximum wind velocity
forecast in the jet stream is depicted by two pennants
and three feathers. The speed value of the pennants
is fifty knots each and the feathers have a value of
ten knots each. Therefore, answer (C), 130 knots is
correct. Answer (A), 80 knots, would be depicted by a
single pennant and three feathers. Answer (B), is
wrong because 103 knots cannot depicted with
pennants and feathers.

9-164   I64
(Refer to figure 20.) What is the height of the
tropopause over Kentucky?

A – FL390.
B – FL300 sloping to FL 400 feet MSL.
C – FL340.

9-164. Answer C. GFDICM 9C (AWS)
All heights on high-level significant weather prognostic
charts are depicted in flight levels. The five sided poly-
gon located over Kentucky indicates the lowest height
of the tropopause. In this example, the tropopause
height is at flight level 340.

9-165   I63
(Refer to figure 12 on page 9-53.) What is the
approximate wind direction and velocity at 34,000
feet (see arrow C)?

A — 290°/50 knots.
B — 330°/50 knots.
C — 090°/48 knots.

9-165. Answer A. GFDICM 9D (AWS)
To determine the wind direction, first consider the
general orientation of the wind direction indicator. This
station indicates a wind from the northwest. The "9" at
the end of the direction indicator is the second digit of
the wind direction rounded to the nearest 10°. In this
example, the wind is from 290°. You determine the
wind speed by adding the barbs on the wind direction
indicator. A flag represents 50 knots, a barb 10 knots,
and a half a barb 5 knots. The wind speed in this
example is 50 knots. Answer (B) is wrong because
330° is not the correct wind direction. Answer (C) is
wrong because neither the direction nor the speed are
correct. Also, the "-48" is not wind speed, but the
observed temperature in degrees Celsius.

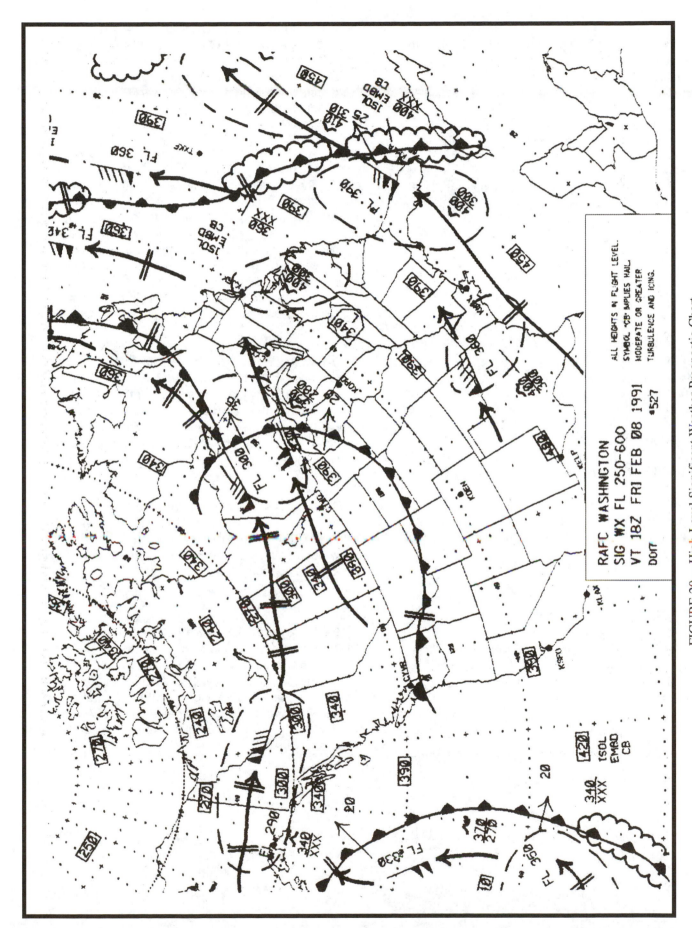

FIGURE 20.—High-Level Significant Weather Prognostic Chart.

9-166   I63
(Refer to figure 12.) The wind direction and velocity on the Observed Winds Aloft Chart (see arrow A) is indicated from the

A — northeast at 35 knots.
B — northwest at 47 knots.
C — southwest at 35 knots.

9-167   I65
(Refer to figure 9 on page 9-38.) What type of thunderstorm activity is expected over Montana on April 4th at 0800Z?

A — None.
B — A slight risk of severe thunderstorms.
C — General.

9-168   I63
(Refer to figure 12.) What is the approximate wind direction and velocity at CVG at 34,000 feet (see arrow A)?

A — 040°/35 knots.
B — 097°/40 knots.
C — 230°/35 knots.

9-169   I63
(Refer to figure 12, arrow B.) What is the approximate wind direction and velocity at BOI?

A — 270°/55 knots.
B — 250°/95 knots.
C — 080°/95 knots.

9-170   I64
(Refer to figure 7 on page 9-44.) The symbol on the U.S. HIGH-LEVEL SIGNIFICANT WEATHER PROG, indicated by arrow G, represents the

A — wind direction at the tropopause (300°).
B — height of the tropopause.
C — height of maximum wind shear (30,000 feet).

9-166. Answer C. GFDICM 9D (AWS)
See explanation for Question 9-165. The wind is southwest, or 230°, at 35 knots. Answer (A) is wrong because the wind direction indicator points to the direction the wind is from. Answer (B) is wrong because both the direction and speed are incorrect.

9-167. Answer A. GFDICM 9D (AWS)
For the correct chart you need to refer to the day 1 convective outlook. The severe weather outlook chart provides a 48-hour outlook for thunderstorm activity. A line with an arrowhead depicts forecast general thunderstorm activity. When facing in the direction of the arrow, thunderstorm activity is expected to the right of the line. Since Montana is to the left of the line there is no thunderstorm activity expected on April 4th at 0800Z.

9-168. Answer C. GFDICM 9D (AWS)
See explanation for Question 9-165. For this question, you must know that arrow A is pointing at CVG. The wind direction is 230° at 35 knots. Answers (A) and (B) are wrong because incorrect wind directions are indicated. In addition, the wind speed in answer (B) is wrong.

9-169. Answer B. GFDICM 9D (AWS)
See explanation for Question 9-165. The wind direction is 250° at 95 knots. Answers (A) and (C) are wrong because they indicate incorrect wind directions, and the speed is wrong for answer (A).

9-170. Answer B. GFDICM 9D (AWS)
The three-digit numbers contained in boxes represent the forecast height of the tropopause measured from Mean Sea Level. Arrow G indicates that the height of the tropopause is 30,000 feet MSL. Wind direction is shown using shafts, pennants and barbs. Areas of moderate or greater turbulence are enclosed by bold dashed lines.

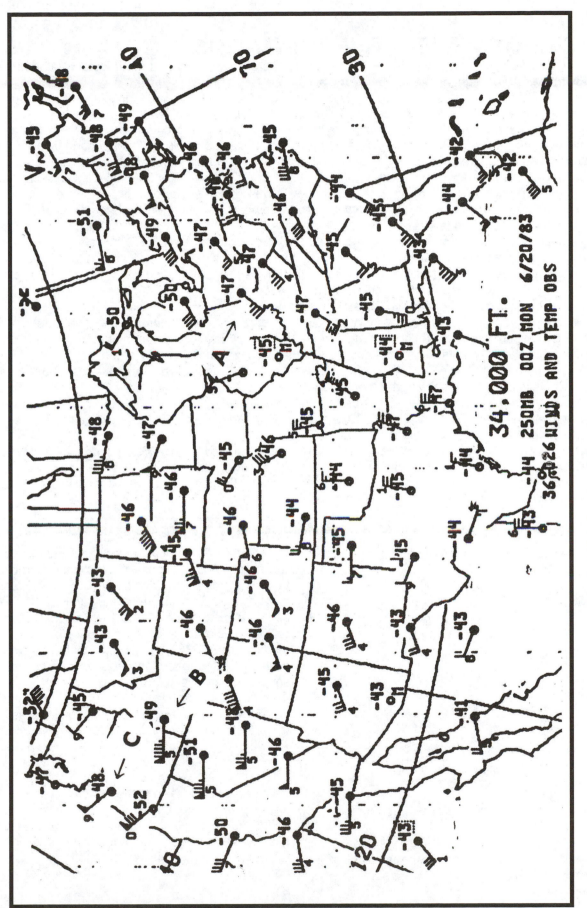

FIGURE 12.—Observed Winds Aloft for 34,000 Feet.

SECTION E
SOURCES OF WEATHER INFORMATION

1. Enroute flight advisory service (EFAS) provides enroute aircraft with timely and meaningful weather advisories pertinent to the type of flight intended, route, and altitude.
2. EFAS is obtained by contacting flight watch, using the name of the ARTCC facility identification in your area, your aircraft identification, and name of the nearest VOR, on 122.0 MHz below FL180.
3. In-flight aviation weather advisories consisting of AIRMETs, SIGMETs, and convective SIGMETs are forecasts that advise enroute aircraft of the development of potentially hazardous weather, and information on volcanic eruptions that are occurring or expected to occur. All in-flight advisories in the contiguous U.S. are issued by the National Aviation Weather Advisory Unit in Kansas City, MO. All in-flight advisories use the same location identifiers (either VORs, airports, or well-known geographic areas) to describe the hazardous weather areas.
4. Convective SIGMETs contain either an observation and a forecast, or just a forecast, for tornadoes, significant thunderstorm activity, or hail 3/4 inch or greater in diameter.
5. A center weather advisory (CWA) is an unscheduled advisory issued by an ARTCC to alert pilots of existing or anticipated adverse weather conditions within the next two hours. A CWA may be issued prior to an AIRMET or SIGMET when PIREPs suggest AIRMET or SIGMET conditions exist. Even if adverse weather is not sufficiently intense or widespread for a SIGMET or AIRMET, a CWA may be issued if conditions are expected to affect the safe flow of air traffic within the ARTCC area of responsibility.
6. AIRMETs and center weather advisories (CWA) provide an enroute pilot with information about moderate icing, moderate turbulence, winds of 30 knots or more at the surface, and extensive mountain obscurement.
7. Weather advisory broadcasts, including severe weather forecast alerts (AWW), convective SIGMETs, and SIGMETs, are provided by ARTCCs on all frequencies, except emergency, when any part of the area described is within 150 miles of the airspace under their jurisdiction.
8. The hazardous in-flight weather advisory service (HIWAS) is a continuous broadcast of in-flight weather advisories over selected VORs of SIGMETs, convective SIGMETs, AIRMETs, severe weather forecast alerts (AWW), and center weather advisories (CWA).
9. A transcribed weather broadcast (TWEB) provides specific information concerning expected sky cover, cloud tops, visibility, weather, and obstructions to vision in a route format. To obtain continuous transcribed information, including winds aloft and route forecasts for a cross-country flight, you could monitor a TWEB on a low-frequency radio receiver. TWEB mostly has been replaced by HIWAS.

9-171   I57

SIGMET'S are issued as a warning of weather conditions potentially hazardous

A — particularly to light aircraft.
B — to all aircraft.
C — only to light aircraft operations.

9-171. Answer B. GFDICM 9E (AIM)
SIGMETs (WSs) are issued for hazardous weather which may be significant to all aircraft. According to the AIM, whether the condition described is potentially hazardous to a particular flight is for the pilot and/or aircraft dispatcher (in Part 121 operations) to evaluate on the basis of experience and operational limits of the aircraft. SIGMET criteria include the following: severe or extreme turbulence, severe icing, and widespread duststorms, sandstorms, and volcanic eruptions or volcanic ash lowering surface and/or inflight visibilities to less than three miles. An AIRMET is issued for weather that may be hazardous to light aircraft. Answers (A) and (C) are incomplete, since the advisory may apply to all aircraft.

9-172   I57

Which meteorological condition is issued in the form of a SIGMET (WS)?

A — Widespread sand or duststorms lowering visibility to less than 3 miles.
B — Moderate icing.
C — Sustained winds of 30 knots or greater at the surface.

9-172. Answer A. GFDICM 9E (AIM)
See explanation for Question 9-170. Answers (B) and (C) are wrong. Moderate icing (answer B) and sustained winds of 30 knots or more at the surface (answer C) are hazards appropriate for an AIRMET, not a SIGMET.

9-173   I56

A pilot planning to depart at 1100Z on an IFR flight is particularly concerned about the hazard of icing. What sources reflect the most accurate information on icing conditions (current and forecast) at the time of departure?

A — Low-Level Significant Weather Prognostic Chart, and the Area Forecast.
B — The Area Forecast, and the Freezing Level Chart.
C — Pilot weather reports (PIREP's), AIRMET's, and SIGMET's.

9-174   I57

Which forecast provides specific information concerning expected sky cover, cloud tops, visibility, weather, and obstructions to vision in a route format?

A — DFW FA 131240.
B — MEM TAF 132222.
C — 249 TWEB 252317.

9-175   I57

What is the maximum forecast period for AIRMET's?

A — Two hours.
B — Four hours.
C — Six hours.

9-176   I54

The Hazardous Inflight Weather Advisory Service (HIWAS) is a continuous broadcast over selected VORs of

A — SIGMETs, CONVECTIVE SIGMETs, AIRMETs, Severe Weather Forecast Alerts (AWW), and Center Weather Advisories.
B — SIGMETs, CONVECTIVE SIGMETs, AIRMETs, Wind Shear Advisories, and Severe Weather Forecast Alerts (AWW).
C — Wind Shear Advisories, Radar Weather Reports, SIGMETs, CONVECTIVE SIGMETs, AIRMETs, and Center Weather Advisories (CWA).

9-173. Answer C. GFDICM 9E (AWS)

PIREPs represent real-time reports from pilots, and they typically contain information on icing, visibilities, turbulence, cloud bases and tops, temperatures aloft, and wind. On the other hand, AIRMETs and SIGMETs provide the most accurate forecast information on icing conditions. Therefore, all three of these reports are valuable for timely and accurate information. Answer (A) is wrong because area forecasts do not provide the most current information on icing, and the low-level significant weather prog chart isn't updated frequently enough to be considered an up-to-date, accurate forecast of icing conditions. Answer (B) is wrong because the area forecast references AIRMETs and SIGMETs containing icing information. In addition, a freezing level chart provides only general information about icing.

9-174. Answer C. GFDICM 9E (AWS)

Transcribed weather broadcasts (TWEBs) are similar to area forecasts (FAs) except the information is in a route format. Information pertaining to forecast sky cover, cloud tops, visibilities, weather, and obstructions to vision are described for a corridor 25 miles to either side of the route. Answer (A) is incorrect because the FA is not in a route format. Answer (B) is wrong because a terminal aerodrome forecast (TAF), only predicts weather information within five to ten miles of specific airports.

9-175. Answer C. GFDICM 9E (AIM)

AIRMETs are issued for the same six areas as the Area Forecasts, and they have a maximum forecast period of six hours. Answer (A) is wrong because two hours is the forecast valid period for a Convective SIGMET. Four hours (answer B) is the forecast valid period for a SIGMET.

9-176. Answer A. GFDICM 9E (AIM)

HIWAS broadcasts include summarized AIRMETs, SIGMETs, convective SIGMETs, AWWs, CWAs and, on occasion, urgent PIREPs. In areas where HIWAS is implemented, you should be aware that ARTCC, terminal ATC, and FSS facilities have discontinued their normal broadcasts of in-flight advisories. Answers (B) and (C) are wrong because wind shear advisories are normally associated with terminal facilities and/or reports and not with enroute weather broadcasts.

9-177   J33
What does the Runway Visual Range (RVR) value, depicted on certain straight-in IAP Charts, represent?

A — The slant range distance the pilot can see down the runway while crossing the threshold on glide slope.
B — The horizontal distance a pilot should see when looking down the runway from a moving aircraft.
C — The slant visual range a pilot should see down the final approach and during landing.

9-178   J35
On what frequency should you obtain En Route Flight Advisory Service below FL 180?

A — 122.1T/112.8R.
B — 123.6.
C — 122.0.

9-177. Answer B. GFDICM 9E (AIM)
RVR is horizontal visual range, not slant range. It is based on the measurement of a transmissometer located near the touchdown point of the instrument runway and represents the horizontal distance a pilot will see down the runway from the approach end. Answers (A) and (C) are incorrect because both include slant range instead of horizontal visual range, or RVR.

9-178. Answer C. GFDICM 9E (AIM)
Unless otherwise indicated, the standard EFAS frequency below 18,000 feet MSL is 122.0 MHz. Frequencies 122.1T/112.8R (answer A) are wrong because they are the frequencies for communicating with Cedar City FSS through the BCE VORTAC. 123.6 MHz (answer B) is incorrect since it is the frequency for the Bryce Canyon FSS.

IFR FLIGHT CONSIDERATIONS

CHAPTER 10

SECTION A
IFR EMERGENCIES

DISTRESS AND URGENCY CONDITIONS

1. The *Aeronautical Information Manual* defines an emergency as a condition of distress or urgency. Pilots in distress are threatened by serious and/or imminent danger and require immediate assistance. An urgency situation, such as low fuel quantity, requires timely but not immediate assistance.
2. In an emergency, you may deviate from any rule in FAR Part 91 to the extent necessary to meet the emergency. ATC may request a detailed report of an emergency when priority assistance has been given, even though no rules have been violated.

COMMUNICATION PROCEDURES

3. During a flight in IFR conditions, do not hesitate to declare an emergency and obtain an amended clearance when a distress condition is encountered.
4. The frequency of 121.5 MHz may be used to declare an emergency in the event you are unable to contact ATC on other frequencies.
5. In a distress situation, begin your initial call with the word *"MAYDAY,"* preferably repeated three times. Use *"PAN-PAN"* in the same manner in an urgency situation.
6. Your transponder may be used to declare an emergency by squawking code 7700.
7. A special emergency is a condition of air piracy and should be indicated by squawking code 7500 on your transponder.
8. FAR Part 91 requires that you report the malfunction of any navigational, approach, or communications equipment while operating in controlled airspace under IFR. In the malfunction report you should include the aircraft ID, equipment affected, the degree to which the flight will be impaired by the failure, and any assistance you require from ATC.

MINIMUM FUEL

9. If your remaining fuel quantity is such that you can accept little or no delay, you should alert ATC with a minimum fuel advisory. Declaring minimum fuel to ATC indicates an emergency situation is possible should any undue delay occur.
10. If the remaining usable fuel supply suggests the need for traffic priority to ensure a safe landing, you should declare an emergency due to low fuel and report fuel remaining in minutes.

INSTRUMENT FAILURE

11. Gyroscopic instruments include the attitude indicator, heading indicator, and turn coordinator. These instruments are subject to vacuum and electrical system failures.
12. During an instrument failure your first priority is to fly the airplane, navigate accurately, and then communicate with ATC.
13. Radar approach procedures may be available to assist you during an emergency situation requiring an instrument approach.
14. A radar instrument approach that provides only azimuth navigational guidance is referred to as an airport surveillance radar (ASR) approach. A surveillance approach may be used at airports for which civil radar instrument approach minimums have been published.

15. In addition to headings, the information a radar controller provides without request during an ASR approach includes; when to commence descent to the MDA, the aircraft's position each mile on final from the runway, and arrival at the MAP.

16. During a precision approach (PAR), the controller provides you with highly accurate navigational guidance in azimuth and elevation as well as trend information to help you make the proper corrections while on the approach path.

17. A no-gyro approach may be requested when you have experienced a gyroscopic instrument failure. Controllers provide course guidance by stating *"turn right, stop turn"*, and *"turn left"* to align you with the approach path. Turns should be made at standard rate until you have been handed off to the final approach controller, at which point they should be made at one-half standard rate.

COMMUNICATION FAILURE

18. You can use your transponder to alert ATC to a radio communication failure by squawking code 7600.

19. During a communication failure while operating under IFR, you are expected to follow the lost communication procedures specified in the regulations.

20. During a communication failure in VFR conditions, remain in VFR conditions, land as soon as practicable, and call ATC.

21. If you lose communication with ATC during your flight, you must fly the highest of the assigned altitude, MEA, or the altitude ATC has advised may be expected in a further clearance.

22. If an approach is available at your clearance limit, begin the approach at the expect further clearance (EFC) time. If an approach is not available at your clearance limit, proceed from the clearance limit at your EFC to the point at which an approach begins.

10-1   J24

While flying on an IFR flight plan, you experience two-way communications radio failure while in VFR conditions. In this situation, you should continue your flight under

A — VFR and land as soon as practicable.

B — IFR and maintain the last assigned route and altitude to your flight plan destination.

C — VFR and proceed to your flight plan destination.

10-1. Answer A. GFDICM 10A (FAR 91.185)

If you experience a communications failure in VFR conditions or if you encounter VFR conditions subsequent to the failure, you should continue the flight under VFR conditions and land as soon as practicable.

10-2   J12

What does declaring "minimum fuel" to ATC imply?

A — Traffic priority is needed to the destination airport.

B — Emergency handling is required to the nearest useable airport.

C — Merely an advisory that indicates an emergency situation is possible should any undue delay occur.

10-2. Answer C. GFDICM 10A (AIM)

Declaring "minimum fuel" is simply an advisory which tells ATC that you can accept little or no delay upon reaching your destination. It does not indicate an emergency, but undue delay may result in an emergency situation. Declaring "minimum fuel" does not mean you will receive traffic priority (answer A), or emergency handling (answer B).

10-3   J21

During an IFR flight in IMC, a distress condition is encountered (fire, mechanical, or structural failure). The pilot should

A — not hesitate to declare an emergency and obtain an amended clearance.

B — wait until the situation is immediately perilous before declaring an emergency.

C — contact ATC and advise that an urgency condition exists and request priority consideration.

10-3. Answer A. GFDICM 10A (AIM)

The AIM defines distress as a condition of being threatened by serious and/or imminent danger and of requiring immediate assistance. In this situation, do not hesitate to declare an emergency immediately and request an amended clearance. Waiting until the situation is immediately perilous before declaring an emergency (answer B) may leave little time for ATC to help. Advising ATC of an urgency condition (answer C) does not mean the same as a distress condition. According to the AIM, an urgency situation is a condition of being concerned about safety and of requiring timely, but not immediate, assistance.

10-4   J14

When may ATC request a detailed report of an emergency even though a rule has not been violated?

A — When priority has been given.
B — Any time an emergency occurs.
C — When the emergency occurs in controlled airspace.

10-5   B08

What action should you take if your No. 1 VOR receiver malfunctions while operating in controlled airspace under IFR? Your aircraft is equipped with two VOR receivers. The No. 1 receiver has Localizer/Glide Slope capability, and the No. 2 receiverhas only VOR/ Localizer capability.

A — Report the malfunction immediately to ATC.
B — Continue the flight as cleared; no report is required.
C — Continue the approach and request a VOR or NDB approach.

10-6   J21

During an IFR flight in IMC, you enter a holding pattern (at a fix that is not the same as the approach fix) with an EFC time of 1530. At 1520, you experience complete two way communications failure. Which procedure should you follow to execute the approach to a landing?

A — Depart the holding fix to arrive at the approach fix as close as possible to the EFC time and complete the approach.
B — Depart the holding fix at the EFC time, and complete the approach.
C — Depart the holding fix at the earliest of the flight planned ETA or the EFC time, and complete the approach.

10-7   J21

Which procedure should you follow if you experience two-way communications failure while holding at a holding fix with an EFC time? (The holding fix is not the same as the approach fix.)

A — Depart the holding fix to arrive at the approach fix as close as possible to the EFC time.
B — Depart the holding fix at the EFC time.
C — Proceed immediately to the approach fix and hold until EFC.

10-4. Answer A. GFDICM 10A (FAR 91.123)
Each pilot in command who is given priority in an emergency by ATC, shall submit a detailed report of that emergency within 48 hours to the manager of that ATC facility, if requested. The key criteria in this regulation is if priority has been given in an emergency, no matter where it happened or when. Therefore answers (B) and (C) are incorrect.

10-5. Answer A. GFDICM 10A (FAR 91.187)
FAR Part 91.187(a) states, in part, that, "The pilot in command of each aircraft operated in controlled airspace under IFR shall report as soon as practical to ATC any malfunctions of navigational, approach, or communication equipment occurring in flight; ..." In the report, you should include the degree to which your ability to operate under IFR in the ATC system is impaired and the type of ATC assistance you may need. Answers (B) and (C) are wrong since a report is required.

10-6. Answer B. GFDICM 10A (FAR 91.185)
FAR Part 91.185(c)(3)(ii) states, in part, that, "If the clearance limit is not a fix from which an approach begins, leave the clearance limit at the expect-further-clearance time if one has been received, ...". Answer (A) is wrong since you should leave the holding fix at the EFC. Answer (C) is wrong since your last clearance, which included an EFC time, is specified in the regulations, and it is the time ATC expects you to depart the fix.

10-7. Answer B. GFDICM 10A (FAR 91.185)
FAR Part 91.185(c)(3)(ii) states, "If the clearance limit is not a fix from which an approach begins, leave the clearance limit at the expect-further-clearance time if one has been received, or if none has been received, upon arrival over the clearance limit, and proceed to a fix from which an approach begins and commence descent or descent and approach as close as possible to the estimated time of arrival as calculated from the filed or amended (with ATC) estimated time enroute." Answers (A) and (C) are incorrect since neither are in agreement with the specific wording of the regulation.

10-8   J24

You are in IMC and have two-way radio communications failure. If you do not exercise emergency authority, what procedure are you expected to follow?

A — Set transponder to code 7600, continue flight on assigned route and fly at the last assigned altitude or the MEA, whichever is higher.

B — Set transponder to code 7700 for 1 minute, then to 7600, and fly to an area with VFR weather conditions.

C — Set transponder to 7700 and fly to an area where you can let down in VFR conditions.

10-8. Answer A. GFDICM 10A (AIM) (FAR 91.185)

If an aircraft experiences a loss of two-way radio capability, the pilot should adjust the transponder to reply on MODE A/3, Code 7600 and continue on the assigned route at the last assigned altitude or the MEA, which ever is higher. The code 7700 is not used for communications failure (answers B and C).

10-9   J24

Which procedure should you follow if, during an IFR flight in VFR conditions, you have two-way radio communications failure?

A — Continue the flight under VFR and land as soon as practicable.

B — Continue the flight at assigned altitude and route, start approach at your ETA, or, if late, start approach upon arrival.

C — Land at the nearest airport that has VFR conditions.

10-9. Answer A. GFDICM 10A (FAR 91.185)

FAR Part 91.185(b) states, "If the failure occurs in VFR conditions, or if VFR conditions are encountered after the failure, each pilot shall continue the flight under VFR and land as soon as practicable." Choice (B) is wrong because it applies if you remained in instrument meteorological conditions (IMC) and did not have an EFC time. Answer (C) is also wrong because, if you are in VMC and can remain in VMC, you can continue; you don't have to land at the nearest airport short of your destination.

10-10   J24

What altitude and route should be used if you are flying in IMC and have two-way radio communication failure?

A — Continue on the route specified in your clearance, fly at an altitude that is the highest of last assigned altitude, altitude ATC has informed you to expect, or the MEA.

B — Fly direct to an area that has been forecast to have VFR conditions, fly at an altitude that is at least 1,000 feet above the highest obstacles along the route.

C — Descend to MEA and, if clear of clouds, proceed to the nearest appropriate airport. If not clear of clouds, maintain the highest of the MEA's along the clearance route.

10-10. Answer A. GFDICM 10A (FAR 91.185)

FAR Part 91.185(c)(2) states, "At the highest of the following altitudes or flight levels for the route segment being flown: the altitude or flight level assigned in the last ATC clearance received; the minimum altitude (converted, if appropriate, to minimum flight level as prescribed in FAR Part 91.121(c) for IFR operations; or the altitude or flight level ATC has advised may be expected in a further clearance." Answer (B) is wrong since it does not specify the assigned route; answer (C) is wrong because you should use the highest choice of altitudes, not just the highest MEA.

10-11   J24

(Refer to figure 87 on page 5-8.) While holding at the 10 DME fix east of LCH for an ILS approach to RWY 15 at Lake Charles Muni airport, ATC advises you to expect clearance for the approach at 1015. At 1000 you experience two-way radio communications failure. Which procedure should be followed?

A — Squawk 7600 and listen on the LOM frequency for instructions from ATC. If no instructions are received, start your approach at 1015.

B — Squawk 7700 for 1 minute, then 7600. After 1 minute, descend to the minimum final approach fix altitude. Start your approach at 1015.

C — Squawk 7600; plan to begin your approach at 1015.

10-12   B10

In the event of two-way radio communications failure while operating on an IFR clearance in VFR conditions, the pilot should continue

A — by the route assigned in the last ATC clearance received.

B — the flight under VFR and land as soon as practical.

C — the flight by the most direct route to the fix specified in the last clearance.

10-13   J18

Where may you use a surveillance approach?

A — At any airport that has an approach control.

B — At any airport which has radar service.

C — At airports for which civil radar instrument approach minimums have been published.

10-14   J18

Which information, in addition to headings, does the radar controller provide without request during an ASR approach?

A — The recommended altitude for each mile from the runway.

B — When reaching the MDA.

C — When to commence descent to MDA, the aircraft's position each mile on final from the runway, and arrival at the MAP.

10-11. Answer C. GFDICM 10A (FAR 91.185)

From the information given, it is not clear where you are holding or where the IAF for the approach is located. However, answer (C) is the best answer. FAR Part 91.185(3) states that, "When the clearance limit is a fix from which an approach begins, commence descent or descent and approach as close as possible to the expect-further-clearance time if one has been received . . .". You should begin your approach at 1015 and squawk 7600 as soon as the radio failure is detected. Answer (A) is incorrect because there is no voice on the LOM frequency for ATC instructions. Answer (B) is incorrect because you begin the approach at your EFC. Whatever your altitude is, you must comply with published minimum altitudes shown on the approach chart. Also, squawking 7700 is no longer part of the lost communications procedure.

10-12. Answer B. GFDICM 10A (AIM) (FAR 91.185)

If your radio fails in VFR, or if you encounter VFR conditions after the failure, continue the flight under VFR and land as soon as practicable. Continuing by the route last assigned by ATC (answer A) applies to continuing the flight in instrument meteorological conditions (IMC). Continuing the flight along the most direct route does not comply with the requirement to remain VFR (answer C).

10-13. Answer C. GFDICM 10A (AIM)

This type of approach requires airport surveillance radar (ASR) and published civil radar instrument approach minimums. Not all approach control facilities have the required radar equipment (answer A). For those airports which have radar service (answer B), radar instrument approach minimums may not be available.

10-14. Answer C. GFDICM 10A (AIM)

The radar controller will inform you when to begin descent to the MDA, advise you of your position each mile on final from the runway, and notify you when at the MAP. If you want the controller to provide the recommended altitude each mile on final (answer A), you must request it. You normally will not be advised when reaching the MDA (answer B) because the controller does not have an exact indication of your altitude.

10-15   Reserved

10-16   J18

During a "no-gyro" approach and prior to being handed off to the final approach controller, the pilot should make all turns

A — one-half standard rate unless otherwise advised.
B — any rate not exceeding a 30° bank.
C — standard rate unless otherwise advised.

10-17   J18

After being handed off to the final approach controller during a "no-gyro" surveillance or precision approach, the pilot should make all turns

A — one-half standard rate.
B — based upon the groundspeed of the aircraft.
C — standard rate.

10-15. Reserved

10-16. Answer C. GFDICM 10A (AIM)

When executing a "no-gyro" approach, all turns before the final approach should be at standard rate. After the aircraft has been turned onto the final approach course, all turns should be half standard rate. In addition, all turns should be executed immediately upon receipt of instructions from ATC. Half standard rate (answer A) is used only after the aircraft is on final approach. Answer (B) is incorrect because regardless of the bank required, all turns should be standard rate before the final approach and half standard rate when on the final approach course.

10-17. Answer A. GFDICM 10A (AIM)

See explanation for Question 10-16. Answer (B) is wrong because groundspeed does not affect the rate at which a turn should be made. Answer (C) is incorrect because all turns are standard rate until being turned onto the final approach course; then, all turns are half standard rate.

SECTION B
IFR DECISION MAKING

1. Accidents involving IFR conditions are roughly 65 percent fatal. Obtaining your instrument rating and maintaining IFR currency greatly reduces your risk for these types of accidents.
2. Accidents are rarely attributed to a single cause, but are the result of a series of poor choices.

SAFE HABIT PATTERNS

3. You should consider filing an IFR flight plan for every flight, and close that flight plan only when a safe landing is assured.
4. Though you work closely with ATC under IFR, you remain the final authority as to the safety of the flight. You may also need to coordinate responsibility with other pilots that fly with you.
5. Flying with a safety pilot to practice instrument maneuvers will help you maintain currency and proficiency.

PERSONAL MINIMUMS CHECKLIST

6. Developing a personal minimums checklist will assist you in determining the feasibility of a particular flight. You should take into account your currency and experience when deciding which conditions you feel comfortable flying in.
7. Five hazardous attitudes affect your decisions, and you should examine your choices to ensure that you make the proper response when one of these attitudes affects your flight.

COMMUNICATION

8. To avoid confusion, be sure to read back all important parts of a clearance, and ask for clarification when there is an instruction you do not understand.
9. Barriers to communication include preconceived notions of upcoming clearances, abbreviated clearances, and words that have more than one meaning.

RESOURCE USE

10. Effective use of resources occurs when you understand and utilize all the people and equipment available to you during a flight.
11. Plan for each IFR flight thoroughly before you leave the ground, including fuel requirements, alternates available, and missed approach instructions. It is also helpful to program any navigation information before engine start. The more you can rehearse ahead of time, the more prepared you will be in the event of a problem.
12. During a high workload situation, identify the most important tasks and make those a priority. Do not allow yourself to fixate on an extraneous issue.

SITUATIONAL AWARENESS

13. Visualization techniques can be used to create a mental picture of the flight overall.
14. You can avoid CFIT by maintaining positional awareness: staying abreast of your altitude, the proper procedures in use, and the terrain surrounding the airport.
15. Loss of situational awareness can occur when pilots are confused by clearances, misunderstand onboard equipment, or do not communicate properly with others in the cockpit.

10-18   J31

Which statement is correct regarding the use of cockpit lighting for night flight?

A — Reducing the lighting intensity to a minimum level will eliminate blind spots.

B — The use of regular white light, such as a flashlight, will impair night adaptation.

C — Coloration shown on maps is least affected by the use of direct red lighting.

10-18. Answer B. GFDICM 10B (AIM)

To maintain night vision, it is important to avoid bright lights before and during the flight. This includes sources of white light such as headlights, landing lights, strobe lights, or flashlights. Answer (A) is incorrect since blind spots are fixed by the internal structure of the eye and cannot be eliminated by lighting. Answer (C) is wrong because direct red lighting will wash out or change the appearance of colors on the map.

10-19   J31

Which use of cockpit lighting is correct for night flight?

A — Reducing the interior lighting intensity to a minimum level.
B — The use of regular white light, such as a flashlight, will not impair night adaptation.
C — Coloration shown on maps is least affected by the use of direct red lighting.

10-19. Answer A. GFDICM 10B (AFH)

Reducing the interior lighting to a minimum level helps you to see outside visual references more clearly. Answer (B) is incorrect since to maintain night vision, it is important to avoid bright lights before and during the flight. Answer (C) is incorrect because direct red lighting will wash out or change the appearance of colors on the map.

SECTION C
IFR FLIGHT PLANNING

FLIGHT PLANNING

1. When you begin the IFR flight planning process, take a preliminary look at factors like weather, airplane performance and equipment, potential routes, and your instrument proficiency that may prevent you from making the flight.
2. Availability of preferred IFR routes, aircraft performance considerations, and fuel economy will influence route selection.
3. Preferred IFR routes beginning with a fix indicate that departing aircraft will normally be routed to the fix via a departure procedure (DP), or radar vectors. Check for published departure or arrival procedures relevant to your intended flight.
4. NOTAMs should be reviewed for items like navaid and lighting outages or runway closures that can significantly affect your flight.
5. Review the A/FD for specific information about departure and arrival airports as well as possible alternate airports that are pertinent to your flight.
6. Begin gathering weather data several days before your flight in order to obtain a general overview of weather patterns.
7. Although weather information may be obtained from numerous sources including newspapers, television, and the internet, these sources should not be considered suitable alternatives to a flight service station or DUATS standard briefing.
8. In case the weather at your intended destination is forecast to have a ceiling less than 2,000 feet or visibility less than 3 miles, you need to file an alternate.
9. A good alternate airport should be far enough away to be unaffected by weather at your destination, be equipped with appropriate communications and weather reporting capabilities, and have more than one approach.
10. The most current enroute and destination weather information for an instrument flight should be obtained from the FSS. Once your weather briefing is complete, you can make your go/no-go decision and begin planning the flight if conditions are favorable.

NAVIGATION

11. For IFR flight, you are required to have working navigation equipment appropriate to the ground facilities to be used.
12. It is your responsibility as pilot in command to make sure that the VOR check has been accomplished within the past 30 days, and the transponder has been checked within the past 24 calendar months. Transponder checks must be entered in aircraft logbooks. There also must be a written record of the VOR test, which includes the date, place, bearing error, and the signature of the person performing the test.
13. The navigation log is a convenient way for you to complete your preflight planning, organize your flight, and provide you with a concise textual description of your flight.
14. You may determine that a Loran C equipped aircraft is approved for IFR operations by checking the Airplane Flight Manual Supplement.

FILING AND FLYING YOUR FLIGHT PLAN

15. Before filing your flight plan, ensure you have all of the blocks in the flight plan form filled in correctly with information needed by flight service to process the flight plan. The information needed includes the correct aircraft equipment code, route, destination, and fuel available information. The point of first intended landing at your destination should be used to compute the estimated time enroute on an IFR flight plan.
16. If you are flying to an airport that does not have an operating control tower, you are responsible for closing your own IFR flight plan by phone through FSS, or by direct communications with ATC.
17. Unless you have better-than-VFR conditions forecast from one hour before to one hour after your ETA at your destination, you must include an alternate airport in your flight plan. To list an airport with a precision approach as an alternate, the forecast at the ETA at the alternate must be at least a 600-foot ceiling and 2 miles visibility.
18. If you actually proceed to the selected alternate, then the landing minimums used at that airport should be the minimums specified for the approach procedure selected.

10-20 J34
Preferred IFR routes beginning with a fix indicate that departing aircraft will normally be routed to the fix by

A — the established airway(s) between the departure airport and the fix.
B — an instrument departure procedure (DP), or radar vectors.
C — direct route only.

10-20. Answer B. GFDICM 10C (AIM)
Preferred IFR routes beginning or ending with a fix usually indicates that aircraft will be routed to or from these fixes via a DP, radar vector, or STAR. If one is not listed, consult the enroute chart to find the most practical route for the flight. In all cases, remember to check applicable minimum enroute altitudes that may be beyond your aircraft's climb capabilities. Answers (A) and (C) may be correct in some situations, but they do not describe how aircraft will normally be routed.

10-21 J15
(Refer to figure 1) The time entered in block 12 for an IFR flight should be based on which fuel quantity?

A — Total fuel required for the flight.
B — Total useable fuel on board.
C — The amount of fuel required to fly to the destination airport, then to the alternate, plus a 45-minute reserve.

10-21. Answer B. GFDICM 10C (AIM)
When indicating the fuel on board, block 12, you should include the total time at normal cruising speed for the usable fuel on board, expressed in hours and minutes. Answers (A) and (C) are wrong because they may not represent the total fuel on board the aircraft. In fact, both (A) and (C) should normally be less than total usable fuel.

10-22 J15
(Refer to figure 1) What information should be entered in block 7 of an IFR flight plan if the flight has three legs, each at a different altitude?

A — Altitude for first leg.
B — Altitude for first leg and highest altitude.
C — Highest altitude.

10-22. Answer A. GFDICM 10C (AIM)
The altitude listed in block 7 for an IFR flight plan should be the requested initial cruising altitude. If you want to change altitude, direct your request to the controller during flight. Answer (B) is wrong because you can only list one altitude when filing a flight plan. Answer (C) is wrong because the highest altitude on your route of flight will often be higher than your initial cruising altitude.

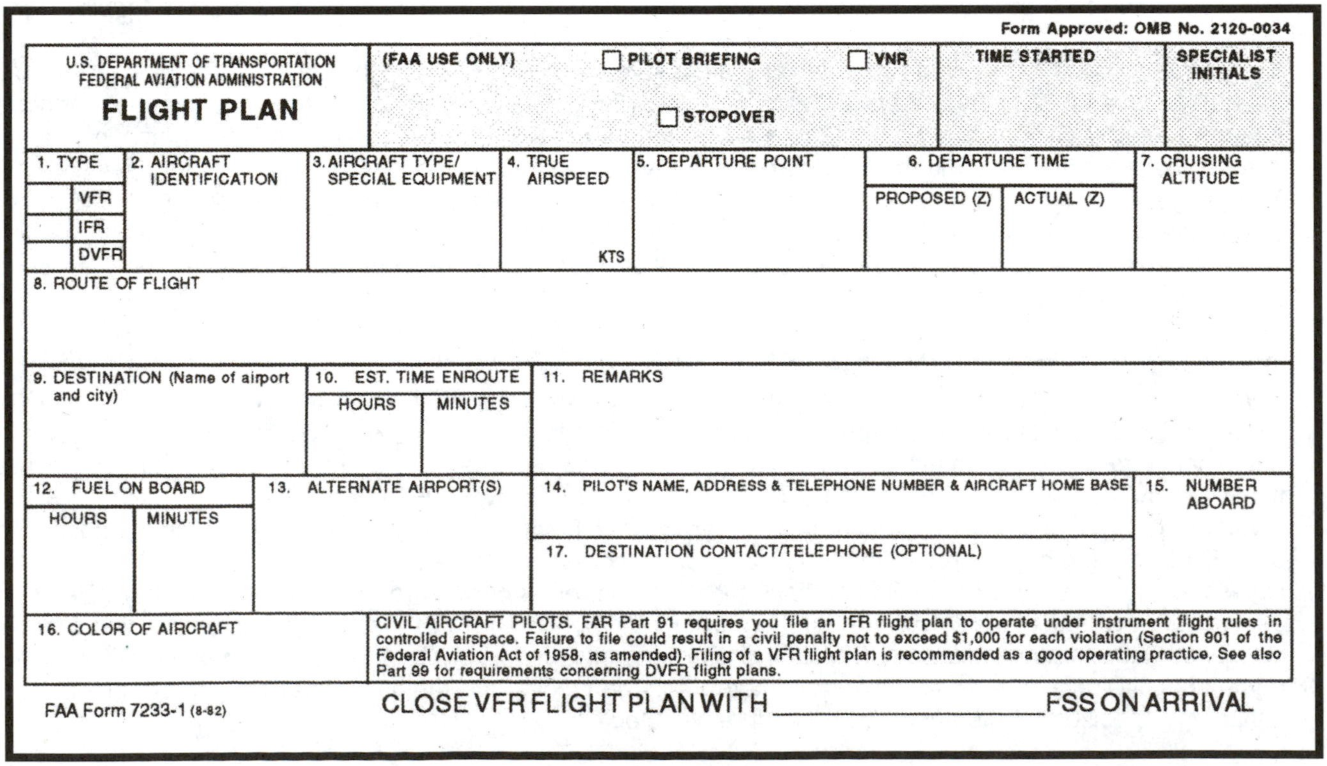
Form Approved: OMB No. 2120-0034
U.S. DEPARTMENT OF TRANSPORTATION
FEDERAL AVIATION ADMINISTRATION
FLIGHT PLAN
(FAA USE ONLY) ☐ PILOT BRIEFING ☐ VNR ☐ STOPOVER
TIME STARTED
SPECIALIST INITIALS
1. TYPE: VFR, IFR, DVFR
2. AIRCRAFT IDENTIFICATION
3. AIRCRAFT TYPE/ SPECIAL EQUIPMENT
4. TRUE AIRSPEED KTS
5. DEPARTURE POINT
6. DEPARTURE TIME: PROPOSED (Z), ACTUAL (Z)
7. CRUISING ALTITUDE
8. ROUTE OF FLIGHT
9. DESTINATION (Name of airport and city)
10. EST. TIME ENROUTE: HOURS, MINUTES
11. REMARKS
12. FUEL ON BOARD: HOURS, MINUTES
13. ALTERNATE AIRPORT(S)
14. PILOT'S NAME, ADDRESS & TELEPHONE NUMBER & AIRCRAFT HOME BASE
15. NUMBER ABOARD
17. DESTINATION CONTACT/TELEPHONE (OPTIONAL)
16. COLOR OF AIRCRAFT
CIVIL AIRCRAFT PILOTS. FAR Part 91 requires you file an IFR flight plan to operate under instrument flight rules in controlled airspace. Failure to file could result in a civil penalty not to exceed $1,000 for each violation (Section 901 of the Federal Aviation Act of 1958, as amended). Filing of a VFR flight plan is recommended as a good operating practice. See also Part 99 for requirements concerning DVFR flight plans.
FAA Form 7233-1 (8-82)
CLOSE VFR FLIGHT PLAN WITH ______________ FSS ON ARRIVAL

FIGURE 1.—Flight Plan

10-23   **J15**
(Refer to figure 1) Which equipment determines the code to be entered in block 3 as a suffix to aircraft type on the flight plan form?

A — DME, ADF, and airborne radar.
B — DME, transponder, and ADF.
C — DME, transponder, and RNAV.

10-23. Answer C. GFDICM 10C (AIM)
When determining the equipment capability suffix to be entered in block 3 of a flight plan, remember that the suffix is based on whether the aircraft is equipped with DME, transponder, TACAN-only equipment, and/or RNAV. Answers (A) and (B) are wrong because ADF and airborne radar equipment have no bearing on determining an equipment suffix code.

10-24   H342

(Refer to figures 21 and 21A, 22 and 22A, 23, 24, 25, and 26 on pages 10-14 through 10-21.) After departing GJT and arriving at Durango Co., La Plata Co. Airport, you are unable to land because of weather. How long can you hold over DRO before departing for return flight to the alternate, Grand Junction Co., Walker Field Airport?

Total useable fuel on board, 68 gallons.
Average fuel consumption, 15 GPH.
Wind and velocity at 16,000, 2308-16

A — 1 hour 33 minutes.
B — 1 hour 37 minutes.
C — 1 hour 42 minutes.

10-24. Answer A. GFDICM 10C (IFH)

In order to determine how long you can hold over DRO, you must subtract the fuel required to get to DRO, the fuel required to get back to Grand Junction, and the fuel reserve 45 minutes). Your total fuel on board is 4 hours and 30 minutes figure 21). Begin by determining your time enroute to DRO and your time enroute back to GJT.

True airspeed ....175 kts.
Cruising altitude...15,000 feet
Variation ....14°E
Wind..230/08

Check Points	Mag Crs	Mag Wnd	GS	Dist	Time
GJT					
JNC					
HERRM	151				:24:00
MANCA	151	216/8	171	75	:26:19
APP/LND	092				:18:30
TOTAL					1:08:49

True airspeed ....174 kts.
Cruising altitude...16,000 feet
Variation ....14°E
Wind..230/08

Check Points	Mag Crs	Mag Wnd	GS	Dist	Time
DRO					
MANCA	272				:14:30
HERRM	333	216/8	177	75	:25:25
JNC	331	216/8	177	35	:11:52
APP/LND					:12:00
TOTAL					1:03:47

The flight to DRO requires 17.2 gallons of fuel (1:08:49 × 15gph = 17.2) and the return flight requires 15.9 gallons (1:03:47 × 15 gph = 15.9). When you subtract the enroute (17.2), return (15.9), and reserve (11.3) fuel required, you will have 23.6 gallons left for holding over DRO (68 − 17.2 − 15.9 − 11.3 = 23.6). This equates to approximately 1 hour 34 minutes of fuel (23.6 ÷ 15 = 1:34). Answer (A) is the closest to being correct. Answers (B) and (C) are wrong because they exceed the time available.

10-25   H342

(Refer to FD excerpt below, and use the wind entry closest to the flight planned altitude.) Determine the time to be entered in block 10 of the flight from GJT to DRO.

Route of flight ....Figure 21
Flight log & MAG VAR.............................Figure 22
En route chart ....Figure 24

FT	12,000	18,000
FNM	2408-05	2208-21

A — 1 hour 08 minutes.
B — 1 hour 03 minutes.
C — 58 minutes.

10-26   H342

(Refer to figures 21, 22, and 24 on pages 10-14 through 10-19.) What fuel would be consumed on the flight between Grand Junction Co. and Durango, Co. if the average fuel consumption is 15 GPH.

A — 17 gallons.
B — 20 gallons.
C — 25 gallons.

10-27   J15

(Refer to figure 27 on page 10-23.) What aircraft equipment code should be entered in block 3 of the flight plan?

A — T.
B — U.
C — A.

10-25. Answer A. GFDICM 10C (IFH)

(Refer to figures 21, 22, and 24 on pages 10-14 through 10-19.) This question requires you to find the estimated time enroute (ETE) for block 10 on the flight plan. Use the flight log (figure 22) to record the necessary information. You'll also need information from the other figures referenced in the question. A first step is to compute groundspeed from each leg of the route using the winds aloft data. Since winds aloft are reported in true direction, you can simplify the problem by converting them to magnetic. Remember, airways are oriented to magnetic north. Then, determine distances and times using all available information to find the total ETE.

True airspeed...175 kts.
Cruising altitude..15,000 feet
Variation ....14°E
Wind...220/08

Check Points	Mag Crs	Mag Wnd	GS	Dist	Time
GJT					
JNC					
HERRM	151				:24:00
MANCA	151	206/08	170	75	:26:28
APP/LND	092				:18:30
TOTAL					1:08:58

10-26. Answer A. GFDICM 10C (AIM)

See explanation for Question 10-25. The total flight time is 1:08:58. With a fuel consumption rate of 15 gph, the total fuel consumed would be 17.2 gallons. Answers (B) and (C) are wrong because they substantially exceed the required amount.

10-27. Answer C. GFDICM 10C (AIM)

By referring to Legend 25 in Appendix 2 you will see that having DME and a transponder with altitude encoding equipment requires an "/A" equipment code. Answer (A) is wrong because "/T" indicates no DME or altitude encoding equipment. Answer (B) is wrong because "/U" indicates no DME.

Form Approved: OMB No. 2120-0034

U.S. DEPARTMENT OF TRANSPORTATION FEDERAL AVIATION ADMINISTRATION **FLIGHT PLAN**	(FAA USE ONLY)	☐ PILOT BRIEFING ☐ STOPOVER	☐ VNR	TIME STARTED	SPECIALIST INITIALS

1. TYPE	2. AIRCRAFT IDENTIFICATION	3. AIRCRAFT TYPE/ SPECIAL EQUIPMENT	4. TRUE AIRSPEED	5. DEPARTURE POINT	6. DEPARTURE TIME		7. CRUISING ALTITUDE
VFR X IFR DVFR	N 123RC	T210N/	175 KTS	GJT	PROPOSED (Z)	ACTUAL (Z)	15,000

8. ROUTE OF FLIGHT

JNC9, JNC, V187, MANCA, V211

9. DESTINATION (Name of airport and city)	10. EST. TIME ENROUTE		11. REMARKS
DRO	HOURS	MINUTES	

12. FUEL ON BOARD		13. ALTERNATE AIRPORT(S)	14. PILOT'S NAME, ADDRESS & TELEPHONE NUMBER & AIRCRAFT HOME BASE	15. NUMBER ABOARD
HOURS	MINUTES	GJT		
4	30		17. DESTINATION CONTACT/TELEPHONE (OPTIONAL)	2

16. COLOR OF AIRCRAFT	CIVIL AIRCRAFT PILOTS. FAR Part 91 requires you file an IFR flight plan to operate under instrument flight rules in controlled airspace. Failure to file could result in a civil penalty not to exceed $1,000 for each violation (Section 901 of the Federal Aviation Act of 1958, as amended). Filing of a VFR flight plan is recommended as a good operating practice. See also Part 99 for requirements concerning DVFR flight plans.
RED/WHITE/BLUE	

FAA Form 7233-1 (8-82)   CLOSE VFR FLIGHT PLAN WITH _____ FSS ON ARRIVAL

AIRCRAFT INFORMATION

MAKE <u>Cessna</u>   MODEL <u>T210N</u>

N <u>123RC</u>   Vso <u>58</u>

AIRCRAFT EQUIPMENT/STATUS**

**NOTE: X= OPERATIVE   INOP= INOPERATIVE   N/A= NOT APPLICABLE
TRANSPONDER: X (MODE C) X ILS: (LOCALIZER) X (GLIDE SLOPE) X
VOR NO. 1 X (NO. 2) X ADF: X RNAV: X
VERTICAL PATH COMPUTER: N/A DME: X
MARKER BEACON: X (AUDIO) X (VISUAL) X

FIGURE 21.—Flight Plan and Aircraft Information.

Form Approved: OMB No. 2120-0034

U.S. DEPARTMENT OF TRANSPORTATION
FEDERAL AVIATION ADMINISTRATION
FLIGHT PLAN

(FAA USE ONLY)	☐ PILOT BRIEFING	☐ VNR	TIME STARTED	SPECIALIST INITIALS
	☐ STOPOVER			

1. TYPE	2. AIRCRAFT IDENTIFICATION	3. AIRCRAFT TYPE/ SPECIAL EQUIPMENT	4. TRUE AIRSPEED	5. DEPARTURE POINT	6. DEPARTURE TIME		7. CRUISING ALTITUDE
					PROPOSED (Z)	ACTUAL (Z)	
VFR							
X IFR	N 123RC	T210N/	175 KTS	DRO			16,000
DVFR							

8. ROUTE OF FLIGHT

V211, MANCA, V187, HERRM, V187, JNC

9. DESTINATION (Name of airport and city)	10. EST. TIME ENROUTE		11. REMARKS
	HOURS	MINUTES	
GJT			

12. FUEL ON BOARD		13. ALTERNATE AIRPORT(S)	14. PILOT'S NAME, ADDRESS & TELEPHONE NUMBER & AIRCRAFT HOME BASE	15. NUMBER ABOARD
HOURS	MINUTES			
			17. DESTINATION CONTACT/TELEPHONE (OPTIONAL)	2

16. COLOR OF AIRCRAFT	CIVIL AIRCRAFT PILOTS. FAR Part 91 requires you file an IFR flight plan to operate under instrument flight rules in controlled airspace. Failure to file could result in a civil penalty not to exceed $1,000 for each violation (Section 901 of the Federal Aviation Act of 1958, as amended). Filing of a VFR flight plan is recommended as a good operating practice. See also Part 99 for requirements concerning DVFR flight plans.
RED/WHITE/BLUE	

FAA Form 7233-1 (8-82)   CLOSE VFR FLIGHT PLAN WITH _____ FSS ON ARRIVAL

AIRCRAFT INFORMATION

MAKE Cessna   MODEL T210N

N 123RC   Vso 58——

AIRCRAFT EQUIPMENT/STATUS**

**NOTE: X= OPERATIVE   INOP= INOPERATIVE   N/A= NOT APPLICABLE
TRANSPONDER: X (MODE C) X ILS: (LOCALIZER) X   (GLIDE SLOPE) X
VOR NO. 1 X (NO. 2) X ADF: X RNAV: X
VERTICAL PATH COMPUTER: N/A DME: X
MARKER BEACON: X (AUDIO) X   (VISUAL) X

FIGURE 21A.—Flight Plan and Aircraft Information.

FLIGHT LOG

GRAND JUNCTION (GJT) TO DURANGO (DRO)

CHECK POINTS		ROUTE	COURSE	WIND	SPEED-KTS		DIST	TIME		FUEL	
FROM	TO	ALTITUDE		TEMP	TAS	GS	NM	LEG	TOT	LEG	TOT
GJT	JNC	JNC9JNC CLIMB V187		230 08				✕			
	HERRM	15,000	151°		175			:24:0			
	MANCA	V187	151°								
APPROACH & LANDING		V211 DESENT	092°					:18:30			
	DRO										

OTHER DATA:
NOTE: TAKEOFF RUNWAY 29.
MAG VAR, 14° E.

FLIGHT SUMMARY

TIME	FUEL (LB)	
		EN ROUTE
		RESERVE
		MISSED APPR.
		TOTAL

FIGURE 22.—Flight Planning Log.

FLIGHT LOG

DURANGO (DRO) TO GRAND JUNCTION, WALKER FIELD (GJT)

CHECK POINTS		ROUTE		WIND	SPEED-KTS		DIST	TIME		FUEL	
FROM	TO	ALTITUDE	COURSE	TEMP	TAS	GS	NM	LEG	TOT	LEG	TOT
DRO	MANCA	V211 CLIMB	272°	230 08				:14:30			
	HERRM	V187 16,000	333°		174						
	JNC	V187	331°								
APPROACH & LANDING		DESCENT						:12:00			
	GJT										

OTHER DATA:
NOTE: MAG. VAR. 14° E.

FLIGHT SUMMARY

TIME	FUEL (LB)	
		EN ROUTE
		RESERVE
		MISSED APPR.
		TOTAL

FIGURE 22A.—Flight Planning Log.

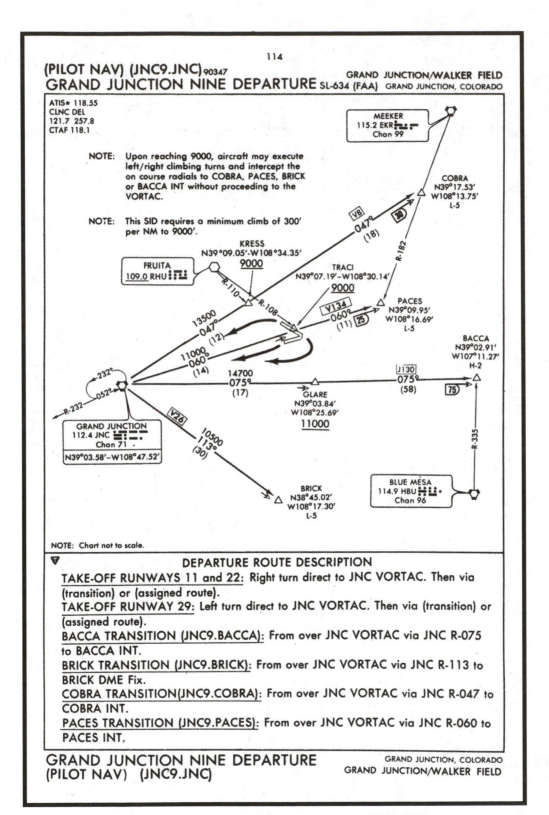

FIGURE 23.—Grand Junction Nine Departure (JNC9.JNC).

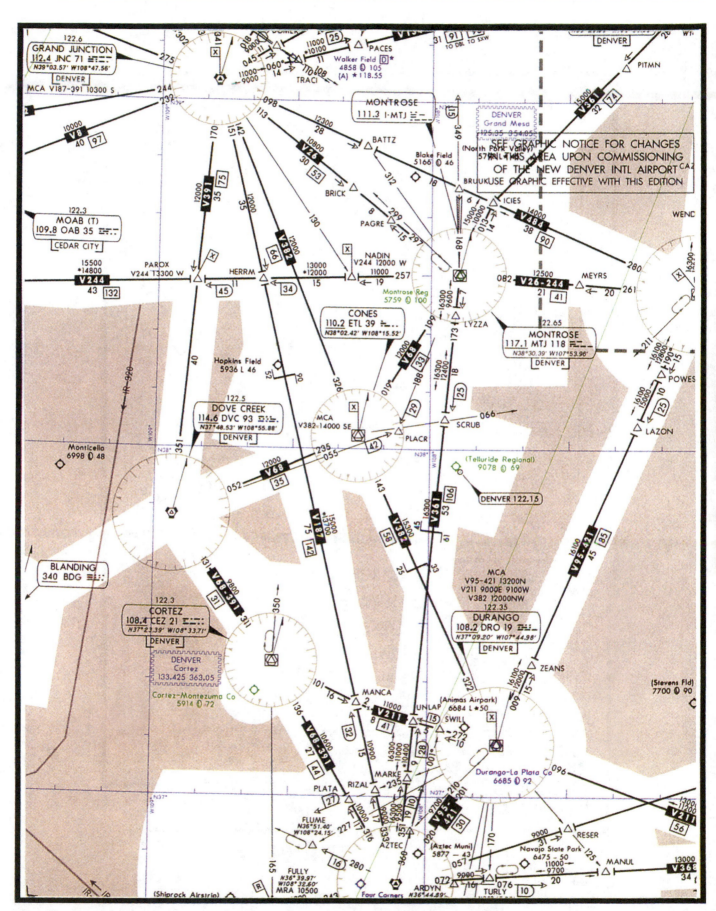

FIGURE 24.—En Route Low-Altitude Chart Segment..

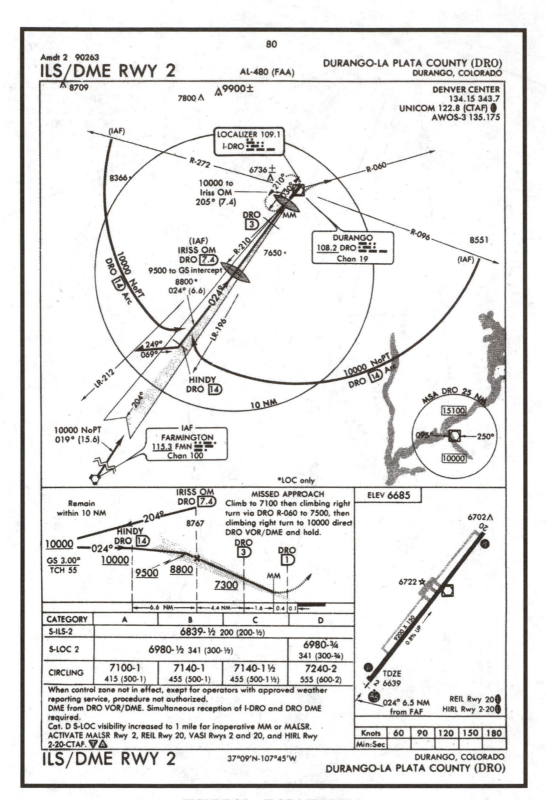

FIGURE 25.—ILS/DME RWY 2.

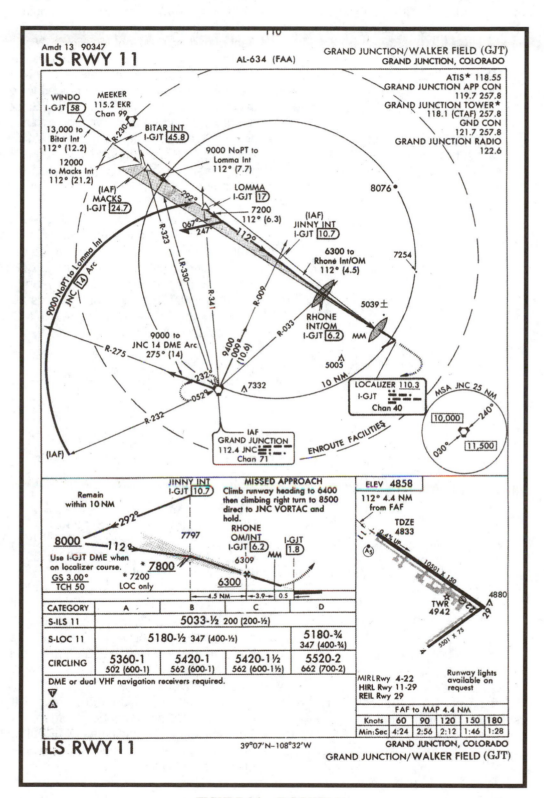

FIGURE 26.—ILS RWY 11.

10-28   H342
(Refer to the FD excerpt below, and use the wind entry closest to the flight planned altitude.) Determine the time to be entered in block 10 of the flight plan.

Route of flight ....Figures 27, 28, 29, 30, & 31
Flight log & MAG VAR...............................Figure 28
GNATS ONE DEPARTURE
and Excerpt from AFD...................................Figure 30

FT	3000	6000	9000
OTH	0507	2006+03	2215-05

A — 1 hour 10 minutes.
B — 1 hour 15 minutes.
C — 1 hour 20 minutes.

10-28. Answer C. GFDICM 10C (IFH)
(Refer to figures 27, 28, 29, 30, and 31 on pages 10-23 through 10-27.) This question requires you to find the estimated time en route (ETE) for block 10 on the flight plan. Use the flight log (figure 28) to record the necessary information. You'll also need information from the other figures referenced in the question. A first step is to compute groundspeed for each leg of the route using the winds aloft data. Since winds aloft are reported in true direction, you can simplify the problem by converting them to magnetic. Remember, airways are oriented to magnetic north. Then, determine distances and times using all available information to find the total ETE.

To compute the time from MERLI to MOURN Intersection, you must determine the length of the 15 DME arc off the OED VORTAC. To do this, take the number of degrees traveled on the arc (333 − 251 = 82), times the number of miles (15), and divide the product by 60. The length of the arc is 20.5 n.m. (82 × 15 ÷ 60 = 20.5). The total distance to MOURN Intersection is 36.5 (20.5 + 16 = 36.5).

True airspeed ....155 kts.
Cruising altitude..8,000 feet
Variation ....20°E
Wind..220/15

Check Points	Mag Crs	Mag Wnd	GS	Dist	Time
MFR					
MERLI					: 11:00
MOURN	333	36.5			:16:13
RBG	287	200/15	153	19	:07:27
OTH	272	200/15	150	38	:15:12
EUG	024	200/15	170	59	:20:49
APP/LND					:10:00
TOTAL					1:20:41

Your total time to Sweet Field is 1 hour, 20 minutes, and 41 seconds. Answers (A) and (B) are wrong because they are less than the time required.

10-29   J15
(Refer to figure 32 on page 10-29.) What aircraft equipment code should be entered in block 3 of the flight plan?

A — I.
B — A.
C — C.

10-29. Answer A. (AIM)
Area Navigation (RNAV) and a Mode C transponder requires an "/I" equipment code suffix. Answer (B) is wrong because "/A" indicates DME but no RNAV. Answer (C) is wrong because "/C" indicates no altitude encoding equipment.

Form Approved: OMB No. 2120-0034

U.S. DEPARTMENT OF TRANSPORTATION FEDERAL AVIATION ADMINISTRATION **FLIGHT PLAN**	(FAA USE ONLY) ☐ PILOT BRIEFING ☐ STOPOVER	☐ VNR	TIME STARTED	SPECIALIST INITIALS

1. TYPE	2. AIRCRAFT IDENTIFICATION	3. AIRCRAFT TYPE/ SPECIAL EQUIPMENT	4. TRUE AIRSPEED	5. DEPARTURE POINT	6. DEPARTURE TIME		7. CRUISING ALTITUDE
VFR					PROPOSED (Z)	ACTUAL (Z)	
X IFR DVFR	N132SM	C 182/	155 KTS	MFR			8,000

8. ROUTE OF FLIGHT

GNATS 1, MOURN, V121 EUG

9. DESTINATION (Name of airport and city)	10. EST. TIME ENROUTE		11. REMARKS
MAHLON/SWEET FIELD, EUGENE, OR.	HOURS	MINUTES	INSTRUMENT TRAINING FLIGHT

12. FUEL ON BOARD		13. ALTERNATE AIRPORT(S)	14. PILOT'S NAME, ADDRESS & TELEPHONE NUMBER & AIRCRAFT HOME BASE	15. NUMBER ABOARD
HOURS	MINUTES			
		N/R	17. DESTINATION CONTACT/TELEPHONE (OPTIONAL)	

16. COLOR OF AIRCRAFT	CIVIL AIRCRAFT PILOTS. FAR Part 91 requires you file an IFR flight plan to operate under instrument flight rules in controlled airspace. Failure to file could result in a civil penalty not to exceed $1,000 for each violation (Section 901 of the Federal Aviation Act of 1958, as amended). Filing of a VFR flight plan is recommended as a good operating practice. See also Part 99 for requirements concerning DVFR flight plans.

FAA Form 7233-1 (8-82)   CLOSE VFR FLIGHT PLAN WITH _____ FSS ON ARRIVAL

AIRCRAFT INFORMATION

MAKE CESSNA   MODEL 182

N 132SM   Vso 57

AIRCRAFT EQUIPMENT/STATUS**

**NOTE: X= OPERATIVE INOP= INOPERATIVE N/A= NOT APPLICABLE
TRANSPONDER: X (MODE C) X ILS: (LOCALIZER) X (GLIDE SLOPE) N/A
VOR NO. 1 X (NO. 2) X ADF: X RNAV: N/A
VERTICAL PATH COMPUTER: NA DME: X
MARKER BEACON: (AUDIO) INOP (VISUAL) Inop.

FIGURE 27.—Flight Plan and Aircraft Information.

FLIGHT LOG

MEDFORD - JACKSON CO. AIRPORT TO HAHLON/SWEET FIELD, EUGENE, OR.

CHECK POINTS		ROUTE		WIND	SPEED-KTS		DIST	TIME		FUEL	
FROM	TO	ALTITUDE	COURSE	TEMP	TAS	GS	NM	LEG	TOT	LEG	TOT
MFR	MERLI	GNATS 1 CLIMB	270°		155			:11:0			
	MOURN	V121 8000	333°			AVER. 135					
	RBG	V121 8000	287°								
	OTH	V121 8000	272°								
	EUG	APPROACH DESCENT	026°								
APPROACH & LANDING								:10:0			
	SWEET FIELD										

OTHER DATA:
NOTE:

MAG. VAR. 20° E.
AVERAGE G.S. 135 KTS. FOR GNATS 1
DEPARTURE CLIMB.

FLIGHT SUMMARY

TIME	FUEL (LB)	
		EN ROUTE
		RESERVE
		MISSED APPR.
		TOTAL

FIGURE 28.—Flight Planning Log.

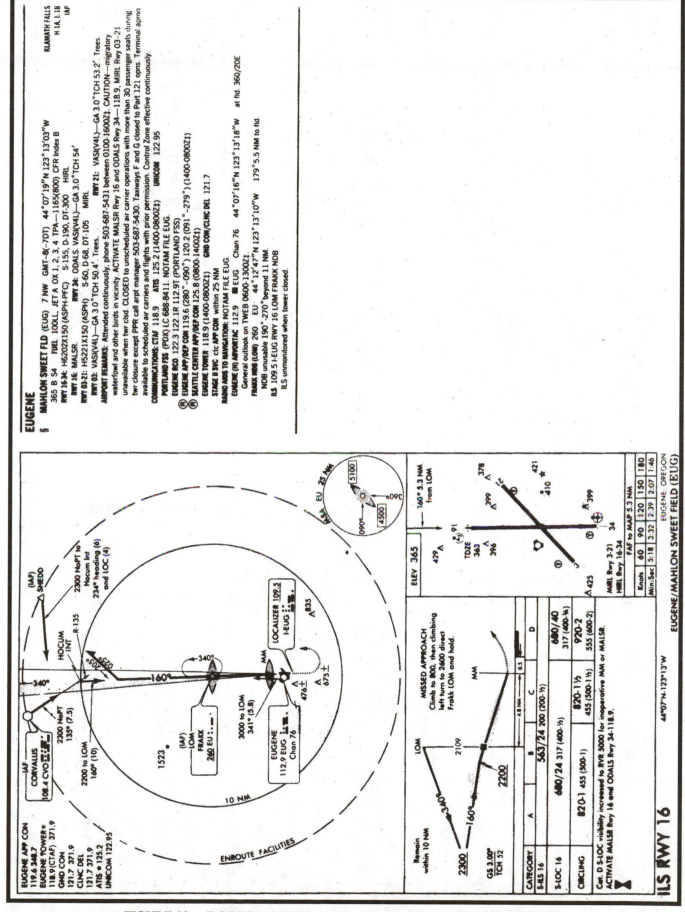

FIGURE 29.—ILS RWY 16 (EUG) and Excerpt from Airport Facility Directory.

GNATS ONE DEPARTURE (GNATS1.GNATS)

MEDFORD-JACKSON CO
MEDFORD, OREGON

DEPARTURE ROUTE DESCRIPTION
(Continued)

MOURN TRANSITION (GNATS1.MOURN): Continue via 270° magnetic bearing from the LMM to MERLI INT, turn right via MEDFORD 15 DME ARC to intercept V23-121 to MOURN INT.

DREWS TRANSITION (GNATS1.DREWS): Continue via 270° magnetic bearing from the LMM to MERLI INT, turn right via MEDFORD 15 DME ARC to DREWS INT.

TALEM TRANSITION (GNATS1.TALEM): Turn left via MEDFORD R-216 to 15 DME Fix thence turn left via MEDFORD 15 DME ARC to intercept V23 to TALEM INT.

HANDY TRANSITION (GNATS1.HANDY): Turn left via MEDFORD R-216 to 15 DME Fix, thence turn left via MEDFORD 15 DME Arc to HANDY DME Fix.

GNATS ONE DEPARTURE (GNATS1.GNATS)

MEDFORD, OREGON
MEDFORD-JACKSON CO

§ **MEDFORD-JACKSON CO** (MFR)   3 N   GMT–8(–7DT)   42°22'21"N 122°52'17"W   **KLAMATH FALLS**
1331   B   S4   FUEL 80, 100, 100LL, JET A1 +   OX 1, 3   CFR Index B   **H-1A, L-1A**
RWY 14-32: H6700X150 (ASPH-PFC)   S-200, D-200, DT-400   HIRL   .5% up S   JAP
RWY 14: MALSR. Trees.   RWY 32: REIL. VASI(V4L)—GA 3.0° TCH 49'. Road.
RWY 09-27: H3145X150 (ASPH)   S-50, D-70, DT-108   MIRL
RWY 27: Road.
AIRPORT REMARKS: Attended continuously. CLOSED to unscheduled Part 121 air carriers operation, without prior
approval, call 503-776-7222. Night refueling delay sunset-1500Zt, ctc TOWER. Rwy 09-27 clsd to acft over 12,500
lbs GWT. Rwy 09/27 CLOSED when tower clsd. Rwy lgts 14/32 operate med ints when tower closed. ACTIVATE
MALSR 14—119.4. Flocks of large waterfowl in vicinity Nov-May
COMMUNICATIONS: CTAF 119.4   ATIS 125.75   UNICOM 122.95
NORTH BEND FSS (OTH) LC 773-3256. NOTAM FILE MFR.
RCO 122.65 122.1R 113.6T (NORTH BEND FSS)
APP CON 124.3 (1400-0800Zt)   DEP CON 124.3 (1400-0800Zt)
SEATTLE CENTER APP/DEP CON 125.3 (0800-1400Zt)
TOWER 119.4 (1400-0800Zt)   GND CON 121.7
VFR ADVSY SVC ctc TOWER
RADIO AIDS TO NAVIGATION: NOTAM FILE OTH.   VHF/DF ctc Medford TOWER
   VORTAC unusable: OED   Chan 83   42°28'47"N 122°54'43"W   146° 6.1 NM to fld. 2080/19E
      160°-165° beyond 35 NM below 8900'   280°-345° beyond 30 NM below 6500'
      198°-205° beyond 35 NM below 8500'   345°-360° beyond 35 NM below 6800'
      250°-280° beyond 25 NM below 6100'
   PUMIE NDB (LOM) 373   MF   42°27'04"N 122°54'44"W   140° 4.5 NM to fld. NOTAM FILE MFR
      LOM unusable 150°-165° and 260°-265° beyond 5 miles.
   VIOLE NDB (LMM) 356   FR   42°23'22"N 122°52'47"W   140° 0.5 NM to fld. NOTAM FILE MFR
      LMM unusable 305°-335° beyond 10 NM. all altitudes
   ILS/DME 110.3 I-MFR Chan 40 Rwy 14 LOM PUMIE NDB. LMM VIOLE NDB. ILS unmonitored when tower closed.
      Localizer unusable inside threshold.

MEDFORD-JACKSON CO
MEDFORD, OREGON

MEDFORD GND CON
121.7
MEDFORD DEP CON
124.3 257.8
ATIS 125.75
CTAF 119.4

ROSEBURG •
108.2 RBG

MEDFORD
113.6 OED 83

LMM
VIOLE
356 FR

NOTE: This SID requires a minimum climb rate of 400' per NM to 4100' for obstacle clearance.

NOTE: Chart not to scale.

DEPARTURE ROUTE DESCRIPTION

Climb direct to the VIOLE ILS Middle Compass Locator (south take-off turn right), then climb on the 270° magnetic bearing from the LMM to GNATS INT, cross GNATS INT at or above 4100; thence via (transition) or (route).

COPPO TRANSITION (GNATS1.COPPO): Turn left via R-216 to 15 DME Fix, thence turn left via MEDFORD 15 DME Arc to COPPO DME Fix.

KOLER TRANSITION (GNATS1.KOLER): Continue via 270° magnetic bearing from the LMM to MERLI INT, turn right via ROSEBURG R-154 to KOLER INT.

(Continued on next page)

GNATS ONE DEPARTURE (GNATS1.GNATS)

ELEV 1331

MEDFORD, OREGON
MEDFORD-JACKSON CO

FIGURE 30.—GNATS One Departure and Excerpt from Airport/Facility Directory.

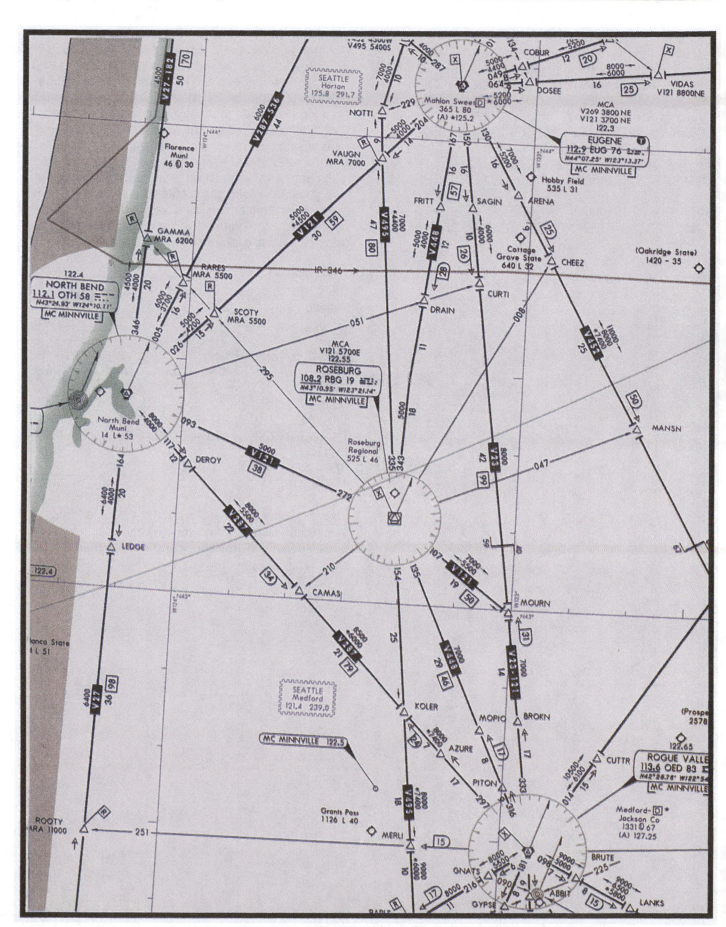

FIGURE 31.—En Route Low altitude chart Segment.

10-30   H342

(Refer to the FD excerpt below, and use the wind entry closest to the flight planned altitude.) Determine the time to be entered in block 10 of the flight plan.

Route of flight ...Figure 32 (page 10-29), 33 (page 10-30), 34 (page 10-31), 35 (page 6-2), 35a (page 6-3), and 36 (page 10-32.)
Flight log & MAG VAR ....Figure 33
RNAV RWY 33 & Excerpt from AFD..........Figure 36

FT	3000	6000	9000	12000
DAL	2027	2239+13	2240+08	2248+05

A — 1 hour 35 minutes.
B — 1 hour 41 minutes.
C — 1 hour 46 minutes.

10-30. Answer A. GFDICM 10C (IFH)

(Refer to figures 32, 33, 34, and 36 on pages 10-29 through 10-32 and 35 and 35A on pages 6-2 and 6-3). This question requires you to find the estimated time en route (ETE) for block 10 on the flight plan. Use the flight log (figure 33) to record the necessary information. You'll also need information from the other figures referenced in the question. A first step is to compute groundspeed for each leg of the route using the winds aloft data. Since winds aloft are reported in true direction, you can simplify the problem by converting them to magnetic. Remember, airways are oriented to magnetic north. Then, determine distances and times using all available information to find the total ETE.

True airspeed	180 kts.
Cruising altitude	8,000 feet
Variation	4°E
Wind	220/40

Check Points	Mag Crs	Mag Wnd	GS	Dist	Time
HOT					
MARKI	221				:12:00
TXK	210	216/40	140	55	:23:34
TXK/BUJ3	272	216/40	155	61	:23:37
BUJ3	239	216/40	142	59	:24:56
APP/LND					:10:00
TOTAL					1:34:07

Your total time to Dallas Addison is 1 hour, 34 minutes, and 7 seconds. Answers (B) and (C) are wrong because they indicate considerably more than the time required.

Form Approved: OMB No. 2120-0034

U.S. DEPARTMENT OF TRANSPORTATION FEDERAL AVIATION ADMINISTRATION **FLIGHT PLAN**	(FAA USE ONLY) ☐ PILOT BRIEFING ☐ STOPOVER	☐ VNR	TIME STARTED	SPECIALIST INITIALS

1. TYPE	2. AIRCRAFT IDENTIFICATION	3. AIRCRAFT TYPE/ SPECIAL EQUIPMENT	4. TRUE AIRSPEED	5. DEPARTURE POINT	6. DEPARTURE TIME		7. CRUISING ALTITUDE
					PROPOSED (Z)	ACTUAL (Z)	
VFR **X** IFR DVFR	N4078A	PA 31/	180 KTS	HOT			8,000

8. ROUTE OF FLIGHT

HOT V573, TXK, TXK.BUJ3

9. DESTINATION (Name of airport and city)	10. EST. TIME ENROUTE		11. REMARKS
DALLAS ADDISON AIRPORT DALLAS, TX	HOURS	MINUTES	

12. FUEL ON BOARD		13. ALTERNATE AIRPORT(S)	14. PILOT'S NAME, ADDRESS & TELEPHONE NUMBER & AIRCRAFT HOME BASE	15. NUMBER ABOARD
HOURS	MINUTES			
		N/A	17. DESTINATION CONTACT/TELEPHONE (OPTIONAL)	2

16. COLOR OF AIRCRAFT	CIVIL AIRCRAFT PILOTS. FAR Part 91 requires you file an IFR flight plan to operate under instrument flight rules in controlled airspace. Failure to file could result in a civil penalty not to exceed $1,000 for each violation (Section 901 of the Federal Aviation Act of 1958, as amended). Filing of a VFR flight plan is recommended as a good operating practice. See also Part 99 for requirements concerning DVFR flight plans.
TAN/WHITE	

FAA Form 7233-1 (8-82)   CLOSE VFR FLIGHT PLAN WITH _____ FSS ON ARRIVAL

AIRCRAFT INFORMATION

MAKE Piper   MODEL PA-31

N 4078A   Vso 74

AIRCRAFT EQUIPMENT/STATUS**

**NOTE: X= OPERATIVE   INOP= INOPERATIVE   N/A= NOT APPLICABLE
TRANSPONDER: X (MODE C) X ILS: (LOCALIZER) X (GLIDE SLOPE) X
VOR NO. 1 X (NO. 2) X ADF: X RNAV: X
VERTICAL PATH COMPUTER: N/A DME: X
MARKER BEACON: X (AUDIO) X (VISUAL) X

FIGURE 32.—Flight Plan and Aircraft Information.

FLIGHT LOG

HOT SPRINGS, MEMORIAL FIELD TO DALLAS, ADDISON, TX.

CHECK POINTS		ROUTE		WIND	SPEED-KTS		DIST	TIME		FUEL	
FROM	TO	ALTITUDE	COURSE	TEMP	TAS	GS	NM	LEG	TOT	LEG	TOT
HOT	MARKI	V573 CLIMB	221°					:12:00			
	TXK	V573 8000	210°		180						
	TXK BUJ3	BUJ3 8000	272°								
	BUJ3	BUJ3 DESCENT	239°								
APPROACH & LANDING								:10:00			
	DALLAS ADDISON										

OTHER DATA:
NOTE: MAG. VAR. 4° E.

FLIGHT SUMMARY

TIME	FUEL (LB)	
		EN ROUTE
		RESERVE
		MISSED APPR.
		TOTAL

FIGURE 33.—Flight Planning Log.

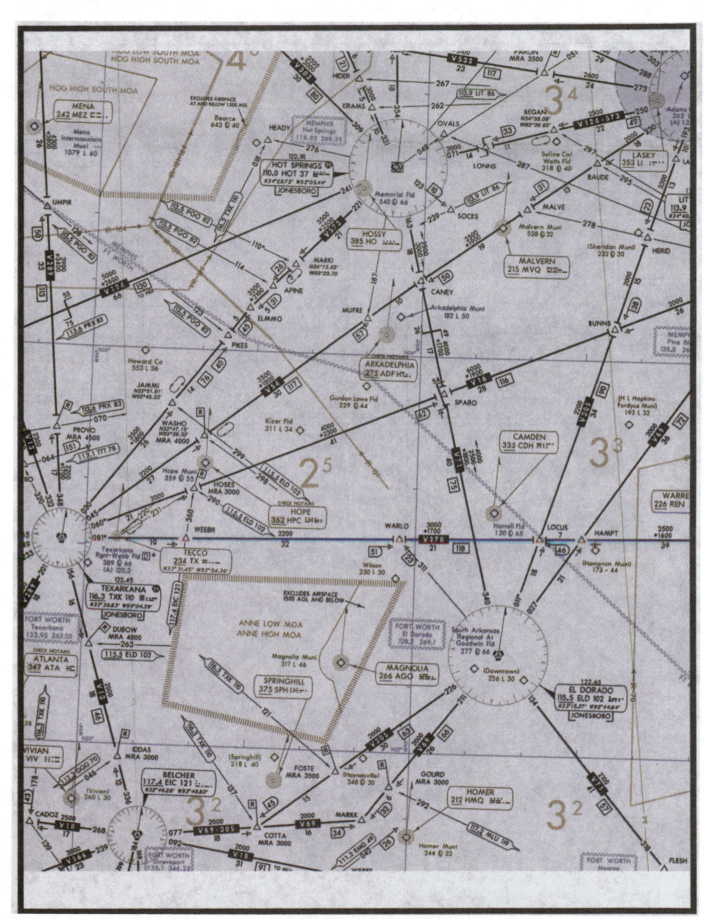

FIGURE 34.—En Route Chart.

TEXAS   1·15

DALLAS

ADDISON   (ADS)   9 N   UTC-6(-5DT)   32°58'06"N 96°50'10"W   DALLAS-FT. WORTH
  643   B   S4   FUEL 100LL, JET A   H-2K, 4F, 5B, L-13C, A
  RWY 15-33: H7201X100 (ASPH)   S-80, D-100, DT-160   MIRL   IAP
    RWY 15: MALSR. VASI(V4R)—GA 3.0°TCH 51'. Thld dsplcd 980'. Ground.
    RWY 33: REIL. Thld dsplcd 468'. Road.
  AIRPORT REMARKS: Attended continuously. Numerous flocks of birds on and in vicinity of arpt. Use extreme care:
    numerous 200' AGL buildings within 1 mile East, and South of arpt, transmission towers and water tanks West of
    arpt. Rwy 33 REIL out of svc indefinitely. ACTIVATE MALSR Rwy 15—CTAF. Rwy limited to maximum gross
    weight 120,000 pounds. Control Zone effective 1200-0400Z‡.
  WEATHER DATA SOURCES: LAWRS
  COMMUNICATIONS: CTAF 121.1   ATIS 126.8 (1200-0400Z‡)   UNICOM 122.95
    FORT WORTH FSS (FTW) TF 1–800–WX–BRIEF. NOTAM FILE ADS.
  ®REGIONAL APP CON 123.9   ® REGIONAL DEP CON 124.3
    TOWER 121.1 (1200-0400Z‡)   GND CON 121.6   CLNC DEL 119.55
  RADIO AIDS TO NAVIGATION: NOTAM FILE DAL.
    LOVE (L) VORW/DME 114.3   LUE   Chan 90   32°50'51"N 96°51'42"W   002° 7.4 NM to fld. 490/08E.
    BRONS NDB (LOM) 407   AD   33°02'40"N 96°52'13"W   153° 4.9 NM to fld.
    ILS/DME 110.1 I-ADS Chan 38 Rwy 15. LOM BRONS NDB. Unmonitored when tower closed.
    ILS 110.1 I-TBQ Rwy 33 LOC only. Unmonitored when twr clsd.

FIGURE 36.—Excerpt from Airport/Facility Directory.

10-31   J15
(Refer to figure 38 on page 10-34.) What aircraft equipment code should be entered in block 3 of the flight plan?

A — A.
B — I.
C — C.

10-31. Answer B. (AIM)
RNAV and a transponder with altitude encoding equipment requires an "/I" equipment code. Answer (A) is wrong because "/A" indicates that you do not have RNAV. Answer (C) is wrong because "/C" indicates you do not have altitude encoding equipment.

10-32   H342
(Refer to the FD excerpt below, and use the wind entry closest to the flight planned altitude.) Determine the time to be entered in block 10 of the flight plan.

Route of flight............................Figures 38, 39, and 40
Flight log & MAG VAR...............................Figure 39
ACTON TWO ARRIVAL ....Figure 41

FT	3000	6000	9000	12000
ABI		2033+13	2141+13	2142+05

A — 1 hour 24 minutes.
B — 1 hour 26 minutes.
C — 1 hour 31 minutes.

10-32. Answer C. GFDICM 10C (IFH)
(Refer to figures 38, 39, 40 on pages 10-34 through 10-36 and figure 41 on page 6-4.) This question requires you to find the estimated time en route (ETE) for block 10 on the flight plan. Use the flight log (figure 39) to record the necessary information. You'll also need information from the other figures referenced in the question. A first step is to compute groundspeed for each leg of the route using the winds aloft data. Since winds aloft are reported in true direction, you can simplify the problem by converting them to magnetic. Remember, airways are oriented to magnetic north. Then, determine distances and times using all available information to find the total ETE.

True airspeed..156 kts.
Cruising altitude ....11,000 feet
Variation ....11°E
Wind...210/42

Check Points	Mag Crs	Mag Wnd	GS	Dist	Time
21XS					
BGS					:06:00
LORAN	075	199/42	176	42	:14:19
ABI	076	199/42	175	40	:13:43
COTTN	087	199/42	167	63	:22:38
AQN	075	199/42	176	50	:17:03
CREEK	040	199/42	194	32	:09:54
APP/LND					:08:00
TOTAL					1:31:37

Your total time to Dallas Fort Worth Airport is 1 hour, 31 minutes, and 37 seconds. Answer (C) is the closest choice. Answers (A) and (B) are wrong because they indicate less than the time required.

Form Approved: OMB No. 2120-0034

U.S. DEPARTMENT OF TRANSPORTATION FEDERAL AVIATION ADMINISTRATION **FLIGHT PLAN**	(FAA USE ONLY)	☐ PILOT BRIEFING ☐ STOPOVER	☐ VNR	TIME STARTED	SPECIALIST INITIALS

1. TYPE	2. AIRCRAFT IDENTIFICATION	3. AIRCRAFT TYPE/ SPECIAL EQUIPMENT	4. TRUE AIRSPEED	5. DEPARTURE POINT	6. DEPARTURE TIME		7. CRUISING ALTITUDE
					PROPOSED (Z)	ACTUAL (Z)	
VFR **X** IFR DVFR	N4321P	C402/	156 KTS	BGS			11000

8. ROUTE OF FLIGHT

DIRECT BGS, V16 ABI, ABI.AQN2

9. DESTINATION (Name of airport and city)	10. EST. TIME ENROUTE		11. REMARKS
	HOURS	MINUTES	
DALLAS FT. WORTH DFW			

12. FUEL ON BOARD		13. ALTERNATE AIRPORT(S)	14. PILOT'S NAME, ADDRESS & TELEPHONE NUMBER & AIRCRAFT HOME BASE	15. NUMBER ABOARD
HOURS	MINUTES			
		N/A	17. DESTINATION CONTACT/TELEPHONE (OPTIONAL)	2

16. COLOR OF AIRCRAFT	CIVIL AIRCRAFT PILOTS. FAR Part 91 requires you file an IFR flight plan to operate under instrument flight rules in controlled airspace. Failure to file could result in a civil penalty not to exceed $1,000 for each violation (Section 901 of the Federal Aviation Act of 1958, as amended). Filing of a VFR flight plan is recommended as a good operating practice. See also Part 99 for requirements concerning DVFR flight plans.
RED/BLUE/WHITE	

FAA Form 7233-1 (8-82)   CLOSE VFR FLIGHT PLAN WITH _____ FSS ON ARRIVAL

AIRCRAFT INFORMATION

MAKE Cessna   MODEL 402C

N 4321P   Vso 71

AIRCRAFT EQUIPMENT/STATUS**

**NOTE: X= OPERATIVE   INOP= INOPERATIVE   N/A= NOT APPLICABLE

TRANSPONDER: X (MODE C) X ILS: (LOCALIZER) X (GLIDE SLOPE) X

VOR NO. 1 X (NO. 2) X ADF: X RNAV: X

VERTICAL PATH COMPUTER: N/A DME: X

MARKER BEACON: X (AUDIO) X (VISUAL) X

FIGURE 38.—Flight Plan and Aircraft Information.

FLIGHT LOG

BIG SPRING McMAHON-WRINKLE TO DALLAS FT. WORTH (DFW)

CHECK POINTS		ROUTE		WIND	SPEED-KTS		DIST	TIME		FUEL	
FROM	TO	ALTITUDE	COURSE	TEMP	TAS	GS	NM	LEG	TOT	LEG	TOT
21XS	BGS	DIRECT CLIMB	DIRECT					:06:0			
	LORAN	V16 11,000	075°								
	ABI	V16 11,000	076°		156						
	COTTN	DIRECT 11,000	087°								
	AQN	AQN2	075°								
	CREEK	AQN2	040°								
APPROACH & LANDING		RADAR VEC-						:08:0			
	DFW AIRPORT	DESCENT									

OTHER DATA:
NOTE: MAG. VAR. 11° E.
(STAR) ACTON TWO ARRIVAL (AQN2)

FLIGHT SUMMARY		
TIME	FUEL (LB)	
		EN ROUTE
		RESERVE
		MISSED APPR.
		TOTAL

BIG SPRING McMAHON-WRINKLE   (21XS) 2SW UTC-6(-5DT).   **DALLAS-FT. WORTH**
H-21, 5A, L-13A, 15B
IAP

    32°12'45"N101°31"17"W
2572 B S4FUEL 100LL, JET A
RWY 17-35: H8803X100 (ASPH-CONC) S-44, D-62, DDT-101 MIRL
  RWY 17:SSALS.PVASI(ASPH)-GA3.0°TCH 41'.
RWY 06-24:H4600X75(ASPH) MIRL
  RWY 24:PVASI(PSIL)-GA3.55°TCH31'. P-line.
AIRPORT REMARKS: Attended 1400-2300Z . For fuel after hours call 915-263-3958. ACTIVATE MIRL Rwy 06-24
  and Rwy 17-35, SSALS Rwy 17 and PVASI Rwy 17 and 24-CTAF.
COMMUNICATIONS:CTAF/UNICOM 122.8
  SAN ANGELOSFSS (SJT) TF 1-800-WX-BRIEF. NOTAM FILE SJT.
  RCO 122.4(SAN ANGELOFSS)
  FORT WORTH CENTER APP/DEP CON 133.7
RADIO AIDS TO NAVIGATION: NOTAM FILE SJT.
  (L) VORTACW 144.3 BGS Chan 90 32°23'08"N 101°10.5NM to fld. 2670/11E.

EXCERPT FROM AIRPORT/FACILITY DIRECTORY (21 XS)

FIGURE 39.—Flight Log and Excerpt from Airport/Facility Directory (21XS).

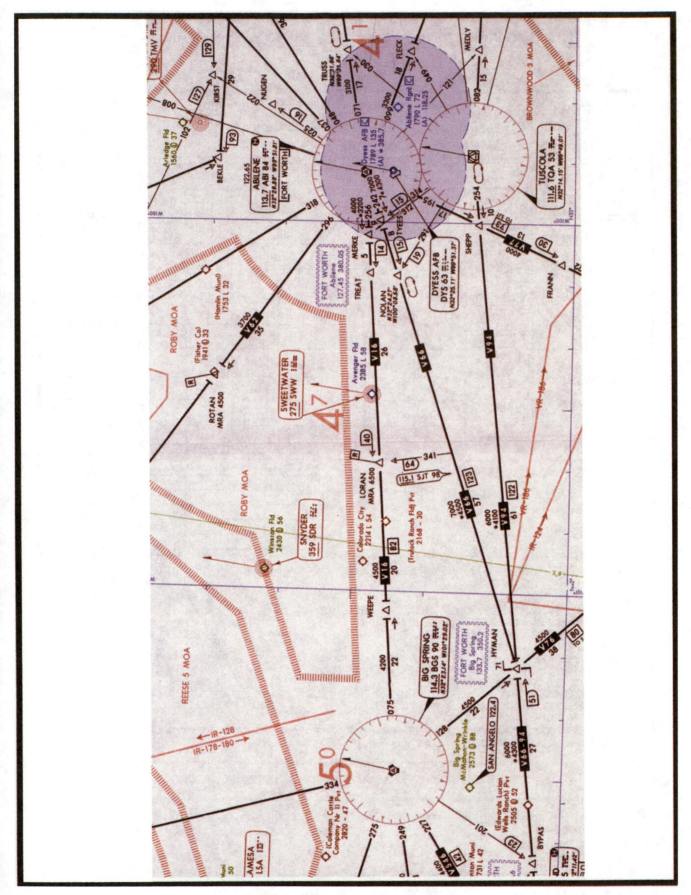

FIGURE 40.—En Route Chart Segment.

ACTON TWO ARRIVAL (AQN.AQN2)   DALLAS-FORT WORTH, TEXAS

ARRIVAL DESCRIPTION

ABILENE TRANSITION (ABI.AQN2): From over ABI VORTAC via ABI R-087 and AQN R-255 to AQN VORTAC. Thence . . . .

EDNAS TRANSITION (EDNAS.AQN2): From over EDNAS INT via AQN R-199 to AQN VORTAC. Thence . . . .

WINK TRANSITION (INK.AQN2): From over INK VORTAC via INK R-071, TQA R-254, TQA R-073 and AQN R-255 to AQN VORTAC. Thence . . . .

TURBOJETS LANDING DALLAS-FT. WORTH INTL, MEACHAM, CARSWELL AFB, DENTON, ALLIANCE: (Landing South): From over AQN VORTAC via AQN R-040 to CREEK INT, thence heading 350° for vector to final approach course. (Landing North): From over AQN VORTAC via AQN R-040 to CREEK INT. Expect vectors at BRYAR INT.

NON-TURBOJETS LANDING DALLAS-FT. WORTH INTL, MEACHAM, CARSWELL AFB, DENTON, ALLIANCE: (Landing South): From over AQN VORTAC via AQN R-033 to RENDY INT. Expect vectors to final approach course. (Landing North): From over AQN VORTAC via AQN R-040 to CREEK INT. Expect vector at BRYAR INT.

TURBOJETS LANDING DALLAS-LOVE FIELD and ADDISON: (Landing South): From over AQN VORTAC via AQN R-040 to CREEK INT, thence heading 350° for vector to final approach course. (Landing North): From over AQN VORTAC via AQN R-079 to BRITY INT. Expect vector to final approach course.

NON-TURBOJETS LANDING DALLAS-LOVE FIELD and ADDISON: (Landing South/North): From over AQN VORTAC via AQN R-079 to BRITY INT. Expect vector to final approach course.

ALL AIRCRAFT LANDING FORT WORTH SPINKS, ARLINGTON, NAS DALLAS, REDBIRD, and PHIL L. HUDSON: (Landing South/North): From over AQN VORTAC via AQN R-079 to BRITY INT. Expect vectors to final approach course.

FIGURE 41A.—ACTON Two Arrival Description.

10-33   J15

(Refer to figure 44.) What aircraft equipment code should be entered in block 3 of the flight plan?

A — A.
B — I.
C — C.

10-34   H342

Determine the time to be entered in block 10 of the flight plan. (Refer to the FD excerpt below, and use the wind entry closest to the flight planned altitude.)

Route of flight......................Figures 44, 45, 46, and 47
Flight log & MAG VAR...............................Figure 45
GROMO TWO DEPARTURE
and Excerpt from AFD ....Figure 46

FT	3000	6000	9000	12000
YKM	1615	1926+12	2032+08	2035+05

A — 54 minutes.
B — 1 hour 02 minutes.
C — 1 hour 07 minutes.

10-33. Answer B. (AIM)

Having RNAV and a transponder with altitude encoding equipment requires an "/I" equipment code. Answer (A) is wrong because "/A" indicates that you do not have RNAV. Answer (C) is wrong because "/C" indicates you do not have altitude encoding equipment.

10-34. Answer B. GFDICM 10C (IFH)

(Refer to figures 44, 45, 46, and 47 on pages 10-39 to 10-42.) This question requires you to find the estimated time enroute (ETE) for the block 10 entry on the flight plan form. Use the flight log (figure 45) to record the necessary information. You'll also need information from other figures referenced in this question. The first step is to compute groundspeed for each leg of the route using the winds aloft data. Since winds aloft are reported in true direction, you can simplify the problem by converting them to magnetic. Remember, airways are oriented to magnetic north. Then, determine distance and times using all available information to find the total ETE.

True airspeed ....180 kts.
Cruise altitude...12,000 ft.
Variation ....20°E
Wind..200°/35 kts

Check Points	Mag Crs	Mag Wnd	GS	Dist	Time
YKM		180/35			
HITCH		180/35		16	:10:00
VOR/COP	206	180/35	148	37	:15:00
BTG	234	180/35	157	53	:20:15
PDX	160	180/35	147	10	:04:05
ARPT		180/35			:13:00
TOTAL					1:02:20

The distances between YKM and HITCH (16), and BTG and PDX (10) are conservative estimates based on the enroute map (figure 47).

Form Approved: OMB No. 2120-0034

U.S. DEPARTMENT OF TRANSPORTATION FEDERAL AVIATION ADMINISTRATION **FLIGHT PLAN**	(FAA USE ONLY) ☐ PILOT BRIEFING ☐ VNR ☐ STOPOVER		TIME STARTED	SPECIALIST INITIALS

1. TYPE	2. AIRCRAFT IDENTIFICATION	3. AIRCRAFT TYPE/ SPECIAL EQUIPMENT	4. TRUE AIRSPEED	5. DEPARTURE POINT	6. DEPARTURE TIME		7. CRUISING ALTITUDE
					PROPOSED (Z)	ACTUAL (Z)	
VFR							
X IFR	N3678A	PA31/	180 KTS	YKM			12000
DVFR							

8. ROUTE OF FLIGHT

GROMO 2, HITCH, V468 BTG, DIRECT

9. DESTINATION (Name of airport and city)	10. EST. TIME ENROUTE		11. REMARKS
	HOURS	MINUTES	
PORTLAND INTL. AIRPORT PDX			INSTRUMENT TRAINING FLIGHT

12. FUEL ON BOARD		13. ALTERNATE AIRPORT(S)	14. PILOT'S NAME, ADDRESS & TELEPHONE NUMBER & AIRCRAFT HOME BASE	15. NUMBER ABOARD
HOURS	MINUTES			
		N/A	17. DESTINATION CONTACT/TELEPHONE (OPTIONAL)	2

16. COLOR OF AIRCRAFT	CIVIL AIRCRAFT PILOTS. FAR Part 91 requires you file an IFR flight plan to operate under instrument flight rules in controlled airspace. Failure to file could result in a civil penalty not to exceed $1,000 for each violation (Section 901 of the Federal Aviation Act of 1958, as amended). Filing of a VFR flight plan is recommended as a good operating practice. See also Part 99 for requirements concerning DVFR flight plans.
GOLD/WHITE	

FAA Form 7233-1 (8-82)   CLOSE VFR FLIGHT PLAN WITH _____ FSS ON ARRIVAL

AIRCRAFT INFORMATION

MAKE Piper   MODEL PA-31

N 3678A   Vso 77

AIRCRAFT EQUIPMENT/STATUS**

**NOTE: X= OPERATIVE   INOP= INOPERATIVE   N/A= NOT APPLICABLE
TRANSPONDER: X (MODE C) X ILS: (LOCALIZER) X (GLIDE SLOPE) X
VOR NO. 1 X (NO. 2) X ADF: X RNAV: X
VERTICAL PATH COMPUTER: N/A DME: X
MARKER BEACON: X (AUDIO) INOP (VISUAL) X

FIGURE 44.—Flight Plan and Aircraft Information.

FLIGHT LOG

YAKIMA AIR TERMINAL TO PORTLAND, INTL.

CHECK POINTS		ROUTE	COURSE	WIND	SPEED-KTS		DIST	TIME		FUEL	
FROM	TO	ALTITUDE		TEMP	TAS	GS	NM	LEG	TOT	LEG	TOT
YKM	HITCH VOR C.O.P.	GROMO 2 CLIMB V468 12,000	206° 206°		180			:10.			
	BTG	V468 12,000	234°								
	PDX	DIRECT	160°								
APPROACH & LANDING								:13.			
	PDX AIRPORT										

OTHER DATA:
NOTE: MAG. VAR. 20° E.

FLIGHT SUMMARY

TIME	FUEL (LB)	
		EN ROUTE
		RESERVE
		MISSED APPR.
		TOTAL

FIGURE 45.—Flight Planning Log.

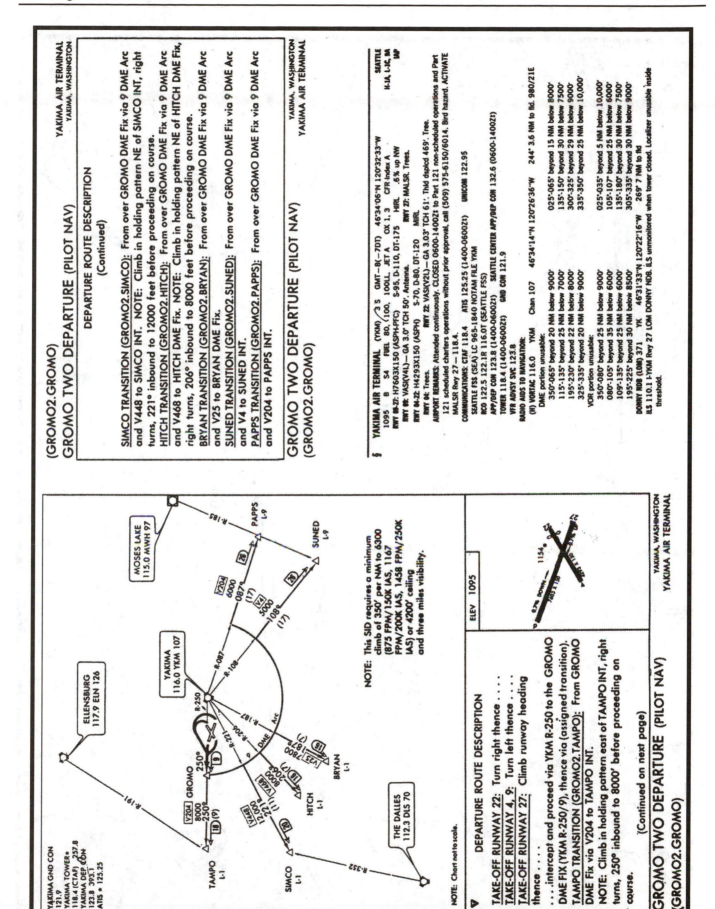

FIGURE 46.—GROMO Two Departure and Excerpt from Airport/Facility Directory.

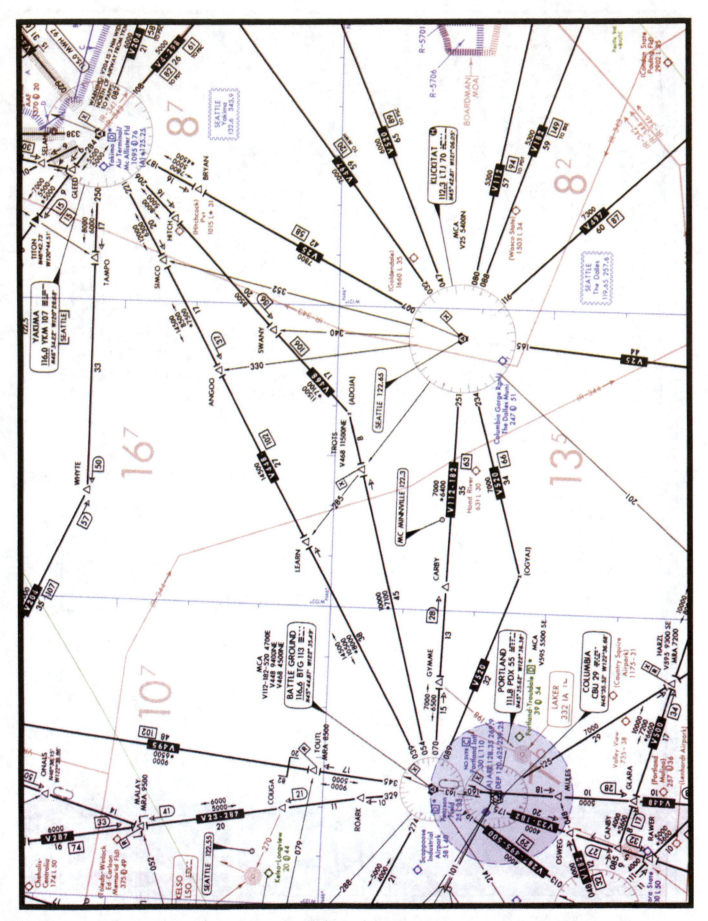

FIGURE 47.—En Route Chart Segment..

10-35   J15

(Refer to figure 50 on page 10-44.) What aircraft equipment code should be entered in block 3 of the flight plan?

A — T.
B — U.
C — I.

10-36   H342

Determine the time to be entered in block 10 of the flight plan. (Refer to the FD excerpt below, and use the wind entry closest to the flight planned altitude.)

Route of flight......................Figures 50, 51, 52, and 53
Flight log and MAG VAR ......Figure 51on page 10-60
HABUT ONE DEPARTURE
and Excerpt from AFD ....Figure 52

FT	3000	6000	9000
SBA	0610	2115+05	2525+00

A — 43 minutes.
B — 46 minutes.
C — 51 minutes.

10-35. Answer C. (AIM)

The aircraft indicated in the flight plan, N2468 is equipped with a Mode C transponder, RNAV and DME. This would correspond with the "I" designation. The suffix "T" (answer A) indicates the aircraft is equipped only with a transponder without Mode C, while "U" (answer B) indicates that the aircraft is equipped only with a Mode C transponder.

10-36. Answer C. GFDICM 10C (IFH)

(Refer to figures 50, 52, and 53 on pages 10-44 through 10-46 and figure 51 on page 10-60.) This question requires you to find the estimated time enroute (ETE) for the block 10 entry on the flight plan form. Use the flight log (figure 51 on page 10-60) to record the
necessary information. You'll also need information from other figures referenced in this question. The first step is to compute groundspeed for each leg of the route using the winds aloft data. Since winds aloft are reported in true direction, you can simplify the problem by converting them to magnetic. Remember, airways are oriented to magnetic north. Then, determine distance and times using all available information to find the total ETE.

True airspeed...158 kts.
Cruise altitude...8,000 ft.
Variation ....16°E
Wind...250°/25 kts.

Check Points	Mag Crs	Mag Wnd	GS	Dist	Time
HABUT	253	234/25			:08:00
GVO	343	234/25	164	6.4	:02:20
MQO	307	234/25	149	54.0	:21:45
PRB	358	234/25	171	26.0	:09:07
ARPT					:10:00
TOTAL					:51:12

Form Approved: OMB No. 2120-0034

U.S. DEPARTMENT OF TRANSPORTATION FEDERAL AVIATION ADMINISTRATION **FLIGHT PLAN**	(FAA USE ONLY)	☐ PILOT BRIEFING ☐ STOPOVER	☐ VNR	TIME STARTED	SPECIALIST INITIALS

1. TYPE		2. AIRCRAFT IDENTIFICATION	3. AIRCRAFT TYPE/ SPECIAL EQUIPMENT	4. TRUE AIRSPEED	5. DEPARTURE POINT	6. DEPARTURE TIME		7. CRUISING ALTITUDE
	VFR					PROPOSED (Z)	ACTUAL (Z)	
X	IFR							
	DVFR	N2468	A36/	158 KTS	SBA			8000

8. ROUTE OF FLIGHT

HABUTI GVO, V27 MQO, V113 PRB

9. DESTINATION (Name of airport and city)	10. EST. TIME ENROUTE		11. REMARKS
	HOURS	MINUTES	
PASO ROBLES MUNI PRB			IFR TRAINING FLIGHT

12. FUEL ON BOARD		13. ALTERNATE AIRPORT(S)	14. PILOT'S NAME, ADDRESS & TELEPHONE NUMBER & AIRCRAFT HOME BASE	15. NUMBER ABOARD
HOURS	MINUTES			
		N/A	17. DESTINATION CONTACT/TELEPHONE (OPTIONAL)	2

16. COLOR OF AIRCRAFT	CIVIL AIRCRAFT PILOTS. FAR Part 91 requires you file an IFR flight plan to operate under instrument flight rules in controlled airspace. Failure to file could result in a civil penalty not to exceed $1,000 for each violation (Section 901 of the Federal Aviation Act of 1958, as amended). Filing of a VFR flight plan is recommended as a good operating practice. See also Part 99 for requirements concerning DVFR flight plans.
GOLD/WHITE	

FAA Form 7233-1 (8-82)   CLOSE VFR FLIGHT PLAN WITH _____ FSS ON ARRIVAL

AIRCRAFT INFORMATION

MAKE Beechcraft   MODEL A-36

N 2468   Vso 52

AIRCRAFT EQUIPMENT/STATUS**

**NOTE: X= OPERATIVE   INOP= INOPERATIVE   N/A= NOT APPLICABLE·
TRANSPONDER: X (MODE C) X ILS: (LOCALIZER) X (GLIDE SLOPE) X
VOR NO. 1 X (NO. 2) X ADF: X RNAV: X
VERTICAL PATH COMPUTER: N/A DME: X
MARKER BEACON: X (AUDIO) X (VISUAL) INOP

FIGURE 50.—Flight Plan and Aircraft Information.

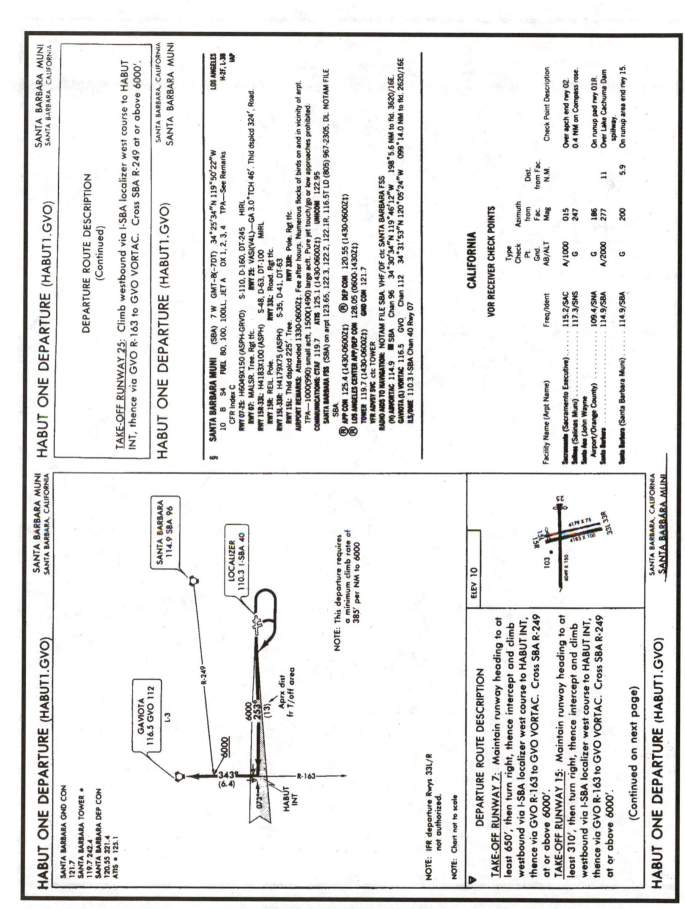

FIGURE 52.—HABUT One Departure and Excerpt from Airport/Facility Directory.

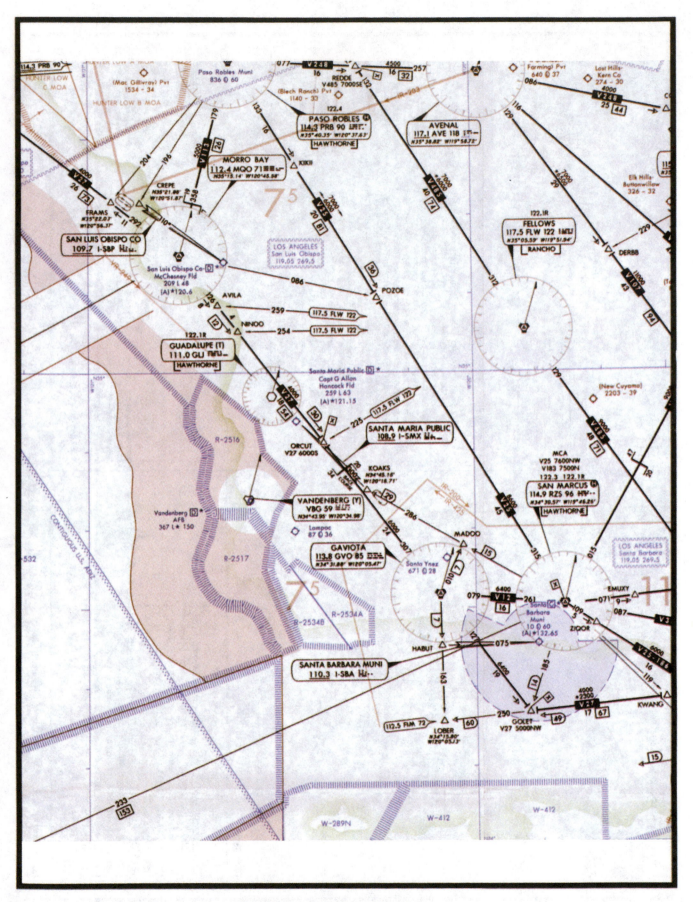

FIGURE 53.—En Route Chart Segment.

10-37 J15
(Refer to figure 69 on page 10-48.) What aircraft equipment code should be entered in block 3 of the flight plan?

A — A.
B — B.
C — U.

10-38 H342
Determine the time to be entered in block 10 of the flight plan. (Refer to the FD excerpt below, and use the wind entry closest to the flight planned altitude.)

Route of flight .... Figures 69, 70, and 71
Flight log and MAG VAR .... Figure 70
JUDDS TWO ARRIVAL and
Excerpt from AFD .... Figure 72

FT	3000	6000	9000
BDL	3320	3425+05	3430+00

A — 1 hour 14 minutes.
B — 58 minutes.
C — 50 minutes.

10-37. Answer A. GFDICM 10C (AIM)
Figure 69 lists the available equipment, and the equipment code entry in block 3 consists of a slash (/) and a letter designation. An aircraft with DME and a transponder with Mode C encoding altimeter meets the equipment requirements for a "/A" designation. The designation "/B" (answer B) does not include Mode C. The designation "/U" (answer C) does not include DME.

10-38. Answer B. GFDICM 10C (IFH)
(Refer to figures 69, 70, 71, and 72 on pages 10-48 through 10-51.) If your calculations are accurate, they will not agree with any of the answers provided. (B) is closest, and is apparently the result when you do not convert true winds to magnetic before performing the calculations. This question requires you to find the estimated time enroute (ETE) for the block 10 entry on the flight plan form.Use the flight log (figure 70) to record the necessary information. You'll also need information from other figures referenced in this question. The first step is to compute groundspeed for each leg of the route using the winds aloft data. Since winds aloft are reported in true direction, you can simplify the problem by converting them to magnetic. Remember, airways are oriented to magnetic north. Then, determine distance and times using all available information to find the total ETE.

True airspeed	128 kts.
Cruise altitude	5,000 ft.
Variation	14°W
Wind	340°/25

Check Points	Mag Crs	Mag Wnd	GS	Dist	Time
4N1		354/25			:08:00
SHAFF	029	354/25	107	24	:13:27
HELON	102	354/25	133	21	:09:28
IGN	112	354/25	138	15	:06:31
COP	100	354/25	133	17	:07:40
JUDDS	057	354/25	115	6	:03:08
BDL					:12:00
TOTAL					1:00:14

Form Approved: OMB No. 2120-0034

U.S. DEPARTMENT OF TRANSPORTATION FEDERAL AVIATION ADMINISTRATION **FLIGHT PLAN**	(FAA USE ONLY) ☐ PILOT BRIEFING ☐ STOPOVER	☐ VNR	TIME STARTED	SPECIALIST INITIALS

1. TYPE	2. AIRCRAFT IDENTIFICATION	3. AIRCRAFT TYPE/ SPECIAL EQUIPMENT	4. TRUE AIRSPEED	5. DEPARTURE POINT	6. DEPARTURE TIME		7. CRUISING ALTITUDE
VFR					PROPOSED (Z)	ACTUAL (Z)	
X IFR	N2142S	C172/	128 KTS	GREENWOOD LAKE 4N1			5000
DVFR							

8. ROUTE OF FLIGHT

DIRECT SHAFF INT., V213 HELON INT., V58 JUDDS INT., JUDDS2

9. DESTINATION (Name of airport and city)	10. EST. TIME ENROUTE		11. REMARKS
BRADLEY INTL. BDL	HOURS	MINUTES	INSTRUMENT TRAINING FLIGHT

12. FUEL ON BOARD		13. ALTERNATE AIRPORT(S)	14. PILOT'S NAME, ADDRESS & TELEPHONE NUMBER & AIRCRAFT HOME BASE	15. NUMBER ABOARD
HOURS	MINUTES		17. DESTINATION CONTACT/TELEPHONE (OPTIONAL)	2
		N/A		

16. COLOR OF AIRCRAFT	CIVIL AIRCRAFT PILOTS. FAR Part 91 requires you file an IFR flight plan to operate under instrument flight rules in controlled airspace. Failure to file could result in a civil penalty not to exceed $1,000 for each violation (Section 901 of the Federal Aviation Act of 1958, as amended). Filing of a VFR flight plan is recommended as a good operating practice. See also Part 99 for requirements concerning DVFR flight plans.
BROWN/TAN/WHITE	

FAA Form 7233-1 (8-82)   CLOSE VFR FLIGHT PLAN WITH _____ FSS ON ARRIVAL

AIRCRAFT INFORMATION

MAKE Cessna   MODEL 172

N 2142S   Vso 33

AIRCRAFT EQUIPMENT/STATUS**

**NOTE: X= OPERATIVE   INOP= INOPERATIVE   N/A= NOT APPLICABLE
TRANSPONDER: X (MODE C) X ILS: (LOCALIZER) X (GLIDE SLOPE) X
VOR NO. 1 X (NO. 2) X ADF: X RNAV: N/A
VERTICAL PATH COMPUTER: N/A DME: X
MARKER BEACON: X (AUDIO) INOP (VISUAL) X

FIGURE 69.—Flight Plan and Aircraft Information.

FLIGHT LOG

GREENWOOD LAKE (4N1) TO BRADLEY INTL. (BDL)

CHECK POINTS		ROUTE	COURSE	WIND	SPEED-KTS		DIST	TIME		FUEL	
FROM	TO	ALTITUDE		TEMP	TAS	GS	NM	LEG	TOT	LEG	TOT
4N1	SHAFF	DIRECT CLIMB	350°					:08:0			
	HELON	V213 5000	029°		128						
	IGN	V58 5000	102°								
		JUDDS2	112°								
	JUDDS	JUDDS2	100°								
	BRISS	JUDDS2	057°								
APPROACH & LANDING								:12:0			
	BDL INTL										

OTHER DATA:
NOTE: MAG. VAR. 14° W.

FLIGHT SUMMARY		
TIME	FUEL (LB)	
		EN ROUTE
		RESERVE
		MISSED APPR.
		TOTAL

FIGURE 70.—Flight Planning Log.

FIGURE 71.—En Route Chart Segment.

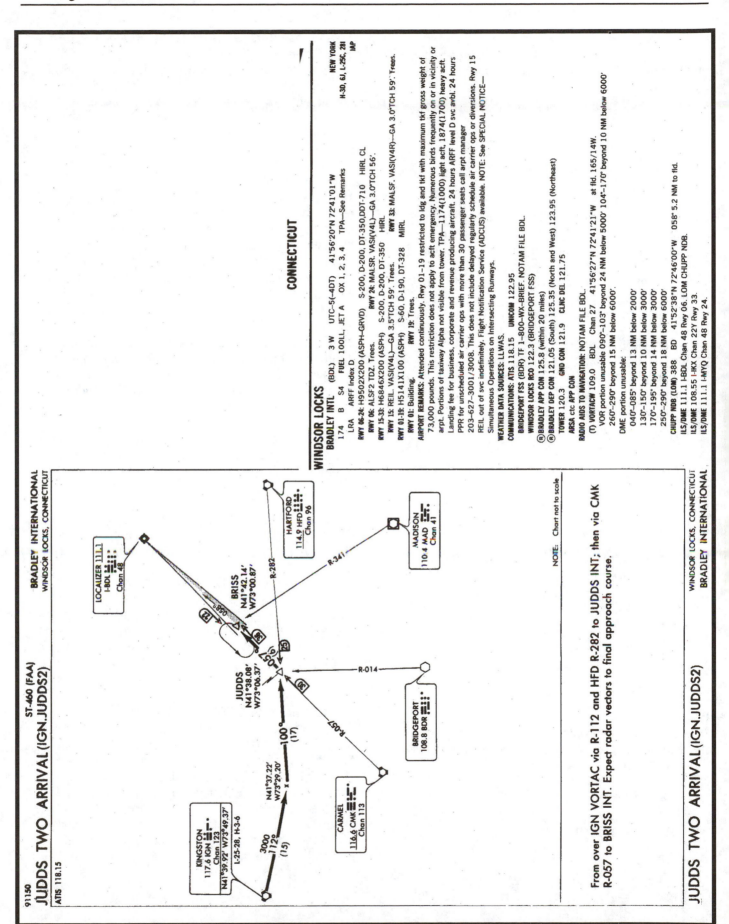

FIGURE 72.—JUDDS TWO ARRIVAL.

10-39   J15
(Refer to figure 74 on page 10-53.) What aircraft equipment code should be entered in block 3 of the flight plan?

A — T.
B — U.
C — A.

10-40   H342
Determine the time to be entered in block 10 of the flight plan. (Refer to the FD excerpt below, and use the wind entry closest to the flight planned altitude.)

Route of flight...............Figures 74, 75, 76, 77, and 78
Flight log & MAG VAR..............................Figure 75
VOR indications and Excerpts from AFD ....Figure 76

FT	6000	9000	12000	18000
BIL	2414	2422+11	2324+05	2126-11

A — 1 hour 15 minutes.
B — 1 hour 20 minutes.
C — 1 hour 25 minutes.

10-41   J15
The most current en route and destination flight information for planning an instrument flight should be obtained from

A — the ATIS broadcast.
B — the FSS.
C — Notices to Airmen (Class II).

10-39. Answer C. GFDICM 10C (AIM)
See Aircraft Equipment Suffixes in Appendix 2. It indicates that for aircraft equipped with DME and a transponder with altitude encoding capability, you should enter "/A" in block 3 of the flight plan. "T" (answer A) does not include DME or Mode C altitude reporting capability. "U" (answer B) does not include DME.

10-40. Answer C. GFDICM 10C (IFH)
(Refer to figures 74, 75, 76, 77, and 78 on pages 10-53 through 10-57.) This question requires you to find the estimated time enroute (ETE) for the block 10 entry on the flight plan. Use the flight log (figure 75) to record the necessary information. You'll also need information from other figures referenced in the question. A first step is to compute groundspeed for each leg of the route using the winds aloft data. Since winds aloft are reported in true direction, you can simplify the problem by converting them to magnetic. Remember, airways are oriented to magnetic north. Then, determine distances and times using all available information to find the total ETE.

True airspeed..160 kts.
Cruising altitude ....11,000 feet
Variation ....18°E
Wind...230/24

Check Points	Mag Crs	Mag Wnd	GS	Dist	Time
HLN					
VESTS	103				:15:00
BZN	140	212/24	151	44	:17:29
COP	110	212/24	163	13	:04:47
LVM	063	212/24	180	20	:06:40
REEPO	067	212/24	179	39	:13:04
BIL	069	212/24	179	38	:12:44
APP/LND					:15:00
TOTAL					1:24:44

10-41. Answer B. GFDICM 10C (AIM)
Planning for an instrument flight should include a preflight weather briefing. This briefing should consist of the latest or most current weather, airport, and enroute NAVAID information. This briefing service may be obtained from an FSS, either by telephone, by radio when airborne, or in person. ATIS (answer A) will have only a destination's flight information, and the Notices to Airmen publication (answer C) may not have the most current information and it does not contain weather reports.

Form Approved: OMB No. 2120-0034

U.S. DEPARTMENT OF TRANSPORTATION FEDERAL AVIATION ADMINISTRATION **FLIGHT PLAN**	(FAA USE ONLY)	☐ PILOT BRIEFING ☐ STOPOVER	☐ VNR	TIME STARTED	SPECIALIST INITIALS

1. TYPE		2. AIRCRAFT IDENTIFICATION	3. AIRCRAFT TYPE/ SPECIAL EQUIPMENT	4. TRUE AIRSPEED	5. DEPARTURE POINT	6. DEPARTURE TIME		7. CRUISING ALTITUDE
	VFR					PROPOSED (Z)	ACTUAL (Z)	
X	IFR	N242T	C310/	160 KTS	HLN			11000
	DVFR							

8. ROUTE OF FLIGHT

STAKK2, V365 BZN, V86

9. DESTINATION (Name of airport and city)	10. EST. TIME ENROUTE		11. REMARKS
	HOURS	MINUTES	
LOGAN INTL. AIRPORT (BIL)			

12. FUEL ON BOARD		13. ALTERNATE AIRPORT(S)	14. PILOT'S NAME, ADDRESS & TELEPHONE NUMBER & AIRCRAFT HOME BASE	15. NUMBER ABOARD
HOURS	MINUTES			
		N/A	17. DESTINATION CONTACT/TELEPHONE (OPTIONAL)	2

16. COLOR OF AIRCRAFT	CIVIL AIRCRAFT PILOTS. FAR Part 91 requires you file an IFR flight plan to operate under instrument flight rules in controlled airspace. Failure to file could result in a civil penalty not to exceed $1,000 for each violation (Section 901 of the Federal Aviation Act of 1958, as amended). Filing of a VFR flight plan is recommended as a good operating practice. See also Part 99 for requirements concerning DVFR flight plans.
RED/BLACK/WHITE	

FAA Form 7233-1 (8-82)   CLOSE VFR FLIGHT PLAN WITH _____ FSS ON ARRIVAL

AIRCRAFT INFORMATION

MAKE Cessna   MODEL 310R

N 242T   Vso 72

AIRCRAFT EQUIPMENT/STATUS**

**NOTE: X= OPERATIVE   INOP= INOPERATIVE   N/A= NOT APPLICABLE
TRANSPONDER: X (MODE C) X ILS: (LOCALIZER) X (GLIDE SLOPE) INOP
VOR NO. 1 X (NO. 2) X ADF: X RNAV: N/A
VERTICAL PATH COMPUTER: N/A DME: X
MARKER BEACON: X (AUDIO) X (VISUAL) X

FIGURE 74.—Flight Plan and Aircraft Information.

FLIGHT LOG

HELENA REGIONAL AIRPORT TO BILLINGS LOGAN INTL.

CHECK POINTS		ROUTE		WIND	SPEED-KTS		DIST	TIME		FUEL	
FROM	TO	ALTITUDE	COURSE	TEMP	TAS	GS	NM	LEG	TOT	LEG	TOT
HLN	VESTS	STAKK2 CLIMB	103°					:15:0			
	BZN	V365 11000	140°		160						
	LVM	V86 11000	110° / 063°								
	REEPO	V86 11000	067°								
	BIL	V86	069°								
APPROACH & LANDING								:15:0			
	LOGAN INTL										

OTHER DATA:
   NOTE: MAG. VAR. 18° E.

FLIGHT SUMMARY

TIME	FUEL (LB)	
		EN ROUTE
		RESERVE
		MISSED APPR.
		TOTAL

FIGURE 75.—Flight Planning Log.

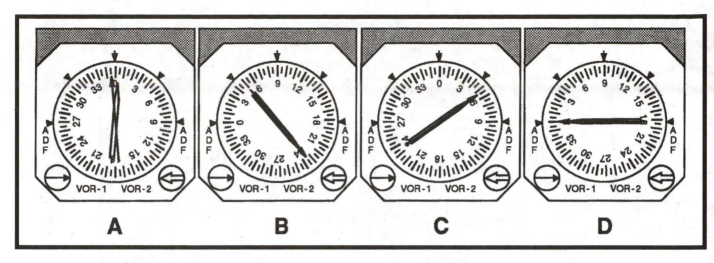

HELENA REGIONAL   (HLN)   2 NE   UTC-7(-6DT)   46°36'25"N 111°58'55"W   GREAT FALLS
  3,873   B   S4   FUEL 100LL, JET A   OX 1,3   AOE   ARFF Index B   H-1C, L-9B
RWY 09-27: H9000X150 (ASPH-PFC)   S-100, D-160, DT-250   HIRL   IAP
  RWY 09: VASI(V4L)—GA 3.0°TCH 45'. Ground.   RWY 27: MALSR. VASI(V4L)—GA 3.0°TCH 55'. Rgt tfc.
RWY 05-23: H4599X75 (ASPH-PFC)   S-21, D-30
  RWY 05: Road.   RWY 23: Fence. Rgt tfc.
RWY 16-34: H2979X75 (ASPH)   S-21, D-30   MIRL
  RWY 34: Ground. Rgt tfc.
AIRPORT REMARKS: Attended 1200-0800Z‡. East 2400' Taxiway C and first 900' Rwy 27 not visible from tower.
  Prior permission for unscheduled FAR 121 operations, Call 406-442-2821. AOE, 1 hour prior notice required,
  phone 449-1569 1500-0000Z‡, 0000-1500Z‡ 449-1024. Twys A;B; high speed and C (between A and D)
  not available for air carrier use by acft with greater than 30 passenger seats. Rwy 16-34 and Rwy 05-23 (except
  between Rwy 09-27 and Twy D) not available for air carrier use by acft with greater than 30 passenger seats.
  When tower closed, ACTIVATE HIRL Rwy 09-27 and MALSR Rwy 27—CTAF, when twr closed MIRL Rwy 16-34
  are off. Ldg fee for all acft over 12,500 lbs. NOTE: See SPECIAL NOTICE—Simultaneous Operations on
  Intersecting Runways.
COMMUNICATIONS: CTAF 118.3   ATIS 120.4 (Mon-Fri 1300-0700Z‡, Sat-Sun 1300-0500Z‡)
  UNICOM 122.95
  GREAT FALLS FSS (GTF) TF 1-800-WX-BRIEF. NOTAM FILE HLN.
  RCO 122.2 122.1R 117.7T (GREAT FALLS FSS)
  APP/DEP CON 119.5 (Mon-Fri 1300-0700Z‡, Sat-Sun 1300-0500Z‡)
  SALT LAKE CENTER APP/DEP CON 133.4 (Mon-Fri 0700-1300Z‡, Sat-Sun 0500-1300Z‡)
  TOWER 118.3 (Mon-Fri 1300-0700Z‡, Sat-Sun 1300-0500Z‡)   GND CON 121.9
RADIO AIDS TO NAVIGATION: NOTAM FILE HLN.
  (H) VORTAC 117.7   HLN   Chan 124   46°36'25"N 111°57'10"W   254° 1.2 NM to fld. 3810/16E.
    VORTAC unusable:
      006°-090° beyond 25 NM below 11,000'   091°-120° beyond 20 NM below 16,000'
      121°-240° beyond 25 NM below 10,000'   355°-006° beyond 15 NM below 17,500'
      241°-320° beyond 25 NM below 10,000'
  CAPITOL NDB (HW) 317   CVP   46°36'24"N 111°56'11"W   254° 1.9 NM to fld.
    NDB unmonitored when tower closed.
  HAUSER NDB (MHW) 386   HAU   46°34'08"N 111°45'26"W   268° 9.6 NM to fld.
  ILS 110.1 I-HLN Rwy 27 ILS unmonitored when tower closed.

VOR RECEIVER CHECK

Facility Name (Arpt Name)	Freq/Ident	Type Check Pt. Gnd. AB/ALT	Azimuth from Fac. Mag	Dist. from Fac. N.M.	Check Point Description
Helena (Helena Regional)	117.7/HLN	G	237	0.7	On Twy E midway between Twy C and Rwy 27.
Kalispell (Glacier Park Intl)	108.4/FCA	A/4000	316	6.4	Over apch end Rwy 29.
Lewistown (Lewistown Muni)	112.0/LWT	A/5200	072	5.4	Over apch end Rwy 07.
Livingston	116.1/LVM	A/6500	234	5.5	Over northern most radio twr NE of city.
Miles City (Frank Wiley Field)	112.1/MLS	G	036	4.2	On twy leading to Rwy 30.
Missoula (Missoula Intl)	112.8/MSO	G	340	0.6	On edge of ramp in front of Admin Building.

FIGURE 76.—VOR Indications and Excerpts from Airport/Facility Directory (HLN).

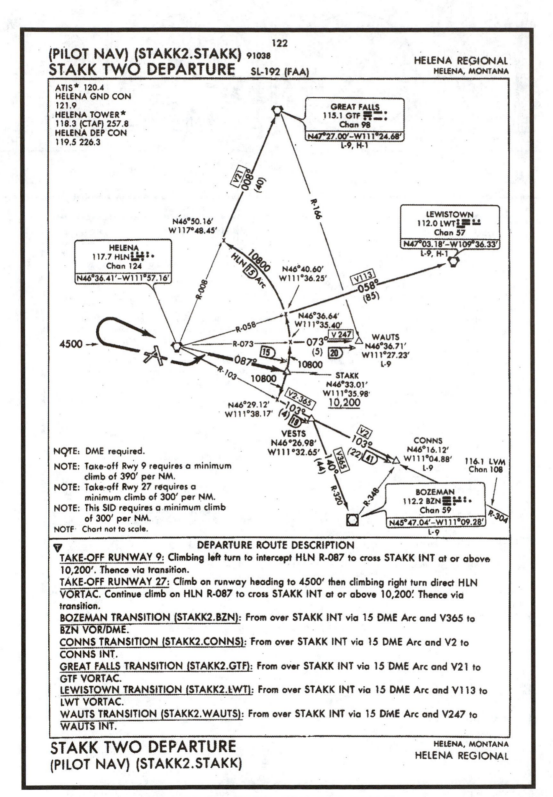

(PILOT NAV) (STAKK2.STAKK) 91038
122
STAKK TWO DEPARTURE SL-192 (FAA)

HELENA REGIONAL
HELENA, MONTANA

ATIS★ 120.4
HELENA GND CON
121.9
HELENA TOWER★
118.3 (CTAF) 257.8
HELENA DEP CON
119.5 226.3

GREAT FALLS
115.1 GTF
Chan 98
N47°27.00'–W111°24.68'
L-9, H-1

LEWISTOWN
112.0 LWT
Chan 57
N47°03.18'–W109°36.33'
L-9, H-1

HELENA
117.7 HLN
Chan 124
N46°36.41'–W111°57.16'

N46°50.16'
W117°48.45'

N46°40.60'
W111°36.25'

V113
058°
(85)

R-166

V21
008°
(40)

HLN 15 Arc
10800

R-008

R-058

N46°36.64'
W111°35.40'

WAUTS
N46°36.71'
W111°27.23'
L-9

R-073

073°
(5)

V 247
20

4500 →

15

087°
R-103   10800

10800

STAKK
N46°33.01'
W111°35.98'
10,200

N46°29.12'
W111°38.17'

V2.365
103°
(4)
19

VESTS
N46°26.98'
W111°32.65'

V2
103°

V365
40°
(22)
41

CONNS
N46°16.12'
W111°04.88'
L-9

116.1 LVM
Chan 108

R-320

R-348

BOZEMAN
112.2 BZN
Chan 59
N45°47.04'–W111°09.28'
L-9

R-304

NOTE: DME required.
NOTE: Take-off Rwy 9 requires a minimum
climb of 390' per NM.
NOTE: Take-off Rwy 27 requires a
minimum climb of 300' per NM.
NOTE: This SID requires a minimum climb
of 300' per NM.
NOTE: Chart not to scale.

DEPARTURE ROUTE DESCRIPTION

<u>TAKE-OFF RUNWAY 9:</u> Climbing left turn to intercept HLN R-087 to cross STAKK INT at or above
10,200'. Thence via transition.
<u>TAKE-OFF RUNWAY 27:</u> Climb on runway heading to 4500' then climbing right turn direct HLN
VORTAC. Continue climb on HLN R-087 to cross STAKK INT at or above 10,200'. Thence via
transition.
<u>BOZEMAN TRANSITION (STAKK2.BZN):</u> From over STAKK INT via 15 DME Arc and V365 to
BZN VOR/DME.
<u>CONNS TRANSITION (STAKK2.CONNS):</u> From over STAKK INT via 15 DME Arc and V2 to
CONNS INT.
<u>GREAT FALLS TRANSITION (STAKK2.GTF):</u> From over STAKK INT via 15 DME Arc and V21 to
GTF VORTAC.
<u>LEWISTOWN TRANSITION (STAKK2.LWT):</u> From over STAKK INT via 15 DME Arc and V113 to
LWT VORTAC.
<u>WAUTS TRANSITION (STAKK2.WAUTS):</u> From over STAKK INT via 15 DME Arc and V247 to
WAUTS INT.

STAKK TWO DEPARTURE
(PILOT NAV) (STAKK2.STAKK)

HELENA, MONTANA
HELENA REGIONAL

FIGURE 77.—STAKK TWO DEPARTURE.

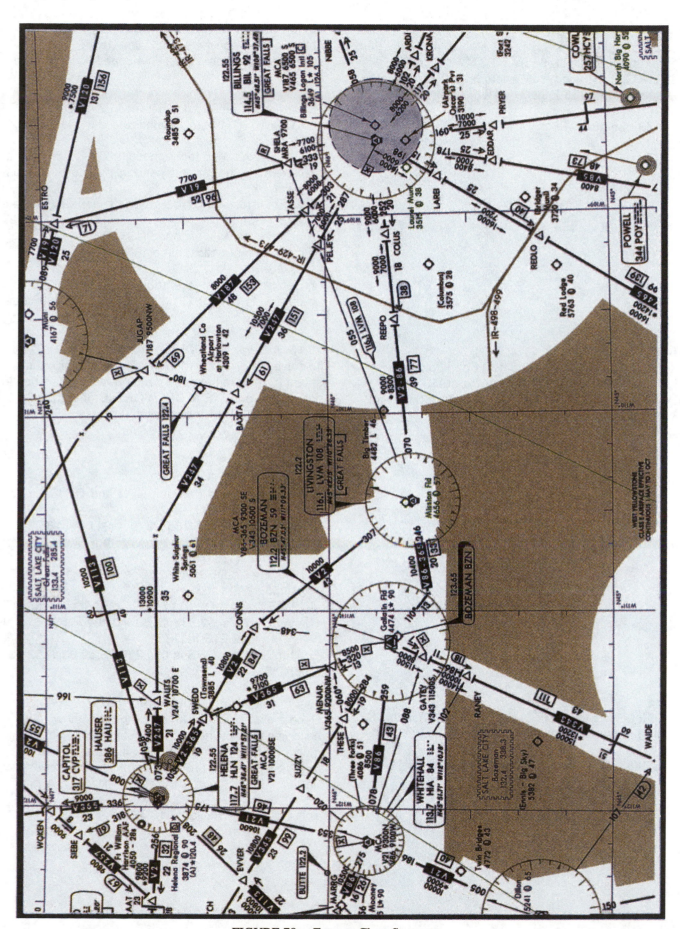

FIGURE 78.—Enroute Chart Segment.

10-42   H342

(Refer to figure 91 on page 5-12.) What should be the approximate elapsed time from BZN VOR to DBS VORTAC, if the wind is 24 knots from 260° and your intended TAS is 185 knots? (VAR 17°E.)

A — 33 minutes.
B — 37 minutes.
C — 39 minutes.

10-42. Answer C. GFDICM 10C (PHB)

This question requires you to calculate the ground-speed and then complete a time-speed-distance problem.

1. Determine the distance between BZN VOR and DBS VORTAC (111 n.m. as indicated in the box near V343).
2. Convert the wind to magnetic (260° − 17° = 243°).
3. Determine the groundspeed using your flight computer.
   a. Enter the wind direction and speed (243° true at 24 kts.).
   b. Enter the true airspeed (185 kts.).
   c. Enter magnetic course 186°.
   d. GS = 171 kts.
4. Determine the time enroute using your flight computer (111 n.m. at 171 kts = 38:57). This is rounded to 39 min.

10-43   H342

(Refer to figure 91 on page 5-12.) Southbound on V257, at what time should you arrive at DBS VORTAC if you crossed over CPN VORTAC at 0850 and over DIVID Intersection at 0854?

A — 0939.
B — 0943.
C — 0947.

10-43. Answer B. GFDICM 10C (PHB)

To solve the problem you must first solve for ground-speed (GS). Use the speed and remaining distance to determine your ETE to DBS VORTAC, then add this to the ATA over DIVID Int. to determine your ETA over DBS VORTAC.

1. Determine GS
   a. (0854 − 0850 = 4 min.)
   b. The distance between CPN and DIVID Int. is 9 n.m. (figure 91)
   c. Groundspeed = 135 kts (9 ÷ :04:00 = 135)
2. Determine distance between DIVID Int. and DBS VORTAC. (110 n.m.)
3. The time to DBS VORTAC is :48:53 (110 ÷ 135 = :48:53).
4. The ETE from DIVID to DBS VORTAC plus the ATA over DIVID is :52:53 (:48:53 + 04:00 = :52:53). This is your total ETE to DBS.
5. The ETA over DBS is 09:42:53 (8:50:00 + :52:53 = 9:42:53).

10-44   B10

If a pilot elects to proceed to the selected alternate, the landing minimums used at that airport should be the

A — minimums specified for the approach procedure selected.
B — alternate minimums shown on the approach chart.
C — minimums shown for that airport in a separate listing of "IFR Alternate Minimums."

10-44. Answer A. GFDICM 10C (IFH)

Once a pilot proceeds to the alternate, it now becomes the destination, and published landing minimums for that approach apply. Alternate minimums (answers B and C) are for flight planning purposes only.

This question is similar to 10-45.

10-45   B10

When making an instrument approach at the selected alternate airport, what landing minimums apply?

A — Standard alternate minimums (600-2 or 800-2).
B — The IFR alternate minimums listed for that airport.
C — The landing minimums published for the type of procedure selected.

10-46   J01

By which means may a pilot determine if a Loran C equipped aircraft is approved for IFR operations?

A — Not necessary; Loran C is not approved for IFR.
B — Check aircraft logbook.
C — Check the Airplane Flight Manual Supplement.

10-47   B10

When a pilot elects to proceed to the selected alternate airport, which minimums apply for landing at the alternate?

A — 600-1 if the airport has an ILS.
B — Ceiling 200 feet above the published minimum; visibility 2 miles.
C — The landing minimums for the approach to be used.

10-48   B10

What are the alternate minimums that must be forecast at the ETA for an airport that has a precision approach procedure?

A — 400-foot ceiling and 2 miles visibility.
B — 600-foot ceiling and 2 miles visibility.
C — 800-foot ceiling and 2 miles visibility.

10-49   B10

What point at the destination should be used to compute estimated time en route on an IFR flight plan?

A — The final approach fix on the expected instrument approach.
B — The initial approach fix on the expected instrument approach.
C — The point of first intended landing.

10-45. Answer C. GFDICM 10C (IFH)
See explanation for Question 10-44. Answers (A) and (B) are incorrect, since they are for flight planning purposes only.

10-46. Answer C. GFDICM 10C (AIM)
Approval of LORAN-C receivers for IFR operations will be documented in the Airplane Flight Manual Supplement, on FAA Form 337 or in aircraft maintenance records, or by a placard in the airplane. Answer (A) is wrong because some Loran C equipment is certified for certain IFR operations. Aircraft maintenance records, rather than the aircraft logbook (answer B), will show whether the Loran C is certified for IFR or VFR operations.

10-47. Answer C. GFDICM 10C (IFH)
When you proceed to your alternate, it now becomes your destination, and you may use the published landing minimums for the approach you will use. Remember, alternate minimums are used only for flight planning purposes. Answers (A) and (B) are incorrect because published landing minimums apply. These answers should not be confused with the IFR alternate airport weather minimums of 600-2 for a precision approach and 800-2 for a nonprecision approach.

This question is similar to 10-44 and 10-45.

10-48. Answer B. GFDICM 10C (FAR 91.169)
To use an airport with a precision approach as an alternate, it must be forecast to have a ceiling of at least 600 feet and a visibility of 2 miles at the estimated time of arrival (ETA). Answer (A) has an incorrect ceiling, and (C) is the minimum ceiling and visibility for an alternate airport with a nonprecision approach.

10-49. Answer C. GFDICM 10C (FAR 91.153, 91.169)
Both IFR and VFR flight plans include the estimated time enroute to the point of first intended landing. Answers (A) and (B) are incorrect because the time enroute is to the airport, not an approach fix.

FLIGHT LOG

SANTA BARBARA MUNI TO PASO ROBLES MUNI

CHECK POINTS		ROUTE	COURSE	WIND	SPEED-KTS		DIST	TIME		FUEL	
FROM	TO	ALTITUDE		TEMP	TAS	GS	NM	LEG	TOT	LEG	TOT
SBA	HABUT	HABUT 1 CLIMB	253°					:08:00			
	GVO	163°R 8000	343°		158						
	MQO	V27 8000	306°								
	PRB	V113	358°								
APPROACH & LANDING		DESCENT						:10:00			
	PRB AIRPORT										

OTHER DATA:
NOTE: MAG. VAR. 16' E.

FLIGHT SUMMARY

TIME	FUEL (LB)	
		EN ROUTE
		RESERVE
		MISSED APPR.
		TOTAL

FIGURE 51.—Flight Planning Log.

FEDERAL AVIATION REGULATIONS

SECTION A
14 CFR PART 61 — CERTIFICATION: PILOTS AND FLIGHT INSTRUCTORS

WHEN AN INSTRUMENT RATING IS REQUIRED

1. The pilot in command of a civil aircraft must have an instrument rating when operating under IFR, in weather conditions less than the minimum for VFR flight, or in Class A airspace. An instrument rating is for any flight on an IFR flight plan even if the flight is in VFR conditions.

2. An instrument rating is required for most commercial operations. A newly certificated commercial airplane pilot must hold an instrument pilot rating to carry passengers for hire on cross-country flights of more than 50 NM and to carry passengers for hire at night.

INSTRUMENT CURRENCY

3. To maintain IFR currency, you must, within the preceding six months, perform at least six instrument approaches, holding procedures, and intercepting and tracking courses through the use of navigation systems. These procedures must be performed and logged under actual or simulated instrument conditions, either in flight in the appropriate category of aircraft for the instrument privileges sought or in a flight simulator or flight training device that is representative of the aircraft category for the instrument privileges sought.

4. After your recent IFR experience lapses, you may not act as pilot in command under IFR. However, you have an additional six months in which to gain the necessary instrument experience, with the help of a safety pilot or CFII, or using a simulator. After that time, you must pass an instrument proficiency check before you can again act as PIC under IFR.

5. An instrument proficiency check must be in the category of aircraft involved, and given by an approved FAA examiner, instrument instructor, or FAA inspector. After successfully completing an instrument proficiency check, you remain current for 6 months even if no further IFR flights are made.

LOGGING INSTRUMENT TIME

6. If a pilot enters the condition of flight in the pilot logbook as simulated instrument conditions, the place and type of each instrument approach completed and name of safety pilot must also be entered?

7. A certificated instrument flight instructor may log as instrument flight time all time during which the instructor acts as instrument instructor in actual instrument weather conditions.

8. When on an instrument flight plan, you may log as instrument time only the time you controlled the aircraft solely by reference to flight instruments.

11-1   A20

No pilot may act as pilot in command of an aircraft under IFR or in weather conditions less than the minimums prescribed for VFR unless that pilot has, within the preceding 6 calendar months, completed at least

A — three instrument approaches and logged 3 hours.
B — six instrument flights under actual IFR conditions.
C — six instrument approaches, holding procedures, intercepting and tracking courses using navigational systems, or passed an instrument proficiency check.

11-1. Answer C. (FAR 61.57)

Six approaches, holding procedures, and intercepting and tracking courses through the use of navigation systems are required. An instrument proficiency check also meets the requirement. Answer (A) is incorrect because there is no time requirement. Answer (B) is incorrect because the term "instrument flight" is not specific, and regulations do not state that any procedures must be accomplished in IFR conditions.

11-2   A24

What limitation is imposed on a newly certificated commercial airplane pilot if that person does not hold an instrument pilot rating?

A — The carrying of passengers or property for hire on cross-country flights at night is limited to a radius of 50 nautical miles (NM).
B — The carrying of passengers for hire on cross-country flights is limited to 50 NM for night flights, but not limited for day flights.
C — The carrying of passengers for hire on cross-country flights is limited to 50 NM and the carrying of passengers for hire at night is prohibited.

11-2. Answer C. (FAR 61.129)

If a commercial pilot is certified without an instrument rating, his/her pilot certificate will be endorsed with a limitation prohibiting the carriage of passengers for hire in airplanes on cross-country flights beyond 50 nautical miles, or at night. Answers (A) and (B) are wrong because the carriage of passengers for hire at night, even within a 50 NM radius, is prohibited.

11-3   A20

What portion of dual instruction time may a certificated instrument flight instructor log as instrument flight time?

A — All time during which the instructor acts as instrument instructor, regardless of weather conditions.
B — All time during which the instructor acts as instrument instructor in actual instrument weather conditions.
C — Only the time during which the instructor flies the aircraft by reference to instruments.

11-3. Answer B. (FAR 61.51)

A certificated instrument flight instructor may log instrument time during that portion of the flight he/she acts as an instrument flight instructor in actual instrument weather conditions. Answer (A) is wrong because the logging of time does depend on the existing weather conditions. Answer (C) is wrong because the instructor is not required to fly the aircraft in order to log time.

11-4   A20

Which flight time may be logged as instrument time when on an instrument flight plan?

A — All of the time the aircraft was not controlled by ground references.
B — Only the time you controlled the aircraft solely by reference to flight instruments.
C — Only the time you were flying in IFR weather conditions.

11-4. Answer B. (FAR 61.51)

You may log instrument flight time anytime you operate an aircraft solely by reference to instruments. This can done in actual or simulated instrument flight conditions. Answer (A) is incorrect because VFR flight is common above an overcast. Answer (C) is wrong since it does not include the regulatory provisions for simulation.

11-5   A20

To meet the minimum instrument experience requirements, within the last 6 calendar months you need

A — six hours in the same category aircraft.
B — six hours in the same category aircraft, and at
      least 3 of the 6 hours in actual IFR conditions.
C — six instrument approaches, holding procedures,
      and intercepting and tracking courses in the
      appropriate category of aircraft.

11-6   A20

After your recent IFR experience lapses, how much
time do you have before you must pass an instrument
competency check to act as pilot in command under
IFR?

A — 6 months.
B — 90 days.
C — 12 months.

11-7   A20

An instrument rated pilot, who has not logged any
instrument time in 1 year or more, cannot serve as
pilot in command under IFR, unless the pilot

A — passes an instrument proficiency check in the
      category of aircraft involved, followed by 6
      hours and six instrument approaches, 3 of those
      hours in the category of aircraft involved.
B — passes an instrument proficiency check in the
      category of aircraft involved, given by an
      approved FAA examiner, instrument instructor,
      or FAA inspector.
C — completes the required 6 hours and six approach-
      es, followed by an instrument proficiency check
      given by an FAA-designated examiner.

11-8   A20

A pilot's recent IFR experience expires on July 1 of
this year. What is the latest date the pilot can meet the
IFR experience requirement without having to take an
instrument proficiency check?

A — December 31, this year.
B — June 30, next year.
C — July 31, this year.

11-5. Answer C. (FAR 61.57)
Six approaches, holding procedures, and intercepting
and tracking courses through the use of navigation
systems are required. An instrument proficiency check
also meets the requirement. Answers (A) and (B) are
incorrect because there is no time requirement.

11-6. Answer A. (FAR 61.57)
If you do not meet the recent instrument experience
requirements during the prescribed 6 months, you
have 6 additional calendar months to meet the
experience requirements. Answer (B) is wrong; it
refers to a landing currency requirement for carrying
passengers. Answer (C) is also incorrect since it
implies you have 12 months after expiration of the
recent experience requirement before an instrument
competency check is required.

11-7. Answer B. (FAR 61.57)
If you do not meet the recent instrument experience
requirements during the prescribed 6 months or 6
calendar months thereafter, you may not act as pilot in
command under IFR or in weather conditions less
than VFR until you pass an instrument proficiency
check. Answers (A) and (C) are wrong because an
instrument proficiency check is all that is required.

11-8. Answer A. (FAR 61.57)
See explanation for Question 11-6.

11-9   A20
What minimum conditions are necessary for the instrument approaches required for IFR currency?

A — The approaches may be made in an aircraft, approved instrument ground trainer, or any combination of these.
B — At least three approaches must be made in the same category of aircraft to be flown.
C — At least three approaches must be made in the same category and class of aircraft to be flown.

11-9. Answer A. (FAR 61.57)
To maintain instrument currency, you must complete 6 instrument approaches. The approaches can be made in the category of aircraft to be used, an approved instrument ground trainer, or any combination of the two. Answers (B) and (C) are wrong because all approaches can be made in a ground trainer.

11-10   A20
How may a pilot satisfy the recent flight experience requirement necessary to act as pilot in command in IMC in powered aircraft? Within the previous 6 calendar months, logged

A — six instrument approaches and 3 hours under actual or simulated IFR conditions within the last 6 months; three of the approaches must be in the category of aircraft involved.
B — six instrument approaches, holding procedures, and intercepting and tracking courses using navigational systems.
C — 6 hours of instrument time under actual or simulated IFR conditions within the last 3 months, including at least six instrument approaches of any kind. Three of the 6 hours must be in flight in any category aircraft.

11-10. Answer B. (FAR 61.57)
Six approaches, holding procedures, and intercepting and tracking courses through the use of navigation systems are required. An instrument proficiency check also meets the requirement. Answer (A) is incorrect because there is no time requirement, and all approaches must be in the category of aircraft, or in a simulator representative of that category. Answer (C) is also incorrect because there is no time requirement for flight in IFR conditions.

11-11   A20
How long does a pilot meet the recency of experience requirements for IFR flight after successfully completing an instrument competency check if no further IFR flights are made?

A — 90 days.
B — 6 calendar months.
C — 12 calendar months

11-11. Answer B. (FAR 61.57)
An instrument competency check satisfies the recent IFR experience requirements for 6 months. Answers (A) and (C) are wrong because the time frames apply to other requirements listed in FAR 61.57.

11-12   A20
What recent instrument flight experience requirements must be met before you may act as pilot in command of an airplane under IFR?

A — A minimum of six instrument approaches in an aircraft, at least three of which must be in the same category within the preceding 6 calendar months.
B — A minimum of six instrument approaches in an airplane, or an approved simulator (airplane) or ground trainer, within the preceding 6 calendar months.
C — A minimum of six instrument approaches, at least three of which must be in an aircraft within the preceding 6 calendar months..

11-12. Answer B. (FAR 61.57)
Before a pilot can act as pilot in command of an airplane under IFR, the pilot must have logged six instrument approaches under actual or simulated instrument conditions, either in flight in the appropriate category of aircraft, or in a flight simulator or flight training device that is representative of the aircraft category. In addition, the pilot must have performed holding procedures, as well as intercepting and tracking courses through the use of navigation systems. Answers (A) and (C) are both incorrect since all approaches can be made in an appropriate category of aircraft, or in a flight simulator, or flight training device representative of the aircraft category.

11-13   A20

What additional instrument experience is required for you to meet the recent flight experience requirements to act as pilot in command of an airplane under IFR? Your present instrument experience within the preceding 6 calendar months is:

1.   3 hours with holding, intercepting, and tracking courses in an approved airplane flight simulator.
2.   two instrument approaches in an airplane.

A — Three hours of simulated or actual instrument flight time in a helicopter, and two instrument approaches in an airplane or helicopter.
B — Four instrument approaches in an airplane, or an approved airplane flight simulator or training device.
C — Three instrument approaches in an airplane.

11-13. Answer B. (FAR 61.57)

Before acting as pilot in command of an airplane under IFR or in weather conditions less than VFR, you must have logged, within the preceding 6 calendar months, at least six instrument approaches, holding procedures, and intercepting and tracking courses through the use of navigation systems. Answer (A) is wrong because no additional flight time is required, nor is it required in a helicopter. Answer (C) is wrong because a total of six instrument approaches must be completed.

11-14   A20

To meet the minimum required instrument flight experience to act as pilot in command of an aircraft under IFR, you must have logged within the preceding 6 calendar months in the same category of aircraft: six instrument approaches,

A — and 6 hours of instrument time in any aircraft.
B — three of which must be in the same category and class of aircraft to be flown, and 6 hours of instrument time in any aircraft.
C — holding procedures, intercepting and tracking courses through the use of navigation systems.

11-14. Answer C. (FAR 61.57)

Six approaches, holding procedures, and intercepting and tracking courses through the use of navigation systems are required. Answer (A) is incorrect because there is no time requirement. Answer (B) is incorrect because all six approaches must be in THE SAME CATEGORY aircraft, or in a simulator representing that category aircraft, and it also incorrectly mentions a time requirement.

11-15   A20

A certificated commercial pilot who carries passengers for hire at night or in excess of 50 NM is required to have at least

A — an instrument rating in the same category and class of aircraft.
B — an associated type rating if the airplane is of the multiengine class.
C — a First-Class Medical Certificate.

11-15. Answer A. (FAR 61.133)

In order to carry passengers for hire at night or in excess of 50 nautical miles, you must hold a commercial pilot certificate with an instrument rating in the same category and class of aircraft listed on the commercial pilot certificate. Answer (B) is wrong because an instrument rating is not mentioned. Answer (C) is wrong because a First-Class Medical Certificate is not required.

11-16   A20

You intend to carry passengers for hire on a night VFR flight in a single-engine airplane within a 25-mile radius of the departure airport. You are required to possess at least which rating(s)?

A — A Commercial Pilot Certificate with a single-engine land rating.
B — A Commercial Pilot Certificate with a single-engine and instrument (airplane) rating.
C — A Private Pilot Certificate with a single-engine land and instrument airplane rating.

11-16. Answer B. (FAR 61.133)

See explanation for Question 11-15. Answer (A) is wrong because it doesn't mention the requirement for an instrument rating. Answer (C) is wrong because you must have a commercial certificate to fly passengers for hire.

11-17   A20

Do regulations permit you to act as pilot in command of an airplane in IMC if you hold a Private Pilot Certificate with ASEL, Rotorcraft category, with helicopter class rating and instrument helicopter rating?

A — No, however, you may do so if you hold an Airline Transport Pilot-Airplane Certificate, limited to VFR.

B — No, you must hold either an unrestricted Airline Transport Pilot-Airplane Certificate or an airplane instrument rating.

C — Yes, if you comply with the recent IFR experience requirements for a helicopter.

11-18   A20

Under which condition must the pilot in command of a civil aircraft have at least an instrument rating?

A — When operating in class E airspace.

B — For any flight above an altitude of 1,200 feet AGL, when the visibility is less than 3 miles.

C — For a flight in VFR conditions while on an IFR flight plan.

11-19   A20

Which limitation is imposed on the holder of a Commercial Pilot Certificate if that person does not hold an instrument rating?

A — That person is limited to private pilot privileges at night.

B — The carrying of passengers or property for hire on cross-country flights at night is limited to a radius of 50 NM.

C — The carrying of passengers for hire on cross-country flights is limited to 50 NM and the carrying of passengers for hire at night is prohibited.

11-20   A20

To carry passengers for hire in an airplane on cross-country flights of more than 50 NM from the departure airport, the pilot in command is required to hold at least

A — a Category II pilot authorization.

B — a First-Class Medical certificate.

C — a Commercial Pilot Certificate with an instrument rating.

11-17. Answer B. (FAR 61.167)

Since an instrument rating is category specific, you may not operate an airplane in IMC without an instrument airplane rating. However, if you hold an unrestricted Airline Transport Rating you are entitled to the same privileges as a pilot who holds a commercial pilot certificate with an instrument rating.

11-18. Answer C. (FAR 61.3)

To operate an aircraft under instrument flight rules or in weather conditions less than those prescribed for VFR, you must hold an instrument rating and meet the IFR recent experience requirements. Answer (A) is wrong because an instrument rating is not required to fly in the segment of Class E airspace formerly known as the continental control area. Answer (B) is wrong because an instrument rating is not required when flying above 1,200 feet AGL, and below 10,000 feet MSL, with a visibility of 1 statute mile or greater in Class G (uncontrolled) airspace.

11-19. Answer C. (FAR 61.133)

In order to carry passengers for hire, you must hold a commercial pilot certificate. In addition, to carry passengers for hire at night or on cross-country flights beyond 50 NM, you must hold an instrument rating. Answer (A) is wrong because you are not limited to private pilot privileges alone. Commercial pilot privileges may be exercised, except for the limitations due to the lack of an instrument rating. Answer (B) is wrong because you cannot carry passengers for hire at night.

11-20. Answer C. (FAR 61.133)

See explanation for Question 11-19. Answers (A) and (B) are wrong because neither a Category II pilot authorization nor a First-Class Medical Certificate are required to carry passengers for hire.

SECTION B
14 CFR PART 91 — GENERAL OPERATING AND FLIGHT RULES

PREFLIGHT PLANNING

1. FAR 91.103 requires that a pilot in command, before beginning a flight, become familiar with all available information concerning that flight. For a flight under IFR or a flight not in the vicinity of an airport, this information must specifically include weather reports and forecasts, fuel requirements, alternatives available if the planned flight cannot be completed, and any known traffic delays of which the pilot in command has been advised by ATC. For any flight, the PIC must determine the runway lengths at airports of intended use, and takeoff and landing distance information for the aircraft.

2. An alternate airport must be listed in an IFR flight plan when the forecast ceiling and visibility is less than 2,000 feet and 3 statute miles (SM), from 1 hour before to 1 hour after the ETA.

3. To list as an alternate an airport that has that has only a VOR approach or other nonprecision approach with standard alternate minimums, the forecast at the ETA must be at least an 800 foot ceiling and 2 SM visibility. If the airport has an available precision approach and you are equipped to fly it, then the required minimums are a 600-foot ceiling and 2 SM visibility.

4. If an airport has no approved IAP, and you wish to list it as an alternate, the ceiling and visibility at ETA must allow descent from the MEA, approach, and landing, under basic VFR.

5. If weather conditions are such that it is required to designate an alternate airport on your IFR flight plan, you should plan to carry enough fuel to arrive at the first airport of intended landing, fly from that airport to the alternate airport, and fly thereafter for 45 minutes at normal cruising speed.

6. Except when necessary for takeoff or landing or unless otherwise authorized by the Administrator, the minimum altitude for IFR flight is 2,000 feet above the highest obstacle over designated mountainous terrain; 1,000 feet above the highest obstacle over terrain elsewhere.

IFR CLEARANCE REQUIRED

7. You may not enter controlled airspace under IFR unless you file a flight plan and receive a clearance prior to entering controlled airspace.

8. You must have an instrument rating and an IFR clearance for flight in Class A airspace, even in visual meteorological conditions (VMC).

9. A pilot on an IFR flight plan is responsible for avoiding other aircraft whenever whether conditions permit.

TRANSPONDER REQUIRED

10. In the 48 contiguous states, excluding the airspace at or below 2,500 feet AGL, an operable coded transponder equipped with Mode C capability is required in all controlled airspace at and above 10,000 feet MSL.

11. In addition to a VOR receiver and two-way communications capability, an operable coded transponder having Mode C capability is required for IFR operation in Class B airspace?

12. ATC may authorize a deviation from the FAR 91 requirement for a transponder in class B airspace, if a request for the proposed flight is made to ATC at least 1 hour before the flight. If an aircraft's transponder fails during flight within Class B airspace, ATC may authorize deviation from the transponder requirement to allow aircraft to continue to the airport of ultimate destination.

13. A transponder is required within and above Class C airspace, and at any altitude within 4 n.m. of the primary airport in Class C airspace.

14. Generally, a transponder is not required for flight within Class D airspace. However, if this Class D airspace is within 30 n.m. of the primary airport within Class B airspace, a transponder is required because it is within the 30 n.m. mode C veil.

OXYGEN REQUIREMENTS

15. If an unpressurized aircraft is operated above 12,500 feet MSL, but not more than 14,000 feet MSL, the minimum flightcrew is required to use supplemental oxygen for the time beyond 30 minutes. Above 14,000 feet MSL, the minimum flightcrew is required to use supplemental oxygen continuously. Above 15,000 feet MSL, oxygen must be available to passengers.

OTHER REGULATIONS

16. The use of certain portable electronic devices is prohibited on aircraft that are being operated under IFR or in certain commercial passenger-carrying operations.
17. A person who occupies the other control seat as safety pilot during simulated instrument flight must be appropriately rated in the aircraft.

11-21   **B08**

Before beginning any flight under IFR, the pilot in command must become familiar with all available information concerning that flight. including:

A — all instrument approaches at the destination airport.
B — an alternate airport on the flight plan and confirm adequate takeoff and landing performance at the destination airport.
C — the runway lengths at airports of intended use, and the alternatives available if the flight cannot be completed.

11-22   **B07**

The use of certain portable electronic devices is prohibited on aircraft that are being operated under

A — IFR.
B — VFR.
C — DVFR.

11-23   **B10**

During your preflight planning for an IFR flight, you determine that the first airport of intended landing has no instrument approach prescribed in 14 CFR part 97. The weather forecast for one hour before through one hour after your estimated time of arrival is 3000' scattered with 5 miles visibility. To meet the fuel requirements for this flight, you must be able to fly to the first airport of intended landing,

A — and then fly for 45 minutes at normal cruising speed.
B — then to the alternate airport, and then for 30 minutes at normal cruising speed.
C — then to the alternate airport, and then for 45 minutes at normal cruising speed.

11-21. Answer C. (FAR 91.103)

For any flight conducted under IFR or any flight not in the vicinity of an airport, the information obtained must include runway lengths at airports of intended use, takeoff and landing distances, weather reports and forecasts, fuel requirements, alternatives available if the flight cannot be completed, and any known traffic delays. Answers (A) and (B) are wrong because you are not specifically required by regulation to be familiar with all approaches at your destination, nor are you required to list an alternate when weather is expected to be above alternate minimums.

11-22. Answer A. (FAR 91.21)

For any flight, no person nor may any operator or pilot in command allow the operation of any portable electronic device on any U.S. registered civil aircraft operated by a holder of an air carrier operating certificate or while under IFR (answer A). There are certain exceptions to this rule such as portable voice recorders, hearing aids, heart pacemakers, electric shavers, and devices that the operator has determined will not cause interference with navigation or communication systems. Answers (B) and (C) are wrong.

11-23. Answer C. (FAR 91.167)

Since the airport of intended landing has no instrument approach prescribed, the pilot has to plan for enough fuel to get to the original destination, an alternate destination, and be able to fly for an additional 45 minutes. Answer (A) pertains to VFR night fuel minimums only. Answer (B) only allows for 30 minutes extra fuel after reaching your alternate airport.

11-24 B10

Except when necessary for takeoff or landing or unless otherwise authorized by the Administrator, the minimum altitude for IFR flight is

A — 3,000 feet over all terrain.
B — 3,000 feet over designated mountainous terrain; 2,000 feet over terrain elsewhere.
C — 2,000 feet above the highest obstacle over designated mountainous terrain; 1,000 feet above the highest obstacle over terrain elsewhere.

11-24. Answer C. (FAR 91.177)

The minimum altitude for IFR flight in mountainous areas is 2,000 feet above the highest obstacle within a horizontal distance of 4 nautical miles from the course to be flown. In all other areas, it's 1,000 feet above the highest obstacle within 4 nautical miles from the course to be flown. Answers (A) and (B) are wrong because they indicate altitudes that exceed those required.

11-25 B11

If the aircraft's transponder fails during flight within Class B airspace,

A — the pilot should immediately request clearance to depart the Class B airspace.
B — ATC may authorize deviation from the transponder requirement to allow aircraft to continue to the airport of ultimate destination.
C — aircraft must immediately descend below 1,200 feet AGL and proceed to destination.

11-25. Answer B. (FAR 91.215)

If your transponder fails while in Class B airspace, ATC may authorize you to continue to your destination, including any intermediate stops, and/or proceed to a place where repairs can be made. Answers (A) and
(C) are wrong because neither permit the flexibility provided by the regulations.

This question is similar to number 11-49.

11-26 A20

If a pilot enters the condition of flight in the pilot logbook as simulated instrument conditions, what qualifying information must also be entered?

A — Number and type of instrument approaches completed and route of flight.
B — Location and type of each instrument approach completed and name of safety pilot.
C — Name and pilot certificate number of safety pilot and type of approaches completed.

11-26. Answer B. (FAR 61.51)

The logbook entries must include the location and type of each instrument approach completed, and the name of the safety pilot for each simulated instrument flight. The number of approaches, route of flight (answer A), and certificate number of the safety pilot (answer C) do not have to be logged.

11-27 B08

What are the minimum qualifications for a person who occupies the other control seat as safety pilot during simulated instrument flight?

A — Private pilot certificate with appropriate category and class ratings for the aircraft.
B — Private pilot with appropriate category, class, and instrument ratings.
C — Private pilot with instrument rating.

11-27. Answer A. (FAR 91.109)

No person may operate an aircraft in simulated instrument flight unless the other control seat is occupied by an appropriately rated safety pilot. Appropriately rated means the safety pilot must hold at least a private pilot certificate with the category and class ratings appropriate to the aircraft to be flown. The safety pilot does not need to hold an instrument rating.

11-28 A20

When are you required to have an instrument rating for flight in VMC?

A — Flight through an MOA.
B — Flight into class A airspace.
C — Flight into an ADIZ.

11-28. Answer B. (FAR 91.135)

All flights in Class A airspace must be conducted on an instrument flight plan by an instrument rated pilot. Answers (A) and (C) are incorrect because flights through a military operations area (MOA) and into an air defense identification zone (ADIZ) do not require an instrument flight plan.

11-29   A20

The pilot in command of a civil aircraft must have an instrument rating only when operating

A — in weather conditions less than the minimum prescribed for VFR flight.

B — under IFR, in weather conditions less than the minimum for VFR flight, or in class A airspace.

C — under IFR in positive control airspace.

11-30   B10

What are the minimum fuel requirements in IFR conditions, if the first airport of intended landing is forecast to have a 1,500-foot ceiling and 3 miles visibility at flight-planned ETA? Fuel to fly to the first airport of intended landing,

A — and fly thereafter for 45 minutes at normal cruising speed.

B — fly to the alternate, and fly thereafter for 45 minutes at normal cruising speed.

C — fly to the alternate, and fly thereafter for 30 minutes at normal cruising speed.

11-31   B08

Before beginning any flight under IFR, the pilot in command must become familiar with all available information concerning that flight. In addition, the pilot must

A — list an alternate airport on the flight plan and become familiar with the instrument approaches to that airport.

B — list an alternate airport on the flight plan and confirm adequate takeoff and landing performance at the destination airport.

C — be familiar with the runway lengths at airports of intended use, and the alternatives available if the flight cannot be completed.

11-32   B11

In the 48 contiguous states, excluding the airspace at or below 2,500 feet AGL, an operable coded transponder equipped with Mode C capability is required in all controlled airspace at and above

A — 12,500 feet MSL.

B — 10,000 feet MSL.

C — Flight level (FL) 180.

11-29. Answer B. (FAR 61.3, 91.135)

To operate an aircraft under instrument flight rules, in weather conditions less than VFR, or in Class A airspace, you must hold an instrument rating and meet the IFR recent experience requirements. Answer (A) is wrong because it does not say you need an instrument rating for flight under instrument flight rules. Answer (C) is wrong because it implies you can fly in less than VFR conditions in Class G (uncontrolled) airspace without an instrument rating.

11-30. Answer B. (FAR 91.167, 91.169)

An alternate airport must be filed if the weather reports and/or forecasts for your intended destination indicate that from 1 hour before to 1 hour after your estimated time of arrival (ETA) the ceiling is to be less than 2,000 feet above the airport elevation or the visibility less than 3 statute miles. In addition, when filing an alternate, the aircraft must carry enough fuel to fly to that alternate plus an additional 45 minutes at normal cruising speed. Answer (A) is wrong because, in this example, an alternate is required. Answer (C) is wrong because the 30 minute requirement applies to helicopter or VFR operations.

11-31. Answer C. (FAR 91.103)

You are required to become familiar with all available information concerning any flight. For all flights not in the vicinity of an airport or under IFR, the information must include runway lengths at airports of intended use, takeoff and landing distance information, weather reports and forecasts, fuel requirements, alternatives available if the planned flight cannot be completed, and any known traffic delays. Answers (A) and (B) are wrong because you are not always required to file an alternate airport.

This question is identical to number 11-21.

11-32. Answer B. (FAR 91.215)

An operable Mode C transponder is required when at or above 10,000 feet MSL, excluding the airspace at or below 2,500 feet AGL. Although a Mode C transponder is required at 12,500 feet MSL and at FL 180, answer B is the most correct because it includes these altitudes.

11-33   B11

A coded transponder equipped with altitude reporting capability is required in all controlled airspace

A — at and above 10,000 feet MSL, excluding at and below 2,500 feet AGL.
B — at and above 2,500 feet above the surface.
C — below 10,000 feet MSL, excluding at and below 2,500 feet AGL.

11-34   B11

If an unpressurized aircraft is operated above 12,500 feet MSL, but not more than 14,000 feet MSL, for a period of 2 hours 20 minutes, how long during that time is the minimum flightcrew required to use supplemental oxygen?

A — 2 hours 20 minutes.
B — 1 hour 20 minutes.
C — 1 hour 50 minutes

11-35   B11

Aircraft being operated under IFR are required to have, in addition to the equipment required for VFR and night, at least

A — a slip skid indicator.
B — dual VOR receivers.
C — distance measuring equipment.

11-36   B11

What is the maximum cabin pressure altitude at which a pilot can fly for longer than 30 minutes without using supplemental oxygen?

A — 10,500 feet.
B — 12,000 feet.
C — 12,500 feet.

11-37   B11

What is the maximum IFR altitude you may fly in an unpressurized aircraft without providing passengers with supplemental oxygen?

A — 12,500 feet.
B — 14,000 feet.
C — 15,000 feet.

11-33. Answer A. (FAR 91.215)
See explanation for Question 11-32.

11-34. Answer C. (FAR 91.211)
When operating an unpressurized aircraft above 12,500 feet MSL, up to and including 14,000 feet MSL, for more than 30 minutes, the flightcrew must use supplemental oxygen. When 30 minutes is subtracted from the 2 hours and 20 minutes, the result is 1 hour and 50 minutes, which represents the time the flightcrew must use supplemental oxygen. Answer (A) does not allow for the 30 minutes and answer (B) allows for more than 30 minutes.

11-35. Answer A. (FAR 91.205)
In addition to the normal equipment required for flight under VFR and night the aircraft must have appropriate two-way radio capability, a gyroscopic rate-of-turn indicator, a slip-skid indicator, a sensitive altimeter, a clock, an adequate electrical supply, a gyroscopic pitch and bank indicator, and a directional gyro.

11-36. Answer C. (FAR 91.211)
The maximum pressure altitude at which you can fly without the use of supplemental oxygen for longer than 30 minutes is 12,500 feet. Answers (A) and (B) are wrong because both are below the maximum cabin pressure altitude specified in the regulation.

11-37. Answer C. (FAR 91.211)
When flying above a pressure altitude of 15,000 feet MSL, each occupant must have supplemental oxygen available to them. Answers (A) and (B) are wrong because only the minimum flight crew are required to use supplemental oxygen at these cabin pressure altitudes.

11-38   B11

What is the oxygen requirement for an unpressurized aircraft at 15,000 feet?

A — All occupants must use oxygen for the entire time at this altitude.
B — Crew must start using oxygen at 12,000 feet and passengers at 15,000 feet.
C — Crew must use oxygen for the entire time above 14,000 feet and passengers must be provided supplemental oxygen only above 15,000 feet.

11-39   B11

To meet the requirements for flight under IFR, an aircraft must be equipped with certain operable instruments and equipment. One of those required is

A — a radar altimeter.
B — a transponder with altitude reporting capability.
C — a clock with sweep second pointer or digital presentation.

11-40   B10

What minimum weather conditions must be forecast for your ETA at an alternate airport that has only a VOR approach with standard alternate minimums, for the airport to be listed as an alternate on the IFR flight plan?

A — 800-foot ceiling and 1 statute miles visibility.
B — 800-foot ceiling and 2 statute miles visibility.
C — 1,000-foot ceiling and visibility to allow descent from minimum enroute altitude (MEA), approach, and landing under basic VFR.

11-38. Answer C. (FAR 91.211)

When flying between a pressure altitude of 14,001 feet MSL and 15,000 feet MSL, the minimum flight crew must be provided with, and use, supplemental oxygen the entire time. Answer (A) is wrong because supplemental oxygen does not have to be provided to passengers until above 15,000 feet MSL. Answer (B) is wrong because crewmembers do not have to start using oxygen until they are above 12,500 feet MSL for more than 30 minutes or at all times above 14,000 feet. In addition, passengers are not required to use oxygen at any time, but, oxygen does have to be available to them once the aircraft is above 15,000 feet MSL.

11-39. Answer C. (FAR 91.205)

In addition to the normal equipment required for flight under VFR and night the aircraft must have appropriate two-way radio capability, gyroscopic rate-of-turn indicator, slip-skid indicator, sensitive altimeter, a clock, adequate electrical supply, gyroscopic pitch and bank, and a directional gyro. The Clock should display hours, minutes, and seconds with a sweep second pointer or a digital presentation.

11-40. Answer B. (FAR 91.169)

To be listed as an alternate airport in an IFR flight plan, current weather forecasts must indicate at the estimated time of arrival at the alternate that the ceiling and visibility will be at least 800 feet and 2 statute miles for a nonprecision approach, such as a VOR. If a precision approach is available the criteria are ceiling 600 feet and 2 statute miles visibility. Answer (A) is wrong because you must have a minimum of 2 statute miles visibility. Answer (C) is wrong because a 1,000-foot ceiling is higher than required and no visibility is specified.

11-41   B10

For aircraft other than helicopters, is an alternate airport required for an IFR flight to ATL (Atlanta Hartsfield) if the proposed ETA is 1930Z?

TAF
KATL 121720Z 121818 20012KT 5SM HZ
BKN030
FM2000 3SM TSRA OVC025CB
FM2200 33015G20KT P6SM BKN015
OVC040 BECMG 0608
02008KT BKN040 BECMG 1012
00000KT P6SM SKC=

A — Yes, because the ceiling could fall below 2,000 feet within 2 hours before to 2 hours after the ETA.

B — No, because the ceiling and visibility are forecast to remain at or above 1,000 feet and 3 miles, respectively.

C — No, because the ceiling and visibility are forecast to be at or above 2,000 feet and 3 miles within 1 hour before to 1 hour after the ETA.

11-42   B10

For aircraft other than helicopters, what minimum conditions must exist at the destination airport to avoid listing an alternate airport on an IFR flight plan when a standard IAP is available?

A — From 2 hours before to 2 hours after ETA, forecast ceiling 2,000, and visibility 2 and 1/2 miles.

B — From 2 hours before to 2 hours after ETA, forecast ceiling 3,000, and visibility 3 miles.

C — From 1 hour before to 1 hour after ETA, forecast ceiling 2,000, and visibility 3 miles.

11-41. Answer C. (AIM) (FAR 91.169)

An alternate airport must be filed if the weather reports and/or forecasts for your intended destination indicate, that from 1 hour before to 1 hour after your estimated time of arrival (ETA), the ceiling is to be less than 2,000 feet AGL and the visibility less than 3 statute miles. In this example, the forecast indicates that from 1800Z to 2000Z, there will be visibility of 5 miles, and broken ceilings at 3,000 feet. From 2000Z to 2200Z, the destination is still forecast to be not less than 2000 and 3. Answer (A) is wrong because ETA ± 2 hours is listed instead of ± 1 hour. Answer (B) is wrong because the ceiling must be forecast to be at or above 2,000 feet.

11-42. Answer C. (FAR 91.169)

See explanation for Question 11-41. Answers (A) and (B) are wrong since they reflect a 2-hour period before and after the ETA versus a 1-hour period.

11-43   B10

For aircraft other than helicopters, under what conditions are you not required to list an alternate airport on an IFR flight plan if 14 CFR part 97 prescribes a standard IAP for the destination airport?

A — When the ceiling is forecast to be at least 1,000 feet above the lowest of the MEA, MOCA, or initial approach altitude and the visibility is 2 miles more than the minimum landing visibiliy within 2 hours of your ETA at the destination airport.

B — When he weather reports or forecasts indicate the ceiling and visibility will be at least 2,000 feet and 3 miles for 1 hour before to 1 hour after your ETA at the destination airport.

C — When the ceiling is forecast to be at least 1,000 feet above the lowest of the MEA, MOCA, or initial approach altitude within 2 hours of your ETA at the destination airport.

11-44   B10

For aircraft other than helicopters, what forecast weather minimums are required to list an airport as an alternate on an IFR flight plan if the airport has VOR approach only?

A — Ceiling and visibility at ETA, 800 feet and 2 miles, respectively.

B — Ceiling and visibility from 2 hours before until 2 hours after ETA, 800 feet and 2 miles, respectively.

C — Ceiling and visibility at ETA, 600 feet and 2 miles, respectively.

11-45   B10

What are the minimum weather conditions that must be forecast to list an airport as an alternate when the airport has no approved IAP?

A — The ceiling and visibility at ETA, 2,000 feet and 3 miles, respectively.

B — The ceiling and visibility from 2 hours before until 2 hours after ETA, 2,000 feet and 3 miles, respectively.

C — The ceiling and visibility at ETA must allow descent from MEA, approach, and landing, under basic VFR.

11-43. Answer B. (FAR 91.169)
An alternate airport is not required for aircraft other than helicopters, when the ceilings will be 2,000 feet above the airport elevation, and visibility will be at least 3 statute miles or higher for a period 1 hour before to 1 hour after the ETA.

11-44. Answer A. (FAR 91.169)
To include an alternate airport in an IFR flight plan, the current weather forecasts must indicate that, at the estimated time of arrival, the ceiling and visibility are at least 600 feet and 2 statute miles respectively for airports with a precision approach and a ceiling and visibility of at least 800 feet and 2 statute miles for airports with a nonprecision approach, such as a VOR. Answer (B) is wrong because the forecasts are for the ETA only, not 2 hours before and after. Answer (C) is wrong because the conditions indicated apply to a precision approach, not a nonprecision approach.

11-45. Answer C. (FAR 91.169)
If no instrument approach procedure exists at your selected alternate, the weather conditions at your ETA must allow you to descend from the MEA and conduct an approach and landing under basic VFR conditions. Answers (A) and (B) are wrong because the indicated weather conditions may not permit a descent from the MEA and an approach under basic VFR. In addition, there is no requirement for VFR conditions to exist from 2 hours before until 2 hours after your ETA.

11-46 B10

For aircraft other than helicopters, what minimum weather conditions must be forecast for your ETA at an alternate airport that has a precision approach procedure, with standard alternate minimums, in order to list it as an alternate for the IFR flight?

A — 600-foot ceiling and 2 SM visibility at your ETA.
B — 600-foot ceiling and 2 SM visibility from 2 hours before to 2 hours after your ETA.
C — 800-foot ceiling and 2 SM visibility at your ETA.

11-47 G10

Which publication covers the procedures required for aircraft accident and incident reporting responsibilities for pilots?

A — FAR Part 61.
B — FAR Part 91.
C — NTSB Part 830.

11-48 J02

When is a pilot on an IFR flight plan responsible for avoiding other aircraft?

A — At all times when not in radar contact with ATC.
B — When weather conditions permit, regardless of whether operating under IFR or VFR.
C — Only when advised by ATC.

11-49 J08

The aircraft's transponder fails during flight within Class D airspace.

A — The pilot should immediately request clearance to depart Class D airspace.
B — No deviation is required because a transponder is not required in Class D airspace.
C — Pilot must immediately request priority handling to proceed to destination.

11-50 J08

In addition to a VOR receiver and two-way communications capability, which additional equipment is required for IFR operation in a Class B airspace?

A —DME and an operable coded transponder having mode C capability.
B — Standby communications receiver, DME, and coded transponder.
C — An operable coded transponder having Mode C capability.

11-46. Answer A. (FAR 91.169)
See explanation for Question 11-44.

11-47. Answer C. (NTSB 830.1)
NTSB 830 contains rules pertaining to the notification and reporting of aircraft accidents and incidents. In addition, NTSB 830 also explains the requirements for the preservation of aircraft wreckage, mail, cargo, and records involving all civil aircraft in the United Sates. Answer (A) is wrong because FAR Part 61 pertains to the certification of pilots and flight instructors. Answer (B) is wrong because FAR Part 91 covers general operating and flight rules.

11-48. Answer B. (FAR 91.113)
When weather conditions permit, regardless of whether an operation is conducted under IFR or VFR, you should be vigilant to see and avoid other aircraft. Flight not in radar contact with ATC (answer A) has no bearing on the pilot's responsibility for collision avoidance. Whether or not you are advised by ATC (answer C), you are always responsible for avoiding other aircraft while flying in VFR conditions.

11-49. Answer B. (FAR 91.215)
Anytime you have an inoperative transponder, you may request an authorization from ATC which will allow you to deviate from the transponder requirement. However a transponder is not required to operate in Class D airspace. You do not have to immediately request clearance to depart the Class D airspace if your transponder fails (answer A). Priority handling is not required if your transponder fails within controlled airspace (answer C).

11-50. Answer C. (FAR 91.131, 91.215)
The applicable FARs state that you must have an operable transponder and it must have Mode C capability. This requirement is in addition to the requirement for an operable VOR or TACAN receiver and a two-way radio. Only these three types of avionic equipment are required for IFR operations in Class B airspace. Answer (A) is wrong because DME is not reqquired in class B airspace (B) is wrong because DME is not required.

11-51   J08

No person may operate an aircraft in controlled airspace under IFR unless he/she files a flight plan

A — and receives a clearance by telephone prior to takeoff.

B — prior to takeoff and requests the clearance upon arrival on an airway.

C — and receives a clearance prior to entering controlled airspace.

11-52   J08

When an aircraft is not equipped with a transponder, what requirement must be met before ATC will authorize a flight within class B airspace?

A — A request for the proposed flight must be made to ATC at least 1 hour before the flight.

B — The proposed flight must be conducted when operating under instrument flight rules.

C — The proposed flight must be conducted in visual meteorological conditions (VMC).

11-53   J08

Prior to operating an aircraft not equipped with a transponder in Class B airspace, a request for the deviation must be submitted to the

A — FAA Administrator at least 24 hours before the proposed operation.

B — nearest FAA General Aviation District Office 24 hours before the proposed operation.

C — controlling ATC facility at least 1 hour before the proposed flight.

11-54   B11

(Refer to figure 91 on page 5-12.) What are the oxygen requirements for an IFR flight eastbound on V520 from DBS VORTAC in an unpressurized aircraft at the MEA?

A — The required minimum crew must be provided and use supplemental oxygen for that part of the flight of more than 30 minutes.

B — The required minimum crew must be provided and use supplemental oxygen for that part of the flight of more than 30 minutes, and the passengers must be provided supplemental oxygen.

C — The required minimum crew must be provided and use supplemental oxygen.

11-51. Answer C. (FAR 91.173)

FAR 91.173 states that "No person may operate an aircraft in controlled airspace under IFR unless that person has (a) filed an IFR flight plan; and (b) received an appropriate ATC clearance." Answers (A) and (B) are inappropriate.

11-52. Answer A. (AIM) (FAR 91.215)

FAR Part 91.215(d)(3) states, "For operation of an aircraft that is not equipped with a transponder, the request must be made at least one hour before the proposed operation." This request must be made to the ATC facility having jurisdiction over the affected airspace. Answers (B) and (C) are wrong since FAR 91.215 does not require the proposed flight to be conducted under instrument flight rules or in VMC.

11-53. Answer C. (AIM) (FAR 91.215)

FAR Part 91.215(d)(3) states, "For operation of an aircraft that is not equipped with a transponder, the request must be made at least one hour before the proposed operation." This request must be made to the ATC facility having jurisdiction over the affected airspace. Answers (A) and (B) are wrong since both include the wrong approval authority and time criteria.

11-54. Answer C. (FAR 91.211)

The MEA eastbound on V520 from DBS VORTAC is 15,000 feet MSL. At cabin pressure altitudes above 14,000 feet MSL, the required minimum flight crew must be provided with and use supplemental oxygen during the entire flight at those altitudes. In addition, the minimum required flight crew must use supplemental oxygen for any part of a flight more than 30 minutes (answers A and B) in duration, above 12,500 feet MSL. At cabin pressure altitudes above 15,000 feet MSL, supplemental oxygen must be available to each occupant.

11-55   B10

An airport without an authorized IAP may be included on an IFR flight plan as an alternate, if the current weather forecast indicates that the ceiling and visibility at the ETA will

A — allow for descent from the IAF to landing under basic VFR Conditions.

B — be at least 1,000 feet and 1 mile.

C — allow for a descent from the MEA approach, and a landing under basic VFR.

11-55. Answer C. (FAR 91.169)

If an airport does not have an instrument approach procedure, the minimum IFR altitude in the area is the MEA. From the MEA, you must be able to proceed VFR to the airport for approach and landing.

SUBJECT MATTER KNOWLEDGE CODES

To determine the knowledge area in which a particular question was incorrectly answered, compare the subject matter code(s) on the Federal Aviation Administration Airmen Computer Test Report to the following subject matter outline. The total number of test items missed may differ from the number of subject matter codes shown on the test report, since you may have missed more than one question in a certain subject matter code.

Title 14 of the Code of Federal Regulations (14 CFR) part 1-Definitions and Abbreviations

A01　General Definitions
A02　Abbreviations and Symbols

14 CFR part 21-Certification Procedures forProducts and Parts

A100　General
A102　Type Certificates
A104　Supplemental Type Certificates
A108　Airworthiness Certificate
A110　Approval of Materials, Part, Processes, and Appliances
A112　Export Airworthiness Approvals
A114　Approval of Engines, Propellers, Materials, Parts, and Appliances Import
A117　Technical Standard Order Authorizations

14 CFR part 23-Airworthiness Standards: Normal, Utility, Acrobatic, and Commuter Category Aircraft

A150　General
A151　Flight
A152　Structure
A153　Design and Construction
A154　Powerplant
A155　Equipment
A157　Operating Limitations and Information
A159　Appendix G: Instructions for Continued Airworthiness

14 CFR part 27-Airworthiness Standards: Normal Category Rotorcraft

A250　General
A253　Flight
A255　Strength Requirements
A257　Design and Construction
A259　Powerplant
A261　Equipment

A263　Operating Limitations and Information
A265　Appendix A: Instructions for Continued Airworthiness

14 CFR part 39-Airworthiness Directives

A13　General
A14　Airworthiness Directives

14 CFR part 45-Identification and Registration Marking

A400　General
A401　Identification of Aircraft and Related Products
A402　Nationality and Registration Marks

14 CFR part 61-Certification: Pilots, Flight Instructors, and Ground Instructors

A20　General
A21　Aircraft Ratings and Pilot Authorizations
A22　Student Pilots
A23　Private Pilots
A24　Commercial Pilots
A25　Airline Transport Pilots
A26　Flight Instructors
A27　Ground Instructors
A29　Recreational Pilot

14 CFR part 71-Designation of Class A, Class B, Class C, Class D, and Class E Airspace Areas; Airways; Routes; and Reporting Points

A60　General-Class A Airspace
A61　Class B Airspace
A64　Class C Airspace
A65　Class D Airspace
A66　Class E Airspace

14 CFR part 91-General Operating and Flight Rules

B07 General
B08 Flight Rules-General
B09 Visual Flight Rules
B10 Instrument Flight Rules
B11 Equipment, Instrument, and Certificate Requirements
B12 Special Flight Operations
B13 Maintenance, Preventive Maintenance, and Alterations
B14 Large and Turbine-powered Multiengine Airplanes
B15 Additional Equipment and Operating Requirements for Large and Transport Category Aircraft
B16 Appendix A-Category II Operations: Manual, Instruments, Equipment, and Maintenance
B17 Foreign Aircraft Operations and Operations of U.S.-Registered Civil Aircraft Outside of the U.S.

14 CFR part 97-Standard Instrument Approach Procedures

B97 General

14 CFR part 105-Parachute Jumping

C01 General
C02 Operating Rules
C03 Parachute Equipment

14 CFR part 119-Certification: Air Carriers and Commercial Operators

C20 General
C21 Applicability of Operating Requirements to Different Kinds of Operations Under Parts 121, 125, and 135
C22 Certification, Operations Specifications, and Certain Other Requirements for Operations Conducted Under Parts 121 or 135

14 CFR part 121-Operating Requirements: Domestic, Flag, and Supplemental Operations

D01 General
D02 Certification Rules for Domestic and Flag Air Carriers
D03 Certification Rules for Supplemental Air Carriers and Commercial Operators
D04 Rules Governing all Certificate Holders Under This Part
D05 Approval of Routes: Domestic and Flag Air Carriers

D06 Approval of Areas and Routes for Supplemental Air Carriers and Commercial Operators
D07 Manual Requirements
D08 Aircraft Requirements
D09 Airplane Performance Operating Limitations
D10 Special Airworthiness Requirements
D11 Instrument and Equipment Requirements
D12 Maintenance, Preventive Maintenance, and Alterations
D13 Airman and Crewmember Requirements
D14 Training Program
D15 Crewmember Qualifications
D16 Aircraft Dispatcher Qualifications and Duty Time Limitations: Domestic and Flag Air Carriers
D17 Flight Time Limitations and Rest Requirements: Domestic Air Carriers
D18 Flight Time Limitations: Flag Air Carriers
D19 Flight Time Limitations: Supplemental Air Carriers and Commercial Operators
D20 Flight Operations
D21 Dispatching and Flight Release Rules
D22 Records and Reports
D23 Crewmember Certificate: International
D24 Special Federal Aviation Regulation SFAR No. 14

NTSB 830-Rules Pertaining to the Notification and Reporting of Aircraft Accidents or Incidents and Overdue Aircraft, and Preservation of Aircraft Wreckage, Mail, Cargo, and Records

G10 General
G11 Initial Notification of Aircraft Accidents, Incidents, and Overdue Aircraft
G12 Preservation of Aircraft Wreckage, Mail, Cargo, and Records
G13 Reporting of Aircraft Accidents, Incidents, and Overdue Aircraft

AC 61-13-Basic Helicopter Handbook

H70 General Aerodynamics
H71 Aerodynamics of Flight
H72 Loads and Load Factors
H73 Function of the Controls
H74 Other Helicopter Components and Their Functions
H75 Introduction to the Helicopter Flight Manual
H76 Weight and Balance
H77 Helicopter Performance
H78 Some Hazards of Helicopter Flight
H79 Precautionary Measures and Critical Conditions
H80 Helicopter Flight Maneuvers

H81 Confined Area, Pinnacle, and Ridgeline Operations
H82 Glossary

FAA-H-8083-1-Aircraft Weight and Balance Handbook

H100 Why is Weight and Balance Important?
H101 Weight Control
H102 Effects of Weight
H103 Weight Changes
H104 Stability and Balance Control
H105 Weight and Balance Theory
H106 Weight and Balance Documents
H107 Requirements
H108 Equipment for Weighing
H109 Preparation for Weighing
H110 Determining the Center of Gravity
H111 Empty-Weight Center of Gravity Formulas
H112 Determining the Loaded Weight and CG
H113 Multiengine Airplane Weight and Balance Computations
H114 Determining the Loaded CG
H115 Equipment List
H116 Weight and Balance Revision Record
H117 Weight Changes Caused by a Repair or Alteration
H118 Empty-Weight CG Range
H119 Adverse-Loaded CG Checks
H120 Ballast
H121 Weighing Requirements
H122 Locating and Monitoring Weight and CG Location
H123 Determining the Correct Stabilizer Trim Setting
H124 Determining CG Changes Caused by Modifying the Cargo
H125 Determining Cargo Pallet Loads with Regard to Floor Loading Limits
H126 Determining the Maximum Amount of Payload That Can Be carried
H127 Determining the Landing Weight
H128 Determining the Minutes of Fuel Dump Time
H129 Weight and Balance of Commuter Category Airplanes
H130 Determining the Loaded CG of a Helicopter
H131 Using an Electronic Calculator to Solve Weight and Balance Problems
H132 Using an E6-B Flight Computer to Solve Weight and Balance Problems
H133 Using a Dedicated Electronic Computer to Solve Weight and Balance Problems
H134 Typical Weight and Balance Problems
H135 Glossary

FAA-H-8083-9-Aviation Instructor Handbook

H200 Learning Theory
H201 Definition of Learning
H202 Characteristics of Learning
H203 Principles of Learning
H204 Level of Learning
H205 Learning Physical Skills
H206 Memory
H207 Transfer of Learning
H208 Control of Human Behavior
H210 Human Needs
H211 Defense Mechanisms
H212 The Flight Instructor as a Practical Psychologists
H213 Basic Elements
H214 Barriers of Effective Communication
H215 Developing Communications Skills
H216 Preparation
H217 Presentation
H218 Application
H219 Review and Evaluation
H220 Organizing Material
H221 Lecture Method
H222 Cooperative or Group Learning Method
H223 Guided Discussion Method
H224 Demonstration-Performance Method
H225 Computer-Based Training Method
H226 The Instructor as a Critic
H227 Evaluation
H228 Instructional Aid Theory
H229 Reasons for Use of Instructional Aids
H230 Guidelines for Use of Instructional Aids
H231 Types of Instructional Aids
H232 Test Preparation Material
H233 Aviation Instructor Responsibilities
H234 Flight Instructor Responsibilities
H235 Professionalism
H236 The Telling-and-Doing Technique
H237 Integrated Flight Instruction
H238 Obstacles to Learning During Flight Instruction
H239 Positive Exchange of Flight Controls
H240 Use of Distractions
H241 Aeronautical Decision Making
H242 Factors Affecting Decision Making
H243 Operational Pitfalls
H244 Evaluating Student Decision Making
H245 Course of Training
H246 Blocks of Learning
H247 Training Syllabus
H248 Lesson Plans
H249 Growth and Development
H250 Sources of Material
H251 Appendix A-Sample Test Items
H252 Appendix B-Instructor Endorsements
H253 Glossary

AC 61-23-Pilots Handbook of Aeronautical Knowledge

H300 Forces Acting on the Airplane in Flight
H301 Turning Tendency (Torque Effect)
H302 Airplane Stability
H303 Loads and Load Factors
H304 Airplane Structure
H305 Flight Control Systems
H306 Electrical System
H307 Engine Operation
H308 Propeller
H309 Starting the Engine
H310 Exhaust Gas Temperature Gauge
H311 Aircraft Documents, Maintenance, and Inspections
H312 The Pitot-Static System and Associated Instruments
H313 Gyroscopic Flight Instruments
H314 Magnetic Compass
H315 Weight Control
H316 Balance, Stability, and Center of Gravity
H317 Airplane Performance
H318 Observations
H319 Service Outlets
H320 Weather Briefings
H321 Nature of the Atmosphere
H322 The Cause of Atmospheric Circulation
H323 Moisture and Temperature
H324 Air Masses and Fronts
H325 Aviation Weather Reports, Forecasts, and Weather Charts
H326 Types of Airports
H327 Sources for Airport Data
H328 Airport Markings and Signs
H329 Airport Lighting
H330 Wind Direction Indicators
H331 Radio Communications
H332 Air Traffic Services
H333 Wake Turbulence
H334 Collision Avoidance
H335 Controlled Airspace
H336 Uncontrolled Airspace
H337 Special Use Airspace
H338 Other Airspace Areas
H339 Aeronautical Charts
H340 Latitude and Longitude
H341 Effect of Wind
H342 Basic Calculations
H343 Pilotage
H344 Dead Reckoning
H345 Flight Planning
H346 Charting the Course
H347 Filing a VFR Flight Plan
H348 Radio Navigation
H349 Obtaining a Medical Certificate
H350 Health Factors Affecting Pilot Performance
H351 Environmental Factors which Affect Pilot Performance

FAA-H-8083-11Balloon Flying Handbook

H400 History
H401 Physics
H402 Basic Balloon Terms
H403 Balloon Components
H404 Support Equipment
H405 Choosing a Balloon
H406 Flight Planning
H407 Preflight Operations
H408 Checklists
H409 Crew
H410 Chase
H411 Inflation
H412 Launch
H413 Approach to Landing
H414 Landing
H415 Standard Burn
H416 Level Flight
H417 Use of Instruments
H418 Ascents and Descents
H419 Maneuvering
H420 Winds Above
H421 Winds Below
H422 Contour Flying
H423 Radio Communications
H424 Deflation
H425 Preparing for Pack-up
H426 Legal Considerations
H427 Propane Management and Fueling
H428 Tethering
H429 Emergency Procedures
H430 Regulations
H431 Maintenance
H432 Earning a Pilot Certificate
H433 Practical Test Standards
H434 Skill Development
H435 What is a Good Instructor
H436 Aeronautical Decision Making
H437 Types of Decisions
H438 Effectiveness of ADM
H439 Glossary

FAA-H-8083-3-Airplane Flying Handbook

H501 Choosing a Flight School
H502 Instructor/Student Relationship
H503 Role of the FAA
H504 Flight Standards District Offices (FSDO's)
H505 Study Habits
H506 Study Materials
H507 Collision Avoidance
H509 Pilot Assessment
H510 Preflight Preparation and Flight Planning
H511 Airplane Preflight Inspection
H512 Minimum Equipment Lists (MEL's) and Operations with Inoperative Equipment
H513 Cockpit Management

H514 Use of Checklists
H515 Ground Operations
H516 Taxiing
H517 Taxi Clearances at Airports with an Operating Control Tower
H518 Before Takeoff Check
H519 After-landing
H520 Postflight
H522 Terms and Definitions
H523 Prior to Takeoff
H524 Normal Takeoff
H525 Crosswind Takeoff
H526 Short-field Takeoff and Climb
H527 Soft-field Takeoff and Climb
H528 Rejected Takeoff
H529 Noise Abatement
H531 Integrated Flight Instruction
H532 Attitude Flying
H533 Straight-and-level Flight
H534 Turns
H535 Climbs
H536 Descents
H538 Slow Flight
H539 Stalls
H540 Spins
H541 Spin Procedures
H542 Aircraft Limitations
H543 Weight and Balance Requirements
H545 Maneuvering by Reference to Ground Objects
H546 Performance Maneuvers
H548 Airport Traffic Patterns and Operations
H549 Normal Approach and Landing
H550 Crosswind Approach and Landing
H551 Short-field Approach and Landing
H552 Soft-field Approach and Landing
H553 Power-off Accuracy Approaches
H554 Faulty Approaches and Landings
H555 Final Approaches
H556 Roundout (Flare)
H557 Touchdown
H559 Basic Instrument Training
H560 Basic Instrument Flight
H561 Use of Navigation Systems
H562 Use of Radar Services
H564 Night Vision
H565 Night Illusions
H566 Pilot Equipment
H567 Airplane Equipment and Lighting
H568 Airport and Navigation Lighting Aids
H569 Preparation and Preflight
H570 Starting, Taxiing, and Runup
H571 Takeoff and Climb
H572 Orientation and Navigation
H573 Approaches and Landings
H574 Night Emergencies
H576 VOR Navigation
H577 VOR/DME RNAV

H578 LORAN-C Navigation
H579 Global Positioning System (GPS)
H580 Radar Services
H582 Systems and Equipment Malfunctions
H583 Emergency Approaches and Landings (Actual)
H585 Airplane Systems
H586 Pressurized Airplanes
H587 Oxygen Systems
H588 Physiological Altitude Limits
H589 Regulatory Requirements
H591 Multiengine Performance Characteristics
H592 The Critical Engine
H593 Vmc for Certification
H594 Performance
H595 Factors in Takeoff Planning
H596 Accelerates/Stop Distance
H597 Propeller Feathering
H598 Use of Trim Tabs
H599 Preflight Preparation
H600 Checklist
H601 Taxiing
H602 Normal Takeoffs
H603 Crosswind Takeoffs
H604 Short-field or Obstacle Clearance Takeoff
H605 Stalls
H606 Emergency Descent
H607 Approaches and Landings
H608 Crosswind Landings
H609 Short-field Landing
H610 Go-around Procedure
H611 Engine Inoperative Emergencies
H612 Engine Inoperative Procedures
H613 Vmc Demonstrations
H614 Engine Failure Before Lift-off (Rejected Takeoff)
H615 Engine Failure After Lift-off
H616 Engine Failure En Route
H617 Engine Inoperative Approach and Landing
H618 Types of Decisions
H619 Effectiveness of ADM

Understanding the Gyroplane-The Abbott Co.

H650 Magic of Rotor Blades
H651 Behind the Power Curve
H652 Beating P.I.O.

FAA-H-8083-21-Rotorcraft Flying Handbook

H700 Glossary
Helicopter
H701 Introduction to the Helicopter
H702 General Aerodynamics
H703 Aerodynamics of Flight
H704 Autorotation
H705 Helicopter Flight Controls
H706 Helicopter Systems

H707 Engines
H708 Transmission System
H709 Main Rotor System
H710 Fuel Systems
H711 Electrical Systems
H712 Hydraulics
H713 Stability Augmentations Systems
H714 Autopilot
H715 Environmental Systems
H716 Anti-Icing Systems
H717 Rotorcraft Flight Manual
H718 Operating Limitations
H719 Weight and Balance
H720 Performance
H721 Performance Charts
H722 Basic Flight Maneuvers
H723 Minimum Equipment Lists
H724 Rotor Safety Considerations
H725 Vertical Takeoff to a Hover
H726 Hovering
H727 Taxiing
H728 Turns
H729 Normal Takeoff
H730 Ground Reference Maneuvers
H731 Traffic Patterns
H732 Approaches
H733 Go-Around
H734 Noise Abatement Procedures
H735 Advance Flight Maneuvers
H736 Reconnaissance Procedures
H737 Maximum Performance Takeoff
H738 Running/Rolling Takeoff
H739 Rapid Deceleration (Quick Stop)
H740 Steep Approach to a Hover
H741 Shallow Approach and Running/Roll-On
        Landing
H742 Slope Operations
H743 Confined Area Operations
H744 Pinnacle and Ridgeline Operations
H745 Helicopter Emergencies
H746 Autorotation
H747 Height/Velocity Diagram
H748 Retreating Blade Stall
H749 Ground Resonance
H750 Dynamic Rollover
H751 Low G Conditions and Mast Bumping
H752 Low Rotor RPM and Blade Stall
H753 Recovery From Low Rotor RPM
H754 Systems Flight Diversion Malfunctions
H755 Lost Procedures
H756 Emergency Equipment and Survival Gear
H757 Attitude Instrument Flying
H758 Flight Instruments
H759 Night Operations
H760 Aeronautical Decision Making
        Gyroplanes
H761 Introduction to the Gyroplane
H762 Aerodynamics of the Gyroplane

H763 Autorotations
H764 Rotor Disc Regions
H765 Retreating Blade Stall
H766 Rotor Force
H767 Stability
H768 Horizontal Stabilizer
H769 Propeller Thrust Line
H770 Gyroplane Flight Controls
H771 Cyclic Control
H772 Gyroplanes Systems
H773 Semirigid Rotor Systems
H774 Fully Articulated Rotor System
H775 Prerotator
H776 Rotorcraft Flight Manual
H777 Weight and Balance
H778 Performance
H779 Height/Velocity Diagram
H780 Gyroplane Flight Operations
H781 Taxi
H782 Blade Flap
H783 Takeoff
H784 Jump Takeoff
H785 Basic Flight Maneuvers
H786 Ground Reference Maneuvers
H787 Flight at Slow Airspeeds
H788 High Rate of Descent
H789 Landings/Crosswind
H790 Go Around
H791 Gyroplane Emergencies
H792 Aborted Takeoff
H793 Lift-Off at Low Airspeed and High Angle of
        Attack
H794 Pilot-Induced Oscillation (PIO)
H795 Buntover (Power Pushover)
H796 Ground Reference
H797 Emergency Approach and Landing
H798 Aeronautical Decision Making

FAA-H-8083-15-Instrument Flying Handbook

      Human Factors
H800 Sensory Systems
H801 Spatial Disorientation
H802 Optical Illusions
H803 Physiological and Psychological Factors
H804 Medical Factors
H805 Aeronautical Decision Making
H806 Crew/Cockpit Resource Management
        Aerodynamics
H807 Basic Aerodynamics
      Flight Instruments
H808 Pitot Static
H809 Compass
H810 Gyroscopic
H811 Flight Director
H812 Systems Preflight
      Airplane Attitude Instrument Flying
H813 Fundamental Skills

Airplane Basic Flight Maneuvers
H814   Straight-and-level Flight
H815   Straight Climbs and Descents
H816   Turns
H817   Approach to Stall
H818   Unusual Attitude Recoveries
H819   Instrument Takeoff
H820   Instrument Flight Patterns
Helicopter Attitude Instrument Flying
H821   Instrument Flight
H822   Straight-and-level
H823   Straight Climbs
H824   Straight Descents
H825   Turns
H826   Unusual Attitude Recoveries
H827   Emergencies
H828   Instrument Takeoff
Navigation Systems
H829   Basic Radio Principals
H830   Nondirectional Beacon (NDB)
H831   Very High Frequency Omnidirectional
       Range
(VOR)
H832   Distance Measuring Equipment (DME)
H833   Area Navigation (RNAV)
H834   Long Range Navigation (LORAN)
H835   Global Positioning System (GPS)
H836   Inertia Navigation System (INS)
H837   Instrument Landing System (ILS)
H838   Microwave Landing System (MLS)
H839   Flight Management Systems (FMS)
H840   Head-up Display (HUD)
H841   Radar Navigation (Ground Based)
National Airspace System
H842   IFR Enroute Charts
H843   U.S. Terminal Procedures Publications
H844   Instrument Approach Procedures
Air Traffic Control Systems
H845   Communications Equipment
H846   Communications Procedures
H847   Communications Facilities
IFR Flight
H848   Planning
H849   Clearances
H850   Departures
H851   Enroute
H852   Holding
H853   Arrival
H854   Approaches
H855   Flying Experience
H856   Weather Conditions
H857   Conducting an IFR Flight
Emergency Operations
H858   Unforecast Adverse Weather
H859   Aircraft System Malfunction
H860   Communication/Navigation System
       Malfunction
H861   Loss of Situational Awareness

Glossary
H862   Glossary

Gyroplane Flight Training Manual-Jean-Pierre Harrison

H660   General Aerodynamics
H661   Aerodynamics of Flight
H662   Rotor RPM During Autorotations
H663   Function of the Controls
H664   Some Hazards of Gyroplane Flight
H665   Precautionary Measures and Critical
       Conditions
H666   Gyroplane Flight Maneuvers

AC 61-27-Instrument Flying Handbook

I01   Training Considerations
I02   Instrument Flying: Coping with Illusions in
       Flight
I03   Aerodynamic Factors Related to
       Instrument Flying
I04   Basic Flight Instruments
I05   Attitude Instrument Flying-Airplanes
I06   Attitude Instrument Flying-Helicopters
I07   Electronic Aids to Instrument Flying
I08   Using the Navigation Instruments
I09   Radio Communications Facilities and
       Equipment
I10   The Federal Airways System and
       Controlled Airspace
I11   Air Traffic Control
I12   ATC Operations and Procedures
I13   Flight Planning
I14   Appendix: Instrument Instructor Lesson
       Guide-Airplanes
I15   Segment of En Route Low Altitude Chart

AC 00-6-Aviation Weather

I20   The Earth's Atmosphere
I21   Temperature
I22   Atmospheric Pressure and Altimetry
I23   Wind
I24   Moisture, Cloud Formation, and
       Precipitation
I25   Stable and Unstable Air
I26   Clouds
I27   Air Masses and Fronts
I28   Turbulence
I29   Icing
I30   Thunderstorms
I31   Common IFR Producers
I32   High Altitude Weather
I33   Arctic Weather
I34   Tropical Weather
I35   Soaring Weather
I36   Glossary of Weather Terms

AC 00-45-Aviation Weather Services

I54   The Aviation Weather Service Program
I55   Aviation Routine Weather Report
        (METAR)
I56   Pilot and Radar Reports, Satellite
        Pictures, and Radiosonde Additional Data
        (RADATs)
I57   Aviation Weather Forecasts
I58   Surface Analysis Chart
I59   Weather Depiction Chart
I60   Radar Summary Chart
I61   Constant Pressure Analysis Charts
I62   Composite Moisture Stability Chart
I63   Winds and Temperatures Aloft Chart
I64   Significant Weather Prognostic Charts
I65   Convective Outlook Chart
I66   Volcanic Ash Advisory Center Products
I67   Turbulence Locations, Conversion and
        Density Altitude Tables, Contractions and
        Acronyms, Station Identifiers, WSR-88D
        Sites, and Internet Addresses

AIM-Aeronautical Information Manual

J01   Air Navigation Radio Aids
J02   Radar Services and Procedures
J03   Airport Lighting Aids
J04   Air Navigation and Obstruction Lighting
J05   Airport Marking Aids and Signs
J06   Airspace-General
J07   Class G Airspace
J08   Controlled Airspace
J09   Special Use Airspace
J10   Other Airspace Areas
J11   Service Available to Pilots
J12   Radio Communications Phraseology and
        Techniques
J13   Airport Operations
J14   ATC Clearance/Separations
J15   Preflight
J16   Departure Procedures
J17   En Route Procedures
J18   Arrival Procedures
J19   Pilot/Controller Roles and Responsibilities
J20   National Security and Interception
        Procedures
J21   Emergency Procedures-General
J22   Emergency Services Available to Pilots
J23   Distress and Urgency Procedures
J24   Two-Way Radio Communications Failure
J25   Meteorology
J26   Altimeter Setting Procedures
J27   Wake Turbulence
J28   Bird Hazards, and Flight Over National
        Refuges, Parks, and Forests
J29   Potential Flight Hazards
J30   Safety, Accident, and Hazard Reports

J31   Fitness for Flight
J32   Type of Charts Available
J33   Pilot Controller Glossary

Other Documents

J34   Airport/Facility Directory
J35   En Route Low Altitude Chart
J36   En Route High Altitude Chart
J37   Sectional Chart
J39   Terminal Area Chart
J40   Instrument Departure Procedure Chart
J41   Standard Terminal Arrival (STAR) Chart
J42   Instrument Approach Procedures
J43   Helicopter Route Chart

ADDITIONAL ADVISORY CIRCULARS

K01   AC 00-24, Thunderstorms
K02   AC 00-30, Atmospheric Turbulence
        Avoidance
K03   AC 00-34, Aircraft Ground Handling and
        Servicing
K04   AC 00-54, Pilot Wind Shear Guide
K05   AC 00-55, Announcement of Availability:
        FAA Order 8130.21A
K06   AC 43-4, Corrosion Control for Aircraft
K11   AC 20-34, Prevention of Retractable
        Landing Gear Failures
K12   AC 20-32, Carbon Monoxide (CO)
        Contamination in Aircraft-Detection and
        Prevention
K13   AC 20-43, Aircraft Fuel Control
K20   AC 20-103, Aircraft Engine Crankshaft
        Failure
K23   AC 20-121, Airworthiness Approval of
        Airborne Loran-C Navigation Systems for
        Use in the U.S. National Airspace System
K26   AC 20-138, Airworthiness Approval of
        Global Positioning System (GPS)
        Navigation Equipment for Use as a VFR
        and IFR Supplemental Navigation System
K40   AC 25-4, Inertial Navigation Systems (INS)
K45   AC 39-7, Airworthiness Directives
K46   AC 43-9, Maintenance Records
K47   AC 43.9-1, Instructions for Completion of
        FAA Form 337
K48   AC 43-11, Reciprocating Engine Overhaul
        Terminology and Standards
K49   AC 43.13-1, Acceptable Methods,
        Techniques, and Practices-Aircraft
        Inspection and Repair
K50   AC 43.13-2, Acceptable Methods,
        Techniques, and Practices-Aircraft
        Alterations
K80   AC 60-4, Pilot's Spatial Disorientation
L05   AC 60-22, Aeronautical Decision Making
L10   AC 61-67, Stall Spin Awareness Training

L15 AC 61-107, Operations of Aircraft at Altitudes Above 25,000 Feet MSL and/or MACH numbers (Mmo) Greater Than .75

L25 FAA-G-8082-11, Inspection Authorization Knowledge Test Guide

L34 AC 90-48, Pilots' Role in Collision Avoidance

L42 AC 90-87, Helicopter Dynamic Rollover

L44 AC 90-94, Guidelines for Using Global Positioning System Equipment for IFR En Route and Terminal Operations and for Nonprecision Instrument Approaches in the U.S. National Airspace System

L45 AC 90-95, Unanticipated Right Yaw in Helicopters

L50 AC 91-6, Water, Slush, and Snow on the Runway

L52 AC 91-13, Cold Weather Operation of Aircraft

L53 AC 91-14, Altimeter Setting Sources

L57 AC 91-43, Unreliable Airspeed Indications

L59 AC 91-46, Gyroscopic Instruments-Good Operating Practices

L61 AC 91-50, Importance of Transponder Operation and Altitude Reporting

L62 AC 91-51, Effect of Icing on Aircraft Control and Airplane Deice and Anti-Ice Systems

L70 AC 91-67, Minimum Equipment Requirements for General Aviation Operations Under FAR Part 91

L80 AC 103-4, Hazard Associated with Sublimation of Solid Carbon Dioxide (Dry Ice) Aboard Aircraft

L90 AC 105-2, Sport Parachute Jumping

M01 AC 120-12, Private Carriage Versus Common Carriage of Persons or Property

M02 AC 120-27, Aircraft Weight and Balance Control

M08 AC 120-58, Pilot Guide for Large Aircraft Ground Deicing

M13 AC 121-195-1, Operational Landing Distances for Wet Runways; Transport Category Airplanes

M35 AC 135-17, Pilot Guide-Small Aircraft Ground Deicing

M51 AC 20-117, Hazards Following Ground Deicing and Ground Operations in Conditions Conducive to Aircraft Icing

M52 AC 00-2, Advisory Circular Checklist Soaring Flight Manual-Jeppesen Sanderson, Inc.

N20 Sailplane Aerodynamics

N21 Performance Considerations

N22 Flight Instruments

N23 Weather for Soaring

N24 Medical Factors

N25 Flight Publications and Airspace

N26 Aeronautical Charts and Navigation

N27 Computations for Soaring

N28 Personal Equipment

N29 Preflight and Ground Operations

N30 Aerotow Launch Procedures

N31 Ground Launch Procedures

N32 Basic Flight Maneuvers and Traffic

N33 Soaring Techniques

N34 Cross-Country Soaring

Flight Instructor Manual-Balloon Federation of America

O10 Flight Instruction Aids

O11 Human Behavior and Pilot Proficiency

O12 The Flight Check and the Designated Examiner

Balloon Digest-Balloon Federation of America

O150 Balloon-Theory and Practice

O155 Structure of the Modern Balloon

O160 Lift-off to Landing

O165 Weather for the Balloonist

O170 Propane and Fuel Management

O171 Chemical and Physical Properties

O172 Tanks

O173 Burners

O174 Hoses

O175 Refueling

O176 Fuel Contamination

O177 Heat Tapes (Coils)

O178 Nitrogen Pressurization

O179 Repairs and Maintenance

Powerline Excerpts-Balloon Federation of America

O30 Excerpts

Balloon Ground School-Balloon Publishing Co.

O220 Balloon Operations

How To Fly A Balloon-Balloon Publishing Co.

O250 Basic Terminology

O251 History

O252 Physics

O253 Equipment

O254 Checklists

O255 Flight Planning

O256 Preflight Operations

O257 The Standard Burn

O258 Inflation

O259 Launch

O260 Level Flight

O261 Ascents and Descents

O262 Contour Flying

O263 Maneuvering
O264 Approach to Landing
O265 Landings
O266 Deflation
O267 The Chase
O268 Landowners Relations
O269 Recovery and Pack-up
O270 Propane: Management and Fueling
O271 Tethering
O272 Emergency Procedures
O273 Skill Development
O274 Crew
O275 What is a Good Instructor
O276 Regulations
O277 Maintenance
O278 Earning a Pilot Certificate
O279 Radio Communications
O280 Appendix 1: Glossary

Goodyear Airship Operations Manual

P01 Buoyancy
P02 Aerodynamics
P03 Free Ballooning
P04 Aerostatics
P05 Envelope
P06 Car
P07 Powerplant
P08 Airship Ground Handling
P11 Operating Instructions
P12 History
P13 Training

The Parachute Manual-Para Publishing

P31 Regulations
P32 The Parachute Rigger Certificate
P33 The Parachute Loft
P34 Parachute Materials
P35 Personnel Parachute Assemblies
P36 Parachute Component Parts
P37 Maintenance, Alteration, and Manufacturing Procedures
P38 Design and Construction
P39 Parachute Inspecting and Packing
P40 Glossary/Index

The Parachute Manual, Vol. II-Para Publishing

P51 Parachute Regulations
P52 The Parachute Rigger's Certificate
P53 The Parachute Loft
P54 Parachute Materials
P55 Personnel Parachute Assemblies
P56 Parachute Component Parts
P57 Maintenance, Alteration, and Manufacturing
P58 Parachute Design and Construction

P59 Parachute Inspection and Packing
P60 Appendix
P61 Conversion Tables
P62 Product/Manufacturer-Index
P63 Name and Manufacture-Index
P64 Glossary-Index

FAA Accident Prevention Program Bulletins

V01 FAA-P-8740-2, Density Altitude
V02 FAA-P-8740-5, Weight and Balance
V03 FAA-P-8740-12, Thunderstorms
V04 FAA-P-8740-19, Flying Light Twins Safely
V05 FAA-P-8740-23, Planning your Takeoff
V06 FAA-P-8740-24, Tips on Winter Flying
V07 FAA-P-8740-25, Always Leave Yourself an Out
V08 FAA-P-8740-30, How to Obtain a Good Weather Briefing
V09 FAA-P-8740-40, Wind Shear
V10 FAA-P-8740-41, Medical Facts for Pilots
V11 FAA-P-8740-44, Impossible Turns
V12 FAA-P-8740-48, On Landings, Part I
V13 FAA-P-8740-49, On Landings, Part II
V14 FAA-P-8740-50, On Landings, Part III
V15 FAA-P-8740-51, How to Avoid a Midair Collision
V16 FAA-P-8740-52, The Silent Emergency

FTP-Flight Theory for Pilots-Jeppesen Sanderson, Inc.

W01 Introduction
W02 Air Flow and Airspeed Measurement
W03 Aerodynamic Forces on Airfoils
W04 Lift and Stall
W05 Drag
W06 Jet Aircraft Basic Performance
W07 Jet Aircraft Applied Performance
W08 Prop Aircraft Basic Performance
W09 Prop Aircraft Applied Performance
W10 Helicopter Aerodynamics
W11 Hazards of Low Speed Flight
W12 Takeoff Performance
W13 Landing Performance
W14 Maneuvering Performance
W15 Longitudinal Stability and Control
W16 Directional and Lateral Stability and Control
W17 High Speed Flight

Fly the Wing-Iowa State University Press/Ames, Second Edition

X01 Basic Aerodynamics
X02 High-Speed Aerodynamics
X03 High-Altitude Machs
X04 Approach Speed Control and Target Landings

X05 Preparation for Flight Training
X06 Basic Instrument Scan
X07 Takeoffs
X08 Rejected Takeoffs
X09 Climb, Cruise, and Descent
X10 Steep Turns
X11 Stalls
X12 Unusual Attitudes
X14 Maneuvers At Minimum Speed
X15 Landings: Approach Technique and Performance
X16 ILS Approaches
X17 Missed Approaches and Rejected Landings
X18 Category II and III Approaches
X19 Nonprecision and Circling Approaches
X20 Weight and Balance
X21 Flight Planning
X22 Icing
X23 Use of Anti-ice and Deice
X24 Winter Operation
X25 Thunderstorm Flight
X26 Low-Level Wind Shear

Practical Test Standards

Z01 FAA-S-8081-6, Flight Instructor Practical Test Standards for Airplane
Z02 FAA-S-8081-7, Flight Instructor Practical Test Standards for Rotorcraft
Z03 FAA-S-8081-8, Flight Instructor Practical Test Standards for Glider

NOTE: AC 00-2, Advisory Circular Checklist, transmits the status of all FAA advisory circulars (AC's), as well as FAA internal publications and miscellaneous flight information, such as Aeronautical

Information Manual, Airport/Facility Directory, knowledge test guides, practical test standards, and other material directly related to a certificate or rating. To obtain a free copy of AC 00-2, send your request to:

U.S. Department of Transportation
Subsequent Distribution Office, SVC-121.23
Ardmore East Business Center
3341 Q 75 Ave.
Landover, MD 20785

LEGEND INFORMATION

ABBREVIATIONS

The following abbreviations are those commonly used within this Directory. Other abbreviations may be found in the Legend and are not duplicated below. The abbreviations presented are intended to represent grammatical variations of the basic form. (Example—"req" may mean "request," "requesting," "requested," or "requests").

abv	above	MSAW	minimum safe altitude warning
acft	aircraft		
AER	approach end rwy	NFCT	non-federal control tower
AFSS	Automated Flight Service Station		
		ngt	night
AGL	above ground level	npi	non precision instrument
apch	approach		
arpt	airport	NSTD	nonstandard
avbl	available	ntc	notice
bcn	beacon	opr	operate, operator, operational
blo	below		
byd	beyond	ops	operations
clsd	closed	OTS	out of service
ctc	contact	ovrn	overrun
dalgt	daylight	PAEW	personnel and equipment working
dsplcd	displaced		
durn	duration	p-line	power line
eff	effective	PPR	prior permission required
emerg	emergency		
extd	extend, extended	req	request
FBO	fixed-based operator	rgt tfc	right traffic
FCT	FAA Contract Tower	rqr	request
fld	field	rwy	runway
FSS	Flight Service Station	SPB	Seaplane Base
hr	hour	SR	sunrise
indef	indefinite	SS	sunset
ints	intensity	svc	service
invof	in the vicinity of	tfc	traffic
LAA	Local Airport Advisory	thld	threshold
idg	landing	tkf	take-off
lgtd	lighted	tmpry	temporary
lgts	lights	twr	tower
med	medium	twy	taxiway
MSL	mean sea level		

LEGEND 1.—Abbreviations.

DIRECTORY LEGEND
SAMPLE

① ② ③ ④ ⑤ ⑥

CITY NAME
  AIRPORT NAME (ORL)   4 E   UTC-5(-4DT)   N28°32.72' W81°21.17'   JACKSONVILLE
  200 B S4 **FUEL** 100, JET A   OX 1, 2, 3   TPA—1000(800)   AOE   ARFF Index A   Not insp.   **COPTER**
                                                                                   H-46, L-19C
⑨ ⑩ ⑪   ⑫   ⑬   ⑭   ⑮   ⑯   ⑰   IAP
                                                                                      ⑦

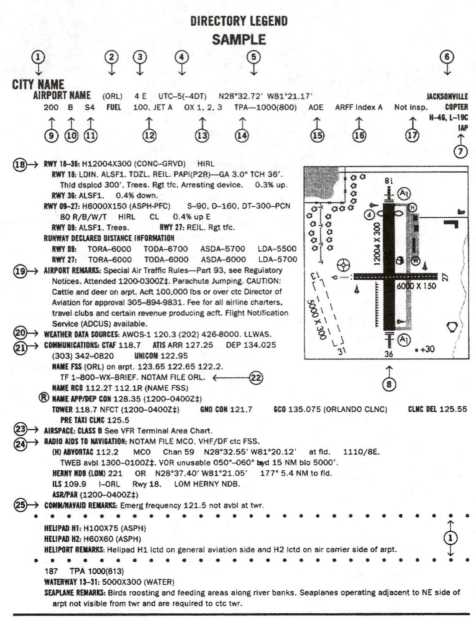

⑱ → **RWY 18-36:** H12004X300 (CONC-GRVD)   HIRL
       RWY 18: LDIN. ALSF1. TDZL. REIL. PAPI(P2R)—GA 3.0° TCH 36'.
           Thld dsplcd 300'. Trees. Rgt tfc. Arresting device.   0.3% up.
       RWY 36: ALSF1.   0.4% down.
     RWY 09-27: H6000X150 (ASPH-PFC)   S-90, D-160, DT-300-PCN
         80 R/B/W/T   HIRL   CL   0.4% up E
       RWY 09: ALSF1. Trees.   **RWY 27:** REIL. Rgt tfc.
     RUNWAY DECLARED DISTANCE INFORMATION
       RWY 09:   TORA-6000   TODA-6700   ASDA-5700   LDA-5500
       RWY 27:   TORA-6000   TODA-6000   ASDA-6000   LDA-5700
⑲ → **AIRPORT REMARKS:** Special Air Traffic Rules—Part 93, see Regulatory
       Notices. Attended 1200-0300Z‡. Parachute Jumping. CAUTION:
       Cattle and deer on arpt. Acft 100,000 lbs or over ctc Director of
       Aviation for approval 305-894-9831. Fee for all airline charters,
       travel clubs and certain revenue producing acft. Flight Notification
       Service (ADCUS) available.
⑳ → **WEATHER DATA SOURCES:** AWOS-1 120.3 (202) 426-8000. LLWAS.
㉑ → **COMMUNICATIONS:** CTAF 118.7   ATIS ARR 127.25   DEP 134.025
       (303) 342-0820   **UNICOM** 122.95
     NAME FSS (ORL) on arpt. 123.65 122.65 122.2.
       TF 1-800-WX-BRIEF. NOTAM FILE ORL. ← ㉒
     NAME RCO 112.2T 112.1R (NAME FSS)
  Ⓡ **NAME APP/DEP CON** 128.35 (1200-0400Z‡)
     TOWER 118.7 NFCT (1200-0400Z‡)   **GND CON** 121.7   **GCO** 135.075 (ORLANDO CLNC)   **CLNC DEL** 125.55
       PRE TAXI CLNC 125.5
㉓ → **AIRSPACE:** CLASS B See VFR Terminal Area Chart.
㉔ → **RADIO AIDS TO NAVIGATION:** NOTAM FILE MCO. VHF/DF ctc FSS.
       (H) ABVORTAC 112.2   MCO   Chan 59   N28°32.55' W81°20.12'   at fld.   1110/8E.
       TWEB avbl 1300-0100Z‡. VOR unusable 050°-060° byd 15 NM blo 5000'.
       HERNY NDB (LOM) 221   OR   N28°37.40' W81°21.05'   177° 5.4 NM to fld.
       ILS 109.9   I-ORL   Rwy 18.   LOM HERNY NDB.
       ASR/PAR (1200-0400Z‡)
㉕ → **COMM/NAVAID REMARKS:** Emerg frequency 121.5 not avbl at twr.
• •
     HELIPAD H1: H100X75 (ASPH)   ①
     HELIPAD H2: H60X60 (ASPH)
     HELIPORT REMARKS: Helipad H1 lctd on general aviation side and H2 lctd on air carrier side of arpt.
• •
     187   TPA 1000(813)
     WATERWAY 13-31: 5000X300 (WATER)
     SEAPLANE REMARKS: Birds roosting and feeding areas along river banks. Seaplanes operating adjacent to NE side of
       arpt not visible from twr and are required to ctc twr.

⑧

All Bearings and Radials are Magnetic unless otherwise specified.
All mileages are nautical unless otherwise noted.
All times are UTC except as noted.
The horizontal reference datum of this publication is North American Datum of 1983 (NAD83), which for charting purposes
is considered equivalent to World Geodetic System 1984 (WGS 84).

LEGEND 2.—Airport/Facility Directory.

DIRECTORY LEGEND

⑧ SKETCH LEGEND

RUNWAYS/LANDING AREAS

Hard Surfaced . . . .

Metal Surface . . . .

Sod, Gravel, etc. . . . .

Light Plane, ...
Ski Landing Area or Water

Under Construction . . . . .

Closed . . . .

Helicopter Landings Area . . . . Ⓗ

Displaced Threshold . . . .

Taxiway, Apron and Stopways . .

MISCELLANEOUS BASE AND CULTURAL FEATURES

Buildings . . . .

Power Lines . . . .

Fence . . . .

Towers . . . .

Tanks . . . .

Oil Well . . . .

Smoke Stack . . . .

Obstruction 5812

Controlling Obstruction . . . . +5812

Trees . . . .

Populated Places . . . .

Cuts and Fills . . . . . . Cut   Fill

Cliffs and Depressions . .

Ditch . . . .

Hill . . . .

RADIO AIDS TO NAVIGATION

VORTAC . . .   VOR . . . .

VOR/DME . .   NDB . . . .

TACAN . . . .   NDB/DME . . . .

MISCELLANEOUS AERONAUTICAL FEATURES

Airport Beacon . . . .   ☆

Wind Cone . . . .

Landing Tee . . . .

Tetrahedron . . . .

Control Tower . . . .

APPROACH LIGHTING SYSTEMS

A dot ' • ' portrayed with approach lighting letter identifier indicates sequenced flashing lights (F) installed with the approach lighting system e.g. Ⓐ① Negative symbology, e.g., Ⓐ Ⓥ indicates Pilot Controlled Lighting (PCL).

Runway Centerline Lighting . . . . .

Ⓐ Approach Lighting System ALSF-2 . .

Ⓐ① Approach Lighting System ALSF-1 . .

Ⓐ② Short Approach Lighting System SALS/SALSF . . . .

Ⓐ③ Simplified Short Approach Lighting System (SSALR) with RAIL . . . . .

Ⓐ④ Medium Intensity Approach Lighting System (MALS and MALSF)/(SSALS and SSALF) . . . .

Ⓐ⑤ Medium Intensity Approach Lighting System (MALSR) and RAIL . . . . . .

Ⓞ Omnidirectional Approach Lighting System (ODALS) . . . .

Ⓓ Navy Parallel Row and Cross Bar . . .

Ⓘ Air Force Overrun . . . .

Ⓥ Visual Approach Slope Indicator with Standard Threshold Clearance provided

Ⓥ② Pulsating Visual Approach Slope Indicator (PVASI)

Ⓥ③ Visual Approach Slope Indicator with a threshold crossing height to accomodate long bodied or jumbo aircraft

Ⓥ④ Tri-color Visual Approach Slope Indicator (TRCV)

Ⓥ⑤ Approach Path Alignment Panel (APAP)

Ⓟ Precision Approach Path Indicator (PAPI)

LEGEND 3.—Airport/Facility Directory.

DIRECTORY LEGEND
LEGEND

This Directory is an alphabetical listing of data on record with the FAA on all airports that are open to the public, associated terminal control facilities, air route traffic control centers and radio aids to navigation within the conterminous United States, Puerto Rico and the Virgin Islands. Airports are listed alphabetically by associated city name and cross referenced by airport name. Facilities associated with an airport, but with a different name, are listed individually under their own name, as well as under the airport with which they are associated.

The listing of an airport in this directory merely indicates the airport operator's willingness to accommodate transient aircraft, and does not represent that the facility conforms with any Federal or local standards, or that it has been approved for use on the part of the general public.

The information on obstructions is taken from reports submitted to the FAA. It has not been verified in all cases. Pilots are cautioned that objects not indicated in this tabulation (or on charts) may exist which can create a hazard to flight operation.

Detailed specifics concerning services and facilities tabulated within this directory are contained in Aeronautical Information Manual, Basic Flight Information and ATC Procedures.

The legend items that follow explain in detail the contents of this Directory and are keyed to the circled numbers on the sample on the preceding pages.

① CITY/AIRPORT NAME

Airports and facilities in this directory are listed alphabetically by associated city and state. Where the city name is different from the airport name the city name will appear on the line above the airport name. Airports with the same associated city name will be listed alphabetically by airport name and will be separated by a dashed rule line. All others will be separated by a solid rule line. (Designated Helipads and Seaplane Landing Areas (Water) associated with a land airport will be separated by a dotted line.)

② LOCATION IDENTIFIER

A three or four character code assigned to airports. These identifiers are used by ATC in lieu of the airport name in flight plans, flight strips and other written records and computer operations.

③ AIRPORT LOCATION

Airport location is expressed as distance and direction from the center of the associated city in nautical miles and cardinal points, i.e., 4 NE.

④ TIME CONVERSION

Hours of operation of all facilities are expressed in Coordinated Universal Time (UTC) and shown as "Z" time. The directory indicates the number of hours to be subtracted from UTC to obtain local standard time and local daylight saving time UTC–5(–4DT). The symbol ‡ indicates that during periods of Daylight Saving Time effective hours will be one hour earlier than shown. In those areas where daylight saving time is not observed that (–4DT) and ‡ will not be shown. All states observe daylight savings time except Arizona, Hawaii and that portion of Indiana in the Eastern Time Zone and Puerto Rico and the Virgin Islands.

⑤ GEOGRAPHIC POSITION OF AIRPORT

Positions are shown in degrees, minutes and hundredths of a minute and represent the approximate center of mass of all usable runways.

⑥ CHARTS

The Sectional Chart and Low and High Altitude Enroute Chart and panel on which the airport or facility is located. Helicopter Chart locations will be indicated as, i.e., COPTER.

⑦ INSTRUMENT APPROACH PROCEDURES

IAP indicates an airport for which a prescribed (Public Use) FAA Instrument Approach Procedure has been published.

⑧ AIRPORT SKETCH

·The airport sketch, when provided, depicts the airport and related topographical information as seen from the air and should be used in conjunction with the text. It is intended as a guide for pilots in VFR conditions. Symbology that is not self-explanatory will be reflected in the sketch legend. The airport sketch will be oriented with True North at the top. Airport sketches will be added incrementally.

⑨ ELEVATION

The highest point of an airport's usable runways measured in feet from mean sea level. When elevation is sea level it will be indicated as (00). When elevation is below sea level a minus (–) sign will precede the figure.

⑩ ROTATING LIGHT BEACON

B indicates rotating beacon is available. Rotating beacons operate dusk to dawn unless otherwise indicated in AIRPORT REMARKS.

⑪ SERVICING

S1:   Minor airframe repairs.   S3:   Major airframe and minor powerplant repairs.
S2:   Minor airframe and minor powerplant repairs.   S4:   Major airframe and major powerplant repairs.

LEGEND 4.—Airport/Facility Directory.

DIRECTORY LEGEND

⑫ FUEL

CODE	FUEL
80	Grade 80 gasoline (Red)
100	Grade 100 gasoline (Green)
100LL	100LL gasoline (low lead) (Blue)
115	Grade 115 gasoline
A	Jet A—Kerosene freeze point–40° C.
A1	Jet A-1—Kerosene freeze point–47°C.
A1+	Jet A-1—Kerosene with icing inhibitor, freeze point–47° C.
B	Jet B—Wide-cut turbine fuel, freeze point–50° C.

CODE	FUEL
B+	Jet B—Wide-cut turbine fuel with icing inhibitor, freeze point–50° C.
J8	(JP–8 Military specification) Jet A–1, kerosene with icing inhibitor, freeze point–47°C.
J8+100	(JP–8 Mil spec) Jet A–1, Kerosene with FS–II*, FP** minus 47°C, with fuel additive package that improves thermo stability characteristics of JP–8.
MOGAS	Automobile gasoline which is to be used as aircraft fuel.

NOTE: Automobile Gasoline. Certain automobile gasoline may be used in specific aircraft engines if a FAA supplemental type cetificate has been obtained. Automobile gasoline which is to be used in aircraft engines will be identified as "MOGAS", however, the grade/type and other octane rating will not be published.

Data shown on fuel availability represents the most recent information the publisher has been able to acquire. Because of a variety of factors, the fuel listed may not always be obtainable by transient civil pilots. Confirmation of availability of fuel should be made directly with fuel dispensers at locations where refueling is planned.

⑬ OXYGEN

OX 1 High Pressure
OX 2 Low Pressure

OX 3 High Pressure—Replacement Bottles
OX 4 Low Pressure—Replacement Bottles

⑭ TRAFFIC PATTERN ALTITUDE

Traffic Pattern Altitude (TPA)—The first figure shown is TPA above mean sea level. The second figure in parentheses is TPA above airport elevation.

⑮ AIRPORT OF ENTRY, LANDING RIGHTS, AND CUSTOMS USER FEE AIRPORTS

U.S. CUSTOMS USER FEE AIRPORT—Private Aircraft operators are frequently required to pay the costs associated with customs processing.

AOE—Airport of Entry—A customs Airport of Entry where permission from U.S. Customs is not required, however, at least one hour advance notice of arrival must be furnished.

LRA—Landing Rights Airport—Application for permission to land must be submitted in advance to U.S. Customs. At least one hour advance notice of arrival must be furnished.

NOTE: Advance notice of arrival at both an AOE and LRA airport may be included in the flight plan when filed in Canada or Mexico, where Flight Notification Service (ADCUS) is available the airport remark will indicate this service. This notice will also be treated as an application for permission to land in the case of an LRA. Although advance notice of arrival may be relayed to Customs through Mexico, Canadian, and U.S. Communications facilities by flight plan, the aircraft operator is solely responsible for insuring that Customs receives the notification. (See Customs, Immigration and Naturalization, Public Health and Agriculture Department requirements in the International Flight Information Manual for further details.)

⑯ CERTIFICATED AIRPORT (FAR 139)

Airports serving Department of Transportation certified carriers and certified under FAR, Part 139, are indicated by the ARFF index; i.e., ARFF Index A, which relates to the availability of crash, fire, rescue equipment.

FAR–PART 139 CERTIFICATED AIRPORTS
INDICES AND AIRCRAFT RESCUE AND FIRE FIGHTING EQUIPMENT REQUIREMENTS

Airport Index	Required No. Vehicles	Aircraft Length		Scheduled Departures	Agent + Water for Foam
A	1	<90'		≥1	500#DC or HALON 1211 or 450#DC + 100 gal H$_2$O
B	1 or 2	≥90',	<126'	≥5	Index A + 1500 gal H$_2$O
		≥126',	<159'	<5	
C	2 or 3	≥126',	<159'	≥5	Index A + 3000 gal H$_2$O
		≥159',	<200'	<5	
D	3	≥159',	<200'	≥5	Index A + 4000 gal H$_2$O
		>200'		<5	
E	3	≥200'		≥5	Index A + 6000 gal H$_2$O

> Greater Than; < Less Than; ≥ Equal or Greater Than; ≤ Equal or Less Than;   H$_2$O—Water; DC—Dry Chemical.

NOTE: The listing of ARFF index does not necessarily assure coverage for non-air carrier operations or at other than prescribed times for air carrier. ARFF Index Ltd.—Indicates ARFF coverage may or may not be available, for information contact airport manager prior to flight.

LEGEND 5.—Airport/Facility Directory.

DIRECTORY LEGEND

(17) FAA INSPECTION

All airports not inspected by FAA will be identified by the note: Not insp. This indicates that the airport information has been provided by the owner or operator of the field.

(18) RUNWAY DATA

Runway information is shown on two lines. That information common to the entire runway is shown on the first line while information concerning the runway ends are shown on the second or following line. Lengthy information will be placed in the Airport Remarks.

Runway direction, surface, length, width, weight bearing capacity, lighting, slope and appropriate remarks are shown for each runway. Direction, length, width, lighting and remarks are shown for sealanes. The full dimensions of helipads are shown, i.e., 50X150.

RUNWAY SURFACE AND LENGTH

Runway lengths prefixed by the letter "H" indicate that the runways are hard surfaced (concrete, asphalt). If the runway length is not prefixed, the surface is sod, clay, etc. The runway surface composition is indicated in parentheses after runway length as follows:

(AFSC)—Aggregate friction seal coat	(GRVD)—Grooved	(RFSC)—Rubberized friction seal coat
(ASPH)—Asphalt	(GRVL)—Gravel, or cinders	(TURF)—Turf
(CONC)—Concrete	(PFC)—Porous friction courses	(TRTD)—Treated
(DIRT)—Dirt	(PSP)—Pierced steel plank	(WC)—Wire combed

RUNWAY WEIGHT BEARING CAPACITY

Runway strength data shown in this publication is derived from available information and is a realistic estimate of capability at an average level of activity. It is not intended as a maximum allowable weight or as an operating limitation. Many airport pavements are capable of supporting limited operations with gross weights of 25-50% in excess of the published figures. Permissible operating weights, insofar as runway strengths are concerned, are a matter of agreement between the owner and user. When desiring to operate into any airport at weights in excess of those published in the publication, users should contact the airport management for permission. Add 000 to figure following S, D, DT, DDT, AUW, etc., for gross weight capacity:

S—Single-wheel type landing gear. (DC–3), (C–47), (F–15), etc.
D—Dual-wheel type landing gear. (DC–6), etc.
T—Twin-wheel type landing gear. (DC–6), (C–9A), etc.
ST—Single-tandem type landing gear. (C–130).
SBTT—Single-belly twin tandem landing gear (KC–10).
DT—Dual-tandem type landing gear, (707), etc.
TT—Twin-tandem type (includes quadricycle) landing gear (707), (B–52), (C–135), etc.
TRT—Triple-tandem landing gear, (C–17)
DDT—Double dual-tandem landing gear. (E4A/747).
TDT—Twin delta-tandem landing gear. (C–5, Concorde).
AUW—All up weight. Maximum weight bearing capacity for any aircraft irrespective of landing gear configuration.
SWL—Single Wheel Loading. (This includes information submitted in terms of Equivalent Single Wheel Loading (ESWL) and Single Isolated Wheel Loading). SWL figures are shown in thousands of pounds with the last three figures being omitted.
PSI—Pounds per square inch. PSI is the actual figure expressing maximum pounds per square inch runway will support, e.g., (SWL 000/PSI 535).

Quadricycle and dual-tandem are considered virtually equal for runway weight bearing consideration, as are single-tandem and dual-wheel. Omission of weight bearing capacity indicates information unknown.

The ACN/PCN System is the ICAO method of reporting pavement strength for pavements with bearing strengths greater than 12,500 pounds. The Pavement Classification Number (PCN) is established by an engineering assessment of the runway. The PCN is for use in conjunction with an Aircraft Classification Number (ACN). Consult the Aircraft Flight Manual or other appropriate source for ACN tables or charts. Currently, ACN data may not be available for all aircraft. If an ACN table or chart is available, the ACN can be calculated by taking into account the aircraft weight, the pavement type, and the subgrade category. For runways that have been evaluated under the ACN/PCN system, the PCN will be shown as a five part code (e.g. PCN 80 R/B/W/T). Details of the coded format are as follows:

(1) The PCN NUMBER—The reported PCN indicates that an aircraft with an ACN equal or less than the reported PCN can operate on the pavement subject to any limitation on the tire pressure.

(2) The type of pavement:
  R — Rigid
  F — Flexible

(3) The pavement subgrade category:
  A — High
  B — Medium
  C — Low
  D — Ultra-low

(4) The maximum tire pressure authorized for the pavement:
  W — High, no limit
  X — Medium, limited to 217 psi
  Y — Low, limited to 145 psi
  Z — Very low, limited to 73 psi

(5) Pavement evaluation method:
  T — Technical evaluation
  U — By experience of aircraft using the pavement

NOTE: Prior permission from the airport controlling authority is required when the ACN of the aircraft exceeds the published PCN or aircraft tire pressure exceeds the published limits.

LEGEND 6.—Airport/Facility Directory.

DIRECTORY LEGEND

RUNWAY DECLARED DISTANCE INFORMATION

TORA—Take-off Run Available
TODA—Take-off Distance Available
ASDA—Accelerate-Stop Distance Available
LDA—Landing Distance Available

⑲ AIRPORT REMARKS

Landing Fee indicates landing charges for private or non-revenue producing aircraft. In addition, fees may be charged for planes that remain over a couple of hours and buy no services, or at major airline terminals for all aircraft.
Remarks—Data is confined to operational items affecting the status and usability of the airport.
Parachute Jumping.—See "PARACHUTE" tabulation for details.
Unless otherwise stated, remarks including runway ends refer to the runway's approach end.

⑳ WEATHER DATA SOURCES

ASOS—Automated Surface Observing System. Reports the same as an AWOS-3 plus precipitation identification and intensity, and freezing rain occurrence (future enhancement).
AWOS—Automated Weather Observing System
  AWOS-A—reports altimeter setting.
  AWOS-1—reports altimeter setting, wind data and usually temperature, dewpoint and density altitude.
  AWOS-2—reports the same as AWOS-1 plus visibility.
  AWOS-3—reports the same as AWOS-1 plus visibility and cloud/ceiling data.
  See AIM, Basic Flight Information and ATC Procedures for detailed description of AWOS.
HIWAS—See RADIO AIDS TO NAVIGATION
LAWRS—Limited Aviation Weather Reporting Station where observers report cloud height, weather, obstructions to vision, temperature and dewpoint (in most cases), surface wind, altimeter and pertinent remarks.
LLWAS—indicates a Low Level Wind Shear Alert System consisting of a center field and several field perimeter anemometers.
SAWRS—identifies airports that have a Supplemental Aviation Weather Reporting Station available to pilots for current weather information.
SWSL—Supplemental Weather Service Location providing current local weather information via radio and telephone.
TDWR—indicates airports that have Terminal Doppler Weather Radar.

㉑ COMMUNICATIONS

Communications will be listed in sequence in the order shown below:
Common Traffic Advisory Frequency (CTAF), Automatic Terminal Information Service (ATIS) and Aeronautical Advisory Stations (UNICOM) along with their frequency is shown, where available, on the line following the heading "COMMUNICATIONS." When the CTAF and UNICOM is the same frequency, the frequency will be shown as CTAF/UNICOM freq.
Flight Service Station (FSS) Information. The associated FSS will be shown followed by the identifier and information concerning availability of telephone service, e.g., Direct Line (DL), Local Call (LC-384-2341), Toll free call, dial (TF 800-852-7036 or TF 1-800-227-7160), Long Distance (LD 202-426-8800 or LD 1-202-555-1212) etc. The airport NOTAM file identifier will be shown as "NOTAM FILE IAD." Where the FSS is located on the field it will be indicated as "on arpt" following the identifier. Frequencies available will follow. The FSS telephone number will follow along with any significant operational information. FSS's whose name is not the same as the airport on which located will also be listed in the normal alphabetical name listing for the state in which located. Remote Communications Outlet (RCO) providing service to the airport followed by the frequency and name of the Controlling FSS.
FSS's provide information on airport conditions, radio aids and other facilities, and process flight plans. Local Airport Advisory Service is provided on the CTAF by FSS's located at non-tower airports or airports where the tower is not in operation.
(See AIM, Par. 157/158 Traffic Advisory Practices at airports where a tower is not in operation or AC 90 - 42C.)
Aviation weather briefing service is provided by FSS specialists. Flight and weather briefing services are also available by calling the telephone numbers listed.
Remote Communications Outlet (RCO)—An unmanned air/ground communications facility, remotely controlled and providing UHF or VHF communications capability to extend the service range of an FSS.
Civil Communications Frequencies—Civil communications frequencies used in the FSS air/ground system are now operated simplex on 122.0, 122.2, 122.3, 122.4, 122.6, 123.6; emergency 121.5; plus receive-only on 122.05, 122.1, 122.15, and 123.6.
  a. 122.0 is assigned as the Enroute Flight Advisory Service channel at selected FSS's,
  b. 122.2 is assigned to most FSS's as a common enroute simplex service.
  c. 123.6 is assigned as the airport advisory channel at non-tower FSS locations, however, it is still in commission at some FSS's collocated with towers to provide part time Local Airport Advisory Service.
  d. 122.1 is the primary receive-only frequency at VOR's. 122.05, 122.15 and 123.6 are assigned at selected VOR's meeting certain criteria.
  e. Some FSS's are assigned 50 kHz channels for simplex operation in the 122-123 MHz band (e.g. 122.35). Pilots using the FSS A/G system should refer to this directory or appropriate charts to determine frequencies available at the FSS or remoted facility through which they wish to communicate.
Part time FSS hours of operation are shown in remarks under facility name.

Emergency frequency 121.5 is available at all Flight Service Stations, Towers, Approach Control and RADAR facilities, unless indicated as not available.
Frequencies published followed by the letter "T" or "R", indicate that the facility will only transmit or receive respectively on that frequency. All radio aids to navigation frequencies are transmit only.

LEGEND 7.—Airport/Facility Directory.

DIRECTORY LEGEND

TERMINAL SERVICES

CTAF—A program designed to get all vehicles and aircraft at uncontrolled airports on a common frequency.

ATIS—A continuous broadcast of recorded non-control information in selected areas of high activity.

UNICOM—A non-government air/ground radio communications facility utilized to provide general airport advisory service.

APP CON —Approach Control. The symbol ® indicates radar approach control.

TOWER—Control tower.

GND CON—Ground Control.

GCO—GROUND COMMUNICATION OUTLET—An unstaffed, remotely controlled, ground/ground communications facility. Pilots at uncontrolled airports may contact ATC and FSS via VHF to a telephone connection to obtain an instrument clearance or close a VFR or IFR flight plan. They may also get an updated weather briefing prior to takeoff. Pilots will use four "key clicks" on the VHF radio to contact the appropriate ATC facility or six "key clicks" to contact the FSS. The GCO system is intended to be used only on the ground.

DEP CON —Departure Control. The symbol ® indicates radar departure control.

CLNC DEL—Clearance Delivery.

PRE TAXI CLNC—Pre taxi clearance.

VFR ADVSY SVC—VFR Advisory Service. Service provided by Non-Radar Approach Control.
   Advisory Service for VFR aircraft (upon a workload basis) ctc APP CON.

TOWER, APP CON and DEP CON RADIO CALL will be the same as the airport name unless indicated otherwise.

㉒ NOTAM SERVICE

All public use landing areas are provided NOTAM "D" (distant dissemination) and NOTAM "L" (local dissemination) service. Airport NOTAM file identifier is shown following the associated FSS data for individual airports, e.g. "NOTAM FILE IAD". See AIM, Basic Flight Information and ATC Procedures for detailed description of NOTAM's.

㉓ AIRSPACE

CLASS B—Radar Sequencing and Separation Service for all aircraft in CLASS B airspace

TRSA—Radar Sequencing and Separation Service for participating VFR Aircraft within a Terminal Radar Service Area

Class C, D, and E airspace described in this publication is that airspace usually consisting of a 5 NM radius core surface area that begins at the surface and extends upward to an altitude above the airport elevation (charted in MSL for Class C and Class D).

When CLASS C airspace defaults to CLASS E, the core surface area becomes CLASS E. This will be formatted as: **AIRSPACE: CLASS C** svc "times" ctc **APP CON** other times CLASS E.

When Class C airspace defaults to Class G, the core surface area becomes Class G up to but not including the overlying controlled airspace. There are Class E airspace areas beginning at either 700' or 1200' AGL used to transition to/from the terminal or enroute environment. This will be formatted as: **AIRSPACE: CLASS C** svc "times" ctc **APP CON** other times CLASS G, CLASS E 700' (or 1200') AGL & abv.

NOTE: AIRSPACE SVC "TIMES" INCLUDE ALL ASSOCIATED EXTENSIONS. Arrival extensions for instrument approach procedures become part of the primary core surface area. These extensions may be either Class D or Class E airspace and are effective concurrent with the times of the primary core surface area.

(See CLASS AIRSPACE in the Aeronautical Information Manual for further details)

㉔ RADIO AIDS TO NAVIGATION

The Airport Facility Directory lists by facility name all Radio Aids to Navigation, except Military TACANS, that appear on National Ocean Service Visual or IFR Aeronautical Charts and those upon which the FAA has approved an Instrument Approach Procedure. All VOR, VORTAC ILS and MLS equipment in the National Airspace System has an automatic monitoring and shutdown feature in the event of malfunction. Unmonitored, as used in this publication for any navigational aid, means that FSS or tower personnel cannot observe the malfunction or shutdown signal. The NAVAID NOTAM file identifier will be shown as "NOTAM FILE IAD" and will be listed on the Radio Aids to Navigation line. When two or more NAVAIDS are listed and the NOTAM file identifier is different than shown on the Radio Aids to Navigation line, then it will be shown with the NAVAID listing. NOTAM file identifiers for ILS's and their components (e.g., NDB (LOM) are the same as the identifiers for the associated airports and are not repeated. Hazardous Inflight Weather Advisory Service (HIWAS) will be shown where this service is broadcast over selected VOR's.

NAVAID information is tabulated as indicated in the following sample:

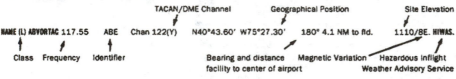

NAME (L) ABVORTAC 117.55   ABE   Chan 122(Y)   N40°43.60' W75°27.30'   180° 4.1 NM to fld.   1110/8E. HIWAS.

Class   Frequency   Identifier

TACAN/DME Channel

Geographical Position

Site Elevation

Bearing and distance facility to center of airport   Magnetic Variation   Hazardous Inflight Weather Advisory Service

VOR unusable 020°-060° byd 26 NM blo 3,500'

Restriction within the normal altitude/range of the navigational aid (See primary alphabetical listing for restrictions on VORTAC and VOR/DME).

Note: Those DME channel numbers with a (Y) suffix require TACAN to be placed in the "Y" mode to receive distance information.

LEGEND 8.—Airport/Facility Directory.

DIRECTORY LEGEND

HIWAS—Hazardous Inflight Weather Advisory Service is a continuous broadcast of inflight weather advisories including summarized SIGMETs, convective SIGMETs, AIRMETs and urgent PIREPs. HIWAS is presently broadcast over selected VOR's and will be implemented throughout the conterminous U.S.

ASR/PAR—Indicates that Surveillance (ASR) or Precision (PAR) radar instrument approach minimums are published in the U.S. Terminal Procedures. Only part-time hours of operation will be shown.

RADIO CLASS DESIGNATIONS

VOR/DME/TACAN Standard Service Volume (SSV) Classifications

SSV Class	Altitudes	Distance (NM)
(T) Terminal	1000' to 12,000'	25
(L) Low Altitude	1000' to 18,000'	40
(H) High Altitude	1000' to 14,500'	40
	14,500' to 18,000'	100
	18,000' to 45,000'	130
	45,000' to 60,000'	100

NOTE: Additionally, (H) facilities provide (L) and (T) service volume and (L) facilities provide (T) service. Altitudes are with respect to the station's site elevation. Coverage is not available in a cone of airspace directly above the facility.

The term VOR is, operationally, a general term covering the VHF omnidirectional bearing type of facility without regard to the fact that the power, the frequency protected service volume, the equipment configuration, and operational requirements may vary between facilities at different locations.

AB	Automatic Weather Broadcast.
DF	Direction Finding Service.
DME	UHF standard (TACAN compatible) distance measuring equipment.
DME(Y)	UHF standard (TACAN compatible) distance measuring equipment that require TACAN to be placed in the "Y" mode to receive DME.
GS	Glide slope.
H	Non-directional radio beacon (homing), power 50 watts to less than 2,000 watts (50 NM at all altitudes).
HH	Non-directional radio beacon (homing), power 2,000 watts or more (75 NM at all altitudes).
H-SAB	Non-directional radio beacons providing automatic transcribed weather service.
ILS	Instrument Landing System (voice, where available, on localizer channel).
IM	Inner marker.
ISMLS	Interim Standard Microwave Landing System.
LDA	Localizer Directional Aid.
LMM	Compass locator station when installed at middle marker site (15 NM at all altitudes).
LOM	Compass locator station when installed at outer marker site (15 NM at all altitudes).
MH	Non-directional radio beacon (homing) power less than 50 watts (25 NM at all altitudes).
MLS	Microwave Landing System.
MM	Middle marker.
OM	Outer marker.
S	Simultaneous range homing signal and/or voice.
SABH	Non-directional radio beacon not authorized for IFR or ATC. Provides automatic weather broadcasts.
SDF	Simplified Direction Facility.
TACAN	UHF navigational facility-omnidirectional course and distance information.
VOR	VHF navigational facility-omnidirectional course only.
VOR/DME	Collocated VOR navigational facility and UHF standard distance measuring equipment.
VORTAC	Collocated VOR and TACAN navigational facilities.
W	Without voice on radio facility frequency.
Z	VHF station location marker at a LF radio facility.

LEGEND 9.—Airport Facility Directory.

TERMS/LANDING MINIMA DATA

IFR LANDING MINIMA

The United States Standard for Terminal Instrument Procedures (TERPS) is the approved criteria for formulating instrument approach procedures. Landing minima are established for six aircraft approach categories (ABCDE and COPTER). In the absence of COPTER MINIMA, helicopters may use the CAT A minimums of other procedures. The standard format for RNAV minima and landing minima portrayal follows:

RNAV MINIMA

CATEGORY	A	B	C	D
GLS PA DA		1382/24 200 (200-½)		
LNAV/ DA VNAV	1500/24	318 (400-½)		1500/40 318 (400-¾)
LNAV MDA	1700/24	518 (600-½)	1700/50 518 (600-1)	1700/60 518 (600-1¼)
CIRCLING	1760-1	578 (600-1)	1760-1½ 578 (600-1½)	1760-2 578 (600-2)

RNAV minimums are dependent on navigation equipment capability, as stated in the applicable AFM or AFMS and as outlined below.

GLS (GLobal Navigation System (GNSS) Landing System)

Must have WAAS (Wide Area Augmentation System) equipment approved for precise approach.
Note: "PA" indicates that the runway environment, i.e., runway markings, runway lights, parallel taxiway, etc., meets precision approach requirements. If the GLS minimums line does not contain "PA", then the runway environment does not support precision requirements.

LNAV/VNAV (Lateral Navigation/Vertical Navigation)

Must have WAAS equipment approved for precision approach, or RNP-0.3 system based on GPS or DME/DME, with an IFR approach approved Baro-VNAV system. Other RNAV approach systems require special approval. Use of Baro-VNAV systems is limited by temperature, i.e., "Baro-VNAV NA below -20 C(-4 F)". (Not applicable if chart is annotated "Baro-VNAV NA".)
NOTE: DME/DME based RNP-0.3 systems may be used only when a chart note indicates DME/DME availability, for example, "DME/DME RNP-0.3 Authorized." Specific DME facilities may be required, for example: "DME/DME RNP-0.3 Authorized. ABC, XYZ required."

LNAV (Lateral Navigation)

Must have IFR approach approved WAAS, GPS, GPS based FMS systems, or RNP-0.3 systems based on GPS or DME/DME. Other RNAV approach systems require special approval.
NOTE: DME/DME based RNP-0.3 systems may be used only when a chart note indicates DME/DME availability, for example, "DME/DME RNP-0.3 Authorized." Specific DME facilities may be required, for example: "DME/DME RNP-0.3 Authorized. ABC, XYZ required."

LANDING MINIMA FORMAT

In this example airport elevation is 1179, and runway touchdown zone elevation is 1152.

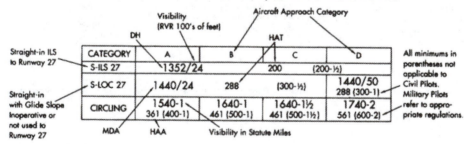

TERMS/LANDING MINIMA DATA

LEGEND 10.—Instrument Approach Procedures Explanation of Terms.

TERMS/LANDING MINIMA DATA

COPTER MINIMA ONLY

CATEGORY	COPTER		
H-176°	680-½	363	(400-½)

Copter Approach Direction   Height of MDA/DH Above Landing Area (HAL)

No circling minimums are provided

RADAR MINIMA

											Visibility (RVR 100's of feet)
PAR (c)	10	2.5°/42/1000	ABCDE	195/16	100	(100-¼)					
(d)	28	2.5°/48/1068	ABCDE	187/16	100	(100-¼)					
ASR	10		ABC	560/40	463	(500-¾)	D	560/50	463	(500-1)	
			E	580/60	463	(500-1¼)					
	28		AB	600/50	513	(600-1)	C	600/60	513	(600-1¼)	
			DE	600-1½	513	(600-1½)					
CIR (b)	10		AB	560-1¼	463	(500-1¼)	C	560-1½	463	(500-1½)	
	28		AB	600-1¼	503	(600-1¼)	C	600-1½	503	(600-1½)	
	10, 28		DE	660-2	563	(600-2)					

Visibility in Statute Miles

All minimums in parentheses not applicable to Civil Pilots. Military Pilots refer to appropriate regulations.

Radar Minima:

1. Minima shown are the lowest permitted by established criteria. Pilots should consult applicable directives for their category of aircraft.
2. The circling MDA and weather minima to be used are those for the runway to which the final approach is flown - not the landing runway. In the above RADAR MINIMA example, a category C aircraft flying a radar approach to runway 10, circling to land on runway 28, must use an MDA of 560 feet with weather minima of 500-1½ .

▲ Alternate Minimums not standard. Civil users refer to tabulation. USA/USN/USAF pilots refer to appropriate regulations.

▲ NA   Alternate minimums are Not Authorized due to unmonitored facility or absence of weather reporting service.

▼ Take-off Minimums not standard and/or Departure Procedures are published. Refer to tabulation.

AIRCRAFT APPROACH CATEGORIES

Speeds are based on 1.3 times the stall speed in the landing configuration of maximum gross landing weight. An aircraft shall fit in only one category. If it is necessary to maneuver at speeds in excess of the upper limit of a speed range for a category, the minimums for the next higher category should be used. For example, an aircraft which falls in Category A, but is circling to land at a speed in excess of 91 knots, should use the approach Category B minimums when circling to land. See following category limits:

MANEUVERING TABLE

Approach Category	A	B	C	D	E
Speed (Knots)	0-90	91-120	121-140	141-165	Abv 165

RVR/ Meteorological Visibility Comparable Values

The following table shall be used for converting RVR to meteorological visibility when RVR is not reported for the runway of intended operation. Adjustments of landing minima may be required - see Inoperative Components Table.

RVR (feet)	Visibility (statute miles)	RVR (feet)	Visibility (statute miles)
1600	¼	4000	¾
2000	⅜	4500	⅞
2400	½	5000	1
3200	⅝	6000	1¼

TERMS/LANDING MINIMA DATA

LEGEND 11.—Instrument Approach Procedures Explanation of Terms.

GENERAL INFO

GENERAL INFORMATION

This publication includes Instrument Approach Procedures (IAPs), Departure Procedures (DPs), and Standard Terminal Arrivals (STARs) for use by both civil and military aviation and is issued every 56 days.

STANDARD TERMINAL ARRIVALS AND DEPARTURE PROCEDURES

The use of the associated codified STAR/DP and transition identifiers are requested of users when filing flight plans via teletype and are required for users filing flight plans via computer interface. It must be noted that when filing a STAR/DP with a transition, the first three coded characters of the STAR and the last three coded characters of the DP are replaced by the transition code. Examples: ACTON SIX ARRIVAL, file (AQN.AQN6); ACTON SIX ARRIVAL, EDNAS TRANSITION, file (EDNAS.AQN6). FREEHOLD THREE DEPARTURE, file (FREH3.RBV), FREEHOLD THREE DEPARTURE, ELWOOD CITY TRANSITION, file (FREH3.EWC).

PILOT CONTROLLED AIRPORT LIGHTING SYSTEMS

Available pilot controlled lighting (PCL) systems are indicated as follows:
1. Approach lighting systems that bear a system identification are symbolized using negative symbology, e.g., ●, ●, ●
2. Approach lighting systems that do not bear a system identification are indicated with a negative "●" besides the name. A star (*) indicates non-standard PCL, consult Directory/Supplement, e.g., ●*
To activate lights use frequency indicated in the communication section of the chart with a ● or the appropriate lighting system identification e.g., UNICOM 122.8 ●, ●, ●

KEY MIKE	FUNCTION
7 times within 5 seconds	Highest intensity available
5 times within 5 seconds	Medium or lower intensity (Lower REIL or REIL-off)
3 times within 5 seconds	Lowest intensity available (Lower REIL or REIL-off)

CHART CURRENCY INFORMATION

FAA procedure amendment number ——— Amdt 11A 99365 ——— Date of latest change
                                            Orig 00365

The Chart Date indentifies the Julian date the chart was added to the volume or last revised for any reason. The first two digits indicate the year, the last three digits indicate the day of the year (001 to 365/6) in which the latest addition or change was first published.
The Procedure Amendment Number precedes the Chart Date, and changes any time instrument information (e.g., DH, MDA, approach routing, etc.) changes. Procedure changes also cause the Chart Date to change.

MISCELLANEOUS

* Indicates a non-continuously operating facility, see A/FD or flight supplement.
# Indicates control tower temporarily closed UFN.
"Radar required" on the chart indicates that radar vectoring is required for the approach.
Distances in nautical miles (except visibility in statute miles and Runway Visual Range in hundreds of feet). Runway Dimensions in feet. Elevations in feet. Mean Sea Level (MSL). Ceilings in feet above airport elevation. Radials/bearings/headings/courses are magnetic. Horizontal Datum: Unless otherwise noted on the chart, all coordinates are referenced to North American Datum 1983 (NAD 83), which for charting purposes is considered equivalent to World Geodetic System 1984 (WGS 84).

LEGEND 12.—General Explanation.

GENERAL INFO

ABBREVIATIONS

ADF	Automatic Direction Finder
ALS	Approach Light System
ALSF	Approach Light System with Sequenced Flashing Lights
APP CON	Approach Control
ARR	Arrival
ASOS	Automated Surface Observing System
ASR/PAR	Published Radar Minimums at this Airport
ATIS	Automatic Terminal Information Service
AWOS	Automated Weather Observing System
AZ	Azimuth
BC	Back Course
C	Circling
CAT	Category
CCW	Counter Clockwise
Chan	Channel
CLNC DEL	Clearance Delivery
CNF	Computer Navigation Fix
CTAF	Common Traffic Advisory Frequency
CW	Clockwise
DH	Decision Height
DME	Distance Measuring Equipment
DR	Dead Reckoning
ELEV	Elevation
FAF	Final Approach Fix
FM	Fan Marker
FMS	Flight Management System
GCO	Ground Communications Outlet
GPI	Ground Point of Interception
GPS	Global Positioning System
GS	Glide Slope
HAA	Height above Airport
HAL	Height above Landing
HAT	Height above Touchdown
HIRL	High Intensity Runway Lights
IAF	Initial Approach Fix
ICAO	International Civil Aviation Organization
IM	Inner Marker
Intcp	Intercept
INT	Intersection
LDA	Localizer Type Directional Aid
Ldg	Landing
LDIN	Lead in Light System
LIRL	Low Intensity Runway Lights
LOC	Localizer
LR	Lead Radial. Provides at least 2 NM (Copter 1 NM) of lead to assist in turning onto the intermediate/final course.
MALS	Medium Intensity Approach Light System

MALSR	Medium Intensity Approach Light System with RAIL
MAP	Missed Approach Point
MDA	Minimum Descent Altitude
MIRL	Medium Intensity Runway Lights
MLS	Microwave Landing System
MM	Middle Marker
NA	Not Authorized
NDB	Non-directional Radio Beacon
NM	Nautical Mile
NoPT	No Procedure Turn Required (Procedure Turn shall not be executed without ATC clearance)
ODALS	Omnidirectional Approach Light System
OM	Outer Marker
R	Radial
RA	Radio Altimeter setting height
RAIL	Runway Alignment Indicator Lights
RBn	Radio Beacon
RCLS	Runway Centerline Light System
REIL	Runway End Identifier Lights
RNAV	Area Navigation
RNP	Required Navigation Performance
RPI	Runway Point of Intercept(ion)
RRL	Runway Remaining Lights
Rwy	Runway
RVR	Runway-Visual Range
S	Straight-in
SALS	Short Approach Light System
SSALR	Simplified Short Approach Light System with RAIL
SDF	Simplified Directional Facility
TA	Transition Altitude
TAC	TACAN
TCH	Threshold Crossing Height (height in feet Above Ground level)
TDZ	Touchdown Zone
TDZE	Touchdown Zone Elevation
TDZ/CL	Touchdown Zone and Runway Centerline Lighting
TDZL	Touchdown Zone Lights
TLv	Transition Level
VASI	Visual Approach Slope Indicator
VDP	Visual Descent Point
VGSI	Visual Glide Slope Indicator
WP/WPT	Waypoint (RNAV)
X	Radar Only Frequency

GENERAL INFO

LEGEND 13.—Abbreviations.

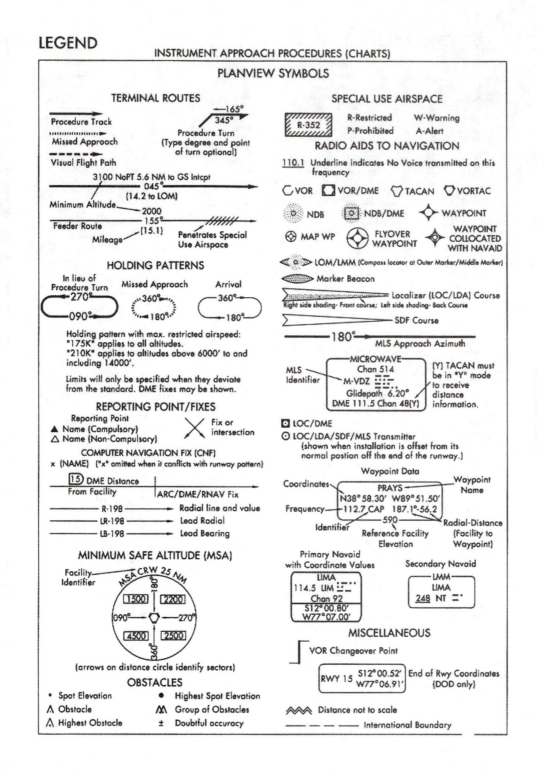

LEGEND
INSTRUMENT APPROACH PROCEDURES (CHARTS)
PLANVIEW SYMBOLS

TERMINAL ROUTES

Procedure Track
Missed Approach
Visual Flight Path

165°
345°
Procedure Turn
(Type degree and point of turn optional)

3100 NoPT 5.6 NM to GS Intcpt
045°
(14.2 to LOM)
Minimum Altitude — 2000
155°
Feeder Route
Mileage (15.1)
Penetrates Special Use Airspace

HOLDING PATTERNS

In lieu of Procedure Turn
270°
090°

Missed Approach
360°
180°

Arrival
360°
180°

Holding pattern with max. restricted airspeed:
"175K" applies to all altitudes.
"210K" applies to altitudes above 6000' to and including 14000'.

Limits will only be specified when they deviate from the standard. DME fixes may be shown.

REPORTING POINT/FIXES

Reporting Point
▲ Name (Compulsory)
△ Name (Non-Compulsory)

✕ Fix or intersection

COMPUTER NAVIGATION FIX (CNF)
x (NAME) ("x" omitted when it conflicts with runway pattern)

15 DME Distance
From Facility

ARC/DME/RNAV Fix

R-198 — Radial line and value
LR-198 — Lead Radial
LB-198 — Lead Bearing

MINIMUM SAFE ALTITUDE (MSA)

Facility Identifier
MSA CRW 25 NM
1500   2200
090°   270°
4500   2500
360°

(arrows on distance circle identify sectors)

OBSTACLES

• Spot Elevation   ● Highest Spot Elevation
⋀ Obstacle   ⋀⋀ Group of Obstacles
⋀ Highest Obstacle   ± Doubtful accuracy

SPECIAL USE AIRSPACE

R-352
R-Restricted   W-Warning
P-Prohibited   A-Alert

RADIO AIDS TO NAVIGATION

110.1 Underline indicates No Voice transmitted on this frequency

◌ VOR   ◻ VOR/DME   ⬠ TACAN   ⬡ VORTAC

⊙ NDB   ⊡ NDB/DME   ◇ WAYPOINT

⊕ MAP WP   ◇ FLYOVER WAYPOINT   ◇ WAYPOINT COLLOCATED WITH NAVAID

◅⊙▻ LOM/LMM (Compass locator at Outer Marker/Middle Marker)

⬭ Marker Beacon

Localizer (LOC/LDA) Course
Right side shading- Front course; Left side shading- Back Course

SDF Course

180° MLS Approach Azimuth

MLS Identifier
MICROWAVE
Chan 514
M-VDZ ⦂⦂
Glidepath 6.20°
DME 111.5 Chan 48(Y)

(Y) TACAN must be in "Y" mode to receive distance information.

◨ LOC/DME
⊙ LOC/LDA/SDF/MLS Transmitter
(shown when installation is offset from its normal position off the end of the runway.)

Waypoint Data
Coordinates
PRAYS
N38° 58.30' W89° 51.50'
Frequency — 112.7 CAP 187.1°-56.2
590
Identifier Reference Facility Elevation
Waypoint Name
Radial-Distance (Facility to Waypoint)

Primary Navaid with Coordinate Values
LIMA
114.5 LIM ⦂⦂⦂
Chan 92
S12° 00.80'
W77° 07.00'

Secondary Navaid
LMM
LIMA
248 NT ⦂⦂

MISCELLANEOUS

⌐ VOR Changeover Point

RWY 15 S12° 00.52'
W77° 06.91'
End of Rwy Coordinates (DOD only)

⩘⩘ Distance not to scale

——— — — ——— International Boundary

LEGEND 14.—Instrument Approach Procedures (Symbols).

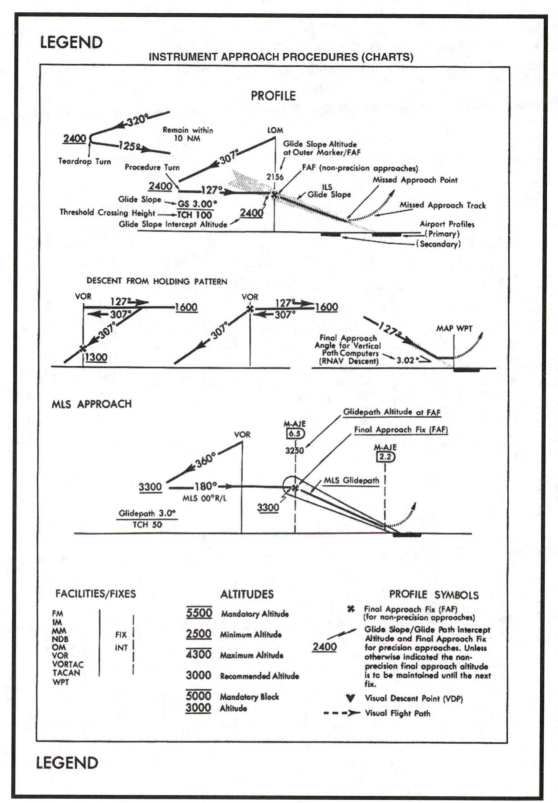

LEGEND 15.—Instrument Approach Procedures (Profile).

INSTRUMENT TAKEOFF PROCEDURE CHARTS
RATE-OF-CLIMB TABLE
(ft. per min.)

A rate-of-climb table is provided for use in planning and executing
takeoff procedures under known or approximate ground speed conditions.

REQUIRED CLIMB RATE (ft. per NM)	GROUND SPEED (KNOTS)						
	30	60	80	90	100	120	140
200	100	200	267	300	333	400	467
250	125	250	333	375	417	500	583
300	150	300	400	450	500	600	700
350	175	350	467	525	583	700	816
400	200	400	533	600	667	800	933
450	225	450	600	675	750	900	1050
500	250	500	667	750	833	1000	1167
550	275	550	733	825	917	1100	1283
600	300	600	800	900	1000	1200	1400
650	325	650	867	975	1083	1300	1516
700	350	700	933	1050	1167	1400	1633

REQUIRED CLIMB RATE (ft. per NM)	GROUND SPEED (KNOTS)					
	150	180	210	240	270	300
200	500	600	700	800	900	1000
250	625	750	875	1000	1125	1250
300	750	900	1050	1200	1350	1500
350	875	1050	1225	1400	1575	1750
400	1000	1200	1400	1600	1700	2000
450	1125	1350	1575	1800	2025	2250
500	1250	1500	1750	2000	2250	2500
550	1375	1650	1925	2200	2475	2750
600	1500	1800	2100	2400	2700	3000
650	1625	1950	2275	2600	2925	3250
700	1750	2100	2450	2800	3150	3500

LEGEND 16.—Takeoff Procedure Charts, Rate-of-Climb Table.

LEGEND

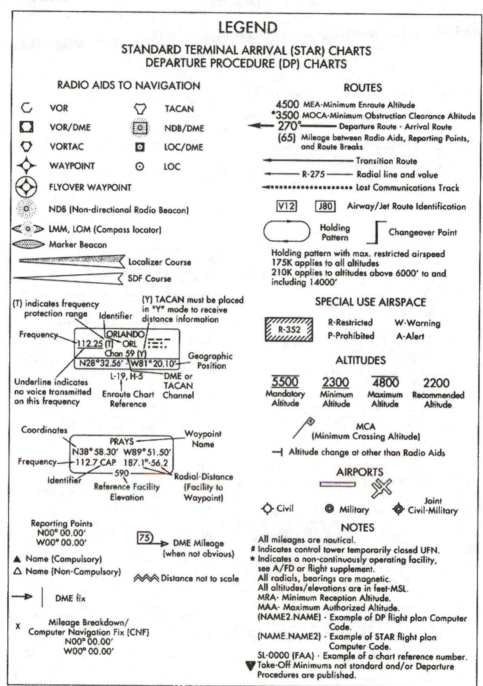

LEGEND

LEGEND 17.—Standard Arrival/Departure Charts.

LEGEND   INSTRUMENT APPROACH PROCEDURES (CHARTS)

AIRPORT DIAGRAM/AIRPORT SKETCH

Runways

| Hard Surface | Other Than Hard Surface | Stopways, Taxiways, Parking Areas | Displaced Threshold |

| Closed Runway | Closed Taxiway | Under Construction | Metal Surface | Runway Centerline Lighting |

ARRESTING GEAR: Specific arresting gear systems; e.g., BAK-12, MA-1A etc., shown on airport diagrams, not applicable to Civil Pilots. Military Pilots Refer to Appropriate DOD Publications.

⌐ uni-directional   ⌐ bi-directional   } Jet Barrier

REFERENCE FEATURES

Buildings...■

Tanks..●

Obstruction..∆

Airport Beacon #..☆

Runway
Radar Reflectors...⟆

Control Tower #...▪

\# When Control Tower and Rotating Beacon are co-located, Beacon symbol will be used and further identified as TWR.

Runway length depicted is the physical length of the runway (end-to-end, including displaced thresholds if any) but excluding areas designated as stopways. Where a displaced threshold is shown and/or part of the runway is otherwise not available for landing, an annotation is added to indicate the landing length of the runway; e.g., RWY 13 ldg 5000'.

Runway Weight Bearing Capacity/or PCN Pavement Classification Number is shown as a codified expression.
Refer to the appropriate Supplement/Directory for applicable codes; e.g.,
RWY 14-32 S75, T185, ST175, TT325
PCN 80 F/D/X/U

Helicopter Alighting Areas Ⓗ ⊞ ⊞ ⚠ ⊞

Negative Symbols used to identify Copter Procedures

landing point............... Ⓗ ⊞ ⊞ ⚠ ⊞

Runway TDZ elevation.................TDZE 123

←—0.3% DOWN

Runway Slope..............................0.8% UP—→

(shown when runway slope exceeds 0.3%)

NOTE:
Runway Slope measured to midpoint on runways 8000 feet or longer.

⊟ U.S. Navy Optical Landing System (OLS) "OLS" location is shown because of its height of approximately 7 feet and proximity to edge of runway may create an obstruction for some types of aircraft.

Approach light symbols are shown in the Flight Information Handbook.

Airport diagram scales are variable.

True/magnetic North orientation may vary from diagram to diagram.

Coordinate values are shown in 1 or ½ minute increments. They are further broken down into 6 second ticks, within each 1 minute increment.

Positional accuracy within ±600 feet unless otherwise noted on the chart.

NOTE:
All new and revised airport diagrams are shown referenced to the World Geodetic System (WGS) (noted on appropriate diagram), and may not be compatible with local coordinates published in FLIP. (Foreign Only)

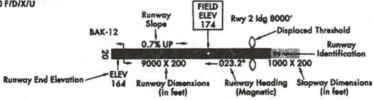

FIELD ELEV 174
BAK-12   Runway Slope   0.7% UP   Rwy 2 ldg 8000'   Displaced Threshold
20   9000 X 200   ←023.2°   1000 X 200   Runway Identification
Runway End Elevation   ELEV 164   Runway Dimensions (in feet)   Runway Heading (Magnetic)   Stopway Dimensions (in feet)

SCOPE

Airport diagrams are specifically designed to assist in the movement of ground traffic at locations with complex runway/taxiway configurations and provide information for updating Computer Based Navigation Systems (I.E., INS, GPS) aboard aircraft. Airport diagrams are not intended to be used for approach and landing or departure operations. For revisions to Airport Diagrams: Consult FAA Order 7910.4B.

LEGEND

LEGEND 18.—Airport Diagram.

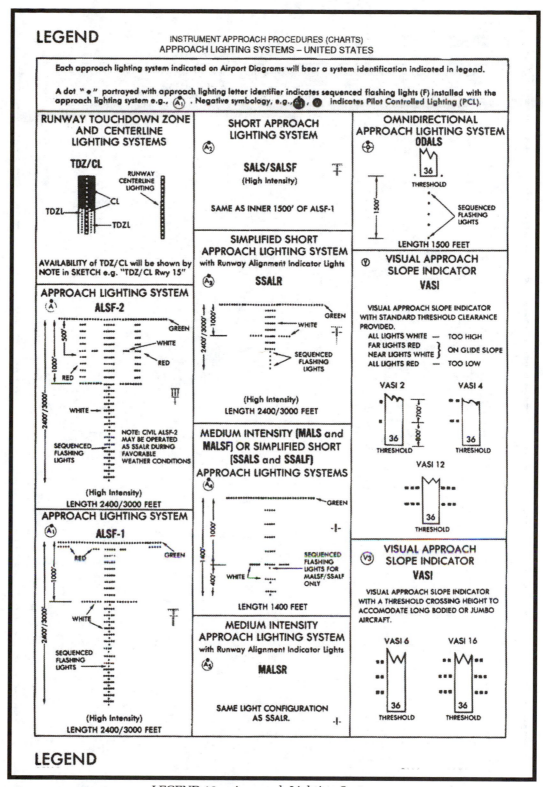

LEGEND 19.—Approach Lighting Systems.

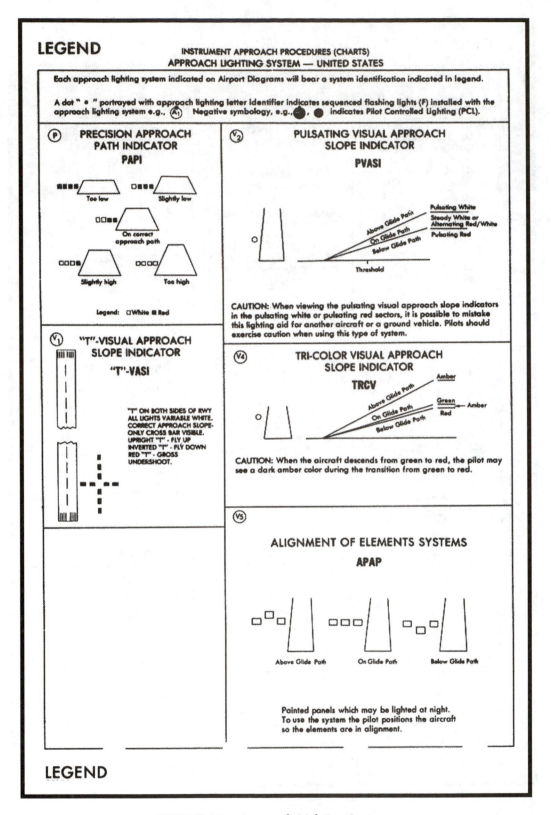

LEGEND 20.—Approach Lighting System.

RATE OF DESCENT TABLE

A rate of descent table is provided for use in planning and executing precision descents under known or approximate ground speed conditions. It will be especially useful for approaches when the localizer only is used for course guidance. A best speed, power altitude combination can be programmed which will result in a stable glide rate and altitude favorable for executing a landing if minimums exist upon breakout. Care should always be exercised so that minimum descent altitude and missed approach point are not exceeded.

ANGLE OF DESCENT (degrees and tenths)		FEET /NM	GROUND SPEED (knots)										
			30	45	60	75	90	105	120	135	150	165	180
2.0		210	105	160	210	265	320	370	425	475	530	585	635
2.5		265	130	200	265	330	395	465	530	595	665	730	795
V E R T I C A L P A T H A N G L E	2.7	287	143	215	287	358	430	501	573	645	716	788	860
	2.8	297	149	223	297	371	446	520	594	669	743	817	891
	2.9	308	154	231	308	385	462	539	616	693	769	846	923
	3.0	318	159	239	318	398	478	557	637	716	796	876	955
	3.1	329	165	247	329	411	494	576	658	740	823	905	987
	3.2	340	170	255	340	425	510	594	679	764	849	934	1019
	3.3	350	175	263	350	438	526	613	701	788	876	963	1051
	3.4	361	180	271	361	451	541	632	722	812	902	993	1083
3.5		370	185	280	370	465	555	650	740	835	925	1020	1110
4.0		425	210	315	425	530	635	740	845	955	1060	1165	1270
4.5		475	240	355	475	595	715	835	955	1075	1190	1310	1430
5.0		530	265	395	530	660	795	925	1060	1190	1325	1455	1590
5.5		580	290	435	580	730	875	1020	1165	1310	1455	1600	1745
6.0		635	315	475	635	795	955	1110	1270	1430	1590	1745	1950
6.5		690	345	515	690	860	1030	1205	1375	1550	1720	1890	2065
7.0		740	370	555	740	925	1110	1295	1480	1665	1850	2035	2220
7.5		795	395	595	795	990	1190	1390	1585	1785	1985	2180	2380
8.0		845	425	635	845	1055	1270	1480	1690	1905	2115	2325	2540
8.5		900	450	675	900	1120	1345	1570	1795	2020	2245	2470	2695
9.0		950	475	715	950	1190	1425	1665	1900	2140	2375	2615	2855
9.5		1005	500	750	1005	1255	1505	1755	2005	2255	2510	2760	3010
10.0		1055	530	790	1055	1320	1585	1845	2110	2375	2640	2900	3165
10.5		1105	555	830	1105	1385	1660	1940	2215	2490	2770	3045	3320
11.0		1160	580	870	1160	1450	1740	2030	2320	2610	2900	3190	3480
11.5		1210	605	910	1210	1515	1820	2120	2425	2725	3030	3335	3635
12.0		1260	630	945	1260	1575	1890	2205	2520	2835	3150	3465	3780

DESCENT TABLE

LEGEND 21.—Instrument Approach Procedure Charts, Rate-of-Descent Table.

INOPERATIVE COMPONENTS OR VISUAL AIDS TABLE

Landing minimums published on instrument approach procedure charts are based upon full operation of all components and visual aids associated with the particular instrument approach chart being used. Higher minimums are required with inoperative components or visual aids as indicated below. If more than one component is inoperative, each minimum is raised to the highest minimum required by any single component that is inoperative. ILS glide slope inoperative minimums are published on the instrument approach charts as localizer minimums. This table may be amended by notes on the approach chart. Such notes apply only to the particular approach catergory(ies) as stated. See legend page for description of components indicated below.

(1) ILS, MLS, and PAR

Inoperative Component or Aid	Approach Category	Increase Visibility
ALSF 1 & 2, MALSR, & SSALR	ABCD	1/4 mile

(2) ILS with visibility minimum Of 1,800 RVR

ALSF 1 & 2, MALSR, & SSALR	ABCD	To 4000 RVR
TDZL RCLS	ABCD	To 2400 RVR
RVR	ABCD	To 1/2 mile

(3) VOR, VOR/DME, VORTAC, VOR (TAC), VOR/DME (TAC), LOC, LOC/DME, LDA, LDA/DME, SDF, SDF/DME, GPS, RNAV, and ASR

Inoperative Visual Aid	Approach Category	Increase Visibility
ALSF 1 & 2, MALSR, & SSALR	ABCD	1/2 mile
SSALS, MALS, & ODALS	ABC	1/4 mile

(4) NDB

ALSF 1 & 2, MALSR, & SSALR	C	1/2 mile
	ABD	1/4 mile
MALS, SSALS, ODALS	ABC	1/4 mile

CORRECTIONS, COMMENTS AND/OR PROCUREMENT

FOR CHARTING ERRORS CONTACT:
National Ocean Service/NOAA
N/ACC1, SSMC-4, Sta. #2335
1305 East-West Highway
Silver Spring, MD 20910-3281
Telephone Toll-Free (800) 626-3677
Internet/E-Mail: Aerochart@NOAA.GOV

FOR CHANGES, ADDITIONS, OR RECOMMENDATIONS ON PROCEDURAL ASPECTS:
Contact Federal Aviation Administration, ATA 110
800 Independence Avenue, SW
Washington, DC 20591
Telephone Toll Free (800) 457-6656

TO PURCHASE CHARTS CONTACT:
National Ocean Service
NOAA, N/ACC3
Distribution Division
Riverdale, MD 20737
Telephone Toll Free (800) 638-8972

Requests for the creation or revisions to Airport Diagrams should be in accordance with FAA Order 7910.4B.

LEGEND 22.—Inoperative Components or Visual Aids Table.

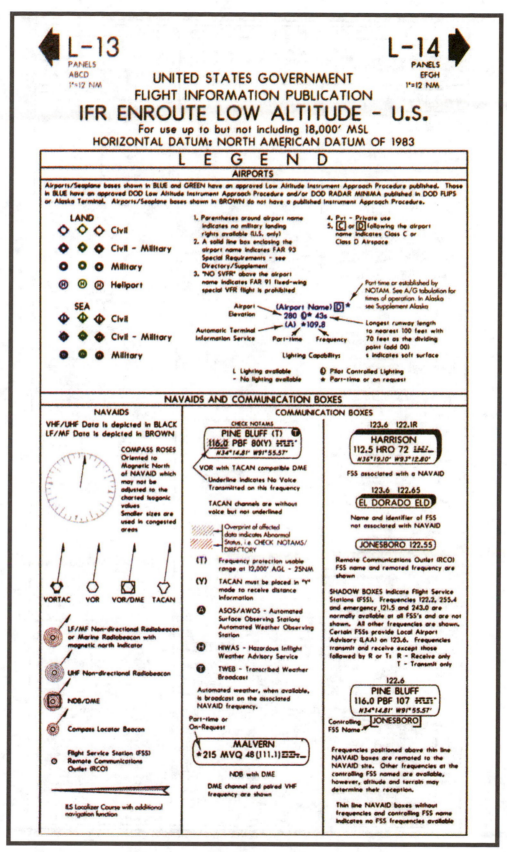

LEGEND 23.—IFR En Route Low Altitude (U.S.).

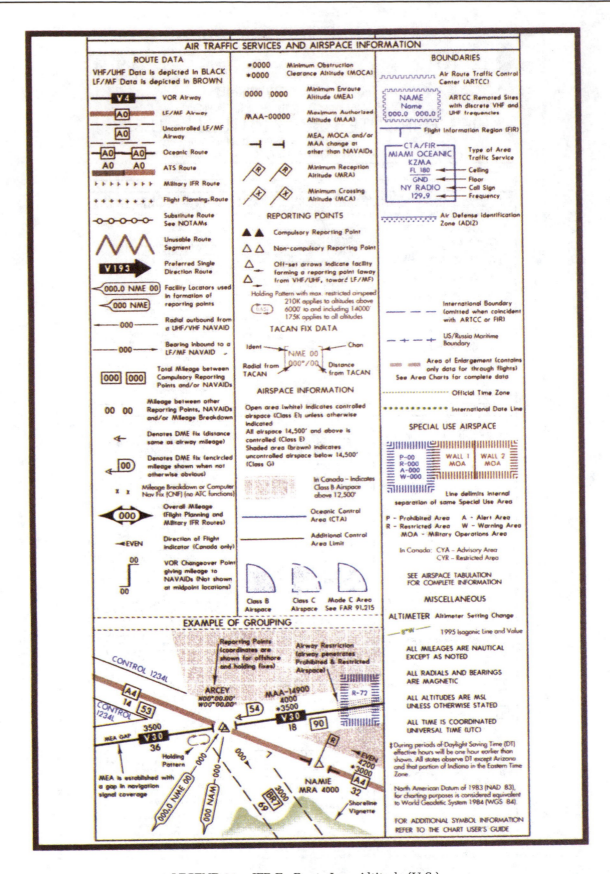

LEGEND 24.—IFR En Route Low Altitude (U.S.).

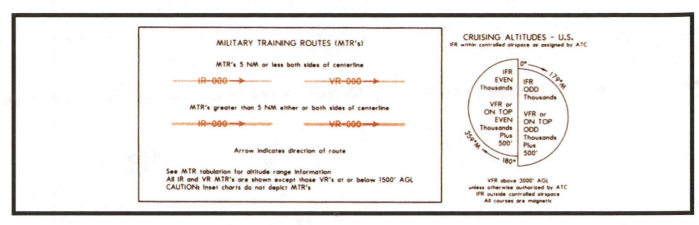

LEGEND 25.—IFR En Route Low Altitude (U.S.).

AIRCRAFT EQUIPMENT SUFFIXES

Suffix	Aircraft Equipment Suffixes
	NO DME
/X	No transponder
/T	Transponder with no Mode C
/U	Transponder with Mode C
	DME
/D	No transponder
/B	Transponder with no Mode C
/A	Transponder with Mode C
	TACAN ONLY
/M	No transponder
/N	Transponder with no Mode C
/P	Transponder with Mode C
	AREA NAVIGATION (RNAV)
/Y	LORAN, VOR/DME, or INS with no transponder
/C	LORAN, VOR/DME, or INS, transponder with no Mode C
/I	LORAN, VOR/DME, or INS, transponder with Mode C
	ADVANCED RNAV WITH TRANSPONDER AND MODE C (If an aircraft is unable to operate with a transponder and/or Mode C, it will revert to the appropriate code listed above under Area Navigation.)
/E	Flight Management System (FMS) with en route, terminal, and approach capability. Equipment requirements are: (a) Dual FMS which meets the specifications of AC 25-15, Approval of Flight Management Systems in Transport Category Airplanes; AC 20-129, Airworthiness Approval of Vertical Navigation (VNAV) Systems for use in the U.S. NAS and Alaska; AC 20-130A, Airworthiness Approval of Navigation or Flight Management Systems Integrating Multiple Navigation Sensors; or equivalent criteria as approved by Flight Standards. (b) A flight director and autopilot control system capable of following the lateral and vertical FMS flight path. (c) At least dual inertial reference units (IRU's). (d) A database containing the waypoints and speed/altitude constraints for the route and/or procedure to be flown that is automatically loaded into the FMS flight plan. (e) An electronic map. (U.S. and U.S. territories only unless otherwise authorized.)
/F	A single FMS with en route, terminal, and approach capability that meets the equipment requirements of /E, (a) through (d), above. (U.S. and U.S. territories only unless otherwise authorized.)
/G	Global Positioning System (GPS)/Global Navigation Satellite System (GNSS) equipped aircraft with en route and terminal capability
/R	Required Navigational Performance (Denotes capability to operate in RNP designated airspace and routes)
/W	Reduced Vertical Separation Minima (RVSM)

LEGEND 26.—Aircraft Equipment Suffixes.

AIR NAVIGATION RADIO AIDS

STANDARD HIGH ALTITUDE SERVICE VOLUME

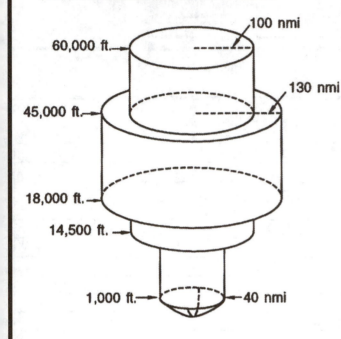

STANDARD LOW ALTITUDE SERVICE VOLUME

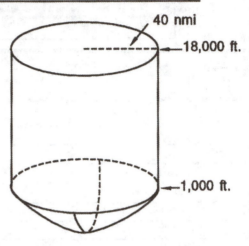

NOTE: All elevations shown are with respect to the station's site elevation (AGL). Coverage is not available in a cone of airspace directly above the facility.

STANDARD TERMINAL SERVICE VOLUME

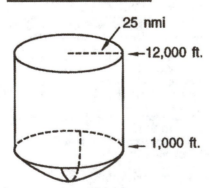

LEGEND 27.—Air Navigation Radio Aids.

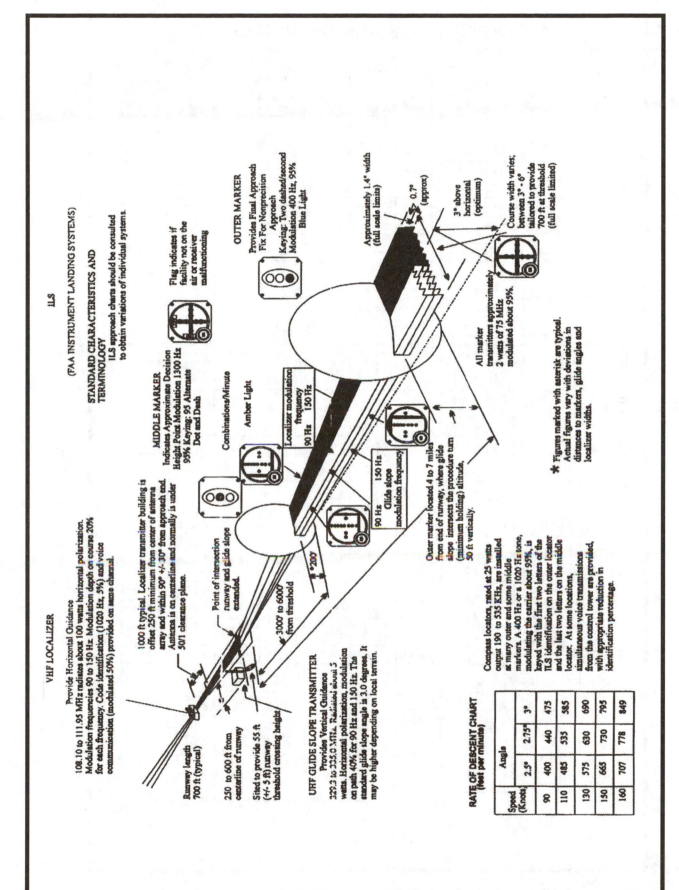

LEGEND 28.—ILS Standard Characteristics and Terminology.

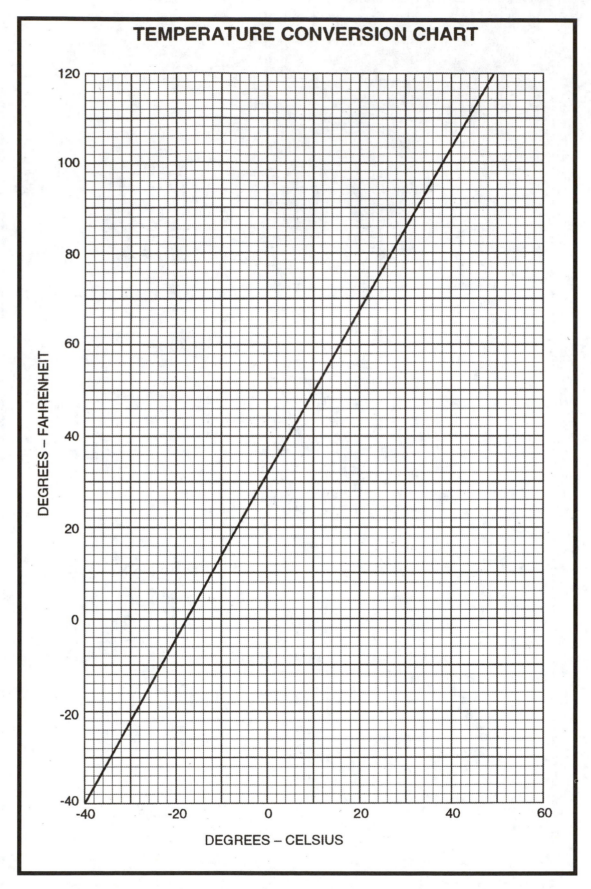

LEGEND 29.—Temperature Conversion Chart.

paving the way.

FliteSchool™ Multimedia Software.

Because the toughest test happens **every time you leave the ground.**

FliteSchool Multimedia Software provides you with a **complete interactive home study course** for passing your FAA knowledge tests, and the tools you need to retain the knowledge you gain, so you can put it to work throughout your flying career.

FliteSchool integrates **complete textual references** to the Jeppesen Guided Flight Discovery® Private and Instrument /Commercial Manuals. You not only get **important test prep information,** you also get access to **greatly expanded reference materials,** including the FAR/AIM.

FliteSchool makes it **easy and fun** to pass your test. By combining carefully selected graphics and computer animation, **difficult concepts become easy** to understand. It also contains all FAA figures and every airplane and helicopter FAA question. It will even generate sample exams. Once you complete the FliteSchool course, you can **receive your endorsement from a Jeppesen CFI** to take your FAA knowledge test.

Jeppesen's pilot training system has been the **leader in the industry** for decades. Now, FliteSchool, with its **comprehensive, interactive multimedia,** computer-based training, will keep you on the cutting edge for decades to come.

For more information about
FliteSchool, visit us
on the internet at
www.jeppesen.com

or call us:

1-800-621-5377
or 303-799-9090
(Western Hemisphere)

+49 6102 5070
(Eastern Hemisphere)

+61 3 9706 0022 (Australasia)

AWARD WINNING SOFTWARE

⫴JEPPESEN
Making Every Mission Possible

JeppPrep Online

JeppPrep is Jeppesen's latest innovation in FAA test preparation. With JeppPrep you can study from the latest FAA questions, continuously updated in our database. JeppPrep is an easy way to ensure you are ready to take an FAA exam.

With the purchase of JeppPrep, you will receive a 60-day period of unlimited study for a particular FAA knowledge exam. If necessary, you can renew for another 30-days for an additional charge.

JeppPrep Features: • Study actual FAA questions at your own pace, on your own time • Review answers and explanations to actual FAA questions • Take sample tests that emulate actual FAA knowledge tests • Efficiently review the results of your practice tests • Compare your performance on several tests • Work with the most current FAA questions • View or print the FAA figures and legends for FAA questions • Private, Instrument, Commercial

Order on the web at: www.jeppesen.com or call 800.621.5377

WB100500 JeppPrep Initial Order – Valid for 60 days $29.95
WB100543 JeppPrep 30-day Renewal $19.95

FAR/AIM Manual (paper)

An excellent study or reference source, the new, larger format includes 14 CFR 135 with complete pilot/controller glossary. Changes are conveniently indicated. Including FAR Parts 1, 43, 61, 67, 71, 73, 91, 97, 119, 133, 135, 141, 142, HMR 175 and NTSB 830, the *FAR/AIM* uses special study lists to direct students to the appropriate FARs. You can check your understanding of the FARs with exercise questions tailored for Private, Instrument, Commercial, and Helicopter. A free Update Summary is available on the internet at www.jeppesen.com.   JS314550 $17.95

Expanded FAR/AIM CD-ROM (includes *FARs Explained*)

The Federal Aviation Regulations are an integral part of aeronautical training. This CD contains applicable portions of Parts 1, 13, 21, 23, 27, 33, 34, 35, 39, 43, 45, 47, 61, 67, 71, 73, 91, 97, 119, 125, 133, 135, 141, 142, 145 (new and old), 147, 183, HMR 175 and NTSB 830. You can search the regulations by part, keyword, or phrase. The FAR/AIM CD-ROM contains: the FARs, FARs Explained by Kent Jackson, FAR Exercises, the AIM and the Pilot Controller Glossary. It also includes SFARs and Maintenance Advisory Circulars as well as FAA-G-8082-11. Both Pilot and Maintenance Regulations are included. Available with a revision service that includes two updated FAR/AIM CD-ROMs following the FAA AIM revisions (two per year). System requirements: PC with 486 or faster processor, 2x CD-ROM drive, Windows 95. Free update summary available on www.jeppesen.com.   JS206350 $29.95

Aviation Weather

This award-winning, 480-page hardcover textbook is extensively updated with the latest METAR, TAF, and Graphic Weather Products from AC00-45E, Aviation Weather Services. Over 500 full-color illustrations and photographs present detailed material in an uncomplicated way. International weather considerations are included as well as accident/incident information to add relevance to the weather data. *Aviation Weather*, by Peter F. Lester, features comprehensive coverage of icing, weather hazards, and flight planning, as well as review questions with answers at the end of the book. The appendices cover common conversions, weather reports, forecasts, and charts, as well as domestic and international METAR, TAF, and graphic weather products.
JS319010 $57.95

Both Bags feature removable headset bags!

B   A

B. The Navigator Bag

The ultimate choice for convenience and flexibility. Contains two detachable headset bags, which can be connected together to form a separate bag. Other features include: Two exterior pockets • 4-way adjustable divider that holds up to 4 Jeppesen binders • Exterior front pocket • 600 denier poly in black or blue. 12"x22½"x8"
JS621213 (black) $99.95 JS621250 (blue) $99.95

A. The Captain Bag

Contains two detachable headset bags, which can be connected together to form a separate bag. Other features include: Removable Transceiver/GPS • 4-way adjustable divider that holds up to 4 Jeppesen binders • Exterior front pocket • Two large zippered storage pockets • 600 denier poly in black or blue.12"x22½"x8"
JS621214 (black) $139.95
JS621251 (blue) $139.95

D

C. The Student Pilot

A great first bag for the student pilot. Features include: Outside pockets • Removable shoulder strap • Double zipper opening • Reinforced bottom • PVC backed 600 denier poly. 10"x5½"x17" JS621212 (black only) $41.95

D. The Aviator Bag

Spacious enough for all of your flight materials. Features include: exterior front pocket • detachable headset and transceiver cases PVC backed 600 denier poly. 15"x6½"x12"
JS621252 (black only) $79.95

E

E. The Protector Headset Bags

Features include: Padded 600 denier poly • Snap-On handle grip • Fits ANR headsets • Single and dual configuration. 12"x2¾"x8"
JS621220 Single (black only) $17.95
JS621219 Dual (black only) $35.95

C

TechStar® Pro

The TechStar Pro combines a 7-function aviation computer and 8-function personal organizer, all in one compact handheld unit. In addition to basic and advanced arithmetic functions, TechStar Pro is designed with 7 main aviation operating modes and 8 organizer modes which offer quick and simple use including:

• Time/Speed/Distance • Altitude/Airspeed • Wind • Weight and Balance • Latitude/Longitude • Timer • Conversions • Telephone/Address • Personal Memo/To Do • Daily Scheduler • Trip Expense Log • Monthly Calendar • Local Time • World Time (128 cities + Zulu time conversions) • Calculator • Approved for use on FAA Knowledge Examinations

JS505000 $89.95

Fuel Tester

Made of clear butyrate plastic to resist cracking, breaking and yellowing. Works with both pin and petcock actuators. Removable splash guard attaches to side for storage. Solid bronze rod actuator prevents breaking and pushing down. Includes hard-tempered, reversible phillips and slotted bit.   JS628855 $13.95

JeppShades

IFR flip-up training glasses replace bulky instrument training hoods. Improved design allows better student/instructor interaction and works conveniently under headsets, while reducing pressure on ears and temples. Flip-up, impact-resistant lens allows convenient IFR/VFR flight transition.
JS404311 $24.95

VFR/IFR Kneeboard

Holds charts, flight computers/plotters, flashlight, pen, pilot notes and more. Features an elastic leg strap with a Velcro closure. The metal clipboard has an additional strap allowing you to use the clipboard independent of the kneeboard.
Kneeboard/Clipboard JS626003 $36.95
Clipboard only with Leg Strap JS626001 $16.95

FREE
Flight Planning Charts
Included! *$6.95 Value!*

Chart Training Videos and DVD

Chart Series Professionally designed and produced, the FlighTime Chart Series Videos and DVD cover Jeppesen enroute charts and approach charts, as well as SIDs and STARs. JS200251 Videos $99.95   JS200300 DVD $79.95

Approach Charts includes a detailed introduction of Jeppesen's approach charts, featuring the Briefing Strip™ format. RNAV and GPS procedures are also covered. JS273268 $37.95

Enroute Charts features Jeppesen four-color enroute charts and is based primarily on US-LO series charts. JS273269 $37.95

Departures and Arrivals presents the unique characteristics of SID and STAR charts. JS273270 $37.95

FliteLog® Electronic LogBook
   A traditional paper logbook feel *(modeled after our Professional Pilot Logbook)*, with the flexibility of a computer program. Available for Windows only.   JM301592 $89.00